Parachutes for Parents

12 New Keys to Raising Children for a Better World

With Aloha, Bobbie Sandoz

Bobbie Sandoz

CB
CONTEMPORARY BOOKS

Library of Congress Cataloging-in-Publication Data

Sandoz, Bobbie.
    Parachutes for parents : 12 new keys to raising children for a better world /
Bobbie Sandoz. — [2nd ed.]
        p.   cm.
    ISBN 0-8092-3025-9
    1. Parenting.   2. Child rearing.   I. Title.
HQ755.8.S29   1997
649´.1—dc21   97-17006
                                                                           CIP

Interior illustrations by Candice Johnston
Cover design by Monica Baziuk
Interior design by Mary Lockwood

Copyright © 1993, 1997 by Bobbie Sandoz
Published by Contemporary Books
An imprint of NTC/Contemporary Publishing Company
4255 West Touhy Avenue, Lincolnwood (Chicago), Illinois 60646-1975 U.S.A.
Manufactured in the United States of America
International Standard Book Number: 0-8092-3025-9

15   14   13   12   11   10   9   8   7   6   5   4   3   2   1

To my parents and sisters who filled my childhood with love and laughter. To my children who inspired me to love them deeply and joyfully without conditions. And to all parents who strive to create loving, laughing, and honorable families and, in so doing, contribute to a more caring and joyful world.

Disclaimer

The suggestions for child management made in this book include the ideas of the author and offer no guarantee of outcomes. Consequently, parents must extract from the material only those parts that resonate for them and assume personal responsibility for whatever guidelines they select. The author and publisher shall have neither liability nor responsibility to any person with respect to any loss or damage caused or alleged to be caused directly or indirectly by the information in this book.

Contents

๑ ๑ ๑

Acknowledgments

෧ ෧ ෧

My love and appreciation go first to my children for their inspiration to my writing *Parachutes for Parents*; my son Tay for his treasured friendship, steady support, clear insights, and editing skills; my daughter Danika for her cherished friendship, loving support, editing help, and author photograph; my daughter-in-law Stephanie for her loving and supportive interest and valued editing help; and my dear friend Tom Sandoz for his boundless belief in me, loyal friendship, enduring support, editing help, and for holding my hand during the roller coaster ride!

I also wish to thank my parents for their support through each stage of my life; my sister and friend Dorothy Bremner for her skilled editing support; my sister and friend Anne Galvan and her husband Ephraim for bringing us our littlest angel Journ; Don Bremner for his loving role in the lives of my children; and my cherished friends who have remained loyal companions and friends of the heart, especially the beloved "Madame Butterfly" birthday adventurers, Prayer Sisters, travel, tennis, theater, lunch, hula, and dolphin friends; and the new and wonderful friends walking the path with me to help create a better world.

Recognition is due Marge Lester as first director of Unity School, whose light guided us through those early discoveries; Jo-Anne Lewis, who first remembered that children can be loved in the middle of their problems; Virginia Beckwith, the first to manifest these ideas in her magical classroom; the other directors and masterful teachers who have so consistently expressed love for the children and in the process have become light beams for us all. Thanks go to my many clients who have shared their hearts, tears, laughter, and personal transformations with me over the past twenty-five years; and special thanks to the numerous parents who have shared with me the profound effect earlier editions of *Parachutes for Parents* had on their families— for they are the reason I stayed the course.

Deep appreciation goes to Candice Johnston for her wonderful skills and loyal help in pulling the book and me together. I couldn't have done it without her!

And, finally, my thanks to NTC/Contemporary Publishing Company and senior editor Susan Schwartz, project editor David Bramer, copyeditor Alison Shurtz, cover designer Monica Baziuk, interior designer Mary Lockwood, and publicist Maureen Musker, for recognizing, preserving, and enhancing the value in *Parachutes for Parents* in such a graciously collaborative manner.

Introduction

ⓖ ⓖ ⓖ

Most of you began your parenting journeys filled with great love for your children and a dedication to doing your best. Yet, more often than not, something goes amiss in the course of parenting, and you find your optimism shifts to frustration and anger at children who don't always cooperate with your dreams of happiness and success for them.

In fact, many of you have confessed in the privacy of counseling how challenged you are by parenting and that you have sometimes questioned having had your children as a result of the problems in raising them. Studies support your impression that child-rearing is difficult and indicate that the majority of you consider it your greatest challenge.

We don't have to look much further than the evening news to realize that your children are deeply affected by the confusion you feel or that we're in a national parenting crisis.

Moreover, today's world mirrors our failure to foster the kinds of beliefs and attitudes that create a caring and gentle world where people live from their higher, more loving and cooperative selves. It's become painfully apparent that we simply don't know how to raise our children or what to teach them. The tragic result is that we have collectively created a disabled society and ailing world, urgently in need of repairs if we're to survive.

This crisis inspired noted biologist Dr. Roger Payne to reflect that man is the only species to have inflicted so many self-destructive acts on itself in so short a span of time. He further predicts that if we continue on this course, we may attain the distinction of being the only species to orchestrate its own extinction.

To respond to this crisis, we must each begin a process of mending our hearts and homes to create building blocks for a healed society. The best way to start is by learning to raise loved and loving, happy, and responsible children to populate a more caring and joyful world. *Parachutes for Parents* offers a unique program that will show you how.

My Personal Search

I was one of those parents who began with high hopes for raising happy children but soon found the job to be more challenging than I had anticipated. Although I thought my status as a professional woman with two graduate degrees in education and child development would protect me from the common difficulties of raising children, I soon discovered that the approaches I had learned were not only misleading but dangerous.

When I sought help, the parenting books and professionals I consulted drew from the same well of faulty information I had been using and made suggestions that worsened the situation. The ideas they offered for loving and encouraging children resulted in mine feeling insecure and addicted to attention. Their systems for teaching cooperative problem solving led mine deeper into their jealousies, competition, and unresolved conflicts. And, their prescription for discipline locked me and my children into an ongoing power struggle. Consequently, I—like others following these guidelines—found child-rearing to be a confusing challenge, and I often wondered why I had bothered to have a family.

Initially, I thought I was the only one struggling with parenting, but I soon learned that others shared my experience. In my effort to find solutions, it occurred to me that child-rearing goes awry because the systems parents work so hard to implement simply don't work. I responded to this insight by constructing something new.

It was during my search for a better approach that I met with a group of parents and teachers at Unity School in Honolulu, Hawaii, who were also seeking new ways to work with children. We explored a number of ideas from our perspectives as parents and professionals as well as people striving to live our lives from our higher selves. What didn't work—no matter how lovely the theory sounded—got tossed, and a number of long-standing assumptions about child-rearing were eliminated. I then wove our discoveries into a more expanded parenting system that would protect children from developing the kinds of problems I was encountering in my adult counseling practice. The initial program was tested at Unity School, and it wasn't long before we realized that our results were profound.

Those children who had been aggressive calmed down; the fearful and dependent ones grew more trusting and confident; those who competed with peers became more connected and cooperative; others who hid their errors developed more comfort with mistakes and openness to admitting and correcting them; and the ones who were angry became more peaceful and loving. All of the children grew uniquely clear-sighted in their outlook on life and their approach to problem solving. We began to take "before" and "after" pictures to chronicle the opening of these children's faces and bodies and the unusual beauty and clarity that emerged as a result of this unfolding process. We gained a reputation in the community, and our waiting list numbered in the hundreds. We not only enhanced the lives of average families, but participated in profound healings with children who had been asked to leave other schools. It occurred to me one day that we had uncovered a new paradigm in parenting!

The Discovery

At Home

As I used this new way of relating to my own children, the energies in our home shifted from resistance and a struggle for control to those of a caring, cooperative family. My children grew in feelings of security and became more self-assured, joyful, and independent as a peaceful energy permeated our home. This is what I had envisioned when I first decided to have a family. The change was so dramatic that it felt like a miracle, and my young children understood and cherished the transformation.

I did not become a perfect parent, nor did my children become perfect children. We still had our problems and disagreements to work out. Yet I was now able to be in the complex and challenging role of parent in a way that allowed me to learn from the various events that surfaced for us; to teach my children to learn from these situations; and to lovingly guide both my children and myself in growing toward slightly better selves as we encountered each experience throughout our journey of life together. As a result of this new style, my children—who are now adults—and I began to treasure our relationships with one another, and we became dear and enduring friends.

Furthermore, I was able to use what I had learned in my new approach to parenting in other relationships and aspects of life. To my surprise, I not only mended my heart in the process of raising my children, I used the parenting journey to uncover a kinder, gentler self and more powerful approach to living.

As a result of my personal search to heal the pain in my own family, I uncovered a system of parenting quite different from the ones traditionally proposed. Because this approach had resulted in such positive changes for me and my children, as well as the families at Unity School, I knew something unique had been discovered, and I wanted to share it with a larger group of people. The opportunity to do this presented itself in a unique way.

At School

Eric came to school as a skinny three-year-old with a pinched face and rounded shoulders. He arrived daily, protected by too much clothing and a frayed blanket tucked under one arm and a stuffed animal under the other.

It was months before he would talk to us, and it took him longer than most to feel safe enough to put away his blanket and stuffed animal. Next, his jacket came off, followed by the extra clothing, and finally a willingness to strip down to his swimsuit and join the others in the playground wading pools.

It was then that Eric felt prepared to peel away the mask that hid his vulnerabilities and allow us to see his hurt and fearful feelings as well as his happy ones. The first time he cried, he choked and coughed while a teacher gently rocked and assured him that it was okay. His first full-bellied laugh began just as cautiously. Eric gradually trusted us to help him express, understand, and cope with his various issues and emotions and to more clearly resolve the problematic ones.

As a five-year-old, in the spring of his last year with us, Eric asked the director if she would teach his parents to treat him at home as he had been treated at school. The director agreed, and the meeting she called to fulfill this assignment gave birth to the parenting classes I taught for over twenty years.

The Larger Community

Since my own children and those of parents in my classes grew increasingly secure and clear, I gained confidence in the importance of my discovery. I expanded my practice to include additional parenting classes, teacher workshops, private family counseling, and consulting in the Honolulu community as well as a number of other states. During the course of these activities, I witnessed innumerable healings in other hearts and homes similar to the one in my own and saw how easily this method helped parents shift in a short span of time from a troubled experience with their children to a uniquely rewarding one. As a result, I decided to share the program with a wider audience by putting my ideas into a book.

Parachutes For Parents

As I sat in a dentist's office a number of years ago, an inner voice told me not to undergo the procedure ahead of me. However, my mouth had already been numbed, and I thought it would be "impolite" to leave. The work I received that afternoon took me a good deal of time, money, and courage to repair.

We are all in the position I was in that day. Our inner voices whisper insistently in our ears of the importance of awakening to our need to make dramatic changes if we're to survive as a society on a planet balanced and healthy enough to sustain us. The time is past for denying this reality or speaking "politely" about the need to heal our collective heart and ailing world—for that's our truth, and we all know it!

Yet if we're to create a cure, we must have the courage to speak openly of the truth that our current approaches to living have not produced good results. It's equally clear that we must discover how to live in the world in an entirely new way.

Marianne Williamson, in her powerful book *A Return to Love* (1992), was the first to fully abandon the traditionally polite voice as she boldly addressed the seriousness of our problem. She offered an equally bold prescription for the miracle that could save us—a collective return to love.

Her daring voice and bestselling book led the way for others to come out from behind the veils hiding their similarly spiritually based beliefs and express themselves more openly. As a result, books probing the larger meaning of life, awakening the principled higher self, and guiding us in the care of our souls and honoring of the earth and its creatures dominate the current bestseller lists.

Deepak Chopra, a successful M.D., was among the first to abandon the comfort of traditional medical parameters in order to share the most recent scientific discoveries that support the beliefs of the spiritually inclined higher self. A number of other doctors and scientists have courageously added their support and documentation to these ideas. Interestingly, once "the road less traveled" was taken by these bold thinkers, they began to experience greater notoriety than their opponents, while awakening within the rest of us the realization that learning to love will offer humanity a more joyful result than the loveless and destructive path we are currently on, yet so adamantly protect.

As we begin to accept these discoveries and prescriptions into our lives and use our various experiences, work, and relationships to hone our ability to love, I offer those among you with children a way to use the parenting journey to activate your heart and bring more love to yourselves, your families, and the world. This particular course for remembering how to love not only invites the millions of you with children to experience love within yourselves and offer it to your children, but helps you to raise wise and loving people to fill our homes and world.

By flooding the children of this world with love from parental hearts saturated with genuine caring we activate the last parachute available to us for stopping the societal fall we are now experiencing. This is our last hope for healing our homes and world.

Therefore, I invite each of you who would like a more loving relationship with your children as well as a gentler, more peaceful, and caring society to join me in taking this extraordinary parenting journey. First, I will awaken in you the value of raising your child as his or her higher self. Next, I will help you to develop a unique attitude toward your children and their problems that will create a foundation for your success in using the simple and effective management system I provide. I will then make you aware that a personalized lesson exists in each of your children's unclear experiences and show you how to identify and clarify the teaching involved. Not only will this critical step provide your children with lessons so clear that they will rarely repeat their troublesome behaviors, it will teach all family members to be wiser, more caring, and responsible people.

And finally, I invite you to enjoy the journey, since once you know how to do it, parenting can be among your richest experiences—and one that leads you joyfully back to love!

> Bobbie Sandoz
> P.O. Box 22509
> Honolulu, HI 96823-2509

How to Use This Book

Parachutes for Parents serves as a comprehensive parenting manual for families throughout their children's growing-up years. It is most effective to read the entire text once; reread the areas most applicable to your family; and consult the Problem-Solving Guide as an ongoing reference. I recommend that you read the text in its entirety, regardless of the ages of your children, since doing so will not only give you a complete picture of how to parent effectively, it will show you how to live your own life more clearly. Keep in mind, however, that the ideas in this book are presented as possibilities. Parents must listen to their own hearts for the wisdom and truth that will guide their lives and parenting journeys.

So that your attention is not drawn from content to pronouns, the pronouns "she" for parents and "he" for children have been seleceted whenever the gender form is unidentified. All case examples are based on composites of several families, and any similarity to any unidentified individual or family is coincidental.

1

Our Parenting Crisis
A Growing and Dangerous Problem

ᎾᎾᎾ

Imbalance can make parenting seem like Mr. Toad's Wild Ride.

ᎾᎾᎾ

Our society is in chaos, due largely to the weakness of our current child-rearing methods. These methods weren't working for me when I was raising my children, and they aren't working for parents today.

Unfortunately, the parenting methods used in our homes, whether effective or not, become the standard for the way we handle children at school; and what we do in our schools permeates our entire society—our businesses, professions, legal systems, and government.

This happens because the concepts we teach our kids, even when they are false, become the foundation for the way we think and act as a society. Thus, anytime our approach to parenting is unreliable, as it currently is, the children we raise in the cloud of our confusion fill our homes and world with the unclarity we have taught them.

We can't keep using this faulty approach to raising our kids or strive simply to rearrange it. It's critical that we stand back instead, reevaluate what we're doing, and start fresh with a new, more workable plan. Only by fully overhauling our present approach to child-rearing can we start the process of healing our homes and world. To begin, we must investigate how we got off track in the first place and what it will take to right ourselves again.

A Twofold Problem

The first error we make in our approach to parenting lies in the faulty notion that the formidable job of child management can be learned by reading a few short books on the subject. In contrast to this odd assumption, we accept the premise that infant and baby care books will be extensive and thorough in their treatment of the importance and methods of nurturing. Yet when the time comes to provide structure and discipline for the growing child, guidance on how to do this is expected to be short, quick, and faddish; consequently, the child management literature has exploded into a mass of books, each treating different, often conflicting, aspects of this complex subject. The result is that advice on structure and discipline is offered in numerous incomplete fragments that fail to guide parents all the way through their child management problems. Thus, although parents are well advised on how to nurture their infants, once their child is mobile enough to challenge his boundaries, they get lost.

Our second parenting error also stems from this early split between our approach to the nurturing and structured parts of parenting. As a result, even when nurturing is in place, learning to add discipline without abandoning nurturing is something few families know how to do. As a result, most parents end up on a pendulum that swings them between their desire to nurture their children and their awareness that they must also provide discipline.

Until parents can figure out how to love their children and discipline them too, their confusion about which to apply, in what doses, and when causes serious bonding breaks as well as a breakdown in discipline. We can see the dangerous results of this unresolved problem acted out with increasing frequency in our homes, schools, communities, and streets.

To reverse this unsettling trend, we must first examine the swinging pendulum, the effects it wields, and what we can do about it. Following this examination, I will provide you with a new road map for the parenting journey that will leave you with a clear understanding of how to handle the child management issues you encounter at each stage of your child's development. The magic of this journey is that once you have completed it, you will not only enjoy restored harmony in your homes, but renewed confidence in your ability to raise a caring and responsible citizen of the world.

Riding the Wild Pendulum

I for one didn't go through two pregnancies and deliveries to introduce chaos and suffering to my life. Yet mixed with the joy my children brought to me were some of my most challenging moments.

Like most parents, I had looked forward to having children and naturally assumed I would be an excellent mother. I dreamed of sweet-smelling, cooing babies and close, warm relationships. Nobody had mentioned that this doesn't always happen naturally or easily. Nor, did they alert me to what an all-encompassing and challenging job parenting can be.

In fact, I had read from the parenting literature that if I simply loved my children and gave them quality time, positive feedback, and ample attention, they would develop with high esteem and a foundation of confidence on which to go forth into the world with ease and success. That certainly sounded logical, and the image of being a nurturing parent with secure, well-adjusted children was an appealing one to me.

However, I soon discovered that children don't always cooperate with this program, and rather than consistently reward loving parents with mature behavior, even nurtured kids are capable of having problems or behaving badly. For instance, your baby might squirm and fuss, rather than nurse peacefully, or perhaps cry for hours instead of sleep when he's exhausted. Your toddler may whine over a toy, run out of control in the supermarket aisles, or throw himself on the floor when he doesn't get his way. And your elementary-aged child might behave shyly, ignore his chores, or lie about homework, while your teen refuses to answer questions cordially or act responsibly. The truth is, kids can be immature and respond with perfectly dreadful behaviors even when you have given them ample doses of freedom and love.

Those of you who believed nurturing would prevent such unpleasantness feel betrayed by these unwelcome behaviors and routinely react with irritation and anger. In response to your anger, you move toward the authoritarian side of your parenting—while nurturing is all but forgotten. You might speak to your child roughly, threaten him with harsh consequences, or perhaps even pinch, pull his hair, push, or hit him. Or, you may withdraw your love altogether in hopes of inspiring him to improve his conduct. In selecting these responses, you strive to marshal the energy of your disappointment and anger for use in herding your child back under control and convincing him that he simply must behave.

After these encounters, you feel remorseful and guiltily swing back to nurturing. Now, forgetting all about discipline, you cuddle and console your child or buy him sweets and gifts to convince him, any scowling onlookers, and yourself that you do, indeed, love him.

The older your child gets and the more mature you were expecting him to be, the more intense your disappointment and anger become when he doesn't match your pictures. This is especially true for parents who have come to view childhood as a race in which their child must achieve early maturation and independence to "win." Those of you still caught in this pattern of swinging between love and discipline by the time your kids are teens will find yourselves wavering between soliciting their elusive friendship and threatening to ground them forever!

It wasn't long after having my own children before I realized that I, too, was ensnared in this continual swing between soft nurturing and angry authority. Because of the disruption it created in my children's development and our relationship, I began to explore how people like myself, with such good intentions to parent well, get caught, instead, in this unpleasant pattern.

How It Works

Most of you are anxious to love your children and begin your parenting journey by offering them ample doses of nurturing. You nursed and rocked your child until he was too big to hold, wiped thousands of tears, and read as many stories or played as many games, all the while striving for patience in responding to his many questions and needs. Those of you with teens have continued to offer your kids love and understanding—as well as the family car—though they rarely notice your efforts in their behalf or respond with appreciation. You have, in short, worked hard to be a nurturing parent.

Yet more often than not, you become dismayed that so much care hasn't resulted in better behavior and higher performance. You discover, instead, that even when you strive to have a loving relationship with your children, they can seem ungrateful and mischievous, if not demanding and tyrannical. As a result, you find yourself in the role of angry disciplinarian, wondering how you got from there to here. It's no wonder that you look and feel like a martyr! "For all I do—this is the thanks I get?"

The answer, unfortunately, is yes. This is because a child is, by definition, immature and frankly unable to show his appreciation for your nurturing by behaving with consistently mature or responsible behaviors. In fact, he will remain immature—no matter how nice you are—as he slowly makes his way through the journey from the dependence of childhood toward adulthood and independence.

Those of you who hoped that the love you provided during this journey would enhance your child's security and esteem enough to evoke precocious, cooperative, and appreciative behaviors feel disappointed and angry when he fails to deliver. Once upset, you shift from nurturing to discipline. And so it goes. You find yourselves swinging back and forth between these two aspects of parenting—the part that starts out loving and the one that is forced to discipline. In fact, a typical parent makes this shift many times within a single day as though riding a wild pendulum, swinging recklessly out of control.

Most of you are more comfortable parenting from the loving side of the continuum, since you've been taught that large doses of nurturing will enhance your child's self-esteem and success. As a result, you resist boundaries for as long as possible—until pushed to use them by an utterly impossible and out-of-control child.

Others of you gravitate to the authoritarian side of the continuum and impose too much control over your child in hopes that your severity will result in good behavior and high achievement. Then you notice that he is withdrawn or tense, and you move over to the nurturing side for a while. Still others waver continuously between these two extremes, using your child's behavior or your own moods and fears to direct you.

And yet another group of you swing back and forth between an intensified continuum punctuated by mother on one end and father on the other. In such cases, mother may assume the more nurturing role, while father strives to enforce discipline. Whenever mother is feeling protective or father behaves too harshly, mother reacts defensively and resists all discipline—even when it's appropriate. Father, in turn, gets fed up with mother's coddling and scolds the children ever more forcefully. The result is a polarization, as the two push each other further along the extremes of the parenting continuum. These polarized roles can also be reversed, with father acting as the overly nurturing parent in contrast to mother's excessive discipline. They can also exist between a parent and grandparent or between parents and teachers, neighbors, or friends. In addition, various ethnic groups have a tendency toward one or the other of these patterns—or swing continuously between the two.

Before you know it, most of you find yourselves making this swing back and forth, while getting increasingly confused about how to strike a balance between loving your children and providing them with structure and discipline.

Not only does the individual parent swing between love and authority, society does too. Because generations of families have shifted between the extremes of nurturing and discipline in their effort to correct the mistakes of their parents, there are times when authoritarianism is in vogue, followed by periods when permissiveness is popular. When one approach to parenting proves ineffective, the following generation corrects back toward its opposite extreme. The majority of books on parenting simply reflect the most current trend in this swing, as one generation of experts strives to offset the imbalance caused by the previous period of advice.

Rather than contribute to this swing between love and structure, I will propose something new that will interrupt the pattern and teach you to balance your parenting. Before presenting this approach, I will first describe the negative effects the current extremes cause for your children and help you to assess where you fall on the continuum. In the following chapter, I will show you how to get off of this pendulum of extremes and try a new, more effective system for raising your children.

The Effects of too Much Control: The Dominated Child

Many of you like to have everything in your life under control as a way to feel secure and work hard to gain dominion over the various elements of your environment. However, you soon discover that although frustrating jobs, friends, and spouses can be either controlled or replaced, kids are not as easy to manage or discard. As a result, you become increasingly forceful, if not rigid, in your effort to gain control over the many problems their immaturity and long journey to adulthood create.

Without realizing it, controlling parents soon overpower their still-fragile developing child. As a result of their discipline being too intense, too frequent, or too early, their child usually shuts down his own personality and lets his forceful parent take over for him. He then views that parent as having great strength, while his own power is denied.

Because such a highly controlled child does not experience being respected, listened to, or believed, he fails to develop a strong sense of self and views lovability and competence as something possessed only by others. As a result, he feels unlovable, diminished, or shamed; becomes fearfully shy and stiff, emotionally paralyzed, or painfully withdrawn; and has more trouble than others venturing forth into life with full participation.

Most children who have been overpowered by strong parents respond with timidity and fear and often become passively compliant in their effort to please others and stay out of trouble. As a result, they develop dangerous lifetime patterns of insecurity and dependence on the power and authority they attribute to everyone but themselves. These are the kids who grow into submissive adults, vulnerable to having their boundaries crossed or even to abuse by autocratic employers, friends, and partners. Yet because they have developed so little internal strength, their efforts to conform to the expectations of their parents and others fall short. As a result, overcontrolled children soon discover that the most effective way to escape displeasing people is by avoiding those activities that might lead to failure or procrastinating over projects they can't otherwise avoid.

In some cases, a dominated child may dare to rebel against his parents' control by engaging in a power struggle to gain more freedom. This struggle rarely appears as a head-on battle, but is more often acted out covertly by using passively resistant behaviors such as eating slowly, "forgetting" responsibilities, or taking all day to clean a room. In more severe cases, the struggle may be expressed in passively aggressive ways such as "accidentally" wetting on the carpet, injuring the family pet, or finding ways to bruise your feelings.

Other children might conform at home but act out when their authoritarian parent is not in view. Because boundaries of conduct and adult values have been so externally controlled for these kids, they not only fail to internalize or claim them as their own, but actively reject them as a way to strike back at the parent who has dominated and hurt them.

In other cases, powerful parents may find that their child is compliant until adolescence, when his increased size gives him the courage to stand up to their authority. Or the child who never dared to rebel may finally escape from powerful parents by destroying all meaningful contact with them once he's an adult. Even more extreme is the child who has been so deeply injured or angered by excessive control that he feels alienated from life and retaliates by sabotaging or destroying his own.

Of course, the effect that overcontrol and dominance will yield not only varies with each child, but depends on the length of time and extent of power and control used to the exclusion of warmth and love.

The Effects of Excessive Nurturing: The Pampered Child

Some parents are, by nature, more easygoing and unstructured and possess a higher tolerance for the unexpected than their more controlling counterparts. In fact, many of you in this category seem to lack nervous systems altogether and can tolerate chaos without flinching as your children are permitted to run about recklessly and whoop loudly all day without regular naps, meals, baths, or bedtimes.

As a result, your kids are either minimally supervised or overly pampered, and you rarely know where your teenagers are or what they are doing. Your children are denied very little, rarely feel frustrated, and have little or no need to struggle for additional freedoms. Consequently, you perceive them as easy to manage and are surprised when others find them unruly and disagreeable. And so, with only a foggy awareness that your lack of discipline creates problems for your children or others, you raise them in an atmosphere of indulgent permissiveness.

Others—perhaps the majority—of you are more naturally inclined toward normal levels of structure, but resist imposing boundaries on your children due to your acquired awareness of the psychological effects of too much control. Because you have concluded from your reading that unthwarted kids will have elevated self-esteem and will be better equipped to achieve success, you have become overly suspicious of discipline. As a result, you slide too far to the other side of the continuum in an effort to avoid any of the unsettling effects of structure.

Yet, anytime authority is so strenuously resisted that nurturing is taken to extreme, you end up slavishly catering to your child's escalating demands in hopes of keeping him quiet and happy—at any price. In this naive attempt to honor all of your child's perceived "needs" in order to avoid dominating him, you become overly indulgent and are soon controlled yourself. In spite of these results, most of you remain stubbornly resistant to seeing that just as too much authority produces serious problems, excessive nurturing has its own set of adverse—even dangerous—side effects. I hope the following information will convince you.

Because the indulged child is rarely required to control his impulses or practice delaying or thwarting gratification, he develops little tolerance for frustration and has no interest in self-control. His unwillingness to put restraints on his desires or behaviors, as he relentlessly imposes his will on others, results in broken boundaries and damaged relationships. If he also fails to sustain the energy and work it takes to achieve basic developmental, academic, and other goals, he suffers from a lack of competence and self-esteem as well. As an adolescent, the indulged child prefers to demand or steal expanded freedoms, rather than earn them, yet lacks the skills required to manage his autonomy responsibly.

Once he's fully grown and ready to leave home, the indulged child is rarely prepared to function as a reliable member of society and remains dependent on others, insisting that they meet his needs. As a result, he's not only unprepared to contribute, but imposes his unruliness and demands on others. Yet he finds them unexpectedly less sympathetic or willing to cater to him than his lenient family has been and soon discovers that he has driven them away. This approach to life becomes progressively more unattractive and less effective with each passing year and results in personal unhappiness as well as an inability to contribute to society.

In reviewing the results, it becomes painfully clear that parents who strive to counter the effects of dominance by avoiding discipline not only injure their child's personal development, but threaten the stability of their societal group. The combination of self-centeredness; poor impulse control; low tolerance for frustration; irresponsibility; poorly developed competence; and an inability to follow the rules, assume responsibility, and get along with others—all leading to low self-esteem—comprise an unexpectedly long list of dangerous side effects for the child raised by permissive parents.

Once again, the effect that overnurturing and indulgence will have on a child is in direct proportion to the length of time and degree they have been practiced to the exclusion of discipline.

Getting off of the Pendulum

As you can see, extremes in either nurturing or structure—or swinging between the two—cause problems in your children's development, their feelings about themselves and others, and the way they behave in the world. To respond to the crisis this pattern creates for our families and society, we must take our first step toward truly effective parenting by getting off of the swinging pendulum!

*Swinging between love and authority results
in damaged development, weakened relationships,
and irresponsible behavior. It's time to get
off of the pendulum and begin anew.*

2

The Pendulum Stops Here

New Beginnings

The First Key:

⊚⊚⊚

Reclaim the higher self.

If we are to interrupt the pattern of swinging between nurturing and structure, we must tame the swinging pendulum and work our way back to balance. Yet to stop the pendulum, we need to understand the forces that drive it.

The Domination of the World Self

The most important key to today's parenting problems lies in our obsession with material success in the world to the exclusion of the loftier pursuits of our higher selves. As a result, we ignore the soul selves our children brought with them to this world while attending only to how they might develop their ego selves for achieving power, status, and material success while they are here.

Thus, once a child's ego self takes root in his being, we teach him to use this part of himself to promote his own self-interest in order to get ahead in the race to the top and that achieving this end will justify whatever means he uses to get there. As a result, skills in manipulation, deceit, and control are viewed as acceptable approaches to life and are subtly encouraged when needed to achieve personal gain.

This goal not only causes the child to put status, power, and money ahead of caring for others, but leaves him feeling separate, anxious, and competitive as he manipulates his world to gratify his personal wanting and secure a position for himself at the top. By programming your child's ego self in this separating, limited, and fear-based manner, it develops into a false self, quite different in its goals from the true self who came to this world to fulfill a larger purpose.

Thus, rather than cooperate harmoniously with others as the higher self proposes, the ego self strikes out on its own in an effort to be the best and have the most in order to feel adequate. Not surprisingly, an ego self using these guidelines not only develops with suspicion, judgment, defensiveness, and separation from others, but is at odds and in conflict with the core of its own true nature.

Because this framework currently dominates our culture and is promoted both at home and school, the ego self usually succeeds in overshadowing the forgotten higher self and its loftier purpose for coming to this world. As a result, the higher self gets parked away on a shelf in the young child's unconscious to sleep throughout the remainder of his childhood and well into adulthood, while the self-centered goals of the ego dominate his life. Thus, the disowned, yet powerful and altruistic, sovereign self is all but forgotten, while the small and helpless ego strives to replace what was lost.

Rather than continue along this uncaring path that leads to our own destruction, it's time that we ask ourselves some deeper questions. Can it be that we have come to this world simply to act like busy ants gathering as many "crumbs" as we can drag to our individual nests? Or, are we here to pursue some larger purpose? Are we here to live from our higher selves, employing good values and high standards in our daily living, or are we here to use the earth and others as our stepping stones to the top? Is our objective while here to serve only the needs of our lower, materially oriented ego selves or to realize the dreams of our more altruistic, spiritually based, sovereign selves?

To find out, we must, as Stephen Covey suggests, carefully define our personal, family, and societal missions and goals before attempting to fulfill them—for only when we know what we care about and wish to achieve will we know how to go about doing it. Moreover, only when our goals for living are identified can we establish clear guidelines for raising our children.

Defining Our Purpose

One morning, as I was on my way to speak at an educational conference in Honolulu, I passed a homeless woman who honored me with a toothless smile and demure wave of her hand. I had previously given money to this injured soul and now reached for my purse to offer her something more.

In the middle of this gesture, I remembered the story of Mother Teresa's response to a disk jockey who wanted to raise money for her projects. After refusing his repeated offers of financial support, she let him know that if he really wanted to help, he could awaken early each morning and go out to find someone who believed they were alienated from society and convince them that they were not alone.

In this response, Mother Teresa suggests that we cannot heal our hearts, our families, or our world by throwing money and material at our problems, but must learn, as she has, to include our hearts in all that we do. With this in mind, I not only gave the woman some money, but took a moment to make a human-to-human connection with her.

Similarly, popular media hostess Oprah Winfrey throws her heart into the gifts of love she sends over the airwaves while discussing everything from yard sales and fashion to racial tensions and the meaning of life. In doing this, she doesn't merely improve her ratings, but sends healing energies to the millions of viewers who have tuned in for their daily hour with her.

What do the saintly nun and talk-show diva have in common? They offer us models of what it looks like to live from the heart of the sovereign self. But, what about the rest of us? Are we living from our higher selves or is this an anomaly to be found in only a handful of saints and sages and one talk-show hostess? If so, what has happened to the higher selves of everyone else?

The answer was made clear to me by an unusual counseling problem a mother presented when her young children asked if they could invite a homeless child to spend a day with their family. This mother did not want to close the hearts of her open and loving children, yet she feared the experience and the problems it posed.

As we spoke, I remembered that all children come to this world angelic and sensitive with their higher selves well intact, including a desire to care for others in this deeper, more meaningful manner. Yet while raising them, we not only ignore this altruistic aspect of their natural state, but mold their personalities to serve only the narrow interests of their worldly selves. This arrangement leaves little room for their higher selves to be encouraged or expressed in a world that fails to value this essential aspect of themselves.

Parents caught up in this race to the top feel pressured to inspire rapid and precocious development in their children and become anxious anytime their offspring falter and lag behind—or get sidetracked by less worldly, more altruistic pursuits. With so much pressure and tension surrounding our children's growing-up process, it's no wonder parents end up on the swinging pendulum between love and discipline as they strive to rush their children past all distractions to the top.

Although some children manage to keep glimmerings of their higher selves alive in spite of so little support for doing so, most forget about this part of themselves until disillusionment with the empty pursuits of the ego awakens this slumbering giant sometime during adulthood—and many never remember it at all. The result is a world filled with only a handful of people living from their sovereign selves, while the rest feel justified in using dishonest and hurtful measures for achieving personal gain and winning the race. The thought is a terrifying one, yet can no longer be denied as we see the results of this shallow and destructive reality acted out in our homes, communities, and world.

Increasingly more children are dropping out of this futile race due to feelings of inadequacy and discouragement. Others become angry and strike out at those they perceive as "winning." The result is a society filled with people swinging between despair and anger. Thus, many become helpless and dependent, while others behave with aggression and violence.

Keeping the Higher Self Awake

Rather than encourage kids to act as rivals pitted against one another, with each grasping for all he or she can get, the new parenting goal would be to inspire children to view themselves as part of a larger whole and to care as deeply about the world and others as they care about themselves. This more altruistic goal would, in turn, permit them to become their personal best, while supporting others to do the same. Only in this way can they put the needs of their societal group first; become caring, cooperative members of the human experience; and unite their power with others for a greater result.

If we adopted this loftier mission, we would raise our children in an entirely different manner. We wouldn't, for example, use episodes of conflict as the only times that we ask kids to consider the feelings of others or the needs of the whole. Nor would we put such things as our own work schedules or their studies ahead of helping them practice their ability to be caring and wise people.

Under the new regime, if a young girl requested permission to pet the turtle at a hands-on aquarium park, rather than teach her to think only of herself by answering, "No, he might bite," her father might suggest that she become sensitive to the turtle's feelings and consult her heart regarding his needs. By learning to do this, she would become more sensitive to the world around her, and her decisions would be more conscious, global, and wise.

Or, if a gang of kids was taunting a child from a minority group, this would not be overlooked or handled superficially, as such things often are.

Instead, it would be viewed as a primary lesson and addressed accordingly and in depth, even if it required that other curriculum be put aside to do so.

Moreover, if we elected to raise our children in a more conscious manner, rather than ask that they sit at school desks all day long and again in the evening to do homework, we would offer more vibrant, participatory educational programs designed to help kids integrate into real life as progressively clearer-minded, more loving and contributing people.

Thus, rather than put human issues aside in favor of offering more self-interest and academia to arm our kids for winning the race, children would be taught how to become more conscious and caring human beings on a daily basis. If we integrated these kinds of lessons into their daily living, we would no longer need to teach values as an afterthought or a separate subject.

Breaking Through to New Beginnings

As we awaken to the needs of our higher selves, the worldly race of the ego subsides; the pendulum driven by this race is calmed; and the disappointment and confusion are lifted from our lives. Under these more natural conditions, we can better examine how a child's personality might form in greater alignment with his higher purpose. We can also more clearly determine how parents might best support that process using a new, more global mission and balanced approach to parenting.

How Personalities Are Formed

Childhood is the journey your child will take from infancy to adulthood during which he moves from his dependency on you toward becoming an independent adult, able to manage his life with autonomy. Following are the components he must develop in order to form the personality he will use for accomplishing this goal and living in the world.

The Wanter and Fulfiller

When your child is first born into the world, he is simply the essence of his pure self—or soul—packaged in a little body. That's why his presence in a room is so enchantingly full and magical, even as he lies there doing absolutely nothing. As such, he is in a pure, angelic state and can be viewed as simply his higher self who has arrived on earth to live a worldly life.

Although he is enchanting during this initial stage of his life on earth, your little angel is primarily a *wanter*, filled with many desires, urges, and needs for living in the world, which he is unable as an infant to fulfill on his own. Thus, he lies on his back and cries to summon your help.

Whenever you are sensitive to his needs and respond with gentle caring, he experiences himself as lovable and loved in a safe and caring world and freely surrenders to your lap and love. This valuing and nurturing of your child keeps his spirit alive and his wanter trusting that life on earth is both safe and fulfilling, while the essence of this encounter is recorded at a cellular level and woven into the fabric of his being. Moreover, the bond he experiences between you creates a biological trigger in him that not only assures his emotional security, but activates the physical and mental development he will need for living in this world.

Yet, as important as this early arrangement is to your child's normal developmental process, it can't last forever. To survive in this world, he must also grow toward independence and adulthood by creating his own method for fulfilling his needs, a coping system I call the *fulfiller*.[1]

As a result, your child's journey from childhood to adulthood becomes a process during which he designs his own personal style—or *personality*—for fulfilling the desires of his wanter and managing in the world. If formed correctly, his fulfiller will enable him to move from a helpless, dependent child to a mature, autonomous adult, eventually capable of fulfilling his worldly needs independently. In order for your child's undeveloped fulfiller to grow and strengthen, you must allow him to go through the time-consuming, often messy process of trying it out, rather than continuing to use only your own fulfiller to do everything for him as you did when he was an infant. (See Figure 2.)

Parental Roles

We can see from this model of how your child's personality forms why your ability to sustain nurturing supports his belief in the value of the "angel"—or soul self—that came to this world, while your willingness to provide him with structure encourages his development of a participating, responsible fulfiller—or personality self—for functioning in this world.

This is why it's so critical to your child's development that you know how to both love and provide structure for him at all times, rather than swing between these two parts of your parenting. In fact, your primary job as a parent is to figure out how to consistently provide both love and limits without

Figure I. Process of Personality Development

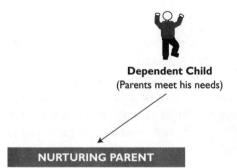

Dependent Child
(Parents meet his needs)

NURTURING PARENT

- Supports child's belief in the value of his higher self

- Triggers physical and mental growth and development of the personality or *ego* self

STRUCTURED PARENT

- Supports development of a responsible personality or *ego* self

- The needs of the higher self are better served when the *ego* self is cooperative and responsible

Immature Adult
(Lacks developed fulfiller)

Independent Adult
(Meets his own needs)

abandoning either, no matter how difficult your child gets or how long it takes him to mature. The following guidelines will show you how to do it.

Balancing Love with Structure

In addition to the nurturing you offer your child, once he grows mobile enough to challenge your boundaries, you must also provide whatever structures and discipline are needed to teach him to use his developing fulfiller with control, safety, responsibility, and competence. This includes furnishing the kinds of limits that will teach him to manage his impulses; sustain the effort needed to succeed in life's goals; and tolerate the pain and frustration that go with whatever rejection, thwarted gratification, or failure he may encounter along the way.

It helps to understand that any resistance your child has to these boundaries simply represents the time it takes for him to adjust to his frustration with limits. Yet it's this very adjustment that helps him to manage the hard parts of life which, in turn, strengthens his ability to "hang in there" and use his own fulfiller, even during the challenging times. Thus, your structures not only support his ability to adapt to limits, but are the catalyst that trigger the internal strength and competence he needs to set coping and responsibility in motion.

As important as limits are to your child's development, continued nurturing is equally important. Thus, you must find a way to add limits to your nurturing program without giving up nurturing. Learning to do this requires that you trust in the genuine power of your child's higher self, rather than feel driven to push and prod his development beyond that of others in order to produce the illusion of a superior worldly self. This can be a challenge for those of you following the old guidelines that value high levels of early achievement, righteousness, and winning as indicators that your child is on course for reaching his potential.

Thus, in order to get off of the swinging pendulum driven by your doubts and fears over whether your child will emerge a "winner," you must not only relinquish the narrow goals of the ego self to the broader ones of the higher self, but must learn to trust that there is already a beautiful "butterfly" within. Once you are able to do this, your parenting will become both relaxed and balanced.

Trusting the Butterfly

Much like a caterpillar, your child will go through many stages of development before overcoming his immaturity and revealing the full grace of the

Figure 2. Diagram of the Individuating Process

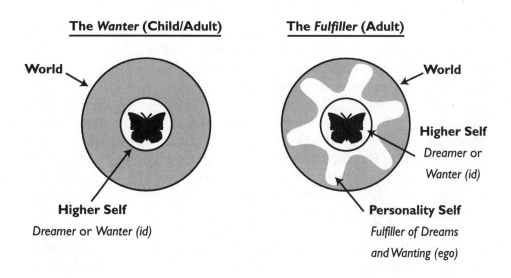

The butterfly represents the spiritual essence, or higher self, of the child born into the world. Because this part of the self carries the dreams and passions, I refer to it as the *wanter*, or in psychological terms, the *id*.

The personality he must form to live on this plane has been drawn around him as a flexible structure depicting the choices he has made and things he has learned from his experiences which, in turn, enable him to fulfill his needs and function in the world. I refer to this personal style of coping or *personality self* as the child's *fulfiller* or *ego*.

matured "butterfly" within. Yet, unless you believe that the precoded beauty of a mature being is already in place and on the way, you become mistrustful of its existence and impatient for it to appear as quickly as possible.

Although it's as futile as pulling up plants to see if they are growing or stomping on a caterpillar for not yet being a butterfly, many of you have trouble accepting the uncertainty of your child's outcome as he slowly works his way toward maturity and adulthood. Instead of having the patience to wait, you feel pressured to have him develop quickly and may poke at his "cocoon" or perhaps tear it open to assure yourself that an adequate "butterfly" is emerging from within.

Thus, rather than wait for your child to unfold in his own time and way, you assume that high levels of early achievement and maturation will ensure his uniqueness and value. As a result, you encourage him to enter the ego race and compete with peers to prove that he's more "special" than they are.

It's this lack of faith in the intrinsic value and ultimate goodness of their child's higher self that causes parents to swing between love and discipline as they push him toward this false version of success, while hypnotizing him with their doubts and fears about his ability to achieve it. Ironically, it's this very program—initially designed to ensure that their child reach his potential—that alters his internal program and interferes with the full attainment of who he was meant to be.

With my own children, I was initially so anxious for the early maturation of their worldly selves to reflect well on them and on me that I pushed them out of my lap and pressured them to appear more grown up than they were ready to be. Not surprisingly, their spirits were wilting, and they were unable to live up to the kinds of precocity I expected.

The pain of seeing them floundering eventually awakened me to the remembrance that children are like blossoms on a tree, some opening early, while others bloom later; yet, all are precoded to be equally beautiful. Thus, I released mine from the ego race and not only became willing for them to develop more naturally and in harmony with their higher selves, but to be the last blossoms to open if that was who they were destined to be.

Although they each lacked precocity in a variety of areas, they grew steadily with happy hearts and thriving spirits under the new regime. As a result of my surrender to their unfolding in their own time and way, I stopped inflicting wounds on their development and interfering with the outcome. My new method of parental guidance not only trusted the butterfly within each child, but encouraged its development by keeping the goals of the higher self awake and active.

Interestingly, in the latter part of their high school years, my children began to blossom in a way that caught me by surprise. I'm grateful I had learned by then to view their personal successes and life journeys as their own, rather than a reflection on me or a boost to my own ego-based pride.

Similarly, it's critical that each of you let go of the current societal guidelines for raising children and learn to trust that just as the caterpillar is destined to become a butterfly, your child has his own magical destiny to fulfill beyond the needs and race of the ego.

Within this context, your primary job is to trust the potential of your child's higher self; look for it daily; and never lose faith in it as he goes through the long process and many stages required for it to unfold. In short, you must learn patience in tending the cocoon of your child's development while waiting for the precoded beauty of his butterfly to emerge.

Once we no longer feel pressured to rush our children's development so that they can win the race, we're free to relax and guide their personality development with increased patience. This patience provides the foundation on which we can merge love with discipline, rather than continue to swing between the two.

Grizzly Patience

In seeking a contrast to our current model of impatient, coercive parenting which swings us between nurturing and structure, the image of a grizzly mother, sluggish and languid as she emerges from hibernation, comes to mind. Because she feels no pressure to engage her cubs in a race to maturity, but trusts their optimal selves to unfold, she's able to remain patient, yet clear, in her handling of them.

Although the grizzly mother lolls about, licks her babies as they nurse, and gently plays or naps with them, her boundaries are strictly defined, and any cub who wanders off is indelicately retrieved by having his entire head engulfed in her large mouth. She's willing—without doubt or guilt—to provide him with a memorable lesson about limits. Yet once he's in bounds again, nursing, cuddling, teaching, and play are gently resumed with no lingering grudges.

The grizzly mother, one of the few animals obliged to spend several years teaching her young to survive, provides us with an equalized model of parenting. She favors neither love nor authority—nor does she swing on an emotional pendulum between these two parts of her nature. Although she's among the strongest of animals, she shows no signs of impatience or anger while disciplining her young; yet her rules remain firm, and broken ones are met with swift repercussions. She may seem indulgent at times, but her cubs soon discover that they are allowed to have as good a time as possible—so long as they remain within the constraints of this very firm but loving mother's boundaries.

The grizzly mother provides a delightful image of how offspring can be handled with firmness and clarity in an atmosphere of warm nurturing. It's time that we embrace her unpressured, noncompetitive model and discover how we, too, can become more trusting, centered, and balanced in our parenting.

Merging Your Child's Higher Self with the Personality He Forms

In order to do what the grizzly mother has done, you must first trust the presence of your child's intrinsic value and loving nature, rather than equate his lovability and worth with early maturation and success in the world by the ego self's standards.

The realization that your child's higher self and innate worth is already in place when he is born and need not be constructed, earned, or competed for frees you from rushing his achievements in order to gain value for him and pride for you. Instead, you can view his development as a more gentle and joyful process during which the intrinsic beauty of the "butterfly" within is recognized, honored, and included in the personality he develops for functioning in the world.

The key is that your child remain connected to the sweet and loving essence of the larger spiritual self and higher aspirations he brought with him so that they can permeate the personality of the smaller world self he must now form. In doing this, his personality becomes an extension of his true soul self—rather than a separate, opposing false self—and brims with the higher self's unlimited energies of love and joy.

A child who weaves the essence of his higher self into the formation of his personality doesn't lose touch with his intrinsic worth and feels no need to reign superior over others in a counterfeit effort to increase his worldly value. When a child is no longer required to gain supremacy in order to experience his worth, his need to compete for dominance and control naturally falls away.

Eliminating these separating energies of competition between children— as well as families, communities, and nations—frees each of us to remain good and loyal friends while keeping our naturally caring, cooperative natures and higher selves intact.

Thus, the goal of this book will be to show you how to raise the higher selves of your children by first getting out of the race and off of the swinging pendulum; trusting that the seed of a beautiful being has already been planted within the essence of your child; and allowing that seed to unfold at its own rate of growth without doubting its potential or interfering with the results.

Getting Started

Although many of you are anxious to learn about discipline, your efforts to manage your children can only succeed if love is consistently present. Thus, prior to addressing structure, I will show you how to cultivate steady feelings of caring in your hearts to ensure the success of your discipline. To accomplish this, I will show you first how to merge love with discipline, then how to love gently from the depth of your heart.

Putting the higher self in charge opens the way for new parenting goals and a restored society.

3

Balancing the Parental Seesaw

Merging Love with Discipline

The Second Key:

⏣⏣⏣

Get into balance by merging love with discipline.

As your child goes through the process of forming his personal style for functioning in the world, your job is to patiently trust his journey without swinging on the pendulum between sweetness and anger. Your goal, instead, is to maintain the equanimity of a grizzly mother as you gently guide your child through the developmental stages of his emerging personality.

Yet the question remains—what in the world does this patience, trust, and equanimity look like in the middle of raising a child? What is your role and how do you guide your child through this daily process without dominating, spoiling, or rushing him; feeling anxious or guilty; harboring anger; or getting confused and ending up back on the pendulum?

The first thing you must learn is how to merge love with discipline—since your ability to offer both at all times is what enables you to remain gently patient, balanced, and wise in your parenting.

Thus, the secret to successful parenting lies in knowing how to combine love with discipline and fulfilling these two goals of good parenting simultaneously. In order to accomplish this, you must learn to love and accept your child in the the middle of his crying, making a mistake, or misbehaving. You must also control and discipline him as needed, no matter how tenderly you are feeling toward him or how much you prefer to avoid conflict. In this way, you encircle both loving and correcting, bring these two opposites together, and execute them in the same moment. This merging of love with discipline enables you to both nurture and guide your child with balance at all times. It was this lesson that dramatically changed my parenting and put me back on course.

My Story: Getting into Balance

I got off to a bad start with my second child. She was on solid foods before she was a month old, a short-lived medical fad that was later discovered to trigger indigestion and allergies. Initially, I felt tender and nurturing toward this daughter I had longed for, but her digestive problems caused her so much discomfort that most of my efforts to love and cuddle her were met with squirmy rejection. She fussed or cried continuously, and I felt inadequate and powerless to help.

Over time, I began to respond to her fussiness with tension, while she reacted to my anxiety with even more crying. We were thrown into a cycle of resistance to one another that prevented us from maintaining our initial bond on a consistent basis. Instead, I had developed the habit of loving her deeply when she was content, but reverting to anger whenever she cried.

Feeling abandoned during those periods when my love was withdrawn, she developed into such an irritable child that sitters and relatives were reluctant to care for her, and her doctor recommended medication for hyper-activity. I realized that things weren't going well and felt anxious about our relationship and her falling behind in the race to maturity.

As time went on, the original cause of our problems faded into the back-ground, and I began to view her as a "difficult" child. I sought literature on "strong-willed" children to corroborate my diagnosis of the problem and held her fussy nature responsible for the struggle between us. This gave me an alibi for the times I felt resistant toward her. Yet I knew in my heart that there was no pardon for not steadily loving my child.

Nevertheless, I remained trapped in this predicament, convinced that my daughter was the source of our difficulties. I expected her, rather than myself, to change and longed for her to become a sweetly cooperative and success-ful child who would be easier for me to consistently love. Needless to say, she didn't change, and there was nothing to alter the unfortunate cycle that ensnared us.

One day it occurred to me that we had many years ahead of us, and that if our relationship didn't improve, it would surely spoil most of my adult years and her entire childhood. I further realized that such a young child couldn't be expected to have the maturity or resources to heal our relationship, and that I would have to behave as the adult and lead the way. It was up to me to find a different approach that would take me off of the continuum between liking her when she was content, then swinging over to disappointment and anger during those times when she was irritable.

What I discovered is that even when she was difficult, I could continue to feel loving toward her, rather than succumb to anger. Once I made the decision not to give up on my loving feelings for her, no matter how much she squirmed or cried, a new willingness to love her as she presented herself in every moment came over me. It was then that I committed to loving my daughter at all times, regardless of how many unhappy moments that might include.

As a result of my new resolve to consistently accept this child, something within me changed. My body no longer tensed in an effort to shield myself from her periods of unhappiness or make them go away. I now included whatever problems she imposed on my day and embraced the reality they offered. With this shift in my *willingness* to experience whatever unpleasantness entered our time together, something powerful happened. My heart fully opened to my daughter, and I was able to experience my love for her—even when she fussed and squirmed or cried for hours.

Soon after this discovery, my daughter lay on her bed having a tantrum over some minor problem, as I sat in an adjoining room. This time I didn't sit there with my usual impatience and anger over her tears, but with a new willingness to embrace this part of our day, no matter how long it took. Once she wound down, I went into her room and lay down beside her. She began to sob quietly as I held her in my arms with genuine love and caring. Within moments, a flood of emotion encircled us, and I knew that our relationship was healed. As I surrendered to my child's crying, she, in turn, yielded to my offer of love, and the result was almost mystical. By learning to sustain my love for her in the difficult moments, I had discovered how to love without conditions. That was my daughter's last tantrum, and the day marked the beginning of a new and wonderful bond between us.[2]

In addition to this problem with my daughter, I was experiencing difficulties handling my two children during those times when they were together. Although I had always enjoyed a smooth relationship with my son and had recently established a good one with my daughter, I still hadn't figured out how to handle the daily squabbles, jealousies, and chaos that developed between them. Thus, anytime they had some problem to resolve, I would lose touch with my tender, loving feelings and swing into my impatient, authoritarian ones.

Because there were so many quarrels to settle, I was habitually angry and had come to feel tense around my children. As a result, I often directed them to find some activity or friend in hopes of gaining relief from their squabbles. I cherished the peaceful hours when they were in school and noticed that my stomach tightened into a knot of resistance whenever their car pool delivered them home to me. I felt bad that having children had become such a challenge, as I had hoped for so much more when I started my family. It frankly worried me that my kids and I might spend the remainder of our years together trapped in this unfortunate dilemma.

I'm grateful it occurred to me that since I had enjoyed so much success with my new approach to handling my daughter, I could combine nurturing with structure while dealing with the problems between my two children. As a result, I adopted an attitude of accepting the many little interruptions, disputes, and problems they presented throughout each day as they surfaced, using whatever guidance, correction, or discipline was called for. The key was that I no longer felt irritated by my children's interruptions to my peace and was able to serenely help them unravel their problems and find appropriate solutions without my usual resistance, disappointment, or anger.

Before long, I could see how this new attitude of combining nurturing with discipline enabled me to love my children all day long—whether they were misbehaving or in harmony. Once this shift was made, the knots in my stomach dissolved, and I felt newly relaxed and comfortable around them at all times. They, in turn, sensed the constancy of my love and were no longer anxious about losing it during those times when there were problems. The effect was swift and powerful and completely transformed their development and our relationship. In fact, my children became two of my most treasured friends—and I became a favorite of theirs.

Initially, I thought I was the only mother in America who had experienced so much confusion about how to parent successfully and assumed that other households were filled with perfect family units. However, during my years as a counselor to a wide cross section of families, I had a chance to observe that people not only experience parenting as uniquely demanding, but that the majority view it as their greatest challenge. I learned from this exposure that parenting creates serious problems for a large segment of otherwise well-adjusted, bright, and successful people.

These observations are confirmed by any number of psychologists, including Louise Genevie and Eva Margolies (*The Motherhood Report*, 1987), who put together a compilation of statistics and trends on how mothers feel about parenting. Many, according to the report, had simply underestimated how stressful, endless, frustrating, and painful a job parenting would be.

As I pondered why so many people find this common vocation so challenging and what the solution might be, it occurred to me that an important part of the answer—merging love with discipline—lay right under our noses! If so, why had this simple solution to such a big problem been completely overlooked?

Merging Love with Discipline: Simple or Challenging?

The concept of being both loving and structured with children sounds simple, even obvious. Yet, if this was true, why wasn't it being used in more families and schools? Why had it been such a key discovery for me in relating to my children? Why has it so dramatically improved the interactions between children and teachers in schools now trying this program? And why has it so thoroughly changed the relationships between parents and children in families who have adopted this approach to parenting? In short, why has such a simple concept produced such startling results for so many people?

The reason is that although the idea of continuously loving a child sounds simple, it's something that most parents have their greatest trouble achieving. This is because very few families have learned to uphold loving feelings for their children in the middle of their daily interactions with them. Or, when they are able to sustain love, they do so at the expense of discipline. It's equally difficult to apply discipline with love, and most parents have simply not mastered these skills.

To reverse this trend and meet the challenge of merging love with discipline, parents must begin by first overcoming their particular barriers to holding love in their hearts while disciplining their children. Following is a list of the most common of these barriers.

Common Barriers to Sustaining Feelings of Love

Most of you understand the value of loving your children, and it's well documented that doing so is critical to their well-being. It's equally clear that a failure to love them will severely damage both their development and your relationship. Consequently, the recommendation that you give children ample doses of love has been prescribed so often that it has become a cliche, which has lost both its impact and meaning. Thus, in spite of its importance, suggesting that you consistently love your children is more easily said than done. Following are a number of attitudes and concerns that interfere with applying this simple piece of advice.

- **Caught in the Race.** Those of you who are anxious to have gifted children and get caught up in the race to catapult them to early maturity feel disappointed and angry when your children exhibit problems. You also have a tendency to push your kids to be goal-directed, busy, and fruitful and resist the unproductive, yet essential, "hanging out," socialization, and play of children. Yet, these attitudes compete with your ability to gently love and accept your child as he is, *before* he is accomplished and mature. Many of you couch the rejection you feel toward your child's immature and difficult moments in statements you have learned such as, "I like you, but not your behavior." Unfortunately, your disappointment, rejection, and anger serve as barriers to feelings of closeness and connection with your growing child, regardless of the words you use.

- **Overdirecting, Correcting, and Teaching.** Many of you get so wrapped up in your roles as teachers and correctors of your children's behaviors that your focus is primarily on what needs to be learned, changed, or fixed. As a result, you not only fail to see or respond to the good things already present in your kids, but forget to make time in your schedules and hearts for nurturing connections with them. Others of you are so caught up in your own race to be the best that you have become whirling dervishes with little time for loving connections with your kids.

- **Self-Absorbed.** Many of you were inadequately loved as children and get lost in your own feelings of emptiness. As a result, you have become so absorbed in attaining enough love to fill your own emptiness that you are unable to focus on giving it to others, including your children.

Common Barriers to Including Structure

Although most of you would like to have well-behaved children, a number of attitudes stand in the way of your comfort with discipline. As a result, a permissive style of parenting is currently in favor, and many of you are reluctant to assert your authority, even when it's clear that your children need more structure. The following barriers to parenting with discipline will help to explain why so many of you doggedly persist in parenting without structure in spite of poor results.

- **Anxious vs. Healthy Attachment.** A growing awareness taught in baby care books of the role bonding plays in a child's security and development has caused many of you to become overly anxious about the attachment process. As a result, rather than create healthy attachment with your growing child, you slide into anxious attachment and overcare, which paradoxically hurts his or her development. For example, many of you lie down with your child each time he naps or goes to bed for the night, not only during his first months of life, but well into his toddler years. Others refuse to leave your children with relatives or sitters and forgo all personal and couple activities in order to remain with them. Working parents understandably like to be with their kids during their time off, but some of you carry this too far and resist spending any leisure time whatsoever without children. Moreover, those of you who have created anxious attachment bonds with your children tend to believe that all crying is detrimental to their development and will do anything to prevent it, including never leaving them. Yet, not allowing a child to experience normal amounts of separation from you blocks the development of his individuating process, which is triggered under normal conditions by opportunities for him to learn that he *can* manage without you for increasingly extended, yet tolerable periods of time.

- **Acquired Discomfort with Discipline.** Many of you who were given too little love as children or too much discipline—or a combination of both—view disciplined children as victims. As a result, you avoid disciplining whenever possible or do so with great reluctance. This happens, in part, because you fail to realize that boundaries don't have to be delivered harshly or without love, but can be administered with equanimity, kindness, and care.

- **Fear of Pain.** Others of you feel so overwhelmed by the hurts of your own childhoods that you fear inflicting pain of any sort on your offspring. As a result, you are so upset by seeing your child "suffer" anytime he resists or cries during his period of adjustment to not getting his way that you back down on limits and consent to his demands.

- **Guilt and Conflict.** Many of you go into conflict or experience guilt whenever you are required to discipline. Thus, even though you want well-behaved kids, you constantly second-guess yourselves by questioning your fairness; whether or not your child will understand; if he really needs discipline; or if he will still like you. By entertaining these questions while you're in the middle of disciplining your child, you fill yourselves with so much conflict, doubt, and guilt that you ultimately back down.

- **Lack of Skills.** Others of you value authority and would like to use more of it with your children, but simply don't know how. Although you attempt a variety of methods, you lack the skills and consistency needed to sustain effective discipline.

■ **Honoring Your Child's Feelings.** Many of you interrupt your discipline in order to honor your child's feelings about it. Since these "feelings" usually represent his unhappiness and protests over the limits and consequences you have set, interrupting your discipline to let him express these complaints merely strengthens his resistance to rules.

■ **Fear of Breaking Your Child's Spirit.** In order to have a disciplined child, you must get him to surrender to the rules required for civilized and cooperative behavior. Yet if you perceive surrender as synonymous with breaking his spirit, you will resist requiring it. Paradoxically, children of parents who resist gaining surrender become resistant and willful, rather than open and spirited as their parents had hoped. This is because their energies have been marshaled against cooperation, rules, and responsibilities, rather than toward a creative purpose or cause. Not only do parents grow weary of these children, teachers must constantly discipline and isolate them and peers have trouble getting along with them. Thus, protecting your child's spirit by avoiding discipline actually backfires, whereas his spirit is strengthened, rather than broken, by normal levels of structure.

■ **The Desire for Democratic Discipline.** Some of you believe so strongly in democratic discipline that you offer your child extensive freedoms and an equal voice before he has learned to behave in a civilized manner or accept responsibility for his decisions. You make repeated requests that he voluntarily agree to your rules and constantly invite his cooperation. However, should he fail to respond, you are left with only wistful suggestions and emotional pleas for altering his behavior. When these also fail to elicit cooperation, you resort to the advice of "experts" who suggest locking *yourselves* in the bathroom. Yet once there, you realize that you have lost control over your dignity and reason as well as your child! The truth is, you can ignore behaviors, give "feeling" messages, and lock yourselves behind closed doors all you want, and your kids aren't necessarily going to respond. Those of you who persist in this approach are left helpless and begging for voluntary cooperation while your kids go progressively out of control.

You then defend your democratic approach to discipline with the argument that it's the "child's body," "his room," or "his life." Yet, upon exploring the logic of this premise, you can see that although a child's body may be "his," you wouldn't allow him to take it into the street, refuse to wash it, or pour drugs into it, whether or not he was able to understand the wisdom of your decision or voluntarily agree to it. Children have not fully developed physically, mentally, or emotionally, which is why they still live in your homes and rely on you for survival and guidance. If they were mature enough to make all of their own decisions and accept responsibility for the results, they would have their own apartments, and you could visit their homes or take them to dinner!

When you give a child too much freedom and independence before he has accepted the rules for responsible living, he fails to learn how to submit to even the most basic requests. Such children are not only endlessly demanding, but highly resistant. They refuse to stop unacceptable behaviors or comply with requests to clean up their messes or help with chores. As a result, they end up being self-centered and rejected by adults and peers alike, as they doggedly pursue "their way." Their inability to push through hard times or discipline themselves to perform unpleasant or difficult tasks interferes with successful performance, which further undermines their self-esteem and happiness. Yet, the idea still persists among parents committed to democratic discipline that these children will develop into bright and spirited young people who will eventually—perhaps magically—agree to behave.

Because children do, in fact, lack maturity, it's essential that you get comfortable with imposing structure and guidelines on them during those periods when they are not yet able to see the larger picture, don't always know what is best for them or others, and are not yet willing to voluntarily accept your guidance, no matter how lovingly it's given. In view of these factors, democracy should be exercised only in those areas of family life that don't involve discipline.

Common Barriers to Including Love with Structure

The greatest parenting challenge lies in being responsible for guiding, teaching, and urging your child toward his best self—which includes the need to notice his mistakes and help him correct them—while simultaneously accepting and loving him as he exists now, before his faults are rectified. Thus, as you strive to accept your child in each moment, while also correcting whatever state of error he may be in, it feels as though you are trying to meet two conflicting goals.

Consequently, even when you have learned to both love your children and impose structure on them, it's hard to grasp the idea that the two can be combined at all times. Following are the primary barriers to this awareness.

■ **Doubting That Love and Authority Can Be Mixed.** Because loving and disciplining a child seem like such opposite experiences, many of you have trouble trusting how well they go together and simply never try it.

■ **The Challenge of Maintaining Loving Feelings During Hard Times.** Many of you have trouble accessing loving feelings toward your children in the middle of the chaotic times or when you are required to discipline. Thus, although you start out with a commitment to love, the moment your child misbehaves you feel disappointed, tense, and angry and withdraw your love as you discipline him. Only after the problem is resolved do you return to your softer, more loving feelings. Yet, as soon as another problem surfaces, the cycle repeats itself, and you are back to swinging on the pendulum.

■ **The Belief That Disappointment and Anger Enhance Discipline.** Much of the literature has taught you to believe that you can't love a child and discipline him at the same time. This concept was reinforced in the 1960s and 1970s with the popularity of behavior modification, a reward system designed to create behavior change. In applying this method with children, attention and nurturing were used as reinforcers for good conduct and withdrawn during times when the child misbehaved. Because a lingering belief in the value of withdrawing love from a misbehaving child continues to influence child-rearing practices, many of you not only fear that kindness to a wayward child will promote disobedience, but that disappointment and anger will motivate him to cooperate.

To the contrary, discipline administered by a disappointed or angry parent is both ineffective and toxic and results in greater management problems. By contrast, the child who feels loved will want to cooperate with the person who cares for him. Thus, anytime nurturing is combined with discipline and rules are clearly enforced in a neutral, loving context, parental effectiveness is greatly optimized.

Merging Love with Authority: What It Looks Like

Each of you will recognize your own personal barriers to loving a child, disciplining him, and merging your love with discipline. Most of you will also see the value in resolving these obstacles to bringing love into your teaching moments and teaching to your loving times—since only then will your teaching be effective, your love fulfilling, and your parenting balanced. To help you achieve these critical goals, the following examples will provide you with models of what love, discipline, and a combination of the two look like.

The Loving Component: A Model for Gentleness

One of my children's favorite adventures when they were little was to visit an assembly of pigeons that gathered daily on a big, open lawn at the Honolulu Zoo. Thus, before a trip to the zoo, they would carefully put together a large bag of bread in anticipation of feeding these feathered friends. Yet upon arriving, whenever they got excited and ran stomping and screaming at the pigeons, the frightened birds would fly away, and my toddlers were left on an empty lawn with a bag full of bread. When I taught them to approach the birds, instead, with quiet care and gentleness, the birds sensed the difference and were more trusting. Only then were my children able to stand in the midst of the flock, feeding and befriending the birds.

It's the same for you in relating to your offspring. Whenever you stomp and shout as you approach your child, you evoke tension and fear in him, and he becomes too withdrawn and anxious to listen. In fact, he becomes so frozen with emotional paralysis that his system shuts out whatever message you had hoped to deliver. To help your child to feel calmer and better able to listen, you will have to approach him with more gentleness and love. Once he feels safe in your presence, he will view you as a trustworthy teacher and friend and will remain more relaxed and open to your love and guidance.

The Discipline Component: A Model for Gentleness

I suspect that we all prefer to fly with an airline pilot who is confident about being the commander of his plane. Such a pilot evokes feelings of security and respect in his passengers, which allows them to relax and not worry about managing the flight. By contrast, if we found ourselves in the plane of a pilot who felt insecure about taking charge and polled the passengers for help with navigating decisions or gave up on his role as commander and locked himself in the bathroom, we would feel understandably disquieted!

The same uneasiness develops in your child when you are unsure of yourself and fail to claim your parental authority. Such uncertainty on your part leaves him feeling unprotected in this big, complex world, and he may withdraw, become hyperactive, or misbehave as a way to express his uneasiness or to force you to draw clearer boundaries around him. Other kids strive to assume a leadership position in order to generate a feeling of strength in their households, much as a passenger—equally unequipped and overwhelmed by the task—might try to fly a plane if the pilot refused to do so. This example demonstrates how claiming your position at the head of the household will evoke feelings of security, respect, and relief in your children. As a result, they will see you as a wise leader and will be better able to relax and surrender to your authority and guidance.

Combining Both Components: A Model for Expressing Authority with Love

My son enjoyed his first summer job as a lab assistant for his high school science department. He loved the staff, his coworkers, the students, and the program. But, most of all he loved the responsibility he was given and the fact that he was treated as a peer by teachers in the department.

The following summer he and his student coworker returned to this rewarding job and, on their own initiative, cleaned out the disordered lab in preparation for another summer of assisting. However, they soon discovered that the new teacher on staff expected resistance from student workers and gruffly barked his requests as if they were orders.

After a few weeks, my son shared the effect this unfriendly attitude was having on him and explained that it evoked a desire in him not to cooperate. He felt as though he would lose some invisible battle if he did what he was ordered to do, whereas during the previous summer when he was cordially asked to do the very same tasks, he wanted to perform them to the best of his ability.

Fortunately, my son viewed this experience as an opportunity to note the contrast between gentle and autocratic styles and made the decision to remain cooperative. However, a younger child, not yet formed, who is similarly bombarded with unfriendly commands would be less equipped to make the same choice and would probably succumb to the urge not to cooperate.

As we can see from this example, when adults lack gentleness in their approach to authority, it seems to the child that he is on an opposing team, and his goal is no longer one of cooperation. It shifts, instead, to an urge to fight, and he looks for ways to upset or outsmart the adult he views as his adversary. Before long, such interactions between adults and children turn into power struggles, with losses and pain for all parties.

By contrast, parents who are at ease with their authority and know how to remain gentle, calm, and caring will have children who feel secure and close to them, see them as friends, and want to cooperate with their boundaries and goals.

Merging Love with Authority: Putting the Parts Together

A child who is inadequately loved not only experiences feelings of abandonment, but becomes pervasively insecure. The dismay he feels may be expressed by passive despair or overly active energy, as he frantically searches for a lap, a reassuring voice, loving arms, or some other sign that he is loved and protected in this large, uncertain world. Other children experience the rejection as an assault on their very being and, if they don't drown in despair, may strike out in anger against its unfairness.

We see this reaction because children simply can't feel peaceful or settle down, much less pay attention to your lessons or rules, until they're secure in knowing that they are loved. I have witnessed many children thought to have attention deficit disorder (ADD) or need medication for hyperactivity settle down and become uniquely peaceful once their parents learned to maintain love for them even during those times when they misbehaved and required discipline.

Similarly, whenever parental structures and boundaries are undefined or lacking, a child feels insecure and becomes overactive as he searches for the parameters of his world. It's as though he is in a swimming pool with shifting sides that give way rather than hold firm, forcing him to focus his attention on where the edges might be during any given moment. Under these conditions, a child understandably becomes frantic as he checks and rechecks his boundaries in an attempt to draw a reliable parameter around himself in which to securely operate.

It has been a remarkable experience for me to witness many overactive and disobedient children, also thought to be hyperactive or to have ADD, relax in a clump of relief once they were given some reliable boundaries. Feeling secure at last, these kids were able to behave appropriately for the first time and enjoy the experience of being in life's "pool" without worrying about the edges.

As a consultant to elementary schools, I have also been asked on occasion to restrain a child who has gone out of control. Whenever these children have experienced my calm strength and clear willingness to impose a boundary on them, they have surrendered as if they had found what they were searching for. Because my limits were imposed with love, which I consciously invited into my heart and directed at the child involved, each one I restrained later sought me out for a hug whenever I visited his or her school.[3]

In order for nurturing to be felt or structure to have an effect, both must be provided simultaneously. Whenever one is utilized without the other, it loses its power and becomes ineffective, as the child, worried and distracted by the absence of the missing component, puts all of his attention on relocating it.

Thus, only when parents succeed in blending love with authority will their child no longer be faced with periods when love has been withdrawn or times when discipline is lacking. As a result, he won't think that he is loved less when he's making a mistake, acting immature, or breaking a rule. And he won't think that he is loved more when he's obeying the rules and behaving maturely. He will be handled differently, but he won't be loved differently. Consequently, he will have the security of knowing that he can rely on both nurturing and structure in his life at all times.

The Effect of Balanced Parenting on a Child's Development

As we have discussed, failing to merge love with discipline interferes with your child's overall potential, whereas offering him a blend of both enhances his maturational process. By reviewing each of your child's developmental stages, you can further see the effect that love merged with discipline will have on specific stages of his development as well as the impact it has when this is lacking.

The Infant to Five-Year-Old Period: The Caterpillar Stage
(The Years at Home, Preschool, and Kindergarten)

The child from infancy to age five is immersed in a world where—much like the caterpillar—he is faced with the challenge of learning about the physical-sensory environment around him.

Most of you are quite patient at the beginning of your child's learning program and tend to forgive his ineptness and mistakes at this juncture. Yet once he gets beyond this initial learning stage, your expectations rise, and you grow less patient with his immaturity and errors. In addition, the child approaching two wants to explore his environment as far as his boundaries will allow and thus tests the limits by waging his first challenges to your authority. Whenever your impatience with his immaturity and challenges goes unchecked, it can create enough tension between you to interfere with his development.

In addition to learning about his physical world and its limits, the young child is working on establishing feelings of security, based on the strength of his relationships, first with Mother, then Father, and finally with his extended family and others. (When Father functions as a primary parent or full coparent, this happens first with him or at the same time as bonding with Mother.) As a result, sometime between two-and-a-half to three years of age, a child whose primary bonds have remained intact will feel secure and at ease in the world, connected to both parents and extended family, and feeling safe enough to develop friendships with teachers, peers, and others.

Parental Goals During the Infant to Five-Year-Old Stage. Your objective during this early stage of your child's development is to establish a relationship with him that embraces both love and authority.

Initially, you will focus solely on loving your child, since your early nurturing will give him an experience of feeling loved and safe during the period when he is only a wanter and has not yet begun to develop his fulfiller.

However, as your child gets mobile and begins to exercise his own fulfiller, your goal must expand to one of continuing to love him—including his ineptness—while administering boundaries and guiding him through his mistakes. When you are able to lovingly contain your child within safe, appropriate parameters, he learns to trust your love and friendship while surrendering to your boundaries and guidance.

Thus, a two-year-old who is grabbing, hitting, and biting or running away must not be disliked but merely restrained until he is ready to cooperate. Similarly, a three- or four-year-old may be allowed to walk on his own at the park or mall so long as he accepts the limits you have set. However, if he breaks those boundaries and touches forbidden objects or darts away, he will lose that freedom and must hold your hand or sit in a cart. Although it may be a challenge to deal with the inevitable crying that results when your toddler loses his freedom, you must have both the courage and loving countenance to face his tears if you are to raise a safely manageable and socialized child. In short, you must learn to stay calm—even if he has a tantrum—while also requiring that he surrender to your limits.

Many of you in this situation lose it on one side or the other. You either ignore the authority side of your parenting, simply because you don't wish to deal with your child's resistance to your boundaries. Or you require that he accept your limits, but do so with disappointed scoldings and anger or even shaming or hitting, as you completely lose touch with the loving component of your parenting.

To succeed in balanced parenting, you must find the courage to calmly thwart or restrain your child, to neutrally endure his tantrum without showing much interest in it, and after it's over, to lovingly help him to understand why he lost his freedom. When this happens, your child not only yields to the love you offer, but surrenders the impulses of his "immature boss" to the management of your "mature boss." This surrender is critical to the normal development of his unfolding personality.

The Reward of Balanced Parenting During the Early Years. When love and authority are in balance during the infant to five-year-old period, your young child feels secure in knowing that he is loved, his world is ordered, and that he is in the care of someone who is strong and wise enough to assume a leadership role with him.

As he yields to both your love and structure, he surrenders the infantile boss of his undeveloped fulfiller to the wiser boss of your matured fulfiller. In this surrender, he is able to let go, accept your guidance, and learn to behave cooperatively as a way to gain and maintain the freedoms he desires.

Once this is accomplished, the remainder of the infant to five-year-old stage will not only be smoother, but will pave the way for an even calmer period from ages six to eleven years. This all sounds so easy—but it only happens when love and authority are in balance!

The Loss That Goes with Unbalanced Parenting. Whenever your love and authority are out of balance during the infant to five-year-old period, your child fails to surrender to either your nurturing or your structure or both. As a result, he not only feels less loved and secure, but refuses to yield to the mature boss of your fulfiller and behaves according to the dictates of the tyrannical, yet immature, boss of his own unformed fulfiller.

Those of you with an unsurrendered child will notice that you are having trouble managing him and may receive your first reports from brave friends and good teachers that he is having some adjustment problems. Many of you ignore these early warnings and rationalize that because your child is young, he will outgrow his problems. In truth, this early feedback is a serious indicator of disharmony in your child's environment, and you would be wise to take heed and bring your parenting into balance.

Joey

By the age of four, Joey had been asked to leave his second preschool. Because he had no rules at home, he ignored them at school as well, and any attempts to structure or control his behavior were met with violent tantrums. Joey was equally unable to function appropriately with peers, since he refused to comply with their limits, and it wasn't long before both teachers and classmates began to reject him.

Extreme amounts of nurturing had thrown Joey's parents out of balance in their parenting. In fact, they were so hesitant to assume authority that they made only meek attempts to dissuade him from his demands before succumbing to doing things his way. Dad played with Joey by the hour, accepting commands of where to stand and what to do and allowing his son to win at every game. Mom cooked whatever meals Joey demanded and capitulated to his orders to lie down with him whenever it was time for him to sleep. Both parents believed that they had no right to impose their will or limits on Joey and were afraid of breaking his spirit or curbing his precocity by requiring that he suppress any of his desires. They even felt a sense of pride in the ways he used to outsmart them and took pleasure in reporting his pranks to friends. Unwittingly these parents had raised an unmanageable, unpopular child who needed a great deal of help to heal this injury to his development.

Fortunately, Joey's parents were so shocked by his second removal from school that it forced them to face the seriousness of his problem. Although they had previously ignored the glares of strangers and warnings of friends and teachers, when Joey became unwelcome at two schools, his parents confronted the fact that their son's "immature boss" had seized control of their entire household. As a result, they worked hard to bring authority into their home and get back in charge. Within a short time, they found the courage to endure their son's tantrums and leave malls, restaurants, parks, and parties whenever he misbehaved as well as calmly hold him to their limits and rules at home. In short, they required that Joey surrender his "immature boss" to the "mature boss" of each of his parents.

The result was remarkable! Within a few months, Joey had stopped all tantrums and was able to accept most directions from adults. He was better able to play with peers and became a happier child with a more relaxed and flexible approach to life. Although Joey had further to go, adding authority to love had offered him a new chance to be a normally socialized child.

The Six- to Eleven-Year-Old Period: Integration and the Chrysalis Stage (The Elementary Years from First to Sixth Grade)

Those of you who failed to establish love and authority with your child during the years from infancy through age five would be wise to do so with your six- to eleven-year-old, since problems resulting from an imbalance in parenting worsen as a child gets older. For those families who successfully established a balance between love and authority during the infant to five-year-old period, your child's development will be as follows.

Similar to the chrysalis stage of a butterfly, the six- to eleven-year-old period represents a time of integrating those things your child has already learned. He is no longer confused about how to express himself; manage daily routines; or manipulate eating utensils, writing materials, or playground equipment. He also knows and accepts his limits at home and school. Once these learning tasks have been accomplished, he has mastered much of what he will need to know about his physical environment for a while. Thus, his primary job during this period will be to further assimilate and synthesize the lessons previously learned as he ventures into the world to try them out in more expanded settings.

Since this stage of your child's development is a time of integration, those of you who established a balance between love and authority during the infant to five-year-old period will experience it as a rather smooth and easy phase. Furthermore, because the six- to eleven-year-old child who has been raised in a balanced framework doesn't challenge his parents very often or vehemently, living with him can be delightful. I don't mean to imply that there will be no problems, since there are always some issues to address throughout a child's development. However, those problems will occur less frequently and can be resolved within the context of a framework that is already in balance.

Teaching Parental Values. Those of you who have created enough balance in your parenting to experience this stage as a smoother, integrative period often think that your job is complete. Others of you believe that your child is primarily formed in the period from infancy to five years old and assume that he won't need much more parenting. As a result, you stop paying so much attention to his needs and shift your focus to increasing your work schedules or other obligations.

This notion is a false one. Although his early learning is indeed behind him, your child's fulfiller continues to develop as he examines his beliefs and searches for ways to express his evolving self. Thus, it's critical that you remain an integral part of your six- to eleven-year-old's life during this formative period, rather than turn so much influence over to chance, television, or peers who may espouse immature, anti-adult ways of coping.

Because the period from six to eleven is a time when your child is comfortable with his continued dependence on you, likes and trusts you, and views you as a worthy teacher, it's an opportune time to deepen your close-ness. You can do this best by sharing yourself, listening to him, and explor-ing such things as how to be a caring person who lives life from the highest self. Since this period offers such a rich opportunity for closeness and teach-ing altruistic values to the high-minded preadolescent, it's critical that you use it productively.

Maintaining Love and Authority. In addition to remaining an active part of your six- to eleven-year-old's life, it's essential that you hold a balance between love and authority in your relationship with him. Consequently, those of you who have already established this in the infancy to five-year-old period must remember to maintain that balance throughout the six- to eleven-year-old stage. To do this, you must guard against the tendency to overlook physical contact and connected times as your child grows bigger and you get busier. You must also protect against becoming so inattentive dur-ing this easier period that you fail to monitor his expanding boundaries or follow through on your rules.

New Challenges to Holding the Balance. Even those of you who have established a balance between love and authority with your infant to five-year-old will find that your six- to eleven-year-old periodically challenges you. This is because even cooperative children sometimes challenge, particularly when they are feeling so good about themselves that they question their need of you. Yet, when you are clear about staying in the parental role and know how to remain calmly in control, such provocations are short-lived.

On the other hand, those of you who are in awe of these challenges or erroneously believe that they are important to your child's development and thus back down from your authority will be plagued with many more tests. You must also remember that anytime your child's immature boss success-fully defies your mature boss, he will try it again. If he continues to be suc-cessful, it won't take long before your naive and immature child will be in control of your household.

Consequences of Failing to Establish a Balance During the Elementary Years. For those of you who never did establish a balance between love and authority during the infant to five-year-old period, the six- to eleven-year-old stage will be more chaotic and problematic. If you are in this category, you will recognize yourselves, since you will be struggling for control and may feel uneasy in the presence of your children. You may also receive new or continuing reports that your child is having adjustment problems outside of your home or notice that he is experiencing rejection from his teachers and peers.

Getting Back on Track. At this point, you have another opportunity to establish a balance between love and authority. However, if this is being addressed for the first time with an acting-out or passively withdrawn six- to eleven-year-old who has developed some bad habits, the task becomes a remedial one and is more difficult to accomplish than it was in the infant to five-year-old period. Challenging as it is, it can—and must—be addressed.

I disagree with the idea that a child's personality is set by this age, implying that little can be done to improve a situation that has gone awry. In contrast to this popular view, I have witnessed countless dramatic changes in short periods of time accomplished by motivated parents, willing to do the work necessary to establish love and authority with their six- to eleven-year-olds.

Kristi

Kristi's mother remained out of balance on the authoritarian side of her parenting until her daughter was eleven. She was a career schoolteacher who ran a disciplined classroom with high standards. As a busy single mother she ran her household in much the same way and was a strict perfectionist who made unreasonable demands on her only child. She scolded and spanked for tasks done sloppily, food left on the plate, and homework done inaccurately. Although structure and discipline were clearly present in this household, warmth and love were seriously lacking.

It didn't take Kristi long to realize that her mother liked her best when she did things right, and she initially strove to please. However, because her mother was always so disappointed and angry, Kristi eventually got discouraged. Since making mistakes only got her into trouble, she began to sidestep all activities that could be done incorrectly. The lower Kristi's performance dropped as a result of her avoidant behavior, the less her mother liked her and the more disconnected their relationship became.

When Kristi, at the age of eleven, received an especially bad report card, her mother flew into a rage, and Kristi ran away from home. At that point, Mother sought professional help and began for the first time to comprehend the need for adding love to her authority. It was difficult for her, but she worked hard to become more gentle and loving. Although Kristi had developed a firm shell of protection, she softened when she saw that her mother was trying. Kristi had a long way to go to regain the confidence she had lost, but once love and authority were in better balance at home, her chances for developing normally were renewed.

The Twelve- to Seventeen-Year-Old Period: Breaking out of the Cocoon (The Junior High and High School Years)

The twelve- to seventeen-year-old is no longer in the calm, easy period of the six- to eleven-year-old, but has entered into a more challenging stage of development similar to that of the infant to five-year-old. Much like the butterfly emerging from its cocoon, the teenager is poised on the edge between dependence and independence, gathering enough courage and skills to take flight into autonomy and freedom. To prepare for this step, he will continue to borrow from your fulfiller for a little guidance, while using and strengthening his own fulfiller ever more vigorously. (See Figure 3.)

This period goes best when it's a cooperative effort between parents and teen in which parents gradually pass the baton of their child's life over to him in a cooperative interplay between them. This is rather easily accomplished anytime parents voluntarily give their adolescent increasing opportunities to practice using his own fulfiller, while providing encouragement and guidance as well as the condition that he use his freedom responsibly.

By contrast, it can go badly when parents are unaware of their adolescent's need to take over the reins of his life, hold onto them too tightly, and require that he fight for every opportunity to make his own decisions and manage his life. It also goes badly when parents turn over the reins too quickly without also requiring responsibility or when they are prepared to turn over the reins, but their teen would rather rebel to gain his independence than accept the baton offered and use it responsibly.

This intense period of learning catches your adolescent by surprise and you off guard. Furthermore, because he has just completed a smooth and easy period and seems so physically mature and capable, you are dismayed to discover how much encouragement and guidance your teen requires at this juncture. Yet, in spite of his need for more help than expected, the twelve- to seventeen-year-old challenges your authority as well as the previously close feelings between you. This rejection of your love and guidance makes it ever more challenging to give him the loving support he actually wants and needs.

Figure 3. Diagram of the Individuating Process

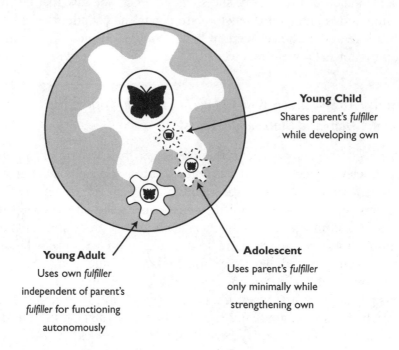

Young Child
Shares parent's *fulfiller*
while developing own

Young Adult
Uses own *fulfiller*
independent of parent's
fulfiller for functioning
autonomously

Adolescent
Uses parent's *fulfiller*
only minimally while
strengthening own

Maintaining Love and Authority During the Junior High and High School Years. Your goal during this period is to stay on duty as a parent while discovering how to preserve whatever love and authority has previously been established. In addition, you must grant your child increasingly more independence based on growing levels of accountability. If you are successful in maintaining this balance throughout the teen years, your adolescent has the gentle, yet clear environment he needs for strengthening his own fulfiller enough to move responsibly toward independence without trauma. Under these conditions the teen years can be surprisingly delightful for both of you.

Failing to Establish or Maintain Love and Authority. On the other hand, families unable to maintain the balance between love and authority are mystified by how fast they lose loving feelings and parental authority as their previously agreeable and loving child becomes sullen, rejecting, sassy, and unco-operative. Once this happens, things go rapidly out of control, and the teen years become disruptive, unhappy ones for the entire family.

Those of you who never succeeded in establishing love and authority at any point along the way will have teens whose "immature bosses" convert during this period to "rebellious tyrants." These teens go ever more out of control at all levels, which creates turmoil and tragedy for everyone involved. The only hope for those of you in this predicament lies in finding skilled professional help to guide you in establishing control balanced with love. (See **Adolescent** entry in the Problem-Solving Guide.)

Peg

Peg's mother lacked authority in her parenting and remained out of balance on the permissive side until Peg was well into adolescence. As a divorced, working parent, full of guilt, she felt compelled to compensate for a missing father and busy mother. She couldn't bear to say "No" to her little girl and pampered her from the time she was young. As a result, Peg learned to rule her household with sassing and tantrums and, over time, developed into an unpleasantly self-centered teenager who was unpopular with peers and adults alike.

When Peg, at seventeen, insisted that her mother not get remarried, her mother stood her ground for the first time in many years. As a result, Peg screamed and pouted for days before running away to the home of a cousin. When her mother still wouldn't bend to her daughter's demands, Peg took an overdose of pills before phoning her mother for help.

After much thought and counseling support, Mother realized that she had to hold to her decision, no matter what tactic her daughter tried. When she visited Peg in the hospital she told her with resolve, "I love you very much and hope you will want to live out the life God has given you—so that we can enjoy more time together; but, if you decide differently, that's your decision—and I do still plan to marry Jim."

Tears streamed down Peg's face as the "fight" went out of her. She had finally surrendered to the reality that she couldn't force her mother—or life—to always go her way. Peg discovered something that day in the hospital that she could have learned years earlier, had her mother possessed the courage to not only love her little girl, but provide her with discipline as well.

Eighteen and Beyond: Independence and the Butterfly Stage (The College and Working Years)

The stage from eighteen and beyond includes the final steps of letting go for the parent and gaining independence for the child.

It's important to understand that once a child has finished his education, he should be a contributing member of society. As such, his metamorphosis from infancy to adulthood is complete, and it's essential that you now set him free to test his wings in the real world without further control.

Only by being independent, using his own fulfiller, and taking responsibility for the results of his choices and life will your young adult discover the strength and power that lie within him to design and create a world of his own, separate from your supervision. Yet even when offspring become adults, friendship and mutual support—or even living together—are available to the degree that it's desired by both parties and is done with mutual respect and as equals.

It's important at this juncture to allow your offspring to fully manage their own lives and permit them to make their mistakes as they find their way. By doing this, the essence of love is maintained while authority is withdrawn. The only thing left for you to offer is love without strings—much in the way you would love a friend or enjoy the flight of a butterfly without directing its course.

The Gift of Unconditional Love

As we have discussed, an essential component for successfully raising children is to take the two parts of parenting—the loving, nurturing component and the structured, disciplined one—embrace them both, and employ the two simultaneously.

Once you have removed disapproval from your parenting and can maintain feelings of love and caring for your child in the same moment you are holding your boundaries or making corrections, you have discovered the secret of truly balanced parenting, epitomized by the gentle grizzly mother. It's this kind of enduring love without conditions that preserves your relationship as you go through the long process of molding, guiding, correcting, and disciplining your child as he grows ever so slowly toward adulthood. In learning to do this, you become patient tenders of the cocoon, while trusting your butterfly to emerge.

It's important to remember that learning to love your child without conditions is a lofty goal that can be accomplished in a moment—or it could take a lifetime! Thus, you shouldn't feel guilty each time you notice yourself swinging on the pendulum between love and authority, but can simply notice it and shift to balance. Meanwhile, it will work best if you view your growing child as a gift who offers you the opportunity to continuously practice this heightened experience of loving unconditionally.

Balancing love with authority while trusting your child's inherent worth encourages him to bring his loving essence to the world through the personality he forms while here.

4

The Good, the Bad, and the Reality

Embracing Life's Agenda

The Third Key:

ඟඟඟ

*Embrace all of life's agenda, including the challenges of
the parenting journey.*

To succeed in blending love with discipline, you must first learn to be happy with your kids during the good times and the bad, since only then will you feel genuinely accepting of your children while in the middle of raising them. In fact, it's this attitude of acceptance that will assure your success in parenting, whereas a failure to learn it will cause everything to go wrong.

Yet mastering this attitude can be a challenge while you're in the midst of child-rearing. In fact, today might have been the day your toddler spilled ketchup on your new carpet, ignored the neighbor who came to play, and sucked his fingers until his visitor left. Then, he resisted taking a bath, but once in, splashed water all over the floor and wouldn't get out. Your elementary-aged child might have teased her brother until he cried, argued with her sister over the front seat of the car, and refused to clean up her messes or do her chores. Your preteen might have procrastinated over your request for help with the dishes or been rude to his grandmother, while your teen stayed up half the night phoning friends instead of doing her homework. You may be wondering why you had children at all and can hardly wait to get this crew to bed. Yet the moment you walk into their bedrooms and see them sleeping as peacefully as angels, your heart melts, and you fall in love with them all over again!

Loving the Sleeping Angel

Why is it that your heart spills over with love the moment you see your children snuggled into bed for the night? It's a very important question, since the answer clarifies why your loving feelings for them so often go awry during their waking hours.

The answer is that it's easier to remember your love for a child once he has surrendered himself to sleep for the night, since in his peaceful slumber he no longer annoys you with his antics. While your child rests, you have no ruined carpets or wet floors to upset you, no teasing, quarrels, or rudeness to distract you, and no resistance to responsibilities and rules to block your tender feelings for him. Whenever you observe your child resting as peacefully as an angel, you are able to sense the essence of his higher self, and your heart softens with love. In the quiet of night, it becomes clear that it's the various behaviors your child selects throughout the day that interfere with the constancy of your love for him.

Loving the Active—Even Rude or Irresponsible—Angel

When parents in my classes first begin to understand the value of being simultaneously loving and structured with their children, the most common question asked is, "How? How do we begin?"

The first step lies in learning to reach deep within yourself and tune into those feelings for your child that most touch your heart—to go beyond his behaviors and look for the angel in the very moment he's racing across the room or refusing to do a chore. In short, your goal is to discover how to feel the same way toward your child while he's awake, busy, and active—or even resistant, rude, and irresponsible—that you do in those moments when he's your sleeping angel.

In order to accomplish this goal of consistently loving your children no matter what problems they create, you must learn to put life with kids on your daily agenda. This demands that you embrace all aspects of living, which includes the unpleasant along with the pleasant. To do this, you must come to terms with the fact that life isn't always going to provide you with trouble-free moments, and that life with children will bring you an abundance of the challenging times.

Parental Illusions

Most of you hold onto the illusion that your time with your kids will be filled with nothing but serenely ordered and pleasant moments. You cling to the fantasy of having a child who wakes up in a cheerful mood and easily pulls on a clean, matching outfit. Next, he makes his bed, feeds the dog, then eats his breakfast with enthusiasm before rinsing his dishes, brushing his teeth, and patiently waiting for his car pool. Once at school, friends swarm around

Figure 4. A Parent's Ideal Agenda

him as he makes sure to treat each one kindly. He returns home with papers full of glowing remarks about his schoolwork and character, chats about his day, and shares his heart. After completing his homework, he practices his music or art before going to sports practice, then spends the remainder of the afternoon entertaining his siblings. When evening comes, he picks up his messes and hops into a tub or shower to prepare for dinner and bed. At the table, he's full of bright remarks and regal manners, and after some family time, is ready to retire. He gets himself to bed, leaving you to reflect on another wonderful day with your well-behaved, bright, and delightfully mature child.

Even parents of teens continue to dream of adolescents who are sensitive and open; voluntarily helpful; academically keen; fun and popular; replete with ambition, talents, and skills; and wonderfully responsible and mature.

In my parenting classes, I ask how many parents started out with this fantasy of the ideal agenda, and they all answer affirmatively. (See Figure 4.) Then, I ask how many still hold onto it, and everyone laughs. Next, I ask how many secretly—at least partially—continue to cling to this illusory image, and most sheepishly raise their hands.

Getting Real

In reality, life is full of moments that go quite well or even wonderfully, laced with those that don't go as well or turn out quite badly. When children are involved, there are considerably more of the difficult times, due to the fact that they are not yet mature. Thus, you can count on a healthy number of unpleasant moments, along with the good times, on your daily agenda during the period it takes your child to grow from infancy to adulthood.

This is why your young child is just as likely to awaken on the grouchy side as on the sweet one. Instead of acting pleasant and cooperative as you had hoped, he has trouble figuring out what to wear, yet objects to every combination you suggest. When he finally makes an unmatched selection, he's so out of sorts that he can't pull up his pants. He then responds to this self-made dilemma by demanding that you help, but screams his displeasure when you do. He later ignores your reminders to make his bed, and you find him playing with the dog instead of feeding him. He may request cereal for breakfast on the morning you have made eggs, or waffles on the day you have made pancakes—but then pushes the food back and forth on his plate, rather than eat it. Moments later, he might shift unexpectedly to a better mood, clear his dish without objection, brush his teeth before any reminders, and pick up his messes while waiting for the car pool.

Similarly, your teen may wake up in a cheerful mood and be helpful and talkative before school. However, he may return home with a cloud over his head and act surly and rude, while procrastinating over his chores and homework.

Most of you resist this more chaotic reality. You didn't order it from life's menu, want no part of it, and hold onto the notion that such difficult times have found their way into the wrong household. Yet no matter how long or strenuously you resist or deny such an unwelcome reality, disagreeable moments continue to appear on a daily basis in the lives of families with children. (See Figure 5.)

The truth of this presented itself to our family one evening during dinner, while our four-year-old entertained a tantrum in her room. Next, she was clinging to the walls and sobbing as she dragged herself for the third time down our long hallway into the dining area and stood tear-stained and pitiful before us. Once again, I "wrestled" her back to her room and returned somewhat disheveled to resume my meal. As another piercing shriek of protest traveled down the hallway, my husband pounded his fist on the table and declared, "Can't I come home after a day's work to a little peace and quiet?!" Our six-year-old son earnestly inquired, "Where did you get that idea, Dad?" My husband paused for a moment before replying, "I don't know where I got it!" And, we all had a good laugh!

Like my husband, most of you react to the chaos in your homes with surprise and shock or become upset when things have gone off course. This part of the day doesn't match your expectations, and you feel disappointed when your illusion is shattered by how children actually behave. You assume something has gone uniquely wrong in your particular household, and your

Figure 5. A Parent's Real Agenda

belief that other families have only sweet, calm moments adds to your disillusionment.

One father, still clinging to his hope for smoother times, inquired during a lecture I delivered to parents of adolescents, "My child still loses things. Isn't there some magical cure for this?" The other parents chuckled knowingly, so I asked the group how many of their kids—even as adolescents—were still capable of misplacing things. Most of the hands went up, cautiously at first. Yet after looking around the room, these parents soon saw how many other hands were also raised, and the realization slowly dawned that their child was not only normal, but typical. In fact, one of the benefits of my monthly class is that it allows parents to see how many other families share the same challenges they have been battling in the privacy of their homes. It becomes apparent in a group setting that most of the problems parents have with their kids represent normalcy rather than a deviation from it. Yet, in spite of the universality of so many difficult moments in the lives of families, the majority of you cling tenaciously to your vision of a trouble-free and tranquil home.

If You Want Peace and Quiet, Don't Have Kids. When my kids were young, I, too, dreamed of the day when discord would subside and life with children would get smoother.

By the time they were four and six, I was a considerably improved parent and my children were calmer and better behaved. Yet, to my surprise, unpleasant moments persisted in our daily lives. Although I was initially disappointed that my keener parenting skills had not eliminated such moments, it eventually registered that no matter how skilled I became, my ideal agenda would never be realized. I could see from my new perspective as a more competent parent that chaotic moments were simply a part of raising children.

Once you confront this reality, you will take your first step toward putting children on the agenda, rather than yearn endlessly for serenity and peace. In truth, if you want only peace, you shouldn't have had children. But, it's too late for that. So, now you must face that children aren't the messengers of peace and quiet, but of life, rich in all of its complexities, confusion, lessons—and joy!

To assist you in absorbing this reality, it helps to remember that children are, by definition, immature and thus—by necessity—are constantly learning new things. This, in turn, subjects them to countless errors, large messes, and noisy disruptions. If you had known in advance how interruptive children would be to the serenity of daily living and had avoided having them, you would have missed the blessings they bring to your life, along with their disturbance to your peace. Now that they're here, the only way to enjoy your journey together is to put their chaos on the agenda.

Including Your Children's Disruptions on Life's Agenda

Those of you wishing to put your children on the agenda must learn to greet their unpleasant moments as expected, even welcome, guests. In doing this, you embrace each disturbance, and the child who brings it, rather than resist these normal aspects of family life. Putting your child and his disruptions on the agenda, in this way, enables you to feel close to him on a consistent basis, without abdicating your love during the difficult times or when you are required to discipline. As a result, he will have an experience of being continuously valued and loved, no matter what's going on.

Once you succeed in putting your children on the agenda, life with them gets considerably smoother. Although you will still be required to address the difficult moments, you will feel better able to do so with a new sense of neutrality and calm. In fact, you will find, paradoxically, that once you are able to stop resisting the problematic times, they will no longer seem like such frequent or disruptive forces in your life.

Embracing the Unseen "Blessings"

In the process of learning to embrace the difficult times with your children you will soon discover that they bring unseen blessings along with their disruptions to your life.

In my case, before becoming a mother, I was quite a perfectionist. I felt strongly attached to my idealized notions of how things should be and was unhappy when life failed to match my expectations. To my horror, my first child projectile vomited every half hour throughout his first year of life. What a contrast to my image of the "perfect" Gerber baby! I was in a perfectionist's nightmare, and I responded by fighting this impossible reality. I simply couldn't believe it was happening to me. Yet, no matter how much I doubted or resisted, it was happening.

Because my resistance caused even more suffering, I was eventually forced to adjust. It was then that I learned simply to wear aprons and carry rags wherever I went and graciously wipe vomit off of public benches, waiting room chairs, and grocery store floors. Before long, I had learned to accept having a child who vomited all over himself, me, the house, the car, and everywhere we went.

The result was that I became a more flexible person, and unexpected events no longer threw me out of balance or triggered feelings of resistance and anger. I had found a new way—quite opposite from the compulsions of perfectionism—to feel peaceful. Thus, in the final analysis, this vomiting child proved to be a special gift of life who helped me to discover inner peace.

Like me, all of you will encounter your share of the unexpected, uninvited, and difficult moments while living with children. Yet if you look for the blessings they offer, these moments can teach you not only to be more adaptable as you go through life, but to accept and love both your children and yourselves in the midst of the error-ridden and difficult times.

As you succeed in putting the unpleasant moments with your child on the agenda, you will learn to sustain a heart connection between you throughout the good times and the bad. This acceptance of your child, no matter what's happening, will enable you to love him throughout each day in the same way you love him when he's your sleeping angel. Such acceptance is the very essence of unconditional love—or love without the condition of everything going smoothly—and learning to love so completely will indeed be a blessing to your life.

Putting the Disruptions of Experience on the Agenda

The late Buckminster Fuller, a great genius of our time, adeptly illustrated the inherent value of one's own experience—either "positive" or "negative"—by pointing out that the child falling from a sofa learns three laws of physics on his way to the floor. We can see from this simple example why experience is the most effective teacher.

Nonetheless, those of you who have not yet put your child on life's agenda aren't as willing to deal with the disruptions that go with his experiences. Rather than allow him to learn from his own frustrating and messy encounters with daily living, you strive, instead, to hand him the lessons you have gleaned from your own experiences. As efficient and tidy as this approach sounds, it simply won't work. Because a child is unable to vicariously discover very much about living from another's experiences, he learns best by plunging into his own encounters, making his own mistakes, and learning what he can from them. Thus, your job will be to embrace the frustration and errors that go with the chaos and complexity of this process as your child dives in and learns from his own experiences.

Including Your Child's Frustrations on the Agenda

Each time your child wants something and must resolve how that wanting will be fulfilled, he's forced to confront that many of his desires will not be fulfilled immediately, if they're fulfilled at all. He must also face that he will be required to rely increasingly more on his own fulfiller to satisfy his wanting.

Not surprisingly, the frustration of adapting to these realities is at the core of much of a young child's temperamental crying, which culminates in the two-year-old's famous tantrums. Yet this kind of crying is not overly significant, since it merely represents the time it takes your child to adjust to being thwarted and does not indicate that you have asked too much or need to alter things to keep him happy. Instead, this period of adjustment must be understood, allowed, and calmly endured if he's to adapt to the normal frustrations of living.

Supporting His Adjustment to the Conflict. Many of you interrupt your child's adjustment periods because you can't stand listening to his unhappiness or believe that it's psychologically damaging for him to cry. You may reward his fussy retreats from coping with excessive checking, concern, or anger; encourage him to abandon difficult tasks; or even let him have his way in order to stop his misery. In doing these things, you not only undermine his effort to make this important adjustment to not always getting his way, but interfere with his ability to push through to the fulfiller side of his personality.

By contrast, if you are able to accept the noise that goes with your child's frustrations and fears as he confronts these struggles between his wanting and fulfilling selves, you give him the time and space he needs to resolve the conflict. In this resolution he not only discovers that he can, with sustained effort, manage things on his own, but that some of his wanting simply needs to be delayed or released. Understanding how this works helps you to see the role your acceptance plays in your child's normal development.

Welcoming Error

When a child is allowed to learn about life from his own experiences, making mistakes will be inevitable. Thus, it's essential to view errors not as enemies to be avoided, but as friends and allies that guide his life.

Yet those of you still caught in the race for high performance or not yet able to put your child's problems on the agenda will view his mistakes as villains. You will then pass this attitude toward errors on to your child by responding to his mistakes with gasps of, "Oh no!" "Watch out!" "Now see what you've done!" or "How many times have I told you to be more careful?!" By doing this, you give the impression that his errors are not welcome, and that if he's going to make them, he will be shamed or reprimanded. It's as though you expect your child to somehow get through life and learn its lessons without making any mistakes.

You are also forgetting that natural laws use error as a teacher, and that the freer your child feels to engage in life's activities without concern about his mistakes, the more he will learn. For example, the child struggling to walk or ride a bicycle experiences being out of balance each time he falls, and the slap on his thigh or gravel in his knee tells him which side he overbalanced on. His job is to get up again without concern about repeating his error and take as many tries as needed to discover the place of balance in contrast to the place of imbalance that he just experienced. In this way, whatever errors he makes in his balancing serve as guideposts for locating where true balance lies. Similarly, the child who pours juice on the table next to his cup has a better sense of where the right place to pour it will be. And the one mushing at his paper with scissors moves away from that unrewarding feeling to locate the sweetness of slicing it correctly. In the same way, the older child uses missed baskets to help him find the basketball hoop and the teen driving on the lane dividers or shoulder of the road uses the bumpy ride to help him relocate the center of his lane.

Whenever you become excited or emotional in the face of your child's mistakes, rather than allow whatever lessons they offer to unfold, you give him the incorrect feedback that he's not a good person during those times when he's in error. Children who experience adult disapproval of their mistakes don't feel free to make them and get anxious or freeze in the face of experiences that might result in error. Moreover, rather than learn whatever lesson their mistake might teach, they become paralyzed by concern over having made it, and all learning shuts down as they focus on ways to conceal the error or avoid repeating it.

A child taught to fear his mistakes will begin to resist participation in daily experiences as a means to protect himself from making them. This avoidant tendency marks the beginning of a breakdown in his healthy personality functioning, since, in his effort to escape mistakes, he also bypasses the opportunities for success that only participation can bring.

It's important to remember that most successful people first experienced a number of failures prior to their achievements and that the famed Babe Ruth not only held a long-standing record for home runs, but for strikeouts as well. We can see from his example that if our children are to succeed, we must not discourage them from stepping into the batter's box of life and risking the errors involved in fully extending themselves.

Removing Anger as a Barrier to Acceptance

Anger is the feedback our bodies provide when we feel that things are not going as we wanted. If we pay attention to what was going on and what we were feeling prior to the anger, the anger serves as a valuable indicator of trouble that can help us to view things more clearly.

However, when we ignore what the anger is trying to show us, and act it out, instead, the anger becomes a mechanism for deflecting the feelings that go with our disappointment over not getting what we wanted, while blaming others for our pain.

Parental Anger

It helps to understand that there are two types of anger. One is the deep anger we feel when life has dealt us a tough blow. In such cases, the anger strives to speak to us about the deep, yet, unacknowledged feelings of hurt, sadness, loss, and despair that go with the painful event. Yet, until we are ready to face the pain of our loss, the anger is what we feel in its place. As such, the anger serves as a buffer from the pain until we are prepared to face it. Eventually, the feelings beneath this form of anger must be allowed to surface in order to be resolved and healed. Thus, anytime this step is not taken, the anger gets stuck and becomes toxic to its owner, while the energy used to push down the pain is experienced as depression.

The second type of anger grows out of our resistance to less serious things that are not going our way. We often hate to examine these issues honestly, even in the privacy of our own minds, since such explorations typically expose our irritations as trivial or based on faulty perceptions. Instead, we elect to express the anger by dumping it on others. No matter which form of anger we are dealing with, once we confront the real issue beneath the anger, it eventually gets resolved.

Parental anger usually falls into the second category and serves the purpose of beating away the hard and painful aspects of the parenting job. Yet because parental anger strives to ward off the disruptions parents encounter while living with children or the pain they feel when their kids are lagging in the developmental race, it interferes with their goal of accepting all aspects of their children and putting them on life's agenda.

Thus, anytime you are filled with parental anger, you must determine why you would rather beat away the issue before you than include it on your agenda and simply experience it. In doing this you can ask yourself such questions as, What is it I dislike about confronting this problem? Is it my generalized fear of unpleasant events or my desire to keep my ideal agenda intact by beating away the unpleasant moments my child brings to me? Or am I concerned about my child or that his immaturity and errors will serve as a reflection on myself? Once these and other questions have been explored, the ultimate question to ask is, How can I use this event to practice embracing the issue rather than continue my resistance to it? An effective time to ask these questions is while your child is on a time-out. It's also helpful to write out your questions and their answers.

Exploring Parental Anger

Most parents falsely view parental anger as a useful parenting tool that will inspire better behavior in a child they assume would do whatever it takes to prevent their fury. This view is erroneously reinforced by their child's initial improvement following one of their outbursts. However, these results are rarely enduring, and kids handled with verbal or physical anger can usually be counted on to repeat their undesirable behaviors. This is because children are often fascinated by the power their misconduct has over their parents' emotions and like to use it against them. Many are also delighted to have so much attention focused on them, even if it's negative, and view the strength of emotion binding them to their parents during these impassioned moments as love. Others are afraid of the anger and become withdrawn and reluctant. Yet they, too, resist cooperation, but do so passively.

Anger Teaches the Wrong Message. When parents react with emotion and anger to some error their child has made, the child is so distracted by the outburst that he fails to notice the lesson accompanying the experience. For instance, if a young girl knocks over a pitcher of milk and her mother becomes enraged, she receives the discouraging feedback that she's a disappointment to others whenever she makes mistakes. What her mother could be accomplishing—if she weren't so busy flailing against reality with her anger—is helping her daughter to determine what went wrong and how she can learn from the experience. Was the pitcher too full or poorly balanced? Was it placed too near the edge of the table? Were her arms waving too wildly as she talked? Only with the help of calm and gentle guidance can a child comfortably face her mistakes and learn from them.

Likewise, anytime your older child or teen exposes information about some trouble he's in, problems with friends, or a failing grade, if you respond with anger, he not only feels ashamed of these normal aspects of growing up, but feels too vulnerable to remain open with you. As a result, he defends against your attacks by concealing his mistakes. This denial of his true self not only interferes with the development of his integrity, it prevents him from knowing himself honestly. Interestingly, most psychological problems result from this avoidance of facing the truth about oneself or feeling the pain of life—most often the pain we feel when we have not yet learned to embrace all of who we are, including our errors.

As we can see, anger as a parenting tool not only fails to motivate better behavior, but causes kids to become defensive and distracted from the lessons they could be learning from life's daily experiences. Parental anger results in a broader societal problem as well, since most people in today's world have learned from angry families to deny and defend their mistakes with omissions, deceit, and blaming, rather than openly acknowledge and learn from them.

Thus, parents would be wise to remember that unexplored, yet expressed, anger serves only as a smoke screen that conceals the truth of things, while preventing the appropriate lesson from being learned or the errors from being corrected. Kevin's story shows how this works.

Kevin's Lesson

Four-year-old Kevin was decked out in his Christmas best on his way to have pictures taken on Santa's lap. However, as luck would have it, upon entering the mall, he noticed a candy store, equally adorned for Christmas, and succumbed to the call of the merchandise within. However, when he tried to sell Mother on the idea, she wasn't interested.

But Kevin was not to be dissuaded and threw himself on the pavement to scream his protest over being so "unfairly treated." As bystanders stared and clucked, Mother stood firm on her decision and quietly strived to talk him out of his tantrum. However, she soon realized that Kevin was out of control and would not be able to recover in time to see Santa. Feeling disappointed and angry at her son for spoiling this special outing, Mother roughly marched him to the car, wrestled him into his seat, and drove home in a state of fury. Once home, she wanted nothing more to do with this child and gave him to his father to put to bed.

The following year, they made another plan to see Santa, and while dressing to go, Kevin inquired, "Do you remember that I didn't get to see Santa last year?" His mother replied, "I certainly do—and do you remember why?" Kevin answered promptly that he did remember, "Because you were so angry!"

Dialogue from Class

FATHER: If I decide to bypass my anger, how is that different than suppressing my emotions?

BOBBIE: Rather than suppress your anger, the goal is to transform it.

FATHER: How can I do that?

BOBBIE: Most of us have been trained to escape our uncomfortable feelings by batting them away with defense, anger, and blame. In order to reverse this trend, we must learn to confront and embrace the feelings beneath the bluster of anger and rest in them long enough to understand and learn from them. Once we begin this process, more of our truths surface so that we can better understand these thoughts and feelings and determine which of them work for us and which ones don't. Once this step is taken, anger is allowed to serve its true purpose and soon dissipates without expression.

ଵଵଵ

Antidote to Anger: The Neutrality of an "Oak Tree." Once you have learned to view whatever unpleasant moments your child brings to your life as a normal part of his development, it no longer seems valid to respond with disappointment, resistance, and anger to his immature behaviors. Instead, you can embrace each moment, shift your awareness to your heart, and remain as unattached and neutral as a referee or "oak tree" in your child's life, simply announcing the cause and effect of his actions as needed.

For example, if your child's behavior requires some contraction of his freedom, you can inform him of his loss in much the way an official of a tennis match lets a player know when his ball has bounced long. In doing this, you become a neutral, dispassionate guide as you help your child to learn from life, rather than a shocked, disappointed, and scolding adult who can't accept that a young child is not fully formed and is bound to encounter some problems along his developmental path. By embracing this attitude, you will find yourself behaving with the grace of an "oak tree"—reliable and strong, yet rooted, centered, and calm.

Interestingly, once you learn to remain neutral, your children will no longer feel a need to hide their errors or defend themselves from blame or attack. By contrast, they will be able to remain relaxed and open and face themselves honestly enough to learn from the situation. In fact, a child handled gently becomes surprisingly interested in where he went wrong and what you have to say about how he can correct his errors and do better next time.

When viewed in this way, we can see that there really is no place for anger in parenting. Yet not getting emotionally excited is a skill that may take some time to develop. Consequently, remaining neutral should be viewed as a goal, rather than something to feel guilty about each time you succumb to anger.

Dialogue from Class

MOTHER: I can't imagine myself being able to get calm enough to act like a referee—much less an oak tree!

BOBBIE: That's a natural reaction when you're first giving up anger as a parenting tool. Yet each time you witness yourself responding with anger and notice its ineffectiveness, you are waking up to your error and getting closer to the time when you will choose neutral refereeing over anger. It's valuable to understand that it takes awhile to retrain oneself, so there's no point in diving into feelings of guilt every time anger takes over. During the period when I was first changing from being an angry parent to a more neutral one, daily meditation helped me to become a calmer individual. Displaying angelic pictures of my children around the house also evoked more soothed, positive feelings toward them. And consciously shifting my awareness away from the irritated thoughts gathering in my head down to my heart—while inviting the calming image of the "oak tree"—helped me to release my resistance and replace it with soft rememberances of my love for my children.

FATHER: What if you start out with anger but don't want to keep going with it? Will it hurt your child if you back down?

BOBBIE: No. In fact, it will help him. Let your child know that you still plan to deal with his behavior but aren't happy with your approach and want to start over without the upset. I discovered that whenever I could acknowledge and drop my anger, my children were very forgiving. It's only when I denied my wrath or blamed it on their behavior that I could see them withdraw and lose faith in my credibility as a guide or teacher. I also invited my children to quietly alert me to my anger anytime they noticed it before I did. In doing this, I openly declared that I no longer believed in anger and was working to eliminate it. Yet if you elect to do this, remember not to allow your child to focus more on your anger than on his behavior. His behavior is the primary problem and must be addressed. Addressing the anger can come later.

ANOTHER MOTHER: If anger and spanking don't work, why is my child always so well-behaved right after a burst of anger and a good whack?

BOBBIE: When a mother such as yourself is unable to elicit cooperation, she eventually gets fed up and switches from nurturing to authority, using anger as a bridge between the two. When her child then succumbs, she thinks he's responding to the anger and spanking, when he's actually responding to her clarity. Because she finally reached the point where she felt annoyed enough to make her meaning clear, he was relieved and felt calmer. It's not because he got hit; in fact, he'll seek revenge for that later! It's because he was wondering where her boundary line was drawn and finally got a clarification. Yet because of her irritation and the swat, he's also confused about his feelings toward her. On the other hand, if she had provided the same degree of clarity but remained loving, he would be free to respond to the clarity, without feeling ambivalent toward her for injuring him.

The Results of Putting Children on the Agenda

As we learn to put our children on the agenda and use their problems and errors as guides for teaching them various lessons, we learn to do the same for ourselves. In the process, we discover through this embracement of life that we gain a personal sense of mastery and peace.

For instance, if I get stuck in traffic, I can sit in my car stewing in the toxicity of my anger, honking at the blocked cars ahead of me, or I can choose to feel peaceful and listen to music or a tape, review the day, or notice the scenery and faces of my fellow travelers. Either way, I'm going to be caught in the traffic. I don't control the traffic, but I can control my response to it by including it on my agenda.

Putting life—and especially life with children—on the agenda is a goal that feels better each time we succeed in achieving it. Learning to also accept ourselves during those times when we fail to consistently accept our children will help us to get better at meeting this goal of acceptance. Each time we improve, we become more accepting of all of life—of our children, ourselves, events, and others. And, over time, we will have mastered the ability to consistently love our children as though they were sleeping angels!

★★★

We can choose peace by embracing both
the easy and the difficult.

★★★

5

At the Heart of the Matter

The Power of Loving Deeply

The Fourth Key:

෧෧෧

Love the essence of your child from the depth of your heart.

Now that you understand the value of embracing all aspects of your child's developmental journey while merging love with discipline, it's time to address what deep love and clear discipline actually look like in the middle of raising a child. Since discipline only works for those parents who are able to experience a continuously loving connection with their child, I will begin by showing you how to love your child in a way that keeps your connection intact.

Loving Deeply

Bonding is a term used to describe the profoundly loving connection that forms between you and your child from the moment of his birth. This connection continues throughout his childhood if it's not interrupted by such things as premature separations, inconsistent loving, or pushing too hard and too early toward maturity and independence.

When I first learned of the impact such deep and continuous connections could have on a child's ability to love himself and others as well as fulfill his potential, an empty hurt awakened in me. Although I had experienced moments of caring connections with my children, our bonding had been erratic, and I yearned for a connection that would go deeper and last longer than the more sporadic ones we had established. Gratefully, my pursuit of that goal led to a profound change in my capacity to love—not only my children, but the essence of life. Here is what I learned.

In spite of our more recent awareness of the power of bonding, many parents still falter in their ability to establish or maintain adequate connections with their offspring. This results in their children feeling insufficiently loved and thus failing to care for themselves and others with fullness or depth. In fact, millions of adults in today's world are working to heal the injuries of having been inadequately loved as children, and the numbers are growing. This is a disturbing notion and may contribute to the profusion of injured hearts, unhappy feelings, and violent acts inflicted on others in our society. As we face this problem, it becomes clear that we would all benefit from greater quantities of love filling our hearts, our homes, our communities, and our world.

Fortunately, my impression is that loving bonds that have been weakened or broken can be recaptured at any time during a child's development. Thus, when parents who have achieved only minimal or average levels of bonding commit—as I did—to deepening their bonds, both their children's development and their parent-child relationships are significantly enhanced. Moreover, when this depth of love is in place, it has the strength to heal the past and assure the future.

The Power of Love

The reason for the dramatic healing and improved functioning that goes with love lies in Robert Bly's theory that we are able to access notably higher levels of intelligence and wisdom by opening and maintaining feelings of love in our hearts. (See Chapter 13.)

Research not only supports this view, but suggests that all levels of function within ourselves and the environment are significantly enhanced when our hearts are actively included. Deepak Chopra reveals how well this works in his account of a group of rabbits who maintained low cholesterol on the same fatty diet given other rabbits who developed elevated cholesterol levels. The variable uncovered was that the man feeding the low cholesterol group had succumbed to holding, petting, and kissing the rabbits, prior to giving them their fatty meal. This demonstration of the healing effect of love offers an explanation for why cardiac patients given pets to love have better recovery rates than those without a stimulus to stir their hearts. This power of love also extends to our environment, as evidenced by the studies Larry Dossey cites in which those plants sent positive and loving wishes flourished while those offered unkind and hateful messages died.

These studies show us that love is both powerful and healing and has the capacity to alter everything it permeates. When we tune into this power, we can see that it is similar to an electrical force, but stronger. Yet it's also gentle, and lives in the same meditative frequency found in nature.

Based on our increasing awareness of the power embodied in the energy of love, our goal must be to learn to keep this extraordinary force more active in our hearts as continually as possible so that our homes, lives, and world can be awash in its curative and creative powers. The blessing of children is that they activate our loving response and thus help us to access the place in our hearts that releases this unseen, yet compelling force.

The Magic of Bonding

In my urge to understand the power of love in parent-child relationships, I discovered that bonding occurs when parents experience deep feelings of love and caring centered within their hearts as they tune into the very essence of their child. The energy of love that gathers in their hearts then overflows to encircle their child, enabling him to feel the presence of this potent force while uniting him with the parent who has sent it. It's as though they have met on a common pathway deep within their hearts, where they bow respectfully to one another in recognition of the connection between their souls.

I realized that I had experienced this meeting of the hearts with my children, but that it had been an encounter that came and went, depending on the moment, their behavior, or my mood. However, with my new awareness of the effect it could have on our relationship and their experience of themselves as loved and loving beings, able to access higher levels of intelligence and wisdom, I began to understand the importance of maintaining this connection between us at a deeper level and on a more consistent basis.

What It Feels Like

We have all heard the story of Saint Francis of Assisi, who was so attuned to life that he attracted wild birds and animals to him. Similarly, Helen Keller was known to stand in the wooded area surrounding her home, feeding untamed birds from her hands. We have also read or heard accounts of people who have befriended animals in the wild or played with dolphins and whales at sea. These individuals all share a love for life so deep that it has opened their hearts and bonded them to it.

We are all able—at various levels—to experience a similarly intense connection to the heart of life. Some of us feel it spontaneously while listening to music, climbing a mountain, or enjoying a sunset or rainbow. Others feel it when soothing an animal, welcoming a newborn, or sharing laughter with friends. Still others are moved even by life's smaller blessings such as the velvety scent of gardenias, the crinkling of an elder's face, or a sparrow bathing in a puddle of rain.

When and How Bonding Happens

Whenever we approach an animal we would like to befriend or hold, we instinctively know that we must win its trust. In response to this knowing, we shift down within ourselves, become very still, and experience a stirring in our hearts much like the purring of a cat. In such moments, we are in a quickened, yet quietly harmonic, state that is compatible with the frequency nature lives in. It's similar to the vibration we sense in the oak tree standing so still yet strong, stars pulsing their pure light, or the magnetism of the ocean as it swells and recedes. It's this same heartfelt atunement to the very heart of life that enables us to befriend wild creatures or feel a bond of love with our children.

Deepak Chopra draws from science to help us understand the reason behind our feelings of union with the rest of life. He describes all aspects of life as part of a large soup in which the atoms and molecules of our essence constantly move in and out of us to join with the essence of the rest of life. The result is a continuous dance of atoms and molecules uniting us in a fluid, yet collective body, mind, and heart.

It's our ability to become aware of this shared essence of all of life and experience our interplay and connection to it that evokes feelings of love and caring and the opening of our hearts beyond ourselves to include others. And it's this deeply felt love in our hearts that weaves the delicate web that bonds us to animals, nature, our children—and, ultimately, to all of life.

Conscious Bonding

Interestingly, we are all able to call upon this unconscious, automatic process and bring it into moments with our children—and others—at will, simply by focusing our awareness in our hearts while in their presence. Thus, the more you remember to drop into your heart in this way, the more your child will sense your reverence for life and love for him. His heart will open, in turn, and he will feel his love for you. Once this exchange is underway, love flows between you—heart to heart—creating a bonded connection.

Some of you are fortunate enough to have experienced bonding from the moment your child was born and continue to deepen and maintain it throughout his growing-up process. Others of you bonded with your child at birth, but then lost the strength of that connection as a result of too much physical or emotional separation as he grew older or by pushing him too quickly toward maturity and independence. And still others of you have yet to experience a deep connection with your child.

For those of you who have never experienced bonding or have lost touch with it along the way, discovering how to achieve and maintain this deep connection with your child is the most important thing that you can do for him and for yourself.

Initial Bonding with Your Young Child

Those of you who understand the bonding process that takes place between you and your child in the first few hours, months, and years of his life are fortunate, since you are continuously aware of the importance of being available and open to this profound experience. As a result of your availability and responsiveness to your child, he learns to trust in your love and becomes attached to you. This, in turn, sets a series of developmental processes in motion, including his ability to surrender to your nurturing and guidance. When bonding continues, it provides the conditions necessary for your child's optimal development. By contrast, anytime this bond is interrupted, the break interferes with his normal patterns of growth.

Bonding Breaks

Many of you will notice that you failed to solidly bond with your children in the first few months and years of their lives due to a variety of breaks in your parent-child relationships. These breaks are not only common in today's society, but range from mild to severe and are caused by such things as delays in physical contact after delivery due to hospital procedures or medical problems; infrequent handling and holding once your baby gets home; colic, illness, and allergies creating tensions between you; excessively early or inappropriate child care or custody placements causing more separation from primary parents than the child is ready to manage; prolonged absence during a vacation or business trip before the child is ready for so much separation; prematurely pushing a child toward early independence; parental impatience and anger; inappropriate custody placements and visitations; personal problems or drug use severe enough to interfere with adequate responding to the child; and verbal, physical, or sexual abuse, causing the child to feel tense and unsafe. The earlier these fractures in the bond with your child occur and the more intense and prolonged they are, the more serious the interruption to the bonding process between you.

Each child will react to these breaks in bonding with varying degrees of detachment as a way to protect himself from the pain of separation that the break has caused. For example, if your child's bonds are only partially weakened, he will respond with milder levels of mistrust and insecurity, often expressed by fussing and crying or getting overly attached to security blankets or toys. If his bonds are slightly more broken, he may avoid eye contact or stare with eyes glazed over in his attempt to withdraw and keep a safe distance from you, whom he now sees as someone he can no longer count on. If your child suffers from more severely damaged bonds, he will manifest even stronger levels of mistrust and separation, sometimes exhibiting sleep problems, including nightmares; hyperactivity; tantrums; or aggressive—even destructive—behaviors. The most disturbing result of these bonding breaks is your child's inability to trust and surrender to your love and the guidance that goes with it.

Continued Bonds

The more bonded you remain with your child throughout the course of his childhood, including his teen years, the more he will trust in you and believe in himself. Because the combination of trust in you and belief in himself creates a foundation of security from which your child goes forth into the world, it's important to both strengthen and preserve the bonds that you created in the early months throughout his entire childhood. This is best done by keeping yourself and your heart open to your child, no matter what's going on.

Keeping Arms and Laps Available. Whenever your child feels nurtured, he trusts that he is lovable and loved in a safe and caring world. This, in turn, allows him to surrender to your love and accept the guidance that goes with it. From this foundation of security and surrender to your guidance, he develops the stability and courage he needs to venture out and away from you into the larger world. You can see this step most vividly when your child first learns to crawl or later to walk and can, for the first time, leave your side and explore the world beyond you. This newfound mobility marks the beginning of his separating—or individuating—process, in which he leaves his feelings of dependence behind as he dares to do some things for himself, begins the process of strengthening his fulfiller, and prepares for his independence.

Yet if you watch closely, you will see that as he ventures forth into the world he often experiences conflict over whether or not he can manage on his own or will still need you. This conflict explains why the baby scooting forward in his effort to reach a toy often puts as much energy into his fussing and crying as he puts into his efforts at scooting or grasping. At this point, he is caught between the possibilities of remaining the dependent wanter who cries to summon your help or becoming his own fulfiller. It's during these times that he returns to connect with you again—or perhaps seek your assistance—before venturing out and trying again. This pattern of going toward independence and returning to dependence goes on throughout his entire childhood, including the teen years and beyond.

Thus, if you pay attention, you will see that each time your developing child is faced with assuming responsibility for some new or difficult task, he typically responds with the same conflict he felt during those early transitions. His lack of confidence in his ability to manage the new activity on his own causes him to retreat or fuss for help, while he simultaneously wants to cope by himself. This is why the toddler struggling to dress himself or tie his laces won't accept the aid his tears have summoned. It's also why your elementary-age child who was begging for assistance with homework or riding his bike becomes agitated when help is offered. And it's why your adolescent acts resistant or pretends disinterest when confronting the conflict he feels over new experiences such as team tryouts, learning to drive, or going on his first date or job interview.

If you are concerned about whether or not your child appears mature and independent throughout his development, you will resist welcoming him back during those times when he's feeling dependent and in need of nurturing. This, in turn, will undermine his belief in himself as well as his courage to venture out further. Thus, although it's important to encourage your child in his explorations into the world toward independence, it's also critical that you welcome him back into your lap and heart anytime he falters or simply feels a need for your love and support. Yet care must be taken during these periods not to join him in his fears, but to calmly trust in his strength and ability to move steadily toward independence as you also allow him to touch base with you as needed.

As my children developed, I initially pushed them toward early independence and made them feel unwelcome during those times when they seemed to need me for things I thought they should manage on their own. I was particularly rejecting anytime they became fussy during these periods of conflict. I also felt uneasy about their continuing desire to sit in my lap as they grew older, especially since others seemed so disapproving of this practice. However, once I understood that neither my children's periods of conflict between pushing forward and returning to dependency, nor their desire for an ongoing physical connection indicated undue immaturity, I reinstated lap-sitting and welcomed them during those times when they wanted to touch base with me. As a result, lap-time and connecting continued for many years as a valuable avenue for bonding between us, and we spent many pleasurable hours connecting in this way. Paradoxically, this renewed access to me and the opportunity for a continuing bond increased my children's confidence and gave them a firmer, more consistent foundation on which their independence was able to develop in a faster, stronger, more genuine way. Following is an explanation of why and how I made that change.

Offering Full Access

In addition to wanting our children to appear precociously mature, we like them to behave independently as early and often as possible in order to help us with living in such a rushed and busy world. Thus, we have come up with the idea that we can most efficiently meet our children's dependency needs by allotting them brief blocks of enriched time, commonly referred to as "quality time."

The Problem with "Quality Time." Although the concept of "quality time" sounds ideal for busy parents in busy times, it actually creates unexpected breaks in parental bonds with their children. This is because each time you anticipate giving your child a block of qualitative time, you feel obligated to go "on duty" and keep him amused, happy, and productive in order to ensure that your time together is special. Consequently, "quality time" is action-packed and goal-oriented, as you relate to your child in a falsely exciting way, perhaps even using an artificially cheerful tone of voice to indicate what fun you are having. Your child, in turn, mirrors back your unnaturalness with goofy behaviors or speaking in equally false tones. The result is that "quality time" unexpectedly alters your relationship and gives it an inauthentic ring, as you and your child "act out" your time together as "special" and "exciting."

Many of you stand in as your child's playmate during "quality time," slavishly mimicking the role of another child. Not only is this practice artificial, it often leads to your compliance to his demands during play which gives your child an artificial picture of how real friends interact. As a result, he becomes confused when actual playmates are neither as flexible nor entertained by his self-centered activities as you have pretended to be.

Other parents who are working or divorced often feel guilty about the limited time they have available for their children and compensate by parceling out segments of "quality time." Unfortunately, special time for those of you in this category often translates to giving your child his way, showering him with gifts, and avoiding the unpleasantness of discipline.

For the most part, the child who receives "quality time" becomes hyper-responsive to attention and behaves in frantic ways to get more of it. Thus, even though he fails to experience the connection he originally sought, he becomes addicted to its replacement and wants progressively more of the energy, focus, and excitement that "quality time" engenders.

Erecting Walls. In contrast to your child's desire for more of this special time together, you are exhausted by its demands and wonder why he never seems satisfied by so much attention! In fact, "quality time" becomes so draining for you that you grow anxious for time off and look for opportunities to steal away. To accomplish this, you unconsciously erect an invisible wall between yourself and your child in hopes of resting for awhile on one side of it, while he entertains himself on the other. In doing this, you alternate between being overly available, helpful, and fun, then hiding behind walls formed by your own activities, breaks, and closed doors. The end result is that there is never a time when your child experiences the more genuine heart connection he was seeking, grows tired of the substitute of "quality time," or feels fulfilled and ready to be alone. There is, in short, no point of satiation, and your child becomes addicted to spending all of his time with you, while you strive to remain behind your wall.

Many of you put off the intensity of "quality time" by erecting your walls at the beginning of your time together. For instance, a father might, upon arriving home, ask his son to wait until he has read the newspaper before playing a game together, while Mom requests that her daughter allow her to lie down for a few minutes before reading her a story. Thus, children who haven't seen their families all day are left to wait awhile longer, because their parents, believing that time together must be special and productive, now put it off until they have the energy required for "quality time."

To your dismay, your child wants full access to you at all times and won't tolerate your walls, either before receiving "quality time" or afterwards. In fact, if your child is blocked from contact—even temporarily—he will persist in reestablishing access in order to achieve a connection and will spend the entire time your walls are up devising ways to break through. He might, for example, slap at Dad's newspaper, bother Mother as she tries to nap, pick a fight with sister, create some mess, or pester and whine the entire time you are on the other side of your wall, struggling for a break.

Eventually, your nervous system gives out, your wall is penetrated, and your child regains access. However, because he was required to misbehave in order to connect, the time is now negative, rather than serene and happy as it could have been at the outset. The experience is neither loving nor bonding, and your child, still unsure of his ability to create a heart connection, clings ever more tightly to your side.

Letting Down the Wall: Access Without Entertainment—But with Cooperation. Those of you ready to release "quality time" must dare to replace it with allowing your child full access to you throughout each day.

Yet the very thought of letting down your walls on a consistent basis will cause many of you to feel quite anxious. Because your entertained child has grown used to demanding your attention and receiving "quality time," you fear that he will never leave your side, once he's allowed full access. What you don't realize is that a child offered access to you is able to be in your presence without overwhelming you with his needs—if the access is given *without entertainment for as long as your child is cooperating.* Here's what it looks like.

Being vs. Doing. Those of you who learn how to allow your child regular access without feeling a need to focus exclusively on him or to keep your time together active and memorable will no longer feel anxious or "on duty" around him. Instead, you will be available to him in the course of daily living, and he will feel free to be in your presence no matter what's going on. Once your child has full access, there will be no further need to make your time together child-centered, qualitative, and special, nor must you continue to suggest that he amuse himself in a separate area when you are unable to play. Instead, you will be able to sit and *be* with him for awhile or continue essential things while allowing him to remain with you or nearby. He can help if he likes, but it won't be necessary, since time together no longer requires *doing* something special, productive, or educational and can simply include a more natural, relaxed time, free of activity. Because the climate you are striving to achieve is one where things will simply feel more real and natural, it's important that your availability to him has no overtones of overprotection, anxiety, or clinging, but feels comfortably easy and relaxed for both.

Anytime your child is free to be in your presence whenever he wants for as long as he is cooperating, he will no longer need to create an excuse or activity, behave dependently, generate a problem, or demand attention in order to get close. He can simply join you where you are to create a connection.

Once you have learned to allow this kind of direct access and can respond with ease to your child's requests for it, he will no longer feel a need to break through a wall to be with you or dominate your time once there. Instead, he will become more relaxed and peaceful in your presence as a result of having achieved the closeness he was after.

Moreover, once "quality time" is eliminated, the time your child spends with you will no longer be so entertaining that your child craves more. Instead, after periods of easy connections or pure "being" time, he will naturally move away to do his own thing. Because you will no longer be engulfed by the demands of "quality time," you won't feel so anxious to bring an end to your time together or put up walls to block the next encounter. The happy result is that you and your child will more comfortably enjoy stress-free periods of natural and real contact with one another whenever you are together, rather than spurts of "special" time, followed by cold walls and uneasy separations.

In contemplation of letting down your walls, many of you fearfully envision your child spoiling each day with one difficult behavior after another. What you must remember is that full access without entertainment only includes access until your child's behavior becomes inappropriate. For example, if your young child is squirming and climbing or fussing in your lap, or your preteen insists on wrestling with the dog under your feet while you are cooking, they temporarily lose their choice to be with you and are calmly removed from your lap or sent out of the kitchen—or if they resist, to their rooms—until they are ready to cooperate. This loss of access is a direct result of your child's unacceptable behavior, rather than your attempt to take a break from him. Under these conditions, there are no walls to keep him from you— only his own behavior. In this way, your child is able to control how much access he has to you and soon discovers that it's in his best interest to behave cooperatively.

In addition, once you have claimed that each of your child's inappropriate behaviors will result in his removal, you will no longer feel controlled by these behaviors and will feel more relaxed and welcoming of his presence.

The final result is that when this full access is available to your child throughout his growing-up years, he will be able to maintain the earlier bond that was established between you when he was first born. A child's ability to count on this connection for the duration of his childhood provides the basis for his continued feelings of self-love and security; higher levels of intelligence; and optimal development and functioning.

The Day My Wall Came Down. I was anxious for my children to mature quickly and believed that giving them ample doses of "quality time" would ensure their rapid development. Yet rather than develop maturely, they became demanding and anxious for more of my time and attention—and my wall became my only protection from being overwhelmed by their needs. However, the more I buttressed my wall, the greater my children's insecurities grew and the harder they tried to break through to me. I tried to appease them with parcels of "quality time," but these allotments were never enough, and they always demanded more.

I noticed one day that whenever I heard my children's car pool turn into our driveway to return them to me, I felt my stomach churn as I rushed about the house in a futile attempt to finish my projects. I knew that the moment they walked through the door the remainder of the day would be spent alternating between "quality time" and walling off their demands for more. I felt bad about my wall and could see that it bewildered my innocent children. They couldn't understand why I put them off or asked that they wait until "later," when "later" always took so long or never came.

Because I could feel the bond between us slipping away, I decided to try something new. I made a promise to myself that I would sit on the sofa and be available to my kids upon their return from school without timetables or distractions. I wouldn't play games or *do* anything special, but would simply *be* there with them as the real, natural me. I resolved to remain available for pure "being" time for as long as they desired without resisting the experience or seeking a break from it. Yet because I had grown so used to attention-demanding children who tried my patience, I worried that this new approach would backfire and that they would never leave my side.

Upon arriving home that day, my children noticed me sitting on the sofa and came over to join me. At first they suggested a number of activities, but I responded with, "No . . . the truth is I'm a grown-up and don't really love to play children's games all afternoon—but I am willing to just sit here and be available to you." I remained there in my adult role as the real me in lieu of the false roles I had previously played of entertainment director, solicitous teacher, or passive playmate.

The two of them sat near me on the sofa, and, not knowing what else to do, they began to chat about their day. They opened up more than usual, and I responded to them as I would to a friend. Rather than feel obligated to make our time together entertaining, I was free to be my real, adult self, and my children had a chance to see me as others do. As a result of spending our time together in this more natural way, I could feel my fear of their demands dissolve, and my heart opened to them with deep feelings of love.

My children sat with me that day for about half an hour before getting up to seek out friends and do their own thing. I was impressed by their more relaxed attitude and willingness to go off and play on their own. Initially, they would check back to see if I was still there for them but soon learned to trust my availability. As time went on, I continued to wave off invitations to play games or do activities, unless I was particularly interested in one. Yet if I happened to be doing something that could be handled later, I would consistently put down the project and be present to my kids. During this period of transition, we discovered how to comfortably *be* together—which marked a significant transformation in our relationship.

Dialogue from Class

MOTHER: Are you saying that your children had access to you even when you were busy?

BOBBIE: Yes. But remember, it was access without entertainment—and until their behavior became inappropriate.

MOTHER: But didn't you deserve to get your work done or take a few moments for yourself, rather than be available to your children every time they wanted to be connected?

BOBBIE: Well, deserve it or not, was I really going to get it? (Laughter) If I didn't let them get to me through the front door, they would have just found a back door to use. Whenever I had previously guarded moments for myself, they never lasted very long and certainly weren't peaceful. Yet when I began to offer my children the same access—without entertainment—that I gave other adults living with me, I no longer felt the need to carve out time for myself or hide behind walls, since, under these new conditions, my children would touch base for awhile and then go off to do their own thing. Although many of you fear that full access will make your children clingy and dependent, the truth is that they will become considerably more independent, so long as your time together is not overly entertaining or exclusively child-centered. Thus, paradoxically, once you allow access, you will get your free moments—not by peeling insecure children from your legs, but by giving them an opportunity to connect with you, since only then will they feel safe enough to leave your side.

ANOTHER MOTHER: I have a two-year-old who wants to sit all morning looking at books, but I get antsy after awhile. Am I cutting him off from access to me when I say I've had enough?

BOBBIE: Although looking at books can feel like a pure "being" state, it's actually an activity or "doing" state, and is okay to do for as long as you like. However, it's not the same as the "being" state I'm describing in which you are available to sit with your child, perhaps even chatting, but without entertaining him or making the time together primarily child-centered. Due to the absence of activities in a true "being" state, your child will be ready to let go of the time together once he feels connected. And, that won't take all day!

MOTHER: How long does it take?

BOBBIE: It varies. But the key is that you fully surrender to having him with you, rather than remain anxious for "being" time to come to an end. Thus, if you're watching the clock, your child will sense that you are not genuinely available and will not only fail to feel the connection he seeks, but will sit there longer waiting to experience it.

ANOTHER MOTHER: What about talking? My seven-year-old likes to be near me, but he asks a million questions, and I can't get anything done.

BOBBIE: This could indicate that your verbal interaction has some attention-demand energy in it which can come from overpraising, overdirecting, and overteaching. It can also come from his awareness that you don't like the questions and his subsequent desire to get you to surrender to them. Do you fall into any of these categories?

MOTHER: I do praise his activities—because I'm concerned about his development.

BOBBIE: That could explain why he's so anxious to keep verbal connections with you going. If you make your exchanges more honest and natural, they will not only be more pleasurable for both of you, he will be less attached to keeping them artificially going. Remember, too, that young children do ask a lot of genuine questions, and it's important that you surrender to being available for answering them.

THIRD MOTHER: I've been making myself available to my child, but he often gets fussy and demanding. How do I respond to these demands during "being" time?

BOBBIE: It's important not to confuse "being" time with overresponding to every whimper or demand. This is where so many parents get into trouble; they think that making themselves available for loving their child precludes drawing limits and holding boundaries. The key is to make yourself available until your child becomes demanding and uncooperative. If this happens, his demands should be ignored, and if they continue, he must be removed.

๑๑๑

Taking the Moments. Time is the greatest gift you can give your children and one that is in short supply in today's busy world. Consequently, those of you who want close relationships with your children must find a way to make time for those moments when they would like to talk or just "hang out" together. There will be times, for example, when your young child will want to discuss a particular problem about a friend, a teacher, or some event at school, or to merely chat or engage in harmless gossip. As he gets older, your preteen or teen may want to go shopping or run an errand together, have a driving lesson, or perhaps go for a run or out to lunch. If you think you can put your child off, stay with your nonessential projects, and get back to him later, you will miss key opportunities to feel close. You must be aware that these natural opportunities for connecting with your child seldom reappear later when you are in the mood or have more time.

Frankly, the best times with children come out of a series of spontaneous moments that have neither been planned nor scheduled. These times, when taken, often evolve into connecting talks and laughter or poignant moments that will be remembered and cherished for years to come. Since there will always be something else to do, if you want to experience these natural moments with your children, you must learn to release your other activities, redirect your focus, and become genuinely interested and available.

One day, I was at my computer, completely absorbed in writing when my son, home from college for the summer, and my daughter, a senior in high school, wandered into my room to chat. I hesitated for a moment before remembering my long-standing commitment to give up the project and be present to them—even though they no longer needed me as they had when they were younger. Our talk that day soon led to wonderfully funny stories about experiences they had enjoyed while growing up, many I had forgotten or never heard. Before long, we were shrieking with the kind of gasping, tearful laughter that locks hearts in a memorable bond. Once again, I was grateful I had taken the moment. The important thing to remember is that it doesn't always turn out this way; but then again it can. Your job is to simply be present to them and available for whatever happens.

Dialogue from Class

MOTHER: My child's teacher suggests that parents set time aside for their children, and I wonder just how to do that or if I am giving enough time to my daughter. After work, I race to pick her up from school, then get home to face the laundry and dinner plus a mother-in-law who wants to talk, and I feel overwhelmed.

BOBBIE: Rather than set aside a block of time for your daughter, it would be more effective to simply be present to her during the drive home and throughout the course of the evening in the same way that you are present to the adults in the family. Treat her as if she's just as important as Dad and Grandma, rather than the one who is in the way and can be interrupted or put aside with promises of "quality time" later to atone for ignoring her. The key is to treat your daughter with the same naturalness and respect you would offer other family members or a friend.

ANOTHER MOTHER: My kids are jealous of each other, so I try to give each of them time alone with me. How do I continue this, without getting caught in the "quality time" trap?

BOBBIE: You can't, and I don't think it's necessary to try. I believe that setting aside special time for jealous siblings intensifies competitive feelings between them, since it perpetuates the idea that they each need as much of your individual focus as they can get. By creating special time alone with each child, you keep their anxiety alive over who can hold your attention and gain the position of preferred child. Offering full access, instead, to all of your kids at once allows them the opportunity to enjoy more natural, "hanging out" time together as a group. This helps them to give up the false idea that they need your undivided attention, while offering them time as a family unit for getting close to one another as well as to you.

FATHER: Don't you think it's important for different family members to have special times together?

BOBBIE: Not necessarily. Besides, these times will evolve naturally on those occasions when you're driving one child to an activity while his siblings are going their separate ways. On the other hand, when these times are planned, they become artificial and create the same false feelings that "quality time" engenders.

ANOTHER WOMAN: Both my husband and I work, and I'm discovering that it's almost impossible to find any moments in the day for my child. I feel guilty about it, but I just don't see any time in the schedule.

BOBBIE: This is a very real and serious problem for today's working parents. (See **Working Mother** in Problem-Solving Guide.) One solution is to make sure that you are fully present to your children during those times when you are together. For example, time spent around the dinner table or in the car offers busy parents important opportunities to be with their kids. However, this only works if you are clear not to infect mealtimes with television or lectures and don't view driving as a time to ignore your child while listening to the radio or fussing over the traffic. These limited, but regular, opportunities open the way for a surprisingly bonded connection to your children if you make it a point to be fully conscious and present to them.

⊙⊙⊙

Sitting Down. Many of you are in a state of perpetual motion, which makes it difficult for anyone to relate to you. Consequently, when your children desire a moment with you, the most effective response is to put your projects aside, sit down, and surrender to being still and present to them. This might include lingering in the car after an outing, hanging out with them on the kitchen floor to pet the family dog, lolling about in the family room, or "being" together on the living room sofa. This kind of time together can include such things as connecting, lap-sitting, and chatting, but does not require that you keep your child entertained and happy or make your time with him educational or productive. The key is that the time feels calm and easy, rather than active or goal-directed.

Although many of you will initially fear the amount of time your child may wish to spend sitting together, you will soon realize that he won't sit there forever and, after connecting, will be content to go on his way. In fact, those of you who learn to sit and "be" with your child will find this new way of relating so comfortable that you will no longer feel anxious for him to move on to his next activity.

It's particularly effective, upon returning home at the end of a day, to sit down and be fully present to your child during those first moments together. Although many of you erroneously believe that you need time for yourselves after a long day's work, it's not realistic to put your child off at this point in the day. Others of you leave the office so late that you feel compelled to begin dinner immediately upon arriving home. Taking a moment, instead, to sit down and allow your child to connect with you, if he hasn't already done so during your drive home, will facilitate a smoother outcome for the rest of the evening.

Permission to Refuse Activities. It's wonderfully freeing to give yourself permission to do only those things with your children that you truly enjoy and refuse doing those things that you don't relish. Whenever you don't wish to join your child in an activity, you can still allow him access by offering him the alternative of sitting down and "hanging out" with you for awhile.

Permission to Enjoy Activities. Granting yourself permission to refuse activities does not mean that you never play another game or enjoy getting silly with your kids again. The important thing is to be real and do only those activities that are mutually enjoyable. In that way, your time together will be genuinely meaningful in a manner that strengthens your bond.

Dialogue from Class

MOTHER: For the most part, I sincerely like to do things with my kids. However, should I have an important chore to do—and one of my kids wants me to do something—how do I say "Wait" without putting up a wall?

BOBBIE: If you are unable to do an activity, it's best not to ask your child to "wait," since he will do just that! In fact, he'll wait right next to you, checking every few minutes to see if you are ready. It's better for him—and for you—to state that you are not available at this time and to give him a clear refusal. This frees him to adjust to that reality and go on to something else. Should you want to do the suggested activity after completing your project, you can check to see if he's still interested.

ᖆᖆᖆ

Real Barriers to Access. Once access without entertainment is established, your child will want to be with you a reasonable amount of time. He won't get overly attached as you may fear, since knowing that he's welcome in your life gives him the security he needs to move away from you and pursue other interests. Thus, on those occasions when you must attend to something or get to work or an appointment, you can simply let your child know that you are unavailable. Although this won't be a problem for the child who has learned to trust general access to you, it's important that you are careful not to put everything into this "essential" category.

A Word About Anxious Attachment and Overcare. Baby care books appropriately emphasize the importance of bonding and attachment. However, a problem develops when parents stop there and are concerned only with attachment, while failing to balance their parenting with structure.

Thus, anytime attachment is valued more than self-management or the individuating process, parents resist the various stages of separation needed to accomplish these important steps toward maturity. This results in anxious attachment on the part of the parent, which then gets transferred to the child and is detrimental to his development.

As a result, anytime a child has not been taught to gradually separate from his parents, he fails to experience himself as strong enough to manage progressively more things on his own without their help, and his need for his family to manage life for him deepens. This not only prevents him from learning to separate and cope on his own, he fails to adjust to not getting his way and doesn't learn to tolerate the pain and frustration that go with normal living. This response can result in poor individuation, a lack of self-help skills, and other developmental delays such as failing to socialize normally.

Thus, although bonding and attachment are important, anxious attachment will backfire. Consequently, parents who find themselves resisting the normal benchmarks of structure, discipline, and separation might want to consider the possibility that they are overdoing their attachment.

Dialogue from Class

FATHER: You hear so much today about the importance of healthy love. How can you maintain a close bond with your kids and still keep your love healthy?

BOBBIE: Healthy love does not include the stressful, fear-based love that you see in overcare or overconcern, nor does it feel invasive or controlling in order to meet the parent's unmet emotional needs. As a result, although you are connected to your child, you are not enmeshed. And because you understand that his life will be separate from yours, you rejoice in his activities and friends apart from you as well as in each step he takes toward autonomy. This is healthy love that you feel no need to hide or withdraw as your child grows in independence.

ⓖⓖⓖ

Summing Up and Looking Ahead

Putting your child—and the confusion he brings to your life—on the agenda, while loving him deeply and continuously, are the keys to keeping the loving part of your relationship in balance. With these in place, your child not only feels free to move out into the world from this base of security, but structure becomes deceivingly simple. In fact, with this foundation in place, you will find that you are able to discipline your child without losing sight of the angel within. The following two chapters will show you how.

★★★

Love is the glue that bonds hearts, inspires a child's surrender to parental love and guidance, and creates the secure foundation from which his independence springs.

★★★

6

Setting Clear Boundaries

Choices and Nonchoices

The Fifth Key:

ᠺᠺᠺ

Set clear boundaries without hesitation or fear.

Let's face it! Nobody enjoys a bratty child. Yet many of you are so uncomfortable with authority that your kids end up being just that.

My observation over the twenty-five years I've worked with families is that most parents are reluctant to control and discipline their children. When I ask in my classes how many parents fall into this category, about 75 percent raise their hands. This lack of discipline in so many homes might explain why studies indicate that there are almost three times more resistant kids than compliant ones in today's society.

The disturbing result of this growing reluctance to discipline is that similar to the super-strains of bacteria we've developed with an erratic use of drugs, we are now developing a super-strain of resistance to rules in our kids due to our unsteady use of discipline. We can see the effects of our reluctance to discipline showing up everywhere with alarming frequency, as increasingly more people grow up without learning to respect limits, control their impulses, or behave in an honest, caring, and responsible manner. In effect, the growing breakdown in requiring socialized behavior in our homes is causing a national crisis in our streets.

If we're to reverse this dangerous trend and raise children who preserve the sweet harmlessness they brought with them to this world, while forming the personalities they will use while here, we must overcome our discomfort with discipline and raise responsible kids, interested in caring and cooperating for the good of the whole. In short, we must learn to set and hold loving, yet effective, boundaries with our children if we want them to tame the impulses of self-interest and function at higher, more responsible levels. It's time that we faced the societal crisis we have created by our failure to discipline reliably and find both the courage and skills to bring it back.

The methods presented in this chapter and the next for establishing and holding clear, yet loving, boundaries offer a discipline style so palatable that even the most confused or fainthearted among you will not only want to use it, but will gain the skills to do so. To begin, you must require that your children surrender to you as the wise and mature head of your household.

Surrendering to the "Mature Boss"

I read an account of a young girl, instructed not to look at the sun during an eclipse, who snuck to her bedroom to drink in a long, deliberate look at it. Later that morning, while on her way to school, this young girl noticed that her eyesight was dimming, and, in a panic, turned to run for home. However, by the time she arrived, no one could help, for she had been permanently blinded by the sun.

As children get older and become mobile, they want to manage everything for themselves and act as "the boss." Yet as you can see from the above example, when children are not fully developed, their naive and "immature bosses" do not always make the best decisions or control their immature impulses. Because of this deficit in judgment, there are times when kids simply must surrender to the more "mature bosses" of their parents to help guide and manage them. Yet kids won't naturally do this unless they have been taught to release the temptations of their own naive impulses. Consequently, learning to surrender the "immature boss" of the child to the "mature boss" of the adult is a critical step in a child's development. Here's why.

Because the analysis, judgment, and decision-making functions of a child's brain are not fully formed until he's fifteen to eighteen years of age, kids aren't able to function at a fully competent level until they are well into their teens. Thus, rather than be impatient with your child for not always having the best judgment or making the right decisions, you must understand that he's not only less experienced than you, but that his brain is still in the process of developing the fullness of its capacity for those higher-level functions.

Consequently, the "immature boss" of your toddler might suggest that he jump into the twinkling water of a swimming pool, whereas your "mature boss" would be able to see his potential for drowning if he acted on this impulse. Similarly, the "immature boss" of your elementary-aged child may suggest that he ignore his homework or be rude to friends, whereas your "mature boss" could see how this would hurt his relationships and life; or the "immature boss" of your teen might determine that it's okay to drop out of school or drive while drinking, whereas your "mature boss" could see the larger implications of these decisions. Due to the discrepancy between the judgment skills of these two bosses, the job falls on you to take control with your more "mature boss" whenever needed to guide your kids through safe and productive childhoods, while also requiring that they conform to reasonable societal boundaries.

Yet in order to do this, you will need your child's surrender to the guidance of your "mature boss" during those times when you must preempt the shortsighted decisions of his "immature boss" that would get him off track and into trouble. If he fails to make this surrender and won't give up the inappropriate desires of his "immature boss," he becomes resistant to your guidance and fights you for control. Not only does this battle interfere with his normal progression toward maturity, it turns his relationship with you—and others—into a battleground.

When a child's resistance goes unresolved and continues into adolescence, it becomes a full-blown rebellion. Thus, in order for your child's development to remain on course, you must succeed in getting him to yield to your authority. The earlier you do this the better.

Parental Responsibilities

Once your child has surrendered his "immature boss" to the guidance and control of your more "mature boss," it's critical that you do, in fact, behave maturely and offer him as much freedom and control over his life as he seems ready to manage. Otherwise, the control your child has yielded to your "mature boss" is now turned against him by an "immature" and controlling "boss," and he may—wisely—reconsider his surrender.

Thus, once your child's surrender is achieved, it's important that you put your authority on a back burner and offer him ample opportunities to enjoy normal, age-appropriate freedoms. It's equally important that you offer him increasing control over his life in proportion to his willingness to handle his freedom responsibly. In effect, the cooperative child must be allowed to express himself as an individual, practice making his own decisions and choices, and experience a life of his own design. In this way, his surrender to your guidance paradoxically results in his being given progressively more control over his life.

When the development of your child's autonomy is handled in this cooperative manner, you no longer feel a need to maintain such tight control, and he no longer feels a need to fight for it. Instead, his surrender frees you to offer him additional opportunities to practice self-management and decision making as he begins to use and strengthen his own fulfiller. Yet on those occasions when he requires guidance, he's receptive to receiving it.

The Importance of Achieving Surrender with Love

The key to gaining your child's surrender is that you do it with love. Only then will your efforts lead to genuine surrender and result in his healthful functioning and a positive relationship between you.

In short, if you hold onto your newfound skills of loving deeply, while simultaneously adding this updated method of clear discipline, you will see profound improvements. The stories of Andy and Brett demonstrate how dramatically this works.

Andy

At the age of five, Andy was diagnosed as hyperactive with a focusing problem. Medication was recommended, but his parents wanted to try counseling first.

In our preliminary sessions, I could see that Andy's parents had deficits in their ability to both love and discipline their son. Their inadequacy in loving him had started with a significant bonding break when Andy was hospitalized soon after his birth. Not understanding what had happened, Mother became irritated by Andy's fussy response to this break and induced Father to join her in viewing him as a "strong-willed" and "difficult" child. In addition to this broken connection, both parents lacked discipline skills, and as Andy grew older, they allowed his boundaries to slide too long, then responded with anger.

I encouraged Mom to let down her wall and allow her son full access to her throughout each day. Although this was unsettling for her, she had tried everything else and was willing to give it a try. I further suggested that she stop her campaign against Andy so that Dad would feel free to love him as well. In addition, I offered both parents specific ways to be clearer, less angry, and more balanced in their discipline and sent them home with a set of parenting tapes to review these ideas.

Within a few months, Andy's parents expressed surprise at the changes they witnessed in their son so soon after they had brought more love and discipline into their parenting. Not only had most of his fussing stopped, he no longer seemed hyperactive and was able to relax and focus. They stopped describing him as resistant and "strong-willed" and now viewed him as a more loving and flexible child. Yet they still couldn't believe so much change had occurred in such a short period of time and wanted to understand better what had happened. Following is an explanation.

When the "Immature Boss" Is in Charge

Any time there's a parental deficit in nurturing, the grieving, often angry child is unable to trust his parents or learn from them how to care for others. In response to this failure to be loved or to love, he erects an emotional wall to protect himself from further rejection and pain. He then refuses to let his parents through this wall to guide him and relies, instead, on his own "immature boss," which naturally behaves in a demanding, disobedient, and childlike manner.

Whenever parents are weak in discipline, their child develops problems similar to the child whose family is deficient in nurturing. Because his parents have not yet learned to take control and be in charge, he, too, lacks an effective "boss" to parent him. As his "immature boss" strives to take charge in the absence of parental control, it fails to do such things as inhibit inappropriate behaviors or act responsibly. As a result, like the unnurtured child, he too, becomes a difficult, "strong-willed" child.

Whether it's a lack of nurturing and bonding or a failure to discipline and control, the results are strikingly similar; and when both are lacking, as in Andy's case, the problem is compounded. The child under these conditions fails to surrender to his parents' love or submit to their control—or both—and refuses to accept them as his "boss." Consequently, he lacks a "mature boss" to guide him in his development and is out there on his own to raise himself. Because such children pay no attention to the limits or guidance of adults, they are often out of control and may incorrectly be given the diagnosis of attention deficit disorder with or without hyperactivity—or ADD(H). As the child caught in this syndrome gets older, he becomes increasingly difficult for his family—and society—to manage. (See **Reactive Attachment and Other Attachment Problems** entry in the Problem-Solving Guide.)

When the "Mature Boss" Prevails

While working many years ago with my own children and others, I discovered that providing unfocused, whiny, and wiggly rule-challengers with a balance between love and discipline brings the missing, yet essential, "mature boss" back into their lives. This not only results in their surrender to love and the increased harmony that goes with it, but allows them to accept external control and thus respond more appropriately to their environment. In short, providing the "difficult" child—sometimes thought to be ADD(H)—

with an adult "boss" who will lovingly, yet firmly, teach him life's lessons enables him to settle down, pay attention, and behave normally once again. The impact of this surrender was made visibly clear to me one afternoon as I worked with a child named Brett.

Brett

One day I was called upon to restrain a six-year-old child who was out of control because he didn't get his way on some minor issue and was attempting to run out of the schoolyard. Brett had been a difficult child to manage, and his teachers were constantly exploring ways to reach him. He was a strong boy, and I was required to use all of my strength to hold him. (See **Safe-Holding** entry in the Problem-Solving Guide.)

Initially, I felt anger rise within me as I struggled with Brett, but then remembered to shift my awareness down to my heart and call forth the love that I knew I felt for him. Once I remembered my love, I was able to feel calm again. Then, as I firmly restrained Brett—while actively remaining in my heart and sending him love—he, too, became calmer.

Next, I slowly released my grip, checking with each release to see if he was ready to surrender to my boundaries. Whenever he would begin to fight me again, with love in my heart, I resumed control. Meanwhile, I softly verbalized to Brett that he would lose freedom each time he fought my boundaries, but would get it back whenever he sat in my lap without resistance.

After forty minutes of struggling and yelling that I wasn't "his boss," Brett allowed his body to go limp, and he melted into my lap. Before long, deep feelings of love flowed between us as we sat in silence for awhile, tears trickling down both of our cheeks. I knew that Brett had surrendered, at last, to my boundaries as he sat there docilely, loving me for possessing the strength and courage to know how to care for him. Gradually, Brett was able to verbalize his acceptance of my control over his immaturity as he now yielded to my love, while playing with my hair and stroking my face. After a period of lingering in my lap, this newly sweet child hopped down, returned to his classroom, and went on to have a better day.

Brett was the first child I held in this way, and I, too, was changed by the experience. The thing that most surprised me was how loving Brett was with me after our encounter and how much more cooperative he became with his teachers and peers.

After this experience, I noticed that whenever I worked with children while holding active feelings of love in my heart along with firm clarity, the child regularly responded with a desire to cooperate. I discovered, however, that my feelings of love had to be as strong as my intent to discipline. And likewise, my intent to discipline had to be as clear as my feelings of love. In short, when I could hold a balance between love and discipline, the child responded quickly and dramatically.

I began to notice that this surrender to discipline felt exactly like my daughter's surrender to love had felt the day I held her sobbing in my arms and offered her love without conditions (see Chapter 3). I also remembered that after my daughter's surrender to love, she, too, had allowed me to be her guide and—without further resistance—had accepted my discipline for the first time.

It occurred to me that the very same issue prevails for both the child whose parents are weak in discipline and the one whose parents have failed to provide adequate love. Because the child under either of these conditions is not able to experience his parents as both loving and firm, he's unable to trust them to act as kind and mature "bosses"—and he strives to fill the void by acting as his own "boss."

Although gaining surrender from your child is the issue—whether it's getting him to surrender to your love or to your discipline or both—your success will lie in your ability to offer genuine love that is balanced with discipline and discipline balanced with love. In this way, the combination of love and structure gives your child something stronger and wiser than himself that he can put his trust in. This trust helps him to feel secure enough to surrender to your love and submit to your control, and he's able, at last, to accept you as his "boss" or guide. He no longer has to be in charge of such a little guy in this large world but can now turn over the role of "boss" to his stronger and wiser parents.

The Results of Gaining Surrender

It's my observation that parents comfortable with requiring their children to acquiesce to civilized boundaries, while also understanding and respecting their need for self-management, end up with congenial offspring who are able to accept rules and conform to normal boundaries without resistance and suffering. Because such kids have a cooperative orientation, they tend to choose amiable friends, make responsible decisions, and live happy and productive lives.

Studies support my observation that children who have made this surrender to adult standards of behavior are actually happier than their resistant counterparts. James Dobson (*Parenting Isn't for Cowards*, 1987) discovered in a survey that compliant children are not only the most cooperative, but get better grades, make superior social adjustments, are less influenced by negative peer pressure, rebel less often during adolescence, have higher self-esteem, and are, as young adults, the most successful.

Once parents understand the benefits of structure and their child's surrender to it, they become more interested in how to create both. In this chapter, I will present my guidelines for establishing clear, fair, and consistent boundaries with children. The following chapter will show you how to achieve your child's surrender to whatever parameters you establish. The key is that you remember while working with discipline to also hold love in your heart.

Setting Boundaries: Establishing Choices and Nonchoices

The first step in providing structure for your child is to clearly determine the boundaries that he will be required to live within. These boundaries can best be visualized by depicting a *circle of choices* containing all of the choices available to him, including what he is required to do as well as what he is allowed to do. Everything outside of this circle represents the *nonchoice zone*, or behaviors, freedoms, and privileges that are not a choice and will not be allowed. (See Figure 6.)

Getting Precise

You must decide exactly what is and what is not a choice for your child, rather than present rules as hazy suggestions or wishful expectations. It helps, for example, when you visualize just how it would look in various settings if your child were behaving precisely as you would like. For instance, if he's calmly playing with some packets of sugar at a restaurant, would that behavior be acceptable? What if he's opening one of them or pouring its contents into his water? What if he's opening all of the packets and sprinkling them over his dinner? (I would personally allow one or two of the packets to go into the water but would then establish a boundary.)

If you have decided not to create a rule about your child playing with the packets, you must refrain from making any suggestions about putting them away, since this would convey a mixed message, including your wish that he not touch them coupled with a license to do so. You must understand that this mixture of signals teaches your child to resist all suggestions you make in the future.

Figure 6. Boundary Line

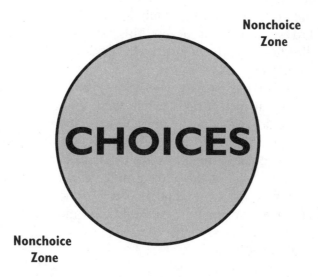

If, on the other hand, it's a choice for him to play with the packets but not to get wild or open them, a tossed or opened packet is precisely where your boundary line must hold. Thus, once a limit is established, it's essential that you stay awake enough to notice the moment it gets crossed, so that you can stop your child from lingering in the nonchoice zone.

Identifying What's Important. Select only those rules that are truly important to you, rather than overwhelm your child with requests for things you don't care enough about to follow through on. Accordingly, each boundary must represent something you're willing to go to the mat on—even if it results in an hour-long tantrum or a major confrontation with your teen. Not only do these more carefully selected boundaries simplify the implementation of rules, they allow your child more freedom of choice and control over daily living.

Careful boundaries further protect you from being like the parent we have all seen who constantly instructs her child on how to do everything: "Use your fork, not your spoon! Sit up straight in your chair! Push your hair out of your eyes. Stop swinging your legs! Don't drink your milk shake! Eat your sandwich first." Not only is this parent offering too many instructions and overcontrolling her child's personal freedom as he eats, she's not going to follow through on any one of these nonessential mandates, should they be ignored or challenged. Whenever instructions are given without enforcement, your child gets trained to stop taking you seriously and becomes dangerously deaf to everything you suggest. This "deafness" continues for the teen who is overdirected in such things as when to study, get off of the phone, take a shower, or go to bed.

Likewise, you should pause before asking your child to do things you don't really care about such as asking your young child to get out of his bath, but then when he doesn't, allowing him to linger. If you "prefer" that he get out but have no real need for him to do so, you would be wise not to say anything about terminating the bath. It's better to allow him more time in the tub—with permission—than allow him to remain there without it. Use it as an opportunity to relax your tendency to overdirect and let it be a swim. What difference does it make if he gets a little wrinkled?

Selecting Your Child's Choices

It's critical that you determine just what choices are available to your child at each stage of his development. Although defining boundaries is an exercise you must individually tailor to your personal style, values, educational standards, and ethnic background, it's important that you know how to create a medium-sized circle that is neither too small and restrictive nor too large and unstructured. Following are some guidelines for creating an appropriate-sized circle that supports healthful functioning.

Parents Who Overcontrol: The Restrictively Tight Circles. Because excessive control ignores the needs of your child and leaves him with too few opportunities to practice the decision-making and self-management needed for healthful functioning, it's critical not to have overly restrictive boundaries.

Yet in spite of the problems, some of you will fall into this category. You are the ones, for example, who tend to require that your child participate only in those activities you consider educational or worthwhile; spend his time and money in accordance with your wishes; eat solely the amounts and types of foods you approve; achieve at high levels in academics and other pursuits of your choosing; or select only the friends you value. Your boundaries are even more rigid if you prohibit child-centered activities and teen opportunities for socialization—or require that your child continually care for siblings or do most of the household chores.

Interestingly, families using such controlling limits don't get the same results as those with more flexible guidelines, since their kids recognize that something is deeply wrong and may respond with active—or passive—resistance, if not rebellion or despair. Thus, parents with dominant tendencies to be in charge of too many aspects of their children's lives must strive to develop more realistic, less rigid guidelines for behavior.

Parents Who Undercontrol: The Gaping Circles. Others of you are undercontrolling and allow your young children to run thoughtlessly and recklessly through malls, bump into others without apology, act cruelly to insects and animals, talk or cry during movies, watch as much television as they desire, or choose any hour or place they like for meals and bedtime. As your children get older, you fail to object to their aggressive back talk or moods, much less ask where they are going or that their bedrooms be cleaned. Those of you with these looser standards simply don't offer your kids enough structure to help them develop in a competent or socially suitable manner.

Parents Who Control with Balance: The Medium-Sized Circles. The goal of balanced parenting is to establish medium-sized circles that offer your children enough structure to assure their safe and appropriate behavior, while also providing them with ample choices and control over their lives. Those of you who accomplish this provide normal, balanced circles in which your children are allowed to freely operate.

Once a balanced circle is established, parents must remain alert to protecting their child's freedoms as he matures by continuously adjusting his boundaries as needed. For example, what is appropriate for the three-year-old is too little freedom for a five-year-old, and what is adequate for the five-year-old is not enough for an older child or teen.

It's equally important that you expand your child's freedom according to his level of responsibility. If, for instance, your child is ten and acts as responsibly as an eleven- or twelve-year-old, he should enjoy the more expanded freedoms of an older child for as long as he's operating at that level. On the other hand, if he's ten and functions at the level of a seven- or eight-year-old, he must be given the more limited freedoms of a younger child, until he's ready to behave more responsibly. Likewise, your reliable teen should be given full management over his affairs, whereas the one still fighting you for control must be given tighter boundaries until his "immature (and rebellious) boss" has surrendered and can be trusted.

An essential guide to use while creating your children's circles of choices is to allow them as much reasonable choice as possible while assuring that they function as responsible members of society. Using the model of the grizzly mother, you can allow your children to have as good a time as possible so long as they stay within your and society's boundaries. It's interesting to note that children adhere most easily to boundaries set in this context, since they recognize their flexibility and fairness.

Establishing Adult-Designated Choices—or Rules. Each circle should contain a number of adult-directed choices—or rules—which your child will be required to adhere to. Following are some guidelines for determining what rules to establish with your particular child.

▶ *Safety and Welfare.* Of primary consideration in establishing rules is the safety and welfare of your child and others. With this in mind, your young child would not be allowed to race across streets or push friends from walls. Nor would your elementary-age child be allowed to practice his martial arts on friends or your teen permitted to drive without a license. Such boundaries would not be in the best interest of your child's or others' safety and welfare. On the other hand, those of you who are overly cautious must be careful not to view everything as dangerous and prevent your child from normal levels of play and exploration.

▶ *Consideration of Others.* It's your job to make sure that your child does not encroach on the personal space, property, or rights of others. To ensure this, your young child would not be permitted to invade the tables of others dining at a restaurant or smear syrup on the table for the waitress to clean. Neither would your elementary-age child be allowed to blast his music on a hike or your teen permitted to park his car on the neighbor's lawn.

▶ *Respect for Nature and Property.* In addition to being sensitive to the rights and needs of others, it's critical that your children also learn respect for property and nature. Consequently, it's important that you teach them never to leave a path of garbage and destruction in their wake but to carefully restore all things used and places visited to their original state. Thus, your young child would not be allowed to leave gum under furniture, nor disturb the homes or lives of insects and plants. Neither would your older kids be allowed to throw litter from the car or leave coals unattended at a camp-out.

▶ *Full-Cycling.* The Native Americans, who were close to nature and its laws, believed deeply in restoring their land to its original order before moving on to new territory. Similarly, the early Hawaiians required that all relationships that had become messy be healed. And educator Maria Montessori taught children respect for materials by stressing the importance of completing the cycles of each activity before going on to the next. We learn from these examples both the value of and means for preserving the land, our relationships, and materials by completing each of the cycles we initiate before switching to new ones. This process is called full-cycling.

Because accepting responsibility for his actions is important to your child's development, it's essential to teach him to clear his path and complete the cycles of his activities—or full-cycle—as he moves through life. Thus, he must be taught to clean his messes, return his materials to their rightful place, restore rooms to their original order, and heal any breaks in his relationships. By doing this, he not only keeps his world and relationships cleaner and clearer, but learns to refine his choices in accordance with their effect on himself and others as well as the environment. Happily, the child who is taught to be conscious of the need to complete the cycles of his activities will move through life with greater awareness, gentleness, and a sense of caring about the land, people, and materials he encounters along the way.

Dialogue from Class

MOTHER: How early can children start full-cycling?

BOBBIE: Children can begin at about two to two-and-a-half years old by putting away each game or puzzle they have used before going on to the next activity. When a child is first learning this, he's usually pretty cooperative. If not, you simply move his hands gently through the motions as you clearly but lovingly talk about what you are doing. It helps to appeal to the young child's natural heart-based sensitivity to things by explaining that the activities want to be tucked back into the shelves where they belong and can feel more cozy and comfortable. Not only does this heighten the child's sensitivity to the importance of keeping our world ordered, it makes the task more conscious and fun. Over time, completing the cycle becomes part of every activity for him.

FATHER: Do you really think a child that young is capable of putting his toys away?

BOBBIE: If you think of it in terms of a movie running in reverse, you will realize that they're just as capable of putting an activity away as they are of taking it out. It's only when a child resists cleaning that those same little fingers that were so dexterously working with his blocks a moment ago suddenly mimic overcooked linguine as they become limp and inoperable! Be aware that resistance only develops when a child frames full-cycling as a negative or difficult thing to do. This decision isn't a natural one and happens only when adults label this part of an activity as challenging or something their child may resist. An important key to success with a young child is to have him put each activity away before beginning the next, rather than allow him to accumulate several messes that will seem overwhelming to him when it's time to clean.

MOTHER: I just go along behind my child to get it cleaned the way I really want it. (Laughter)

BOBBIE: The problem with this is that your child realizes his effort was lacking—even when you do this out of his view—and that's the conclusion he develops about his abilities. It's better to lovingly take the time to show him how to restore things fully to their original condition. The goal is to teach him to easily include this part of life as an habitual response.

A SECOND MOTHER: After I taught my child to full-cycle his own messes, he began to question why he had to clean up messes that weren't his own.

BOBBIE: This does create a point of confusion for young children unless we take time to explain the difference between our own individual messes and the work we do for the common good of our community, in this case, the family unit. You must teach him that in a family, there are numerous community chores in addition to each person's individual messes, and every family must decide which of its members will do the various tasks needed to keep the family functioning.

▶ *Honoring Your Child's Needs and Rights.* Your children's need for exploration, socialization, fun, and a healthy degree of control over their own choices and lives must be honored. For example, it's important for kids to have ample opportunities to spend undirected, playful, and fun time with their siblings and friends. It's equally important that they be allowed to practice doing things for themselves and others at every opportunity. And it's essential that their need to be in charge of such things as what they will eat and wear, how they will spend their time and money, and which friends, interests, and activities they will pursue be acknowledged.

By honoring the needs and rights of your kids, you will bypass the kinds of mistakes many parents make. For example, one mother failed to honor her son's right to enjoy free time and play by insisting that he read a book whenever he was free; a dad failed to honor his ten-year-old's need to practice managing things on her own when he wouldn't allow her to place the call to order a family pizza; another mom failed to honor her preteen's need to select her own clothes and bought her daughter's school wardrobe during a business trip; and another dad failed to respect his teen's time by ordering that he do the dishes in the middle of the family's favorite sitcom, rather than ask that he do them during the commercials or following the program.

▶ *Age-Appropriate, Socially Acceptable Behavior.* In selecting your child's choices, you must determine what would be considered acceptable, age-appropriate behavior for a child at his stage of development, rather than base his options on what you can personally tolerate. For example, some of you are comfortable with your child climbing over the neighbor's furniture, hanging on clothes racks at shopping malls, or kicking the airplane seat of the passenger in front of him. Others of you fail to notice if your child has such problems as bad breath and body odor or talks with his mouth full. You are simply oblivious to the unattractive, overactive, or outright obnoxious behaviors of your children. Thus, rather than use your own excessively high levels of tolerance for deciding your child's parameters, you would be wise to utilize the combined feedback of friends, neighbors, and teachers in determining acceptable boundaries for your child.

Then again, there are others of you who have no tolerance whatsoever. You simply don't like to deal with anything and always say "No" to your child, even when his requests and behaviors are age-appropriate and acceptable to others. Your children are not only expected to sit unrealistically still and upright in chairs and never interrupt adult conversations, but are scolded for normal behaviors like soiling playclothes, getting silly with friends, or talking loquaciously during dinner. Your teens are expected to visit friends only when their parents are home, are not allowed to have their own guests in their bedrooms, and must call you every time they make a move while spending a day with friends. Because your kids are thwarted from pursuing the normal activities of childhood, you would be wise to observe the common freedoms of other well-behaved and responsible kids and get your boundaries into more realistic perspective. For another measure of appropriateness try imagining how comfortable you would feel if your child acted in any given manner publicly. If the behavior would likely be intrusive to others or would cause your child rejection, you are not being fair to allow it, unless you clarify that this particular behavior would only be tolerated at home. If the behavior seems acceptable in public, allow it.

Establishing Child-Centered Choices—or Freedoms and Privileges. In addition to the boundaries and rules that a child is required to use, each circle of choice also contains those freedoms and privileges he would like to have which his parent is willing to allow. Following are some guidelines to use when determining which of these privileges to grant your children.

▶ *Willing and Able.* In addition to the criteria already established for adult-based rules, two additional components are needed for deciding what privileges your child will be allowed: 1) your child's *willingness* and 2) his *ability* to assume responsibility for whatever freedoms he would like to have. Thus, anytime your child is both *willing* and *able* to accept responsibility, his choices are expanded.

However, if he is either unwilling or unable, those choices are not available to him. For example, your child might be willing to light the barbecue but may not be able to manage it safely. At other times he's able to do some activity, but is not yet willing to do it responsibly. He might, for instance, understand the procedure for crossing streets, biking to the mall, or driving a car, but is not yet mature enough to use the rules consistently and is thus not ready for those freedoms. In such circumstances, your child is told that as soon as he's willing to remember the rules, he will be allowed that privilege.

The child raised in this way experiences a great deal of control over his life, since he can regulate the expansion or contraction of his liberty with his choice of behaviors. Not surprisingly, it's this very control over his freedom that inspires a child's willingness to select increasingly responsible and cooperative behaviors.

By contrast, the child who is handled in an arbitrary manner and is told that he can't bike to the park until he's older has no idea what steps he might take to earn that freedom or how he can gain control over his activities and life. Such a child might sneak to the park, since there is no alternative plan he can use to gain this expanded freedom he sees so many of his friends enjoying.

At other times, your child is both willing and able, but you remain unwilling for him to try something new as a result of your own rigidity or fears. This is highly frustrating to a child who is ready for more responsibility, and it breaks down his trust in you as a good manager with a genuinely "mature boss." Consequently, those of you who are overly cautious must learn to let your child demonstrate his willingness and ability to do increasingly more things.

Dialogue from Class

FATHER: What do you do if your child is unwilling to do something that's a required rule?

BOBBIE: Whenever your child is unwilling to cooperate with a rule such as cleaning his room before breakfast, all freedoms stop until he becomes willing to do so. On the other hand, if some privilege such as spending the night with a friend is being offered on the basis of his willingness to first wash the dog, then only that additional freedom is withheld if he's unwilling to do the task.

Getting Specific. To create clear, specific boundaries for your child, it helps to mentally go through his day and visualize or write down exactly what his choices are and what they are not. For example, what are his options when he's dressing, making his bed, eating, cleaning up messes, watching television, napping, snacking, doing homework, participating in extracurricular activities, eating at a restaurant, playing with friends, or doing chores?

Is he free, for instance, to make his own clothes selection for various activities, and, if so, may he choose anything or are there guidelines? Is he required to make his bed, and, if so, at what age does this begin and what time of day is he asked to do it? What happens if he doesn't do it? Exactly what happens if he refuses to eat? Does he get another selection? Is he allowed to leave food on his plate or skip an entire meal? May he lie on the floor at a restaurant? What about sitting in Dad's lap after his meal? How about wiggling in his chair, leaning back in it, or standing up on it? Is he required to clean his messes as he goes? Or, is he allowed to repair the damage at the end of each day? What happens when he needs reminding? What if he refuses? Is he allowed to watch as much television as he likes? If not, what precisely are his guidelines? Can he walk around the house with his thumb in his mouth? Or must he do this in his room? At what age—if ever—will this be controlled? Is he required to take a nap? If so, for how long? What if he doesn't sleep? What if he fusses? May he lie in his bed and play quietly or read during nap time, or is he required to sleep? What about at bedtime? Is he allowed to select his own clothes when shopping, or do you purchase things without his input? Is he free to snack whenever he likes? If so, may he eat anything in the house, or is he required to select from certain foods? Can he help himself, or does someone have to serve him? Does he leave his dishes for you to wash, or does he clean up after himself? Is he required to complete his homework? If so, when and where will it be done? How is it handled if he procrastinates? What happens if he says he doesn't have homework and it turns out that he did? What happens if he doesn't turn in completed assignments? Is he required to learn some skill such as a musical instrument? If so, can he choose the particular instrument, or is that selected by you? Is he obliged to practice? For how long? What time of day? Is he allowed to stop taking lessons or stop practicing? Is he allowed to participate in sports? Is he required to participate? If so, is he free to select the sport, or must he play the one you prefer? Is he allowed to quit? Is he free to play or socialize with friends after school? If so, does he play before or after homework? What chores is he required to do? What happens when he needs reminding? What happens if he delays or refuses? What if he argues about his chores? What happens when he name-calls, yells, swears, or pouts? Will he be allowed to get his driver's license when he's of age? If not, what conditions must he meet? Will he be allowed to go to dances and parties or out with friends at night? If so, at what age? What will his curfew be? Will it be flexible or firmly set? Will it expand with age? With responsibility? Will it contract if the terms are not met? Who plans his summers? Is he required to do something that will stimulate growth or be productive? Or, will he be allowed to do nothing if desired? Will he be required to work when he's of age? What will happen if he doesn't get around to securing a job? Does he get an allowance? If so, how much? Is he required to do anything to earn it? Which of his expenses must it cover? Is he allowed to spend the remainder as he chooses? What happens when he fails to meet his financial responsibilities? Is he allowed to have his own opinions about politics, race, and religion, or is he required to think as you do? What happens if he disagrees or refuses to conform to your ideas?

The following parameters for determining morning routines, cleaning guidelines, and the assignment of allowances and chores offer a model of how much detail is required for establishing clearly defined boundaries in these particular areas. (Refer to the Problem-Solving Guide for guidance in other areas.)

▸ ***Morning Routines.*** Morning goes better for dawdlers if you establish a routine, preferably illustrated on a visual chart for them to use as a guide.

My preference is to let children know that they're free to leave their bedrooms only after they have dressed, made their beds (beginning at about four years of age), and have fed any caged animals that live in their bedrooms. Once these chores are completed, they're free to leave their rooms and join the family for breakfast (preferably sitting and talking as opposed to watching television). When breakfast is finished, teeth must be brushed and articles gathered before your child is free to read a book or play a game while waiting for his ride to school.

If he elects not to complete his dressing and misses breakfast, it's important to be clear that his ride will leave, whether he is ready or not. Thus, at this juncture, he may grab his clothes and, if you're uncomfortable with letting him go hungry, a dry piece of toast—as opposed to something more exciting—in order to dress and eat on the way. Once in the car, you can calmly reflect how much easier it is to dress at home in order to get his hair right, eat a good meal, and get his mouth smelling fresh— and that you are sure he'll do better tomorrow.

If you remain calm and friendly and don't take any more interest in his delay than that, he will eventually correct this pattern. If he loves school, you can let him go late or miss it if he didn't do his chores. However, if attending school is tentative for your child, it's better to let him go; but when he returns home, make sure that he's not free to do anything else until his chores are completed.

▸ ***Cleaning.*** It's important to create a clear structure for when and how various cleaning tasks will be accomplished during each stage of your child's development. For example, it's best to require that young children clean each mess they make before going on to the next. This helps them to view an activity and its cleanup as a unit and trains them in the habit of regularly cleaning after themselves. Once your child accepts this cycle of activity without resistance, he can be allowed to make several messes in an area and required to clean only when he's ready to leave the vicinity.

When your child can be relied on to clean these messes—without reminders—for a period of at least a year, he can then be given an expanded boundary to operate within such as cleaning within his own time frame, yet sometime before the end of each day for as long as this is working. A child who is succeeding with this level of maturity may then be allowed to clean his bedroom once a week rather than daily, as long as he handles it sometime before the designated time and day and doesn't turn his room into a pigsty between cleanings.

However, if your child is offered the expanded freedom of cleaning his room only once a week, but then fails to conform to this looser boundary, he must be returned to the more controlled structure of cleaning his room on a daily basis—or if that isn't working, on a mess-by-mess basis.

You can learn from a mistake I made with my daughter in the cleaning department. Initially, I required that both of my children's rooms be cleaned daily in order to establish the habit of regular cleaning. I then offered them the opportunity to operate at the next level of maturity and clean their rooms on a weekly basis. Because my oldest had established a daily cleaning routine which he had used for about a year, he continued to clean regularly with only a little additional work on Saturdays for dusting or picking up.

On the other hand, my youngest child was still disinclined toward cleaning and had barely established a reluctant daily routine at the time she was offered the more expanded boundary. Consequently, when the tighter structure requiring her to clean daily was removed, not only did her daily cleaning pattern collapse, she was unprepared to meet the new standard of weekly cleaning. Unfortunately, I didn't adequately address this issue, and due to a weak plan plus my inconsistency in handling it, room-cleaning became a problem for her until adulthood, when she made a new decision about a desire for order in her own home.

By contrast, I had been unusually clear with this same child about making her bed and cleaning her guinea pig cage each morning before leaving for school. In fact, one morning when she slipped off without doing this pair of chores, because she had been so resistant to cleaning, I elected to make a point. Thus, I went to her school to bring her home. When she saw me, her eyes grew wide and she blurted out, "I didn't make my bed or change Soapy's cage!" I calmly replied, "That's right, and when you don't get your chores done, you're not free to be at school—so you'll have to come home with me to get them handled for today, but I'm sure you will remember tomorrow."

And, indeed, she did! The rest of our day at home together was friendly but boring (with no television), and to this day,—although the guinea pig has long since expired—she wouldn't think of walking out of the house without first making her bed. Yet the rest of her room for years looked like something only a fellow piglet could appreciate. It would have confused anyone who had not heard this story to walk into her room and see the carefully made bed amidst the mess! But, it's a good story to demonstrate the effectiveness of so clearly holding a boundary and the ineffectiveness of letting one go.

▶ ***Community Chores.*** In addition to personal chores, I would require a child to do community chores in order to contribute to the running of the family household. These would include helping with such things as yard work, kitchen duties, and general housework, rather than only the personal responsibilities of cleaning his own bedroom, doing his personal laundry, or caring for his individually owned animals.

Although I would allow a child to select which chores he wanted to do, he would be required to select at least one small community chore (such as setting the table or folding the towels) while he is still young. I would increase his contribution to at least two medium-size chores (such as emptying the trash, raking the leaves, or washing the dog) as he gets older and at least one of the larger chores (such as vacuuming, mowing the lawn, or doing the marketing) for a teen.

▶ ***Allowances and Chores.*** My personal preference is to establish allowances based on your child's contribution to community chores. I suggest linking your child's allowance to his chores not only to serve as a motivator for getting them done on time but to teach him that money is something we get in exchange for energy. This establishes that his money is earned, rather than doled out to him and gives him full ownership of his funds and the freedom to spend—or waste—them as he chooses, except in ways that would break family rules or values.

Once your child's chores and their compensation are assigned, I would pick a time when these needed to be accomplished. My preference is to require that the young child complete both personal and community chores on Saturday morning prior to leaving the house for the day's activities. As he gets older and more responsible, I would allow him to determine when he wanted to do his chores, but require that they be done sometime before a predetermined time, such as Sunday afternoon.

Anytime a chore is not completed by its deadline, your child would not only lose the payment assigned for that chore, but all freedom to do anything else (except for other commitments and responsibilities) until the chore was completed. If he failed to complete his chores by the time assigned on the expanded program, in addition to losing payment and freedom, he would be returned to the more restrictive Saturday morning program for awhile longer.

Once you can count on your child to function as a fully responsible, contributing family member, you can allow him to schedule his chores into his week without any time frames or deadlines.

Communicating Boundaries

During a trip to Hong Kong, I found the people there so disciplined that I inquired about how their children were raised. A well-versed father gave my question considerable thought before replying, "The key lies in 'teaching' a child what is expected of him rather than 'punishing' him for not doing it." In listening to this prescription, I realized that Western parents would be well advised to communicate clearer pictures of desirable behaviors to their children as well.

Making Your Boundaries Visible

Once you have decided which boundaries to use, it's important to transmit the message to your kids by making the images that go with your limits equally clear and visible to them. Although you can't possibly anticipate every situation a child might encounter, the goal is to create as clear a picture of his boundaries as possible, rather than give vague and wistful messages along the way of "Be good," "Behave yourself," or "Settle down." In short, the first step in holding boundaries is to clearly define whatever parameters you have decided upon. By remembering to do this, you will no longer find yourself in situations like the one created by the mother in the following example.

When Mrs. King arrived with her daughter, Megan, at a friend's house and saw an area of harmless low-level rocks, leading to some larger, more dangerous ones above, she quickly calculated to herself, "I'd rather Megan didn't play on those rocks because I'm concerned that she'll go too high and get hurt," so she called out to her daughter as she ran off to play, "Don't go near the rocks!" When she later noticed Megan on the low-level rocks, she thought to herself that it would be okay, so long as she didn't go any higher. However, since her actual rule was never clearly stated, and she wasn't enforcing the vague one she had tossed out, Megan began to experience confusion. She realized that she was playing on the forbidden rocks and that her mother saw her. Yet her mother evidently didn't mean what she said, since she wasn't enforcing her rule. As a result, Megan felt free to explore the higher rocks as well. When Mrs. King noticed this, she yelled to her daughter, "I told you not to climb on those rocks!" However, because Megan assumed, once again, that Mother didn't mean what she said, she continued to climb on the high rocks, which were now seriously endangering her safety.

It would be a clearer message, and one that more honestly reflects her true boundaries, if Mrs. King had said in the first place, "You may play on the low-level rocks, but it's not a choice to go any higher than the crack on the gray rock leading to the bigger ones." Because that message would have clarified for Megan as well as herself exactly where her boundary lay, she would have been more likely to both notice and hold it, in the event it got crossed.

Getting Your Child's Attention

When communicating boundaries, it's essential that you get your child's full attention. This doesn't happen if you call out your rules to him from another room or as he's going out the door or off to play. Not only should you and your child be within a few feet of one another, you must give each other your attention. This works best when both of you stop your other activities and perhaps even sit together to assure that your communication is clearly given and clearly received.

Speaking from the Heart. Whenever you are giving your child instructions about boundaries, if you speak from your heart, he will be more likely to hear them with his heart and respond accordingly. Thus, offering gentleness, warmth, and kindness, while providing boundaries or responding to broken ones, keeps things calm and peaceful as you administer and address your limits. Keeping your awareness—and breathing—focused in your heart further softens and protects you from becoming rigid, dominant, and controlling while managing your rules. Yet it's also critical that you do not misinterpret speaking from the heart to mean speaking with uncertainty.

Agreements: Having Your Child Restate His Boundary. Not only is it important that you clearly state your boundaries, it's useful to have your child reflect them back to you. By actively expressing what he agrees to do in this way, your child confirms that the message was both received and understood and that he consciously accepts responsibility for doing what was asked of him.

Requiring that your child state his boundaries is especially helpful on those occasions when you want him to agree to certain terms prior to expanding his freedom. For example, before your child is allowed to ride his bike around the neighborhood, he must be clear that his limits include wearing his helmet, looking both ways at intersections, and riding near the curb. Thus, it would be prudent to ask your child precisely what he plans to remember if he is to keep his new freedom. In this way, you help him to become aware of exactly what responsibilities he is accepting. If he holds to the parameters he has agreed to—and you must stay alert to make sure that he does—then he's permitted to maintain his expanded freedom. If not, he temporarily loses this freedom and is given a chance in a few hours, days, or weeks to see if he is ready to restate his parameters and agree to hold to them. Restating boundaries is particularly useful with kids who claim not to hear their rules or regularly "forget" them.

Using the Language of "Choice." Boundaries are best communicated to young and elementary-aged children by using two simple phrases: "That's a choice" and "That's not a choice." This uncomplicated language gives them a sense that there are many options and choices in life, while at the same time indicating that some things will be designated nonchoices. For example, rather than give the child who wants to light the barbecue imprecise messages such as, "Not now, son," or "Dad will light it later," it's preferable to simply state that lighting the barbecue won't be a choice for him tonight and why. Because children function best when messages are given as directly and clearly as possible, the direct—yet gentle—statement, "That's not a choice, sweetheart," will make it easier for him to begin to absorb and accept that reality.

In addition to pointing out those things that are not a choice, you can help your child to see where his remaining choices lie. For example, although you are not always required to provide substitute activities when nonchoices occur, alternate options do help your child to maintain a sense of control, rather than feel unduly frustrated by too many blocked choices. Thus, you might offer him the alternative of laying the fire and, in that way, help him to experience more control over his life as well as an opportunity to participate in this activity of interest to him.

In other situations, it may not be a choice whether your child does something such as his homework or a chore; however, he may be offered the choice of when he does it, where, and under what conditions. He might, for example, have the option of doing his homework at the dining room table while eating a snack or alone in his room with music blaring. Or he may be allowed to do his chores on Friday afternoon or Sunday morning or with the help or companionship of a sibling or friend.

Sometimes a child's choices have been narrowed to a simple choice between walking cooperatively to his room for a time-out or being carried—or to accept being in his room peacefully or to continue to resist it. By reflecting these options, your child can be taught that regardless of the circumstances, he always has enough choice in the matter to maintain some measure of control.

Viktor Frankl, while a prisoner in a concentration camp, discovered that his captors could take away his clothes, his dignity, and even his family, but they could not remove his choice of how he would react or feel within himself. Interestingly, children also discover the power to choose how they will feel as a result of parents using this language of choice which subtly, but persistently, reinforces the idea employed by Viktor Frankl that there are always some choices in life. They learn through this use of language that although they must sometimes accept doing things they don't like, they always maintain control over their emotional state by choosing their internal response to each situation.

Four-year-old Savanah, who loved this system and the language of choice, was overheard talking to Muffin, the family dog, who was looking at her longingly as she ate a cookie. She looked back at him with the courage more parents ought to muster and calmly said, "Muffin, I know you want this cookie, but that just isn't one of your choices." Savanah understood that some things are simply "not a choice," and she was helping Muffin adjust to that idea!

Dialogue from Class

MOTHER: I've read that we shouldn't ever say "No" or "Don't" to children. I like "That's not a choice" better, but it still seems like a euphemism for "No."

BOBBIE: Although I much prefer the softness of "That's not a choice," I would rather see parents say "No" or "Don't" to children than skirt the issue of boundaries. How will children know where their boundaries lie if adults are so afraid to mention them that they keep them vaguely wrapped in feeling statements?

FATHER: Don't you think "That's not a choice" sounds a bit like jargon?

BOBBIE: Some parents worry about that initially, but then get over their discomfort when they discover how well their child responds to it.

MOTHER: Whenever I suggest that my five-year-old sit quietly at the doctor's office, she won't do it. It's not a choice for her to refuse, but I can't figure out how to get her to do it.

BOBBIE: When you ask her to sit with you, is it clear that it's a requirement, or does it sound more like a request?

MOTHER: It probably sounds like a request since I say, "Would you like to sit next to me and read a book?" or "Would you like to thank Susie's mother for the party?" And she always says, "No."

BOBBIE: Do you see what the problem is? In your mind it's not a choice to refuse. Yet you're presenting it as a choice. It would be more effective to say, "Sweetheart, you need to sit quietly next to Mom. You can either sit in my lap or by yourself in the seat next to me." It's also important never to say such things as, "I would like you to sit here next to me; can you do it now?" or "That's not a choice, okay?" since this implies that the child has the final say over the matter. Simply say, "You'll need to sit here, sweetheart." or "That's not a choice."

MOTHER: That does sound clearer, but what if she still refuses?

BOBBIE: Then neutrally let her know, "You have a choice to put your body here by yourself or have Mom do it for you."

MOTHER: And if she refuses?

BOBBIE: You calmly escort her body next to you, and if she has a tantrum, you restrain her in your lap until she settles down.

MOTHER: But what if she makes a horrible scene and never settles down?

BOBBIE: Because it's important not to let her resistance work for her, you must continue to sit calmly in the doctor's office holding her, even if she makes a big fuss about it. Or you can take her into the hallway if you prefer until she settles down. The key is not to give in to her demands because you are embarrassed and want the crying to stop. Incidentally, other families in the doctor's office and other public places would do well to support those parents who have the courage to discipline their children by giving a wink or thumbs-up, rather than stare at them as if they were abusive parents. On the other hand, in situations such as at a movie or restaurant where it would be untenable for others if you allowed your daughter to scream, it's important that you calmly remove her to an area outdoors or to the car—or home—where she can have her tantrum without disturbing others.

ANOTHER MOTHER: How do you get kids to say thank you?

BOBBIE: Because we can't force children to speak, I prefer not to set up "pleases" and "thank yous" as a requirement that I can't enforce. Instead, I would privately say, "Let's thank Susie and her Mom for inviting us to their party—so that they will know we had a good time." Then, I would cheerfully model my "thank yous" for him. If he joined in, that would be great. If not, I would not struggle over whether or not he said them. I would simply restate when we got to the car the importance of letting the host know that we enjoyed ourselves, both to support their feelings about their party and to ensure being included again.

If a child persisted in refusing to say thank you at parties, I would require that he write a thank you note in lieu of a verbal response. This can be enforced by not allowing him to proceed with other activities until it has been completed—with a good attitude. An effective way to develop the habit of saying please and thank you is to ask the young child just learning to express his requests to say please before giving him what he has asked for and then cheerfully asking that he say thank you without making an issue if he fails to do so.

The Nonchoice Zone

Whenever your child goes past the line that defines his circle of choices, he crosses over his boundary into the nonchoice zone. At this point, it's your job to stop all activity and return him to his circle of acceptable behaviors once again.

To do this, you must initially return him to an even smaller circle than his original one. (See Figure 7.) Only then will he view venturing into the nonchoice zone as a problem for himself that he would rather avoid in the future. You might, for instance, sit your child out of a game or remove him

Figure 7. Diagram of Contracted Boundary

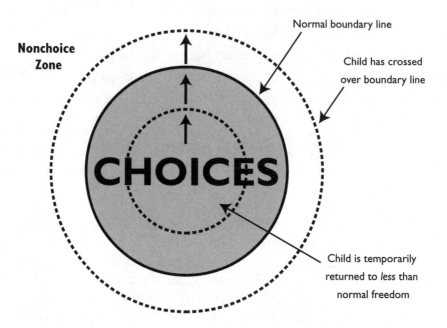

to his room. Or, if you are in public, you may require that he hold your hand, sit on a bench or in a shopping cart, or return to the car until he can cooperate; if he refuses, you would be wise to take him home to another family member, relative, friend, or a sitter while you return to the activity. Your job, at this juncture, is to teach him that he is simply not allowed to go forward with his life until he can surrender to your boundaries.

Each time your child tests his boundaries and is held to them in this way, he learns that rules are real and that you can be trusted to follow through on what you say. As a result, he eventually learns that it's in his best interest to respect the boundaries you have drawn and remain voluntarily within his circle of acceptable choices. (See Figure 8-E.) Once this is accomplished, it will feel easy and comfortable to have your child with you in all kinds of situations.

Time in the Nonchoice Zone

Each time you fail to respond to your child's crossed boundaries, he not only learns that boundaries aren't stable, but that you can't be counted on to stick

Figure 8. Variously Held Boundary Lines

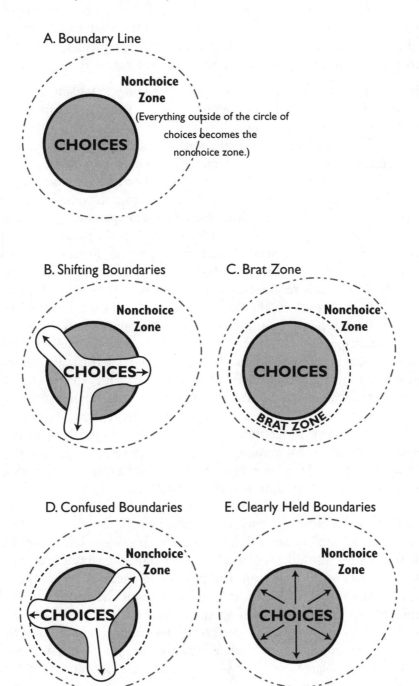

A. Boundary Line

Nonchoice Zone

(Everything outside of the circle of choices becomes the nonchoice zone.)

CHOICES

B. Shifting Boundaries

Nonchoice Zone

CHOICES→

C. Brat Zone

Nonchoice Zone

CHOICES

BRAT ZONE

D. Confused Boundaries

Nonchoice Zone

←CHOICES

E. Clearly Held Boundaries

Nonchoice Zone

CHOICES

by your rules. As a result, he doesn't trust the validity of your rules and continues to check each one as it's presented. Following are a number of ways many of you fail to consistently stick to your rules while your child remains in the nonchoice zone, constantly checking his parameters, as he becomes increasingly confused about where they lie. (See Figure 8.)

When Boundaries Shift. Children periodically try to expand their boundaries by using such tactics as delaying, ignoring, sassing, crying, or perhaps even boldly refusing to cooperate.

Whenever these tactics coincide with your concern about your child's unhappiness with his rules; your feelings of insecurity in holding him to his boundaries; or when you are feeling more tired or tolerant, you might allow your child to succeed in pushing his boundaries into the nonchoice zone. As a result, his original boundary line shifts and the expanded line becomes his new boundary for a period of time. (See Figure 8-B.) For example, if Mother allows young Jana to run around the table when she's supposed to be sitting to eat, the original boundary line Mother was holding has shifted. The confusion Jana now feels requires that she check her boundary line once again to determine where it actually lies. Consequently, in the following moment, or perhaps a few hours or a day later, Jana will run around the table again to see what happens. If Mother—in a clearer mood this time—requires that Jana sit down to eat, Jana's boundary will have shifted back to its original position once again. Because she will be unsure which of the two boundaries is the operational one, she will feel compelled to test them again. Similarly, if Father bans twelve-year-old Adam from the television set one day for messing up his VCR programming, but then ignores it when he sees him watching a program that evening, Adam's boundaries are shifting and he isn't sure whether Dad's TV is off-limits or not. As a result, he will feel compelled to check that boundary until it stops shifting.

Whenever your child lives with shifting boundaries, he will get confused. Because he won't be able to trust your rules, he will feel a need to check each time one is declared to see if that particular boundary will hold on this particular day. As a result, he will awaken every morning wondering what form his boundary lines will take and will proceed to check on where they are for the day. Only when the line indicating his circle of choices stabilizes will he stop challenging it and begin to accept its limits. (See Figure 8-E.)

The child who busily checks and rechecks shifting boundaries in this way is unfairly viewed as a troublemaker. However, on closer analysis, we can see that he's not to blame, since he is simply acting as he must in accordance with the reality of what happens in his family when boundaries are crossed. In short, he has been trained not to trust boundaries as they are presented, since they may shift if challenged. He's quite simply living by the rules of his household as they presently function, and his boundary-checking makes perfect sense. It's important, therefore, that parents and teachers not become confused—or angered—by a child's continuous challenges, since he's merely trying to establish a clear and stationary circle within which he can relax and operate comfortably. Instead, they can help him to stop this behavior by giving him a clear boundary that he can count on to hold. Once they do this, he will stop checking.

Creating Resistance—The Willful or Brat Zone. If you allow your children to linger in the expanded area just outside of your declared boundary line, a dotted line encircling your desired boundary represents the actual operative circle you hold. I refer to the zone this line creates as the *willful* or *brat zone*, since it falls outside of the desired boundary and seeps into the non-choice zone. Kids allowed to "hang out" in this area are continuously on the edge of boundaries and view breaking the rules as working for them. Because they have been repeatedly trained to resist their rules, they develop an increasingly strong desire to rebel against doing what they are asked. Before long, they are perceived as stubborn and bratty and are sometimes referred to as "strong willed." Not surprisingly, these are the kids who become increasingly difficult as they get older and often have the most tumultuous adolescent years. (See Figure 8-C.)

In many cases, these children aren't breaking specific rules, but are simply oozing out of bounds. They may wiggle and poke too exuberantly, speak too loudly at inappropriate times, infect rooms with aggressiveness or moods, and dally too long when asked to do something or ignore instructions altogether.

In other cases, their rule-breaking is more defiant. Such a child might run away from his family at the mall, grab things he has been asked not to touch, or turn on the television when called for dinner. The older ones sneak in extra calls after telephone hours, ignore curfews, or lie about their homework. They are not bad kids—as they often seem—but are merely doing what they have been trained to do, while their parents ignore their rule-breaking or strive ineffectively to coax them back within the parameters of their original boundaries.

Whenever you fail to handle broken limits in this way, you teach your kids to resist subsequent instructions and rules, and they become progressively more defiant, bratty, stubborn, and willful. (See Figure 8-D.)

Dialogue from Class

BOBBIE: Those of you with children who constantly push their circles out or linger in the willful or brat zone, what motivates you to resist holding your boundaries?

FATHER: We're afraid to come down hard on them.

MOTHER: I'm afraid I'll lose my children's friendship or that they will like my ex-husband more than me if I'm the disciplinarian.

ANOTHER MOTHER: It's such a hassle to deal with, and I hate to lose the peace.

A THIRD MOTHER: I'm still hoping they'll figure it out for themselves because I really don't want to deal with it. Also, if I follow through, I'll have to go home too! (Laughter)

ANOTHER FATHER: My threats are too severe, and I don't really want to have to follow up on them.

FIRST MOTHER: I think I'm being a good mom when I say, "Please don't act this way, honey, because . . ." and then I give another explanation. But I honestly don't understand why a child wouldn't respond to a polite request to do something!

BOBBIE: Look at it from your child's viewpoint for a moment. Let's say that you ask him to get off of the skating rink, but he ignores you. So you spend the next ten minutes reminding him to get off, then give him a couple of stern warnings. Meanwhile, your child has succeeded in hanging out in the willful or brat zone as he skates for an extra fifteen minutes before you reach the point when you really mean business. Since he will probably experience a scolding—at most—when he finally gets off, the price for skating considerably longer is well worth paying. In short, his resistance has worked very nicely for him.

FIRST FATHER: I have to admit that the longer I delay, the more my child messes around. Then, I end up getting angry and destroy the peace I was trying so hard to hang on to.

BOBBIE: That's an excellent point. Not only is it clearer for your child when you stick with your boundaries, you are better able to hold them with neutrality if you don't wait so long.

FIRST MOTHER: How do you get a child out of the brat zone?

BOBBIE: Your willingness to follow through on your rules is the primary thing that can turn your child's resistant response around. For example, when a mother tells her child not to eat the grapes at the supermarket, but then looks the other way as he stuffs more into his mouth, she's allowing him to hang out in the willful or brat zone. Instead of waffling on her boundary, she should deal with his defiance the moment she notices him eating more grapes. If he refuses at that point to stay next to her or hold her hand, he should be taken to the car—or perhaps home—until he stops resisting. Even though that shopping day could prove unpleasant, the child handled in this way won't eat grapes the next time he's in the market.

MOTHER: But what if he hates marketing and wanted to go home?

BOBBIE: Whenever leaving a place accomplishes exactly what your child wanted, calmly take him home to another family member, relative, friend, or a sitter, and return to the activity. Although he may have wanted to go home, most kids don't expect to be dropped off while you continue with your day. In fact, it would be a good time to go somewhere interesting or out to lunch, and don't be afraid to let him know what he missed. Parents often resist taking this step, but it's an effective way to show your child that you won't put up with his misbehavior just because he's ready to go home, and that if he wants to stay with you, he will have to behave.

MOTHER: What if he likes staying with the relative or sitter?

BOBBIE: Make sure that the person taking care of him understands that he has lost his normal freedoms due to a lack of cooperation and is, therefore, not allowed to watch television or be entertained. If his time at home is duly boring, he won't want to repeat it. Also, if your child genuinely dislikes going with you to do errands, offer him the option of staying home with a caretaker if he's young or by himself for short periods if he's older and ready to remain alone. Be careful not to allow daytime television viewing, or some children will choose staying home over everything else. (See **Television** in the Problem-Solving Guide.) If you need—or want—to take your child with you, be prepared for it to take longer, since the only leverage you will have to gain his cooperation under these circumstances is sitting him on benches along the way, until he's ready to cooperate—while calmly reflecting that it will go faster if he chooses willingness versus resistance.

ANOTHER MOTHER: What if I can't afford a sitter?

BOBBIE: Every parent must make some arrangement for alternative care for their children. Not only is it good for parents and their kids to have some separate recreational time from one another, backup care is occasionally critical for implementing discipline. In this regard, if relatives, friends, or neighbors are unavailable for trading child-care services, a sitter must be considered for the few times it will take for your child to realize that you have alternatives to putting up with uncooperative behavior. If you resist this expenditure, you could end up with even greater costs such as the cost of living with an out-of-control child, including the cost of counseling or other therapeutic services.

FIRST MOTHER: I don't have the time to deal with all of these detours.

BOBBIE: If I could show you on a graph the amount of extra parenting time required for parents who fail to hold their boundaries, it would stagger your imagination. The truth is, holding your boundaries is one of the greatest time-savers you have available to you!

Ineffective Responses to Broken Boundaries. Following are fourteen of the most commonly used parental responses to broken boundaries that fail to hold a child to his rules and encourage his resistance.

▶ *Ignoring.* Many of you have been taught that children will stop undesirable behaviors if they are ignored, and you're hopeful that this gentle and easy parenting tool will work. However, ignoring only works when a behavior such as fussing is specifically designed to get your attention, control your emotions, or cause you to back down on a rule. Unfortunately, there are many other behaviors and broken boundaries that bring their own rewards and—if ignored—will continue and get worse. For example, a child who refuses to do what you have asked, has clearly broken a boundary and cannot be ignored.

▶ *Explaining, Reasoning, and Arguing.* Endless explanations, logical arguments, and patient reasoning are commonly used by those of you who are reluctant to discipline. You explain to a child who has deliberately crossed your boundaries why that line was created in the first place. Or you debate the validity of your rules while your child lingers in the willful or brat zone, throwing out rebuttals to each of your arguments. Yet these explanations and arguments are completely irrelevant, since the only valid response to a child who has crossed your boundaries is to get him back within his circle.

Thus, if you create a rule that your child may not climb on the wall surrounding your yard, it's okay to explain your reasoning for the rule when you first give it. However, once established, he must obey that rule, whether or not he understands or accepts your reasoning. The real issue at this juncture is not his knowledge of heights and danger, but his willingness to surrender to the guidance of your "mature boss." Those of you who restate explanations and reasons for your limits in order to gain your child's compliance train him to mind your rules only after he understands and agrees with their logic. Of course, you must discuss heights and falls at some point, if you haven't already, but never as a way to convince your child to cooperate while he's in the middle of resisting his limits. The fact is, he must first adhere to your boundaries, whether or not he understands or agrees with them. Explanations come later.

Dialogue from Class

MOTHER: I feel that my rules are quite lenient, but my eight-year-old daughter argues with me every time I say "No" to something, and I can't figure out how to get her to stop.

BOBBIE: If she's a persistent arguer, interrupt her challenge and offer her a *crossroads* choice: to stop arguing or go to her room. If she persists, you must follow through with removing her.

MOTHER: But then she tries to hook me into more arguing while I'm trying to get her to her room, and I seriously don't know how to deal with it.

BOBBIE: The key here is not to respond at all, since your mission is to get her to go to her room and accept remaining there for a period of time before engaging in any further discussion. Remember, anytime you find it necessary to put your child in her room, it's because she has already stepped out of line and is on her way to banishment. Such a child is in no position to barter or reorganize the rules! Consequently, this is not the time for a reasoned discussion, and interacting with her will only draw you into an argument. Although communication must always follow a time-out (see Chapter 8), it's inappropriate to discuss the problem before your child has first accepted her contraction of freedom. Thus, you need to let your daughter know that you are willing to hear her input after she learns to accept your guidance, but for now, she must simply practice accepting your decisions.

ANOTHER MOTHER: My daughter lures me into a discussion with comments like, "You're a mean mother," "You don't love me," or "I hate you."

BOBBIE: These remarks aren't personal and merely represent your child's last, desperate effort to distract you from your mission of getting her to her room and holding her to your boundaries. Such comments are completely insignificant, and it's important that you not bite the bait and feel hurt or insist that you do love her. If you continue to hold your boundaries in a neutral, yet clear context, your child will have an *experience* of your ability to love her in the middle of the chaos. As a result she will be able to maintain her love for you and know that she is loved as well—even if she doesn't want to admit it! This is far more effective than interrupting your discipline to debate whether or not you love each other.

▶ *Reminding, Restating, Warning, Counting, Threatening.* A certain amount of reminding is natural and necessary for young children still learning to manage routines and responsibilities. However, anytime you find yourself repeatedly reminding your child to behave or you notice that you are restating your rules—then warning, counting, or threatening as a means to elicit his cooperation—you aren't facing the fact that your child has already broken a rule and should, at this point, be disciplined rather than coaxed.

For example, you might calmly remind your ten-year-old to take his shower, but then return to your adult conversation and ignore his lack of responsiveness. Later, when you notice that he's still watching television, you may repeat yourself by asking, "How many times do I have to tell you to get into the shower?" You then begin two-minute warnings or issue the ultimate of warnings, "Johnny, I'm warning you!" As you get closer to really meaning it, you use anger to signal your child that he'd better respond. At this point, you might count to five or ten, but if that doesn't work, you may threaten a spanking or loss of some privilege such as a birthday party or the family vacation! At last, after fifteen minutes of resistance and extra television viewing, your child finally responds.

Not only does this repeated reminding delay your follow-through, it teaches your child to rely too much on your leadership, rather than develop his own initiative to direct him. This explains why children who are regularly talked through each step of what they need to do feel overdirected and react by responding slowly, passively, or not at all to directions.

Dialogue from Class

MOTHER: What about restating rules with a young child?

BOBBIE: Whenever your child is first learning to cooperate, you will need to restate his rules. Yet anytime you repeat a rule, it's important to also make sure that he responds to it, even if he's young and is just learning about boundaries. If you merely restate your rules without also enforcing them, your child will develop the unfortunate habit of ignoring instructions and resisting boundaries.

MOTHER: At what age can you assume that your child understands his rules?

BOBBIE: This is something that happens gradually. With a young child of about ten or twelve months old, you simply remove him with a restatement of the boundary. If he cries, calmly allow that, but continue to hold your boundary. If he resists, you can neutrally restrain him in your lap until he surrenders and is ready to cooperate. Once his resistance has passed, return him to his normal freedoms with a restatement of the boundary. As he gets to be twelve to sixteen or eighteen months old, you will notice that he is understanding more of what you are requesting of him. Although you may need to remove him to a playpen or behind a gated doorway due to his increased mobility and strength of resistance, the plan is still the same. He gets gently removed and restrained until his resistance has passed. When he seems ready to cooperate, he is returned with a restatement of the boundary. By the time he's eighteen to twenty-four months old, you will notice that your child understands most of what you ask of him, and crossed boundaries are more clearly defiance. Again, you calmly contract his freedom to a lap, playpen, or gated room until he's ready to cooperate.

ANOTHER MOTHER: You don't give any warnings at all, once your child knows a rule?

BOBBIE: You do restate it, but you do so while also following through to make sure the consequence happens, rather than simply as a reminder that may or may not be adhered to. Thus, the young child still learning rules is removed from the area, while the older, defiant one loses his freedom for a period of time. Only in this way does your child begin to learn that rules count. If he decides to test a rule, that's an unfortunate choice he made which he must now pay for. On the other hand, when your child is crossing over the boundary of a rule that is set by degrees—such as how much he's wiggling in his chair or how boisterous he's getting in the living room—you can use a technique I refer to as a *crossroads choice*. With a crossroads choice, you offer your child a choice between two options such as, "You have a choice to calm your energy or leave this area." In this way, you ask him to make a clear and conscious choice in that moment. If he gets calm, he may stay. If not, he must leave. If he settles down for awhile but then resumes the overactive behavior, he's not given another crossroads choice, but is removed.

▶ *Chasing the Toddler.* Many of you make the mistake of thinking that you can't communicate boundaries to your young, newly mobile toddler and end up chasing him, instead. This creates a bad precedent for your authority as it puts your toddler in charge, running randomly here and there, while you chase after him. It's important to realize that toddlers are able to understand boundaries when given repeatedly and followed through on consistently.

Thus, you might draw a circle in the sand at a beach; a line in the dirt at a park; or you can create an area defined by sidewalks or benches in which your toddler is free to run. If he should run past that area, you must bring him back and hold him in your lap until he accepts your restraint. You can then show him the boundary again and offer him a new chance to remain freely within it. This is repeated until he voluntarily holds to the line. Once his impulse to run beyond his boundaries is under control, you are no longer required to chase after him to keep him in bounds. Although the lines are less clearly drawn on a zoo outing or at a shopping mall, you must create some picture of what you expect. The child who then runs ahead must be brought back and is required to hold hands, sit in a cart, or be held until he's willing to stay within his bounds.

▶ *Martyrdom, Guilt, Hinting, Pleading.* Resist the temptation to get your children to behave by evoking feelings of guilt or pleading for assistance because you are so overworked or emotionally burdened. Rules must simply be required, rather than manipulated or begged for, and using a martyred style creates feelings of burden and depletion in your child which he will carry into adulthood. It also puts you into a powerless position of begging for cooperation, rather than requiring it. Those of you who are single, working, or emotionally depleted must be particularly careful not to succumb to this seductive style of asking for cooperation.

▶ *Fear.* Even stronger than guilt is the use of fear to get your child to do what you want. For example, some of you threaten that a stranger might nab your child if he doesn't stay with you, the boogie man will get him if he doesn't come when called, or he will be locked in the movie theater or restaurant if he doesn't cooperate when you are ready to go. Not only does this style create anxiety in your child, it's simply not honest. Furthermore, those of you who try this are using the power of your child's fear to herd him from place to place, rather than simply claiming your authority and requiring that he do as you ask. The worst result of this approach is that it genuinely worries your child and can trigger intense anxieties and fears.

▶ *Negotiation.* Parents often get into trouble by negotiating with a child who has not yet learned to surrender to his limits. This is extremely confusing for him since, while he's in the middle of learning to accept rules, he is simultaneously allowed—even encouraged—to resist them! By doing this, you inadvertently teach your child to resist and debate rules, rather than cooperatively yield to following them. As a result, anytime he's presented with a boundary, he will ask to do it a different way, try something else first, or agree to it only if you will first meet certain conditions. Unfortunately, a child handled in this way becomes extremely resistant and, upon entering school, attempts to negotiate the rules of his classroom as well as those set by peers.

Only after your child is clear that he must comply with his rules is he ready to go to the next level of development known as negotiation. Once ready for negotiation, he may be offered an opportunity to discuss his rules, share his own viewpoint about them, and occasionally renegotiate his boundaries. He must be aware, however, that there will still be times— even after these discussions—when you won't agree to his ideas, and he will be required to surrender to your final decision.

Dialogue from Class

FATHER: What if you feel you have made a rule too quickly and don't want to follow through on it?

BOBBIE: If you catch this before your child breaks that rule or resists conforming to it, then it's okay to retract it. However, once he has begun to resist a rule or has crossed its boundary, that would be a bad time to reconsider its validity, even if you don't like the rule.

MOTHER: When do kids surrender to rules?

BOBBIE: Some accept boundaries as early as two to two-and-a-half and others may still be putting up a mild fuss until four. However, a child who continues to strongly challenge his rules after three or regularly challenges them after four is probably not being handled with clarity.

ANOTHER MOTHER: At what age do you usually start to negotiate?

BOBBIE: Although your child must have the verbal skills and maturity of a three-and-a-half- to four-year-old, the key is that he has learned to surrender to his rules for at least six months. Thus, I probably wouldn't begin negotiations with a child under four. Also, timing is important. For instance, if your child has just been asked to come in from play, that's not a good time to open up negotiations. On the other hand, once he's already indoors, it's okay for him to calmly discuss the possibility of playing longer. If you are receptive to changing your request, an adjustment can be made, whereas if you're not, he must accept that playtime is over.

FATHER: What if a child knows how to comply with his rules but negotiates aggressively?

BOBBIE: A child must understand that anytime discussions are brought up in an aggressive manner, he loses all opportunity to get a boundary changed, whereas if he discusses the matter calmly, he maintains a reasonable chance for an adjustment. I like to let kids know that if they're aggressive and rude in their effort to get their way, they have a 100 percent chance of being turned down, whereas if they're appropriate and polite, they have a 100 percent chance of being heard and a fair chance of getting what they want.

꧁꧂

Brock

Brock was a bright child who came to school as a two-year-old. We could see the beginning stages of resistance forming early in his personality and tried to warn his parents about negotiating all of their rules. However, these well-educated people were committed to letting Brock express his views on every subject—including rules—and he could argue boundaries with the facility of a lawyer. As a three- and then as a four-year-old, he was having increasingly more trouble accepting the limits of his classroom as well as the boundaries his peers required. By the time he was five, his parents reluctantly faced that he had become an extremely resistant child who had tantrums at every turn, had made no friends, and was not even displaying the intelligence we knew he possessed, except when he was arguing over a rule.

Finally, his parents accepted our suggestion to stop negotiating. Although they initially had to interrupt his constant argumentation by sending him to his room, Brock gradually improved and was able, after several months, to stop his urge to negotiate and to comply with his rules. Even though teaching a resistant child to surrender to his boundaries at five is a difficult task, it's a great deal harder at eight, ten, or twelve and often fails at fourteen or fifteen.

▶ *Bargaining and Bribing.* The worst tools you can use to get your child to cooperate are to bargain with him or offer a bribe, since these techniques teach him that resistance not only buys stolen time in the nonchoice zone, but will bring him treasure as well!

Dialogue from Class

MOTHER: How would it be to tell my son, "If you practice the piano, then I'll let you go outside and play."

BOBBIE: I would rather see you use different language such as, "When you finish your responsibility—in this case practicing the piano—then you're free again." I would not want to hold out play as a special bargaining chip and would prefer that play be viewed as one of your child's normal freedoms, rather than something you withhold until he has particularly pleased you.

ANOTHER MOTHER: What if I point out to my child that I made him his favorite cookies, so he owes me a favor in return.

BOBBIE: A comment like that successfully uses guilt to evoke cooperative behaviors in a child, grateful for being loved and cared for and anxious to please his mother. However, this tactic also teaches him to feel guilty and responsible for the feelings and happiness, not only of Mother, but of others as well. Such guilt is extremely crippling, since the child raised with it will find it difficult to reject the unreasonable, and even unjust or unhealthy, demands of others. In addition, it's important that parents do things like baking cookies for their children with no strings attached and make the enforcement of rules a completely separate matter.

ANOTHER MOTHER: When we're at the shopping mall I let my daughter know that if she cooperates, ice cream will be the last thing on our list before going home. Is that a bribe? (Laughter)

BOBBIE: With or without ice cream, your child must learn to surrender to your rules. If she doesn't, she must sit on a bench until she gains control over her impulses. If she gains control, then it's okay to finish the shopping trip, which may or may not include ice cream. The key is not to mention the ice cream while you're in the middle of gaining her cooperation, since the two should remain separate issues.

▶ ***Screaming and Yelling.*** Many of you will resort to yelling and screaming to get your child to cooperate. At this point, your message is, "I mean business," and young children will often capitulate. However, as your child gets older and more desensitized to your yelling, he will see that you have also lost emotional control. Although you may mean business, you're not sure how to make it happen, and he can sense the helplessness behind the noise you're making.

▶ ***Making Hasty, Restrictive Decisions.*** Many of you make hasty, overly restrictive decisions which force your child into a position of having to plead, or worse, break unreasonable rules merely to gain normal privileges. Those of you with a tendency to block too many of your child's ideas or reject most of his requests would do better not to say "No" so quickly and view his behaviors and requests more flexibly.

In this regard, I once observed a young mother playing at a swimming pool with her five-year-old daughter. With the aid of floaties, the child was enjoying jumping from the side of the pool into the water, then scrambling up the ladder and jumping in again. After one of her jumps, she used a wide gutter to climb out of the pool. She easily got one foot on the ledge and was on her way out when her mother hastily suggested, "Don't climb there—you'll fall!" On closer examination, this was an unnecessary request, since even if the child did fall, her injury would have been minimal, and learning to climb from the gutter designed for an alternative exit from the pool was a worthy challenge. Already growing deaf to her mother's directions, the little girl ignored this suggestion and successfully finished climbing out at the gutter. Mother seemed to realize that her mandate was unnecessary and said nothing, while her daughter continued to use the gutter for the rest of her swim. Although there was no ugly struggle between them, Mother's boundary had been ignored, and, over time, such hasty decisions and lack of follow-through will get in the way of clear boundary-setting.

▶ ***Tolerating Delayed Cooperation.*** Many of you are so relieved by the time your child gets around to following your directions that you ignore his prior delays and resume normal freedoms without any repercussions. As a result, he grows used to delaying his response to your requests and ends up in the willful or brat zone. It would be more effective to create some loss for the child who fails to respond in a reasonably prompt manner in order to make this form of resistance a less appealing option for him.

Dialogue from Class

FATHER: What do you mean by reasonably prompt?

BOBBIE: It's important that your child respond to your requests, for example, by getting out of a swimming pool when asked; but it's equally important that you not get rigid. In other words, it would be acceptable for him to dive under the water a few times on his way to the ladder or take a few moments to say good-bye to his friends. However, it would not be acceptable if he turned his back on you to dive under water and stay there, come up for a quick breath, and dive down again to get out of earshot of further requests for compliance.

MOTHER: How do you handle it when your twelve-year-old finally paddles his surfboard to shore after you've been signaling him to come in for the past twenty minutes—and you know that he saw you but pretended not to?

BOBBIE: He should not be free to go forward as if nothing happened, but must experience some contraction of his freedom and acknowledge his mistake before resuming normal activities. You might, for example, have him sit with you on the beach for the same amount of time he delayed getting out of the water, before releasing him to have lunch or join his friends.

ⓖⓖⓖ

▶ *Making Excuses.* Offering excuses for your child's misbehavior such as he's "too tired," "hungry," or "not feeling well" erroneously teaches him that he doesn't have to accept responsibility for his behavior unless he's feeling tip-top. As a result, he learns to put his energy into finding excuses to justify his lack of cooperation, rather than simply behave responsibly. Over time, such a child ends up in the willful or brat zone with an array of excuses for being there.

▶ *Allowing Uncooperative Behavior in Public.* Many of you have trouble holding boundaries in public, since you don't want to deal with your child's resistance in front of others. By doing this, you teach him that rules don't count in public settings or when others are around. This causes him to be on his worst behavior and in the willful or brat zone during those times when you would most like to count on him. When rules get changed to accommodate such situations as visiting, shopping, or eating out, your children learn to behave dreadfully in public! It's essential to use your rules under all circumstances, so that your kids will understand that their boundaries will follow wherever they go.

Dialogue from Class

FATHER: How do you get your child to cooperate on airplanes?

BOBBIE: When rules are held consistently at other times, a child will rarely present a problem in such places as airplanes, since he knows that he can trust the parent sitting next to him to mean what he or she says. Thus, the best way to handle public situations that might otherwise become a challenge is to offer your child the kind of discipline program he can count on at all times. If he still challenges you in public—even if it's on an airplane—you must follow through. If you have been consistent before boarding the plane, his period of resistance will be briefer. If not, your child's crying could be extensive. In either case, I recommend that fellow passengers salute those parents who stick with their rules; listening to an hour of crying during the flight will be better for them than another rule-breaking citizen in their midst.

☙❧☙

▶ *Boundaries Broken by Degrees.* Be alert to boundaries that are broken by degrees. For example, when your child becomes increasingly noisy in the living room or rambunctious at a restaurant, there's a point at which he crosses the line from acceptable, fun-loving play to obnoxious behavior. Thus, rather than shoosh at your kids as if they were pesky insects whenever they start to get out of line, present a crossroads choice the moment you notice that a behavior is becoming a problem. You may, for example, offer your child the option of calming his energies and staying with the group or continuing to escalate them and losing his freedom to remain in the area. If he then decides to go over the line drawn for him, you must respond appropriately.

Consistency: What It Is, How to Do It, and Why It Helps

Only by consistently holding your child to his rules in a clear, neutral, and confident manner will he eventually lose all interest in challenging his limits and become one of those easygoing children parents yearn to have. Thus, it's important never to declare a boundary unless you are willing to deal with whatever it takes to implement it. Only in this way does your child learn that you mean what you say, are firm about your boundaries, and can be trusted to enforce them. In short, consistency is the key to your child's ability to learn that he must surrender to your boundaries.

Conciously Changed Boundaries. Consistency does not require that you be rigid, nor does it imply that your rules can never be changed. Instead, it includes flexible boundaries that can be expanded, not because you feel pushed by a resistant child to alter them, but because it seems like an appropriate thing to do. Therefore, it's not the rules that must be consistent, but you as the parent in holding whatever boundaries you have selected for that point in time. For example, if a child who has already learned to accept limits would like to stay up later one night to watch a television special, you could respond with, "Sure, we can change your bedtime for tonight and let you retire at the end of the program." It never confuses a child who accepts boundaries when we change one of his rules, either temporarily—for tonight's TV program—or permanently to a new bedtime of 8:00. However, if your child has not yet learned to accept his parameters and is whining and fussing to expand them, it's essential that you not give way to a new boundary.

Becoming Consistent After a Period of Inconsistency. Whenever you have previously had a wavy circle but then decide to hold it firmly in place, your child will initially be confused and wonder why you aren't letting your boundaries balloon out as you used to. As a result, he will act worse and work harder than ever to get you to return to your old way of capitulating to the larger, expanded circle.

If you then decide that firm boundaries aren't working and give in to his efforts to break them down, he will learn from the situation to resist even harder each time you attempt to reestablish your rules. If you later firmly hold your boundaries for several days, but then give in and let them go again, your child will become even more confused, and it will take considerably longer for him to believe in boundaries.

By contrast, if you're able to weather your child's initial storm and calmly stand firm in sticking to your newly held boundaries, he will eventually settle down and accept the new standard. Once you remain completely consistent, after about three to five days for some children and up to one or two weeks for others (depending on the amount of prior confusion and degree of present resolve), your child will begin to see that you are, in fact, holding to your boundaries—and he will stop checking them at long last. Because it's such a relief for him to no longer be required to figure out this confusing puzzle, your child will visibly relax as he surrenders to consistently held rules.

Dialogue from Class

MOTHER: My problem comes after my child has surrendered to my clearer boundaries and has been acting like such a good kid for awhile—but then I loosen up my rules and resist giving consequences again.

BOBBIE: When children are behaving well, we hate to break the positive spell by having to discipline. As a result, we are often reluctant to deal with that next infraction of the rules. We think, instead, of how delightful he has been and how much we hate to start nagging at him. However, once he sees that our boundaries aren't holding, he begins to push on them again. If we continue to remind and nag or give more chances, he loses confidence in our ability to hold boundaries for extended periods of time.

ANOTHER MOTHER: I often tell my teen that he's restricted for the whole weekend, but then he's so good I would love to let him off the hook.

BOBBIE: It actually works best when the expansion and contraction of your child's freedom is flexible, like an accordion. Thus, the moment a child is not being responsible he should lose all of his freedom, but once he accepts full responsibility for his behavior and has shifted back to a cooperative mode, it's okay for him to regain part of his freedom.

MOTHER: Won't he think he can act badly whenever he wants, if he doesn't have to pay the full consequence?

BOBBIE: It would depend on what he did. If he's a resistant kid who belligerently defied your boundaries, sneaked off to some clearly forbidden activity, and was not contrite, then I would require that he pay the full price. But if he's basically a cooperative kid who regretted his decision and fully acknowledged his error, I would reduce the time allotted for his restriction, while making it clear that his acknowledgment was the thing that had won him part of his freedom back. In such cases, a chore is sometimes used as penance before returning the child's freedom to him. In other cases, if a child's problem stemmed from something like a sulky attitude, I would simply let him know that he wasn't free to do anything until he surrendered his negative position. Since no rule was broken, once the mood was released, he would be free.

MOTHER: I'm not clear what they learn when they're allowed to get out of part of their consequence.

BOBBIE: They learn that cooperation works. Children who know that they have a chance of being released from a portion of their restriction are more motivated to act cooperatively, face the problem, acknowledge their part in it, and do some penance in the form of a chore. And that's what we want from them. Still, parents must not be naive in accepting shallow or guiltless apologies from persistently uncooperative kids. With these harder cases, it's important to set tough consequences that match the degree of defiance and hold out for thoroughly talking out the problem, sincere acknowledgments, and full ownership of responsibility before reducing any sentences. Yet even with these kids, if you do attain acknowledgment and contrition from them, it's critical that their honesty, surrendering, and remorse be rewarded.

★★★

Fair boundaries create the frame within which families, communities, and nations live cooperatively in peace.

★★★

7

Holding Boundaries

Gentle Truths and Firm Consequences

The Sixth Key:

ଔଔଔ

Hold all of your boundaries with courage and kindness.

Boundaries are of no use unless you know how to maintain them. Yet many of you have lost both your courage and ability to hold the limits that you have set for your children. Unfortunately, this results in an outright struggle for control in your homes which often leads to your kids ruling the roost. The consequence of this breakdown of boundaries is unpleasant households filled with unmanageable kids which, in turn, is fueling society with growing numbers of uncooperative people. The need for families to do better in holding their boundaries is becoming dangerously clear!

How Boundaries Work

Each time your child comes up against a boundary that conflicts with his desires, he is faced with a choice. He can either ignore the rule and fulfill his desires or respect the boundary and control his urges. If he elects to ignore the boundary and succeeds in getting his way without repercussion, he won't learn to control his immature impulses. On the other hand, if he yields to temptation, but then experiences pain and loss for breaking the rules, he will be more likely to exercise impulse control in the future.

This process of how children learn to control their untamed impulses was made visible to me by a two-year-old who had been removed from his class-room for biting a playmate. It was clear that he didn't like being banished from the group and was delighted when he was allowed, in due course, to return. Later that day, when he again wanted a toy already occupied by another child, he bared his teeth and approached the unsuspecting child's arm. He then paused a few inches from the chubby appendage, mouth agape, as he reconsidered. His jaw slowly closed, and he looked around for another toy. This child had successfully controlled his impulses.

Once impulse control is mastered, your young child no longer sinks his teeth into the arms of peers who thwart him, nor does your elementary-aged child fight with his friends for control over their games or resist his rules at home. Neither does your teen swear at the umpire or sulk when he loses a game. Instead, these kids have learned to manage their immature impulses and are on their way to becoming appropriately socialized. Yet this level of self-control only develops in children whose parents know how to hold the boundaries they have established in their homes.

To support parents in mastering this skill, the remainder of this chapter provides specific steps needed to effectively hold boundaries.

Nine Steps for Handling Crossed Boundaries

Regardless of the reasons for broken boundaries, a parent's responsibility is to bring wayward children back within their operative circles and impart a feeling within them that they wish they had never ventured over the line. Thus, your job is to engender in your children a feeling of regret over broken boundaries similar to the one expressed in the ad, "I could have had a V-8!" To accomplish this, you must provide the kinds of emotional pain and loss for broken rules that your child would want to avoid in the future. Thus, by flooding your child with pain when he's breaking rules and pleasure when he's cooperating, you motivate him to select increasingly better choices. The following steps provide a summary of how to accomplish these goals.

Step 1: Put the Problem on the Agenda

Rather than be surprised and disappointed or wonder how some problem with your child found its way into your life, you must face that it did happen and will probably happen again in the next few hours, days, or weeks. Consequently, it's important that you not get sidetracked by your resistance or anger, but accept that parenting problems will be a part of each day and put this one on the agenda to be embraced and handled to the best of your ability.

Step 2: Stop Everything to Address the Problem

The moment there's a broken boundary, you have a problem on your hands and must stop everything in order to address it. Thus, rather than deal with escalating resistance, get back in charge of your child immediately. You can begin by stopping all activities, contracting your child's boundaries to less than his original freedoms, and gaining his cooperation before allowing him to resume normal activities. The more you respond in this way, the fewer problems you will have with your children and the more effective it will be for you in the long run.

By contrast, if your child is repeatedly reminded to simply return to his original boundary such as walking with you at the mall, sitting politely at a restaurant, or coming home at the appointed time, he would enjoy a period of stolen freedom before being returned to what he was supposed to be doing in the first place. Because this would result in no losses for him, he would most likely repeat his uncooperative behavior in order to steal additional moments of expanded freedom.

Step 3: Remain Firm but Neutral

For many of you, using your authority means drawing from the intensity of your frustration or anger to get yourselves in the frame of mind to mean business. However, this kind of power not only distracts your young child's attention away from his problem, but may create enough tension and emotional "freezing" in him to interfere with his grasp of the lessons involved. As your child gets older, this form of authority usually causes him to stiffen his will and brace himself against you. Because this blustery form of dominance provokes so many problems for kids, true parental strength is better drawn from a calm and caring heart. Thus, it's always best to allow the neutral clarity of the "referee" or "oak tree" within you to be in charge of holding boundaries with your children.

Step 4: Identify the Problem—Immaturity or Defiance?

Except on those occasions when a child is justifiably resisting unfair boundaries, anytime he resists or breaks his rules, it's due either to immaturity or defiance. Identifying which it is will help you to know how to respond. Following is an explanation of the difference.

Immaturity

The immature child still learning to cope with being thwarted by his boundaries typically cries during those times when he wants something that is off-limits to him. Until he learns to accept the frustration that boundaries impose, he will noisily balk at his restrictions, in part to express his dismay, but also in hopes of convincing you to give in to his demands. Whenever you are able to calmly hold your ground in these situations, your child eventually accepts his rules and visibly surrenders.

This is best demonstrated by the young child who has a fit over something he thinks he must have and wails anywhere from a few minutes to an hour—or more—while checking periodically to see who's taking note of his plight. However, if he can't get anyone worried about his unhappiness or how long he has been crying, he suddenly stops and looks around as if to say, "Oh, well—I guess this isn't working." With that insight, he gathers himself together and goes cheerfully on to his next endeavor.

The child who is simply frustrated by something he is not yet able to manage may also have a fit over it. In such cases, he's not crossing a boundary but, nevertheless, needs to be handled with care. Although many parents run over to help such a child in order to bypass his frustration and stop the crying, allowing him the time he needs to adjust to his frustration is more effective. Thus, allowing him to first cry it out, then reflecting that he has other options such as asking for help is useful. Once he is calm enough to do this, it's important that you are responsive. If he made this request prior to crying and you ignored him, you must let him know that he did the right thing and that it was you who failed to respond. Then, do better next time.

Making His Adjustment to Blocked Boundaries. During the period when your child is first learning to surrender to his limits, he will discover that an important part of growing up is to accept his frustration over boundaries without making such a big deal out of it. In view of this process, we can see that the duration of a child's crying merely represents the time it takes him to *adjust* to a particular limit. Thankfully, kids who live with boundaries that hold firmly, no matter how long they fuss, eventually learn that cooperation is the norm and that they can accept parameters without so much drama.

Thus, anytime your child is crying during his period of adjustment to blocked boundaries, the only thing for you to do is to understand the purpose and value of his tears as he makes this important adjustment. Then stand back and let him go through it.

Stepping out of the Bounds of "Preferred" Behaviors. It's also a matter of immaturity—not defiance—that causes your child to step over the line of "preferred" behaviors when he's doing such things as crying; making messes; wetting his pants or bed; biting his nails; sucking his thumb; leaving his bicycle outdoors overnight; losing things; forgetting to take his lunch or homework to school; getting too boisterous; not cleaning his room; failing to do his chores to satisfaction; ignoring his homework; leaving his messes; not thoroughly washing the pots on his night for dishes; failing to tend to his hygiene; slouching or mumbling; forgetting to write thank-you notes; playing music too loudly; arguing or fighting with siblings or a friend.

These and other behaviors emerge simply because your child, even as a teenager, is not yet grown up enough to consistently produce "preferred" or mature behaviors. Understanding this helps to make it clear that annoyance and anger are inappropriate responses to his immature behaviors and serve only to damage your child's spirit and undermine his belief in himself.

Yet because you do need to respond in some way, it would be useful to gently address each immature behavior in a way that helps your child to safely confront and learn from it. Thus, anytime he steps outside the parameters of mature behavior, gently bring him back within the circle and show him what would be a more effective behavior. Initially, you will simply teach him what is preferred—and why—and then guide him to do it.

However, should he persist in not doing some preferred behavior and elect, instead, to continue to "forget," you can improve his remembering by making the forgetfulness a problem for him. For example, the child who has left his dishes in the family room must be interrupted from play or other activities to handle his duties, plus given another chore to repay you for the inconvenience of having to remind him. Likewise, the one who has lost yet another jacket must participate in both the effort and cost of replacing it.

The more consistently you provide your child with some inconvenience or lesson which has been connected to his immature response, the sooner he will mature. Even so, it's important to understand that it will take much repetition and many years before your child is fully developed.

Defiance

Whenever your child refuses to cooperate or behaves defiantly—rather than immaturely—discipline takes on a completely different tone. Thus, anytime your child refuses to cooperate with your rules or requests, you must sit up, take note of his defiance, and go on duty the moment you become aware of it. You don't have to get nasty, but you do need to respond!

For instance, if your child has been asked to retrieve a bicycle, throw out the trash, or go to bed, whether he passively continues with his own activity, openly complains and refuses to budge, or angrily objects to being "bossed," he has deliberately crossed your boundary. Such behavior is clearly defiant and requires immediate—yet calm—handling. If you fail to respond, he will become progressively more defiant. Yet if you meet the challenge, things will improve rather easily and quickly.

Be aware that the child who has learned to accept the rules of your home prior to his adolescence will more naturally yield to your boundaries during his teen years as a continuation of what he has already learned. The nice result is that his habit of easy cooperation becomes a stable foundation from which his sense of responsibility and independence will gradually emerge.

By contrast, those of you who have waited until your child's preteen or teen years to establish your authority have given yourselves a larger challenge and will probably require professional help to resolve it. It's critical for families in this position not to delay any further, as your ability to bring your adolescent under control at this late date is already in jeopardy.

Step 5: Create Loss and Pain for Broken Boundaries

Whenever your child repeatedly defies you and succeeds in spending a good deal of his time in the nonchoice zone, it's because he hasn't been given a clear enough connection between breaking rules and experiencing the kind of loss and pain he would want to avoid in the future. For this reason, it's important not to merely return a child who has broken the rules to his original boundary, but to bring him back to *less* freedom than he was previously enjoying. (See Figure 9.)

Thus, the younger child who has run ahead at the park or mall is not merely brought back to you, but loses his original freedom to walk by himself and must now hold your hand. A child unwilling to settle down at a restaurant must be taken to the car to wait (with supervision) or be taken home while others remain to eat. And the teen who has returned home unduly late from an outing without calling should lose car privileges for a period long enough to bring him feelings of loss and pain.

Upon experiencing these losses, your child begins to understand that defiant moments in the nonchoice zone do not, in fact, bring pleasure, but lead to a loss of freedom and privileges. The pain he feels over these losses is what will motivate him to renew his interest in cooperating. Thus, it's critical that parents not worry about the hurt their child feels over these losses or try to reduce his pain in any way—since it's the pain he experiences that will cause uncooperative behaviors to feel aversive to him.

Step 6: Decide What Losses to Impose on Your Child

One of the most important yet challenging aspects of discipline is deciding what losses will create enough feeling of pain for your child that he will actively strive to avoid them in the future. Following are a number of options.

Figure 9. Diagram of a Contracted Boundary

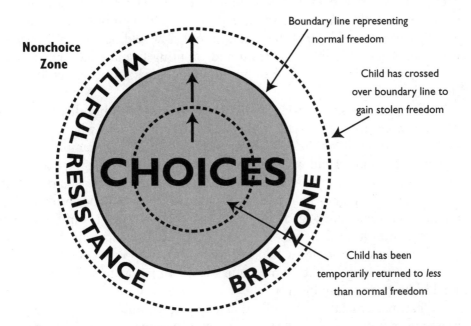

Nonchoice Zone

Boundary line representing normal freedom

Child has crossed over boundary line to gain stolen freedom

Child has been temporarily returned to *less* than normal freedom

WILLFUL RESISTANCE

BRAT ZONE

CHOICES

Allowing More Natural Consequences

Natural consequences—or nature's results—are happening all of the time and offer your child innumerable opportunities to learn from his choices which behaviors work well and which ones to avoid. For example, when a child rollerblades down a slope too fast and falls, he evaluates that event. If he got hurt, he will probably decide to take more care while rollerblading.

We can see from this example that Mother Nature is more willing to inflict loss and pain on a child than his more protective parents. She is known, for example, to provide broken bones for careless climbers, hungry stomachs for picky eaters, a loss of friends for bossy companions, and chills for children who have dressed too lightly. Furthermore, she never gives a child second chances or conflicting messages about what will work for him and what will not. Because her consequences are so reliable, children raised by Mother Nature become alert and learn quickly if they are to survive.

Unfortunately, today's parents often find Mother Nature too harsh and thus interfere with her plans. Granted, there are times—as in the case of a young child ready to dart into the street or fall off some precipice—when it's essential to block nature's plan, as the results would, indeed, be too devastating.

In addition, many of nature's consequences are equally wise to thwart because they can be overly discouraging to a child. For example, if your generally responsible junior high schooler has slept through his alarm and is in jeopardy of missing an important team tryout, it would be proper to awaken him. The value of making the team and profiting from whatever growth it would stimulate is worth more to him than the lesson of being cut for oversleeping.

A problem arises, however, anytime you have trouble distinguishing between when it's appropriate to thwart nature's plans and when it's not. In today's world, most families err on the protective side. For example, many of you save the young child who has repelled his peers from feeling the pain of his loneliness by allowing him to watch television after his friends have gone home to escape his self-centeredness. You take an extra jacket or provide your own for the elementary-aged child who habitually forgets his in your effort to protect him from the cold. You rush a forgotten science report to school to prevent your junior high schooler's grade from dropping a notch. And you make false excuses for the teen who has failed to report to work in order to shield him from losing his job.

What makes matters worse is that you give confused messages by providing the entertainment, jacket, report, or excuse one moment, then chastising your child for his immaturity and forgetfulness the next. In the end, your admonitions and insults prove harsher and more difficult for your child than the boredom, chills, dropped grade, or lost job he would have experienced at nature's hands.

Thus, a more effective method would be for you to first determine which natural consequences will teach your child the important lessons life has to offer without overwhelming him with too much failure or injuring him beyond repair; then, have the courage to allow Mother Nature's pain to do the teaching for you.

Reflecting Nature's Lessons. Your only job following a natural consequence is to calmly reflect the lessons it offers your child. This is particularly appropriate during those times when he's complaining about the inconvenience of some result he must endure. For instance, if he's fussing about the cold in a movie and asks for his father's jacket, Dad can respond with, "I'm sorry that you forgot your jacket, son, but I don't want to be cold for the next few hours, so I'm going to hang onto mine. You may snuggle up to me if you like, and maybe you'll remember to bring yours next time." Even if the child catches a cold, the cold is more appropriately his than Dad's and becomes a natural part of his consequence.

Using Logical Consequences

Logical consequences are the results parents create when they want their child to realize that a particular behavior is not going to work for him but are unwilling to allow him to experience the severity of the natural consequence connected to it. Thus, a logical consequence is substituted anytime a natural consequence might prove too *harsh*, as in the case of a child being hit by a car after running into the street; too *discouraging*, as in the case of failing to enjoy a valued activity due to not knowing how to sign up for it; too *subtle*, as seen by the effect poor hygiene and grooming may have on relationships; or falls too far into the *future*, such as the impact poor grades will have on a child's college and career choices.

Whenever you elect to bypass a natural consequence, you must replace it with either additional teaching or an effective logical consequence that is not too severe, yet is strong enough to motivate your child to select more productive behaviors in the future.

Teaching. In many cases, when you interrupt a natural consequence, the best response will be to teach your child more about the situation, motivate him to want to respond differently, and then show him how. For instance, the child who is about to miss a sign-up for a valued activity due to his lack of knowledge of when, how, and where to do it can be taught how to obtain such information. The one needing improved hygiene and grooming can be tactfully shown why and how to address this. And the one whose grades need improving will do better if he's both motivated and shown the way to improve, rather than scolded or punished for not yet knowing or caring how.

Designing Consequences. On the other hand, there will be times when you will need to replace nature's consequence with a logical one of your own in order to help your child learn a lesson that he has not yet absorbed from nature's feedback or your teaching and guidance.

In order for the logical consequences you design to help your child notice the connection between a negative behavior he has selected and its unrewarding result, it's best when your logical consequences have the following components.

1. Your child is given a loss or contraction of some of the freedoms and privileges he highly values each time he crosses a boundary.

2. The loss your child is given causes him to feel as though he created a problem for himself, rather than for his family or others.

3. The loss occurs as soon after the event as possible; if you can't do it in that moment, do it in the next available moment that you are free to address it.

4. The loss selected is as clearly related to what just happened as possible.

5. Your child is flooded with enough loss, pain, and feedback that crossing boundaries feels aversive and is something he will want to avoid experiencing in the future.

With these components in mind, picture Sara deciding that she doesn't want to clean her room as directed and sneaking out to play, instead. If she is interrupted from play as soon as this is noticed—to pick up her room plus do an extra chore to repay her father for reminding her—Sara will not only fail to gain extra play time, but will lose her normal privileges during the time it takes her to do the extra chore. Thus, her decision to avoid cleaning will have given her—rather than her father—a problem, and she will probably discontinue making similar choices in the future. If Father further announces that Sara has lost her choice to play for the rest of the day, she will experience additional pain as a result of her decision to disobey. With so much loss occurring so soon after she skipped out to play, it's unlikely that Sara would feel good about her decision or want to repeat it.

By contrast, if Sara's messy room is ignored while she's allowed to play all afternoon, because the natural consequence of a dirty room is too vague and distant, Sara will probably conclude that it worked for her to ignore her parents' requests. Moreover, if Sara's decision to disobey is not addressed, she can be counted on to disobey again. She may also decide that messy rooms aren't as bad as her family had warned and thus choose to live "happily ever after" in one! Similarly, if Sara is allowed to play all afternoon, but is then scolded upon returning home, she might conclude that the scolding was a small price to pay for the freedom she enjoyed and that going out to play worked quite well for her. She may further draw the most dangerous conclusion of all: that her parents don't know how to get her to respond to their requests.

Dialogue from Class

MOTHER: How old should a child be before you start to give him consequences?

BOBBIE: When a child first defies what you want him to do, you can let him know that his behavior is unacceptable. When he's very young, stating that the activity is not a choice, then distracting and redirecting him will be enough to get him to stop. However, there will come the day, when your child will challenge you with some unwanted behavior. For some children, this begins at nine or ten months while having his diaper changed, whereas for others, it doesn't begin until the child is mobile enough at fifteen or eighteen months to get into a wide array of things. Once the challenge begins, it's helpful to give the child some contraction of his freedom. For example, the child refusing to cooperate with a diaper change can either be restrained until you are finished diapering him or put in a playpen without toys for a minute before you return to try again. The older one can be removed from his high chair if he's throwing food or to the playpen for a little longer if he's refusing to accept a boundary.

MOTHER: I have trouble thinking of consequences to use. An example is that my daughters share a bedroom, and the seven-year-old hid her big sister's underwear the other morning. Needless to say, it resulted in a chaotic morning for everyone, but I couldn't figure out what to do about it.

BOBBIE: At least she has a sense of humor! If you think in terms of determining what consequence would make your daughter feel as though she had given herself—rather than you or her sister—a problem, you can determine some loss she would care about. You might, for example, calmly prevent her from going into their shared bedroom for the rest of the day—or longer if she's as much of a rascal as it seems—since she's not using the rules required to be there. That would turn the situation around to make her feel as though she—rather than her sister—was the one with the inconvenience. Before reinstating her freedom, I would also clear with her to make sure that she viewed her decision to hide the underwear as a choice that didn't work for her. (See Chapter 8 on Clearing.)

ⓖⓖⓖ

Guidelines

Because so many parents report that thinking of consequences is one of their greatest challenges, the following guidelines are designed to stimulate some ideas.

- **Practice Responsiveness**. Anytime your child refuses to respond when asked to do something, it's best not to keep restating your instructions while he continues to ignore you. Instead, stop everything and require that he "practice" being responsive until it comes more easily to him. For instance, if he ignores your request to brush his teeth, calmly require that he practice stopping his other activities and walking to the bathroom a number of times until he can do this without delay or resistance. If he refuses to practice, give him a time-out until he's ready to cooperate. A child who has been handled in this manner will experience a loss of control over the situation each time he resists responding to requests and will be more careful in the future to actively cooperate.

- **Backup Consequences**. Although consequences are most effective when they fit naturally into a situation, parents are often at a loss to come up with tidy outcomes. Thus, it's helpful to draw from a stack of previously created cards designating general losses for your child on those occasions when you can't find one to match the event. These might include such things as a loss of television or stereo privileges for an evening or weekend; a loss of freedom for the social child to play with friends for an afternoon or day; a loss of phone privileges for a day or two; the loss of using the family car for a day or weekend; and so forth. Whenever you get stuck, simply refer to these cards for an idea. Note that I have drawn only from extra privileges, rather than those activities designed to develop a child's talents or fulfill his responsibilities to others. In fact, I never remove such things as sports or other pursuits as general consequences, since these activities help him to grow in responsibility. These would only be at risk on a one-time basis if a child was refusing to cooperate just prior to leaving for the activity.

- **Zero Tolerance vs. Three Strikes and You're Out**. Some experts suggest flashing cards similar to the ones used in a soccer game in which a child is shown a warning card for his first infraction of the rules, then a second card, and on the third one he's given a consequence. It's more effective to give children a consequence for their first infraction of standing rules, since this protects against erroneously teaching them that initial rule-breaking will be condoned. Because tolerating rule-breaking strengthens willfulness and a lack of cooperation, I strongly advocate *zero tolerance* of broken boundaries, in which kids are asked to pay the price for their first step over the line. Only then will they experience boundary-crossing as aversive for *them* and learn that rules are not something to be toyed with or challenged.

- **The Accordion.** Just as you want your child to associate aversive feelings of pain and loss with his choice to cross your boundaries, you also want him to associate pleasure, gain, and freedom with the choice to surrender to life's rules. Therefore, it's critical that parents not only flood their child's awareness with pain when he is defiant, but fill it with pleasure during his periods of cooperation.

  A good way to implement this idea is by looking for ways to create losses for him as soon as he has crossed a boundary; then, give some of it back when he surrenders to your rules. In this way, you not only associate pain with crossed boundaries, but flood your child's awareness with an experience of gain for his cooperation. I refer to this system of contracting a child's freedom during defiant periods—then returning it when he's cooperating—as the *accordion*, since the child's freedom pushes in and out in accordance with his willingness to cooperate. The key is to keep the accordion moving, rather than stuck on normal freedoms for both the cooperative and uncooperative child.

  Thus, when an elementary-age child, still requiring homework supervision, does his assignments without resistance one evening, this might earn him some expanded privileges. For example, in addition to maintaining his normal freedom to do his work in the evening, rather than right after school, he may also be free to watch approved television programs, talk as long as he likes on the phone, or engage in some family activity. In this way, the accordion of freedoms is expanded beyond his normal ones to further encourage his responsibility. By contrast, if he resists his homework, the accordion must contract to the point that he loses the option of watching television or talking on the phone that night as well as the freedom to do his homework in the evening the next day. Such an accordion not only discourages uncooperative behavior, it encourages being responsible.

- **Extra Consequences for Resistance.** Anytime a child resists doing what he is asked with delays, arguments, or refusals, he must pay an additional price for his resistance. Only by doing this will he lose his appetite for resistance and learn, instead, to respond with more willingness and cooperation. The effectiveness of doing this is demonstrated in the story of Sonja, who had fits every time her parents asked her to do something. They would wait out her tantrums, talk to Sonja about it, and require that she complete the original task requested before regaining full freedoms. Yet it wasn't until they required that an additional consequence be paid specifically for her resistance that Sonja lost interest in having these otherwise rewarding, attention-getting episodes prior to doing tasks requested of her.

Step 7: Achieve Surrender with Resistant Children

From the time your child is able to scoot away from you until he is independent and ready to be on his own, you must know how to get him to do as you ask. Every child will challenge his parent's authority from time to time throughout his development, and the bigger he gets, the tougher this challenge can be—especially for those of you who have been inconsistent in holding your boundaries and unclear about who is in charge.

Thus, anytime your child refuses to do as you ask or submit to some consequence you have designed, you must achieve surrender. The key is that both you and your child understand that he is simply not free to resume normal freedoms and activities until he has worked through his resistance and has responded to whatever was originally requested of him.

For example, anytime a child is actively fussing about cleaning up his messes or passively sitting there rather than doing it, you don't need to insist that he stop complaining and begin the task; you can simply remain clear that he's not free to resume normal freedoms until he has done so. Then, don't worry about how long it takes him or what losses he incurs. And don't try to talk him into getting past his resistance. In fact, the less interested and involved you are in how long it takes, the sooner he will see that his resistance hurts his life rather than yours. He should not be allowed to participate in any activities other than meals, hygiene, and rest, or ones requiring responsibility until he has surrendered to the rules. The younger your child is when you deal with his resistance, the sooner he will learn to let go of it.

Dialogue from Class

FATHER: Are there some kids who are so strong-willed that they never do surrender?

BOBBIE: When you do your part correctly, by balancing love with holding your children to responsible boundaries, they are all able to surrender. By contrast, when parents begin to hold their child to the rules, but then get overly concerned about his missing out on things or worn down by his resistance, and thus give in, the child becomes ever more oppositional. These cases are difficult to overcome, particularly when a parent and child have practiced this pattern for years and the child knows that he can wear his family down.

MOTHER: My child will eventually do what is asked, but he never lets go of the resistance he feels about it.

BOBBIE: Resistance starts out as posturing used to get out of doing things. If it works, it becomes a habit. If not, the resistance disappears and willingness remains. Adjusted people *choose* to be in life—including the hard parts. By contrast, poorly adjusted people cultivate internally strong feelings of resistance that cause them to suffer over every task which, in turn, makes their lives miserable. Consequently, it's important that your child learn to release his resistance and choose doing those things that he will be required to do anyway. You can help him to do this by pointing out that although he doesn't have control over everything asked of him, he does have control over how he will feel about doing things. If he chooses to resist, he will suffer, whereas if he decides to willingly let the basic requirements of life be okay with him, he will feel considerably better. To help him learn this, I might also wait until he had released his resistance to doing the chore asked of him before allowing him to do it.

Time-Out

Anytime your child refuses to cooperate with one of his boundaries or a consequence that you have delivered, you must remove him to his room—or an alternate place—where he will be required to remain until he has fully surrendered and you invite him out. This full contraction of your child's freedom is referred to as a *time-out* and has constituted the foundation of discipline since it was introduced as an alternative to spanking in the early 1970s.

Whenever possible, it's best to begin disciplinary measures by finding a way other than time-out to contract your child's freedoms. For example, a child breaking the rules of a card game can be asked to sit out for a couple of hands. However, if this doesn't work and the child resists conforming to your contraction, then it's important that you move him to time-out. Also, on those occasions when you are unable to determine an alternative contraction of freedom to time-out, you simply begin with that.

If your child fails to conform to time-out by refusing to go to his room—or running out of it once put there—you have lost control and must begin immediately to regain it. Since time-outs are a gentler form of discipline than the spankings they replace, those of you who view them as unkind or feel squeamish about using them end up relinquishing all authority and are left with no discipline whatsoever. Ironically, it's this very reluctance to discipline that puts a struggle for control in the foreground of your relationship with your child, and you end up dispensing more anger, threats, yelling, and spanking than parents who are comfortable with discipline. Consequently, those of you who have not yet faced the importance of claiming your authority would be wise to do so and can begin by mastering the use of time-outs.

Following is a sequence of effective steps for parents with children who challenge their time-outs.

1. Getting Your Child to His Room. The first step toward accomplishing a successful time-out with a reluctant child is to physically get him to his room. It's preferable, of course, if he responds to your calm, yet firm directions.

However, if he refuses to comply, and you are forced to physically get him to his room, so be it. Although emotionalism is considerably less effective in gaining control than clear, firm intention and can even trigger a stronger challenge from your child, your goal during these times is to use whatever strength you require to gain his surrender. Consequently, you must employ whatever style works best for you in accomplishing that mission with your particular child. Thus, it's perfectly acceptable for you to use a strong, even stern, tone at this point whenever such intensity is needed to gain your child's cooperation. This tone will be more effective for those parents who have not overused it for nagging about less important issues.

Don't attempt to discuss this contraction of your child's freedom with him during this step, as he has already crossed over his boundary, is not cooperating in getting to his room, and is in no position to bargain for his freedom. Promises of cooperation in the future are insignificant, since he is presently facing the result of a boundary he has already crossed. If he chooses differently in the future, that will be to his benefit, but it has nothing to do with the consequence he is presently facing.

Anytime you allow your child to argue with you while you are in the middle of holding him to his limits, he not only becomes disrespectful, resistant, and unmanageable, but fails to develop the essential skills of surrender, cooperation, and responsibility. Thus, it's important that you not be concerned with honoring his feelings or ideas at this juncture, since these will merely be related to his resistance and need not be discussed. Any valid feelings or thoughts that remain after a child's resistance has passed and he has fully surrendered can be discussed during a period called *clearing* which follows his time-out. (See Chapter 8 on Clearing.)

When an older child, too big to physically handle, refuses to cooperate, you must remind him of his dependence on you by letting him know that if he plans to live under the protection of your household, he will be required to follow the rules. This must be done with genuine love for your child held actively in your heart, combined with a willingness to let him test his own rules in the larger world if he's unwilling to use the ones in your home. When you speak from the heart—even while holding these firm boundaries—you invite your child to respond from his heart, and your chances of reconnecting are significantly enhanced.

Whenever you expect a strong challenge to your requirement that a child follow the rules of your home, you would be wise to maintain or reestablish your control at a time when another parent, relative, or friend is around. Again, this must be done with calm neutrality and love in your heart.

Very few kids will continue to push a challenge under such conditions, unless you have employed entirely too little discipline much too late and have lost all influence over your child. In such cases, parental control has been severely damaged, and you are in critical need of professional help and/or joining a support group such as "ToughLove." (See **Adolescent** entry in the Problem-Solving Guide.)

If you feel physically threatened, you can call your local police requesting help with an "unmanageable" or potentially abusive child. In some cases, it may be necessary to leave the house in order to safely make this call. The key is to confront the issue until it's resolved, rather than continue to ignore the seriousness of your problem. Once you are out of crisis, recommit to balancing love with discipline in your parent/child relationship, using professional help as needed.

Dialogue from Class

MOTHER: What if your child is yelling about how mean you are or that he wants to live at his friend's house?

BOBBIE: Either ignore him completely or let him know that you will discuss it later; then, get him to his room without further response.

These comments are simply diversionary tactics and represent his effort to make you doubt your action and back down.

MOTHER: What if it's his father he wants to live with?

BOBBIE: Again, don't talk about it until he has surrendered to time-out, has accepted his part in the problem during clearing, and has reconnected with you. Then, if he still wants to live with his father—and this is a viable option—that's the time to discuss it.

ANOTHER MOTHER: My three-year-old is one of those kids who is entirely too happy in her bedroom, but I'm having trouble getting her to sit in a chair.

BOBBIE: I would suggest that you forget the chair and let her take her time-outs in her room again. A playpen for the younger child and the bedroom for an older one are the easiest places to regulate time-outs and don't require your involvement to keep your child there. I don't think you need to worry about a child being too happy in his bedroom surrounded by security objects and toys. Remember, we are not trying to frighten, hurt, or punish kids. We're merely showing them that their behavior has cost them control over their freedom to choose which of the rooms in the house they are in for awhile. Most children don't like to lose control over selecting which room they are in. In fact, it helps to remember that if your child really wanted to be in his bedroom more than the family room, that's where he would have been in the first place. So don't let him fool you by acting like his bedroom is just the place he most wanted to be.

On the other hand, there are children who don't seem to care about being given a time-out and are thus not learning from the situation. Others are unusually resistant and are sometimes destructive during time-outs. In these cases, clear out an unused room or safety-proof a bathroom and use that more austere and less destructible area for time-outs.

FATHER: My son can last for hours in his room because his TV and computer are in there.

BOBBIE: First, I would never put a television set in a child's bedroom, since unlimited access to it can seriously distract him from his own development and life. Thus, I would use his misbehavior as an excuse for removing it permanently. I would also temporarily remove all such things as telephone receivers and computer games from a child's room whenever he's on a time-out.

MOTHER: My eleven-year-old refuses to go to his room and shoves me when I try to make him do as I ask.

BOBBIE: How do you respond when he shoves you?

MOTHER: I try to talk him out of it or just leave the area until he cools down. I'm divorced, so I don't feel I can control him.

BOBBIE: Can you see what's happening? You're not only accepting his abuse, you're allowing all control to slip away. Because you will need to have your authority intact to finish raising him, you would be wise to reestablish control. The first step would be to simply claim the feeling of strength and clarity within yourself. Next, with calm neutrality and a gentle but confident voice, let him know that he needs to go to his room and that he will have a chance to air his grievances after he has calmed down. Drop eye contact and move slightly away from him in order to give him some space to make his decision. Most kids will back down at this point. If not, you will have to let him know that you are serious. You can do this by informing him that he's not welcome to stay in your home without following the rules. If necessary, enlist the help of someone else—a neighbor, partner, friend, member of a group such as "ToughLove," to be there when you take a stand; or call them—or even the police—for help if you are underway, and he refuses to either go to his room or leave the house. Remember that it's critical to your child's development and your future together that you stop being afraid of claiming your authority. Throughout this challenge, remember to stay in your heart in order to call on your own strength as well as to keep you in a neutral—even loving—frame of mind.

   Be aware that most kids are significantly more cooperative after their parents have taken a stand like this, especially when it's done with love. You must also be aware that parents who back down at this juncture end up surrendering even more control to increasingly unruly kids who take over their households and may even act abusively toward their parents. If you are still unable to gain control, seek professional help.

2. Keeping Your Child in His Room. When a child is first learning about time-outs, he must stay in his room until invited out. Moreover, any invitation to come out of his room should not be extended until he has fully accepted his time-out and has remained there without objection for the required period of time.

Anytime a child resists this arrangement, you must find a way to keep him in his room. Yet because it's important not to shut a very young resistant child behind a closed door, it works best to restrain him in a playpen or in his room with a tall gate across the threshold or two gates stacked one above the other if he's able to climb over one gate. This allows him to see you but not to escape.

Once your child is old enough to climb over whatever barriers you have established, you must have a plan for keeping him in his room. Following are some guidelines for retaining the resistant older child in his room. (See Figure 10.)

Whenever your child cooperates and accepts staying in his room, he may remain there—with his door open—until he is invited out. Although he's allowed to cry for as long as he likes, if his crying is resistant—which it usually is under such circumstances—his time-out will begin only after his crying has stopped. You can let him know that it's okay if he prefers to cry for awhile and stay in his room a bit longer to accommodate the time needed to do so.

Or if he prefers, he can skip the resistance, begin his time-out immediately, and remain in his room for a shorter period of time. Either before the problem has started or during a period called *clearing*, you can show him on a timeline how resistance extends his period of banishment. (See Figure 10, Option #1.)

If his crying is genuinely sad, be aware that you may have been unfair in your assessment of the situation. Or he may be feeling the pain of his loss, in which case you reflect to him that his choice to break the rules didn't work very well for him. On the other hand, he may be holding a distortion that prevents him from seeing his part in the situation, which you must help him to examine during *clearing* once he has completed his time-out. (See Chapter 8.)

It's important that you remain neutral and not be concerned if your child resolves to cry, even if he does so with resistance. He's simply adjusting to his frustration about the limits of his boundaries and—in some cases—may be trying to get you to back down; if you don't get emotionally involved in this activity, he will eventually wind down and stop. Because it's essential

Figure 10. Time-Out Guidelines

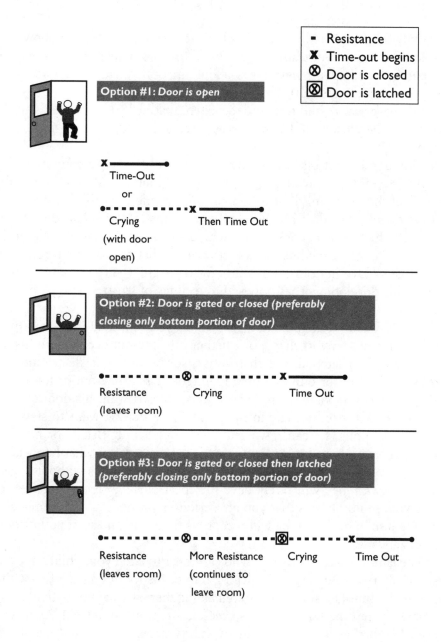

never to walk into a tantrumming child's room to request that he stop crying or ask how he is doing, all checking on a younger child to assure his safety must be done discreetly.

Only if he has tried to leave his bedroom should a child be shown subsequent time-out procedures, since you don't want to provide a generally cooperative child with new ideas about uncooperative behaviors that he might use. (See Figure 10, Options #2 and #3.)

Whenever your child resists to the extent that he leaves his room, his door must then be closed, and if he leaves a second time, latching it is a good option.

Although it's not essential, some parents will feel more comfortable taking this step if they buy or construct a Dutch door that allows the top third or half of the bedroom door to remain open while only the bottom section is closed and latched. If a child climbs over this arrangement, then the top portion (which can be constructed with a window) can also be closed and latched. Whichever method is used, it's critical that parents do it from a neutral place of love held in their hearts for their child and a conscious desire to help his development, as opposed to feelings of frustration, lost patience, and anger. (See Figure 10, Options #2 and #3.)

You may draw a diagram of Figure 10 for your child in order to help him see that he's not only in charge of whether his time-out occurs with his door open, closed, or latched, but that he is also the one who determines if he stays in his room for only the time required for his time-out or for a longer period to accommodate his resistance. If he doesn't want his door closed or latched, he will need to stay in his room. If he doesn't want to stay in his bedroom for long, he can resist and cry about it only briefly or not at all. The key is for him to understand that he is in control of what happens.

Those of you who are able to clearly follow these steps without anger or additional warnings will rarely have to repeat closing or latching the door. Once your child realizes that you are serious—yet neutral and calm—about keeping him in his room, he will accept his time-out, and your authority will be reestablished.

The fainthearted among you who can't bear to latch your child's door may use the alternative of calmly returning him to his room repeatedly—without discussion—until he surrenders to remaining there. Explain once that his freedom will be returned only after his time-out has been completed. Parents who have tried this say it can take as many as fifty times or more and that it's only successful if you are able to remain completely calm.

Other parents prefer to stand on the outside of the door to hold it closed, but I fail to see the difference between this and latching it—except that the parent is not free and the child knows it!

In my experience, those parents who bravely latch their child's door—or calmly return him the required number of times—are the most successful in gaining clear-cut, no-nonsense control over their children, while those who resist this step often spend years squeamishly resisting taking control.

A word of caution. A child who resists going to bed should never have his door closed or latched. Because bedtime is a time when your child is adjusting to separating from you for the night, settling down, and surrendering to sleep, it's best to have a night-light on while calmly returning him repeatedly to his room. Yet it should also be noted that the child who has been required to accept your directions and boundaries in the light of day is less likely to put up a fuss about going to bed at night.

Dialogue from Class

MOTHER: I can see from my child's behavior that I have to face this step—but it seems abusive to me.

BOBBIE: When angry parents throw their children into their rooms and lock their doors with hate and loathing in their hearts, such acts are, indeed, abusive and generate feelings of abandonment in a child. By contrast, I'm recommending that calm, neutral parents close and latch doors only if necessary to keep uncooperative children in well-lit, airy bedrooms for reasonable periods of time, until they can settle down and accept the idea that their parents are in charge. When done this way, it will not feel abusive to either the parent or child.

ANOTHER MOTHER: Wouldn't it be easier to just spank the child?

BOBBIE: Unfortunately, spanking uses hitting as a means for gaining control over a child. Although I consider parental dominance essential to discipline, I believe it's equally important that it be established by genuinely mature parents acting older and wiser than their children and able to dispense discipline in a neutral, caring manner. This not only prevents damaging the child in the process of establishing control, but allows him to trust his parent's wisdom and guidance. By contrast, the hurt of a spanking, as well as the negative feelings connected to it, invariably cause a child to feel violated which, in turn, damages his ability to fully trust in the wisdom of his parent's "mature boss" or guidance.

A THIRD MOTHER: What do you do if your child starts pulling his room apart while he's in there?

BOBBIE: This only happens when you have delayed taking control with your younger child and are now trying to get him to surrender after he has spent several years practicing his resistance. There are two options to use at this juncture, depending on the age of your child and the level of resistance and destruction. You can calmly require that he clean the mess after he has settled down and you have cleared with him. Or if your child is resistant to cleaning and/or continues to be destructive, use a safety-proofed, less destructible bathroom or some other unused area for his time-outs.

3. Beginning the Time-Out. Once your child has stopped his resistance and crying, you can begin to clock the amount of time you want him to remain there. Although some experts suggest keeping a child in his room a minute for every year of his age, I usually double, triple, or more than quadruple that, depending on the child, his age, and the situation. Thus, a child under two might be required to remain in his playpen or room for only a minute or two after his crying has completely stopped, whereas a two-and-a-half-year-old might need to stay anywhere from three to five minutes or more once his crying has stopped. A three-year-old might stay from five to fifteen minutes or more and a four-year-old from about five to twenty minutes or more. A child from five to six years old who is still resisting might be required to stay as long as twenty to thirty minutes after his tantrum is over. A child seven to eight and older might be required to remain in his room for up to thirty to forty minutes.

The shorter times are appropriate for the younger child just learning to manage his time-out without crying, whereas the longer times are more effective for a child who will be motivated to cooperate if he's excluded from the group for awhile. The time a child is kept in his room must be long enough for him to experience a loss of freedom, but not so long that he's overwhelmed by the experience or becomes desensitized to it.

It's important not to walk into a child's room the instant he stops crying, as he hasn't had enough time to consciously face that he has been given a time-out for a few minutes. On the other hand, the goal is not to punish, but to merely have your child notice that his freedoms have been contracted, and that he has lost—rather than gained—both freedom and control as a result of the methods he was using.

In addition, children three years of age and older who are resistant during their time-out must be given additional grounding or other losses once their time-out is over in order to pay for the resistance they waged—since only then will they lose their appetite for fighting these periods of restriction. For example, a resistant young child might be grounded from play for the rest of the afternoon, or an older one might lose the opportunity to talk on the phone that evening. I rarely make grounding last for more than a day for young children or a weekend for adolescents, unless the older child has done something very serious; in such cases grounding may take up to a month or more in order to break the pattern of associating with rebellious friends. (See Chapter 12 for more specifics.) Moreover, if a child who is not a regular resister is genuinely remorseful and cooperative, he may get off early from grounding after paying at least part of his penance.

Dialogue from Class

MOTHER: What if your child stops crying for a moment, but starts again when you go into his room?

BOBBIE: See if he's able to wind down the crying and begin to talk or if he's determined to wind it back up. If he is still resisting—as opposed to quietly sobbing some additional emotion upon seeing you—then you will have to leave the room again, calmly letting him know that you will return when he's ready to talk. If he's sincerely expressing emotion with genuine tears—rather than more resistance–allow that. You may even want to sit with him and begin your talk by reflecting to him that learning about not always getting our way can take some time to accept, but that you can see he's getting adjusted to the idea.

ꙮꙮꙮ

4. Voluntarily Returning When Ready to Cooperate. The child who accepts parental control and has demonstrated his willingness for a number of months to go to his room cooperatively—without resistance or crying—is no longer required to wait for an invitation to come out, but may voluntarily return whenever he feels ready to clear things up with you (see Chapter 8 on Clearing). Under such conditions, your child might remain in his room for just a moment or for a longer period of reflection, depending on what he decides. However, should he come out prematurely, claiming that he's ready to talk, but then acts resistant, he must be sent back to his room and now loses the chance to leave voluntarily.

Step 8: When Problems Repeat, Examine What You Are Doing

Anytime a child's problem is repeating, it's due to the fact that the way you and others are responding to the problem is reinforcing for the child. You can uncover which responses are serving as maintainers of the problem by recording everyone's reactions and examining what it is about them that is causing your child to want to repeat the behavior. (See Chapter 9.)

Step 9: Motivate Your Child to Want to Do Better

Unless a child can see the cost to him of his behavior, he simply won't change. Thus, any child who has been given a time-out, whether he resists or is cooperative, should not be allowed to return to the rest of the house or resume normal activities without first sitting down to face what happened, what price it cost him, and what he can learn from the situation.

Consequently, even though it's rarely taught in parenting programs, *clearing* with your child after his time-out and then selecting and teaching the right lessons connected to the problem are the most important parts of your discipline program. The following two chapters will teach you how to take these crucial steps.

A child's surrender to parental love and guidance is critical to his well-being and the well-being of society.

★★★

8

Clearing

Pathways to Clarity

The Seventh Key:
◉◉◉
*Clear and learn from each mess
along the pathway of your life.*

One of the biggest errors in parenting is the practice of sending reluctant children to their rooms to "think about" what they have done, then foolishly letting them out—with only a reprimand—to resume their normal freedoms and privileges.

What most of you fail to realize is that your child has, indeed, gone to his room to "think about" what happened and usually concludes that you are a mean-spirited and cruel parent to have treated such a sweet and blameless child so unjustly! Instead of thinking about where he has gone awry, he spends his time of banishment building a case against you and conducting a trial in his mind to prove your culpability. It's no wonder that, once free, he recoils from the likes of you to further nurse his anger and close his heart, while waging alliances with other family members against you.

Whenever your child is allowed to shrink from acknowledging his transgressions in this way, you not only miss the opportunity to hold him accountable for his actions, but encourage his denial and avoidance of the truth. As a result of not owning up to his errors, he fails to see what needs correcting or what he might learn from his mistakes. Thus, he is no clearer after his banishment than he was before it.

This common tendency to allow our children to deny the truth of their actions mirrors how we handle transgressions in our larger society as well. As a result, a denial of responsibility for crossed boundaries has become increasingly more tolerated in all aspects of our lives. To reverse this, we must find a way to more thoroughly address and repair the problems between us if we're to heal our spirits and reopen our hearts to each other. Yet because we don't practice this level of integrity in our daily lives, we no longer know how to do it, and healing our injuries and violations to one another has become a lost art.

The problem is rooted in the importance we place on being right at all costs in order to be the best, achieve the most, and win the race of the ego. To accomplish this, we teach our kids that it's okay to deceive in order to protect their "righteousness"; that using others may be required in their rise to the top; that concealing their dishonesty and betrayals is acceptable when needed to preserve relationships; and that fixed denial, false blame, and aggressive communication are useful tools for the ego that seeks domination, rather than collaboration. The overall result of living in a world that has become so tolerant of deception is that we often feel as though we are surrounded by double agents, each wondering what our colleagues and friends are *really* thinking and doing.

Our growing unwillingness to admit to the truth of things and accept responsibility for our actions and errors not only damages our relationships and emotional health, it's endangering our societal order. In effect, our growing lack of integrity in so many areas of our lives is destroying us, and learning to tell the whole truth and nothing but the truth is the only antidote that can help. It's time that we begin!

Healing Our Lives with Honesty

In order to heal the injuries between you and your children, as well as others, a conscious effort must be made to expose the truth about every event that has created a problem between you. To do this, you must go to your heart with sincerity to scan for the complete truth about what happened—including all of the shadowy wisps of unfavorable and embarrassing information. Only by doing this will you admit to your transgressions and face when and how you have injured the heart of another person. You must then acknowledge when your lack of kindness or responsibility has brought them pain and sincerely apologize for your infractions without distortion or defense. Only by doing this do you free others to reopen their hearts to you once again and relate to you with renewed trust and candor. This experience, in turn, brings clarity and love to your own heart and life. Yet in spite of the importance of taking these steps, it's something that is rarely done in today's world.

A group of governors from various states in search of a system that would achieve these kinds of results for use in family court mediation recently met in Hawaii. They were drawn together to examine why Ho‘oponopono,[4] a unique method for settling disputes used by the early Hawaiians, had worked so well. Here is what they learned.

Hawaii's Gift of Clarity

Because good relationships and bonded hearts were of such importance to the early Hawaiians, they developed an unequaled system of group counsel called *Ho'oponopono*, which facilitated their ability to relate to each other in a unique and caring way that preserved integrity, clarity, and the bond of love among them. In this system, societal members were asked during periods of conflict to voluntarily expose the full truth of their feelings and actions; to care deeply about the effect of their behavior on the environment and others; and to look for ways to make amends, ask forgiveness, forgive, and release all problems that had developed between them.

In examining these criterion for settling disputes, it becomes instantly clear how easy it could be. Yet if settling disagreements is as easy as these guidelines suggest, why are we having so little success in settling them in our homes, communities, nations, and the world? The reason quite simply is that we do not include the step of voluntarily exposing the full truth of our feelings and actions during conflict resolution.

In fact, if we look carefully, we will see that in contrast to the early Hawaiians' view that societal members must voluntarily offer full exposure of the truth, the right to conceal incriminating information is protected by the Fifth Amendment of the American Constitution. When we examine this difference, we can see that the key to the success of the Hawaiians' system lay in their unwillingness to conceal any information whatsoever. Instead, they understood the importance of testifying against themselves if they had, in fact, done something wrong and valued—even insisted on—bringing all transgressions into the open to be exposed and healed. In short, because they prized the truth, they behaved honorably; and this combination enabled them to unravel their problems and set them free.

They further believed that anytime there was some misunderstanding or transgression between two people, negative energies would bind them together in an invisible web of unclear energy, and this web could only be released by having an honorable examination of the matter, anchored in integrity.

In order to accomplish this, a Ho'oponopono counsel or group meeting was developed as a means to clear up misunderstandings and "set things right." Every individual involved in the misunderstanding was required to come to the counsel with an attitude of sincerity and a willingness to search his heart for the "very spirit of the truth." Since the witness of the higher self and God were also included by invitation through prayer at the opening of the meeting, deceit could not be sanctioned, and truth became the foundation on which the success of Ho'oponopono rested.

Next, the discussion period would begin, offering each participant an opportunity to provide information about his own conduct, share his viewpoint, and fully express his attitudes and emotions. A helping-healer or respected family elder would guide the meeting by directing each person to share his viewpoint while mediating any problems that might arise.

Everyone in attendance was committed to listening—without interruption—to the various parts shared by others and dealing honestly with each layer of the issue as it surfaced. This process prevented individuals from glossing over problems with premature or shallow apologies before sincerely facing the full effect of their transgressions. If the leader felt that participants were not being sincere, he or she would call it to their attention and ask that they tell what had *really* happened or express what they *genuinely* felt within their hearts. Furthermore, whenever there was more than one layer to a problem, the leader would guide the group in getting to its core.

In addition to honestly clarifying the issues, the first transgressor had a responsibility to the group to offer sincere acknowledgement of his error and true motives for his behavior. He was also expected to offer his sincere regrets, some gesture of compensation, and an appeal for forgiveness. Secondary transgressors followed this admission by disclosing their own confessions of wrongdoing, revenge-taking, grievances, grudges, and resentments. Whenever possible, arrangements were made for restitution as a means to repent and ease the losses that had been suffered.

Because the early Hawaiians viewed a wronged person who elected to hold tightly to his or her anger and get caught in nonforgiveness as making a mistake equal in gravity to the error of the original transgressor, anyone who held onto negative feelings was considered an equal contributor to the problem. Thus, whenever a transgression had been fully acknowledged and discussed, and forgiveness was sincerely asked, the person transgressed against had a responsibility to forgive the transgression. In doing this, he was required not merely to suppress his negative feelings but to fully release them from his heart.

Once a transgression was successfully *acknowledged* and *forgiven*, the problem—and the energies attached to it—were considered to be dissolved. Thus, the problem no longer existed and the matter was not to be discussed again. The meeting closed with a prayer of gratefulness for getting clear and being in harmony once again with the forces of nature and one another.

This system is considered among the best devised for resolving differences and maintaining good relationships. However, to use it, we have to tell the truth. What better place to start than in your own home.

Clearing

Clearing is a system I have drawn from the model and wisdom of Ho'oponopono for use in keeping your relationships with your children clear.[5]

Clearing teaches your child not only to investigate the true cause of his problems and how to resolve and release them, but why a particular problem is in his life and what lessons it has to offer him. A child is also taught during the clearing process that if he is to draw the correct conclusions from a problem, he must examine the problem honestly without concealing or denying any aspect of his part in it. He must learn, instead, to trust the value of fully exposing his mistakes, acknowledging his transgressions, and taking responsibility for his actions without resistance or drama. This process is key not only to helping a child become a clearer and more cooperative person, but to becoming his best and most loving self. The same is true for you.

The Rationale

To understand why clearing is so important, you must first understand that any problems, consequences, or time-outs that your child has experienced will teach him absolutely nothing about how to improve his behavior or life unless he is also required to face the lessons contained in the experience. In order to do this, he must openly discuss the problem, explore exactly what happened, honestly confront why he was given a consequence—either by his family or by life—and determine what his part in the problem has truthfully been. Simultaneously, the person with whom he is clearing is required to be equally sincere in searching his heart for the truth of the matter and determining his part in the problem.

Children raised with clearing are unusually open, honest, clear-seeing, and loving. They are also spared the need to later pry off facades of defense, deceit, and denial or reopen hearts that have been closed to the truth and others. Moreover, they learn to perceive problems as events showing them where they are still unclear about how to live life more effectively and what they can do to improve and grow in wisdom.

The happy result of a child understanding the lessons that go with his difficulties is that he will be less likely to re-create that particular problem again. Instead, he will develop life skills, improved clarity, and an understanding of how to live from his higher self. He is also released from the negative energies that surround any conflicts he has had with others and is thus free to resume his life with a clear and open heart.

The Requirement

Anytime your child has failed to behave responsibly, has been given a time-out, or has caused some disruption in your family or his other relationships, he is required to *clear* before regaining his freedom to reenter family life or resume normal privileges. Likewise, whenever you have behaved in a manner that has caused your child to shut down his spirit and close his heart to you, you have a responsibility to clear with him so that he can feel safe and open with you once again.

During clearing, your child is required to sit with you, his siblings, friends, and any others involved in the problem in order to talk things out until it feels completely clear between you. This is true even if he was not the initiator of a problem, since he has a responsibility to listen to those who wish to clear their transgressions with him as well.

The Setting and Tone

Clearing is not a time for scoldings, lectures, recriminations, or recitations on how disappointed you feel about your child's immaturity or misbehavior; nor is it a time to elicit quick apologies or promises that he will never make such errors again. Instead, it's a close, connecting time filled with warmth and is designed to explore the truth of what happened, what can be learned from the experience, and how to best remedy the problem and clear up whatever negative feelings it generated.

To establish a friendly, cooperative atmosphere, it's important that you and your child sit together in a neutral place such as on the living room sofa, while giving your full attention to the clearing experience. You can allow him to sit in your lap or snuggled up to you, if he wishes, or to simply sit nearby. Touching during clearing helps both of you to remember that it's a time for reconnection and bonding, rather than one of struggle and separation. Approaching clearing from your heart in a soft and gentle manner invariably melts your child's heart and is your greatest ally in helping him to feel safe enough to reopen his spirit and get clear with you once again.

If you are to effectively teach your child not to deny his mistakes, you must also provide a model of nondefensiveness and easily admit to your own errors. Many of you will find it difficult to back down on a hasty or poor decision or acknowledge that your impatience, anger, faulty perceptions, or poor communication has contributed to a misunderstanding. Yet clearing can only work when you are able to be open and honest enough to fully expose your own weaknesses and errors. Even more important, clearing becomes abusive if your goal is to be right, rather than to genuinely examine the true source of the problem.

It's essential that you maintain a pleasant, supportive attitude throughout the clearing process, as this helps your child to experience truthfulness and acknowledgment as safe and rewarding. You must further understand that as your child feels safe with you and secure enough to face his part in a problem, he will acknowledge his mistakes and correct them accordingly. Thus, in order to be effective, clearings must include the elements of kind and loving parents talking to valued friends rather than dominant adults bossing naughty children into guilty regret and submission. Moreover, parents must take care not to become overly controlling or to turn clearings into power struggles.

Before starting, each person is asked to get quiet, consciously shift awareness to his or her heart, and speak from a place of honor. For families comfortable with their spiritual connection, a moment of meditation or prayer and a request for spiritual guidance greatly enhances the process. For those not yet comfortable with this, I would remind you of Marianne Williamson's realization one day that God could create something as beautiful and awe-inspiring as the ocean; yet she couldn't even make a soufflé! I have personally found new power in my life by subordinating my own fragile, yet pretentious world self enough to invite the "Ocean-maker" to be on my team. Whether or not you include a higher power, be sure to include your own higher self. This will protect you from becoming dominant and controlling during the process.

The Discussion

Once you and your child are settled and ready for a discussion of the problem, you must bring your most neutral, sovereign self to the clearing and communicate with your child in a calm and loving manner. You can assure him that your goal is not to uncover "who is to blame," but to discover what went wrong and how to find a solution. By not focusing on who is right or wrong or good or bad, you let your child know that you are not there to judge or condemn his feelings or actions, but are on his side throughout the discussion in helping him to become his best self.

Furthermore, you need not feel pressured to provide quick solutions, since—as with math—the process of getting to the answer is just as important to your child's learning as the ultimate solution. A thorough clearing can take anywhere from fifteen or twenty minutes to an hour or more.

Getting to the Core of the Problem. It's important to diligently guard against the urge to handle the matter quickly and superficially when serving as the mediator in a clearing. Strive, instead, to calmly and gently guide children all the way through each layer of their problem and uncover the core belief that provoked them to behave as they did. For example, if an overly sensitive child has been teased by a more aggressive playmate, it won't help either child if the teaser gets reprimanded, while the one who was teased is consoled. Because both children have something to learn that is not yet clear for them, it's important that you handle their problem at a deeper level. In this case, the teased child is unclear about how to deal with teasers and may need help in learning not to be so sensitive or how to withdraw his dramatic reaction which the teaser finds so reinforcing. On the other hand, the teaser needs to understand the true effect that teasing and aggression will have on his own popularity as well as how to heal his urge to annoy and hurt others. Thus, rather than deal with the superficial layer—the teasing—you can be immensely more helpful if you guide both children toward a greater understanding of the underlying dynamics of their problem.

Communicating Sensitively. To understand each layer of a problem, you must communicate with your child sensitively while speaking—without interruptions—one at a time. It further enhances communication when you ask careful questions designed to engage your child's mind and lure his thinking processes into the discussion. To do this, you must replace parental lectures and monologues with the kinds of Socratic, reflective questions, gently asked, that will encourage your child to communicate his way to clearer conclusions.

It's particularly important that you listen carefully and intuitively, while striving to uncover the source of the problem as well as what is not presently understood by one or both of you about how to live life harmoniously. (For more information on how to listen, consult Chapter 11 on Communication.)

Acknowledging Transgressions

Your willingness to lay down your defenses, put your own truths on the table, and acknowledge whatever errors you have made offers enormous relief to your child—and others—in knowing that you can see the same reality they do. This, in turn, enables them to trust in you once again and reopen their hearts to you. Once a disagreement is no longer an issue of who is right or wrong, there is no battle to win or pride to save, and it's easier to remain in your heart and admit to the truth, including whatever mistakes are involved. Because this is the key to keeping relationships open and clear, it's critical that you not only learn this for yourself, but teach your children to acknowledge their errors and transgressions along the way.

Often, your child merely needs to practice admitting that it was his behavior—rather than unkind parents—that cost him a consequence or a time-out. Verbally expressing this teaches him to accept responsibility for his actions and develop the habit of facing personal truths. Only when he can honestly accept his part in a problem will he experience appropriate remorse and want to fix whatever needs adjusting in his approach to life.

On other occasions, he will be asked to acknowledge his part in a misunderstanding with another child. For example, the teen who has excluded his friend from activities must admit to his unkind behavior before clearing can get underway and closeness resumed. If, instead, he denies what he has done or blames his friend's behavior for his own cruel acts, his friend feels even more betrayed and is confused by the denial of what he or she knows to be true. Whenever people attempt to rebuild a friendship on the shaky soil of denials, their relationships lack trust. By contrast, full acknowledgment of whatever mistakes were made allows hearts to genuinely reopen, trust to return, and closeness to resume.

Whenever you sincerely acknowledge your part in a problem, children are quick to forgive and reopen their hearts. Thus, anytime your child is having trouble responding to your efforts to clear, you would be wise to examine if you have some unacknowledged part in the matter and, if so, to promptly acknowledge it. It's useful, even when you are the secondary transgressor, to be willing to be the first to acknowledge. This not only creates a model of acknowledging for your child, but helps him to trust in you and surrender to examining his part in the problem.

Dialogue from Class

MOTHER: Whenever I try to clear with my child, he turns the problem around and accuses me of being mean. He's very effective at making me feel guilty for disciplining him. How do I stop this?

BOBBIE: It's important to be clear first within yourself and then with him that he's the one who caused his contraction of freedom. If he had chosen to cooperate, he could have maintained his freedom, but since he chose differently he gave himself a problem. Your clarity will not only help him to see the truth, it will help you to release your guilt. You can also check yourself to see if you were abrupt or angry, since a disapproving attitude causes children to focus on your poor temperament and then view your treatment of them as the source of the problem. If your temper was poor, you must acknowledge your failure to be your best self, without blaming your child's behavior for your shortcomings. You must also clarify that you still need to deal with his behavior, but would like to begin again in a better frame of mind.

ANOTHER MOTHER: My nine-year-old doesn't mind staying in his room, but he hates to talk about the problem.

BOBBIE: Kids who don't want to talk about their problems usually dislike admitting to errors or taking responsibility for them. It might help to approach your child gently and let him know that you are not looking for someone to blame or scold but merely want to determine what went wrong and how to best correct it. Be sure not to let him off the hook until he is able to surrender to talking about his problem.

MOTHER: I'm also asking for some assurance from him that he won't do that behavior again, but he resists agreeing to anything.

BOBBIE: I wouldn't bother to ask for that. It's not realistic to have a child promise that he will never cross his boundaries in the future. That would be equivalent to my asking the parents in this class to promise that they will never get angry with their kids again. He's going to cross your boundaries, so just forget about the promises. If he repeats this particular behavior in the future, deal with it at that time, but for now, your goal is to help him get clear that it didn't work for him this time.

FIRST MOTHER: If I sense that my child is still holding a grudge against me, even after we have cleared, should I let it go if he's able to integrate with the rest of the family?

BOBBIE: I almost never walk away from an incomplete clearing. Even if it takes up to an hour or more, it's essential that you get all the way through the problem before your child is free to resume normal activities. Yet you must also make sure not to turn it into a power struggle that takes all day or ends in an impasse. If your child is having a good deal of trouble acknowledging, reevaluate your certainty of his part, and, if appropriate, help him to accept the idea that he at least shares some of the responsibility for the problem. He may need to take a break to think about it, or to write or draw his part in it. If that's the case, you can postpone discussing it further until later that evening or the next day—perhaps in a family meeting. You will know it's clear when he's willing to talk openly, can honestly face his own responsibility in the matter, and is able to genuinely surrender any negative emotions he was feeling toward you.

A THIRD MOTHER: What do you do when you ask what they did to cause their problem and they say they forgot, and you don't know if they really did or not?

BOBBIE: Children don't forget but say that they do as a way to avoid responsibility. You can take your child back to the moment of his transgression and ask what he was hoping would happen, just to get him started. If he still refuses to talk, let him know that because he's not ready, he will have to wait on the sofa awhile longer and that you will check on him later to see if he's more willing to discuss the problem. If he has another fit at this point, have him return to his room for another time-out.

MOTHER: What if he says he's ready to talk just as I start to leave?

BOBBIE: If this happens one time, then it's okay to begin your talk. However, if he says he's ready but then withdraws again or doesn't fully participate in the discussion, you will have to leave him sitting there for awhile before checking to see if he's truly ready.

MOTHER: What if it takes a long time before he's ready?

BOBBIE: That's not a problem. Just go about your business and get a few things done. But if it's taking more than one try, let him know that you are going to do a bigger chore before checking on him again. Then, allow him to sit there for fifteen minutes or so before returning to see if he's prepared to clear. If he calls out that he's ready during that time, he still has to wait, since his initial unwillingness to cooperate lost him the opportunity to be in control of the timing of your talk.

MOTHER: What if he keeps calling that he's ready?

BOBBIE: Once he has been told that it's not a choice to call, doing so becomes a broken boundary and he will have to go back to his room for another time-out. He's allowed to wait on the sofa only if he's cooperating. If he's calling from his room, simply ignore him and begin clocking his time-out after all calling has stopped. You can go to his room to explain how this works if it's his first time; but do this only once. Otherwise, explain it again during your clearing.

ANOTHER FATHER: What do you do when kids say they "don't know" to things you know they have the answer to?

BOBBIE: "I don't know" usually means, "I'm not willing to know what's going on with me or to take responsibility for it, and I'd rather feel confused." If you suspect that he's avoiding the issue, don't beg for cooperation. Let him know, instead, that he will be free to try again when he's ready to face the problem and talk about it.

MOTHER: My son fell asleep while he was sitting on the sofa waiting.

BOBBIE: That's not uncommon. Going unconscious is another way to avoid taking responsibility for one's behavior. Let him sleep, but don't allow him to do anything once he's awake until he has cleared with you. If it's nighttime, put him to bed, but don't let him do anything in the morning until after he has cleared.

ANOTHER MOTHER: What if two children need to clear something and one is ready but the other doesn't want to talk?

BOBBIE: The child who is cooperating can be excused until the uncooperative one is ready, whereas the uncooperative child is not free to go anywhere until the misunderstanding has been cleared. You will be amazed by how quickly the uncooperative child shapes up when he sees this development!

FATHER: How do you clear with a two-year-old?

BOBBIE: You can clear with a child that young by taking him over to the forbidden object and saying, "It's not a choice to touch the stereo. Are you ready to remember?" Then allow him to be free again to decide what choice he will make about touching it. If he doesn't touch it, he has learned the lesson and is clear about it. You can let him know that he's getting the idea and can remain free. If he touches it, he will need to be restrained or given a time-out. At the end of the restraint or time-out, restate your boundary and see what choice he makes. Calmly repeat this cycle until he no longer touches the object.

ANOTHER MOTHER: My five-year-old sobs so hard whenever he's in his room on a time-out that by the time I get there he seems too frenzied and disoriented to cope.

BOBBIE: Allow that to happen. If he's not ready to talk, wait until he is. Let him know that you will return when he's more willing to take responsibility.

MOTHER: But what if he cries again?

BOBBIE: That's fine. You can start all over with the tantrum phase of the problem.

MOTHER: (Confused look)

BOBBIE: You seem to be a little worried about the frenzy he gets himself into.

MOTHER: I'm afraid he'll never understand why he's been sent to his room.

BOBBIE: The reason he doesn't understand is because you are beginning your talk before he has completed his resistance. You're probably not trusting that he can get calmed down enough to assume responsibility, so you're accepting minimal levels of cooperation and surrender from him.

MOTHER: You're right! I honestly don't think he can get back in control once he gets so frenzied. And it frightens me.

BOBBIE: You're falling for his theatrical presentation of how hard this is for him and believing that he's not capable of taking responsibility for settling down to talk. What do you do while he's in this disoriented state?

MOTHER: I wait in another room, but I can hardly stand it. So, the minute he calms down, I go into his room and find his face all puffy and his body completely wilted. Then, when I start to talk to him, he can't seem to focus on what we're talking about. He stares at the ceiling while he gasps and sobs.

BOBBIE: This kid is good! I suspect we'll be seeing him at the Academy Awards someday. (Laughter) It sounds like you need to wait a little longer after he has calmed down before going into his room and attempting a communication. Once he has finished with his dramatics, get him to transfer to the living room sofa rather than talk in his room. The key is not to begin a communication until he's ready to talk as a recomposed five-year-old.

FATHER: What if we're running late for an activity and we need to clear something?

BOBBIE: Whenever possible I would choose clearing over the activity. This helps children to see that clearing is a priority and that you are serious about requiring them to be clear with their family before regaining their freedom to be with the rest of the world. If a child is particularly anxious to get to an activity, you can let him know, "You have a crossroads choice to make at this juncture. You can keep struggling with this and make our clearing take a long time, or you can choose to work this out cooperatively and make it go faster. It's completely up to you how long it takes, but you're not free to go to your activity until we have cleared." Choosing clearing over other activities becomes even more important on those occasions when a child has been particularly difficult, since sending an uncooperative child out into the world invariably leads to additional problems.

MOTHER: What if he has baseball practice?

BOBBIE: If he loves to go to practice, I would require that he clear before going. Unless of course he's still tentative about playing ball; in which case I would clear afterwards.

MOTHER: What if it was a game?

BOBBIE: If the team needed him, I would have him fulfill his responsibility to the team. However, if the team had other players to fill in, I would require an eager player to clear first and a reluctant one to clear later.

MOTHER: If he doesn't get himself together in time to report to the game on schedule, should I make him miss it?

BOBBIE: No. The moment he has cleared, he's free! Don't punish him for taking awhile; instead, reward him for getting it together in time to possibly play. In fact, your job is to be on his side and get him to the field as soon as possible. It will then be up to the coach to determine if he plays, without any suggestions from you. Because you were so supportive, if the coach does bench him, he will be able to see that he—rather than you—created the problem.

ANOTHER MOTHER: What if I'm the one who has an activity, but we need a clearing?

BOBBIE: Whenever parents must be somewhere, it's important to release everyone to go their separate ways with the understanding that clearing will be the first order of business once the family is together again. This is also important to do when your child has a responsibility to fulfill, such as a music lesson or scout meeting. However, if his activity is simply one of pleasure, and he is still unwilling to clear, you can get a relative or sitter—if needed—while other family members are free to resume their activities. It's important that an older child, who would not normally need a caretaker, be in the care of a relative or friend if he's not behaving responsibly enough to be on his own.

A THIRD MOTHER: Clearings with my five-year-old all seem so shallow. He quickly admits to what he did and that's the end of it. I don't know where to go from there.

BOBBIE: In order not to allow your child to rush you through clearings, slow everything down and hold out for a more thorough acknowledgment. Then take time to carefully explore what motivated his transgression, what he's unclear about, and how he might look at things differently in the future. Remember, your goal is not to get back to normalcy as quickly as possible, but to teach your child whatever he needs to know about how to become a more harmonious family and societal member.

MOTHER: But how do I get him to slow down enough to really care about hitting the baby?

BOBBIE: Let him know that his quick apology didn't feel real and that you are more interested in his true feelings—even if they are ones of jealousy and anger at the baby for being so cute and taking up so much of your time and attention, or if he simply wanted to get a reaction from you or the baby or both. Draw pictures of the situation as you talk about his worries regarding your interest in the baby, or what reaction he was hoping for. It's important not to plant ideas—for example, of jealousy—that are not real in this particular child, or to make such feelings seem special or a cause for extra concern and attention. When you reflect your hunches in this neutral, clear way, a deeper, more honest conversation is underway. (See **Sibling Rivalry** entry in the Problem-Solving Guide.)

Forgiveness and Releasing

Once a transgression is admitted; sincere regrets are expressed; and reparations—when appropriate—are made, the wronged party must search his heart for forgiveness.[6] Because this is such a critical step toward bringing clearing to completion, the responsibility now falls on the person doing the forgiving to let go. If he refuses to forgive, feelings are blocked from healing, and the problem cannot be released. Thus, responsibility for a new transgression shifts to the person unwilling to forgive.

Children are uniquely capable of forgiveness in the face of an acknowledged error, since they have not practiced the habit of holding onto anger for as many years as their adult counterparts. For example, should the teen who was unkind to his friend admit to that behavior and acknowledge his own insecurities that provoked it, the rejected friend's feelings are now congruent with reality. He feels relief because what he knew to be true is now out in the open to be aired and honestly discussed. He has the opportunity to hear the cause of his rejection as well as any regret his friend felt about doing it. In the face of the truth, his trust reopens, forgiveness spills easily from his heart, and he's open to repairing the relationship.

Once acknowledgment and forgiveness are accomplished, the matter is forgotten and the individuals involved are freed from the pain of misunderstanding and unclear energies between them. With all barriers removed, they are free to feel close again.

The Effect of Clearing

Similar to the results of Hawaii's Ho'oponopono, the wonderful results of raising children with clearing are that it teaches them to

- Speak openly about their feelings and problems while allowing others to do the same
- Face the truth of their actions and accept responsibility for their errors

- Ask forgiveness when appropriate
- Release negative feelings toward those who desire forgiveness
- Keep their hearts open and honest and their relationships honorable and clear
- Learn from their mistakes
- Feel more loving toward themselves and others

A Simple Vision

Parents who have learned the skill of clearing are grateful for knowing how to heal relationships and maintain bonded connections with their children, family, and friends. As more of us learn to do this, we build a world based on the level of integrity that the early Hawaiians used when they created a sanctuary for the loving energy of *aloha*, which came to be known throughout the world as "Paradise."

*The more we bring our truth into the light the clearer
we become for ourselves and the world.*

9

Life Sculpting

Teaching Clear Lessons for Effective Living

The Eighth Key:

ⓖⓖⓖ

*Use the unclear moments to teach what is not presently clear about
how to live life more harmoniously.*

Our challenges and problems are not meant to serve as obstacles to our happiness but as life's way of showing us those things that are not yet clear for us. In fact, each problem we face provides us with a personalized lesson we would profit from learning and offers an important opportunity for getting clearer about how to live our lives more effectively. The same is true for our children. Thus, rather than strive to avoid facing our problems, we can view them as opportunities for learning life's lessons.

Using Problems as Opportunities for Learning

To help your child examine the important lessons connected to his particular problems you must first perceive each challenge he encounters as *a window of opportunity for showing him what he does not presently know about how to live life more harmoniously.*

By viewing your child's problems in this new, more useful way, it will be easier for you to embrace and welcome them as starting points for the lessons he must learn. (See Figure 11.)

With this shift in perception, your goal will no longer be to hurriedly stamp out his problems in order to restore momentary peace. You can focus, instead, on looking for the lessons contained in each situation and allow the problem to point the way to what is not yet clear for your child that must be addressed and learned.

Clearing is a good time to sift through your child's various problems to examine the lessons they are exposing. You can begin by investigating the beliefs and expectations he has formed about himself and about life that are

Figure 11. Using Problems as Lessons

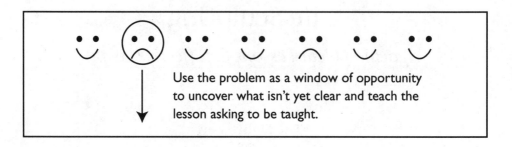

Use the problem as a window of opportunity to uncover what isn't yet clear and teach the lesson asking to be taught.

now causing him to respond in a problematic way. You can then help him to unravel and release these faulty viewpoints and replace them with new, more effective ideas.

For example, kids squabbling over an activity reflect that something is not yet clear for them about how to live life more harmoniously while playing with other children. If you fail to understand this, your goal will be to eliminate their noisy behavior and regain your peace and quiet as quickly as possible. In dealing with their problem in this superficial way, you might put the offending activity on a shelf and separate your children. Unfortunately, this response not only bypasses the deeper lessons each child could have learned about playing agreeably with friends, but because your children are no clearer about how to resolve their differences, you are no closer to your desired peace.

Thus, rather than bat the problem away, it would be more effective to teach your kids how to control their urges to take things that are in the possession of others, how to handle the aggression of those taking things from them, and how to replace this struggle over objects with less focus on material things and more valuing of people and friendships. In this way, your children not only learn to behave more effectively, but include their higher selves in their approach to living. The key is that you uncover and teach whichever lessons are most relevant to the particular children you are helping.

Using the Themes and Patterns Contained in Problems to Uncover Appropriate Lessons

Anytime the lessons connected to a child's problem are not addressed, similar problems will surface in his life, producing a repeating theme or pattern. Whenever such a pattern develops, it helps to examine what it is that draws this kind of problem to this particular child on a recurring basis and what he needs to learn from the situation in order to resolve the problem and stop the pattern.

For example, if your child is afraid of aggressive children and strives to avoid dealing with them, he will find bullies in his life at every turn until he learns to handle them. Although he may initially believe that appeasing bullies, hiding from them, or wailing about their torture will be his best defense, he will eventually notice that these styles draw more bullies to him. This is because aggressive children are delighted by peers who whimper helplessly, while succumbing to being controlled, rather than respond with strength. Thus, only after being helped to see the lessons that bullies offer him will your child confront his fears and stop reacting with so much apprehension and drama. Interestingly, once his fear of aggressive kids and his desire to avoid them are confronted and resolved, bullies will no longer be drawn to him, and they will cease to be a factor in his life.

After learning how to explore the themes or patterns of a child's problems as a way to understand what isn't yet clear for him, one family decided to change their method of handling a conflict their eleven-year-old daughter was having with her school friends.

Rather than suggest that she ignore their unkind remarks or look for new friends as they had in the past, they helped her to face her own unclear patterns of behavior. To do this, they sat down with a drawing pad to diagram her long-term habit of pouting whenever she didn't get her way. Next, they illustrated how both they and her classmates had previously strived to humor her into better moods, but that neither they nor maturing peers were willing to put up with her attitude any longer. They helped her to see how her pouting and anger were pushing friends away, rather than attracting the attention she sought, and that her increasing unpopularity was not a result of unkind schoolmates as she was professing, but of her own patterns of behavior. Thus, rather than salve their daughter's feelings and smooth things over as they had done in the past, these parents now showed her how a change in her own behavior would reap more effective results with her friends.

Dialogue from Class

MOTHER: My child seems to be developing a pattern of throwing things when he doesn't get his way—and I would like to know what he isn't understanding when he hurls his cup at me, just because his father pours his juice when he wants me to do it.

BOBBIE: Your child is throwing his cup because he doesn't know something about how to live life more effectively. What do you think it is that he doesn't know?

MOTHER: He doesn't know that he can't throw things at people just because he doesn't get his way. But I don't know why he doesn't know that because we talk to him about it all the time!

BOBBIE: Even though you repeatedly restate a rule for your child—or even scold him for breaking it—he won't believe that it isn't a choice until the day comes when breaking that rule impacts on *him* in some way.

MOTHER: Are you saying that he really doesn't know that he can't throw things?

BOBBIE: If he's still throwing them, it means that he doesn't trust the message, since he has been told repeatedly that he can't throw things; yet when he does—except for your anger—nothing happens. As a result, he doesn't know how to compute the information you offer him. You're going to have to do more than just scold if you want him to learn that throwing things is not only discouraged, but won't be tolerated. For instance, if he were calmly removed from the table each time he threw something—regardless of whether or not he was finished eating—do you think he would continue to view throwing dishes as an effective behavior?

MOTHER: No, he wouldn't like that.

BOBBIE: But if he throws a cup and the whole family becomes distraught, while he sits in the center of all that excitement eating his dinner, will it seem like an effective behavior?

MOTHER: (Pause, then laughter) Now I see what you mean!

BOBBIE: Be aware that your upset will serve as a maintainer of his unpleasant behaviors if he decides that he likes being the center of attention or enjoys controlling your emotions.

MOTHER: If I start removing him from the table when he throws things, how long will it take for him to figure it out?

BOBBIE: Am I to assume that you will be doing this both calmly and consistently? (laughter) Your calm consistency plus the quality of your clearing will be the deciding factors. After each removal, he must be required to look at what he was hoping to accomplish by throwing the cup (Were you trying to get me to pour your juice?); to notice if throwing the cup worked in getting him what he wanted (Am I pouring your juice?); or if it worked against him (Not only am I not pouring your juice, you're not even sitting at the table). Next, you can help him to decide if he wants to continue throwing cups when he doesn't get his way about who pours for him, or if he's ready to accept his father doing the pouring. If you take the time needed to do a complete clearing, while remaining calm and helping him to see how he created a problem for himself, he will probably stop the behavior. If you don't take the time, you can be sure that he will repeat that behavior and many others like it.

How Patterns Get Started

Once we understand the importance of using problems to teach our children what is not yet clear for them, we must teach them how to replace their unclear patterns of behavior with more effective ones. To do this, we must first understand how patterns of unclear thinking and behaving get started and how they can become clear again. The stories of two men help us to see how this works.

In *Seven Stories of Christmas Love* (1987), Leo Buscaglia describes what an inordinate brat he was being during one holiday season. Although his mother had warned him that the Christmas Angel didn't bring her bounty to brats, but left a peach stick, instead, for hitting their legs, he failed to take heed and pursued his obnoxious behavior. Then, to his horror, he discovered on Christmas morning that the Christmas Angel had, indeed, brought him the promised stick, while his stockings and shoes lay barren beside the stuffed ones of his brothers and sisters. He collapsed in despair in his mother's arms and noticed that she, too, was crying as she comforted him, as did his father and even his siblings, who offered to share their gifts with him. His mother gently reflected that he could have been good if he had wanted, but this year had chosen to be bad instead, leaving the Christmas Angel no other choice. She helped him to understand how the Angel reminds us that we always get what we deserve, and even when the lesson hurts, it teaches us what is right and wrong, and thus we get better every year. Although his punishment was strong, he also felt loved and forgiven and knew that he would be given another chance.

As a young child, this internationally known teacher, writer, and lecturer experienced a strong dose of discipline, given with a heart full of love by parents willing to let him feel the pain of his choices. It's clear that he made a significant life decision that day, not only to behave with greater responsibility, but that love could be trusted. Leo Buscaglia's life certainly bears the fruit of his conclusions.

Yet these deductions contrast with those made by my uncle under similar circumstances, the results of which I witnessed as a young girl growing up. I felt particularly sad each holiday season as this uncle would recount the story of his sixth Christmas in Europe, when his father had singled him out from his many brothers and sisters to leave coals and a stick for beating him in his stocking. Whenever we inquired about what he had done to deserve such a gift, he would furrow his brow and reach back in time for the answer but could never remember anything specific—only that his father did not like him. This recollection always filled his eyes with tears, which he would blink back in embarrassment. Whenever I was with him, I could feel the weight of hurt anchoring this man's heart, even on those occasions when he would gleefully sing in full voice as he drove a carload of kids to the movies. It seemed as though he was determined to give children the love they deserved.

Not surprisingly, I watched over the years as this lovely man slipped into a chasm of compulsive drinking and self-destructive behaviors. It was clear that he, like Leo Buscaglia, had made an equally significant vow on Christmas day, but his decision bore very different fruit.

How is it that these two men, given such similar gifts as children, drew entirely different conclusions from their experiences? To understand, parents must recognize that the variation between the decisions children draw from similar events lies not only in the results of the event, but in how they are presented, as well as the conclusion each child elects to take from his individual experiences.

Leo Buscaglia concluded, for example, from the gentler presentation of his consequence that love was available to him no matter how he behaved, but that life offered sweeter results when he was cooperative. As a result, he trusted his own lovability, loved his family in return, and elected to behave in the manner his parents modeled for him as a responsible individual. This combination of conclusions brought a great deal of richness to his life. By contrast, my uncle concluded from his gift, offered without love or explanation, that his father simply didn't like him and that something must be terribly wrong with a child who failed to evoke his father's love. His subsequent belief in his unlovability and lack of value brought deep pain to his life and served as a barrier to his happiness.

We can see from these examples how the conclusion that each man drew from his eventful Christmas was used as a foundation for the life he built for himself.

How It Works: Sculpting Our Lives by the Decisions We Make and the Choices We Select

The various decisions we select from the events in our lives work together to create our patterns of thinking, which are, in turn, converted to energy and stored in our cells and neurology. Once a pattern of thinking is stored, it functions automatically and serves silently within us as the basis for our *expectations* of how life will treat us. Moreover, each pattern of thought and expectation selected strongly influences the choices we subsequently make.

This is why each decision we make about life's events will have such a profound influence on our lives. Moreover, the younger a child is and the more trauma and pain—or bliss and joy—surrounding the events of his life, the more intensely he will drink in the conclusions he draws and convert them to strongly held beliefs. These stronger beliefs are then stored even more intensely and deeply in his neurology and thus more actively influence his future expectations and choices.

As we can see, all of the conclusions a child draws from his life events will be acted out and built upon unless they get erased or reprogrammed at some later point in time. Thus, anytime a child's decision is a good one, it will enhance his life; but, whenever it's faulty, it will cause him recurring, accumulative injury. Because these patterns work together to create the life we see before us, anytime we don't like the shape of the life we have designed for ourselves, we must reexamine the patterns of thinking, expecting, and behaving that have set those results in motion.

It's important that parents be conscious of this ongoing decision-making process in order to guide their children in drawing the kinds of conclusions from life's events that will most support their lives. To do this, they must be aware of the decisions their children are forming while they are still fresh and new, as this allows faulty conclusions to be challenged and reconsidered early, before years of commitment and defense have had time to develop around them. For example, the young child who regularly resists his naptime is in the process of deciding that resistance to things required of him will result in his getting out of them; the elementary-age child refusing to do his homework is drawing the conclusion that there are no meaningful repercussions for avoiding these kinds of tasks; and the teen swearing at his parents is concluding that disrespectful behavior toward others will be tolerated. Because these decisions will not work well for the child who has made them, they must be interrupted and revisited.

Thus, each time your child encounters a problem, it's important that you notice the effect the consequences you provide—or reflect—will have on his decisions. It's also important that you take the time to teach him how to examine the lessons involved; alter whatever faulty viewpoints he is holding; and frame things differently whenever that is needed to keep his approach to life clear. To do this, it helps to know that each problem your child is having today can be traced back to some previous faulty conclusion he has drawn. Likewise, any faulty conclusions he is now forming will result in new or continued unclarity in his approach to life.

Thus, in order to help your child uncover and reconsider any outdated or faulty decisions that are influencing him to select mistaken behaviors, you must first understand what decisions he has made; what expectations he has developed; and what behaviors he is now selecting, based on his earlier conclusions. To do this, spend a week or so recording exactly what is going on.

Charting a Child's Decisions and Choices: the ABC's, D's, and E's

By using an "ABC" plus "D" and "E" format[7] to chart your child's problematic behaviors, you can determine what history or *antecedents* have motivated his selection of ineffective *behaviors*; what results or *consequences* follow; what conclusions or *decisions* he is drawing from those results or consequences; and how his deductions might influence his *expectations* and future choices for managing his life. Only by doing this can you get past the surface layer of problems and understand the real issues.

"A": The History or *Antecedent*. There is always some *antecedent*—or combination of historical factors—present in a child's life that have influenced his selection of a problematic behavior. Antecedents can be made up of strongly significant things such as a bonding break between the child and his parents; an erroneous decision the child has made about some earlier event; a negative view that others hold about the child; a divorce in the child's family; the death of a loved one or pet; a new sibling; rejection at school; or a combination of several of these historical factors.

Or the antecedent might be something only mildly significant such as a mild bonding break between the child and his parents; a typically congenial parent in a bad mood; a moderately unworkable decision the child has made in the past; a minor fight with a friend; the first day of a school year; a change in plans; or a combination of one or two of these. Some antecedents are long-standing historical influences, while others include only the event that happened just prior to the child's selection of a troublesome behavior. At times, antecedents include both long-standing and recent historical factors.

In many cases, the antecedent to problem behaviors is simply that the child has not yet been taught how to live life more cooperatively or how to surrender to not getting his way.

To uncover the antecedents that go with your child's various problems, ask yourself what kinds of things in both his long-standing and recent history might be influencing him to select these problematic behaviors.

As you investigate the various antecedents and their influence on your child's behaviors, you must pay attention to the previous decisions he has made and how those decisions are now influencing his current selections of behavior. In doing this, you may discover that a friendless child (*antecedent*) who has been dawdling over breakfast (*behavior*) has drawn the conclusion from his history that missing his ride to school will enable him to bypass the rejection he receives from his peers in that setting (*antecedent*). Or that same child might have discovered that failing to do his homework (*behavior*) results in being required to stay in the classroom during recess (*consequence*), which saves him having to find friends on the playground. Thus, in this case, the consequences serve to protect the child from facing his fears. As a result, he will not only continue to dawdle over breakfast and ignore his homework, but will fail to address his real problem.

As you can see from this example, you must use your awareness of your child's history as well as his conclusions about it to help you determine the best course of action for assisting him through his problem. For example, it would be useful to help the friendless child who is missing his ride to school or not doing his homework to make new decisions about his ability to develop friends, rather than continue to believe that avoiding the pain is his best solution. This would be more helpful than responding to only the surface layer of his problem by speeding up his morning routine or devising a study schedule for him to follow.

"B": The Problematical *Behavior* Your Child Has Selected. Most of you are understandably concerned about whatever unworkable *behaviors* your child may be selecting—such as dawdling, whining, hitting, biting, tantrums, rudeness, sulking, withdrawing, procrastinating, lying, or stealing—and would like to help him correct them.

Charting these behaviors helps you to more clearly define problem areas by noting specifically what your child does and how many times a day he does it. Such a record of his activities over a period of a week or two provides concrete information about the seriousness of his problematic behaviors.

For example, if you view your child as easygoing, but have received reports that he is causing trouble at school, you may discover by charting his behavior that he has been picking on his siblings and friends more than you had perceived. It's also possible to discover from charting that a child thought to be aggressive is not the instigator of hostile acts, but is appropriately defending himself from the aggression of others. Thus, charting will show that, in some cases, assumptions about your child are unsupported; in other cases, they prove to be true.

A charting journal further helps you to uncover and understand the historical antecedents that have motivated your child's selection of the problem behaviors as well as the results or consequences that are encouraging him to continue to use them.

"C": The *Consequence*—or Result. The result or *consequence* of your child's behavior will teach him to either repeat that behavior or avoid it in the future. Whenever a child likes the consequences of his behaviors, those results will cause him to repeat a behavior and are thus called *maintainers*. By contrast, if he does not like the result or consequence, it will discourage him from pursuing the behavior. As a result, anytime your child is repeating a behavior, it's because there is some result—or maintainer—that the child likes. In view of this, it's important that you carefully select the kinds of results for problematic behaviors that will make your child wish that he had made a different choice. You will also want to uncover and eliminate any consequences that are serving as maintainers of unwanted behaviors.

Charting both the *antecedent* and the *behavior* exhibited will help you to see what results—or *consequences*—would be the most likely to discourage unwanted behaviors and which ones would be most likely to serve as maintainers. Reviewing the information in this context will help you to improve your selection of the kinds of consequences that will discourage unwanted behaviors.

If, for example, a popular (*antecedent*) schoolgirl dawdles in the morning (*behavior*), an effective result would be to allow her to miss her ride to school for that day (*consequence*). Because such a child would prefer to be at school with her friends (information you have from the antecedent regarding her popularity), she would most likely speed up her morning routine the following day, and her dawdling problem would be resolved.

On the other hand, if her brother, who is having academic trouble (*antecedent*), dawdles (*behavior*) and is allowed to miss his ride and stay home for the day (*consequence*), that result would fulfill his secret wish to avoid school and the possibility of academic failure (his way of protecting himself from the pain of the antecedent that is active in this situation). Thus, although staying home would discourage his sister from dawdling, it would maintain that behavior in him. Consequently, it would be better to design a different consequence to help this particular child get back to school and face his fears, while also helping him to uncover solutions to his problems with schoolwork. For instance, an alert mother would ignore the issue of dawdling altogether (at least for the moment) and deliver her son to school late, if necessary. On the way, she might gently talk to him about things he can do to get more comfortable with schoolwork as well as ways she and his teachers might support him in solving this problem. Meanwhile, if lateness becomes a habit and continues to be a problem after the core issue is resolved, it can be addressed at that time.

"D": The *Decision*. Your child will always make some *decision* about the results of his various choices and actions. If his choices seem to be working, he will decide that they are of value and will continue to make them. If not, he will decide against those choices and select new behaviors.

As you will see from your journaling, these decisions create the foundation on which your child's life is built. Thus, anytime you are striving to help him to live life more effectively and from his higher self, you must examine which decisions he is currently drawing, or has already drawn, from life's experiences that simply aren't working.

For example, a shy child (*antecedent*) who has mustered up the courage to raise his hand in class (*behavior*) but is then ignored or chided for his answer (*consequence*), will very likely conclude that risk is dangerous (*decision*). This deduction will, in turn, cause him to pull back and withdraw even deeper into his timidity.

By contrast, another equally withdrawn child (*antecedent*), who has also gathered his courage to speak in class (*behavior*), may receive additional support and warmth from his teachers and peers that day (*consequence*). This child would most likely decide that risk worked well for him and continue in his newfound openness (*decision*). Thus, an alert parent of a shy child would be wise to not only arrange easy social experiences that would bring him more success, but ask teachers to watch for opportunities to encourage outgoing behaviors in him, not by praising, but by responding to his contribution; she could then guide him in drawing the kinds of conclusions from these experiences that would encourage him to feel more outgoing.

Because of this decision-making process and its importance to what a child learns from his experiences, it's critical that you pay attention to your child's decisions and help him to ward off any faulty conclusions that he may be drawing about how life works. For example, when a teen gossips about her friend, that is an event for both girls, and they will each draw some conclusion about it, based on the consequences they experience. The maligned child may elect to let it go in order to stay out of conflict, while leaving the gossiper to conclude that her behavior had worked well for her in bonding with the other girls. Thus, the adult in this situation would be wise to help the maligned girl to see that her passivity had not helped her to avoid the problem as she had hoped and to guide her in talking openly to the gossiper in the presence of the others. In this way, she can unmask the deceptive behavior, rather than allow it to go unexposed and thus continue. The adult can then openly reflect to the gossiper how ineffective gossiping is in gaining the trust of others or keeping their friendship. Only in this way will both girls be motivated to draw more honest and workable conclusions from this event and learn from it how to behave more effectively.

Adults who take the time to guide children in seeing beyond the illusory results of their decisions and actions to more clearly perceiving the truth of the matter help them to make better choices in the future. Thus, by talking to your child about the choices—and patterns of choices—that he's making, what results those choices are creating for him, and which of his decisions will truly support his life, you help him to make increasingly clearer, more effective choices. Moreover, each time you succeed in helping your child to draw more accurate deductions, his future choices are based on a foundation of truth and clarity, rather than inaccurate distortions.

"E": The *Expectation*. The decisions your child makes about life work together to create a collective pattern of thinking. This pattern, in turn, causes him to view the future with certain expectations of what will happen, based on the beliefs that he has adopted. These expectations not only serve as his filter for how he perceives new experiences, but pull expected experiences to him. Consequently, it's critical to not only know what your child's negative expectations are, but to help him to replace them with more optimistic possibilities.

Using *Significant Antecedents* to Uncover What Is Not Understood. The key decisions that your child has made about the various events in his life become *significant antecedents* for him, which, in turn, influence his choices significantly. Thus, a good way to uncover what your child does not yet understand about how to live life more effectively is to explore the significant related antecedents—or events and attitudes—that were in place in his life prior to the problem.

For example, when fourteen-year-old Mike was sent to his room for tormenting the cat the third day in a row, his mother assumed that the recent divorce in their family was serving as a significant antecedent for him, as divorce usually does. However, when she inquired during their clearing about his adjustment to the divorce, she discovered that he had decided that he preferred the new level of family peace to his parents' previous quarreling and that he was enjoying a better relationship with his dad than he had experienced prior to the divorce. Yet during their talk, he also shared that he was having trouble making friends at his new school. Thus, in Mike's case, the more significant antecedent was his change in schools, rather than the divorce, and what wasn't clear for him was how to make friends in a new setting. Once Mother understood this, she was able to address the real problem, rather than nag at Mike to leave the cat alone or continue to worry about his adjustment to the divorce.

When seven-year-old Denise argued every time her mother corrected her, the significant antecedent for Denise was her dislike of making mistakes. Her intense vow never to make errors was instilled during her younger years when a baby-sitter, intolerant of mistakes, lived in their home. During this period, Denise learned to defend her answers, even when they were wrong. Thus, in

Denise's case, what wasn't clear was the knowledge that errors are important to learning. In light of this significant antecedent, rather than turn their conflict into a struggle over who is right or wrong, Mother wisely helped her daughter to work on getting more comfortable with mistakes and making a new decision about them.

In the case of junior high schooler Mark, who held younger brother Doug in a body lock until he cried, the antecedent was simply that his brother had been bugging him, as opposed to a more significant one of having problems with friends, as his mother first thought. In view of this antecedent, Mark's response was understandable, and it soon became apparent that it was Doug who needed guidance on how to live life more harmoniously. Doug's significant antecedent was that he had gotten away with teasing an older brother without repercussion in the past. Thus, what wasn't clear for him was that it doesn't really work to pick on people—particularly bigger ones.

Quite often, as in Mark's case, the antecedent (fighting with brother) is the obvious one that has taken place just prior to the event. Thus, probing for more historical or significant antecedents is not always appropriate and should only be done when it appears that something deeper has stimulated the problem, as in the cases of Denise's long-term fear of error and Mike's lack of skills in making new friends.

Helping Your Child to Understand How His Choices Impact on **Him**

The best way to motivate your child to learn more positive patterns of behavior is by showing him how his undesirable behaviors have created a problem for *him*, rather than for you or others. You can do this by asking a series of questions to help your child see what he did to cause this problem for himself and what changes he can make that will offer him better results in the future.

For example, eight-year-old Greg wanted the family to switch their television program and kicked over a chair when he realized that they had no intention of doing so. During their clearing, Dad asked, "What happened, guy? How did you end up in your bedroom while the rest of us were in the family room?" When Greg answered that he didn't know, Dad offered a suggestion. "When you wanted to look at cartoons and the rest of us kept watching the ball game, did it help to kick over the chair?" Greg shrugged, so Dad continued, "Are you watching the cartoons, now?" When Greg conceded that he wasn't, Dad inquired, "Are you watching any television at all, or did you lose your freedom to even be in the family room?" As Greg reluctantly acknowledged that he wasn't with the group, Dad used the moment to reflect the impact Greg's behavior had on *him*, "Did that work out the way you had hoped, or did you end up alone in your room, while the rest of the family stayed together watching television?" Greg agreed that he would rather have been with the family watching television, so Dad helped him to turn this observation into a better decision for the future by asking, "What could you do differently next time to keep your freedom to remain with the family?"

Once Greg is able to face that chair-kicking wasn't useful to him, Dad can help him to explore what it is that he needs to learn in order to live life more harmoniously. For example, he might ask, "What will work better for you when you want to do one thing, but everyone else wants to do another?" He might also explore whether this problem surfaces for Greg at school and how he handles it in that setting. Dad can further help his son to learn that in order to be part of a larger group, he must sometimes surrender his individual choice of activities, rather than insist on always getting his way. In short, what isn't yet clear for Greg is how to integrate with a group during those times when he's not getting his way.

Creating Images Helps Children to Anchor Their Lessons in Symbols and Metaphors

You can effectively improve the patterns of behavior your child selects by making the unclear patterns more visible for him. This is best done by using examples, stories, and visual illustrations to create mental images for the child. Not only are these powerful teaching tools, they help children to both learn and remember various lessons by anchoring their understanding of a concept in an image that calls up the essence of the larger message learned. For instance, Denise's mother can help her daughter to understand the importance of mistakes by discussing what her baby brother learns about balance each time he falls while learning to walk. This creates a picture in Denise's mind of her brother walking and falling and the acceptability and importance of his errors during that learning process.

These images can be made even more visible by illustrating them to create a picture-story. Such pictures would not only pull young children into communication in the same way a storybook does, but would provide visual aids that help them to remember the lessons learned. For example, Denise's mother might draw a series of pictures of her baby brother walking, then falling, then walking again until he masters the skill, contrasted with another series of him still sitting on the floor as he gets absurdly older due to his unwillingness to make further attempts at walking after his first fall. Such a drawing not only helps Mother to convey this idea with increased simplicity and clarity, but can be hung on the refrigerator as a holographic reference to the idea that mistakes are an important and natural part of learning.

Similarly, diagrams and cartoons can be used to engage the interest of an elementary-age child. For example, nine-year-old Linda, who was losing friends as a result of being so dominant, was open to correcting herself only after seeing a cartoon strip of what had been happening. Her teacher had drawn a series of images of three different girls who had befriended Linda thus far that year, but then got tired of watching her control all of their activities and went off to find new friends. The last frame was of Linda alone, controlling the games that no longer existed without friends around to play them. Seeing this image made an impression on Linda that enabled her to let go of controlling everything and focus more on tending to her relationships.

Putting It All Together

Following are some examples of how you can put your child's problems on the agenda, embrace his errors, and use each episode as a window of opportunity for teaching him what isn't yet clear. Notice how the adults in these models blend love with discipline as they show their child how his faulty decisions and choices of behavior have impacted on him, rather than others. Note, too, how the unclarity that motivated each child's transgression is uncovered, often by exploring the antecedents. At times this unclarity is fairly obvious and easily seen, whereas at other times it's more complex and trickier to uncover. Also note how often visual images are used to support the lesson.

Clearing with a Child Who Has Broken a Boundary

When Jacob's freedom was contracted because he failed to follow the rules, his clearing went something like this:

FATHER: All right, my friend, why did I call you over to walk with me?

JACOB: Because I was running too far ahead of the group.

FATHER: That's right. And did that work for you? Are you the first one out on the trail?

JACOB: No.

FATHER: Are you even walking with your friends at all—or are you having to walk with me?

JACOB: Walk with you.

FATHER: Is that what you wanted?

JACOB: (Sarcastic laugh) No . . . !

FATHER: Well, I'm sorry that you made the decision to break my rule, but the result is that you've lost your choice to hike with the kids until after lunch, since I can't trust you to follow the rules.

JACOB: (Now crying) But I want to be with my friends! I'll stay with the group. I promise . . .

FATHER: I understand how disappointed you must feel, but staying with the group is no longer a choice, since you *already* broke the rule. But I suspect that you'll stay with the group after lunch, so we'll give it another try then and see how you do.

JACOB: Can't I have one more chance?

FATHER: You already used your chance, son. You knew the rule and you took a chance and broke it anyway, right?

JACOB: (Reluctantly) I guess.

FATHER: Did that work for you to take a chance on breaking the rule?

JACOB: No.

FATHER: Does it work for you in other settings?

JACOB: (Pause) It works with Mom sometimes—because she's nicer.

FATHER: (Laugh) Yes, she is nice. And I think I'm being nice in a different way to teach you that life works better when you follow the rules. Have you noticed that breaking rules works with Mom because she hates to see you miss out on things—but that other people are more willing to let you suffer when you break the rules?

JACOB: (Pause) I guess.

FATHER: When you take the chance on it working, you also take the chance
          that it won't work. It certainly didn't work out very well today, did
          it?

JACOB: (Pause) Not really.

FATHER: What do you think will work better for you this afternoon?

JACOB: Staying with the group.

FATHER: (Putting his arm around Jacob) You've got it, my friend. I suspect
          you'll have a better afternoon.

ଡ଼ଡ଼ଡ଼

In this discussion, Father's consequence not only caused Jacob to wish
that he hadn't crossed his boundary, but made it clear that he was the one
who had caused his own contraction of freedom. Moreover, even though
Jacob already knew that he had lost his freedom, being required to express
his responsibility in the matter helped him to face what had really gone
wrong.

Father then made his son aware of the deeper lesson involved by reflecting the previous unclear *decision* he had made that everyone will treat him
with the same concern his mom demonstrates when he breaks the rules
(antecedent). In this interaction Dad realized that *what was not clear* for Jacob
was that breaking rules doesn't work. To reverse this, Dad's consequence and
reflection of what happened will motivate Jacob to release his earlier, *faulty
decision* that he can break rules and replace it with the clearer, *more effective
decision* that it is in his best interest to follow rules. Notice, too, how Mom's
unclarity in handling rules can be exposed without undermining her.

Clearing with a Child Not Tolerating Frustration

If Nikki is sent to her room because she is sulky and angry over not getting
something she had hoped for, the clearing might go something like this:

MOTHER: What was it you were so angry about, sweetheart?

NIKKI: I wanted you to buy me those boots!

MOTHER: Yes, I noticed that you really wanted those boots, and when I said
          "No," you sulked all the way home and then slammed both doors

when we got here. Did all of that pouting and slamming work for you? Did I run out to buy you the boots?

NIKKI: (Giving a slight laugh) No, but I still want them . . . (pause) Cheryl has that style.

MOTHER: I know—it's pretty tough when Cheryl has the boots you want and I still say "No," but I wonder what else you could do when you want something really badly and I stick with saying "No."

NIKKI: But why can't I have them?!

MOTHER: It's important for you to understand that I don't plan to buy you everything you see and want or think you have to have. And I'm certainly not going to buy you everything Cheryl has. You're just going to have to get used to my saying "No" some of the time. Now, what can you do to handle it better? You really want the boots, the answer is "No," and sulking and anger aren't helping. What might help?

NIKKI: I don't know . . .

MOTHER: If you keep wishing for the boots and fussing or pouting over them, will you get them?

NIKKI: No.

MOTHER: Will you get more happy or less happy while you're nursing your anger about it?

NIKKI: Less happy.

MOTHER: I agree. When I'm in a hurry to leave the mall but you and Cheryl are still finishing your ice cream, should I throw myself on the ground and start screaming?

NIKKI: No way!

MOTHER: Should I hang my head and pout?

NIKKI: No! You would look stupid.

MOTHER: So you would agree that when things aren't going our way, we need to figure out how to adjust to the way they are going?

NIKKI: I guess.

MOTHER: Are you willing to stop fussing about the boots and let it be okay that I'm not going to buy them?

NIKKI: I suppose . . .

MOTHER: Do you think you're ready to manage that?

NIKKI: (Pause) Yeah. (Another pause) I can manage.

☉☉☉

Mother noticed that *what wasn't clear* for Nikki was that she had not yet surrendered to the reality that she will occasionally be thwarted in getting what she wants. By directly confronting Nikki with the truth that she will be frustrated from time to time, rather than distracting her with alternative plans or focusing her attention elsewhere, Mother helped her daughter to fully face and tolerate her pain. This allowed Nikki to see that the solution to her problem lay in drawing a new conclusion about learning to accept, rather than resist, such frustrations.

Note, too, that Mother does not give confused messages by indicating that she has no time or money to buy the shoes, but tells her daughter honestly that she simply has no intention of buying her everything she wants or that her friends have—even if she did have the time and money to do so.

In this example, the antecedent is that Nikki had decided at some juncture that resistance (*behavior*) worked and would cause her mother to back down and buy the shoes. However, Mother not only resisted buying the shoes (*consequence*), she reflected the true effect that Nikki's fussing had on her own happiness. This consequence and reflection helped Nikki to draw a new, more effective conclusion about her reality that brought her up to date with mother's new clarity in sticking to her limits.

Clearing Misunderstandings Between Children

Parents often add to the confusion of their children's misunderstandings by asking them to each explain their side of a story. Since the adult wasn't there to witness the problem, each child seizes the opportunity to deny responsibility for his part of the problem or twist the truth in hopes of influencing the adult to act as a judge and to rule in his favor. Such children end up honing skills of deceit and denial in order to defend their position, rather than practice honestly facing reality and acknowledging their part in the conflict.

What isn't clear for these kids is their belief that the goal in life is to deny the truth of things as a way to get what they want, based on the historical effectiveness of this approach.

The new framework, called *clearing*, used for resolving misunderstandings in which each child is asked to sit and talk to the other—rather than the adult—offers very different results. Under these circumstances, children calm down and become more honest while looking into the eyes of their friend who, in contrast to the adult, was at the scene of the "crime" and already knows the truth of what happened.

If the children begin to interrupt one another, become too excited, or need help or clarification, the parent or teacher intervenes as a guide in order to keep the communication even and clear. To further enhance truthfulness, the adult then lets both children know that there is no "good guy" or "bad guy" to pursue but merely a misunderstanding to clear up. She is soft and gentle with both children and may put her arms around them as they talk. This demonstrates that she is neither taking sides nor is she against the child who started the problem.

Under these conditions, the adult can more easily evoke the truth from both children as they work together to discover what might be learned from this situation and how to live life with greater effectiveness. There is no punishment or consequence awaiting the child who owns up to being the first transgressor. Only his willingness to openly discuss the problem, fully acknowledge his part in it, and make amends are required.

When children get to the point in their communication at which the problem is clarified for the adult, she joins their discussion in order to lead them toward a solution—only if they seem unable to manage doing this on their own. At this point, she also highlights the true consequences of the children's behaviors so that they can draw clearer conclusions from their experience.

Exception: when a child regularly bullies other children or has clearly broken an important rule such as pushing others from playground equipment, the children he has transgressed against are not required to clear with him. Instead, he sits out for a period of time and then clears with an adult before regaining his freedom.

Timmy and Johnny

One day two five-year-olds approached me, each hoping to win me over to his side of a conflict. Timmy looked very much the injured party as he sorrowfully told me how Johnny had hit him. Johnny looked guilty and was braced for the boom to fall. When I had the two boys sit down to face each other and talk about it, here's what transpired:

TIMMY: (Holding his arm where he'd been hit) You hit me, and it *really* hurts, you know!

JOHNNY: Well, you knocked over the town I'd been working on for a long time.

TIMMY: (At first Timmy looked at me, holding his arm with a pitiful look on his face to further play on my sympathies, but when I asked him to talk to Johnny about it, he looked back and replied) I know.

JOHNNY: That wasn't very nice, and it made me sad to see everything all broken down.

TIMMY: (Downward glance) Umm.

BOBBIE: What was it you were hoping would happen when you knocked over Johnny's Legos, Timmy?

TIMMY: I wanted to play with Johnny.

BOBBIE: Johnny, when Timmy knocks over your Legos, do you feel like you want to play with him, or get away from him?

JOHNNY: Get away—and hurt him.

BOBBIE: Timmy, did it work for you to knock over Johnny's Legos? Did it make him feel like your friend and want to play with you, or did it make him feel against you and want to get away from you?

TIMMY: Get away.

BOBBIE: That's right, Timmy. You're catching on fast! Would you like to be Johnny's friend, or do you hope that he doesn't like you and won't want to play with you?

TIMMY: Be his friend.

BOBBIE: Johnny, do you feel closer to Timmy after he knocked over your town, or less close?

JOHNNY: Less close. I don't like it when people knock my things down, and I don't want to play with him anymore.

BOBBIE: Timmy, did you hear that? What is Johnny telling you about how he feels when you knock over his Legos?

TIMMY: He doesn't like me.

BOBBIE: That's right. Timmy, do you think knocking over Johnny's town helped you to get what you wanted, or did it make things worse?

TIMMY: Worse. (Pause) But he *never* plays with me.

BOBBIE: Okay. That's important information. You like Johnny, but he never lets you play and being left out feels pretty bad. But knocking over Johnny's Legos didn't work out very well either, did it?

TIMMY: No.

BOBBIE: So, what else could you try that might work better and help you to get closer to Johnny?

TIMMY: Ask him if I can play?

BOBBIE: Do you think he might say "Yes," or might he say "No" like he usually does?

TIMMY: Probably "No."

BOBBIE: Is that why you knocked over his town, instead of asking him?

TIMMY: Yeah.

BOBBIE: Since knocking over the Legos didn't help, and asking to play doesn't usually work, why don't you ask Johnny what might work for you?

JOHNNY: (Strongly reacting) I don't like to play with Timmy because he always plays so rough, and he messes everything up!

BOBBIE: Did you hear that, Timmy? The reason Johnny won't let you play is that he doesn't like rough play. Johnny, explain to Timmy how you feel about rough play and what kind of play you like better.

JOHNNY: You always hit and knock things down. That's why I don't like to play with you.

TIMMY: (Looking distraught with eyes downcast)

BOBBIE: Timmy, look at Johnny, hon, and face what he's saying to you. It's important, "secret-type" information that can help you to understand why so many of the kids say they don't like playing with you. Do you like being left out like that?

TIMMY: No, it makes me really angry!

BOBBIE: You seem to be very worried that nobody will ever play with you, Timmy.

TIMMY: (Firmly) I am, because they never do!

BOBBIE: Well, it seems to me that they don't want to play with you because you're always so angry. Is the anger coming from your worry about the kids letting you play, or is it about something else?

TIMMY: About the kids saying I can't play.

BOBBIE: (Diagramming the discovery of children retreating from Timmy's anger, then Timmy expressing more anger, and children retreating even further from the anger) That's interesting, since the reason they say you can't play is because of all the anger. What would happen if you stopped making yourself so mad by all of that worrying about getting to play? I wonder what would happen if you paid more attention to how to play gently than to your anger? Do you think the kids might let you play? (Diagramming how this might look on paper with Timmy approaching play with a smile and gentle hands, while children feel safe and thus include him)

TIMMY: (Pause) I guess.

BOBBIE: Would you like that, or do you like getting people mad at you and then feeling sad and angry about it?

TIMMY: (Longer pause) I think I would rather play.

BOBBIE: (Using antecedent information she already knew about) Is it a hard choice—since you're so used to getting your mom and dad mad at you all the time that it seems like the more familiar and easy thing to do?

TIMMY: (Looking at Bobbie full face) My Dad gets mad a lot.

BOBBIE: Is he just mad inside himself, or do you try to get him mad?

TIMMY: He gets mad at my Mom too.

BOBBIE: It sounds like he's mad a lot of the time. Do you like it when he's mad at you?

TIMMY: No, it scares me.

BOBBIE: Do you realize that even though you don't like it, it's sort of what you're used to and part of why you try to get the kids unhappy with you? (Diagramming matching pictures of Dad getting mad at Timmy next to a picture of Timmy getting mad at the kids and then bothering them, plus a third picture of the kids getting mad at Timmy) Can you see that you've gotten so used to people getting mad at home that you're trying to keep that same picture going at school?

TIMMY: (Looking at the picture)

BOBBIE: Would you be willing to build a different world and feeling when you're at school? In fact, would you be willing to play with the kids without all of that anger today or without trying to get them angry at you in the same way your dad does? (Changing the second picture of Timmy's face and hands to a friendly one with the kids holding out their hands to include him)

TIMMY: (Pause) Yeah.

BOBBIE: Do you know how to do that?

TIMMY: (Shrugging his shoulders) I guess.

BOBBIE: Johnny, you have lots of friends. What if you showed Timmy some of the friendly things that you do to help you attract all of your friends?

JOHNNY: (Pause/reluctance) Okay.

BOBBIE: Timmy, would you be willing to copy the way Johnny plays for the rest of your playground time so that you can learn how to play gently and make more friends?

TIMMY: Yeah.

BOBBIE: Would you also be willing to try something new and let the kids feel happy with you?

TIMMY: (Pause/slight laugh) Yeah.

BOBBIE: Johnny, would you be willing to show Timmy your friendly behavior for the rest of playground today?

JOHNNY: Okay, but if he's angry again, I don't want to play with him ever again.

BOBBIE: Timmy, did you hear that? You're running out of chances with Johnny.

TIMMY: Uh-huh.

BOBBIE: Would you be willing to forget about all of that anger, since it's not been a very good buddy for you after all?

TIMMY: (More committed to the idea) Yes.

BOBBIE: Do you boys feel clear with each other now? Does it feel friendly between you?

TIMMY: Yes.

JOHNNY: Me too.

ⓖⓖⓖ

We can see from this more complex example how adults can help children to reexamine the previously faulty deductions they have made that have become part of their history—or antecedent—which are now motivating unclear behavior. To do this effectively, it's important that adults not be in such a hurry to reprimand the child who hit, ask for shallow apologies, or offer simple solutions such as "asking to play." Instead, they can guide the children involved all the way through the layers of their misunderstanding and, in so doing, help them to unravel any prior faulty conclusions that are causing their current lack of clarity.

Using Clearing to Heal Family Dynamics

At eight years of age, Gina was becoming increasingly unpopular at school and was having outbursts of door-slamming anger at home. She was reported to concern herself at school with fairness, while tattling on other children for breaking the rules; and, her playground time was spent trying to control the children, rather than play with them. Her parents came to counseling when Gina's teacher suggested that something deeper might be wrong.

For a deeper problem like Gina's, the discussion period during clearing, following an outburst of anger, is a good time to probe the issue—since the child is required under these circumstances to discuss the issue before regaining his or her freedom.

In teaching Gina's parents how to use the clearing to uncover and heal their daughter's problem, I explained this important distinction: they should first make it clear that although Gina would not be allowed to impose her unhappiness on the rest of the family with moods or door-slamming, she would be free to openly express whatever was bothering her in a more appropriate manner. And because she had used the door-slamming method, she would now be required to examine what was wrong before regaining her freedom.

In further discussions with Gina's parents, I discovered that Gina had complained throughout the years about their failing to hold her younger brother to the rules, while requiring that only she follow them. When I inquired about the truth of this accusation, her parents admitted to letting five-year-old Jason slide on doing his chores or having to face consequences when he misbehaved. Thus, I suggested that once Gina was able to acknowledge that door-slamming was the thing that had caused her to be sent to her room, that Mother reflectively interpret (see Chapter 11 on Communication) the following ideas, based on information we had from Gina's history or *antecedent*:

"Does it seem to you as though we ignore Jason's rules, while making you do all of your chores and be the only one who has to go to your room when you've misbehaved?"

Knowing that Gina would avidly concur with this, Mother could then acknowledge the truth of this previously denied reality with: "Honey, I agree with you that we have babied Jason too much, while always asking you to be responsible. I can understand why that doesn't feel good to you and why it would look as though we aren't being fair." She could then playfully add, "We have always done that because he was the 'baby'—but at five years of age, it's time that we face how big he is and hold him to the rules, too!"

This nondefensive explanation and acknowledgment would give Gina some immediate relief in knowing that her mother could now see the reality that had been so obvious to Gina all these years. That, in turn, would help Gina to feel safer in disclosing herself to her mom and offer renewed hope of accomplishing more honest communication and problem-solving between them. Mother could then go on to inquire, "Do you suppose that you're so worried about the kids at school minding their rules because we haven't made Jason mind them at home?"

Again, Gina would probably agree and possibly add additional information to this suggestion. After giving Gina ample time to express her reaction to this observation, Mother could again acknowledge, "Now I can understand why you are always so worried about how rules really work in life, and I can see why you would want someone besides yourself to have to follow them! I can also see why this has made you feel pretty frustrated and upset with everyone."

After giving Gina time to respond, Mother can draw a picture of her at school with friends who turn away each time she tattles on them and reflect, "Can you see that even though we have mistakenly taught you to worry too much about rules, it doesn't make the other kids feel close to you when you act like their policewoman at school?"

She can then explore with Gina which school friends are well liked and what qualities they have that everyone enjoys. She can also ask which girls Gina would like as friends and offer suggestions and help for getting closer to them. And finally, she can share with Gina that they will begin to hold her brother to the rules of the household, so that at least at home, following the rules will apply to everyone.

We can learn from this example how parents can first anticipate what lessons their child needs to learn—based on information revealed by the child's behavior, antecedents, faulty decisions, and current choices—then create a plan for their next clearing to teach the child clearer patterns of thinking and behaving.

Clearing with Preteens

Generations of women have reported being deeply hurt by their junior high school girlfriends. It seems that this is a period when young girls, fearful that they will fail to be the prettiest and most popular in their class, will periodically turn on friends in an effort to secure their own tenuously held position with the group.

As a result, most preteen girls live in constant fear of being the person under attack, and many initiate an offensive to protect against this occurrence. Consequently, this period of development is fraught with deceit and betrayal as well as the anxiety and anger that result from these traumas. In spite of the prevalence of this problem, I have yet to see adults address it adequately or with the goal of helping the girls involved to confront their faulty patterns of thinking on which the problem is based.

My recommendation is that incidents of this type of early adolescent ganging should be handled more thoroughly by calling a full group clearing—using the model of Ho'oponopono as outlined in Chapter 8—in which each girl is helped to release her faulty decisions and achieve increased clarity about how to get along.

During the clearing, each girl must be given an opportunity to explore her faulty conclusions about competition and jealousy as well as expose her motivation for engaging in ganging against a member of her social group. When given such an opportunity, many girls will reveal that they did not want to join in, but feared that they would be the object of ganging if they failed to do so. This creates an opportunity for the adult to discuss such things as faulty group thinking motivated by fear as well as the various problems generated by the race of the worldly ego self, which triggers rivalry among peers.

It's important that the adult guiding the clearing openly explore the girls' true feelings toward the initiators of the ganging, since most girls secretly don't feel close to them. As with the bully, the girls who initiate the ganging would benefit from realizing the true effect of their unfriendly behavior.

Such a discussion might conclude with ways to stand up more honestly during this period of insecurity for what is genuinely felt in one's heart; dismantle the power of the unkind girls; and more clearly honor those with the kindness and courage to act as their higher selves.

We can see from this deeper approach to handling this prevalent preteen problem that such issues can be used to teach our kids what is not clear in their approach to life and what would be clearer. In this particular case, the girls can be taught to release the faulty view that engaging in ganging will help them to maintain their own popularity and replace this false idea with a renewed belief in the value of living as kinder, clearer, more responsible world citizens.

Clearing with Teens

Parents of teens can use clearing to teach important lessons, since clearing is a time when their adolescent is required to participate in discussions on touchy topics.

For example, one father used a clearing—following his son's grounding for being rude when his friends were visiting—to point out that adolescent friends are made to feel uncomfortable when their host is unkind to his parents. He then asked his son to use his own powers of observation to notice how much more teens enjoy those homes where the host has a good relationship with his family and the adults make friends with the kids. He also asked that he notice that these friendships can't develop when the teen host is rude to his family.

A mother used a clearing—after restricting her daughter for ignoring her curfew on a first date—to enter into a discussion about how her daughter handles sexuality in the early stages of a relationship. When she realized that her daughter had not created her own standard and was responding to the wishes of her dates, she had an opportunity to discuss her daughter's needs from a feminine point of view. As a result, they had a good discussion about how much better relationships work for young women who not only hold a higher standard of conduct, but establish solid, mutually responsible, and long-standing friendships or even consider waiting until marriage before entering into sexual relationships. Such discussions must be parallel and two-sided, however, and completely devoid of accusation or a preachy, dominant approach in order to be effective.

Now that you know how to help your children uncover what is not clear for them in their pattern of thinking, expecting, and behaving and replace these faulty patterns with clearer lessons for growing up with clarity, I will introduce you to some updated lessons that can help to create more harmony in your homes and a clearer, more loving world for us all!

The decisions we take from life's experiences create our patterns of thinking and behaving; these, in turn, sculpt the life we see before us. When the patterns of thinking and behaving are clear and attractive, so is the sculpture.

★★★

10

Lessons in Wisdom

New Ideas for a Better World

The Ninth Key:

ⓖⓖⓖ

Teaching clear lessons will bring clear results.

Understanding the value of teaching children the lessons attached to their problems is key; yet knowing what to teach is even more crucial.

Unfortunately, many of the societal lessons currently taught both at home and at school are more habitual than helpful and often serve to shut down the enthusiasm and spirit of the child, while putting his higher self to sleep. He then spends much of his adulthood trying to awaken from his unconscious slumber to recapture the dream he came to this world to fulfill.

Whenever we find ourselves asleep to our higher selves and higher purposes, the result we create is much like the one Woody Allen encountered during one of his films. In this memorable clip, the actor boarded a train filled with depressed passengers, portrayed in black and white to amplify their drab affect and clothing. After quickly surveying this disquieting scene, he glanced out the window to discover with relief that there was another train across the tracks filled with rosy-cheeked people, laughing and talking among themselves in full Technicolor. Yet just as he realized that he wished to disembark his black-and-white train and board the colorful one, it left the station!

We can all relate to not wanting to sleep through our lives or make the kinds of choices that will put us on the "wrong" train—or, if we did board the wrong train, we would want to awaken in time to remedy the situation. And we especially want our children to stay alert enough to create a life for themselves on the "right" track. Yet if we look out the window of our lives to view the world we have created, it appears that we have, in fact, been asleep at the controls for quite some time and now find ourselves dramatically off course. The question is, how did we end up on a track that doesn't fulfill our missions or dreams, and how do we find our way back to a more awakened and meaningful experience?

Teaching the Right Lessons

The first step in getting back on course lies in our understanding that we are the ones who have created the path we find ourselves on with the ideas and attitudes we have adopted for ourselves and then taught to our children. Thus, although we would all like to live in a more caring and joyful world, we often embrace and then teach our children the very lessons that prevent this from happening. In fact, rather than inspire our kids to fully participate in life as mutually caring friends, while behaving responsibly toward one another, we teach them the kinds of self-focused and achievement-oriented lessons that result in their comparing themselves to others, then feeling insecure, separate, jealous, and competitive. These feelings, in turn, convert to behaviors steeped in manipulation and rivalry, which can often lead to aggression—or even violence.

The best way to correct this problem would be to awaken from our collective slumber for long enough to examine what it would require to get off of the black-and-white train going in the wrong direction and board the train of our dreams headed for a better world.

With this in mind, parents and teachers would be wise to not only pay more attention to the daily homilies they offer children, but to some of the habitually taught lessons that result in getting our kids off track. Thus, before automatically teaching them the common societal lessons of "winning is everything," "keep it fair," "no fighting," "do your homework," and "share your things," consider if these instructions actually contribute to their clear development and creation of a better world. We can begin this process of examination by considering the true results of these five commonly taught axioms and what lessons might be more useful. The key while reexamining these currently accepted ideas is to ask the question—"Will this lesson serve the larger purpose of my child's higher self?"

Lesson 1: "Winning is Everything"—a Societal Belief that Results in Fear of Effort, Error, Failure, and Pain

Throughout a child's development, he is faced with many new experiences that offer him an abundance of opportunities for both success and failure. Because these events are initially unfamiliar and require new skills, he may fear them on first encounter. For instance, a young baby may worry about his first bath or the falls and bumps he experiences while learning to walk. An older child might fear his first attempts at riding a bicycle, understanding math, or spending the night with friends. And the teen may fear team tryouts or going on his first date. Yet even though unfamiliar events evoke normal feelings of uneasiness in both children and adults, the fear is meant only to help us become more alert and prepare for the new experience. When viewed in this context, we are able to more easily confront the fear and penetrate whatever barriers it creates for us.

This moment of confronting our fears can best be seen in the child standing on the edge of a diving board for the first time, looking down at the water below with fear pounding in his heart. (See Figure 12.) Under normal conditions, children will make the decision to accept the fear as a part of life and carry it in their hearts as they leap to the water below. In this risk-taking act, they discover the excitement of full participation and realize that their fears have dissolved by the time they reach the water. The very act of jumping shows them how to overcome fear—even transform its energy to exhilaration—as they succeed in one of life's many experiences. By confronting their fear and experiencing the jump and its accompanying success, their feelings of internal power are strengthened. As a result, any reluctance they might have had to facing the risks that go with participation is conquered, and their enjoyment of fully immersing in life is protected.

However, when children have been made to feel afraid of participation or the effort, error, rejection, and pain that it can bring, they will look at the water below, overrespond to the fear, and allow it to dictate their shrinking from the experience. As these children retreat to the stairs to escape the dreaded plunge, fear expands in their minds and hearts.

That childhood jump offers a metaphor for how children negotiate their fears in the face of the programming they have received, and the way they manage will depend on what they have been taught. Those who have learned to embrace their fears—including whatever mistakes, rejection, or hurt they experience—will value participation, even when things are new and unpredictable, and mistakes are a possibility. These are the kids who will jump with abandon, learn from their results, and become enthusiastic participants in life's offerings.

Once immersed in the participatory side of life, a child's fear dissolves and pleasure takes over as he experiences the successes that go with involvement. He soon realizes that the choice for participation offers him abundant opportunities to learn from his experiences, which include effort, failure, and pain as well as the successes, pleasure, and skill-building he seeks.

By contrast, children pushed by parents in the race to the "top" develop fears about "making it" and "winning." Because they are often criticized for

Figure 12. Choosing Between Avoidance and Participation

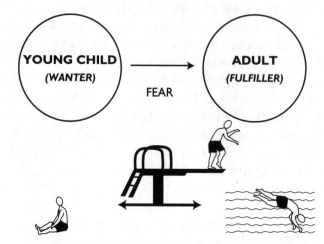

The Illusion: Avoidance will offer an easier road.

<table>
<tr><td>← EASY ROAD</td><td>HARD ROAD →</td></tr>
</table>

AVOIDANCE	**PARTICIPATION**
Retreats from Fear	**Pushes through Fear**
• Avoids life	• Participates in life
• Resists life's activities	• Chooses life's activities
• Hides from effort, error, rejection, and pain	• Exposed to effort, error, rejection, hurt, and pain
• No opportunity for success, growth, aliveness, fulfillment, and joy	• Exposed to opportunity for success, growth, aliveness, fulfillment, and joy
• Fear intensifies and feelings of resistance, inadequacy, helplessness, immaturity, dependence, powerlessness, and low self-esteem develop	• Fear dissolves and feelings of competence, adequacy, strength, maturity, independence, personal power, and high self-esteem develop
• Experiences the emptiness of avoidance	• Experiences the fullness of participation

The Reality: The signs have been switched.
Avoidance turns out to be the hard road.

<table>
<tr><td>← HARD ROAD</td><td>EASY ROAD →</td></tr>
</table>

their choices and mistakes by families concerned about their position in the race, they learn to dread effort, error, rejection, and pain. As a result, they become fearful of jumping and retreat, instead, down the stairs to the illusory "safety" of the avoider's corner. Although this seems like a good place to hide from the challenges required of life's participants, this corner is so devoid of opportunities for success or fulfillment that it ultimately proves harder than the participator's side they were striving to escape. Over time, these children become the resisters and avoiders in life, fearful of venturing out, and are left with narrow options and empty feelings of inadequacy and dependence. What these avoiders and resisters fail to notice is that without participation, there are no opportunities for success and the feelings of competence and joy that go with them. In short, the corner that shields them from fear, effort, error, and pain becomes a lonely place to hide from life's offerings.

The key to getting back on the track of full participation lies in dissolving the separating energies created by the idea that life is a competition among isolated individuals, all striving to be the best in order to "win." If we would replace this fragmenting, fear-based goal for living with working together to create a better world, our kids could reconnect with their passion for life and desire to be full participants in a mutually supportive and joyful global experience.

Some parents take the desire for their children to reach the top to another level. Not only do they want the best for their kids, they want them to have everything without experiencing any of the difficulty or pain involved in attaining it. As a result, they teach their kids to be overly careful; side with them against the "unfairness" of life's difficulties; protect them from normal amounts of pain; and allow—even encourage—them to resist the usual effort and work that are a natural part of a full life. Not surprisingly, these children grow excessively fearful of normal amounts of difficulty and learn to withdraw from the activities that require effort.

Consequently, children of protective parents also retreat to the stairs to avoid jumping into life with full participation. Yet with each retreat they grow increasingly timid, while reluctance, resistance, avoidance, and procrastination become their primary ways of coping. In the end, the overprotected child also lacks a toughness of spirit and the ability to push through barriers to meet his goals and soon finds himself among the other avoiders and resisters on the "wrong train."

The fortunate child who has been taught that fear and pain are a normal part of life and can be confronted, welcomed, and even embraced will barely notice the newness of his experiences. Such a child will easily, even eagerly, push through his fears to the other side, particularly when he is provided with stepping-stones to success when needed. Once there, his fear will dissolve as he willingly immerses himself in life's adventures. As a result, he becomes progressively more comfortable with new experiences, as fear fades into an imperceptible backdrop of his life. Once he's free of the fear, he returns to his more natural state of jumping into life as a full and joyful participant for the mutual benefit of all.

Lesson 2: "Keep It Fair"—The Problem with Trying to Keep Life Fair

Another concept that many parents mistakenly teach their children is that life is fair and even. Not only does a child promised a fair deal feel betrayed when life doesn't deliver, the anticipation of having things equal results in jealousy and competitive feelings between siblings and peers. This is especially true for children engaged in the societal race to the "top" and concerned about their position in life relative to others.

Although we engage our kids in this race, we simultaneously strive to protect them from the pain of not being first by espousing fairness. Yet fairness in this context is usually defined as both the child's and his parents' hope that he will have as much or more than others, rather than a genuine concern about fairness for all of humanity.

Thus, anytime you attempt to keep things "fair" for only your child as a way to prevent the normal pain for him that goes with life's inequities, he becomes increasingly more concerned about this false version of "equality"; as a result, he begins to carry an invisible set of scales in his head to help him determine who is getting more than he has received. If you worry along with him about real or imagined injustices or try to make them up to him, he further believes in the validity of his worries and becomes ever more anxious and unhappy.

A child's constant measurement of the "fairness" of life and his effort to keep things "equal" or better for himself causes him and his siblings to guard against one of them receiving more love or possessions than the other. This, in turn, provokes additional disruptions and discipline issues in the home. One mother became aware of how far out of control this concern had gone when she found herself putting a few more Cheerios into her son's bowl to appease his anxiety over the extra cereal he accused his sister of getting. Then, when his sister saw additional Cheerios going into her brother's bowl, her anxiety was similarly aroused, and she, too, began to fuss for more Cheerios!

It's better to face your children at the outset with the reality that each of them will have an entirely different life experience from others. Some will be more attractive or have nicer clothing or more artistic talents, while others will possess greater athletic skills or superior academic strengths. And some mornings, one child will simply have more Cheerios in his bowl than his siblings.

When parents can give up their own attachment to making life "fair" and "even," they release their children from the anxiety of measuring life's equality. This, in turn, allows them to enjoy siblings and friends—including their successes—while viewing their own fulfillment as a separate matter to be addressed and pursued. Even more important, it releases each child from adopting the faulty view that his glass is half empty and that he will never have enough in life. This, in turn, frees him to appreciate what he has and to live life with a grateful heart.

Dialogue from Class

MOTHER: My eight- and nine-year-old sons like to trade off on who empties the top and bottom of the dishwasher to assure that they will have an equal number of dishes to put away each week. They have also been rotating who sits in the front seat of the car for years. Now, I can see that we all need to get rid of the scales, but I particularly hate the front seat business, since they have an argument about who sat there last every time we get in the car. Unfortunately, they are pretty attached to rotating it, and I can't see how to eliminate this pattern.

BOBBIE: You can begin by announcing that you previously made a mistake in trying to keep everything even and will no longer supervise rotating the front seat of the car. You can further point out that if they were to take the bus, they wouldn't expect fellow passengers to rotate the better seats among themselves, but would have to accept whatever seats were available at the time they boarded. Let them know that from now on you will handle the car seating in the same way in order to help them practice dealing with life in a more realistic manner.

MOTHER: But what if one gets there first and the other tries to push him out?

BOBBIE: Let them know that the car won't go anywhere until they can accept that the first person to the seat is the one who has claim to it. If one child is trying to push the other one out and won't stop, explain that he's not free to ride in the car until he can accept the rules.

MOTHER: What if he keeps pushing?

BOBBIE: Give him a crossroads choice: to accept the rules or go into the house. If he keeps pushing, have him go into the house and let him know that you will return to clear with him after taking his brother to school. When you return, ask him what behavior caused his delay in proceeding to school. See if he's ready to face that you are no longer rotating the front seat and that he will have to accept that reality if he wants to ride in the car.

MOTHER: You just let him be late to school?

BOBBIE: If he likes school, I would let him go only after clearing, or if he takes too long to clear, I would let him miss altogether. However, if he was a reluctant student, I would drive him to school and let him know that we would clear that afternoon upon his return home, but that he would have an additional consequence as a result of not clearing cooperatively that morning.

MOTHER: What if he cooperated when he heard that?

BOBBIE: I would proceed with the clearing for as long as he was truly cooperative.

MOTHER: What if he refuses to cooperate and I want to leave him at home but don't trust him there alone while I'm at work?

BOBBIE: Working parents must develop backup child care for those times when their child is unwilling to comply and needs to stay at home. For those who can't afford a professional sitter, find a relative, friend, neighbor, or a church or temple member with whom you can arrange to trade sitting time. Be aware that parents who don't have such arrangements and are forced to send uncooperative kids to school or leave them at home alone end up with kids who continue to push further out of bounds.

ANOTHER MOTHER: Isn't it good to teach children to be fair in life?

BOBBIE: Absolutely. Being genuinely fair in our approach to life is an essential quality, but it's one that emerges when we learn to care deeply about others from our hearts, rather than by receiving equal portions of life's bounty. In fact, children who have been indulged in their concerns over equal distribution of material things feel jealous of peers and become competitive with friends whom they perceive as having more than they do. This, in turn, creates a barrier to feelings of closeness and friendship, rather than a caring interest in others. In order to engender true feelings of caring, we must seek daily opportunities to inspire the opening of our hearts and those of our children. Only then will we have the kind of genuine fairness that flows from a loving heart and fulfills the purpose of our higher selves.

Sibling Rivalry

By working overtime to prevent your older child from feeling jealous of the new baby or keeping the amount of love, time, and purchases fair and even between siblings, many of you provoke additional tensions and discipline problems in your homes.

In fact, the more you worry about the jealousy your first child may feel toward his new sibling, the more anxious and jealous he becomes. You must remember that billions of children have been required to accept brothers and sisters into their homes and have survived the experience. Thus, more important than worrying about your firstborn's insecurities is planning ways to include him in welcoming the new baby—not as a way to bypass his jealousy—but because it will be natural and fun to do so. Studies show that children allowed to hold the baby and genuinely connect with him right from the beginning become as bonded to their siblings as their parents are. Enabling this bond to take place will eliminate most of the initial feelings of separation and jealousy between siblings.

Similarly, the more you take in stride the differences in time or money you spend on your children, the more relaxed they will feel about it. The key is that each child learns from his history with you to trust your love, whether you are with him or with his sibling. In effect, you want him to learn from experience that your love for one child does not threaten or diminish your love for another. He learns this best when you openly love all of your children, rather than secretly, anxiously hope that each child won't notice your love for the others.

Dialogue from Class

MOTHER: How can we guide our son through his jealous feelings of the new baby when they arise?

BOBBIE: By talking openly about it on those occasions when you see his jealousy being expressed, you help him to confront his fears as well as dispel any distorted conclusions he might be forming. For example, if he's acting babyish or aggressive, rather than subtly reject or openly punish him, it's more effective to say, "You seem to be worrying that I might love the baby more than you and thinking that if you hurt her or act like her it will make things better." You can then listen carefully for clues in his response about how he is seeing things and help him reorganize whatever false viewpoints he's holding that fuel his jealousy.

MOTHER: How do you do that?

BOBBIE: The most common falsehood that drives a child's jealousy is the belief that you have only enough love in your heart for one child, and that if you love the baby, there won't be enough love left for him. Ironically, this fear gets triggered by parents who are concerned about openly loving the baby. As a result, their older child senses from their anxiety that their love for the baby will threaten him in some way, and he begins to worry about it as well.

You can help your child to release this erroneous idea by first releasing your own anxiety over it. You can then draw pictures while reflecting his feelings with, "You seem worried that when I love the baby I might not have enough love left for you." If he acknowledges jealous feelings, you can guide him toward a more accurate understanding of how love works by asking such questions as, "When you are petting the cat, do you run out of love for the dog? Or, when you're with Grandpa do you still like me? Does your love for the family stay in your heart while you're at school? When you are with school friends, do you stop loving your cousins? And can you see that when I'm petting the dog I still like you, and Dad, and the baby? Did you realize that love works the same way for me when I'm changing the baby's diaper, nursing her, or just being with her—that I still like you, and Dad, and Grandma, and the dog? In fact, when you think about it, can you see that people who have lots of relatives, friends, and pets in their lives actually develop more love in their hearts in order to include all of the extras?" (A diagram of this might demonstrate that a heart used for loving more than one person not only gets more practice but expands in size and power in order to generate all of the love needed for the kids, grandparents, friends, and family pets.) Yet even while helping your older child to release his mistaken ideas about the limitations of love, I would remain matter-of-fact, rather than join him in his concern about how much love he is getting or argue frantically against his doubts.

ANOTHER MOTHER: How do I handle it when my three-year-old insists on hurting his baby sister?

BOBBIE: Clearly let him know that he has full access to you, even when you are dealing with the baby, so long as his behavior is calm and cooperative. However, if his behavior becomes unruly, and he pinches the baby or crowds her out of your lap, then his behavior—not your love for the baby—will cause him to lose the chance to be with her for awhile. Moreover, since you are still tending to her needs, he will lose the chance to be with you for awhile as well—but you are confident that after a short break, he will do better.

MOTHER: Won't that make him feel more insecure and angry at the baby?

BOBBIE: He will feel even more anxious if you allow him to hurt her, since that would make you a less reliable mother who doesn't protect her offspring. Thus, rather than worry about his feelings, it's better to address the broken boundary by calmly saying, "I can see that you're not willing to follow the rule to not hurt your sister, so you aren't free to be in the same room with her for awhile. After you have spent some time in your room, we'll have a talk to see if you feel ready to follow the rules."

   If you don't bend over backwards to prove your love to a doubting child, but lovingly carry on with life, he eventually experiences your continued love for him by virtue of the fact that he is allowed as much access to you as the baby has, so long as his behavior doesn't cause him to lose that option. Yet this only happens if you remain calmly connected to him while delivering the rule. On the other hand, if you get angry, you introduce a very real and tangible concern about your ability to love him regardless of the conditions, and he will become increasingly anxious about holding your love.

MOTHER: Won't the talk with you after his time-out motivate him to get into more trouble just to have this special kind of time with you?

BOBBIE: When children have little or no access to their parents, opportunities to talk become very meaningful and will be pursued, even if a price must be paid to have them. However, when children have full access to their parents, additional opportunities to connect are not as important as preserving full access. To assure that your child is clear about this, you can ask during clearing, "Did you want to be close to me or have some special chat time together? And do you realize you could have been close to me just by asking if we could snuggle or if I would sit and talk with you?" The key is to respond when your child makes a direct request for your time; then he won't have to create a problem to get a response.

A THIRD MOTHER: If I tell my daughter to go to her room when she's acting jealous, she accuses me of not loving her and preferring her brother.

BOBBIE: How are you presently handling that?

MOTHER: Well, I hate to have her think that I don't love her, since I know that's precisely what she's worried about, so I try to assure her that I do love her.

BOBBIE: Assuring your child that she is loved at this juncture not only distracts you from getting her to her room, but increases her fear, since it makes you seem as though you are worried about the matter as well. Therefore, only if she brings it up again during clearing would you need to address the subject as a genuine issue. At that time, it's important to search your heart for the truth, and if the accusation is true, to consciously work to correct it. On the other hand, if it's not true, and your child is simply caught in the mistaken idea that she needs all of your attention or requires that you stop loving the baby in order to prove your love for her, then you must help her to adopt a more realistic viewpoint.

MOTHER: If I'm honest, I do prefer my younger child to the older one because she acts so jealous that she has become unappealing to me.

BOBBIE: Jealous children do behave most unattractively. Yet even though your negative feelings toward her are understandable, her only way to improve will be if you can see her innate value once again and commit to loving her.

FOURTH MOTHER: My older child seems very angry at his younger sister and says it's because we baby her.

BOBBIE: Do you baby her?

MOTHER: (Pause) I would say we probably do—since she's four years younger than he is.

BOBBIE: Parents often instigate negative feelings between siblings by babying the younger child and expecting only the older one to mind the rules or behave responsibly. I've seen many cases in which the younger child acts badly; yet should the older one attempt to deal with this, either by restraining the younger child, excluding her from his room or play, or by outright hitting her, the parents scold the older child, while requiring nothing of the younger one. Not only are such parents leaving all of the discipline to their older child, they fail to back his efforts to keep the younger one in bounds. Unfortunately, this teaches the younger child to be a pest, while causing the older one to resent her. Parents who handle things in this manner inadvertently prevent close feelings between siblings and cause their older child to justifiably feel that his parents favor the "baby."

MOTHER: That sounds like our situation exactly. I can see that I have protected the younger child, but haven't dealt with my older child's needs. What do I do now?

BOBBIE: If you will begin to hold your younger child to her boundaries, you will see a big improvement in their relationship. For example, if she's not minding the rules while in her brother's room, she should lose her choice to be in there for the remainder of the morning or day. Not only is it your job to involve yourself in holding the boundaries, but to allow your son to restrain his sister without getting scolded.

MOTHER: I haven't wanted him to act like her parent, so I tell him to let me handle it.

BOBBIE: But then if you fail to address the problem, it's not getting handled at all, and your son feels like her victim with no viable tools for handling her.

MOTHER: That's what he's been trying to tell me, and he has really grown to dislike her.

BOBBIE: If you put yourself in his position, you wouldn't like her very much either. It's always best to allow your older child to deal with his younger sibling, unless he's too aggressive to do so responsibly. During clearing you can point out to your daughter that it didn't work for her to tease or hit her older brother. You can further help her to identify what she wanted from him. For example, did she want her way, or was she after his attention or help; or was she trying to get him into trouble? If her desire is appropriate, help her to get it met in other ways. If not, help her to release it. By doing this, your younger child will no longer get away with pestering or hitting her older sibling, while standing aside as he gets into trouble for reacting. The result of taking the time to do this is that your younger child behaves better, your older one no longer needs to react, they like each other better, and there is considerably more harmony in your home.

FIFTH MOTHER: Do you think it helps to give each child his own special time?

BOBBIE: I suspect this actually intensifies feelings of separation and jealousy between siblings, since it creates an unnatural promise of time alone with parents and keeps each child worried about preserving that privilege. Realistically, the child's world now includes a sibling, and the sooner he makes his adjustment to that reality, the sooner he will be able to include his sibling in his heart and world. In truth, the more you all do together, the closer the siblings will become and the better the family will feel as a unit.

FATHER: Isn't it natural for siblings to bicker and fight while they're growing up?

BOBBIE: I don't subscribe to the idea that kids will struggle with one another indefinitely without growth or resolution just because they are siblings. Parents often teach this belief and foolishly brag about how much they quarreled and fought with their siblings. This isn't a necessary arrangement and can easily be improved by parents who hold a higher standard and know how to handle it effectively. In this regard, it's important to understand that if we give up on getting along with family members, we might as well give up on any hope for brotherhood and peace. With this in mind, parents can remember that each squabble their children have represents something one or both of them don't understand about how to get along with others harmoniously. It's critical that parents not simply endure problems with the idea that they are normal, but use each incident as a window of opportunity to teach what isn't yet clear for their kids about how to live life more effectively.

When children are taught that things must always be kept fair and even, their siblings and peers become competitors, rather than friends; as a result, each is damaged in his ability to genuinely rejoice in the success of the others. By contrast, children not trying to keep things fair and even enjoy both the friendship and good fortune of others and can focus, without distraction, on living their lives and fulfilling their dreams.

Lesson 3: "Don't Fight," a Rule That Contributes to Disharmony

One of the most confusing lessons adults teach children is not to fight, no matter how badly another child is behaving. Because we are so uncomfortable with the battles of children, we angrily chastise them for their squabbling or banish them to their rooms or the principal's office. Ironically, this reaction not only prevents children from learning the lessons their squabbles offer, it keeps them fighting more and longer than if they were left alone to work things out for themselves.

If we take a closer look at what childhood fighting is all about, we can see that it's simply a part of our kids' growing-up process. In fact, it looks very much like the developmental wrestling of all of the toddlers from the animal kingdom and includes such things as posturing and minor scraps designed to define and defend boundary lines between "my yard" and "your yard." If we seek to understand why such a developmental stage exists, it becomes apparent that fighting prepares our children to claim their own personal boundaries at a deep, cellular level within themselves.

When parents stop these scrimmages, make them seem more dangerous and hurtful than they actually are, or offer children unrealistic alternatives such as using their "words" to defend their "yards," they interrupt this important learning experience.

Those of you who do this not only interfere with your child's awareness of where his territorial boundaries lie, but prevent him from discovering how to stay in his own territory as well as protect it, should it become necessary to do so. Moreover, your interruptions cause your children's quarrels to go unresolved and thus escalate in number and duration.

By contrast, children who have been allowed an opportunity to wrestle with siblings and peers while growing up discover—at the experiential level of learning so important to youth—that they can manage their own territorial domain. This allows them to internalize feelings of personal strength and competence in their ability to take care of themselves, and these feelings are then programmed into their neurology.

Paradoxically, once a child feels adequate enough in his capacity to protect his boundaries and hang onto his belongings and rights, he feels safe around others—even when they are aggressive—and has no need to behave aggressively toward them; yet he feels strong enough to stand up for himself, both verbally and physically, when provoked. We can see from this result that childhood fighting is not the precursor to violence that adults fear, but is merely a natural developmental stage that allows children to discover internal feelings of strength.

When the value of youthful battles is understood in this new light, it becomes apparent that adults can be more helpful to a child's development by eliminating the mandate that "fighting is against the rules." This does not mean they must teach kids to fight; they can simply refrain from teaching them not to.

Using Childhood Battles to Help Both the Passive and Aggressive Child Achieve Balance

Many of you teach your children never to fight in hopes of contributing to a more peaceful world. Yet when the children you have taught to be submissive get to preschool, they have no way to deal with the sizable number of peers who grab their toys or push them out of lines and tell them what they can and cannot do. By the time they get to elementary school, these rule-minders encounter even more rule-breaking tyrants in control of the classrooms and playground and feel compelled to submit to their demands in order to stay out of fights and adhere to school rules. In junior high and high school, these kids are faced once again with aggressive peers heckling them in the hallways, swiping their lunches, homework, money, and belongings.

Consequently, parents must be aware that anytime they separate young children who are struggling over boundaries, with a reminder "not to fight," the issues of dominance and submission never get resolved and their kids will remain out of balance. The weaker child—or the one I refer to as the *underclaimer*—has failed to learn that he has a right to hold his ground or how to do it. Because he has no tools for dealing with bullies, he grows increasingly fearful and passive, while his dependence on adults to protect him deepens.

Meanwhile, the dominant child—or *overclaimer*—has successfully intimidated the weaker kids and knows he can do so again anytime the adults aren't watching. Furthermore, because he hasn't explored alternative ways to feel internally secure, he continues to use aggressiveness and control as a way to feel big and strong.

Because of these poor results, my goal in the face of childhood battles is not to focus on the fight as the issue, but to guide both children toward a better understanding of how to resolve their conflicts. I do this by helping the submissive child to develop the strength and courage he needs to claim more; then, as he gets stronger, the aggressive child becomes motivated to back off and claim less. As each achieves improved balance within his personality, he becomes more appropriately assertive in life. The aggressive child stops invading the boundaries of others, while the passive one no longer submits to unreasonable demands. In this way, the two of them work together to create a more balanced community and world.

Terry

Terry, a seventh grader, finally stood up to the school bully, which resulted in a fight between them. Typically, both children were sent to the principal's office to settle the problem. Although the principal realized that the bully was at fault and hated to punish Terry, he felt obliged to enforce the school's rules. Thus, he suspended the bully for a week, due to his past record, while suspending Terry for only one day, since the fight had been his first. Although

Terry's mother was initially pleased when the principal realized that her son was not at fault, both she and her son were left with an unclear message regarding how he was expected to stand up for himself in these kinds of situations.

The principal would have provided a clearer lesson to both boys if he had offered the bully a more honest message such as, "I guess the other kids are tired of your controlling behavior and are no longer willing to put up with it. And since we are all trying to give you the message that it's not acceptable to overclaim your boundaries, I'm going to suspend you from school for a week."

Thus, rather than have a "no-fighting rule" that requires enforcing, it would be more effective to make it clear to both boys that since Terry was not the aggressor, he had not done anything out of line by protecting himself and did not require disciplining. In this way, although aggressiveness would not be condoned, responding to an attack would be allowed.

Whenever I work with children who are fighting, I never offer the mandate, "Don't fight," since there will be times in a child's life when it's appropriate for him to protect himself. Instead, I might say something like, "It looks like there's a problem here. What's going on?" I then take the time needed to guide both children in discovering who wasn't clear about how to live life harmoniously.

Dialogue from Class

MOTHER: I have an overdominant two-year-old and a very sweet, but definitely more submissive, child who is four. I'm always telling the four-year-old that he has to understand that his brother is just a baby, and I try to set up a special area for him; but I feel like I'm sidestepping the problem, and it's not getting any better.

BOBBIE: I would reverse this and allow the four-year-old to protect himself. Not only will this allow your two-year-old to experience some natural feedback when he oversteps his boundaries, it will help your four-year-old learn to stand up for himself. In this way, both of your children will get into better balance.

ANOTHER MOTHER: In our family the six-year-old sister is always overclaiming. The eight-year-old brother would have no trouble dealing with it, but I don't want him to deck her, so I tell him not to hit. Then we put her on time-out, but she's still very aggressive.

BOBBIE: Actually, when parents stop interfering with their children's fighting, the children rarely hurt each other but simply do what is needed to hang on to their toy or get the other child out of their space—unless, of course, they have been overexposed to violent media or are developing abnormally and need to be handled differently. Under normal conditions, it's only when a child's anger has built up over time as a result of being thwarted from protecting his territory that we see him overreact. In your case, your interference with natural consequences for his sister and then giving her time-outs is not only frustrating for your son, but is forcing you to be overly involved in this problem. As soon as you allow the natural course between them to unfold, she will back off and stop pestering; he will like her more; and, they will ultimately be better friends. Incidentally, it's important that you remain watchful while they make this adjustment, yet interfere only if needed for their safety.

A THIRD MOTHER: I'm very uncomfortable with the idea of my son being allowed to hit his little sister.

BOBBIE: Is your son generally aggressive toward her or does he only hit when she's being a pest?

MOTHER: Well, it's pretty much when she has been a pest, but I'm still uncomfortable with him hitting her at all.

BOBBIE: How do you presently respond?

MOTHER: I scold him and tell him that he can't do that no matter what she has done.

BOBBIE: What other options do you offer him to deal with her pestering?

MOTHER: I tell him to use his voice with her.

BOBBIE: Does that work for him?

MOTHER: Not really. It doesn't work for me either! (Laughter) But then I ask him to tell me about it, rather than take matters into his own hands.

BOBBIE: What do you do when he tells you about it?

MOTHER: I remind her to stop pestering.

BOBBIE: Does that stop her?

MOTHER: Some of the time . . . at least for awhile.

BOBBIE: But not really?

MOTHER: I guess you could say that.

BOBBIE: So basically your son has no truly reliable way to deal with his sister that is effective or enduring?

MOTHER: I never thought of it that way.

BOBBIE: As long as you protect her, she will continue to frustrate her brother to her heart's content, since she pays no penalty whatsoever.

MOTHER: I can see that now. So, what else can I do?

BOBBIE: You would be wise to tell him that you have made a mistake by controlling his response. If you are comfortable with taking this step, you can let him know that you will allow him to deal with her but that he must do so responsibly in order to keep this freedom. Then, it will be up to you to make sure that he does. You must also tell your daughter that you no longer plan to protect her from her brother's response to her pestering, and if she wants to keep it up, she does so at her own risk.

FATHER: In our home, we have the opposite problem. My son seems to feel aggressive toward his sister and—without provocation—likes to hurt her.

BOBBIE: Do you only require responsibility from him, or do you require her to mind the rules as well?

FATHER: She has to mind the rules and is very responsible, but he is less mature and has trouble accepting rules. To tell the truth, I think he's jealous of her successes.

BOBBIE: Then, it's your son who holds the mistaken viewpoint. When an older child is the one picking on a younger sibling—unprovoked—he should be removed immediately, without discussion, each time he is unfriendly or aggressive. However, you must be careful to do this neutrally, rather than treat him as the "bad" child in contrast to his "good" sister, as this will only deepen his desire to behave badly in order to remain consistent with his identity as the "bad" kid. When an aggressive child's freedoms are consistently contracted each time he oversteps his bounds, the aggressive behavior impacts on him, and he soon loses his enthusiasm for it. Again, it's important during clearing to neutrally help him to surrender to the rules as well as to the reality that his sister is here to stay. You can further help him to understand that her successes don't prevent him from succeeding and that it's only his fear of trying that holds him back.

Also, by the way you speak of the contrast between them, you might want to look at the possibility that you prefer her due to her "goodness," since he could be cooperating with your impression that only she is the good and lovable child. This leaves him with no other option but to act out your expectation of him as the "bad," unlovable kid. This can be pretty discouraging and might be the key to why he's behaving the way he is. It's important that you honestly investigate your feelings and begin to focus on his innate goodness and lovability as well.

FOURTH MOTHER: What do you do if a child actually hauls off and hits the other child harder than you are comfortable with?

BOBBIE: It would depend on the circumstances. Once I'm aware of a fight of this magnitude, I would calmly interrupt it by saying, "I can see that we have a problem here," rather than get excited about the fight and focus on the hitting. Then, during clearing, I would listen very carefully with an ear to understanding why that child felt the need to hit so hard. Was he frustrated by so many past experiences with this pesky child? Does he harbor envy? Has he been overexposed to violence in the media? Does he erroneously believe that aggression will make his life work better? If he was being overly aggressive, I would contract his freedoms substantially; whereas if he was dealing with a pesky child, I would allow that child to experience the pain of battle as part of life's natural feedback. Once I understand the situation, I always respond according to who is not holding a clear viewpoint, rather than who has been hurt the most.

FIFTH MOTHER: Do kids ever get too violent as a result of not being taught to stop fighting?

BOBBIE: It's my observation that allowing puppy- and kitten-type struggles from an early age—while also offering guidance on the lessons involved—actually leads to greater balance and peacefulness, rather than the violence parents fear.

MOTHER: What makes kids get so aggressive?

BOBBIE: I believe that stimulation from aggressive media images—including the news—inspires abnormal levels of violence in today's kids by falsely depicting aggression as a normal—even "heroic"—part of everyday living and a quick solution to frustration. This could explain why studies show that kids who watch a lot of aggressive and violent cartoons and videos while young, or violent movies and videos as teens, become more aggressive in their interactions with others.

FATHER: How do you decide when to interrupt a fight?

BOBBIE: If a fight constitutes a pretty mellow struggle, and the children seem as though they can work it out by themselves or have not asked for help, I would let it go, while watching from a distance to be sure that it doesn't shift into a more intense fight that could result in injury beyond what would be appropriate for a childhood battle. Also, if I were to observe a tough bully attacking a timid child who was standing with limp arms in awe of his aggressor, I would interrupt the fight immediately. On the other hand, if a historically passive child was successfully standing up for himself, I would let it go for as long as he was holding his ground.

SIXTH MOTHER: What should I say when my child tells me that Johnny hit him at school that day, and he wants to know if he should hit him back. I wanted to say, "Yeah, deck the kid," but of course I didn't and just told him to try to stay out of fights.

BOBBIE: First of all, I would explore with him what was honestly happening. Was he overclaiming with Johnny, or was Johnny overclaiming with him? If he was overclaiming, I would help him to see that aggression didn't work for him. But, if Johnny was in error, then I would want my child to know that he had a right to respond. Yet I would also teach him to do so with a neutral feeling in his heart, rather than filled with anger and hate. By showing kids how to do this, we teach them to hold their boundaries in the same neutral and unattached way that we are learning to hold ours with them.

FATHER: I'm interested in how this relates to what we are taught spiritually in terms of carrying love in our hearts rather than feelings of retaliation.

BOBBIE: That's a wonderful point. In fact, I like to teach kids that they can keep another child out of their space while simultaneously holding loving feelings for him in their hearts and that learning to do this constitutes real power! Because it's natural for young children to struggle as a way to learn about territorial domain, in its unspoiled form, this struggle is conducted without any feelings of malice. Moreover, children discover through this experience that they can manage their own territory, but that the territory of others should be respected. However, when we interfere with this developmental process, some children take on false feelings of being vulnerable and unsafe, while others get carried away with the illusion of their power and dominance. Ironically, both feelings can lead to a sense of imbalance and fear that results in aggression between them. On the other hand, when this developmental experience is allowed to run its natural course without adult interference, any need to protect domain is handled without fear, anger, or malice. It's simply handled.

It's also important to remember that when we raise our children to be their higher selves, they develop into more caring people, and all conflicts over who is right, who is more special, who is in control, or who has the most possessions are naturally replaced with an interest in how to make life more harmonious for everyone.

Helping the Passive Child

Young children who have been taught not to fight are forced into the unrealistic position of remaining immobile while others take their things or push them around. Their efforts to employ adult suggestions such as "using their words" prove ineffective with peers who already know what other children want from them but don't wish to conform. This unsuccessful dilemma causes the rule-minding nonfighters to feel increasingly timid and insecure around their overclaiming peers. When they are later given permission to stand up for themselves, many of these children have simply forgotten how. Therefore, it's helpful to support them in rediscovering their strength and courage. Following is a model for how to do this.

Chris

I was observing a classroom of four-year-olds one day as an aggressive child grabbed some Play-Doh from a boy named Chris. To my surprise, Chris flashed the aggressive child a big, plastic smile and quickly found something else to do. When I asked Chris if he liked having his Play-Doh taken, he assured me that he did like it and gave me one of his false grins as well. Chris was a passive child, and I could see that he really didn't feel strong enough to confront the bully or protect his territory. I ignored his feigned happiness and let him know that I would show him a way to feel stronger. I then taught him to hold on tightly to his Play-Doh and push my hand away as I tried to grab it. Because his grip was so limp, I took him aside with a stuffed animal which I pushed into his space while he practiced pushing it away. Eventually, his response was firm and clear. A few days later, he had an opportunity to use his new skill, and I watched as he successfully held onto a puppet, while another child tried to pull it from his hands. After that experience, he was quite pleased with himself and flashed me a real smile. Although Chris never started a fight, he was no longer the victim of aggressive children.

Dialogue from Class

MOTHER: I taught my eight-year-old child not to fight when he was younger. Would that explain why he's on the timid side now?

BOBBIE: It certainly could. When children haven't learned from their own experience how to handle aggression, they often become the victims of aggressive children. If another child pushes your son in the hallway, for instance, or demands that he do some errand or risk getting beaten up, what choices does he realistically have? How would you expect him to handle such a situation?

MOTHER: Why couldn't he get a teacher's help?

BOBBIE: There are several reasons why this approach is unrealistic. For one, teachers aren't always in the hallways or on the playground when children most need them, and they certainly aren't at the bus stop or along the walk home from school. Furthermore, by the time a child is eight years old, he's no longer willing to get his teacher's help—even if she is nearby—and suffer being teased as a "sissy" or "tattletale." Also, a child who summons adults to protect him fails to gain the experience of protecting himself, which, in turn, causes him to continue to feel weak and fearful. Bullies can easily detect an insecure countenance in a peer and will select that child out of the group to dominate and control. It's only when a child knows that he's able to manage for himself that he develops an internal feeling of strength and safety in the world and projects an aura of confidence. Once this assurance is integrated into his personality and neurology, other children sense that he is no longer an easy target and discontinue picking on him.

Helping the Bully

Paradoxically, the bully wants to be in control, not because he is so big and strong, but because he doesn't feel as powerful as he would like. As a result, the bully is not only insecure, but primarily concerned about himself and has not yet developed the capacity to care about his peers. Consequently, it's ineffective to appeal to his sense of responsibility toward the feelings of others as a way to get him to stop his aggression.

Thus, rather than look to a bully's conscience to motivate better behavior, it's more effective to contract his freedom in a way that impacts on him each time he attacks another child. In this way, the bully experiences creating a problem for himself, which is something he would rather not do. Therefore, instead of telling the bully how hurtful his behavior is to others or asking him how he would like it if they treated him that way or to work it out with the child he's tormenting, it's best to simply remove the bully for awhile.

While clearing with such a child, it's important to help him to see how the bully role has failed to get him the things he wants. For example, it's valuable to reflect that he is neither in control of the games nor the children while he's sitting on a time-out and that other children will avoid playing with him altogether if he continues to overclaim. It's also useful for adults to occasionally sit with the bully during his time-outs in order to gently point out the more effective behaviors of his cooperative peers.

Anytime a bully is identified, it's important that his family and teachers help him to reaccess his higher self, since he is overinvested in his world self and getting ahead of others. Once his heart and higher self are opened, he will feel more genuinely caring toward others, and his own esteem and confidence will be raised.

Teasing

Most adults deal with teasing by imploring the teaser to stop tormenting others as a way to protect his poor victims and reestablish peace. Unfortunately, this usually worsens the problem, since it reinforces the teaser to know how much he is frustrating his victims as well as the adults who can't get him to stop.

When we ask a teaser to stop his antics, for instance, or inquire how he would like it if someone did these things to him, we reinforce how successful his teasing has been. He's perfectly aware of how much his tormenting irritates and hurts, which is precisely why he is doing it. Thus, pleading with him to stop annoying others is futile and only serves to encourage his unpleasant behavior.

Like the bully, the teaser is not concerned with the needs of others and does not respond to an appeal to his conscience. Therefore, when a teaser is persecuting a considerably younger child, the teaser can be removed for generally unfriendly behavior. However, because this approach requires adult intervention, it's preferable when the teased child can also learn to take the fun out of it by not reacting. Yet it won't help to suggest that the child being teased "simply ignore" his tormentor, since this idea is too abstract for a young child. Thus, to help him understand how effective ignoring can be, it's best to act out the scenario with puppets, having some of them pleasing the teaser with upset reactions, while others disappoint him with no response at all.

It's also important that adults not respond with dislike against teasers and bullies nor side with their victims, as this worsens the problem. Our role is to neutrally guide all children toward increased balance and clarity.

Dialogue from Class

MOTHER: Whenever I overhear my child's guest controlling all of the equipment or telling my child that he must watch him build a fort, I go nuts. How do I deal with this without seeming to take my own child's side?

BOBBIE: When guiding children, it's valuable to view each one as if he were your own; thus, rather than take sides, it's better to focus on what is not presently understood by one or both children. In this case, both children are holding a mistaken viewpoint. The guest—or overclaimer—believes that it's acceptable to hoard all of the equipment while your child—the underclaimer—doesn't believe that he's strong enough to object to that arrangement. Your job is to help both children clear up their faulty ideas about how life works. It's important neither to feel angry at the aggressor, nor side with the victim—even when he's your own child. Not only is this an ineffective way to help the aggressor clarify his erroneous viewpoint, it causes the underclaimer to see himself as a victim who relies on adults to protect him, rather than accept responsibility for his part in the problem. Therefore, you will be a more effective guide if you ask your child if he's happy about simply watching his guest play, or if he would rather not play with someone who is hoarding all of the equipment. By asking this, you give your child permission to stand up for himself and draw boundaries around what he is willing to endure. If your child says that he would rather not play with such a friend, you can gently reflect this to his guest in order to help that child see the true consequence of his manner of play. If the guest indicates that he would like to return, you must lovingly help him to see that his present behavior will not very likely gain him another invitation, but that if he's willing to behave differently he would be more likely to get invited again. You must also help your child to see that he can change the situation by reclaiming some of the equipment, rather than passively accepting his guest's commands not to touch anything. You can further help your child to see that it would be balancing and good for both children if he felt ready to do this and would protect their opportunity to play more enjoyably together.

ANOTHER MOTHER: How do you know when to step in and help?

BOBBIE: Adults should step in to help whenever they observe a struggle that children can't seem to work out independently or without consequential injury. In addition, they must always respond to kids who have asked for assistance, rather than send them back to "work it out for themselves," since children who feel capable of doing this would not have summoned help.

VIOLENCE

In odd contrast to our efforts to interfere with the puppies-and-kittens style of fighting practiced by children, we allow kids to be bombarded with violent media images known to stimulate aggressive behaviors in children.[8]

In fact, the abundance of media images graphically depicting struggles between the "good" guy and the "bad" guy teach our children to feel separate from and fearful of others. Once afraid, they identify with the false power and dominance of the superhero and his weapons as the only way offered to tame the dangerous world these images have created in their minds.

Although all children are influenced by these images and the desire they stimulate to respond aggressively to the "bad guy" with "power" and "weapons," kids who have not yet surrendered to parental love or discipline and have problems with holding socialized boundaries are even more affected. Moreover, teens exposed to the genre of music that whispers negative messages in their ears or video images tempting counterculture behavior are not only desensitized to unfriendly behavior, but are drawn into rebellion, drugs, unbounded sexual exploration, and violence by these subliminal messages.

Interestingly, when we juxtapose the abundance of these negative ideas and images with the understanding that whatever we put into our minds is what we are going to create, it becomes clearer that we are the ones creating the violent world we see before us.

The irony is that although we allow our kids to repeatedly hear and view these violent media images, they are not allowed during real-life interactions to physically prevent a sibling or peer from overstepping his boundaries. They are asked, instead, to "use their words," even though their requests for appropriate behavior from peers with no interest in acting responsibly are completely ineffective.

Not surprisingly, we extend this same method of dealing with broken boundaries to our larger society as well. Instead of utilizing our legal system to effectively hold boundary-breakers accountable for their choices, we resist making it worth their while to stick with the rules, while repeatedly warning and restating our preferences for how we would like them to behave. I suspect the reason we find it so difficult to simply and neutrally hold societal boundaries is because we were taught as children to feel that something is wrong with keeping aggressors in their own yards. Yet after failing to manage either our personal or societal yards at each juncture along the way, we eventually get sick of the growing number of transgressors, and, over time, nurse our anger to the point that we develop a taste for retaliation. As a result, we come up with extreme proposals for defending ourselves with weapons, vigilante retaliation, and death penalties!

Perhaps we could regain our sanity around the aggression and violence issue if we would:

- Calmly, yet clearly, require that our children surrender to boundaries, in order to help them become the kind of adults who will understand and accept the importance of boundaries to societal order. If we succeed in this goal, our children will grow to be adults who will feel no conflict about holding the boundaries of their adult world, either with their children or others, and the entire society will become more respectful and responsive to the rules of the group.

- Allow our children to more naturally hold their own boundaries with their peers while they are young, so that they will carry within their personal neurological programming the energy of knowing how to manage their "yards" and feel safe in the world. This more natural and honest approach to aggression among children will not only enable them to better resolve their differences along the way, but will keep them and others in better balance. If they do this with neutral—even loving—hearts and follow each encounter with clearing, they will be able to sustain genuinely connected feelings between themselves and others while serving the higher self.

- Teach children at times other than when there is a specific conflict to be more heart-based and caring—not only of one another—but of the earth and its life-forms.

- Eliminate the bombardment of so many negative audio and media images by simply disallowing them in our homes and holding firmly to that boundary with the confidence that it will strongly benefit—rather than hurt—each child whose family has the courage to do it.

In taking these steps, we create an opportunity to rapidly rebalance ourselves, fully clear each misunderstanding as we go, and allow more room for the positive energies to grow and manifest in our world.

Lesson 4: "Do Your Homework"—How Homework Damages Self-Esteem and Family Relationships

The question I am asked most often is how to get kids to do their homework. This question is a challenging one for me, since I not only fail to see the educational value of so much work to be done during the child's time at home following a long day at school, but see how destructive it can be to a child's self-esteem and his family relationships. In fact, the majority of the parent-child relationships that I observe breaking down begin with battles over homework.

Moreover, children often learn to ignore this overwhelming chore that just keeps coming like the Energizer Bunny. Because kids often get away with this approach to homework, they develop a serious habit of resistance to addressing assignments, which, in turn, results in a lifelong habit of procrastination.

Rather than continue this national ritual that produces questionable results, I would rather see kids spending more of their after-school hours pursuing music, art, dance, and athletic skills—or simply enjoying time with siblings, friends, and family.

Thus, families must ask themselves if they truly believe in this commonly accepted custom of assigning children reams of homework, which parents must then strive to get them to do during the few hours they have to spend together. If parents share my concerns about this practice, they would be wise to join forces and recommend that their schools cut back on the amount of homework assigned to children of all ages. This would allow our society to recapture some of the lost family time so important to the development of a child's social values as well as to his enjoyment of life. In fact, this is a good time for all of us to reexamine the kinds of lessons our children are being taught in school and what results those lessons actually reap for us in form-ing the world of our dreams.

Yet when homework is a responsibility assigned to a child by his school, his failure to address it creates other problems. Consequently, even if you agree with my view, until workloads have been reduced, it's important to help your child succeed in addressing them. (Consult **Homework** in the Problem-Solving Guide for how to do this.)

Lesson 5: "Use Your Words" and "Share Your Possessions"— Rules that Cause Feelings of Separation

Another concept commonly taught to children is the requirement that they share their things as a means to cultivate giving hearts and cooperative play. Yet rather than result in the sociable play among peers that it's designed to develop, requiring that a child surrender his possessions often backfires and provokes closed hearts, relentless squabbling, and a need for adults to more closely monitor children under their charge. Even more important, required sharing causes peers to feel less safe with one another and, thus, interferes with bonding and friendship among them. This would explain why studies show that required kindness is not as enduring as the kindness that spills naturally from the fullness of a child's heart.

Noticing the Struggle

One day, while overhearing my children play with neighborhood friends, I recognized my error in viewing required sharing as a viable method for teaching cooperation. We lived on a street full of kids, with large numbers of them at my house much of the time. Although I enjoyed having the chil-dren around, I didn't like the constant bickering over games and toys or their regular reporting that someone had played with an item for too long or wasn't sharing.

On this particular day, it occurred to me that the sharing concept these children had been taught simply wasn't working. Instead of acting in the coop-erative manner sharing was supposed to inspire, they were continuously quarreling over toys. From that day forward, I not only stopped asking chil-dren under my management to take turns and share their activities, I began to challenge other parents and teachers to reassess the results of required shar-ing. Were they finding that kids responded to this rule with loving cooper-ation, or did it create anxious hoarding and competitive attitudes among peers? While observing children with these questions in mind, I noticed the following kinds of interactions.

Jennifer and Laurie

Jennifer had selected a purple marker and was enjoying watching the colorful liquid slide from her pen onto the paper as she formed designs and drew pictures. Then Laurie, noticing how much fun Jennifer was having with the purple pen, felt jealous of her pictures and remarked, "I need that pen. You've had it too long . . . and you have to share, you know!" When Jennifer continued to use the pen, Laurie called out, "Teacher, Jennifer won't let anybody use the purple pen . . . and I need it." The teacher looked critically at Jennifer and responded with, "All right, Jennifer, you may use the pen for three more minutes, but then it's Laurie's turn." From that moment forward, Jennifer's experience of the pen was spoiled. Her teacher was now timing her remaining use of it as Laurie anxiously awaited her turn. I could see Jennifer's heart close as her shoulder curled over her desk in an effort to shield the pen and herself from Laurie. Sharing had failed to evoke the loving, cooperative attitude it was designed to create in Jennifer, and had, instead, increased her feelings of tension and concern about losing the freedom to complete her experience.

If we stop to consider what the clearest lesson would be for this particular situation, we can see that Laurie is the one who needs to make an adjustment in order to live life with greater clarity. Thus, the teacher ought not to have indulged Laurie's jealousy by requiring that Jennifer give up the pen. Instead, she would have provided a clearer lesson by asking Laurie how she might better cope with the feeling of wanting something that was already occupied and unavailable. Once adults drop the required turn-taking that obligates children to surrender their activities to peers requesting a turn, the solicitors learn to surrender their yearning for things already in use and refocus their attention on available activities. Kids raised with this approach more naturally apply the basic rules of assertiveness, including an awareness of how to ask for only those things that are not in use, while honoring the rights of others to say "No," as well as their own right to refuse the requests of others.

It's interesting to note that we don't use this rule of required sharing in the adult world. For instance, if my friend and I occupied good seats at a popular movie or restaurant, the usher or waiter wouldn't arrive halfway through the evening to announce that we would have to relinquish our places to another group in five minutes. The others would be expected to find seats that were still available. We wouldn't use such an unreasonable rule in the adult world; yet we impose it on children, thinking that it will magically open their hearts and inspire them to feel more loving and caring toward others.

Whenever this rule has been reconsidered and thrown out, adults are not only relieved from supervising who has had what activity and for how long, but the tensions among children over sharing and waiting turns completely dissolve. As a result of feeling less stressed about activities and more relaxed around their peers, kids form deeper, more connected and caring relationships in which voluntary, unsupervised sharing has a greater chance of spilling more naturally and often from the fullness of their hearts.

Jill, an active seven-year-old, learned this lesson the hard way. She was having trouble making friends at her new school, just as she had at her former one. Thus, her teacher recommended that she "use her voice" instead of her hands whenever she behaved aggressively with the other children. Unfortunately, this wasn't helping Jill to understand the real issue, and the other children didn't like her bossy voice any more than they had liked her aggressive hands. Consequently, peers at this school began to avoid her, just as they had at the last one, and she was confused by the lack of popularity that had followed her. Only when Jill was faced with the clearer, more workable conclusion that she needed to control her desire to use all of the toys, rather than adjust her style for getting them, was she able to experience the relief of giving up her need to control everything. As a result of this simple change, Jill finally understood how to play in a manner that attracted friends to her.

Learning to Play Together

In contrast to the child who has been forced to surrender his things to peers, the child who is encouraged, but not required, to allow peers increased closeness to him and his activities will gradually feel safer and more connected to them.

Dialogue from Class

MOTHER: What if a child doesn't seem to mind sharing a toy or playing together with it?

BOBBIE: That would reflect both his interest and comfort in playing with others and would certainly not constitute a problem. Moreover, if a child was interested in joining an activity (as opposed to taking it over), I would tell him that he could check to see if his friend would like to play together; if not, he would have to look for something else. Also, if Laurie accepted that the pen wasn't available and went on to do something else, once Jennifer was finished, I might point out to her that it would be thoughtful to let Laurie know that the pen was now available.

ANOTHER MOTHER: What if Jennifer keeps the purple pen for the entire art period?

BOBBIE: That would be fine. When sharing is not required, children no longer hold onto activities beyond their normal period of interest in them as a means to torture other children waiting a turn. Consequently, if Jennifer was interested enough in the purple pen to use it all period, that would be perfectly acceptable.

MOTHER: Don't you think that's asking too much of Laurie?

BOBBIE: Our fear of seeing children experience any discomfort is what causes us to overpamper them. Not only can Laurie survive the period without the purple pen, her character will be strengthened by doing so.

A THIRD MOTHER: My eleven-month-old tries to take whatever the three-year-old has, and the three-year-old says, "No, that's mine." I agree that it's rightfully his, but I don't know how to deal with the eleven-month-old. Should I distract her with her own toys?

BOBBIE: Your job will be to help the eleven-month-old learn to control her impulse for touching everything the three-year-old has, much in the way you would help her to control her impulse to touch your stove or stereo. You can direct her attention to her toys or a community toy, but if she persists in focusing on the occupied toys of the three-year-old, then you will have to remove her to another area or a playpen for awhile until she catches on to what is being asked of her. Interestingly, I find that when an older child is made to feel that his things are safe from a younger sibling, he no longer feels a need to protect his space and hoard his toys; instead, he gets relaxed around the baby and is more inclined to want to play together and share from his heart.

FATHER: If we always tell a child that he doesn't have to share, won't it stop him from voluntarily wanting to do it sometimes?

BOBBIE: It's important that adults not say, "He doesn't have to share the toy" but use the language of, "That toy is occupied now . . . If Johnny wants to use it together with you, that would be fine and would help the two of you to feel closer, but if he's not ready to do that, you will need to look around for something that's free."

FATHER: Is there any time when you would ask a child to share his things?

BOBBIE: Yes. Anytime a child is hosting a guest at his home, he must make certain toys available for use as community toys while his friend is there. Also, when a child gets to be about three or four I would introduce the idea of passing his unused items on to charity. In the case of hosting a friend, the sharing would be required (see following section on visiting friends), whereas with charity it would be encouraged, but voluntary.

Nonrequired Sharing at School

When sharing isn't required at school, children are allowed to play with any one of the community toys or activities they have selected until they are finished. Once a child voluntarily puts the item he is using away, it's regarded as free again and available for others to use.

Anytime a child is playing in a group activity, such as the block corner or in a ball or tag game, other children may join in without asking his permission. Although it would be against the rules to rearrange the projects or games others are creating, they would be permitted to cooperatively join the games or play in the same general area and use the unoccupied equipment.

Dialogue from Class

MOTHER: What if a child stays on a brand-new swing or bike for the entire playground period and never frees it for the other children?

BOBBIE: It's best not to be tempted to impose any restrictions even on the biggest or newest bikes. If we don't make the new bike even more special by timing it, children will adjust more quickly to its newness and will eventually feel ready to get off.

ANOTHER MOTHER: My child is rather shy and is the type who will never get a chance on a bike if his teacher doesn't help him.

BOBBIE: Whenever teachers help timid children to gain turns on the bikes, those children are never faced with the reality that timidity doesn't work very well in life. Thus, rather than supervise bike-sharing, it's more effective when adults teach a timid child to be more alert and courageous in getting to the bikes.

☙☙☙

Nonrequired Sharing at Home with Siblings

When sharing is not required at home, personal possessions owned by various family members are not used by others without permission. On the other hand, nonpersonal things are considered community property and are available for use any time they are not occupied by another family member. One exception to this would be if the owner carelessly leaves his personal things in the community area on a regular basis. In such cases, a natural consequence would be that his things are subject to community use. I would probably not use this rule for an item rarely left in the community area by a generally responsible child.

Nonrequired Sharing at Home with Guests

Before friends come to play, it helps to discuss what will be expected of the host. For example, he needs to understand that his guest won't have his own possessions with him and will expect to use the activities and toys at their house in the same way he would use them at school. Consequently, any treasured toys that your child doesn't feel ready to have included as community activities must be put away before his guest arrives. All other things will be treated as community property.

It's important to further prepare the host ahead of time to remain calm while his guest plays with his things, since other children will not want to play at his house if they are expected to stand by and watch him control all of the activities and toys. If he's in conflict about allowing his guest to use his possessions, he must consider whether or not he would simply prefer the afternoon alone, playing with the toys all by himself. If that's the case, it would be better not to invite friends over until he feels ready to handle their use of his things. In this way, your child is not forced to share his toys with guests and is in control of doing so only when he feels ready. By the same token, he must realize that he's not free to have guests over until he's ready to take that step. I would help such a child to look at the reality that friendships are more rewarding than toys, and that learning to let other children use his things opens the door to valued friendships.

Dialogue from Class

MOTHER: What if a child prefers to play with his toys rather than have a friend over?

BOBBIE: Children who select toys over friends usually have parents who have purchased too many toys, spend a great deal of time acting as their children's playmates, or allow their kids to watch indiscriminate amounts of television. Because such children are so highly entertained by their toys, parents, and television, their motivation to get along with peers is damaged.

MOTHER: That's me! (laugh)

BOBBIE: If you require that your child entertain himself more often, he will gradually develop an interest in learning to get along with his age-mates. It's also helpful to teach him the value and pleasure in feeling connected to others and making friends.

MOTHER: What if he planned to have his toys serve as community toys, but then when his friend arrived, decided he couldn't face sharing them?

BOBBIE: He must then choose between controlling the toys and having his friend stay, but it can't be both. If he wants to keep his friend there, he must accept that part of friendship is surrendering control over all of the toys.

MOTHER: What if he chooses the toys?

BOBBIE: I would let him choose that. But then I would calmly make sure that the rest of his afternoon was spent only with toys, so that he would have an opportunity to experience the true result of his choice without other distractions. This would give him an opportunity to understand in greater depth the result of the choice he made.

MOTHER: What if he gets fussy, and I can't stand it; is it okay to let him go to the park or watch television?

BOBBIE: I wouldn't. I think it's critical that he experience the boredom that comes when he's unwilling to take the steps required to get along with peers. If you distract him from his boredom, he won't learn the lesson and will continue to rely on you and the television to entertain him.

ANOTHER MOTHER: What about the other child? Is it fair to send him home?

BOBBIE: I would gently share with the guest that my child wasn't feeling ready to share his toys, but that next time he would be ready and they would have a better time together. It's important not to be angry or degrade your child in any way, as you want to preserve his friend's feelings of comfort in your home as well as his interest in playing with your child at a later date.

A THIRD MOTHER: What do you do if the visiting child is attached to the sharing rule?

BOBBIE: I would explain our family rule to the child and let him know that it's the one used while playing at our house, but that when playing at his house, he can choose which of the two rules he likes best.

☺☺☺

Developing Caring and Cooperation

Once we release the outdated lessons that life must be fair, fights are not allowed, and sharing is required as our primary prescriptions for evoking caring in our children, we must seek new ways to convey this important message.

The answer to how to do this came to me one day as I witnessed a mother interrupt her twin daughters' special encounter with a pair of dolphins swimming in a hotel lagoon. She instructed her girls first to wash the sand from their feet, then to notice a tree in bloom, and finally suggested that they go upstairs to shower and return later to watch the afternoon dolphin show. This mother missed seeing that the pair of dolphins had singled her girls out and had been swimming back and forth in front of them flirting and playing only with them, while the rest of us looked on. The girls were enchanted by this interplay and—although they complied with each of their mother's suggestions—were visibly distraught by her interruptions to their unique experience.

I realized that this mother was not "tuned in" to the deeper essence of her environment and strived, instead, to manage the surface of things. It occurred to me as I watched that we all need to learn how to be more consciously attuned to the world around us and experience its essence from our hearts. Only in this way can we be in touch and moved by life, allow it to stir our hearts, and feel love and caring from deep within ourselves for the world we live in, its creatures, and people. The best place to begin is by teaching our children this wonderful skill.

This ability is best taught by taking heartfelt moments with our children to pause and look at flowers, insects, or animals, while sensing the essence of life flowing through them, rather than unthinkingly walk past them or stamp out their tiny, fragile lives. You can further teach your children to carry the harmless bugs that make their way into your home back outdoors to find their families or begin life anew. It's also helpful when you take care not to interrupt any of your children's interactions with others by directing them to say "Hi," or suggesting that they tell about an activity or story. Allow time and space for them and the other person or animal to develop their own relationship.

In addition, you can sensitize your kids to young children, older people, peers, the hungry and homeless, different races, endangered species, and other animals by pointing out their attractiveness and vulnerabilities as well as their universal desire to be appreciated and loved. You can further help them to find ways to actively care for others by involving them in caring gestures and "random acts of kindness" which you can plan together and act upon.

Each time we sensitize our children to looking at the world and listening to it from their hearts, while joining us in acts of caring, giving, and kindness, true urges to love, care, and share will develop from deep within them.

We can further teach our children that our internal feelings and attitudes as well as our behaviors are magnets that draw similar people and experiences to us. Thus, if we are judgmental and attacking, we will find ourselves dealing with the judgments of others. If we fill our minds with violent images, violence will become an increasing presence in our world. By the same token, if our hearts are filled with the bliss of gratitude, love, and giving, we will find ourselves surrounded by appreciative, kind, and generous people and joyful, heartfelt experiences.

Once we understand how this works, it becomes clear why a child who has been taught to feel and act gently toward life, experience compassion and caring for its variety of people and creatures, and send ripples of love forth into the world will naturally and genuinely become a more loving friend. Using this approach, rather than prying his hands open to give up treasured toys to jealous friends, is more likely to encourage a child's heart to genuinely open and his caring for others to develop honestly. In this way, he develops as his higher self.

The "Right" Train

Once our kids know how to jump into life and become fully immersed in helping to create a better, more loving world for the collective whole, we can trust that they are on the "right" train headed for a fulfilling life in a joyful, Technicolor world.

The "right" train can be found through illumination
of the unclear places.

★★★

11

Communication

The Bridge That Bonds

The Tenth Key:

ⓖⓖⓖ

Heart-centered communications connect us to one another.

One sunny morning as I observed a classroom full of kindergartners coloring in their workbooks, Kenny looked out the window for a moment before reaching into his color box for a yellow crayon. Clasping his tongue between his lips, he began to fill in the sky portion of his picture. However, his concentration was soon interrupted by his teacher's cheerful voice insisting, "Oh no, Kenny! The sky isn't *yellow*! You'll need to find your *blue* crayon for the sky!" Kenny looked crushed, then confused, but after one last glance outdoors, did as he was told.

This denial of Kenny's perception disturbed me, and I looked out the window to see if I could understand what this five-year-old had seen. As my eyes followed the direction Kenny's had taken, I was startled by how much yellow the morning sun was casting across the sky and over the mountains. The sky was, indeed, bursting with a golden light that Kenny's teacher had failed to notice. I was troubled by this unfortunate experience in Kenny's day and wondered how often adults fail to validate the deeper perceptions, ideas, and feelings of children before bombarding them with opinions of their own.

Because adults can learn so much from the fresh perceptions of children, it's important that they take care not to automatically alter all youthful ideas to match their own, but strive, instead, to understand them. This continues to be important as a child reaches adolescence, since studies show that the reason teens listen more to their peers than to adults is because their friends understand them in a way that their parents have failed to achieve.

Consequently, it's important to remember that redirecting a child's view of things is a big responsibility that should be undertaken only when his outlook is distorted in a way that would be harmful to himself or others. When his view is simply fresh and new—as Kenny's was—it must be heard deeply, honored fully, and allowed not only to stand, but to influence. In fact, learning to truly understand your children and teens is the very thing that will assure your continued communications with them.

In order to distinguish when to accept your child's views and when it's appropriate to redirect them, you must first listen to him closely enough to understand what he is expressing. Thus, during this phase of communication, you must refrain from imposing your own ideas and expectations of how you would like him to think or feel and allow him, instead, to reveal who he is and how he views things. To succeed in this, you must learn the skills of deep listening and perception needed to achieve understanding.

Achieving Understanding

The primary purpose of all communication is to gain an understanding of another's viewpoint in order to see and feel the same pictures he sees or feels and vice versa. It's through this mutual sharing of perceptions that genuine closeness and true understanding are felt.

Experiencing this level of understanding allows us to go beyond our limited, individual viewpoints and discover the larger world our combined perceptions create. It's as though we each stand on opposite peaks of the same mountain looking into a common valley below. While one person may see a grove of trees on the mountainside across from him, the other may see a small village, nestled into the hills.

One view is not correct while the other is wrong; both are valid and simply reflect different aspects of reality. Thus, the goal is not to struggle over whose perception is correct, but to share these differing views with each other so that both parties can form an image—and understanding—of the larger whole. To do this, we must gather more information about what the other person is seeing, try on what it would be like to view things from his vantage point or feel the way he does, and allow his information to blend with our own understanding of things.

To accomplish this level of understanding with your child, you must have faith in the depth and quality of his perceptions and be open to learning from them, not only about how he thinks and feels, but about life in general. When you are able to do this, your child feels uniquely valued and takes pleasure in sharing himself with you. Unexpectedly, your view of life is deliciously expanded in the exchange, and you both emerge more fulfilled.

Developing the Art of Listening

How you behave during communication with your children determines exactly what and how much they will share with you. If you resist the urge to interrupt, defend, dominate, and control communications, but listen carefully and respond sensitively, you become privy to their secrets; if not, you obstruct opportunities for meaningful communication and connection.

Establishing a Listener. The most serious breakdown in communication comes when there are two speakers and no listeners. The person speaking wants to be heard and understood, but finds it impossible to hold the attention of his listener.

Because most "listeners" are so anxious to share their own opinions or defend against the fragments they have managed to hear, they interrupt the speaker before he is finished. The speaker, in turn, becomes increasingly anxious to complete his ideas and intercedes to regain the floor. The result is that there are two speakers vying for an audience with no listeners to be found. This difficulty gets magnified when adults use dominance to require that their child be quiet and listen, while he sits in silence, yearning to speak and be heard.

The solution to this dilemma lies in the listener learning to remain in the role of listener for as long as it takes to fully receive the message being delivered. Thus, parents must learn to become true listeners and require that their children do the same. Those of you who would like to accomplish this goal must consciously choose to be good listeners, remain in that role for as long as needed, and bypass all urges to interrupt or take over the function of speaker. In effect, the goal of communication is to understand first; being understood comes later.

Deep Listening. Once we see the value of listening carefully enough to understand the views of our children and others, we must determine how to do it. I was fortunate in making this discovery as a counselor in which my primary role was that of careful listener. What I learned from my counseling experience was that getting very still and shifting into my heart enabled me not only to hear the words of others, but to tune into their hearts as well. In this way, I learned to sense even more of what they were feeling and saying.

As I later practiced this skill with children, I was amazed to discover how keen their perceptions can be, how insightful their understanding, and how exquisitely magical their humor and wisdom become when we truly listen.

I began to realize that the more I could understand children—and others—at this heart-based, intuitive level, the more open and caring I felt toward them. I further discovered how wonderful people are and how much we all want simply to be understood and accepted. This level of listening not only made others feel understood and safe, but in the presence of it, they responded from a higher, more honest and heartfelt place within themselves. As a result, I learned from these encounters that being a true "understander" was the greatest gift I had to offer another individual, particularly a child.

Over time, it occurred to me that if everyone could learn to listen from his or her heart, we would all enjoy a deeper level of communication with one another. I then examined the heart-centered style of communication I had learned in order to share it with others and came up with the following observations.

▶ *Being Available.* It's important to be available during those periods when your child is interested in communicating, since you won't be able to recapture his open and available moments at a later time. It's also important to convey the message that you have unlimited time and patience for listening to whatever your child has to offer, no matter what his level of development or ability to express himself. This availability shows your child that you not only care about him, but are interested in what he has to say.

On the other hand, should your child misuse your availability and strive to engage you continuously in senseless and silly conversation or endless imagined stories, be clear when you have lost interest and feel free to disengage. Your availability is meant to be for genuine communication and mutual pleasure, rather than to sentence you to the role of audience for an unnatural performance. Thus, your availability only works when your child shows up as his real and genuine self.

▶ *Paying Attention.* Good communication with your child begins when you are willing to put aside all reading and projects, turn off the television, and sit with him for an unlimited period of time. It's essential that you not interrupt your child while he is speaking with such things as offering more food, answering the telephone, or, if you are en route somewhere, fussing about the other drivers. Staying focused on your child in this way communicates that he is valuable to you and will take precedence over life's small distractions.

▶ *Breaking the Interruption, Defense, and Denial Habit.* Next to impatience, the most common and serious communication error parents make is to interrupt their child while he is still speaking in order to complete his sentences, correct his details, respond with comments of their own, ask questions about what he is saying, promote an opposing viewpoint, defend their own actions, criticize him, boss and scold, or otherwise minimize and deny his reality in some way. Such interruptions and denials not only cause a child to feel invalidated and unheard, they put him in an impossible environment in which the truth he sees is invisible to others. This experience can be so frustrating that he verbally withdraws, and his family—completely unaware of how their interruptions have silenced him—puzzle over why he is so closed and barely speaks.

If you wish to keep communication with your children open, you will need to stop interruptive behaviors, hurried problem-solving, and denials and defenses; then, put your own thoughts on a shelf and listen with a mind quiet enough to hear your child deeply.

Listening With a Quiet Mind and Open Heart. Listening with a still mind requires that the listener not only refrain from audibly interrupting the speaker with his own thoughts and opinions, but quiet the busy chatter and endless judgments within his head as well.

During this process, the listener becomes indifferent to his own thoughts or feelings and puts them momentarily on a shelf to make way for the ideas of the speaker. To accomplish this, he must consciously shift his awareness away from the busy chatter in his head and move it to his heart, then focus on the feelings it carries. As a result of this shift, the listener's heart softens his judgments toward the speaker, while his mind gets quiet enough to receive whatever information the speaker has to offer. His only remaining job is to sit calmly with a still mind, using his heart as his receiver.

It's most exciting when we listen in this manner to children, since a child's way of perceiving an event or experience can be so fresh and interesting—as was Kenny's impression of the yellow sky.

▶ *Intuitive Listening.* Truly deep listening is synonymous with intuitive listening. Although most parents listen intuitively to their children while they are still young and preverbal, they later allow this skill to diminish or atrophy altogether once their child learns to talk. Happily, you can reawaken this intuitive ability by becoming more interested, attentive, quiet, and receptive again, rather than remaining primarily opinionated, questioning, critical, combative, judgmental, or interruptive in your communications with children. The key is to practice listening with a gentle heart and quiet mind which, in turn, opens you to more sensitive, telepathic communication.

Dialogue from Class

Mother: I'm often angry when communicating with my kids, and I feel very cut off from all feeling between us, except for my irritations.

Bobbie: That's because feelings of irritation and anger cloud the sensitivities that would otherwise allow you to passively receive the feelings of your child and thus act as a shield over your heart. Whenever this happens, deep listening is blocked.

Mother: Even if I wasn't angry, I'm not sure that I would know how to listen more deeply.

Bobbie: When you are first practicing deep listening it helps to consciously shift down to your heart and remember your love for your child. This puts you into a soft and gentle receiving state, in contrast to the active, judgmental, combative state of disappointment, irritation, and anger. From that quieter, more receptive place of caring and compassion, you can ask what is happening or what might be worrying or confusing your child. Only in this way can you deeply understand the mysteries and magic hidden within him that he is now ready to reveal.

Getting All The Way To Understanding. Once we are open and listening deeply, we can pull the information we hear through the gears of our minds, the beat of our hearts, and the tenor of our emotions. By thus weaving the child's world into our own, we more fully share his perception of things. In this moment we have become the *understander*.

Responding

Once a communication has been accurately perceived and understood, it's the listener's turn to speak. Thus, anytime you have both heard and understood your child, you're free to respond to what he has shared.

When responding, the key is to look for ways to support your child for having shared his truth with you. Thus, whether he needs help in expressing an emotion, resolving a problem, adjusting a viewpoint, conducting a clearing, or simply chatting and sharing himself, it's essential that you respond with a consistently supportive, nonthreatening style. The thing to remember is that speaking with blame or attack invites defense and counterattack, whereas speaking gently from your heart invites your child's heart to remain open and to respond in kind.

Pulling Scarves

Anytime your child shares some information with you, rather than pounce on it with critiques, judgments, lectures, or admonitions, allow his information to rest safely on the table between you. This not only helps your child to feel safe in exposing himself to you, it encourages the kind of open and honest sharing that leads to increased feelings of understanding and connection between you. Thus, your primary job during communication is to simply enjoy your child's information and take genuine interest in it.

I like to think in terms of using any pieces of information a child offers as the tip of a scarf that can be pulled from a magician's hat in order to gain access to more of the child's thoughts, feelings, and insights. I am most effective in pulling information from a child when I ask the interesting kinds of Socratic or inquiring questions Barbara Walters or Larry King might ask in an interview. If I then use the material offered in response to my questions to stimulate more questions, good discussions, and a mature exchange of ideas—even if we gently disagree—the child will want to tell me more, and we become closer in the exchange.

Whenever I encounter an unclear point of view that needs unraveling, I continue to use the Socratic style of inquiry, while designing my questions to patiently lead the child, as he strives to respond to each inquiry, into seeing his own error of logic. This gentle approach allows him to feel safe enough to see the error of his thinking as it methodically unfolds before him. Once he can see the error, he becomes open to selecting new, more effective conclusions about the way life works.

Perception-Checking and Reflective Interpretation

When communicating about troubling emotions or problems, more sensitive and careful forms of communication such as *perception-checking* and *reflective interpretation* are required. Here's how they work.

Once you have given your child an opportunity to thoroughly express his point of view regarding some sensitive issue or problem, your job is to *perception-check*, or determine whether or not you have perceived his message correctly.

It's ineffective to ask him direct questions such as, "Why did you do that?" Or, "What's bothering you?" The truth is he doesn't know, and that's what he'll tell you. If he had that much understanding of his feelings and actions, he wouldn't be behaving badly or be in need of your help. You must strive, instead, to formulate your hunch about what you think your child is expressing and convert it to a simpler, more direct message. Then, without judgment or a personal reaction, reflect your hypothesis back to your child and wait for him to validate it, make small corrections in it, or let you know that you have misunderstood him altogether. By having him either validate or refine what you believe you have heard, you hone the accuracy of your listening and get as close as possible to holding the same picture your child is holding. This process is repeated until your child experiences being understood. Only then is this part of the communication complete.

Once you have fully understood your child's message, you can trade roles with your child, and it becomes your turn to express your point of view. Whenever he fails to understand you accurately, teach him how to perception-check by asking him to repeat back to you what he thinks he heard, then wait for your agreement or correction. This exchange of roles goes back and forth between listener and speaker until everyone feels completely heard and fully understood. Not only does this process eliminate misunderstandings, it stimulates additional communication as your child corrects the reflections you have offered or shares what he has heard from you.

Whenever your child is unable to fully verbalize the complexity of his feelings, reflective interpretation provides a tool you can use to dig deeper. In *reflective interpretation*, you not only draw from the information provided by your child, but incorporate whatever else you know about him and his antecedents to develop your interpretation of the situation. You might, for example, review his prior conclusions about life; what has been going on more recently for him; or, you might simply observe his behavior, facial expressions, body language, and general attitude to help you assess what he is currently experiencing.

You then synthesize this information and reflect back a selection—or "menu"—of hunches and hypotheses that you believe might describe his viewpoint or problem as you would interpret it. You also offer him an alternate possibility for each of your hunches, which gives him a full range of suggestions to choose from. You might, for instance, ask a child concerned about making errors, "Are you worrying that I might be upset if you make a mistake? Or is it that *you* don't like it when you have made an error? Or are you worried that the other kids might laugh if you mess up?" Unless you interpret the situation for the child in this manner, he is often unaware of what is troubling him or how to express it. Thus, reflective interpretation not only opens up communication between you and your child, but offers him an opportunity to get clearer about his own feelings.

Whenever you combine deep, intuitive listening with perception-checking and reflective interpretation during clearing or problem solving, your child can learn from his problems, while feeling understood and close to you in the process.

Avoid Common Communication Errors During Responding

Following are a number of erroneous responses parents make that not only convey negative messages to their child, but interfere with his ability to communicate in a clear and open manner.

- **Flattening Versus Probing.** Some of you mistakenly close off communication, rather than probe enough to explore the deeper feelings and conflicts involved, simply because you are uncomfortable with these more intense aspects of communication. Thus, rather than flatten feelings or rush too quickly to solutions, you would be wise to spend more time examining your child's ideas and feelings on a subject. You can do this best by pulling the tip of every scarf he offers.

- **Changing the Subject.** Parents often get their feelings hurt by what their child says to them, then change the subject from what the child is expressing to what they want to say. Part of becoming a good listener is to learn not to filter what you hear through your own feelings, since that changes the subject from what your child is experiencing to what you are feeling. It will be more useful for you to get calm, reduce your own sensitivity to what is said, and use the communication as an opportunity to learn what your child is thinking and feeling.

- **Lecturing.** Some of you view parent-child communications as times for lecturing your child in hopes that he will absorb your ideas and values. Not only does this technique fail to effectively teach your child, it trains him to endure communications with you, rather than view them as rewarding.

- **Defensive Communication.** Defensive communication begins when one person interjects an impatient or angry tone of voice into the communication in order to defend himself, while blaming, criticizing, or attacking the other person. Once this is initiated, the other person is left with the options of accepting the defense or attack; counterdefending or counterattacking; withdrawing from the communication; or going to his heart as he calmly waits for the attacker to back down. More often than not, this person selects counterdefense and counterattacking, which escalates the defensive style of communication between them and blocks all opportunity for clarity.

Thus, the person who first notices what has happened would be wise to gently hold up his or her hand in a gesture inviting peace and suggest that they use the Heartmath technique of "freezing," or stopping, then "switching" their awareness from their heads to their hearts. This shift can more easily be made in the heat of battle by remembering something from nature that is easily and deeply loved. During freezing, each person can take note of what is happening and their part in it, then recommit to facing and telling only the truth about the matter. Once this is accomplished and both parties feel peaceful again, they can resume their conversation. Some people will need more time to get calm, and can ask for a short break. However, this break need not be lengthy and should not be used as a time to mentally pursue the anger. Moreover, a time must always be arranged for meeting again within a half hour or so—rather than leaving the communication open-ended and unresolved.

■ **Expressing Disappointment and Anger.** Nothing threatens a child's spirit or the positive feelings between parent and child more than disappointed and angry communications. Consequently, those of you who are angry should calm down, get back into balance, and embrace the reality of what is happening in your child's world. Only then will you be in a position to lovingly help him face and strengthen the areas in his development that need addressing. (For more information on anger, see Chapter 4.)

■ **Overencouraging the Expression of Emotion.** Because we have become aware of the negative effects of blocking our genuinely painful emotions or tucking uncomfortable ones away, adults often encourage children to express their feelings, even during those times when their emotions are filled with distortions, blame, and attack or are being used to get their way on something. It's not uncommon, for instance, to hear parents in the middle of disciplining say to children who are yelling at them, "It's okay to be angry."

Yet encouraging kids to express their aggressive feelings, especially while asking that they adjust to not getting their way, creates a conflicting message. Thus, parents would be wise to distinguish between when a child's emotions are distorted or aggressive and need not be encouraged, and when it would be valuable to help him sort them out. Yet, regardless of what they conclude, it's critical that all feelings surrounding discipline be aired only during clearing.

Dialogue from Class

MOTHER: So, we don't have to listen when our kids are screaming at us about their feelings?

BOBBIE: No. Good communication does not include indulging a child in yelling or speaking aggressively. There are very few people outside of a family unit who will tolerate such hostile communication, and you do your child a disservice to teach him that it's an acceptable style of communication. Even when he does succeed in getting his way by using anger with people who fear this emotion, he will ultimately lose the relationship as well as his opportunity to function as his higher self. Thus, it's all right for him to express emotion— even strong emotion—but it's not okay to attack or "dump" his angry feelings on others.

☉☉☉

■ **Abusing Privileged Information.** Many of you block open and honest communication by failing to treat whatever information your child has voluntarily exposed with respect.

All information a child shares must be considered privileged and can neither be used against him nor told to others without his permission. For example, if your child or teen voluntarily tells you that he is getting a late start on a science project, it would be improper to require that he cancel his weekend plans to work on it. In this case, your only job will be to offer friendly ideas and support in creating a plan for getting it done. It's also important to acknowledge him for facing the need to address it, rather than continuing to ignore it. Similarly, if he complains of a teacher's rudeness or his coach's anger, it's inappropriate for you to call the teacher or coach to extract explanations or apologies. Whenever you misuse your child's confidences in this way, he will not only stop sharing information with you, but will find ways to deceive you instead.

The less dominance, preaching, and control you use and the more you invite your child to participate in parallel communications, the safer he will feel about sharing his world and inviting your guidance.

- **The Problem with "I" Messages.** Many of you have been taught to communicate with children by expressing your feelings about his behavior in the form of "I" messages. Although this concept is designed to create gentler communication between parent and child, problems develop when feelings are used to express rules and boundaries.

Dialogue from Class

FATHER: I've been telling my six-year-old how I feel about his behavior by saying such things as, "Daddy has trouble reading the paper when you run your trucks over my toes." Then when he keeps doing it, I get annoyed because he isn't caring about my feelings and needs.

BOBBIE: That's a perfect example of a situation that requires communicating your boundaries, rather than your feelings, and it's important not to confuse the two. Your son is either allowed to run the trucks over you or he's not, and it's your job to clearly make a selection and then communicate which option you have chosen. An explanation of the feelings that brought you to this conclusion can be offered separately, once he has surrendered to the rule.

ꙮꙮꙮ

- **The Problem with Planned Praise and Attention.** It's commonly believed that consciously planned praise and attention will encourage children to perform at higher levels, an idea that particularly appeals to busy families trying to spur their kids to the top as efficiently as possible.

    This notion became popular as a result of behavioral experiments, performed initially with animals and later with retarded and emotionally disturbed children. In these experiments, positive reinforcement proved useful in breaking through the defective systems of brain-damaged or disturbed children by enabling therapists to capture their attention for long enough to encourage desirable behaviors. In essence, these techniques produced important breakthroughs for a specialized population that could not otherwise be reached.

    Due to the high level of success in working with injured children in this way, it was theorized that positive reinforcement programs would work equally well in shaping desirable behaviors and accelerated performance in the general population of children. However, a number of problems in using this system with normal children have emerged that were not anticipated. In fact, we can now see that consciously planned praise and attention not only interfere with a normal child's development and positive feelings about himself, but have replaced other forms of more genuine connection and communication between adults and kids. As a result, I view self-conscious, yet condescending praise as a serious deterrent to more authentic communication, genuine acknowledgment, and meaningful bonds with children.

Following are some of the reasons this kind of praise interferes with natural communication and hinders the opportunity to go deeper.

Planned Praise Deposes the Internal Reinforcer. When you observe a young child absorbed in some activity such as art, you can see genuine excitement and feelings of competence gathering within him which, in turn, fuel his enjoyment of that activity. These internal feelings of real and natural pleasure serve as the child's internal reinforcer, which not only keeps his interest in an activity alive, but gives birth to his passions.

Anytime you interrupt a child to praise his picture or other activity in hopes of inspiring him to do it more often or better, you disconnect him from his own internally reinforcing experience and cause him to focus, instead, on how you and others feel about what he is doing. These intrusions eventually extinguish his inner fire by training him to ignore its feedback in favor of the response of others. This leaves his self-esteem vulnerable as he relies primarily on the unpredictable and often inaccurate, external assessment of others in his effort to feel good about himself. Once a child's internal motivator begins to atrophy in this way, he gets separated from his inner self, and his energy becomes frantic as he searches for the external praise of others to fill the emptiness that remains. Before long, it becomes difficult to connect and communicate with such a frantic, attention-seeking child.

Dialogue from Class

MOTHER: I have a six-year-old daughter and seven-year-old son who are addicted to my watching everything they do. Whenever they are swimming and I'm not giving them my attention, they start calling, "Mom, Mom, watch me jump." I'll say, "Oh that's very good!" and then go back to my reading.

BOBBIE: Wouldn't it be more honest to say, "I'm not really watching you now, because I'm reading my book."

MOTHER: Then they would say, "But look what I can do," and quickly jump into the water. So I find it easier to just say, "That's great!"

BOBBIE: Your children's constant requests of you to watch indicate that they are hooked on attention. Be aware that this is a learned "need," since kids don't really require that we look at them all of the time. Unfortunately, once they develop this addiction, they get disconnected from their own experience and become more intense and "hyper" in their search for the attention of others.

MOTHER: Yes, I've noticed that. It's as though they can't enjoy one jump without me watching; yet they're so busy calling to me that they're not paying attention to what they're doing.

BOBBIE: Yes. When children behave like this, their performing energy makes it harder for others to connect with them, which is, ironically, the very thing they are striving to achieve when they call for attention. I suggest that you wean your kids from this addiction by facing them with the reality that you will watch them swim from time to time, but only as you are moved to do so, rather than in response to their calling. You can offer to have them sit with you if they want to connect, but let them know that if they prefer to continue swimming, they will have to do it without insisting on an audience. In this way, you help them to give up the need for external responses so that they can reconnect with their own enjoyment of swimming.

ANOTHER MOTHER: How would you relate this to a younger child who has just mastered a toy by getting the ring over the knob?

BOBBIE: When a young child first accomplishes a new task, he will often look to us to check our reaction, not so much for exaggerated adulation, but to see if he is on the right track and has succeeded in the goal. If we nod and smile our enthusiasm and simply say, "All right!" he knows that he has met the goal and that we are happy for him in his accomplishment. Yet this response should neither be consciously planned nor so overdone with whoops and hollers that it lacks in naturalness; neither should it overshadow his own internal feedback so much that he remembers more about our praise than his experience.

ම‍ම‍ම

Planned Praise Treats Normal Behavior Abnormally. When praise is used as a reinforcing technique, too much of it is given too easily for ordinary activities that would not normally merit acclaim.

By making such a fuss, you train your child to expect great adulation for normal behaviors. He then becomes an unnatural performer, self-centered, plastic, and show-offy, while constantly sneaking glances to see if others are observing. Whenever his audience has lost interest, he insistently demands that they "Watch, one more time!" as he frantically wiggles and shakes to hold the spotlight. Although most adults politely respond with, "Very good," there is nothing special to watch, and if the truth were known, they find the praised and attention-seeking child somewhat tedious.

Deals, bargains, and rewards are even stronger reinforcers used to elicit better behavior or higher performance from children. Yet anytime we reward age-appropriate levels of cooperation or participation in life, we imply that being good or working hard is so unusual that we must offer gifts to encourage it. Once kids realize that adults will reward them for average behaviors—or worse—pay them to stop abnormal ones, many resist normal behaviors or purposely develop abnormal ones, then require that adults pay to get them to behave! In fact, one eight-year-old was overheard telling his younger sister that if she was really bad, the adults would give her stickers to shape up and cooperate. Bright kids often up the ante for good behavior and, as they get older, will even add threats of suicide as their highest stake of all.

It has been my observation that children do better when the basic rules of life are presented as commonplace, rather than special, and are expected to be adhered to and obeyed, rather than praised and rewarded when followed.

Dialogue from Class

MOTHER: How do I handle it if my daughter seeks some kind of acknowledgment or praise for a picture she has drawn?

BOBBIE: If she says, "Look at my picture," it's not realistic to say, "I don't want to comment on that." It's okay to say, "It's a great picture" or "I'm impressed" if indeed you are. However, if you have previously trained her to be addicted to external reinforcement, it's helpful to also begin to wean her from the desire to be praised. You might, for instance, respond with, "How do *you* like your picture? You had such a pleased look on your face while you were painting it; was there a feeling inside you to match that look?" In this way, you help her to tune back into her own experience and the inner feelings associated with her internal reinforcer. One wise teacher responds to the kids who call for her attention by covering her eyes with her hands and asking, "Is it still fun?"

When planned praise is dropped from the program, children stop expecting compliments for every little thing they do and lose interest in seeking so much acknowledgment outside of themselves. This frees them to focus on their own internal feelings about themselves and the things they accomplish as well as to take more interest in others. In doing this, they remain connected enough to their own feelings that they fall in love with themselves and thus with others. This is the path of the higher self and the true source of self-esteem.

FATHER: I like to let my daughter know that I think she's bright so I tell her how smart she is. I can see that I'm making her so self-conscious about it that she's starting to feel concerned about making mistakes.

BOBBIE: Actually, singling a child out as brighter than others often backfires, since children who are made to feel that they are especially smart feel pressured to perform at uniquely high levels. This pressure can lead to a fear of failure and a desire to withdraw from activities altogether. It's better to more naturally enjoy a child's brightness by talking to him about interesting things.

TEACHER: What if it feels natural in a classroom setting to say, "That coloring is beautiful, Justin!"

BOBBIE: Then say it by all means, and know that such comments can be very real. It's always okay to mention a child's strengths during those times when it spills from your awareness and heart and is not done deliberately as part of a planned program to motivate him.

However, any time you notice that you are offering planned praise and deliberate comments on what a good job a child is doing with the goal of encouraging his performance, then you are probably manipulating him to be better or do more. The ironic result of trying to get a child to do more artwork is that he will probably do less. Anytime a child's awareness has been drawn away from his artwork and given to the audience, he is no longer as immersed in his painting, unless someone else is watching. Once he's more caught up in the praise than his painting, he may lose his potential for becoming an artist.

ꙮꙮꙮ

Planned Praise Teaches Conditional Love and Acceptance. Programmed attention, praise, and reward subtly serve as evaluative judgments of a child's performance and are given conditionally, whenever he is error-free or has pleased the adult. In effect, planned praise says, "I like you because . . ." and "I'm more interested in you when . . . ." As a result, the consciously praised child is left with the impression that people are happier with him when he's surpassing others than when he's making mistakes. For the child in the middle of a long-term learning curve, this can be a rather discouraging proposition.

In addition, parents who use planned praise and attention to reinforce a child often use their opposites—ignoring, withdrawing, criticism, and anger—to discourage unwanted behaviors. Either way, conscious praise and attention—or the withholding of it—give a child the impression that successful behaviors and getting ahead make him more desirable, while errors cost him his position at the top and threaten his lovability.

Carl Thorenson and his associates from Stanford's School of Education discovered that people with "Type A" personality patterns—possessing an impatient, hostile, and angry orientation toward life—had childhoods in which love was contingent on being good, obeying the rules, doing well in school, or excelling in some sport or activity. Because their parents used praise and criticism to improve their performance, these people felt that they were loved as children not for who they were, but for what they did.

As we can see from this discovery, the child who grows up with praise and reward—and the conditional acceptance they imply—develops a fear of judgment and criticism, as well as the errors that evoke them. His subsequent concern about making mistakes and his drive to be "perfect" interfere with his ability to establish close communications and warm relationships with the parents who serve as his critics, the peers he competes with, or—when he is grown—the partners and children he views with such a critical eye.

In short, the negative effects of the conditional acceptance that planned praise engenders are both far-reaching and hurtful.

Planned Praise Causes Performance Anxiety. I once read a poem about a passerby admiring a young centipede crawling along the bank of a ditch. When he asked the centipede to explain how he managed all of his legs, the centipede began to focus on how he did it and, before long, was on his back at the bottom of the ditch.

Whenever a child is in the process of learning a new skill, any personal attention focused on his abilities will create enough pressure to push him into error, whereas a child who is already adept feels supported by the cheering and does better. This explains why spotlights placed on a child's developing skills in an effort to reinforce his interest in the activity often backfire by causing him—like the centipede—to become self-conscious, overly anxious, and concerned about the results.

Planned Praise Feels False. Because conscious praise comes from the head rather than the heart and is designed to secure improved performance, it has an inauthentic, Teflon quality to it that feels manipulative and false.

I suspect that only the young, socially naive child initially falls for the attention that goes with praise and seeks more of it due to its shiny, glittery appearance. However, as he matures and seeks more sophisticated reflections of himself, the growing child senses that the heart is missing from conscious praise and feels embarrassed by the ego-based manipulation that goes with it.

Accordingly, if a child has offered to help with something like the family chores, a more authentic form of reinforcement than praise would be to chat and laugh while working together so that both of you would look forward to more such encounters.

Dialogue from Class

MOTHER: I praised my resistant seven-year-old for sweetly feeding our kittens, but she was annoyed by my comments and said that she didn't want me to know she was doing it.

BOBBIE: Praise with a purpose can make us feel self-conscious about our behavior and also implies that because we did it right this time, we are obligated to do it that way in the future. This would not be happy news for a resistant child! I think it would be more reinforcing to let her have her experience with the cats without intrusion, since the time spent with them would be naturally reinforcing; then, after allowing her a period of time with them by herself, you could slip yourself into the scene to join her in holding and petting them for awhile.

☉☉☉

Planned Praise Teaches Children to Undervalue the Internal Reinforcer and Overvalue the External One. "When a pickpocket meets a saint, he sees only his pockets; yet when a saint meets a pickpocket, he sees only his heart." As revealed in this saying, how others see us—whether positively or negatively—for the most part has no real bearing on who we are and is merely a reflection of how they view the world. As a result, the praise we receive merely represents the ability of others to see value in us and, at most, is pleasant but unessential to our lives.

Therefore, it's important that we not train our children to view attention and praise—or a lack of it—as a source of significant information about themselves on which to base a positive or negative self-image. If we help them, instead, to keep their internal reinforcer alive and active within themselves, they will always know what feels right for them and when to continue, and they can take that internal reinforcer with them wherever they go.

Once the internal reinforcer is safely in place, it's fun to support others and to be supported. This is most rewarding when done mutually for the joy of giving and receiving, rather than as a program designed to manipulate one another to continue certain behaviors.

Dialogue from Class

BOBBIE: How many of you as adults think it's important that others acknowledge you and that you do the same for them?

CLASS: (Most hands)

MOTHER: But after you're grown, nobody bothers to give it to you anymore.

BOBBIE: That's often true . . . yet whenever we've been trained as children to expect it, we feel hurt and disappointed when it's lacking. Thus, a key problem with external reinforcement is that it won't last. Once parents are out of the picture, the rest of the world is not as interested in your reinforcement program. How many of you as adults can honestly say that a lot of people remember to reinforce you for what you do? How many people are paying that much attention to your lives?

CLASS: (No hands; nervous chuckles)

BOBBIE: No hands at all? I suspect we all get a little acknowledgment along the way, but it's certainly not at the level we have been taught to expect. I read a statistic that estimates if someone is very close to you, they will think of you about 2 percent of the time. And these are your nearest and dearest! We can see from this small percentage that children taught to rely on reinforcement from others will be sorely disappointed and may spend much of their adulthood feeling betrayed and angry at friends for not fulfilling this false promise.

ⓖⓖⓖ

Authentic Acknowledgment. Even though a deliberate use of praise and attention calculated to improve a child's behavior offers questionable results, you should not feel tongue-tied or reluctant to express your genuinely positive observations and feelings about your kids. In fact, authentic moments of honoring the essence of your child, cheering his efforts, taking joy in his accomplishments, and genuinely acknowledging the depth of his being are essential to a truly heartfelt interaction with him. Moreover, anytime feelings of acknowledgment and support are real and spill from your heart, they bathe your child in the energies of love and support, which are, in turn, both powerful and healing.

I merely caution you not to use the false version of planned attention, praise, and reward as a way to consciously encourage your child to behave or perform better.

Communicating with Children as Friends

Whenever there are no problems to be solved, immature viewpoints to redirect, or praise to be dispensed, the best communication response is to talk with your children in the same way you would talk to friends.

Children particularly enjoy having us relate to them as companions, telling poignant, funny, or embarrassing stories about ourselves or ones from our childhood and past. They love to hear us relate things that we have overcome or accomplished or to tell about our present goals, jobs, and friends. They also enjoy discussing likes and dislikes as well as current affairs or the latest movies and events. They further respond to provocative questions about such things as what the purpose of life might be, who dreams their dreams, or how to solve problems facing family, friends, schools, communities, nations, and the world. Kids also feel connected to their parents through their mutual enjoyment of nonjudgmental "village" gossip about the experiences of family and friends or people in the news.

In addition, planning a picnic or party, discussing what pets to adopt, deciding which family excursions and trips to take, and exploring personal aspirations capture the attention of most kids. You can also inspire values in your children by using interesting anecdotes and stories from real life to demonstrate various lessons along the way, so long as you don't turn every discussion into a lecture or sermon.

Kids particularly feel heard when you can understand such things as their desire to spend time with their friends, talk on the telephone, have their plans and activities remain flexible, and enjoy opportunities to "goof off" or simply "be."

All communications must be done in a parallel manner that is respectful of your child as a valued, interesting person, rather than one to be bossed, directed, scolded, coerced, or corrected. By the same token, it's equally important not to speak to him in the condescending, high-pitched, sing-song style so often used by adults when talking to young people. It's valuable, instead, to treat your child with the same degree of respect and consideration a friend or colleague would be given, and to view him as a treasured friend who has come to live in your home for a couple of decades. A child who feels honored in this way will want to share himself with the person who sees his value.

These friendly, nonproblematic interactions provide uniquely connecting times and are every bit as important to communication as those times when you are required to help your children acquiesce to boundaries, adjust an erroneous viewpoint, or solve some problem. Yet before we can succeed in communicating with kids as friends, we must first create both the time and setting to do so.

Intrusions to Family Communications

Excessive amounts of television, toys, and computer or video games are the most intrusive factors in family life today and interfere with positive interactions and communications between parents and their children. Not only do these activities make many kids hyperactive and aggressive, they disconnect them from their own hearts, families, and friends while putting their attention on the material world. Thus, you would be wise to seriously curb the number of toys your children have and the amount of time they spend with video and computer games or in front of television. It's equally important that these be turned off when friends are over or guests are visiting, so that they don't interfere with communications or connections with these important visitors.

Getting Kids Back: Create Some Form of the Old Neighborhood

I grew up on a sugar plantation in Hawaii in the 1940s and 1950s. There were loads of kids from various ethnic groups who played together in a community equipped only with a park, activity center, and roads for biking to our various destinations. The rest was up to us, and we found ways to interact from dawn to dusk. This process taught us to imagine, design, and create countless activities and adventures. We not only organized ourselves to play every game and sport imaginable, but healed injured animals, produced plays and aquacades, and learned a variety of skills from one another. But most important, we learned over the years how to work out our interpersonal problems and became mutually supportive friends.

Because this had been such a special experience, I refused to surrender to what I saw developing for my young children when we lived in a hilly neighborhood filled with children who rarely came out to interact with others but opted, instead, to watch television or play with their toys in isolation. I set out in search of a neighborhood filled with kids in a flat area. Once there, we welcomed all of the gang as well as their forts, games, and noisy laughter into our home, yard, and pool. I had re-created the community I grew up in, and my kids had the same opportunity I had enjoyed to nurture their friendships and develop the social skills and ability to get along with others that is so lacking in today's world.

I challenge each of you not to succumb to the current pattern of using toys, television, and computer or video games to raise children, but to create some alternative form of a participatory environment for your kids.

Body Language and Tone for Communications and Connections

The way we use our bodies and voices can communicate love and honoring of our children.

- **Physical Closeness During Communication.** Mr. Jones shared how he had stood before his seven-year-old son after Saturday's soccer game, calmly delivering a commentary on the importance of trying hard, even when the going gets tough. His son seemed intent on what he was saying, and Mr. Jones assumed that his new, calmer approach to this subject was working. When he asked his son if he had any questions, the boy inquired, "Why do you have hairs in your nose?" This father learned the hard way that it's better during communication to get down to a child's level in order to establish a closer connection with him. The first rule is to be in the same room with your child. Once this is established, closer physical and emotional connections contribute to the success of more meaningful conversation. Following are some ways to achieve this.

- **Eye Contact.** Eye contact not only creates a connection between you and your child, it allows you to look into the hearts and souls of one another and thus enhances honesty and responsibility in your communications and clearings. Nevertheless, it's important to invite, rather than insist on, eye contact—since a demand for this form of connection creates the opposite effect. Games such as stare-downs involving prolonged eye contact can help shy and timid children learn to tolerate this level of closeness for longer periods of time.

- **Body Contact.** Not only does physical closeness keep you and your child connected, it's good for his physical health and emotional well-being. It also strengthens the bond established between you and says, "I'm on your team," "I care about you," and "I love you." Thus, you would be wise to maintain this connection on a regular basis through lap-sitting; sitting side-by-side; an arm around your child's shoulder; walking arm in arm; a hug or kiss; painting over his facial features with your fingers or a makeup brush; playing with his hair; or giving him back, head, or foot rubs.

- **Voice Contact.** An impatient, annoyed, or aggressive tone of voice interferes with safe and open communication between you and your child, whereas a friendly one creates a feeling of closeness. In addition, such things as pet names evoke feelings of endearment and gentleness between family members as does simply saying, "I love you!"

Dialogue from Class

MOTHER: Aren't there times when it's appropriate to show some irritation in your voice?

BOBBIE: Be aware that an irritated tone of voice will always interfere with calm neutrality and worsen the situation during communication. However, a strong voice tone may be needed to convince a defiant child to get back in bounds; if so, use it. Then, return to your calm demeanor and voice during clearing.

Creating Time Together

When asked what would make family life better for them, both young children and teens consistently responded that they would like more time with their parents. They often point out that their parents work hard to provide the family with more material things, but that what they would really like is more closeness.

Feelings of closeness and connection simply have no opportunity to develop between family members who are never together or who allow the time they do have to be interrupted by television, newspapers, and projects. Families who are close make a point of setting time aside for sharing such things as regular meals, family activities, meetings, traditions, and vacations. The key is to find common interests that both parents and kids enjoy and use them to bridge connections and close relationships. Following are some ideas for enhancing family connections.

- **Morning and Evening Routines.** One way to connect with young children is to allow them to come into your bed as the morning dawns or, as the family is rising for work and school, to go into their room to sit on the edge of their bed. This offers a good opportunity for morning foot or back rubs and head scratching as well as a time to chat about last night's dreams or the day's plans as they awaken.

  Evenings also offer a variety of ways to connect with your children. You might, for example, do such things as serve dessert in the living room and use this time and setting for conversation, reading, or family games.

- **Driving.** Travel time in the car on the way to and from activities and school offers a great opportunity to connect with your child, since neither of you are distracted by other interests or obligations. This works best when the radio is turned off or down low to a music station.

- **Dinnertime.** When my children were young, I was blessed by a friend who encouraged me to establish a pattern of eating as a family—without television—on a nightly basis. What she said made sense, especially since I had so many fond memories of my own childhood dinner table in the days before busy schedules, reams of homework, and television took over family life. Thus, I took her advice and gratefully spent my children's growing-up years enjoying our best conversations over family dinners. I then noticed that other families I considered to be close had also established a pattern of eating together on a regular basis. It became clear that dinnertime offers the best regular opportunity for family members to come together at a relaxed, open-ended time for personal sharing, playful humor, a commentary on the day's news, political or philosophical discussions, and talking about values. This only works, however, when you treat your children like important dinner guests, rather than use the time for nagging, interrogations, math drills, or lectures. It's also important that everyone remain at the table for as long as conversations are continuing. Families that can't be together for dinner due to parental work schedules would be wise to get together for another regular meal or find an alternative time together.

- **Other Connecting Times.** Families remain close when they set time aside to go on various excursions together such as to museums, concerts, movies, or plays; going out to breakfast, lunch, or dinner; going on hikes, picnics, or camping trips; taking evening walks; shopping or bargain hunting; playing a sport; having relatives or friends over for dinner; or simply enjoying a game of cards, Scrabble, backgammon, or dominoes. Gardening, cooking, baking, or jointly washing the dishes, dog, or car provide additional opportunities for connection as do other projects and activities done together, including watching quality television. The key is to find common interests that you and your children enjoy and then use them to help build connections and close relationships.

- **Traditions.** Traditions create another focal point around which families can feel connected and bonded. These can include such things as a favorite meal or outing every Friday night; Sunday barbecues with friends and neighbors; community projects; theater and restaurant outings; watching sports events or television specials; and planning annual events such as vacations and holiday celebrations. Each family would be wise to establish a number of traditions that everyone looks forward to implementing.

- **Trips and Vacations.** Trips generate highly bonding experiences, simply because they represent times when your family is forced to be together for an extended period of time in unfamiliar settings. Consequently, no matter whether the trip goes as planned or includes a series of unexpected events or even calamities, it will create bonding between family members and provide special memories to reminisce and laugh over in the years to come.

- **Family Meetings.** Meetings are highly bonding for families, as they bring everyone together to express gratitude, connect with one another, clear up problems, develop personal and family mission statements and goals, create plans, and consider how family members might become their best and highest selves.

Regular meetings are best, since a number of things will surface as a result of gathering together to discuss family matters. At the very least, a meeting should be called when there are problems to be aired or an involved plan—such as a family vacation or move—needs to be designed.

A good format for family meetings is to go around the circle—perhaps using a talking stick—and give everyone a chance to share his or her view-point on the subject being discussed. During this period, all views are con-sidered valid and none are criticized or discounted. When everyone has finished talking, the best ideas will naturally surface and the others will fall away, though parents retain the final say.

Another helpful tool is to have all family members express what they can do to make theirs a better family. The key to being all that you want to be individually and as a family is to focus on what is wanted, rather than what is not wanted.

Meetings can begin with rituals, which might include such things as lighting candles; drinking tea or cocoa; and sharing what each family member is grateful for, what each appreciates about life and each other, and what each hopes to achieve in his daily life at a higher level or how to contribute to strengthening the family, community, nation, and world. Meetings can end with meditation or prayer, with family members asking for help in becoming their highest and best selves and family.

- **Family Prayer.** Although 80 to 90 percent of people believe in a higher power and a world beyond their material senses, most fear openly speak-ing of these beliefs. This began with an overzealous reaction to the sepa-ration of church and state, which was never intended to separate us from our souls, but was meant only to keep specific forms of worship out of government affairs. This separation of people from their spiritual essence, combined with a belief in a reality based only on what we can experience with our five senses resulted in a denial of the higher, spiritual self, while we pursued only our more limited and powerless worldly selves. Now that scientists have used both microscopes and telescopes to uncover a world beyond the perceptions of our limited senses, we are slowly reclaiming the unseen world along with our spiritual essence and the higher power behind it. As we return to an interest in our souls and higher selves, we are uncov-ering such things as the power of prayer, best described in Larry Dossey's *Healing Words* (1993). Thus, families would be wise to tap into this power by joining together in regular group prayer in behalf of family, friends, and the world.

The Strength of the Family is the Strength of the World

We have all walked into homes inhabited by people radiating warmth, wisdom, solace, and joy. They create the kinds of families that wrap their arms around you and entice you to kick off your shoes and stay forever. These are the families and homes we all dreamed of having as children or creating for ourselves as adults. And these are the families that can, in turn, create the foundation on which to build the kind of society we all yearn to live in. The way to create such families can be found more easily than expected by observing the patterns found in "goose sense," dolphin synergy, and tribal cooperation.

Blending "Goose Sense" with Dolphin Synergy and Tribal Cooperation. An unfortunate side effect of living in a society focused primarily on the development of the ego self and striving to win the race of worldly status and material gain is that we engage in the kinds of competitive endeavors that render us islands, each watching out for our own individual needs. Since replacing man's natural patterns of collaboration with individualism has made life's journey a great deal harder for us, we would be wise to draw from the sense of a goose in learning to work together once again.

For example, rather than each striving to fly on its own, geese take turns in the lead position, providing a wind break for the others. They also stay with tired or sick geese for as long as needed and cheer by honking from the rear for those in the lead. By working together and sharing responsibility for leadership in this manner, the group is able to fly longer distances than any individual goose could manage.

Similarly, the more evolved dolphins not only move as a unit, also taking advantage of drafting, shared leadership, and group formations to protect the babies, but base decisions on the needs of the group and cooperate with each other in a variety of other simple, yet synergistic ways—such as massaging each other and working together to chase off aggressors—which supports their ability to live in peaceful play and joy.

Our fascination with human's ability to also live cooperatively made a bestseller out of Marlo Morgan's book, *The Mutant Message Down Under* (1991), which described a small tribe that did such things as rotate leadership among all tribe members. This fascination has further stimulated a sifting through the histories of other groups and tribes in our search for the essence of cooperative living. Hopefully, this search will reveal how the village can come together to help us raise our children and live as our higher selves.

What these flocks, pods, and tribes show us is how we can strengthen our family units and societal village by relinquishing our self-centered goals of winning the race to a commitment to communicate deeply, cooperate fully, and share responsibility for the good of the whole. As we succeed, the village, in turn, helps us to raise our children and live from our higher selves. In short, as we consult our hearts and strive to live a life that honors our higher selves and the higher selves of others, we will not only find this approach to life more harmonious to our collective needs, but easier and more joyful.

The Rewards of Good Communication

The gift of time; gentle communication with love and caring in your hearts; a genuine interest in your child; a belief in his ability to be bright and interesting; and a willingness to create a cooperative family unit and live synergistically from the higher self are powerful ways to love a child!

★★★

Good communication bridges hearts through understanding.

★★★

12

Teen Angels

Enjoying Your Adolescent

The Eleventh Key:

☺☺☺

Clarity during the adolescent years results in a time of friendship, joy, and celebration of your emerging adult.

The teen years are famous for being extremely trying if not impossible, and parents brace themselves for this challenging period as their children approach adolescence. Yet this final stage of development can and should be the most enjoyable one of all for both teens and their parents!

The secret to making this happen is for you to maintain a balance between love and authority throughout the adolescent years—since it is only when an imbalance develops that families are thrown into turmoil. Yet because teens often act as if they no longer need their parents and thus feel free to defy their authority or reject their love, it's a challenge for families to maintain loving, connected feelings with them or sustain the authority that was once established. As a result, only those of you who established a balance between love and authority in your child's earlier years and have been able to maintain that balance during his adolescence will succeed in having pleasant years with your teens.

In contrast to these fortunate parents, others of you never figured out how to maintain loving feelings for your younger child; nor did you take control once he developed enough to challenge your rules. To your dismay, you are now discovering during his teen years that he is not only failing to outgrow his difficulties as you had hoped, but is getting worse, instead.

With this history of imbalanced parenting as a backdrop, the problems you now face have the potential to become severe enough to lead to tumultuous, if not tragic, adolescent years. Those of you in this unfortunate category will benefit by carefully reading the earlier sections of this book, since your challenge at this point will be to heal old injuries and learn the basics of parenting with balance.

For those parents who have been overcontrolling, your only hope for a second chance will come from your willingness to be friends with your teen, to be the first to acknowledge what part you have contributed to the problem, and to gently invite him to join you in a fresh start. If you continue, instead, to be dominant and controlling, his spirit will remain closed to you as his will stiffens even more vehemently against everything you stand for and want from him. By contrast, if you approach him from a place in your heart with gentleness, a willingness to heal, and an invitation to communicate, he will respond in kind.

For those of you who have been too permissive, you must now face the problem this has created and find the courage at this juncture to add discipline to your program.

And for those of you who have wavered between permissiveness and dominance, you must now learn how to stop this swinging and approach your teen with balance. This chapter will provide you with guidelines on how to do this.

Only after this remedial reading and work is done will you be ready to create the cooperative partnership discussed in this chapter for supporting your teen's emerging independence.

The rest of you, at least partially, succeeded in establishing a balance between love and authority in the earlier years, but then let it slip when your child became a teenager. You either failed to keep your adolescent on life's daily agenda or submitted to his rebellion—or both. The unfortunate result is that those of you who were doing reasonably well during your child's prior stages of development now watch helplessly as closeness slips away and balance is lost. You are the families we hear so much about as you struggle unexpectedly through sad, often bitterly unpleasant years with your teens.

The goal for those of you in this category is to determine how to regain and strengthen the balance between love and authority that you once achieved during your child's earlier years and apply it throughout his adolescence. However, to succeed in this important objective, you must first discard two popular myths about the teen years that interfere with your ability to stick with balanced parenting.

Myth #1: Adolescents Don't Need Their Parents

Although most of you are braced for a "difficult" period during the adolescent years, you simultaneously visualize your teen as independent and not needing—even rejecting—your support. This view is reinforced by his larger size and "cool" affect, which make him seem as though he neither wants nor needs much support or guidance from you. Unfortunately, this faulty impression is responsible for much of the turmoil during the adolescent years, since teens do, in fact, both want and need the gentle support and clear guidance of a mature adult figure more than they would like to admit. To help you remember this important point, think of your adolescents as no more precocious or powerful than the "fluffy birds" they actually are.

Fluffy Birds

My husband occasionally enjoys eating his lunch in the park amidst the peacefulness of nature. One day, several scraps fell from his sandwich to the ground around his feet, and within a few moments, he noticed a pair of small, sleek birds fending off a group of other birds as they busily gathered the crumbs. Next, he saw them run over to some nearby bushes where they delivered their hard-earned meal to a pair of larger, fluffy birds squawking loudly for food, but making no effort to gather any.

My husband laughed to himself as he identified with the sleek, overworked birds busily providing security for their oversized and fluffy, yet unemployed, offspring. He shared his experience that evening with his own sizable teenagers, and from that day forward, endearingly referred to them as the "fluffy birds"!

This story offers a wonderful metaphor for the period from twelve to seventeen years of age when it seems as though the adolescent is so large—often outsizing his parents—that he should be able to manage life by himself. He then promotes this view by making proclamations of maturity or using "adult" behaviors such as drinking and smoking or becoming sexually active; yet if you look more closely, you will see that your teen continues to rely on his family for security and survival and is not as grown-up or independent as he would like you to believe.

In truth, if your adolescent were as fully mature as he looked—or pretended to be—he would be ready to live apart from you and provide for his own needs. Yet, like the fluffy birds, he is considerably more dependent than he looks or acts! This discrepancy between your teen's pseudo-mature appearance and behaviors and his actual level of development is not only confusing, but may cause you to ignore and underparent him or capitulate to his demands for more autonomy. You then feel disappointed and angry when he fails to demonstrate the maturity he was claiming to possess or that you were expecting.

Jeremy

Jeremy, a junior in high school, walked into my office with an arrogant attitude that made it clear that he felt no need for counseling and had consented to come only to regain his use of the family car.

Initially, he maintained his cool, distant attitude, but eventually let down his guard and confided in me that he had been hurt a few years earlier by failing to secure a position on his school football team. Since most of his friends had made the squad, this exclusion from the team had caused him to feel isolated, not only from the sport he had dreamed so long of playing, but from his buddies as well. Yet because he gave the impression that everything was "cool" and nothing bothered him, his parents and coaches had not understood his need for more help in getting through such a big disappointment. Neither had they noticed that Jeremy had lost the opportunity to maintain contact with the friends who were on the team and that his new friends were among the unmotivated, drug-using crowd. Nor had they perceived that Jeremy, with all of his bravado, had not only lost his confidence and friends, but was slipping into a drug-induced fog that was robbing him of both his ambition and identity. In fact, Jeremy's parents had required that he come to counseling only because his grades were slipping. They had been fooled by his large body and suave affect and had no awareness of the internal anguish the child within was experiencing.

Thus, behind the illusion of the adolescent as fully grown, looking "cool," and ready for full independence can lie a very different reality. Like Jeremy, most adolescents confronting so many new and challenging tasks—along with the effort, disappointments, and rejection required for independence—feel a great deal of insecurity which they hide behind a mask of overconfidence.

Meredith

Meredith was a cooperative girl with a close relationship to her mother, who had single-parented her from infancy. Yet once she developed into a beautiful young thirteen-year-old, a group of older boys pursued her friendship. The boys smoked marijuana regularly, were often truant from school, and rather than address schoolwork and activities or get a job, they hung around the shopping mall for diversion. Meredith was not only flattered by the attention of these boys, but was taken in by the illusion of their maturity—based on swearing, smoking, and lying to their parents. It wasn't long after her alliance with this group that Meredith dropped her other school friends, let her grades fall, and began to demand freedoms beyond what was appropriate for her years.

Initially, Mother was also taken in by the illusion of precocity in Meredith's affiliation with this pseudo-mature group and, rather than take a stand against her insistence on more freedoms without responsibility, Mother acted helpless as her daughter went progressively out of control.

Behind the Illusion

Adolescents like Jeremy and Meredith are not only unequipped to match your view of them as fully grown, mature, and autonomous, they are deeply challenged by having to acquire so much new and complex information in preparation for genuine maturity and independence.

In fact, as a teen faces this challenge, he must do so without the full maturity or experience needed to always make the best decisions. Moreover, because his brain development will not reach its full capacity until he reaches somewhere between the ages of fifteen to eighteen, he will often seem disorganized, forgetful, and lacking in good sense or sound decisions. This helps to explain why so many teens fail to utilize the more complex brain functions required to envision the consequences of risk-taking behavior or understand why they must begin now to lay the groundwork for their futures.

In contrast to this reality, many of you have fallen for the illusion of precocity that your teens project and thus fail to provide them with the kind of clear-cut authority, balanced with love, that they will need during this important stage of their development. Furthermore, many of you who have grown accustomed to the more easygoing six- to eleven-year-old period expect even more of a break from your child-rearing duties during the adolescent years. In fact, tired after so many years of parenting and interested in picking up the pieces of your own lives, you often welcome the prospect that your teen won't need much help.

As a result, a good number of you are completely unprepared for how much time it will actually take to address the needs of your adolescent. In short, you are *braced* for the teen years, but you are not *prepared* for them!

To get prepared, you must first dispel the myth that your kids won't need you during their adolescent years, but will, in fact, require that you parent them in much the same way you did when they were younger. You can begin by putting them back on the agenda.

Putting Your Teen Back on the Agenda

I first became aware of how much my resistance to teenage errors had been building when I pulled into my driveway one morning to find my fifteen-year-old vacuuming his newly purchased, second-hand car. What caught my attention was my vacuum swiveling about in the middle of a grease spot on the garage floor, while he focused on the interior of his dilapidated car. My initial reaction was one of irritation as I asked myself in disbelief how he could be so unaware.

Fortunately, it was a long driveway, so I had time to get a grip on my emotions—and tongue—and tune into the situation from his point of view. Only then could I see that he was trying to be responsible by vacuuming his car, but did not yet have the experience to keep the canister out of the grease.

By the time I got to him, I noticed that he was feeling quite independent and pleased with himself, and I was grateful that I had not interrupted the moment with insults. Instead, I playfully said, "I see that you're beautifying your car, as well as can be expected for one of its vintage—and I can also see that you are new to vacuuming. Have you noticed, yet, that the canister is in the grease?" We both laughed as his eyes moved to the mess and he apologized with horror equal to mine for his error. In turn, I forgave and consoled him while explaining how to clean the canister, which he promptly did. Not only was he able to learn everything from the experience that he needed to know, the encounter was bonding for us, rather than separating.

Prior to that moment when I watched my son drag my vacuum through the grease, I had felt justified anytime my patience with my teenagers' many little errors ran out. Although I had learned to accept the mistakes of my young children, I had not expected so many from my adolescents, and the older they got, the less accepting I felt when things went wrong. I knew that my disdain was supported by my husband, who glanced at me knowingly on so many of these occasions, and I knew that I was supported by just about every parent of teenagers across America!

Yet regardless of how much support I had, my irritable attitude began to affect my children's confidence in themselves as well as in me. The more impatient I became, the more defensively they responded, and friction eroded what had been a previously close connection between us. I was frankly annoyed by the persistence of their immaturity, and they began to lose faith in me as a supportive friend, willing to guide them all the way through their maturational process.

As I began to reassess my behavior, I could see that my annoyance was a result of my unwillingness to have my teenagers make the kinds of errors they were, in fact, making. Not only had I failed to notice how many new responsibilities they were successfully managing, I was judging their periodic mistakes as careless and irresponsible. As a result, my voice was resistant and grouchy as if to say, "How dare you make so many errors!" or "When will you ever grow up?" Anytime they acted unsure, scattered, forgetful, or simply lacking in good sense as adolescents are prone to do, I responded with scorn. I had become, once again, unwilling to have unpleasant moments on my daily agenda.

And so I found myself right back where I had been when I was first learning to accept my toddlers' spilled juice and my elementary-age children's lost jackets. Now, my tolerance would have to include such things as lost jewelry and dents in the car! It became apparent that I would need to embrace all of their errors before I could offer the support, friendship, and gentle guidance my teens so desperately needed during this final stage of their development. To do this, I had to remember that they didn't wake up each morning and set out to do their worst, and that my job would be to develop patience with the best they had to offer. Putting my son back on the agenda that day reminded me of how well acceptance works while addressing problems and providing lessons. And so I committed, once again, to weaving my children's errors into daily living. (See Figures 4 and 5 depicting the ideal and real parenting agendas in Chapter 4.)

It's critical that each of you also remember to keep your oversized, often immature, adolescents on the agenda at all times, rather than resist the disruptions they bring to your lives or the errors they make during this period of their development. As with younger children, whenever you resist your teen or approach him with control and demands, his will stiffens with defiance, and he feels and acts against you.

By contrast, your continued acceptance invites his cooperation and desire to get along and learn the lessons contained in his problems; thus, it's essential that you remain heartfelt, embracing, patient, kind, and gently supportive during this final period of raising your child.

Sasha

Mrs. Smith came to see me about the deterioration of her previously good relationship with her twelve-year-old daughter. This mother was a popular high school teacher who got along well with her students and had envisioned herself managing equally well with Sasha during her teen years. Consequently, when their relationship began to unexpectedly fall apart, Mrs. Smith assumed that she had underestimated the difficulties of hormones and rebellions and was hopeful that counseling would help to get her daughter back on track.

However, as I explored the changes in their relationship, it became apparent that Mrs. Smith was the one who had provoked their problem by responding to Sasha's immaturity with impatience. Not only was she annoyed by her daughter's ineptness with new situations, she became irritated each time Sasha left things out of place, procrastinated on chores and other responsibilities, or was slow in getting ready for activities and school. Mrs. Smith had expected more of her daughter by this age and was impatient for her to grow up faster.

As a result, she tried to push Sasha into maturity with lectures and scoldings. When that didn't work, she expressed disappointment and anger at her daughter's lack of maturity. Sasha responded to these attacks with defensiveness and anger and wanted nothing more to do with her mother. By the time Mrs. Smith came for counseling, she and her daughter were engaged in a classic parent/teen struggle that was threatening their previously close relationship—and Sasha was in the early stages of forming alliances with a rebellious group of school friends.

I began by helping Mrs. Smith to see that Sasha's ineptness was not only developmentally normal, but typical, and that Mrs. Smith would have to face the reality that she had at least five more years of active parenting ahead of her. If she wanted to continue to enjoy a good relationship with her daughter, she would be required to parent with the same love, support, and patience she had offered in the earlier years.

I further pointed out that all people, including children, want to feel a part of a caring group, and when family fails to fulfill this need, the mobile teen will find a replacement. Thus, anytime parents fail to be loving with their kids, their teens will make their peer group primary. Once these peer clusters—or substitute family groups—are formed, kids trust these units more than they trust their parents and will offer more loyalty to them than their families. If these units are made up of kids who are also rebelling against their families, they become highly dissident groups, promote anti-adult activities, and can even become gangs. This is why it's so critical that you always pay attention to whom your kids are selecting as friends—particularly when you are in conflict with your child.

By contrast, when families are loving and their teens feel connected to them, their peer group is still important, but is less likely to be primary. Furthermore, kids belonging to families who are able to maintain feelings of closeness and connection throughout the teen years are not as attracted to the kinds of peer groups that form around anti-adult attitudes and rebelliousness.

Since irritation, disappointment, scoldings, and attacks were already turning Sasha against her mother during this early stage of her adolescence, it became obvious to Mrs. Smith that she had no choice but to try my advice. She committed to putting her daughter back on the agenda and maintaining the loving part of her parenting.

Several months later, I received a note from Mrs. Smith, reporting how easily she and Sasha had gotten back on track, once she understood the importance of putting her daughter's final stage of development on the agenda. She was pleased by how simple the solution to a problem going rapidly out of control had been and encouraged me to share this "uncomplicated piece of advice" with others.

In addition to rejecting the myth that teens don't need their families, parents would be wise to dispel the equally dangerous myth that their teens must go through hormone-driven rebellions in order to attain maturity.

Myth #2: The Expectation of Raging Hormones and Adolescent Rebellions

The commonly accepted view that hormones drive adolescent rebellions seems to me a rather silly notion that becomes dangerous to the development of our teens. In fact, I suspect that this popular myth actually triggers rebellions in large numbers of teens who would otherwise go through adolescence with ease. Here's how it works.

Hormones

For the past few decades we have unquestioningly accepted the concept that adolescence is a period in which young people must contend with hormones so potent that they will have very little, if any, control over their emotions. Some authorities go so far as to suggest that adolescent behavior can at times mimic emotional illness. Consequently, parents have been advised to be patient with this stage of developmental disequilibrium and not expect too much in the way of "normal" emotional behavior from their adolescents.

I have never been able to figure out what families were expected to do or where they might hide while their kids went through this extended period of emotional instability. Furthermore, I have encountered very few adults or teens who have actually reported experiencing the onset of hormones as the emotionally disruptive event it has been touted to be.

Nonetheless, we have so thoroughly accepted this diagnosis of adolescence that we have come to expect an emotional rollercoaster ride during the teen years. As a result, because both parents and their teens are programmed to expect "hormone-driven," disruptive behavior, teens act badly and parents fail to respond normally. Thus, parents excuse the inexcusable in their developing adolescents by tolerating sullen moods, arrogant rudeness, and aggressive communication in the belief that their teen is unable to control his emotions. The effect this concept has had on parenting the adolescent in the past few decades has been enormously disruptive.

Rebellions

In conjunction with the hormone theory, the hypothesis that adolescents must rebel against their families in order to achieve the individuation on which their independence and maturity will rest has also gained momentum in the past few decades. As a result, parents have been led to believe that rebellion will actually enhance their teen's emerging identity and independence from family and that he will fail to take this healthy step toward maturity unless he goes through a period of objecting to parental guidance.

Because the adolescent is thus expected to defy his family's boundaries and standards, parents respond with passive paralysis as they watch their teen demand, rather than earn, expanded freedoms. Meanwhile, the adolescent allowed to do this obtains only an illusion of independence, since he is still not prepared to manage life responsibly or on his own, yet reigns superior and dominant over the "foolish and stupid" parents who protect and support him.

This dreaded expectation of what the adolescent rite of passage involves makes the overgrown "fluffy bird" appear more ominous than fearful—as an imposing, oversized chick doing as he pleases, rather than sitting hesitant at the edge of his nest, seeking parental guidance on his preparations for flight. No wonder we have become confused by the paradox of what we so often see: an immature fledgling, not yet ready to fly, who, nevertheless, dominates the nest and defies the parent who feeds him!

The idea of allowing our teens to spend four to six years practicing antisocial behavior and aggressive communication in preparation for becoming adults, rather than rehearsing mature, responsible behavior seems like an absurd way to prepare for maturity. Perhaps it's time that we reexamine this illogical theory and try something new.

The Reality of the Teen Years

As a teenager, I had not experienced hormone-induced emotional instability, nor had I gone through a period of rebellion against my family's rules or values. Yet I considered myself to be a mature, well-adjusted, and independent young adult by the time I was ready to leave home in my early twenties. For me, this adjustment had been a gradual one of taking on progressively more responsibility while assuming the expanded freedoms that went with each new level of maturity. This period had been neither tumultuous nor painful, and I certainly felt no need to fight for the opportunity to be more independent. My parents were equally ready to let me assume more self-management and responsibility and enjoy the freedom that went with these steps toward maturity.

Furthermore, as an emerging adult, I had no problem deviating from some of the values my parents held that I considered limiting or outdated, but I also realized that I would have to wait until I no longer lived in their home before fully acting on these differences. I later compared my personal impressions with others and found that most adults in my age-group had experiences to match my own.

In reviewing the history of adolescent development, I discovered that the concept of rebellion as useful was a new and faddish notion that was not used in earlier times. In light of this history, combined with the poor results this idea was creating, it became apparent that encouraging teens to fight for their independence, rather than earn it, was not only providing a false road to maturity, but a destructive one.

I also noticed that during this period, kids were learning to be disrespectful and rude to others; to break family and societal rules; to go *against* things, rather than be *for* something; and to resist all that maturity and adulthood stood for as a way to prepare for their own maturity and eventual adulthood. It became apparent that it would be wise to return to the earlier, less chaotic, and more successful method of dealing with adolescence in which parents handed over the baton of a child's life to him in accordance with his willingness to manage it with responsible maturity. It became clear that practicing maturity would be a better way to achieve maturity.

After many years of sharing this insight with families and supporting them in bypassing this apparently needless rebellion, I read a study[9] conducted a decade ago out of Stanford University that concurred with my theory. This study concluded with the observation that even though psychoanalysts promote the idea that puberty must be a period of tension and turbulence if the adolescent is to achieve independence from his family, studies of the normal population failed to support this idea.

Although a few more recent studies demonstrate that young adults who remain close to their parents are psychologically healthier than those who break away, the word is getting out slowly.

Granted, there are some adolescents who must rebel from severely dysfunctional families in order to attain normal human rights and freedoms or to save their spirits and sometimes their lives. Although recognizing the plight of these kids is critical to an understanding of adolescent behavior, this group does not provide an appropriate model for the development of teenagers in normal families.

I have had numerous parents thank me for helping them to bypass the grief of teenage rebellion by encouraging them not to put up with it. Each family was amazed by how easy it was to suppress the mutiny in its early stages and return to normal family life, once they realized that the rebellion could be quelled without psychologically harming their child. Not only were the adolescent years made easier for these parents, their teens matched the results of James Dobson's study in which cooperative children and teens seemed happier, more mature, and more personally successful than their uncooperative counterparts.

Quelling the Teen Rebellion

Throughout his adolescence, your child will periodically challenge your authority, even when your levels of control are appropriate and handled fairly. During these times, your responses will set the tone and determine whether or not you are able to maintain a position of leadership in your home or will begin the process of losing control.

Unfortunately, many of you still view these uprisings as necessary and purposeful and thus allow your adolescents to be rude and demanding in their approach to claiming independence. As a result, you allow them to speak with contempt and anger, refuse requests made of them, ignore responsibilities, and impose a variety of messes and problems on other family members. Some of you are afraid to stand up to your teens for fear they will run away from home. Others want to address the challenge, but lack the skills needed to do so and resort to screaming matches with your teens, instead.

Whenever you respond to your teen's rudeness and rebellion with such helplessness, you collude with his view of you as weak and lacking. This causes your teen to falsely see himself as dominant and superior to such defective parents, and he loses his perspective regarding the truth of your role as the competent provider and elder of his family unit. Moreover, because it's not possible for a teen to feel truly good about himself while treating family members badly, his own self-respect will diminish as well.

As an alternative, I suggest that you wake up and take notice whenever an attitude toward you begins to form and respond to these teen challenges with greater strength. As you do this, the goal will be to remain loving and nurturing, while also staying in charge of the household. If we review your adolescent's previous challenges, it will be clearer why and how you must do this.

Prelude to the Teen Challenge

Although the adolescent rebellion is the one most talked and written about, in truth it represents only one of many challenges a child poses to his parents throughout his development. By reviewing these recurring challenges, we can see what a normative pattern of challenge looks like, as well as what it is designed to accomplish when handled effectively and what happens when it's not.

The Challenge of the "Terrible Twos." A child wages his first challenges to his parent's authority when he is merely two years old, since that's the age when his newfound mobility exposes him to so many novel things that he would like to have and do, much of which his parents can't allow. Those desires that get thwarted are frustrating to the young child, and he uses his growing strength and determination—usually in the form of tantrums—to persuade his family to yield to his demands.

Uncertain parents make a grave error by allowing their toddler's resistance and crying to dictate the rules. In doing this, such families are soon controlled by his tyranny as they scurry about to keep him happy in order to prevent him from throwing his next tantrum. As a result, he fails to make his adjustment to normal levels of frustration during this critical period of his development.

By contrast, more secure parents who meet their two-year-old's challenges with courage and strength not only help him to accept their rules, but discover that once they take control, he is able to yield to their authority without further confusion or drama. As a result, he makes a normal adjustment for a child of his age to the frustrations that boundaries impose. Once this is accomplished, he becomes a more cooperative child, willing to accept the parameters imposed by his family.

More Encounters. The child from three to eight years old, who has either become used to having his way or periodically gets tired of earning freedom through responsibility may try a shortcut to independence by attempting to steal it. This usually occurs during those times when he is feeling more confident and rather full of himself, questions his parents' right to tell him what to do, and challenges their authority with bold pronouncements of, "I won't do it," and "You can't make me!"

Parents who never established their authority with their younger child, or hang onto it only tenuously, may naively relinquish it altogether during this period, whereas competent parents will hold fast to their authority. Like the two-year-old, the three- to eight-year-old is relieved when his parents demonstrate the strength to remain in control and confidently maintain their position as the managers of their home. In fact, parental strength at this juncture allows these children to maintain their earlier adjustment to the common frustrations and boundaries of life and proceed normally in their development.

By contrast, children who succeed in gaining control of their families fail to make this critical adjustment to normal limits. As a result, their ability to get along with others or "hang in there" during the hard parts of life suffers. In some cases, they may even develop overly resistant and rigid behavior patterns related to their need to be in charge.

From Nine to Eleven: Preadolescence. When nine- to eleven-year-olds challenge their parents, their behavior is typically viewed as "adolescent," and they are often proudly referred to as, "nine years old—going on sixteen."

This attitude was expressed by a competent mother with a ten-year-old who came to counsel with me on another matter. Toward the end of our session, she mentioned that her daughter occasionally refused to cooperate with her, and she wanted some feedback on how to handle it. She shared that she had already told her child, "We're going to have to work this out, Tessa, because as you approach your teens it's only going to get worse!" I pointed out how she was making noncooperation and rebellion sound like very grown-up, "teenage" behaviors to this ten-year-old child. I further noted that this very pronouncement of the coming rebellion to children from nine to eleven unnecessarily contributes to a collective expectation that teenagers will rebel as a normal part of adolescent development.

And Again at Twelve to Thirteen. When my son was twelve, I asked him to go to his room for some infraction. Instead of going as he usually did, he walked toward me, looked me in the eye, and said, "Now that I'm bigger than you are, you can't make me go to my room anymore." Although I realized that I had triggered this reaction with a bossy tone of voice, I was, nonetheless, stunned by this response from my generally cooperative child. Fortunately, I listened to the internal impulse that said it would be a turning point in our relationship if I backed down and that I would have to proceed with the care of an "oak tree." Thus, I shifted to my heart and remembered my love for him as I firmly, yet calmly, let him know that it was not a matter of who was stronger but a matter of who was the head of the household—and since he was not yet paying for his own support, he was still dependent on our care and would have to live by our rules. I further let him know that when he was independent enough to create his own household, that's when he would be eligible to design the rules for his family.

When he balked some more, I gently told him that if he truly felt mature enough to strike out on his own, I would be happy to be his friend, help him to pick out his apartment and furniture, and have him over for dinner. But if he wanted to live with us—as most twelve-year-olds would—he would have to live by our rules. I concluded my statement by letting him know that he could think about it in his room for awhile and we would talk about it later. I then broke eye contact and retreated a bit to make it easier for him to back down. He hesitated for a moment, but then turned to go to his room.

I was grateful in that moment for the many years he had experienced my even strength in holding boundaries, as I knew that backdrop had helped him to realize that I would stick to the rules as presented. I was also grateful that I understood the importance of remaining calm and gentle, as aggressiveness on my part at that sensitive juncture would have pushed him out the door.

One day a few years later, when my daughter was thirteen, she began to behave like the stereotypical teenager. She acted as if I had truly "lost it" and believed that she was above even speaking to someone so "stupid" as I had apparently become. She used dour moods and irritable annoyance to block any warmth between us, and I could feel our previous friendship slipping away. When I realized what was happening, I lovingly let her know that if she continued to behave that way, she would be confined to the house, as I did not intend to impose on the larger society someone who could not figure out how to behave in a responsible, civilized manner with a group of people as small as our family of four. She spent quite awhile in her room without access to a telephone for complaining to friends of my "ridiculous" requirements. I remained calm and sweet, yet clear about my limits. Once she realized that she was going nowhere, she became receptive to a clearing. (See Chapter 8.)

During our clearing, she shared with me that she thought the rebellious behavior was expected of her. She had seen it in the movies and on television, saw friends getting away with it, and decided that she would feel more a part of her peer group if she behaved that way. I let her know that I considered the concept a myth and believed that it hurt the personalities of young people allowed to behave so badly toward their families. We talked more about it, and although she made subsequent attempts at using moods and resistance to get her way, she understood that rebellious behavior as a part of adolescence would not get her very far in our household. I simultaneously made it clear to her that she could enjoy ample freedoms so long as she was friendly and cooperative as well as responsible and open with me.

Standing up to these challenges was pivotal to bypassing the adolescent rebellion with my teenagers. The key is that I challenged their faulty perception that they had achieved independence and could manage without me—and, by offering to have them reconsider this belief, they were reminded of their dependence on me and elected, instead, to accept my rules and guidance.

Meeting Each Adolescent Challenge

Whenever you capitulate to your adolescent's demands, your authority is seriously undermined. Both you and your child realize that he is no longer required to do anything he doesn't voluntarily agree to, and you are left with the powerless tools of pleading, bargains, guilt, threats, or martyrdom as your only hope of enticing him to behave responsibly.

Consequently, the moment you are challenged by your teen—whether his attitude is unfriendly; he's refusing to conform to your rules; or he's not being open and honest in his communications—you must wake up and go on duty as a full-time parent. Nothing should take precedence over reestablishing your authority and requiring his cooperation; and your teen must not be free to go anywhere or do anything until you have done so.

Those of you who foolishly ignore these challenges, tiptoe around them, or go about your business before dealing with an uncooperative teenager give him an opportunity to experience being in charge for long enough to develop a taste for it. As a result, you will find it even more challenging to get him back in line after this delay. The more days, weeks, months, or years this delay lasts, the worse it gets.

By contrast, stopping a teen in his tracks while you reclaim control makes it clear that his freedoms and activities will be based on his cooperation, rather than on pushed or broken boundaries.

The Power of Restriction to Gain Surrender. Once you face the need to confront your teen's rebellion, regular time-outs or longer restrictions—often referred to as grounding—will be critical tools to use on those occasions when he challenges you. During these restrictions, you can let your child know that he's not free to connect with anyone outside of his family, either in person or by phone, during nonscheduled, normally free times until he has surrendered to cooperation and rules. This restriction can take anywhere from an afternoon to up to two to four weeks.

Appropriate Levels of Control

Paradoxically, once your authority has been reestablished, you and your teen will be free to relate as equals again; thus, it's only during those times when your authority is being challenged that you are required to assume a dominant position. It's critical to remember that this control is meant only to maintain cooperative behavior and does not extend to matters that involve your adolescent's personal choices for his own life.

To assure this, you must vigilantly seek opportunities to pass the reins of your teen's life to him in accordance with his ability to manage them with responsibility and take them back temporarily only if he misuses his freedom. You must also listen objectively to whatever appropriately communicated feedback he offers during those times when he feels that your controls are too tight and, if needed, make the appropriate adjustment.

Exceptions: Anytime parents abuse their children in any way, whether verbally, sexually, and/or physically, their control can no longer be viewed within the parameters of normal and appropriate parental control. Thus, rather than strive to gain control as normal families must do, abusive families must seek help, instead, to heal and correct their abusive behavior.

Dealing with "Attitude"

The first step kids take in pushing their boundaries is by developing a bad attitude toward you. This may show up as superiority, disdain, moods, a sharp voice tone, or silence. The key is for parents to understand that although a bad attitude is more subtle and harder to detect than broken boundaries, it could mark the beginning of a rebellion if allowed to continue.

Dialogue from Class

MOTHER: My teens find my husband and me so unpresentable that they want us to hide in the bedroom when their friends come to visit. Is this normal teen behavior or is it the beginning of a rebellion?

BOBBIE: Most kids will try this, and it could lead to rebellion if not addressed. Therefore, it's important not to collude with their image of you as "unacceptable" closet cases to be hidden when adolescent guests arrive. Not only does this undermine your teenager's respect for you and open the way for a rebellion, it interferes with the comfort of his guests as well. In truth, teenagers feel most comfortable in those homes where the parents are visible and friendly to guests, asking questions about how the teens are doing, what activities they are involved in, what their summer, work, travel, post–high school or college plans include, and what careers they hope to pursue. Teenagers enjoy and benefit from time in homes where they are loved by adults interested in them, and it's unfair for a child to block this friendship between his parents and friends. Thus, it's important not only to share this idea with your teens, but to refuse to collude with their efforts to get you out of the way.

Once this is established, after chatting with teen guests for awhile, you can provide your adolescent and his guests with a feeling of freedom from being observed by withdrawing from the group. In addition, it helps when you make an effort to keep up with the times and not become so frumpy, inebriated, cranky, or out of touch that your child would understandably rather hide you or be at another home than expose you to his friends. It's also critical that you not boss your child or act "parental" when his friends are around, as this demeans and embarrasses him and makes him want to withdraw from his family.

ANOTHER MOTHER: My fourteen-year-old is becoming increasingly sullen and rude at home and says that she can't stand us.

BOBBIE: How are you handling that?

MOTHER: Well, we don't know what to do. I guess we're skirting the issue and hoping it's a normal behavior.

BOBBIE: She is continuing this behavior because you're allowing it by not responding. Therefore, I would require that she remain in her room, without access to a phone or TV, until she is willing to act pleasantly toward other family members. It won't take long for her to figure out that rudeness is not working for her. When she's ready to cooperate, have a clearing, and once she has surrendered, return her freedoms to her.

MOTHER: What if during clearing I find that she really does have some legitimate complaints?

BOBBIE: It's important to let her know that you are always available to hear her views on any subject so long as she communicates them in a direct and honest manner as opposed to a sulky or rude one. Once she has acknowledged her attitude, it's a good time to ask if she has some unresolved feelings about a family member or the way the family functions—or something else in her life that is not working out as she had hoped. Although this invites an open discussion, don't assume there is always a problem behind every sulk, as many adolescent moods are simply a result of teenagers believing that they no longer like their parents or want to deal with them. If the adolescent does address some issue, it's important to move into the role of a good listener and discuss the issue both fully and fairly and with a willingness to make adjustments if what she says has merit. (See Chapter 11 on Communication.)

A THIRD MOTHER: My child is marginally polite, but what bothers me is that she refuses to communicate to us on anything more than the most basic, rudimentary level.

BOBBIE: I have found that the current tendency to tolerate minimal levels of communication in adolescents is one of the primary causes of a gradual breakdown of the family unit during the teen years. Parents who do this believe that they are showing respect for their teenagers' rights to privacy but are actually allowing them to hide behind withdrawn, often dishonest, and rude communications.

MOTHER: That's exactly what it feels like, but when I complain, my daughter insists that we are the only people she can't talk to and that she doesn't have this problem with her friends.

BOBBIE: Although some families provoke uncommunicativeness in their kids by acting too bossy, others get shut out simply because their adolescent feels it's the thing to do. Whatever the reason, it's essential to reverse the pattern not only by addressing your part in it, but requiring open communication from your teen as well.

In your case, you must help your daughter to see that you don't have problems with your friends either, and that communication at home is a different matter for both of you. It's important to help her understand that the way a person behaves in the privacy of her home reveals the personality that is the most closely aligned to her real, most unguarded self. Thus, as she becomes more intimate with friends or a partner and is no longer putting her "public" self forward, her more natural self—the one she uses at home—will eventually surface. That's why it's so important to practice being our best selves while in the privacy of our homes with immediate family members.

MOTHER: My daughter believes that I have no business knowing where she's going or who is going with her.

BOBBIE: This erroneous idea develops during the early teen years when kids encounter other adolescents who are not held accountable to their families, and they want you to adopt this negligent standard as well. In fact, this attitude is often an early sign that your child is running around with an unsupervised crowd. Thus, her objection lets you know that it's even more critical that you be aware of what is going on. Consequently, it's vital that you stick with your standards for meeting her friends and checking in with their families from time to time. Then, if you discover that the group is rebellious, it's important to restrict her time with them, particularly if the resistance and rebellion are rubbing off on her.

MOTHER: I think my daughter would welcome my breaking through her moods, since I suspect that she misses our prior closeness. My husband and I have been so frightened of this attitude since it started that we creep around like unwelcome guests in our own home!

BOBBIE: I would call a meeting, acknowledge your part in it, and gently announce your plan to start fresh by more clearly requiring that she get through her teen years with friendly communications.

FOURTH MOTHER: Although my daughter hasn't rebelled against our rules, she's very critical of me and complains that I'm not up-to-date. I can see that I really do irritate her, but I don't know what to do.

BOBBIE: One aspect of kids growing older includes their increasing ability to perceive the weaknesses of family members. This can make parents, who were once thought to be all powerful, now seem overly weak and vulnerable, and the child becomes angry that his parents aren't stronger. Because these feelings of disappointment in his parents are experienced at a vague, unconscious level, they can slowly erode what was previously a good relationship.

MOTHER: What's the best way to handle it?

BOBBIE: Help your daughter to understand that her expanded perception is a normal outgrowth of her increased maturation and ability to perceive people more fully. However, she must also realize that this expanded perception doesn't justify discounting you, anymore than she would discount herself or others just because she has discovered some weaknesses in them. It's also important that you not collude with your teen's perception that you can do nothing right. Instead, help her to understand that regardless of how she elects to view you, she will be required to behave in a friendly and considerate manner as long as she's living in your home.

Addressing Broken Rules

Another way that teens push their boundaries is by passively ignoring responsibilities such as chores and schoolwork or openly defying their rules. Because they are now bigger and have more fully developed fulfillers of their own, they no longer feel so dependent on you and have more courage to oppose your suggestions for what to do and when. Because many of you simply don't know how to get resistant teens to cooperate, your adolescents discover during this period that it's easy to ignore and break boundaries and that you don't know what to do about it.

The key is to understand that you must deal with these issues right from the outset before your teen determines that you no longer know how to handle him and develops a taste for disobedience. Consequently, you must lovingly, yet clearly, bring him back into line the moment he begins to communicate aggressively, ignore responsibilities, or break your rules. Yet it's critical to remember to do this with gentleness, since approaching your teen with bossiness and dominance will only cause him to harden his feelings toward you and brace himself for a battle. Thus, you must deal with him, but do so in a heartfelt manner filled with enough gentleness that it won't trigger resistance or a rebellion.

Whenever you fail to hold the line with bad attitudes and broken rules, it usually leads to escalating problems, including such things as lying, stealing, and drug use, as well as verbal and sometimes physical abuse. As a result, you will find yourself in the untenable situation of working hard to provide shelter and support for your emerging adult, while he not only refuses all responsibility and contribution, but gets way off track in his own development, often becoming a dangerous family member.

Confronting Deceit

Unfriendly behavior and rule breaking are visible behaviors that parents can clearly see and respond to accordingly. On the other hand, deception is a more difficult form of rebellion to perceive and is, consequently, the behavior parents most often fail to notice or rectify in its early stages. Moreover, because we live in a world where deceit is so commonplace, parents erroneously view it as a form of privacy.

Unfortunately, once deception enters into the picture, communication begins to seriously decline. If this trend is allowed to continue, it not only hurts your child's development but causes a breakdown of parental control and destroys all hope for a genuine relationship between you. As a result, it's critical that deception not be tolerated in any form or at any time. You must also adhere to this standard.

To accomplish this, it's important that you remain awake in your communications with your child or teen, stay alert to any inconsistencies you notice in his explanations or behavior, and be willing to check out suspected deception immediately and thoroughly. You must also explain that any truth voluntarily offered will be honored and that anything shared will be safely discussed without fear of repercussion. Once this is established, you must not allow your adolescent to refuse to discuss a topic or problem or get away with shallow responses or insincere and defensive excuses.

Furthermore, I would be concerned if a child behaved secretively or was overly protective of his privacy. Although it's important to give teens plenty of room for their own thoughts and time alone or with friends, it has been my experience that kids who are not engaged in questionable activities are perfectly comfortable with a general sense of openness and honesty and don't spend the majority of their time behind closed doors.

Dialogue from Class

MOTHER: How do you know when you are being lied to?

BOBBIE: There are always clues telling us when a communication is incomplete or insincere, but parents often ignore these signals, in part to avoid confronting the problem before them. In fact, that's the purpose denial serves; it keeps veils and curtains over a truth we are afraid to confront. Sometimes, we simply don't want to face that our child isn't doing well or that he's involved with drugs or is lying to us. I've seen many parents, for example, who have run across drugs in their child's belongings, inquire about their discovery, then naively believe the alibis their teen offers of holding the drugs for a friend or only trying them once. I've known other parents who have called the home where their child was spending the night only to discover that the other family knew nothing about it. Then, when their teen offered weak and confusing excuses of changed plans, they gobbled up his story with foolish relief.

FATHER: Our son often calls us with fibs about why he's delayed in getting home and eventually pushes it to the point that he's so late he has to spend the night.

BOBBIE: Do you let him stay over when it gets to that point?

FATHER: Yes.

BOBBIE: What would happen if he asked directly if he could spend the night?

FATHER: We would probably say "No."

BOBBIE: Always?

FATHER: Pretty much—because we feel he's always pushing us further than we want to go.

Bobbie: Can you see that the lying is working for him better than the truth?

Father: (Pause) Now I do.

Bobbie: I would let him know that from now on the only way he will have a chance to extend his time will be to tell the truth, whereas if he lies, he will have to come home immediately and be grounded for the remainder of the weekend as well.

I would also ground for a whole weekend whenever lied to, but offer generous freedoms to kids who are open and honest. This works well in motivating kids to prefer honesty to lying.

Father: Do you have to give them everything they want so they'll be honest?

Bobbie: No. But I think many parents unnecessarily thwart their kids by saying "No" too often. This kind of an overbearing and controlling attitude not only frustrates kids, but discredits parents. You will find that if your freedoms are generous, your child will be more likely to trust and accept your boundaries, rather than discount them as unrealistic and then constantly strive to sneak around them. Thus, if you view his friends as a positive influence, I would let him enjoy ample time with them.

If you view them as a negative influence, you can limit his time with them, especially during those times when he's not cooperating. In fact, a good consequence for an uncooperative child is to separate him only from the group that is influencing his resistance to rules, while allowing him to connect with his cooperative friends during this period of restriction. If you elect this option, it's important that you explain the logic behind it.

Responding to Serious Rebellion

The worst problems are presented by those teens who were allowed to behave belligerently throughout their early childhoods and middle years or were allowed to rebel for an extended period of time after first becoming adolescents.

Bringing these kids back under control will be considerably more difficult and usually requires counseling support as well as help from organizations such as ToughLove or Boys Town designed to assist families in getting rebellious and troubled teens back on track. (See **Adolescent** entry in the Problem-Solving Guide.) Those of you with such kids would be wise to face your challenge at a time when you have the backup help of a partner, friend, relative or a member of your church, temple, or other support group. Also, remember to approach these teens from your heart with an offer of love and kindness, since this approach helps to open the way for making peace and becoming friends once again, rather than deepening the battle.

Dialogue from Class

MOTHER: I have a belligerent teenager I need to get back in control, and I am getting ready to face it. But I'm divorced and don't know what to do if he crosses me at a time when I don't have a friend around. To be honest, he's a lot bigger and stronger than I am, and I'm afraid to confront him, which puts him completely in control.

BOBBIE: As you already know, the worst thing that can happen in parenting is for you to lose control in your relationship with a child who is still dependent on you. The best thing to do under these conditions is to reclaim your position as head of your household. If you don't have family who can back you up once you commit to doing this, join a support group or enlist the aid of counseling services or even the police, if needed, to help you manage your child. As difficult as it is to face getting this kind of help, you must reclaim your position as the head of your household, or this problem will only get progressively worse.

ANOTHER MOTHER: What if I tell my seventeen-year-old that she needs to conform to the rules in order to live in our home, and she decides to move out?

BOBBIE: When love and fair boundaries are in place and this option is offered with genuine caring, most teens won't take you up on it. In fact, the purpose of presenting this alternative is to remind the teen who is trying to seize control of his household of his dependency on his parents and to get him off of his superior attitude and dominant position. Thus, if your daughter decides to go, it's either because you have allowed her to resist and rebel for too long and she deeply believes in her superiority and dominance; or your behavior is too frustrating or controlling for her to deal with any longer.

MOTHER: I would have to say that we have been quite angry, and our rules have been pretty rigid for some time. It all started when we were so disappointed in her poor study habits in junior high. Yet the more we took away, the worse she got, and now we're in a mess.

BOBBIE: In cases like yours, where you have provoked a rebellion with too much disappointment, anger, and control, I would recommend that you call a family meeting with the goal of acknowledging your errors, apologizing for getting off on a negative tangent, and then designing a program that would put everyone back on track. You can also let your daughter know that once these changes have been made and the family rules are back in balance, that she will be expected to surrender to them.

A THIRD MOTHER: In our case, I honestly believe that we have been kind and that our rules are fair, but we have mistakenly allowed our daughter to resist everything throughout the years and have tolerated her rebellion because we thought it was a normal part of adolescence. Now that she's so deeply into resistance, I honestly believe that she would move out if we pushed it.

BOBBIE: I would explain that because in the past you have failed to require her to surrender to boundaries, her development has suffered, but that you would like to work together to correct this problem—perhaps with the help of a professional. Gently reflect the importance of her knowing how to accept rules in order to get along in the world and be a well-adjusted and emotionally mature person. You can point out any areas in her life—such as studies, sports, activities, or friendships—in which her inability to conform to boundaries has hurt her. Then let her know that from this point forward you will do your part to correct the problem by calmly following through on your rules.

MOTHER: I think she might respond to that, since she has had some problems with her friends as well. But what if she still refuses to cooperate with us just because that's her habit—then what do we do?

BOBBIE: If she still refuses to cooperate, you will have to let her choose between cooperation and making her own way. If she decides to move out, I would do all I could to get her into a foster home, a well-run shelter, or with a family that values structure and rules, rather than on the streets or with a family that is lacking in rules with rebellious children of their own.

MOTHER: What could I do if she insisted on moving in with an unstructured family or living on the streets?

BOBBIE: Kids won't push it that far unless they have been overly influenced by rebellious friends; you have been impossible to deal with; you have tolerated deceit and rebellion for quite some time; they are on drugs; or a combination of these. When you get to this most serious point of the adolescent crisis, you must strengthen your parenting skills, heal past problems, and establish new ground rules with your child. It's extremely difficult to be in this position, and any of you who find yourselves there are well advised to get all of the help you can from professional counseling, family members, support people, churches and temples, public and private therapeutic and drug rehabilitation programs, or the police if necessary. Your last hope is to find a way to *lovingly* reclaim your *authority* and bring your family back into balance. Because you will need the parenting skills that you have lacked until now, you can begin this step by reading the earlier chapters of *Parachutes for Parents*.

MOTHER: Wouldn't it be less risky to keep my daughter at home and not push the issue?

BOBBIE: This is very tempting, since you don't know what she will choose if challenged, and a teen who has left home is truly vulnerable. Thus, pushing the conflict to that point is a personal choice that each family must make for themselves—as well as accepting full responsibility for the results of their choice. Yet allowing an uncooperative teen to remain at home is an equally untenable option, since the longer he's not required to surrender to life's rules, the worse he gets and the more trouble he will have remaining in school; attracting and keeping nonrebellious friends; staying off of drugs; or holding down a job. Too often, frightened parents keep their rebellious teens at home, limping along in a nonfunctional manner, rather than face the seriousness of the problem, take a stand, and begin to require responsibility from him. If it were my child, I would muster up the courage to face the problem, rather than create an illusion that his faulty program was working by continuing to subsidize it. If it got to the point where he decided to fend for himself, I would lovingly let him know that he was welcome back at *any* point he was ready to follow the rules, and that I would like to stay in touch and plan a time to meet.

If a child elects to leave in anger as opposed to working together to find an alternative place to live and either staying in school and/or getting a job, parents have the option of calling the police to have him picked up and put into the "system" of public programs designed to help such teens and their families get back on track. Although this assures the teen's safety, the system is not always effective in resolving the larger problem; yet it can also provide the best alternative and last hope, depending on the quality of the programs in your particular area. Regardless of how parents proceed at this point, the key is to keep trying, rather than give up on their child, while simultaneously holding him lovingly in their hearts as well as to their boundaries and rules. In my experience, among the families who have confronted this in a clear, yet loving, manner, only a few of their kids opted to leave, and most of these eventually returned. Since premature independence did not prove easier for them than the rules of their family, life's true consequences were not to their liking. Once all of these options—and their consequences—have been carefully considered, each family must decide for themselves what course they will choose and accept full responsibility for the results.

FATHER: Aren't parents legally responsible for their minor children?

BOBBIE: Yes, but most kids aren't aware of this when considering whether to live by your rules or strike out on their own—unless you have foolishly brought it to their attention. Remember, that the reason you offer this choice is to remind your child of his dependency on you. The expectation is that he will choose to accept your rules, and most do. However, if a child decides to leave, he usually turns to friends, who eventually get tired of caring for him, and he will typically return in due course. Nonetheless, it's your responsibility to find out where a teen who has left your home is and to make sure that he is, in fact, safe. If you are unable to locate him, it's important that you call the police, who will, once they find him, attempt to return him to you. Yet without his surrender, nothing has changed. Thus, it's critical not to allow the system to coerce you into taking your child back at this point; you must insist, instead, that you are happy to cooperate, but that the child is beyond your control and you are unable to manage him without their services and help. There are laws in most states that provide help for parents of children beyond their control, so find out what these laws are and insist that you are given the help available to you. This is both yours and society's chance to get this child back on track, so don't get pressured into aborting this opportunity.

FATHER: What if you know your kid is on drugs?

BOBBIE: If a rebellious teen is also using drugs, it's essential to get treatment for the drug problem first, since drugs not only trigger serious rebellions, but are key to maintaining them. Because all efforts to help a person on drugs will fail, the drugs must be addressed first. Another option for families with deeply rebellious kids is to send them to a special program designed to help the child confront his faulty approach to life while he is separated from the influence of rebellious peers and substances. (See **Adolescence** entry in Problem-Solving Guide for referrals.)

FATHER: What if you can't get them to go to these programs?

BOBBIE: You can gently let them know that in order to continue to live in your home, they will have to face their problem and get some help—and that you would be happy to support them in getting to the right program. Some families with extremely rebellious, drug-addicted kids have had them forcibly enrolled in these programs and then allowed the influence of the program to take over. This works best when such programs have been court-ordered. These options are tough, but you are in a difficult position if your teen is on drugs, since letting him continue to do drugs while living at home without intervention is an equally painful option.

FATHER: Isn't that too controlling?

BOBBIE: Yes, it's controlling. But these kids are in serious trouble and require meaningful intervention. The problem is that the entire family system is stuck in a pattern of allowing such a teen to remain dependent and subsidized while refusing to be responsible. It's clear that this combination needs to be interrupted. Consequently, loving, yet highly structured, programs offer them their greatest hope for getting back on track. The other option is to release such a child and hope that life will teach him what he needs to know to get righted again before he provokes society to incarcerate him indefinitely. It's a very difficult decision each family will have to make for themselves.

Remaining Firm and Clear, Yet Loving

Anytime your adolescent challenges his boundaries with resistance, deception, or outright rebellion, you must present yourself as someone who neither cowers nor has a fit, but is firmly—yet lovingly—in charge. It's important that you tell him what is required with a voice filled with both conviction and kindness, rather than act fearful or helpless with statements of, "I don't know what I'm going to do with you" or "You've gotten too big for me to handle." By the same token, you can trigger more resistance by being overly controlling and dominant. Therefore, it's most effective when you shift to your heart and remain neutral, yet strong. Yet it's also important that you feel free to consult your own inner voice to guide you in using whatever style will work best with your particular child. If you must employ a powerful—even stern—approach, then so be it. Your first priority is to reinstate your authority. Once that has been accomplished, connected feelings can be reestablished during clearing.

Using Clearing to Heal

A critical step to take with an adolescent, once authority has been reestablished or claimed for the first time, is *clearing*. (See Chapter 8.) During clearing, it's essential that you listen calmly without interruption to the things your teen is trying to express. Quite often, he does have legitimate complaints about too much dominance or your lack of understanding his need for freedom to be with nonrebellious friends or his need for control over his life during those times when he is being cooperative. Thus, it's important that you allow this information to sink in—without defense or continuing the old battle—and be willing to make changes where needed.

Your willingness to address any part you have played in the conflict is the key to reopening communication and has helped many teens who would like to be friends with their families to back down, get out of their rebellious mode, and make a fresh start. Thus, even if your transgressions are secondary to his, be the first to acknowledge your part. Those of you who remain stubbornly righteous and return to your efforts to win the old battle will cause your child to meet your resistance with resistance of his own. In short, if you get too controlling without balancing your authority with love, you will invariably lose the child. Thus, only after offering love, while fully acknowledging your own mistakes, can you effectively require that your teen face his errors and responsibilities as well. Yet this step must always be confronted and taken, rather than avoided, even if your teen has settled down, following your own acknowledgements. In short, the key is to acknowledge first; then, gently require that he do the same.

The Purpose of Adolescence

Now that we have established that resistance and rebellion are not what the adolescent years are meant to include, let's examine what purpose adolescence serves and how you might help your child to fulfill that purpose.

Once you are clear about keeping your teenager on the agenda, yet rejecting any rebellions he wages, the stage is set for a period in which you are loving and fair while your teen is politely cooperative. Under these conditions, both you and your adolescent can work together toward the common goal of helping him to achieve individuation and maturity as he takes his final steps toward independence. In short, the adolescent years are simply a continuation of your child preparing to manage increasingly more of his life while you carefully and deliberately hand him the baton for doing so on his own. (See Figure 13.)

Thus, rather than serve as a confusing and chaotic period as it has so often been promoted to be, the adolescent stage of development should simply include the following components:

- An adolescent faces many new experiences which he must handle increasingly on his own. As he succeeds in managing each experience, his skills and confidence grow. In this way, each event—and the lessons and successes he gains from managing it—contribute to his belief in his ability to handle life independently.

- To augment their adolescent's development, wise parents not only allow him to assume progressively more self-management, but nudge him—

Figure 13. Achieving Independence

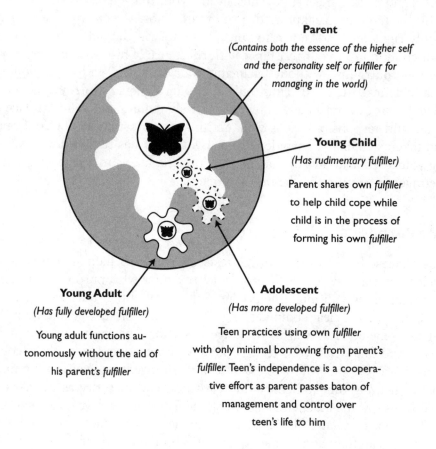

Parent

(Contains both the essence of the higher self and the personality self or fulfiller for managing in the world)

Young Child

(Has rudimentary fulfiller)

Parent shares own *fulfiller* to help child cope while child is in the process of forming his own *fulfiller*

Young Adult

(Has fully developed fulfiller)

Young adult functions autonomously without the aid of his parent's *fulfiller*

Adolescent

(Has more developed fulfiller)

Teen practices using own *fulfiller* with only minimal borrowing from parent's *fulfiller*. Teen's independence is a cooperative effort as parent passes baton of management and control over teen's life to him

when needed—toward each new step, while supporting him in handling it on his own. Increasingly, their role becomes one of teacher and motivator, as they not only rejoice in their teen's new activities and friends, but take pleasure in his ability to function with increasing maturity and independence.

• Not only is the adolescent adjusting to accepting new levels of responsibility, his parents are faced with releasing their management of his life. In this way, achievement of the teen's independence becomes a cooperative effort in which parents let go of the reins of their child's life as he picks them up to guide and direct it on his own. (See Figure 14.)

Figure 14. Teen Participation vs. Avoidance *or* The Technicolor Train vs. the Black-and-White Train

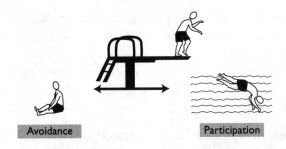

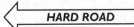

Participation

The Illusion: Avoidance will offer an easier road.

← **EASY ROAD**   **HARD ROAD** →

Avoiding full participation in life offers teens the illusion that life is easier as they:	Teens can fully participate in life only if they are willing to:
• Avoid risk • Look "cool" • Take it easy • Avoid criticism • Avoid responsibility • Avoid rejection • Resist error and failure	• Face fear • Be enthusiastic • Participate • Face criticism • Accept responsibility • Risk rejection • Embrace error and failure

The Reality: The signs have been switched. Avoidance turns out to be the hard road.

← **HARD ROAD**   **EASY ROAD** →

By not participating, a teen loses the opportunity to:	By participating, a teen has the opportunity to:
• Resolve fear • Develop competence • Believe in himself • Keep doors to his future open • Develop a long-term community of friends • Succeed	• Resolve fear • Develop competence • Believe in himself • Keep doors to his future open • Develop a long-term community of friends • Succeed

After high school, it becomes clear to the avoiding teen that the signs have been switched. His community of avoidant friends has dissolved; he has developed no talents; nor has he opened doors to his future. As a result, he's often alone, battling such things as hopelessness, depression, or addiction problems, and, before long, he notices that he's on the black-and-white train. By contrast, the participating teen has not only confronted his fears and gained maturity, he finds himself on the Technicolor train.

The Role of the Teen: Confronting New Experiences to Prepare for Independence

For the first time in his life, your adolescent will be challenged by many new experiences such as managing the selection, tryouts, and fulfillment of his activities; learning to drive, passing his test, and maintaining a vehicle; finding and keeping summer and part-time jobs; maintaining his grades; socializing with both sexes; addressing his sexuality; and developing and preparing for postgraduation plans.

Facing the Fear. Many teens are intimidated by having to manage so many new experiences increasingly on their own. Although it's hard to admit, they sometimes miss their parents' help with signing them up for things, monitoring their responsibilities, planning their social events, and helping them unravel problems with teachers, coaches, and friends.

Others have not yet learned to accept taking risks, working hard, or dealing with rejection and are overly concerned with errors, criticism, and pain. This results in their reluctance to jump from the "diving board of life" into the participatory side of experience, where they are forced to confront their fears, face the risks of the unknown, and accept responsibility for life's feedback and normal levels of pain. (See Figure 14.)

Many deal with their fear of participation by retreating to the "stairs" of life in order to avoid the risks and pain that "jumping in" might produce. They drop out of activities and neglect their studies, while striving to make their withdrawal look like the best of choices. They claim that school and teachers are boring and that everything is too dumb to bother with. Bright kids use more philosophical excuses for their avoidance. Others hide from life's challenges behind deceit, truancy, and running away. And still others withdraw into alcohol and drugs to create an illusion that everything is fine, while they numb themselves to life's normal pain.

Once down the stairs, the avoidant child hates to admit to diminished feelings of adequacy, continued dependence, and low self-esteem or that the avoider's corner is an empty place, devoid of lasting pleasure and leading nowhere.

As a way to bring meaning to their choice, many teens convert their avoidance to resistance and become "rebels without a cause." They strive to make their resistance the "cool" thing to do and lure others into the group to join them in their retreat into nonparticipation. Over time, the avoider's corner becomes a "club" where its members experience a sense of community, so long as parents are supporting them and subsidizing their rebellions, while they contribute very little to their own lives or the lives of others. What they fail to see is that once out of high school, their community disbands, and they are left empty-handed with few skills, talents, or choices and no place to go. Many of them will also be strapped by drug addictions, babies to raise, or both; others will develop the serious emotional problems that kick in after a few years of drug use—which are little known to high school students in the early stages of drug experimentation—but are well known to health professionals who see the long-term results, often leading to psychiatric care, hospitalization, or worse. As a result, these kids notice too late that the signposts indicating that avoidance would be the easier path were, in fact, switched and that they are on an empty, challenging, and extremely painful road. In short, they find themselves in drab settings on life's "black-and-white train." (See Figure 14.)

The more fortunate adolescents who push through their fears; confront the work that goes with participation; handle new situations on their own; and meet with success or survive whatever rejection or failure they encounter, develop their talents and grow in feelings of inner strength and confidence. Not only does their fear dissolve upon taking the plunge, such teens are on the road to full participation, maturity, unlimited independence, and a significantly more fulfilling adulthood. In contrast to the avoiders, they have found the path alongside other fellow winners on the Technicolor train.

Whenever I have shown teens how their lives compare to the child on the diving board—as they stand at a crossroad deciding whether to withdraw from life's activities in order to avoid the effort, errors, and pain or jump into full participation with a willingness to go through whatever it takes to be there—they have shown surprising interest. When I ask them to consider what the options look like further along each of the paths, they quickly see that the avoider's corner dissolves upon high school graduation, with few interesting options remaining—while the path of participation is more expansive and rewarding.

Since so many of our kids end up in the avoider's corner, we would be wise to create additional signposts along the way indicating where and how teens might find the more fulfilling road. We can do this by putting more of our attention and resources on those kids who have selected the road of participation, rather than make them wait so long, as we presently do, for vague and dubious rewards. We can, for example, provide more immediate reinforcers such as extra privileges; truly exciting activities; meaningful ways to participate in such things as helping to restore the environment and rebuild our society; and more free time to those students who are acting responsibly. In this way, we make it clearer that the road of participation, even with its extra risks and work, is the one filled with excitement and meaning as well as the opportunity for success and fun. Similarly, we owe it to all kids to make it clearer to the avoiders during their high school years that the path of avoidance is not only problematic, but dangerous.

The Parental Role: Maintaining Balance While Supporting Independence

The responsibility of parents during the adolescent period is to remember to keep their child on the agenda, remain loving and friendly, and uphold fair rules, while supporting their teen's independence. In short, they must continue to maintain a balance between love and discipline while allowing, supporting, and rejoicing in their teenager's movement toward independence.

Loving Teenagers. As discussed earlier, keeping your adolescent on life's daily agenda is the first step in maintaining a loving relationship with him. Following are other ways to strengthen a loving connection with your teen.

▶ *Finding Time.* Although you often don't expect older kids to want to spend time with you, most teens value being with their families. Therefore, preserving such things as family dinners, outings, meetings, traditions, and trips contributes to connecting times with teenagers. It's also important to continue to be available for moments with your adolescent when they arise, since these times become increasingly rare as he achieves progressively more autonomy. (See Chapter 11.)

▶ *Gentle Communication.* Because adolescents are capable of communicating on a level comparable to adults, it's particularly important that you see them as equals and not talk down to them in a dictatorial or bossy manner. Only when your teen is crossing boundaries must he be reminded that you are still in charge—and even this must be done with calm neutrality. When boundaries are not involved, all communications should be parallel.

Once this is established, taking care to understand things from your teen's point of view and valuing what he sees, feels, and says—in the same way you would with a friend—enhances your bond with him. (See Chapter 11 on Communication.) Anytime such communications are underway, only if you notice that your child holds some unclear view about how life works do you strive to help him to release it and adopt a more effective viewpoint. However, you must make sure not to mistake a failure to agree with you as an unclear viewpoint, since unclear viewpoints are only those that are injurious to the child or others in some way. For example, if your daughter's boyfriend breaks up with her, and she decides that love will never be available to her again, that particular belief would constitute a fear-based, faulty conclusion that would be hurtful to her life. If, however, she rejects your view that making money is more important than following a less lucrative, yet passionate, career interest, that is simply a difference in viewpoint, rather than a faulty conclusion.

▸ *Offering Support.* You can help your adolescent by gently nudging him toward new experiences and challenges whenever his urge to avoid them seems stronger than his desire to participate in life. By understanding his fear of new encounters and talking openly about the normalcy of such feelings, you can help him to realize that his fears are common to everyone, including his fellow adolescents. This reduces his aversion to fearful feelings and helps him to see that participation in spite of them leads to maturity and a reduction in fear, whereas avoidance results in deeper feelings of insecurity, powerlessness, and fear. (See Chapter 10.)

However, once your adolescent seems to be managing on his own, it's important that you step aside and allow the new experience to generate its own reinforcing results.

Dialogue from Class

MOTHER: Whenever I notice that my ninth grader is withdrawing from the challenge of new activities, I try to encourage him, but when that doesn't work, what can I do?

BOBBIE: If your teen is avoiding an activity because he doesn't feel secure enough to participate, you can help him to find ways to feel safer. You can, for instance, talk to him about the importance of facing his fears throughout adolescence as well as look for ways to make the more challenging tasks a little less formidable. For example, my son was interested in volleyball but failed to make the junior varsity team his freshman year and spent an extra year along with several other freshmen on the intermediate team. That summer, he had an opportunity to practice with the JV and varsity teams combined, something he was excited about, yet reluctant to try. Because I was aware of his concern about being on the court with the varsity players, I talked to him about the value of overcoming his fears as well as keeping the doors of opportunity open. In addition, I offered to drive him to these practices, knowing that it would be a little easier for him to attend if he didn't have the additional obstacle of finding a ride or taking the bus.

MOTHER: How did that work out?

BOBBIE: He made the JV team and went on to play varsity and college volleyball. But the real success was the effect it had on his confidence and ability to confront his fears.

MOTHER: How far would you have gone if he had said "No"?

BOBBIE: I would have accepted his decision. Once a teenager has been told that participation—rather than avoidance—is the path to maturity and support has been gently offered to assist him in facing his fears, the choice still remains his. If his reluctance wins out, I would strive to help him uncover less threatening activities that he might feel more comfortable trying.

⊚⊚⊚

Loosening the Reins. Many of you falsely believe that you can avoid problems by keeping tight controls over your adolescents and allowing them only narrow parameters of movement. Yet these boundaries don't match the purpose of the adolescent period during which the teen is supposed to be increasing the management of his own affairs in preparation for independence.

Others require a demonstration of "responsibility" from their teen before giving him normal adolescent freedoms. Yet because they view teen responsibility as an error-free existence, rather than one of practicing new levels of self-management—including the mistakes required to achieve it—it's almost impossible for their teen to satisfy their requirement.

Since teenagers are at a level of maturation in which they are poised for the next step of independence, within them lies a strong and vital urge to manage more and more of their own lives. Consequently, only those of you with fair rules who allow your teen the freedom he needs to learn to manage his own life, explore his own interests, and practice decision-making, create an environment in which his urge for independence can flourish and his need for rebellion subsides.

It's essential, therefore, that you gradually relinquish the management of your child's life as he assumes progressively more responsible ownership of it and temporarily contract his freedoms only when they are being misused. In this way, your teen has a chance to practice responsible autonomy before leaving home.

Whenever you thwart this critical step toward independence by continuing to make all of your teen's decisions, you not only frustrate him, but may trigger a rebellion.

Roger

Roger was a late developer with average grades, a handful of friends, and very few activities. However, at the beginning of his junior year his braces came off, he filled out physically, grew emotionally, and was gaining confidence in many areas. As a result, not only did his grades improve, but he was making more friends and had secured a position on the swim team. Unfortunately, his mother continued to relate to him as a younger, less mature child and did not understand the importance of releasing the reins of his life to him. She continued to monitor his return home from school immediately after swim practice, required that he keep his phone calls brief, made sure that he was settled down to study shortly after dinner, and insisted that he be in bed in time for a good night's rest. She was not facing that these were all things Roger should now be managing on his own in preparation for assuming full control over such decisions after graduation. As a result, Roger began to resist his mother's control and was becoming more and more irritable with her. This caused her to view him as an uncooperative teenager, and it wasn't long before they were in conflict.

One Saturday afternoon, Roger's swim team was having its final meet with an awards banquet to follow. Roger had been out of school for a week with the flu but felt well enough on Saturday to manage his event and the banquet. However, Mrs. Green saw things differently and refused to let him go. After an extended argument, Roger became so furious that he stormed out of the house, walked to the pool, swam his event, and went to the banquet in borrowed clothes.

Although Roger's behavior was clearly defiant, Mrs. Green's behavior was even more problematic. She had seized control over a decision that should have been Roger's to make. Instead of frustrating her son by blocking his freedom to participate in an activity so important to him, she should have surrendered this decision to Roger to practice making decisions on his own. She might have let him know that she supported him in finding ways to meet his needs, while suggesting that he consider how to do so without jeopardizing his health. She could also have cautioned that if he decided to swim he might want to shower and change right after his event and return home as early as possible from the banquet. However, after providing her input, she would have been wise to leave the final decisions to Roger. She should also have allowed him to experience the results of any foolish decisions he might have made in this regard—even if they included getting sicker. By doing this, she would have gained his trust in her as a reasonable parent, and he, in turn, would be more likely to listen to her opinions. Instead, Mrs. Green triggered rebellious behavior in a previously cooperative adolescent by seizing too much control over his decisions and freedom.

Passing the Baton: Requirements for Teens

Rather than do what Mrs. Green did, parents must release control, while requiring that their teens adhere to some basic, appropriate boundaries. These boundaries should very simply include:

- Behaving in a friendly manner toward his family and others
- Accepting a short list of reasonable and fair rules and responsibilities
- Communicating in an open, honest manner with his family and others at all times

The key is for parents to keep requirements short, fair, and reasonable, but to then require full acquiescence to them.

Passing the Baton: Requirements for Parents

Parents must take particular care to provide appropriately generous boundaries that continue to expand as their adolescent develops his capacity to voluntarily cooperate and assume increasing responsibility. In order to keep the expansion of your teen's boundaries appropriate, you must hold him in your heart with caring and view him with respect. In order to do this effectively, parents can use the following guidelines.

- **Guideline #1:** *Are boundaries formed in such a way that the needs of the adolescent are genuinely valued and taken into serious consideration?*
    When you fail to allow a cooperative teen the same liberties his well-adjusted peers enjoy, you lose credibility and tempt him to sneak around your rules in order to achieve normal levels of freedom. For example, many of you use arbitrary guidelines such as requiring that your teen be

home unrealistically early; conform to outdated ideas about fashion; delay normal experiences such as learning to drive; and block opportunities to participate in normal teen functions. You tie such privileges to things like the calendar or your teen's grades, rather than his level of cooperation. This not only prevents him from participating in normal adolescent experiences at a time when his peers are enjoying them, but frustrates his opportunity to demonstrate responsibility as a way of gaining expanded freedoms. Those of you in this category are often overly fearful for the safety and well-being of your child and fail to face the necessity of letting go. Following are some examples of these restrictive parameters and how they can backfire.

► *Grades*. Grades can be a point of contention around which parent and teen struggle and often cause a breakdown in their relationship. This happens when parents want their kids to get higher marks in hopes of keeping doors open to their futures. But their teenagers are not always internally motivated or don't know how to structure themselves to get the desired grades. When parents get impatient or fight over this topic, it only makes matters worse.

Thus, I recommend that parents shift to their hearts, remain as neutral and calm as an "oak tree," and invite their teen to join them in examining what his academic and other goals are, how he can best meet these goals, and what help he might need from his family. They can also help him to face what doors are open to him with his present grades and which ones would open if his marks went a notch higher. The goal is to remain friends while providing help. By keeping communication friendly and open, parents have their best opportunity to influence. From this position, they can offer to establish a study hall, give study advice, help to organize a planner, or provide tutoring assistance if wanted and needed.

Dialogue from Class

FATHER: Do you ever take control and require that your child study for a certain amount of time?

BOBBIE: This is an option families might use for their child's junior high years, his freshman year, or sometimes even the first half of his sophomore year to teach him how to study and develop an ingrained habit of doing so. I would only do this with a second semester sophomore or junior if he agreed that he required help and was willing for me to structure a study hall for him, since a child that age needs to begin to take ownership of his own studies. Yet even when this step is taken with the younger teen, the child should be included in selecting his study hall time and place. Also, your willingness to be nearby for questions or to offer a snack makes this step more palatable.

FATHER: Should I require that my son quit basketball until he can get his grades up?

BOBBIE: Many families—as well as some school programs—require that a teenager maintain a specific grade average before granting him the freedom to participate in a variety of extracurricular activities, including such things as sports, artistic pursuits, committee work, and driving.

Yet on closer analysis, we can see that requiring a child to have enough maturity for his grades to improve *before* allowing him to participate in outside activities blocks his opportunity to be involved in the very things that would contribute most to his maturation. For example, playing sports and joining activities help teens to overcome their reluctance to take risks and try new things. These activities also help them to get comfortable with participation and the errors that accompany it. They further help kids to become more disciplined; develop organizational and social skills; discover their strengths and talents; and improve their self-esteem—all qualities they need to perform well academically. Moreover, participating in these activities exposes kids to other involved and motivated peers who are likely to positively influence them.

Many adults—including myself—were not academically mature early on, but due to playing a sport or starring in an activity, went on to mature in this and other arenas and have full and productive lives. In most cases, their academic skills later improved as a result of the maturity and skills they gained from participation in their outside activities. In fact, many famous and inspiring people fall into this category. As a result, I am strongly opposed to the currently popular practice of basing the opportunity for participation in extracurricular activities on academic performance.

☉☉☉

Cliff

Cliff was class chairman of one of his school fund-raisers when I met him in my capacity as a parent chair. Initially, I found him to be somewhat immature, but as our committee work progressed, he developed more social and leadership skills. Consequently, I was surprised when he didn't show up for our last few meetings, which were critical to our overall fund-raising success as well as to his experience as an emerging leader.

I was dismayed to learn later that Cliff had been required by his parents to drop this activity as well as his position on the wrestling team because he had received an interim report, indicating the possibility of a grade lower than his usual "B" in one of his classes. Not only had this gesture blocked his positive participation in both activities, his parents were forcing him to renege on his responsibilities to his team and committee. This was, understandably, discouraging for Cliff, and I was not surprised when I later heard that all of his grades had slipped even further by the end of the semester.

☺☺☺

▶ ***Driving.*** Many parents make a similar mistake in determining when to allow their teenager to drive. They unwisely ignore his intense interest in learning this skill at the time when he first becomes eligible for it. Instead, they attach conditions such as improved grades or nonspecific levels of maturity before allowing him to get his permit, believing that this will inspire him to do better in school or behave more responsibly. Not surprisingly, the teen who is unable to meet such vague conditions and must, therefore, postpone his driving and the passage into maturity it represents loses an important growth experience, and his maturation is delayed.

To his parents' surprise, such a child is unwilling to face the challenge of driving at a later date when his parents have changed their minds and would like him to pursue it. In such cases, because the teen was denied participation in this rite of passage at the time when his friends were going through it, he lost the intensity of interest in it that was pushing him to confront his fears about organizing and managing it.

Once this period of heightened interest in driving and the teen's willingness to push through his fears in order to attain the skill have passed, he often shifts into avoidance of the challenge. When understood in this light, it appears that learning to drive ought to be encouraged, rather than delayed, in all teens—with the exception of those who are highly irre-sponsible and rebellious. The key is to require extensive lessons, which include such things as guidelines for safety and driving with maturity, as well as basic driving skills. Be aware that car privileges can always be tem-porarily withdrawn whenever teens are not behaving responsibly which, in turn, motivates most teens to cooperate with their parents in order to protect this valued privilege once it is attained.

▶ *Socializing.* Allowing a teen ample opportunity to be with his friends not only honors his individual needs, but helps him in his social develop-ment. Although many parents prefer to see their adolescent engaged in pursuits they consider more "productive," interacting with cooperative and motivated friends strengthens the very skills that are most crucial to his overall confidence, success, and competence. In fact, parents must understand that a child lacking in social skills has very little opportunity for success—even if he is academically keen.

▶ *Curfew.* Rather than impose curfews that thoroughly frustrate the coop-erative adolescent, parents can work out time frames in such a way that both the teen's needs and those of his family are respected. Personally, I am always more interested in how much a child is trusted and what kinds of activities he's involved in than what time it is. The trusted child will do the right thing no matter how late it is, and the unreliable one will do the wrong thing no matter how early it is. Consequently, a curfew works best when it's viewed as a guideline for helping teenagers deter-mine when it's reasonable to wrap up an evening and return home, rather than an instrument to keep them out of trouble. A good gauge to use when selecting approximate times is to find out when other responsible teens from his peer group are required to be home as well as what the safety challenges in your geographic area include.

Used in this way, a teen can work out his evening plans and develop a realistic estimated time to return home. I prefer that this be an approx-imate time, rather than a rigid one and allow for reasonable delays and changes in plans. However, if the teen is delayed and will be home more than fifteen to twenty minutes after the estimated time, he should call so that family members are not left wondering if he has a problem.

If I received a call from a trusted teenager asking for an extension to talk longer, go to a friend's house, or spend the night, I would grant it, unless there was a specific reason not to. In this way, the teen is given ample freedom to enjoy his activities without being frustrated by rigid parents and inflexible time frames for returning home. It must be clearly understood, however, that only when a parent has an open, honest, and friendly relationship with a responsible adolescent will such a flexible curfew benefit the child and not be abused. A teenager who is not yet cooperative or open and honest would be given more restrictive curfews, which would expand only as he became more open and responsible.

The teen must also understand that he doesn't have to be out as late as his estimated time. Thus, it's important to teach him that when the evening has wound down, it's best to break it up and get home, rather than drag it out until the time designated for being home—perhaps even spoiling the memory of a pleasant evening.

Dialogue from Class

MOTHER: What do you do about a child who fools around after soccer practice and gets home later than he's supposed to?

BOBBIE: If a child is expected home at 6:30 following practice, but is having a wonderful conversation with a friend, he shouldn't be made to feel as though he will turn into the proverbial pumpkin if he completes his talk. It's important to trust your child to act responsibly, rather than lack respect for his judgment in handling such things. When reliable kids are allowed to manage their own time, they don't feel a need for extra freedom and thus have no desire to struggle with you over boundaries or abuse the parameters set for them.

FATHER: How long would you allow for this extra time after practice before feeling the privilege was being abused?

BOBBIE: I think a half hour gives a child plenty of time to enjoy his friends and finish conversations after practice. If something caused a longer delay, it would be important for him to call home to relieve parental worry and release the family to proceed with dinner.

ANOTHER MOTHER: What if a sixteen-year-old always comes home a little later than her estimated time?

BOBBIE: I wouldn't be concerned if she returned within the fifteen to twenty minutes you have established as an outside time before a call is required.

MOTHER: But it seems to me that she's abusing her time by always coming home fifteen minutes later than estimated.

BOBBIE: I wouldn't worry about a teenager coming home that late even if it was on a regular basis, since that's not terribly "late." Try to think of your own ability to return home within fifteen minutes of your estimated time, and you will understand better why a responsible child might return home later than expected. Yet if she is not truly responsible and always pushes the rules, or if she seems to be manipulating the system and arrives fifteen minutes or more after the estimated time on a regular basis, it would appear that she wasn't appreciating that the system was designed to help her to be as flexible as possible in her time management. In that case, I would let her know that she was undermining my trust in her ability to work with me on a fair curfew and that I might have to give her a more restricted time if she didn't want to stay within the spirit of the more lenient one.

MOTHER: What would you do if your child came home forty-five minutes late and had not called?

BOBBIE: I would contract his freedom for the following weekend and would return it again the weekend after that if I felt he had successfully cleared with me and was ready to live within the spirit of the rule.

ANOTHER MOTHER: What if I don't trust my child enough to give him as late a curfew as his friends have?

BOBBIE: Is your mistrust based on his behaviors or on your general lack of trust?

MOTHER: It's my fear about what might happen.

BOBBIE: If your lack of trust is based on fear rather than his behaviors, it would help to remember that an unjustified reluctance to release control over a child's freedom actually provokes the teenager to sneak around the rules in order to gain normal freedoms. Under these conditions, trust never has a chance to develop. Therefore, you would be wise to release your fear and start with more generous freedoms, which you can always cut back if your child misuses them. In that way, you learn to adjust to his being out at night while he enjoys normal freedoms.

A Third Mother: What if your child has done a number of sneaky things, and you really don't have an honest relationship with him?

Bobbie: Teenagers should not be free to go out until they have cleared with their families and honesty has been reestablished between them. If parents know that their child is untrustworthy but gloss over the underlying problem and allow him to maintain all of his freedoms, there will always be problems. Thus, only after your child accepts responsibility for his mistakes and commits to honesty and openness can you offer him his freedoms once again.

Father: How do you prevent peer contact when your child has his own telephone?

Bobbie: I would remove the receiver from his room until his restriction was over and we had completely cleared. Incidentally, when socially oriented kids lose contact with their peers, you would be amazed by how quickly they are willing to get their act together to clear with you.

Fourth Mother: My child resists the idea of calling me each time his plans change. Isn't this a reasonable request?

Bobbie: With the younger child from thirteen to fourteen, I would want to know the friends involved and have a clear idea of the plan beforehand as well as a call each time they moved from one setting to another. However, if a trusted child of fifteen or sixteen moved from a pizza shop to somebody's home nearby without it being part of the plan, I would not expect a call unless he was running late on his time. By the same token, if the fifteen- to sixteen-year-old was going to drive some distance or do something drastically different than originally planned, I would want a call. Yet with the older child of seventeen or eighteen who had established good trust and credibility with me, I would only expect a general plan and time frame and would not expect to be called about changes unless he was running unduly late.

■ **Guideline #2:** *Are boundaries formed in such a way that the cooperative adolescent maintains as much control as possible over his choice of friends?*

Is your responsible teen free to select his own friends, or is he required to spend time only with friends you consider suitable? Even if his friends aren't good students or highly motivated, as long as they are cooperative and nonrebellious, your adolescent must be given the freedom to have them as friends so long as he is behaving responsibly. He can be told, for example, that if he's able to maintain his family standards and rules, he can preserve the option of spending time with friends whose standards are somewhat different. Remember that allowing your teen to freely choose his friends in accordance with his willingness to do so responsibly is preferable to assuming that he won't be responsible and thus over-controlling his selection of friends from the outset.

If however, these friends are strongly rebellious or if his closest friends or the majority of them are prone to be anti-adult and rebellious, you must be aware that such kids will teach their friends to become rebellious as well. Thus, it's essential that you pay attention and gently intercede at the outset if your teen is being led astray by resistant kids. If you delay such an intervention, your child will have had time to identify with the rebellious kids, and interceding after this has happened becomes very challenging if not impossible. Once you determine that intervention is needed, here is how to proceed.

First, remain calm and friendly while checking to see if your child would like help in getting out of these relationships and finding more cooperative friends, since this is often the case.

If not, strive to befriend and influence the negative friends and see if your child will accept—without rebellion or going underground—spending time with them only when more positive friends are included or activities are home-based. These two measures can serve to positively influence the rebellious friends, rather than have them negatively influence your child as well as others in the group who are still interested in cooperation.

If the relationship has gone too far and your teen is unreceptive to these measures, use the consequence of restricting him from spending time only with his rebellious friends anytime he is rude, has a bad attitude, goes underground, or behaves rebelliously. During these restricted periods, encourage connections with other, more cooperative and participatory friends, but do this subtly, rather than in a manner that will turn your child against these kids. Meanwhile, remain loving toward your teen, preserve—or reestablish—your relationship with him, and take measures to help him to feel better about himself. This is a logical time to have your doctor screen for drugs as well, since rebellious friends and drugs almost always go together. If drugs are involved, seek professional help. If your teen seems to be accepting this arrangement and is reconnecting with his nonrebellious friends during this period, keep the program in place for as long as it's working, since this break not only gives him an excuse for time away from the rebellious kids, but can serve as a permanent break in the relationship with them—especially if you don't bring up the subject or inquire about the rebellious kids. If, on the other hand, your teen is committed to his rebellious friends, make sure not to allow them to resume time together until your child is willing to fully acknowledge the problem, show genuine concern about the direction this group is headed, and fully clear and resume good feelings toward you. Then, if after resuming time with them, he becomes antisocial again, repeat the restriction from this crowd, but for a longer period of time.

The sooner you become aware of a relationship or a cluster of friends who are having a negative influence on your teen, the better success you will have with intervention. Whenever a disruptive friendship is allowed to go on for too long or involves a number of negative friends, those relationships can lure your child so far off course that you may not be able to bring him back. Thus, if the approach outlined here is not strong enough and your teen is committed to a rebellious group of friends, seek professional help to assist you in getting things back on track before they go any further out of control. (See **Adolescence** entry in the Problem-Solving Guide for resources.)

Dialogue from Class

FATHER: You hear so much about the negative influence of peers, but I read an article questioning it. Do you think it's real?

BOBBIE: Absolutely. Rebellious peers who are off the beaten track create a traffic pattern large enough to make their activities seem normal to the kids who spend time with them. As a result, even cooperative kids lose their perspective about what is right and wrong. Before long, they view these abnormal activities as the norm and their parents' standards as overly restrictive. Once this shift in perspective happens, teens push to participate in these activities. One year I had three separate families who didn't even know one another come into counseling at different times of the year as a result of their daughters making friends with a girl I will call Toni. Each of these girls had previously been only slightly resistant at home but became outright rebellious after befriending Toni.

MOTHER: Why aren't positive friendships as influential as the negative ones?

BOBBIE: Actually, they are. Involved, cooperative peers coax their friends to participate in various activities, and they also provide a model of participatory, agreeable behavior. You are often less aware of this highly valuable influence, since it isn't causing a problem, but your child's friends always influence his development, whether positively or negatively. It's one of the reasons I so strongly support socialization with positive peers as a critical part of a child's healthy development.

FATHER: Wouldn't it be hard for a child to be required to stop seeing his friends, even if they are a bad influence?

BOBBIE: My experience is that nonresistant kids who have gotten in with the wrong crowd often welcome help in making a change. However, kids with a history of their own resistance tend to be more committed to rebellious friends and would need more understanding and support if they are required to change. The key is to act early if you think your child is being negatively influenced by his friends, as it gets increasingly difficult to separate them as time goes on. The first thing you must do is heal any break in your own relationship, since feeling against family causes teens to look to their peers as replacements for family. Next, you must tell him that you realize it's not easy to make new, more responsible friends, but that you will assist him in taking that step. For example, I would help him to look for a team or an activity to join—or take lessons in something that he's interested in to help him meet new friends. Or you might support his going to a special camp program over the summer to help him build his confidence. You can also assist him in planning ways to connect with peers that he would like to befriend but hasn't had the courage to approach. If things have gone too far and are out of hand, I would even look into his changing schools and starting over.

MOTHER: Isn't giving him lessons and sending him to camp or helping him to change schools pampering him?

BOBBIE: I have often seen parents resist such efforts and expenditures on behalf of their children, thinking that their kids can survive going off track, just as they did when they were young. Yet times are different, and most of today's side roads are harder to work back from than they used to be. What these same families later realize is how far things can go, and they often end up in a therapist's office, spending equal if not greater amounts of time and money trying to dig their child out of a hole. Personally, I would do all I could to prevent the bigger problem.

MOTHER: How would you handle it if your child gave you information about his friends using drugs?

BOBBIE: First, be aware that only a generally cooperative child would voluntarily share such information with you. Furthermore, because it's so essential that you never misuse information voluntarily given by your child, it would be important to simply move into a discussion about how your child felt about having friends trying drugs and how he could best manage such a situation. I would also encourage my child to share his thoughts about experimenting with the drugs; then, after allowing him time to share his own viewpoint, I would give him information about why I felt it was a problem for him and his friends. (See **Drugs** entry in Problem-Solving Guide.) Although I would discreetly look for ways to encourage him to connect with more responsible kids, as long as my teen was remaining open and honest as well as cooperative with me, I would refrain from forbidding him to see these friends. Instead, I would continue to use our open communication as my opportunity to influence, while staying alert to signs of drug use.

FATHER: What if you suspect that he's getting into the drugs himself?

BOBBIE: If you suspect drug use, rather than ask him about it, take the initiative to get information from other sources, including asking his doctor for a drug test, since denial goes hand in hand with drug use. If you discover that he is getting involved with drugs, you need to take control and—with professional assistance—make sure that he gets help.

MOTHER: Is there anything we can do to prevent our kids from getting in with the wrong crowd in the first place?

BOBBIE: Building strength in your family is the best way to prevent rebellious peers from penetrating your teen's world, since he will be more attracted to what you provide in your home if it's positive. It's also useful to discuss the problems of rebellious friends with your teens in contrast to the benefits and power of being part of a cooperative family and community of friends. In doing this you disempower nonparticipation and rebellion, while highlighting the advantages of cooperation. Thus, rather than act as if rebellious teens are strong and powerful or acting "mature," your job is to disempower their activities. Figure 14 offers a diagram that disempowers avoidance and rebellion, which you can share with your teens.

- **Guideline #3:** *Are boundaries formed in such a way that the cooperative adolescent maintains as much control as possible over his personal choices regarding his interests, activities, and life?*

   Is your teenager allowed to select his own activities and follow his personal interests, or is he required to meet your needs and expectations of him? For example, is he free to pursue social and extracurricular activities, or is he required to focus primarily on academics? Is he allowed to choose the committees, arts, sports, or jobs he would most like to join, or do you control those choices for him? Is he treated respectfully as a person when it comes to making important decisions about his life such as a school change, family move, job, career, or college choice, or is he bossed into agreeing with your choices for him or told of these decisions after you have already made them? Only when a teen is free to follow his heart and pursue things of interest to him will he genuinely immerse himself in life's activities, commit to them with vigor, and meet with success.

- **Guideline #4:** *Are boundaries formed in such a way that the cooperative adolescent maintains as much control as possible over the management of his own time and affairs?*

   Is your responsible teenager given the freedom to organize when he will be with friends, involved in activities, studying, or meeting other responsibilities, or do you organize and control the timing and management of these affairs for him?

   It's insulting to an adolescent to have the details of his life controlled by his parents, and it feels like a violation of his personal rights when he's not free to organize his activities and time according to his own needs and moods. Accordingly, the adolescent should control such things as his time after school or on the telephone; when and where to study (by the time he's midway through his sophomore year at the latest); how to dress (so long as he's clean and appropriately groomed); when to practice or for how long; what to eat, how much, and when; and when to go to bed.

Anna

When Mother brought sixteen-year-old Anna in for counseling, she realized that their relationship was deteriorating; yet she was surprised when Anna's only complaint was that Mother interrupted her moments of relaxation or time on the phone with friends to tell her to straighten her room, practice the clarinet, or study. Interestingly, the information soon surfaced that Anna was a top student, played the clarinet in her school band, and was not even overly messy by Mother's own admission. Thus, it became clear that this mother was a fairly controlling parent who had gotten into a bad habit of overdirecting all of her daughter's activities without realizing how irritating this behavior might feel to a responsible adolescent.

Dialogue from Class

MOTHER: What if Anna wasn't so responsible? Would Mother's directions have been more appropriate?

BOBBIE: Not for a child of sixteen. Part of the maturational process is learning to organize one's own time, even if mistakes are made in the process. With the less organized and responsible teen, it's more effective to gently offer help in the form of organizers and study help, rather than continue to impose your control.

FATHER: Does this include kids with rebellious attitudes, or are you referring only to cooperative kids who are just not getting their schoolwork done?

BOBBIE: That's an important question. It's essential that parents understand that expanded levels of self-management are offered only to cooperative kids; rebellious ones must first submit to the basic rules of their families. In this regard, it's helpful to both reflect and demonstrate to rebellious kids that they are enjoying less freedom than they would if they were cooperative. It's also important to give them expanded freedoms as they begin to demonstrate more responsibility. In short, when responsibility is high, supervision must be low. When responsibility is low, supervision must be high.

ⓖⓖⓖ

Letting Natural Consequences Stand. As your teen is given increasing control over the management of his life, it's important that you allow the "natural" consequences of his choices to be his teachers, since those are the events that will most closely simulate adulthood.

For example, the adolescent who oversleeps should be allowed to experience being late to class or missing his activity; the one who delays ordering his team uniform should be stuck with the task of finding a place that can take his late order; the one who is unwilling to study must be allowed to fail a course; and the one who quits his job must be allowed to go without funds. Although it's often painful for parents to stand by and watch their teen reap his harvest, nagging at him to bypass his errors or interceding with the results of poor decisions blocks his learning.

Dialogue from Class

Mother: When my daughter doesn't get enough sleep, the natural consequence is that she's grumpy the next day, but I feel I have to pay the price as well.

Bobbie: It's very important to remember to keep whatever problems a teen selects with him, rather than allow them to be pushed on you. If your daughter is acting grumpy, it would be valuable to say something like, "Honey, I realize that you're feeling a bit short due to a lack of sleep, but you will have to impose that on yourself in your bedroom rather than on the rest of the family. So, unless you feel ready to be cheerful enough to remain in the family room, you need to be in your room until your mood has changed."

ⓖⓖⓖ

- **Guideline #5:** *Are boundaries formed in such a way that the adolescent understands that he's preparing for full adulthood?*

Is your teen aware that as he goes through this period, he's preparing for the time when he will be on his own and fully responsible for meeting all of his own needs? If he elects to go to college and his parents are able to help finance it, he will have an extension before being fully on his own. If not, he will begin his emancipation upon graduation from high school. Having this awareness helps the adolescent to not only plan more carefully, but to keep his grades up in order to secure a better job or keep his college options open. This awareness also facilitates handing over the reins of his life, since his increasing interest in his own future and how he will manage by himself frees his parents to withdraw their involvement.

Dialogue from Class

MOTHER: What if a child seems to lack any interest whatsoever in addressing his future?

BOBBIE: After making sure that the problem didn't stem from the influences of rebellious friends and/or drugs, I would want to make it very clear to my teen that I was going to let him assume responsibility for his future, but that I was also willing to let it be his problem if things didn't turn out as he had assumed they would with no effort on his part. I think parents make a mistake by not making it clearer to teens that they will be on their own after graduation, unless they go to college, which, in some cases, makes them eligible for an educational subsidy and four-year delay in assuming full independence. This helps kids to get more involved either in planning for college or for managing their independence.

ⓖⓖⓖ

Letting Go

Once your adolescent surrenders to his guidelines—including a pleasant and cooperative attitude, acceptance of responsibility, and open communication—you must be ever vigilant for ways to open up as much freedom and self-destiny as he can handle. Whenever there is mutual respect for your authority combined with an understanding of his desire to be progressively more in control of his life, there's no need for a power struggle between you. As a result, letting out the line can be a gratifying adventure for both of you.

Nothing is more important to your adolescent's final step into independence and maturity than your ability to voluntarily let go and grant him the freedom to function without your help. This is a challenging step for parents who have spent so many years sharing the use of their own fulfiller to co-manage their child's life. (See Figure 13.) Yet successfully taking this step allows their teen to release his feelings of dependency on his parents without having to push them away in anger or feel guilty for abandoning their help. With the reins thus fully slackened, your young adult is able to pick them up and assume full responsibility for the direction and course of his life. He is on his own, and the transition from dependence to independence is complete.

It's important to note that a child's independence need not preclude a continuing—even close—relationship with his family; thus, experts who label an ongoing relationship with family as unhealthy, or cause parent and child to feel guilty about maintaining such a connection, work against the goals of our higher selves in our effort to achieve healed, bonded relationships with everyone throughout the world. The notion that independence requires a splitting off from family was challenged by the chaplain who spoke at my son's baccalaureate services at Duke University in the spring of 1990. He suggested that the American concept of "breaking" from family as a means to gain maturity and independence leaves us with a nation of isolated and lonely nomads, severed from their bonds with family as well as the history, support, and love that family represents. The key is that once the initial period during which the newly independent adult feels overly sensitive about any parental feedback has passed, a continuing relationship between them becomes a parallel one in which neither parent nor child is dominant or submissive; instead, both are fully equal partners in friendship.

Releasing the "Fluffy Birds." Several seasons after discovering his "fluffy birds" in the park, my husband came across some other birds making quite a commotion. This time, a young and fluffy, oversized bird was darting at his sleek mother's beak with continuous, insistent chirps. My husband took heart as he observed the mother bird dispassionately ignore her demanding offspring, and make it plain for all to see that this able-bodied youth would be on his own from now on. My husband was getting close to the time when he would release his own "fluffy birds," and he appreciated the model of unflappable courage this mother bird offered.

When the time comes to let go, it's our most important moment in parenting . . . and we must allow the big "fluffy birds" to take our love into their hearts and fly on their own if they are to make their final trek across the last and most crucial bridge from childhood to adulthood.

Adolescence is the final bridge from childhood to adulthood which can,
if balanced with love and structure, offer a gentle crossing.

13

The Last Parachute

Tending the Human Garden

The Twelfth Key:

ⓖⓖⓖ

The last parachute for saving our families and society is hidden in our hearts. It will be our job to figure out how to find and open it. We can begin by practicing being our sovereign selves, while teaching our children to do the same.

America's First Lady, Hillary Rodham Clinton, strives to awaken her country's slumbering conscience regarding our children with frank words in her book, *It Takes a Village to Raise a Child* (1996).

In her effort to shake us awake, Mrs. Clinton points out that even though our national rhetoric claims to value children, we, in fact, treat their lives as if they did not matter. She further notes that the issues of children are generally viewed as soft and worthy of being tended to only by the soft people of our society—usually women. Yet she argues that the issues of children are not soft, but hard—in fact, the hardest issues we face, and that how we face these issues and what happens to our children will affect our present and our futures.

Regardless of your politics, these daring claims ring true. What happens to our children does, indeed, affect our present and our future. Yet in spite of the truth of this rich observation, it remains painfully clear that we have not yet found a parenting style that raises people who care enough about the world and each other to live together in harmony. As a result, we are not doing a very good job. In fact, a recent survey indicates that 90 percent of Americans admit to lying regularly; that there is an undeniable sense that something is terribly amiss in the American heart; and that in the areas of basic human concerns such as honesty, race relations, safety, equality, civility, and responsibility, the American community continues to decline, while its soul becomes progressively tattered.

Although as a young nation, America led the way in reaching for the dreams of the sovereign self, over time we have lost track of those earlier ideals. Now, after years of ignoring our more elevated goals and focusing, instead, on less lofty pursuits, we find ourselves in a world we never meant to create.

The crisis of the soul that we are now reaping as a result of this shift in focus suggests that the time has come to revisit our earlier dreams. Not only would the revival of our more altruistic goals bring increased clarity and joy to our homes, it's the very foundation on which our survival rests. Yet to rekindle our dreams, we must first understand what snuffed them out.

Faulty Goals Reap Faulty Results

In our search to understand when and how our dreams were lost, we must examine what in the American way of viewing things caused us to lose track of our original purpose and arrive at this low point in our social history. Yet we don't have to look very far, for the answer is all around us.

It seems that at some point along the way we began to raise our families within the context of valuing the interests of the smaller, materially oriented ego self more than those of the larger, heart-based and spiritually inclined higher self. This, in turn, triggered an erosion of our more benevolent goals for living and led to a gradual overthrow of the higher self by the lesser concerns of the ego self.

The consequence of this shift in focus away from our spiritual essence is that most of what we currently pursue is connected to the material and economic interests of the limited and self-centered ego self and ignores the nobler, more global interests of the wiser sovereign self.

Over time, this narrow focus on the material world has influenced our parenting goals, which are now steeped in teaching children to stop at nothing to rise to the top, rather than cultivate and fulfill the deeper more humanitarian pursuits of life. As a result, we ignore our children's questions about where they came from, why they are here, and what happens afterward in favor of teaching them how to win the ego's race to superiority during their brief stay on earth. Yet in spite of our disinterest in these vital questions, they offer us an opportunity to discover the kinds of goals that would enable us to live as our higher selves in alignment with our larger purpose.

Because we have failed to take an interest in these more meaningful goals, we have also failed to sincerely support the schools our children attend or pay attention to the kinds of lessons they are taught—much less adequately reward the teachers who tend their souls, simply because schools are not entrepreneurial in nature.

In spite of these shortcomings, it seems that we have proudly, often aggressively, peddled this erroneous model for living to others throughout the world. Yet the unfortunate result of this spreading approach to ego-based living is that we are becoming a world society of self-centered and isolated individuals. As a result, we throw aside love, caring, and cooperation along with integrity and responsibility in order to compete with one another for power, status, and money in our businesses, communities, nations, and world—regardless of how much these practices hurt each other and our world home. What can be done to reverse this powerless, soul-free, and dangerous trend?

Weaving the Threads of Our Salvation: Creating New Goals

It seems that many people are tiring of the world we have created and would like to do better; yet they simply don't know how.

Marianne Williamson offers us a beginning step in her claim that in order to live in the world of our higher selves we must let go of the illusionary one that our egos have created. Yet to release the old world and bring in the new, we will have to begin now to live from our higher selves in each moment and to hold others accountable for doing the same. In order to do this, we can no longer use the outdated measuring rods of power, status, or material gain as our guides to daily living. We must have the courage, instead, to release these outdated idols and replace them with new ways to empower one another, while living each moment with integrity and caring about the good of the whole.

To begin, we can change our currently shallow and limited parenting goals to ones that assign primary importance to the higher self of each child right from the beginning of his or her life. The role of the worldly ego self could then more appropriately be subordinated to one of helping the higher self fulfill its nobler pursuits.

To do this, it's essential that parents recognize the importance of not allowing their child's soul self to be put aside to wither, while only his ego is encouraged to develop in isolation and as a separate self, but to weave the qualities of the higher self into his personality as it forms. By doing this we not only bring our personalities into alignment with our souls, but act as channels for bringing heaven to earth. Only in this way can the essence of the goodness we bring with us when we are born be shared with the earth while we are here. Yet to meet this ultimate of goals, we must all more carefully tend the human garden.

Tending the Human Garden

We can each begin to more vigorously tend the human garden by relating to our children in the heart-centered manner presented in this book, while teaching them to do the same. In doing this, we take the first step toward bringing more love to the world and, in so doing, weaving the threads of our salvation. The purpose of this chapter is to offer you both the motivation and means for doing so.

Crumbs and Ripples and a Hundred Monkeys

I once read a book about a child who was brutally injured by her parents and was placed in a Catholic home where nuns cared for her the rest of her life. The book was written by a priest who had spent time daily talking to this child as she was growing up, even though she was mute and never responded. One evening, as he considered what more he might do for her, he realized that his small contribution to such a painful life could only amount to a few crumbs. Nevertheless, he took heart in the thought that if everyone who crossed her path would take a moment to offer a crumb or two, perhaps in her lifetime it would amount to a small piece of cake.

One day, shortly after her sixteenth birthday, this young girl walked into the priest's office and, without warning, spoke to him for the first time. He was deeply moved and wept openly. As he watched her walk back across the lawn to her room, he remembered his hope for this child and realized that the crumbs in her life had, at last, amounted to a small piece of cake.

I was touched by this story and, since reading it, have strived to offer at least a little something to each child I encounter, in hopes that my small gift might contribute to their lives. In doing this, I have become increasingly connected for brief moments to those children whose paths have crossed mine and have learned to see the same value in them I originally saw only in my own offspring.

What I have learned from these encounters is that the effect is circular; each time my heart opens—much like a music box opening in my heart—and sends forth love, the more love I receive in return. In the interchange, I not only connect with my own higher self, but with the higher selves of the children before me—and I am deeply moved by the experience. Whenever

I practice this heart-centered connection, I experience blissful glimpses of my link to all people, the earth, its animals, and all of life.

Once I became aware of this connection to life, I was able to enjoy unexpected moments of it in a variety of settings. One that particularly surprised me happened during a series of snorkeling expeditions during which my heart had become so filled with love for the fish, mantas, turtles, and dolphins before me in the pristine waters off of my island home, that these seafarers would stop and turn toward the energy I was emitting. Then, they would come closer, gaze into my eyes, or even circle around me, while sending me beams of love in return. It became visibly clear to me in these magical moments that the invisible power of the love we send forth from our hearts into the world truly affects the receiver in profound ways that we are just beginning to uncover and experience. Here's how it works.

Our Collective Creation

The writings of bestselling authors Deepak Chopra, Wayne Dyer, Larry Dossey, and others, draw from the discoveries of contemporary scientists to explain how our choices influence our world due to the far-reaching effect our energies have on others.

It seems modern scientists have discovered that we live in a large, common soup made up of atoms and molecules that we inhale and exhale in a constant exchange with the environment and other people. Although these atoms and molecules have the same structure, they adopt different forms to accommodate variations in the individuals who "use" them; consequently, the atoms and molecules we inhale are transformed in accordance with the beliefs we have adopted to make up our personal reality.

It has further been discovered that the choices we make, both visible and unseen, are then copied by our neighbors in a way that produces a rippling effect more far-reaching than previously understood. Thus, it's this sharing of matter, combined with our choices for using it, which are then copied by our neighbors and again by their neighbors, that cause humankind to act as a collective body and a collective consciousness. Now that we understand how this works, we can see that as our neighbors and their children make higher choices and get better, so do we; the reverse is also true.

Because of this, there are no limits to what can be created, once we get clear about the choices we want to select. As a result, your child can be whatever he wishes to become; your homes can be filled with as much harmony as you desire; and the world can be as peaceful as we dare to dream. We need only to join our minds and hearts in consistently focusing on the kind of world we would like to create. Yet as simple as this sounds, joining our minds and hearts in a common positive cause has been a challenge for humanity.

To overcome this challenge, we must simply release our focus from negative thoughts and limited expectations and unite, instead, in kind thoughts, words and deeds if we want to create a gentler, more joyful world. We can learn to do this by first opening our hearts through the process of loving our children more clearly and deeply, then sharing our opened hearts with others and the world around us.

Using the Parenting Journey to Open Our Hearts

My hope is that each of you will help to weave more positive energies into our world by using *Parachutes for Parents* to stimulate the opening of your own hearts as you offer the various children in your lives meaningful cakes—crumb by crumb. This can be done simply by putting them on life's agenda; loving them deeply without conditions while holding their boundaries with equanimity; then, offering gentle guidance in clarifying and communicating whatever is not yet clear for them.

I believe that you will discover through this process—as I and others have—that the material presented in this book for steadily loving your children in the middle of the daily problems of raising them has the capacity to mysteriously inspire you to value all of life, tap your inner wisdom, and see the sacred in the ordinary—even difficult—moments. The opening of your hearts that will result from this experience will further deepen your connection with your children, yourselves, and others. This, in turn, will open the way for you to be your best parent and highest self.

Learning to maintain deeper bonds with our children in this new and profound manner not only enables us to keep our own hearts open, stirred, and active, but the loving energy we send to our children enhances their lives in a powerful way. Moreover, in the process of gathering love within our hearts to send forth to our children, our bodies and homes are bathed more abundantly in love, which, in turn, saturates our communities and world with more of this surprisingly potent force. This force, when present, mysteriously brings us to a new level of wisdom that can be accessed only through the stirring of the heart.

Consequently, loving our children and others in this new and deeper manner brings us the very power we were hoping to attain but failed to manifest in the race to supremacy that our small ego selves are so fond of pursuing.

Thus, through loving, we uncover the soft, yet intense, power and wisdom of our higher selves lying quietly within. In short, whenever we surrender the powerlessness of the small ego self to the magnetism of the larger sovereign self, we tap our own greater wisdom and discover how to create a better world.

Yet although an increasing number of informed people recognize the truth of this, they question if we can transform the world the ego has created into a world the higher self would design in time to ensure our survival. Gratefully, there is a phenomenon called "The Hundredth Monkey"—or attainment of critical mass—that would allow a concerted commitment to loving to result in a rapidly healed society and transformed world—even though we are dangerously late in getting started.

Critical Mass and the Hundredth Monkey

In 1952, on an island in Japan, scientists dropped sweet potatoes into the sand to a group of monkeys being studied. Although the monkeys liked the potatoes, they disliked the taste of the sandy dirt; however, a young monkey named Imo discovered that she could resolve the problem by washing her potatoes in a nearby stream. Soon her mother and several playmates began to copy her behavior, and before long other monkeys followed suit. By 1958, the scientists had counted X number of monkeys that they referred to as ninety-nine who now washed their potatoes prior to eating. When the next—or hundredth—monkey copied the potato-washing behavior, a strange phenomenon was observed. Not only did all of the remaining monkeys on the island begin to wash their potatoes, monkeys on nearby islands started washing theirs as well. At that juncture, the concept of potato-washing had reached critical mass as described by Einstein and thus penetrated the collective consciousness of monkeys in general.[10]

This story explains the truth of Ilya Prigogine's theory that our reality is a result of the various choices, which, once initiated, act as ripples reaching out to influence the choices of others. This pattern of ripples continues until enough others have been influenced by the initial choice to culminate in a new wave of reality. What's encouraging is that we can influence the patterns we produce in our lives, families, and the world by the ideas and actions we select and the waves we set in motion. This theory also helps us to better understand why such things as random acts of kindness as well as good wishes and prayer sent to others and our world have been proven to produce powerfully healing results. Thus, by consciously plunging our minds and our hearts into more uplifting attitudes and conduct, we can generate a series of positive waves and collectively create better times for ourselves and the world.

Only now are modern scientists uncovering the basis for this phenomenon as they discover such things as how a photon behaves. It seems that whenever one of these basic elements of life selects a behavior such as moving left or moving right or spinning, the surrounding photons copy the behavior selected by the first photon. Then other photons, both nearby and far away, copy what the surrounding photons have mimicked, and a new pattern of behavior—or wave of reality—is created.

This demonstrates that there lies an urge deep within the force of life to copy what is already in place or has become newly initiated. This is the basis for the emerging scientific theories that all reality is a result of the various choices which, once initiated, act as ripples reaching out to influence our own future choices as well as the choices of others around us. This pattern of ripples continues until enough others have been influenced by the initial choice to culminate in a new wave of reality, or *fractal*, as Jean Houston refers to these repetitious patterns of becoming.

These various fractals or waves that gather to create the next reality show us why both positive and negative beliefs and expectations as well as periods of good times and bad develop as patterns in individual lives, families, nations, and the world. It also explains why scientists involved in long-term studies of chimpanzees in their natural habitat are now observing a new phenomenon of aggressive and murderous chimp behavior, including the formation of violent gangs. These behaviors and gangs are so similar to those found in our society that it suggests that the influence we have on one another extends to other species. These rippling, expanding patterns of behavior further explain why our current focus on so much negativity in the news, on television, and at the movies is generating a swell of newly dark fractals and harmful activities in today's world.

As we can see, each time we make a higher choice in the way we think or behave, similar to the photon that has elected to spin and is copied in his spinning by surrounding photons, we are copied by others. And, like the photons as demonstrated visibly for us by the monkeys, we, too, create a rippling effect that is both powerful and far-reaching. What is encouraging is that we can influence the patterns we will produce in our lives, our families, our nations, and the world by the ideas, expectations, and actions we select today and the subsequent ripples and waves those choices set in motion. Thus, by consciously releasing the negativity so commonly pursued by the petty—often ghoulish—interests of the small ego self and plunging our minds and hearts into the loftier, more positive attitudes and conduct of our higher selves, we can consciously generate a series of more uplifting waves and collectively create better times for ourselves and the world. The key is that we begin. Yet the question remains, will we do it? Through this process, our hope for creating a better world is empowered by the synergy of the group members copying each other in positive energies and thus working together to dream a common dream as well as fulfill it. Thus, in the simple act of collectively surrendering the limited ego self to the magic of the unlimited higher self, we can easily restore our society and create a caring and joyful world.

The Last Parachute

Prophets and sages say that humanity will have to get its act together in the next five years or perish. It is, indeed, five minutes to midnight in the garden of good and evil!

What will you choose for yourselves and your children? What kinds of fractal patterns of becoming are you now setting in motion for your families, businesses, communities, and world? Are they ripples of caring and kindness, cooperation, clarity, and joy? Or are they waves of manipulation and injury, uncaring, darkness, and despair?

The Wisdom of the Heart

The final parachute that could save us from a societal crash is hidden in our hearts. It will be our job to first uncover how to access it; then, keep it stirred and active; and finally to tap the universal wisdom it holds in safekeeping for us when we are ready to use it. This parachute is made from the unseen, yet powerful, force of love.

What is it about the force of love that is so powerful that it not only stimulates healing and growth, but higher levels of wisdom? Robert Bly offers the answer to these questions in his claim that we have three centers of intelligence—the two hemispheres located in the brain that serve the affairs of the smaller ego self with all of its worries and concerns over the details of life as well as the beliefs it holds so firmly that it will send its children to war to defend them—even though these beliefs change every few years. Then, there's the larger hemisphere of *knowing* located in the heart, which directs the higher self. This center of intelligence is confident in its deeper, unchanging truths and principles, yet feels no need to defend them. It also becomes increasingly more activated in individuals whose hearts have been opened by love and caring. As a result, it is only by becoming more loving that we can gain access to this well of intelligence and become mysteriously wiser.

Thus, as more of our hearts open, our collective mind expands, and we are immersed in both love and wisdom, or the essence of the higher self. Like fragrance riding on molecules across a room to brush against the nostrils of its occupants, these wise and loving energies will also travel invisibly across our living rooms, communities, nations, and world to bathe everything gently in love, wisdom, and joy.

Therefore, in the simple choice to love our children and others more profoundly we not only interrupt the negative fractals currently flooding our planet, but succeed in fulfilling the purpose of our lives by becoming vehicles for the power of love to saturate the world.

Thus, as each of you begins now to raise the higher self of your child from the higher self of your own being, a flood of potent and healing energy of love and wisdom will be sent across this earth ripple by ripple. In this collective act we create new patterns of becoming and bring heaven to earth. In so doing, we open a window of hope that can save our children, ourselves, our society—and our world. We need only a few crumbs, some uplifting ripples, and a hundred monkeys.

For those of you on a parenting journey, you can practice opening this golden parachute hidden in your hearts by using the twelve keys for raising children presented in this book and summarized on page 346. In this way, you use your parenting journey to open your hearts and tap the powerful force contained in the loving energies it stores.

Don't Let Up

I leave you with an excerpt from the transcript of Buckminster Fuller's last public appearance. "Bucky," as he was affectionately called, was one of the great geniuses of our time and was not only brilliant, but caring and kind. Like Einstein, he was known to gain many of his insights through meditation and would often slip into a few moments of silence with his eyes closed and hands clasped prayerfully in front of his heart, while standing on stage before his audience. He would then slowly open his eyes as he returned to his audience, hands still clasped, to share the new piece of wisdom he had just accessed.

During Bucky's last talk, the healthy octogenarian predicted after one of these contemplative moments that he would die with his wife, who was already very near death. Here are his very last words to us.

"So, darling, beautiful people, I think humanity does have a good chance of passing this examination . . . I think it's touch and go . . . but I think we are going to make it. But, don't let up! Don't let up, or we won't make it. Keep at your integrity more than ever in all your lives before. So, thank you darling people."

Buckminster Fuller died six days later lying next to his wife of sixty-six years who, in turn, died shortly thereafter.

It takes only a few crumbs and ripples to save a child
and a hundred monkeys to save a world.
"So, darling, beautiful people . . . don't let up!"

Twelve New Keys to Raising Children
for a Better World

ⓖⓖⓖ

Key 1:   Reclaim the higher self.

Key 2:   Merge love with discipline at all times.

Key 3:   Embrace all of life's agenda.

Key 4:   Love the essence of your children deeply.

Key 5:   Set clear boundaries without hesitation or fear.

Key 6:   Hold all boundaries with courage and kindness.

Key 7:   Return to clarity following each problem.

Key 8:   Use unclear moments to teach what isn't clear.

Key 9:   Teach clearer lessons for clearer lives.

Key 10:   Bond through heart-based communications.

Key 11:   Teach teens maturity through practicing maturity.

Key 12:   Teach children to live as their higher selves.

Meditation

Healing your Parent-Child Relationship

This meditation can be taped in its entirety—or in parts—and played to guide you in meditation. Musical selections such as "The Pachelbel Canon" can be used as background.

Sit comfortably in a favorite chair, close your eyes, and feel your body become relaxed as it surrenders into the chair—much like you would surrender your body to the water if you wanted to float. (Pause)

Feel your focus shift out of your head into your heart. (Pause) Tuck into your heart a favorite animal, person, or aspect of nature that easily evokes loving feelings within you. (Pause)

Notice your essence becoming increasingly light as the loving feelings within your heart expand and transform to light, then merge with a larger shaft of light, which slowly lifts you upward. Enjoy the experience of your lightness as you float higher and higher toward the source of all light, while looking down at the problems of the earth below you fading farther and farther away. (Pause)

Once there, look around for any guides, mentors, or laps to hold and comfort you as you work with your child. Become acquainted with these helpers or—if you like—settle into the Universal lap that's offered.

Now bring the image of your child before you and look deeply into his or her eyes. What do you see? Pause while looking into the heart and soul of this child to see who is there and what he or she wants and needs. Allow yourself to feel from your heart and experience whatever comes to your awareness.

What part do you play in the life of this child? What does he or she need from you? Are you willing to give it to him or her? What fears and conflicts do you feel about helping this child? (Pause to experience your fears, rather than run from them as you usually do.) Talk to these fears, since they have information that can help you. Why are they there? In what way are they trying to protect or help you?

Now ask what you can do to heal these fears, become more connected to your child, and better guide his development. Ask for the additional help of your higher self in accomplishing this healing. (Pause for as long as you need to receive the images, symbols, and directions offered. Then follow the instructions given.)

Note any remaining barriers you feel toward your child as well as the doors that guard your heart to protect you from the pain and fear he or she evokes in you. Become willing to experience these emotions and confront their message as you slowly release these doors to open to your child once again. Experience your heart as if it were the bud of a flower ready to slowly, but fully, open to include and embrace your child and welcome him back into your heart. (Pause for as long as needed to feel the doors release and your heart open.)

When all the barriers have melted away and you feel ready to connect with your child once again, allow him to sit on your lap. Have your child surrender his weight into your body—much as you surrendered yours to the chair. Have his higher self and other guides help him with this if he's afraid. You can help him, too, by letting him know that you are ready to nurture and care for him and that it's now safe for him to surrender to your love. If appropriate, apologize for not having done this in the past. Put your attention in your heart and carefully tuck this child sitting on your lap into a place in your heart where he will feel fully embraced and comforted.

Notice yourself becoming so filled with love that it not only bathes your own being, but washes through and over the child sitting in your lap and tucked into your heart. This loving energy soon sends forth so much caring into the room, then your neighborhood, city, state, country, and world that they become saturated as well. Once the entire world is bathed in this accepting energy and light it begins to reach to the outer edges of the universe— while you and your child sit peacefully at the center of its peace. Joyfully, you feel yourselves lifted higher and higher by its power. You notice a rocking motion as you hold and rock your child, while you, too, are held and rocked by a Universal Parent. Both of you feel safe enough to fully surrender to the gentle arms that hold you and loving heart that embraces you. This is the connection you have both yearned for, and you peacefully surrender to it.

After resting in this place of bliss for as long as desired, gently bring your awareness back to the room and gradually open your eyes.

★★★

Problem-Solving Guide

᪥᪥᪥

The Problem-Solving Guide is designed to help parents with specific parenting problems as well as offer general child-rearing information. It will also serve as a reference for locating various topics in the text. Some entries are brief while others extend for several pages.

Abduction. Adults must assume full responsibility for protecting young children in public places and provide information about self-defense as soon as (but not before) the child gets old enough to be in these places without adult supervision. Even then, the information must be given in a context that doesn't create anxiety in your child. See **Strangers** for details on how to do this. See **Abuse**; **Assertiveness**; **Post-Traumatic Stress**; **Strangers**

Absent Parent. Sometimes a parent is not available to a child either physically and/or emotionally. Although this will always create a significant loss for the child, this loss can be ameliorated by good handling. See **Absent Parent** subentry under **Divorce**

Abuse. Child abuse is equivalent to the murder of a soul and as such should no longer be tolerated in our hearts, our homes, or our society. Not only does the abuser rape the spirit of the child with each act of abuse, society enables these acts by failing to provide adequate protection for the abused child.

Even current laws that require reporting by parents and counselors are often more punitive toward those trying to help the child than toward his or her persecutor. Moreover, once a report is made, inadequacies in the system often result in the child becoming more vulnerable to his or her persecutor, who is now angry, yet more careful to hide the crime, while continuing to have full access to the child.

It's time that we confront how many children live in terror in their own homes, striving as best they can to deal with serious and persistent trauma at the hands of their own families. The solution lies in holding our child protective programs and courts more accountable to children than to the "rights" of nonresponsible and abusing parents who whittle away the very core of our children's souls with each act of abuse.

More subtle forms of abuse can be observed in angry and critical parents; parents who are neglectful and uninterested in their children; and ones who have inappropriate relationships with them, including ones with sexual overtones, a preference for one child or a dislike for another, or babying one while mistreating another. Whenever one parent is in any way abusing or endangering a child, it's essential that the other parent act as the child's advocate. As advocate, this parent must get immediate outside help, rather than act as a co-abuser or collude with the abusing spouse to keep the violations a secret. The sooner the advocating parent openly confronts the reality of what has happened and demonstrates that it will not be tolerated, the better chance the abusing parent has of facing and addressing this tendency to abuse before it becomes a habitual response or further damages the child.

Physical Abuse. There are two forms of physical abuse. One involves the loss of emotional control and excessive spanking used by parents who are having trouble controlling their child. The best way to stop this more manageable form of abuse is to commit to not spanking your child and learn, instead, to use the discipline style described in Chapters 6 and 7. Anger management classes can also help parents who are having trouble managing this control on their own.

The other form of abuse is distinguished by its unpredictability. Because this form reflects the internal state of the abusing parent, unrelated to the child's behavior, a child cannot control the abuse by improving his behavior. As a result, his behavior often becomes confused, if not chaotic.

Within the framework of this second form, there are many categories of abuse, each reflecting the level of personal immaturity of the parent.

The most visible form of physical abuse is family violence, either between spouses or directed at any one of the children. Both forms of family violence leave a child with intense feelings of abandonment, rejection, and unworthiness that create serious developmental problems for him.

Symptoms to look for in physically abused children: Child has bruises, welts, burns, fractures, lacerations, bite marks; is wary of adults or physical contact with them; is jumpy or startles if adult makes an unexpected gesture; gets apprehensive when other children cry; shows extremes in behavior between aggressiveness and withdrawal; is frightened of parents or reports being injured by them.

Sexual Abuse. Nonphysical sexual abuse is the form of abuse in which a parent openly treats the child of the opposite sex as his or her little boyfriend or girlfriend. This way of relating to a child is both inappropriate and confusing, as it offers the child a spousal relationship between him and his parent, rather than a parent-child connection. Nonphysical sexual violations create a framework in which the child may later become a physical partner as well.

Physical sexual violations against a child constitute a less visible but more extensive form of abuse, since the violations are a "secret" between a "trusted" parent or relative acting as a "special friend" to the child. Each violation can be sexually stimulating for the child, while at the same time a violent invasion of his personal, physical, and emotional boundaries. As a result, sexual violations generate intense feelings of guilt and confusion about love for the child which, in turn, cause serious difficulties for him in his adult life and relationships. Parents who were dominated and controlled by their families as children—whether in the form of violence or sexual abuse—often do the same to their own offspring or marry spouses who will do it for them. This may be due to the model they saw while growing up; the low self-esteem that results from such violations; the deep feelings of victimization and a subsequent need to be the one in control; and/or the unresolved anger and rage that typically seethes within the sexually violated person.

Symptoms to look for in sexually abused children: Child has torn, stained, or bloody underclothing; frequent bladder infections; signs of redness, cuts, pain, or itching in genital or anal area; walks as though injured in genital or anal area; masturbates excessively; has sores around mouth; demonstrates overt sexual acting out; relates to others with extreme levels of anger and rage or aggression; is oppositional; acts withdrawn and regressed; shows resistance or fear of being alone with certain individuals or in certain environments; resumes wetting or bedwetting after training is complete; has nightmares; has poor peer relationships; is unwilling to participate in activities, particularly ones involving physical contact; has depressed affect; daydreams or stares excessively, dissociates, or alters consciousness, identity, or motor behavior as a defense against pain; uses weight gain or skin eruptions to prevent being attractive; develops eating disorders used to gain control over some aspect of life; has suicidal ideation or attempts; commits delinquent acts or runs away; reports being sexually abused by parent or caretaker. Many children have been so frightened by threats of what might happen if they tell, they remain silent or deny abuse, even when asked. Thus, anytime a child breaks through his or her fear to seek help with abuse, be sure to take that child seriously.

Neglect. Neglect ranges from not caring for a child properly to not caring about him at all. A serious, yet common form of neglect in today's society includes the neglect of children required by law to visit parents of divorce who are not interested enough in the children to help with expenses or act responsibly, yet claim parenting "rights" for visitation.

Symptoms to look for in neglected children: The neglected child is consistently unwashed, ragged, and dirty; hungry, begging or sneaking food; steals things as symbols of "love" to fill the void; is lacking in supervision for extended periods of time or when doing dangerous or delinquent acts; is constantly tired or listless; has unattended physical problems; is overworked or kept from attending school; is left on his own unattended. The child neglected during custody visitation returns from visits drained; depressed; whiny; clingy; fearful of separation; plagued with sleep problems and nightmares; and is resistant to future visits.

Psychological Abuse. Parents who impose psychological abuse on children do so by imposing their own immature, confused, and unmet needs on their children. This may take the form of excessive control, domination, and diminishing of the child, or it may include trying to get the child to take care of the emotional needs of parents, particularly following divorce.

Psychological abuse includes excessive control, guilt-inducing remarks and behaviors, putdowns, name-calling, vulgar language, and double messages. The child who experiences psychological abuse is either overly compliant and passive or extremely aggressive, demanding, and rageful; behaves in an inappropriately adult manner (manages household and cares for siblings) or an inappropriately infantile manner (constantly rocks, sucks thumb, whines); wets self or bed, even after training; either lags in physical, emotional, and intellectual development or is unusually mature and self-sufficient; has depressed affect and may be "accident-prone" or overtly attempt suicide. See **Assertiveness**; **Authoritarian Parent**; **Bonding**; **Post-Traumatic Stress**; **Reactive Attachment and Other Attachment Problems**

Academics. Parents often put so much focus and pressure on their children's studying that it causes a breakdown in the parent-child relationship. See **Academics, Accelerated**; **School, Adjustment Problems**; **Study**

Academics, Accelerated. Adults must be careful about putting children in accelerated academic placements that offer more work than inspiration, as many children falter in these programs and lose the confidence that originally earned them the placement. When children are put in situations beyond their ability to perform successfully or in ones that require excessive work, the child's spirit as well as his original gifts may get buried. See **School, Adjustment Problems**

Acceptance. Acceptance is a key to good parenting. See Chapters 3, 4, and 5

Access. Full parental access—without entertainment—enhances parent-child relationships. This closely simulates a return-to-nature relationship in which the child who initiates access to his parents—by going to them as opposed to whining for them to come to him—is not rejected; yet neither does he become the center of attention. Consequently, the relationship between parent and child has a natural, nondemanding essence to it, and the child feels free to return to independence after connecting with his parents for awhile. See **Bonding**; **Carrying**; **Contact**; **"In-Arms" Period**; **Lap-Sitting**; See Chapter 5

Accident-Prone. Often the child who is undervalued and overcontrolled is not in charge of his life and thus feels and acts like a victim. Such children are candidates for becoming accident-prone. If a child seems accident-prone, it's helpful to determine: 1) if he is feeling the need for additional nurturing; 2) if he seems anxious to reestablish family unity by bringing members together in order to tend to his emergencies; 3) if he uses illness or accidents to distract himself from the pain of life; 4) if he seems to punish himself whenever he is made to feel overly shamed, guilty, and unlovable; or 5) if he has learned to use accidents and illness as a way to worry and control parents and/or get extra intensity and attention directed his way. Wise parents of such a child will begin to trust his value and abilities more and give him increased opportunities to make choices, solve problems, and handle things on his own. In addition, they will withdraw attention and sympathy for his complaints, injuries, and illness and help him to focus, instead, on how he can experience his power and take charge of the kind of life he would like to have. See **Abuse**; **Antecedents**; **Bonding**; **Illness**; **Reflective Interpretation**; *School Phobia* sub-entry under **School, Reluctance to Attend**; Chapters 5, 7, 9, and 10

Acknowledging Transgressions. The ability to acknowledge transgressions is critical to keeping relationships clear. See Chapter 8

Active Listening. Active listening requires that the listener play as active a role in the communication process as the speaker. This includes listening actively, then feeding back to the child what you believe he is trying to express, including his feelings in a situation as well as his thoughts about it. Active listeners begin with phrases like, "What I hear you saying is __"; "You seem to be feeling __"; or "You seem to think __"; then wait to hear back from the speaker if they got it right. Reflective interpretation is a more comprehensive form of active listening that includes feeding back the listener's interpretations, assumptions, and hypotheses about the speaker's communication. See Chapter 11

ADD(H). See **Attention Deficit Disorder (with Hyperactivity)**

Adjustment Difficulties. See **"Challenging Child"**; **School, Adjustment Problems**

Adjustment Period. Whenever a child cries over not getting something he wants, his crying represents his adjustment period to being thwarted and includes the time it takes him to accept not getting his way. Your job is to simply let him have the time he needs to cry it out and make this adjustment. See **Crying**; **Tantrums**; See Chapter 7

Adolescence. Adolescence can and should be a pleasant, cooperative period in which parents allow their teen to take progressively more charge of his life. (See Chapter 12 for how to do this.)

General Support Programs for Teen Development. Boys Town offers a comprehensive counseling and referral service available for children and teens in trouble as well as their own residential program and a twenty-four-hour national hotline 800-448-3000; SuperCamp Learning Forum, 1725 Pacific Coast Hwy., Oceanside, CA 92054-5319, 800-285-3276, offers an excellent motivational program for youth; Winner's Camp Foundation, 1292 Maleko Street, Kailua, HI 96734, 808-263-0177, fax 808-261-3429, offers a comparable program to SuperCamp; On The Edge Productions, 970-884-2988, provides rope course challenges throughout the United States for various child, teen, and family groups desiring personal growth.

Support Programs for Parents of Normal and Moderately Troubled or At-Risk Teens. Boys Town offers a comprehensive counseling and referral service available for children and teens in trouble as well as their own residential program, twenty-four-hour national hotline: 800-448-3000; ToughLove, P.O. Box 1069, Doylestown, PA 18901, 215-248-7090, helps parents reestablish their authority; SuperCamp 1725 Pacific Coast Hwy., Oceanside, CA 92054-5319, 800-285-3276, offers an excellent motivational program for youth; Outward Bound provides challenging outdoor experiences to stimulate personal growth, Colorado Outward Bound, 945 Pennsylvania St., Denver, CO 80203-3198.

Crisis Programs for Seriously Troubled Teens. Boys Town offers a comprehensive counseling and referral service available for children and teens in trouble as well as their own residential program, twenty-four-hour national hotline: 800-448-3000. In addition, there are a number of programs designed to deal with the highly rebellious adolescent who doesn't like conforming to rules. Many of these programs are necessarily "tough," but must also contain an equally loving component. Make sure you thoroughly understand and agree with the techniques used in these programs before enrolling your child in one. Begin with recommendations from Boys Town for locating the right program to match your child's needs.

Private Residential Treatment Center for Chemical Dependency. Hazelden, Center City, MN, 612-257-4011, ext. 4646. Programs such as this can also offer information on how to find alternative programs.

Other resources. Other resources for help include: local mental health centers and associations; information and referral agencies in your city; Alcoholics Anonymous; Narcotics Anonymous; your local hospital's human resources department; and your family physician or personal therapist. See **Individuation**; See Chapter 12

Adoption. Adoptive parents give a gift not only to the child they choose to raise but to all of us for their care of a child in need of a home. Adoptive parents face all of the challenges the rest of us do and more. The ideal is when they are able to begin their program of caring for the child as early as possible in order to give him the same beginning we all strive to give our children. When this is not possible, it helps to heal any traumas their child has experienced due to prior bonding breaks by giving him abundant doses of love. However, this love must also be tempered and balanced with discipline.

It's valuable never to treat the adoption as a secret so that the child understands his circumstances right from the beginning as his language develops. It's helpful to indicate to your adopted child that although his way of getting to this planet was through his biological parent, that the plan was for him to be with you. It's imperative to impart to him the understanding that he was unable to remain with his birth parents due to their inability to care for him, rather than any lack in him. It's critical that you realize during those times when he's upset with you and claims he should have stayed with his birth parents that all children strike out during these times with declarations of dislike and hate. Thus, rather than take it personally, continue with your boundaries and only talk about it if he brings it up as a sincere issue during clearing. The most you can do for your adoptive child is to raise him with the clarity and balance recommended in this book. See **Bonding**; **Reactive Attachment and Other Attachment Problems**; See Chapters 5, 6, and 7

Advocate. See **Abuse**

Agenda, Putting Your Child on the. See Chapters 4 and 7

Aggressiveness. Aggressive behavior indicates something is not presently clear for a child and must be adjusted. Thus, parents should not only contract the aggressive child's freedoms, but determine what's motivating his behavior. When children are aggressive it is usually due to a faulty belief they hold that aggression will give them more—more toys, more power, more safety, more friends. Thus, after removing an aggressive child from others for long enough to make him feel a loss and a desire to reenter the group, it's critical to examine his beliefs with him. Once his faulty decision or belief is exposed, it's helpful to explore the illusion in the belief and lead him toward a better conclusion about how he can get the things he wants from life. For example, aggressive children may have been handled with excessive anger and dominance; may have gotten their way so much that they are unable to adhere to appropriate boundaries; may not have accepted the loss of their family unit to divorce or a relative to death; may have suffered a severe enough bonding break from their parents that they fail to surrender to adult guidance; and/or may have watched excessive amounts of television depicting aggressive images. When aggression is severe and persistent, other physiological and psychological traumas must be considered. See **Abuse**; **Bonding**; **Bully**; **"Challenging Child"**; **Serious Behavioral and Psychological Problems**; **Television and Video**; **Violence**; See Chapters 1 and 10

Agreements. When using agreements, parents ask their child to consciously agree to the terms required for additional freedoms. For example, a child wishing to go to the movie with his older brother is allowed to do so if he agrees to accept his brother's authority. However, should he break the agreement, he is returned home and may try again in a few weeks or so. Agreements are not made when a child is *required* to do something. For example, a child in a doctor's office is not asked to agree to be good, since being at the doctor's is a requirement, rather than an expanded freedom. In such cases, parents must assume that their child will cooperate and, if he doesn't, his freedoms are contracted until he is ready to do so.

Alcohol. See **Drugs**

Allergies. Allergies can agitate a child's nervous system and negatively affect his behavior. To help prevent allergies from developing, take care not to introduce solid foods to a baby until he has the enzyme production necessary to digest them at about six months of age.

Symptoms. Children with allergies are often pale with dark circles under their eyes; are prone to mucous congestion; have sensitive skin that welts easily; or have sores and rashes, a smooth tongue, and pitted nails. Other children become overactive—or lethargic—after eating certain foods and many children with symptoms of hyperactivity and/or attention deficit disorder are plagued with allergies irritating their nervous systems. It's as though their itchy rashes and hives have expressed internally rather than externally. Although parents with difficult children should be alert to the possibility of allergies, these must not serve as an excuse for unacceptable behavior. Instead, both the underlying allergy *and* problematic behavior must be addressed.

Treatment. An excellent method for helping a child with allergies is to rotate small amounts of the foods bothering him into his diet once every ten days, as this allows his own immune system to gradually develop a tolerance to the offending foods, without being overwhelmed by them. Determine if your milk-sensitive child is able to tolerate milk products containing acidophilus added specifically for allergic children. It's also helpful to ask the allergic child to invite the troublesome food into his body as a "friend" that will agree with him, since his beliefs as well as his willingness to take responsibility for including these foods—without a hyperactive response—will increase his freedom to enjoy them. Using the same premise, it's important not to talk about his allergies and program him to believe that his body will always react to certain foods. Vitamin supplements, regular exercise, generous amounts of lap-time for the young child, and touch and love as well as a general state of well-being and happiness will improve your child's immune system. This, in turn, helps the food-sensitive child to respond to ingested foods with greater harmony and strength. It's also helpful to suggest the possibility of outgrowing allergies—as so many children do—so that your child will not assume that this potentially temporary imbalance must be permanent. Homeopathic and other desensitization treatments might be helpful.

Allowance. My preference is to assign monetary compensation for the community chores as well as dock part of a child's allowance whenever reminders and prodding are needed to get him to do them. This arrangement in part simulates the real world of work for compensation and offers realistic feedback for the child who is not yet willing to contribute. Once chore assignment and compensation are established, it's best to give a young child the full amount he will earn each week and the older one his full amount every two to four weeks, so that he can practice the management of his money in progressively larger blocks of time. Docked amounts can be deleted from the full allotment. It's critical not to control the child's spending choices, except when they are dangerous or against family rules or values, and there should be no guilt or strings attached to the money given. When a child makes mistakes or overspends, he should not be given additional money but made to experience the problem his mismanagement has created. When his purchases are shallow and unfulfilling, better values can be taught and reflected without coercion or control. His financial mistakes and their consequences are what teach him—

over time—to manage money more effectively. See **Money Management**; **Work**; See Chapter 6

Anger. Anger is the resistance we feel against those parts of life we don't want on the agenda, including our own mistakes, the mistakes of others, and any unpleasant or hurtful events we did not order and do not wish to experience. Even when anger seems justified, such as when we have been unfairly treated or our losses seem overwhelmingly painful and unjust, if we hold onto the resistance, it converts to the more toxic feelings of resentment and revenge or depression. Because these energies are held tightly within our hearts, they weaken our bodies and lead to powerlessness in our emotions and lives. However, if we learn to give way to our resistance and embrace all of life's realities, we are set free from the continuous, ongoing pain created by our resistance to the original event. In short, to get free from resistance and anger or the depression they cause, we must be willing to let life be what it is—and was—rather than what we wanted it to be. Moreover, giving up our wish for the perfect past and perfect future sets us free to live fully—and joyfully—in the present.

Parental Anger. Parental anger directed at a child gives him the message that his parents feel resistance toward him and his behaviors. In short, anger tells a child that who he is isn't currently acceptable. Not only does this approach fail to motivate a child, it paralyzes and depletes his spirit. Thus, parents quick to anger would be wise to reframe the way they look at their child's problems and transform their resistance to his immaturities into acceptance of his current stage of development. Moreover, when anger is viewed as a defense against facing the painful parts of life, parental anger can be understood by investigating what it is about the child that the parent doesn't want to face. Thus, rather than beat away the feared behavior with a "stick of anger," parents can learn, instead, to calm down, shift their awareness to their heart, embrace the truth of what's happening, and lovingly help their child to address and strengthen the areas in his development that are presently weak and problematic for him. They can simultaneously look at the underlying fears within themselves that evoked such a strong reaction.

Child Anger. Not only can anger hurt us internally, it negatively affects the way we relate to the world and others. In truth, there are very few people outside of a family unit who will tolerate hostile communication; thus, we do our children a disservice to teach them it's an acceptable way to respond to life's unwelcome moments. If a child wants to talk about something, but is being nasty or is using his anger to blame and attack others, his parents must require that he first exhibit some impulse control before he's free to continue. Once he's willing to manage his anger, it's acceptable for him to express emotion—even intense emotion—but it's not okay to attack or "dump" his feelings of resistance on others or blame them for his pain. When we require children to control their aggressive impulses in this way, they are better able to access and express their more pure, underlying emotions. Thus, once a child is settled down and willing to express himself appropriately, it's critical that his parents listen to whatever he has to say.

Under these conditions, parents are able to guide their child in getting to the real feelings behind his anger by reflecting, acknowledging, and asking questions about the powerlessness, betrayal, hurt, loss, or sadness that he's feeling. Once his emotions are embraced, welcomed, and identified, he too can begin to transform the way he views the situation. In some cases, he must come to terms with a painful reality, whereas in others, he will need to clarify and alter some distortion he's holding. See **Embarrassment**; **Respect**; **Rudeness**; **Sassing**; See Chapter 4

Animal Care. Children become kinder and sweeter when they're taught to care about animal life and other living things, including insects. Animals are a particularly good avenue for developing a child's sensitivity to life, since they are so appealing and cuddly. It's important to teach your child how to get his energies calmed, approach an animal quietly, pick him up in a way that doesn't hurt him or the child, hold him so that he's comfortable, and gently pet and scratch his body in ways that he particularly likes. Adults must supervise a child's interactions with animals until they're sure that he's both willing and able to relate to them in the manner required. If a child fails to follow the rules for kindness to animals and gets too rough, he must be removed from contact with all pets for a period of time. If the pet he bothered is in the family room during this period, the child will have to find another room to use for awhile. Before he's free to resume contact, he must do something nice for the pet. If it's a second offense, his removal should be longer. Children can also be taught to be kind to insects and learn not to randomly destroy those who are living outdoors in their own environment as well as how to save the ones indoors that can be caught and returned to nature. See Chapters 8 and 10

Animals, Hurting/Tormenting. If a child's abuse of animals is persistent after he's been taught to be kind and gentle, this can be a sign of a deeper unhealed trauma that has converted to intense feelings of anger and a more serious problem. Thus, professional help should be sought. See **Animal Care**; **Professional Help**; **Serious Behavioral and Psychological Problems**

Anorexia Nervosa. See *Eating Disorder* subentry under **Eating Problems**

Antecedents. Antecedents include those things that have happened in a child's life prior to the behavior being examined and may be a contributing factor to his current problem. See Chapters 7 and 9

Anxiety. Anxiety results anytime there's an event that has aroused the fight or flight response. When a trauma is big and the anxiety is intense, the mechanism for processing pain may freeze and fail to finish its job. Thus, the person becomes emotionally frozen at that juncture and may cope by returning his thoughts repeatedly to the original experience—or a similar one—in an effort to redo the event, stabilize it, and make it turn out more manageably. These "flashbacks" are often converted to repeated thoughts or behaviors designed to remedy the original trauma by being better prepared for it, responding differently, or fulfilling what wasn't fulfilled in the original setting. When viewed this way, most psychological defense mechanisms appear to be the repetitive ways we go back to prior traumas in our lives in an effort to repair the pain of the past. Unfortunately, this mechanism of "going back to repair the problem or pain"— although designed to reduce our anxiety—actually increases it, since it sustains a resistant response to the original event.

These repetitive behaviors often get triggered by some stimulus in the environment that reminds us of the original trauma. Thus, prolonged anxiety may occur as our fear of a triggering event develops. Also, because these triggers tend to become more and more generalized, the fear expands and begins to infect all areas of life. When the fear intensifies and becomes more generalized and expanded, a fear of the feeling of fear itself develops and the individual feels crippled by fear as well as his fear of it. When this secondary fear sets in, the individual attempts to avoid triggering his fears by limiting his activities and range of thoughts and emotions. This avoidance of tasks, thoughts, and emotions takes a great deal of energy, which in itself creates further anxiety. In order to gain control over so much anxiety, the individual may further attempt to bind it up in more frequently repeated (obsessive) thoughts of the original event or of a symbolic form of it or by repetitive (compulsive) activities such as hand-washing, counting, checking, touching, cleaning and straightening, or eating. Once these obsessive-compulsive mechanisms designed to defend against so much fear are in place, the fear becomes further trapped with no opportunity to get processed and cleared.

Because so many things in today's world trigger anxiety for children, parents should be aware of how this mechanism works and help their child unravel it in its early stages. Only when we can relax and embrace the original event are we free from our fear of the initial pain as well as our anxiety producing resistance to it. This relaxation helps to unlock the frozen mechanism for processing the pain and allows it to finish flowing through to resolution. Thus, when a child seems to have recurring anxiety (or nightmares) and/or attending obsessive thoughts or compulsive behaviors his family should seek professional help.

To prevent your child from being overwhelmed by anxiety, guard against focusing your own thoughts on fear-evoking possibilities; also, protect your child from absorbing the fearful events and thoughts channeled through the media. See **"Challenging Child"**; **Compulsive Behaviors**; **Obsessive Thoughts**; **Post-Traumatic Stress**; **Professional Help**

Anxious Attachment. Some children go beyond a desire for natural bonding and anxiously desire, instead, to remain connected at all times. This often happens when parents are so concerned about their child's needs that they pass anxious feelings about normal periods of separation onto their child. Thus, parents unwilling to leave a child from four to six months for brief periods, one from seven to ten months for slightly longer periods, ten months to three years and older for occasional evenings, and three years and older for longer periods, including at least part-time day classes and programs or full preschool by three-and-a-half to four, would be wise to consider their own anxiety about separation which, in time, could create feelings of anxious attachment in their child. See **Baby-Sitters**; **Bonding**; **Individuation**; **Separation Anxiety**; See Chapter 5

Arguing. Parents who find themselves continually arguing with their children have a discipline problem that needs correcting, while parents arguing between themselves over the children have a parent role problem. See **Parent Roles**; See Chapters 6 and 7

Artistic Pursuits. Artistic and other pursuits are every bit as valuable as academics and should be as enthusiastically encouraged by parents. See **Extracurricular Activities**; **Musical Instruments**; **Practicing**; See Chapter 10

Assertiveness. Children can be taught from an early age to use the basic assertiveness formula for making requests of others: often it's all right to ask for something so long as you are not only clear that the person you are asking has a right to refuse your request, but that you express this understanding prior to making the request. Should they not want to give you what you have requested, it's critical that you not be angry or hold grudges against them for honoring what was right for them in the situation. Neither is it your business to question their reasons for refusing your request in order to measure their standards against your own. A truly assertive individual understands that the other person has a right to use his own values and needs for determining his response. Likewise, when someone requests something of you, you have the same right to decide whether or not you want to accommodate him, even if he doesn't understand your decision or agree with it.

Understanding this formula helps children feel more comfortable about making requests of others, accepting refusals to their own requests, and refusing unreasonable requests made of them. It also helps to protect them from accepting the control—or abuse—of others. Knowing how to do this from a young age helps children to stand up for what they believe and feel, rather than succumb so easily to group pressure. See **Fighting**; **Overclaimer**; **Peer Clusters**; **Peer Pressure**; **Underclaimer**; See Chapter 10

Attachment. See **Anxious Attachment**; **Reactive Attachment and Other Attachment Problems**

Attention. See **Attention-Demand Child**; See Chapters 4 and 11

Attention Deficit Disorder (with Hyperactivity) (ADD[H]). The attention deficit disordered or ADD child has a specific disability in his capacity to focus. He is easily distracted and has trouble staying with a number of tasks (particularly those he's not highly interested in or particularly good at) for long enough to complete them. He also has trouble listening to others and frequently interrupts them with his own thoughts or ideas. Because of his lack of skill in staying focused and receiving information, his perceptions are often not as keen as they would otherwise be, and his ability to learn is impaired.

He may be a calm, cooperative child who is simply unable to sustain his focus on things, or he may also be hyperactive. Because hyperactivity has come to be associated with nonfocusing, fidgety children are often incorrectly diagnosed as having attention deficit disorder with hyperactivity, or ADD(H). On the other hand, some true ADD kids may go undiagnosed simply because they are not hyperactive.

Children with true ADD have problems attending and focusing for long enough to learn from life in a normal way. These children may or may not also exhibit either true hyperactive responses or "learned hyperactivity," the overactive behavior seen in children whose parents are out of balance in either the love or discipline side of their parenting or both.

I suspect the diagnosis of ADD with hyperactivity, or ADD(H), is often erroneously made with children manifesting "learned hyperactivity." Because the symptoms of ADD, which include such things as "often fidgets with hands or feet or squirms in seat"; "often leaves seat in classroom or in other situations"; and "often has difficulty waiting turn" are similar to those of a child raised without balance, it's difficult to distinguish between the two problems. When an incorrect diagnosis is made, parents fail to work toward achieving the balance between nurturing and authority needed to help the child with "learned hyperactivity" calm down and get more focused.

Similarly, I suspect the diagnosis of ADD is incorrectly made with children manifesting "psychologically induced nonfocusing," which is often seen in children who are tense as a result of such things as bonding breaks, overdirection, and overly harsh discipline, since these children can look quite similar. As a result, I believe that the first step in working with a hyperactive or unfocused child or one who appears paralyzed is for his parents to achieve this balance. In short, they must make sure to offer him a bonded connection, rich with "being" time, while simultaneously requiring that he adhere to boundaries. Creating this balance removes the child's reactions to a lack of love or a lack of discipline and makes what is left of his problem easier to diagnose.

Furthermore, the true ADD child, the truly hyperactive child, and the child with "learned hyperactivity" all lack impulse control, including control over their urge to interrupt even themselves. This lack of control could be at the root of their problems or a symptom of them and may explain why a low dose of Ritalin (a central nervous system stimulant that would make anyone more alert and attentive) appears to help the child unable to hold his attention on things. In either case, impulse control is a critical tool for these kids to develop and one that must be addressed at the outset, preferably without drugs at this juncture. Thus, by getting parenting into balance with generous amounts of "being" time offered and impulse control taught, the most common overlays to the child's underlying problem can be removed. After this is accomplished, children still unable to calm down and/or focus for long enough to process and assimilate information remain as candidates for 1) true hyperactivity or 2) ADD with or without hyperactivity. Only then would I recommend the current medical courses of action indicated for such cases described below.

The true ADD(H) child's inability to attend is usually at the core of a cluster of other learning disabilities which are persistent and severe. These children have often had difficult gestations and births or for some reason have soft neurological damage that interferes with their learning process. As a result of their learning problems, they develop poor self-images, have problems with learning social and academic skills, and demonstrate behavioral problems with parents, peers, and teachers.

Possible Causes and Prevention. Although research is inconclusive regarding the causes and prevention of true ADD(H), the brains of these children appear to be affected in some way. In many cases, the cause of this is clear, especially when active drug use by parents or gestation and birth problems were present. In other cases, it is less clear, as in cases involving prior drug use by parents or exposure to toxins. Another currently popular theory is that excessive amounts of television viewing at too early an age is disabling the attention span mechanism of these young brains due to the flicker phenomenon created by the use of multiple cameras during production which, in turn, results in overestimation of the child's sensory system.

The child who appears to have true ADD(H) should have a complete neurological workup and assessment of such things as neurological damage, prenatal history, exposure to drugs and medications, environmental poisoning, food sensitivities, and any other toxins that may be affecting his nervous system. It's critical that parents of a child suspected of having true ADD(H) become fully informed about such things as the quality of their child's drinking water, what chemicals, including pest repellents and garden sprays, are in his home and school environments, and what waste sites or electrical charges he may be exposed to. Parents and schools would be well advised to read *Is This Your Child?* by Dr. Doris Rapp (1992) and *Staying Well in a Toxic World* by Lynn Lawson (Noble Press).

Once a diagnosis is made and all prevention—including such things as detoxing his environment—has been implemented, helping the attention deficit disordered (ADD) and/or truly hyperactive child can be a long-term challenge which families must adjust to if they are to optimize his development. It's important to neither overprotect such a child nor use his disorder as an excuse for not coping. It's also very damaging to get angry at him for his frustrating and often disruptive problems. In addition to any special programs required for such a child, parents can further help their truly hyperactive and/or ADD children by not only holding them in their laps and hearts, but to lovingly hold them to clearly defined boundaries as consistently as possible.

I would like to caution parents not to view an ADD(H) diagnosis as an easy solution to the challenges they have experienced with their child. Although medication often appears to be the easiest answer to this problem, if their child is, in fact, unfocused due to a lack of balanced parenting, learning to get balanced will be easier in the long run than dealing with the long-term side effects of medication.

Parents with children who have true ADD may wish to treat it without drugs, and increasingly more doctors are helping with this alternative. Other doctors have specialized in this disorder and are up-to-date on which drugs are the most helpful with the least number of side effects. Alternatives to explore include Phytobear Vitamins which studies show to be helpful to some ADD(H), learning disabled, and emotionally impaired children, 800-626-9374; Dilantin which has been helpful with some impulsivity and other ADD(H) symptoms, 714-851-1550; and Homeopathy Centers: 503-761-3298, 206-776-4147, and 703-548-7790.

Whether you use drugs or not, the key is to teach the ADD child impulse control, whether it is control over his impulse to interrupt himself or others or to behave in a manner that is outside of the rules. The best way to do this is to watch him closely enough to catch him starting to go with an inappropriate impulse; then stop him in the middle of this decision and offer him a crossroads; do this by giving him an opportunity to notice what he was about to do and to choose again. If he controls the impulse, he keeps his freedom; if not, he loses it. Help him to see the difference during clearing by using visual diagrams and be sure to follow through on the consequence of whatever choice he makes. See **Allergies**; **"Challenging Child"**; **Focusing**; **Impulse Control**; **Overactive Energy**; **Praise**; **Television and Videos**; **Thoughtforms**; **Touch**; See Chapters 4, 5, 6, 7, and 11

Attention-Demand Child. Children who have received excessive praise, criticism, or a combination of both learn to believe that their worth is dependent on pleasing others, and they become addicted to receiving praise, rewards, and attention from adults. Other children become addicted to "quality time" and seek more of this highly entertaining activity. Both groups become so addicted to the time and attention of adults that they are perceived as attention-demand children. Wise parents of attention-demand children must learn to withdraw so much "special" playtime and attention and to avoid praise and criticism. Instead, they can help their child to get in touch with his internal reinforcers and sense of worth by guiding his focus back to his own good feelings about himself and his actions. See **Praise**; **Pride**; See Chapters 4 and 11

Authoritarian Parent. Authoritarian parents tend to be on the extreme end of the strictness continuum. They like their own opinions, have little or no interest in the ideas of others, and use dominance to control the lives of their children. They tend to make personal selections for the child, force him into activities and endeavors of interest to them, and intrude on his personal time and projects to get things done their way. Not only do they control every decision, but often do so in a demanding, autocratic manner. Their law-and-order attitudes seem overbearing, and their lack of respect for how well children can think and contribute is apparent. Discounting a child's needs in this way can be a precursor to physical or sexual abuse. Authoritarian parents were usually raised this way and have not yet interrupted this unfortunate pattern by healing themselves or putting together a better parenting package. What they must realize is that parents can be in charge and require that rules be followed without excessive dominance. See Chapters 2, 3, 6, and 7

Authority. Authority is critical to balanced parenting. See **Rules**; See Chapters 1, 2, 3, 6, and 7

Avoider. See **"Challenging Child"**; **Critical**; **Resistant Child**; **Shyness**; See Chapter 10

Babies, Development. See **Development, Baby**

Babyishness. Babyishness is a form of passive behavior. See **Baby Talk**; **Passivity**

Babyproofing. See **Exploring**

Baby-Sitters. Baby-sitters can be family members, friends you exchange with, or someone you hire. Baby-sitters not only support parents in maintaining their important relationship as a couple, but help children to get comfortable with separating from their parents and relating to others. You may want to begin early with live-in or regular sitters with whom the baby feels secure from the outset. Or, if you wait until he's older, it's best to acquaint him with a sitter before he's five months old, since he begins sometime between five to eight months to get more suspicious of strangers and at nine months to feel a bit anxious around new people. If the child will be left for longer periods, this should only be done with a sitter he knows well and feels comfortable with. If their stay together will be shorter, once the sitter and child have had about a half hour to get acquainted, you can leave. The first departure should be during the day for a fairly brief period, which allows your child to experience that you have left but will also return within a time frame manageable for him. Once he has adjusted to this amount of time, you can leave for progressively longer periods. This teaches him to gradually learn to cope with increasingly longer absences. Once a child is adjusted to a daytime sitter, his parents can leave in the evening, giving him enough time to consciously experience being with a sitter before they leave. A child must *always* know when he is being left so that he can confront the experience and make his adjustment. By contrast, the child who awakens from a nap or in the night to discover that his parents are missing without having told him that they were going will feel abandoned and betrayed and will experience a loss of control over when they might leave him again. As a result, he will not only feel more fearful and insecure in general, but will be more fussy and concerned about separating from them. Leaving when children are eating or listening to a story helps many to accept the separation, whereas others will cry no matter how well the departure is planned. In such cases, it's best for parents to be matter-of-fact and continue on their way with an assuring, "We'll see you later." Even preverbal children intuitively understand the essence of such a confident message. If his parents are comfortable with leaving him, a child will be more likely to trust that it's okay.

Baby-sitters should always be carefully selected and screened and come highly recommended so that parents can be confident that their child is in safe, caring, and capable hands during their absence. Once a detailed selection process is made, attention must be paid to how the sitter handles the child, how the child is adjusting to the experience, and how he reacts when he sees the sitter again. Although most children prefer to be with their parents and may protest their departure, any signs of genuine fear or aversion to the sitter must be noted. Parents must also pay attention to their own intuitive voice, and if it's saying "No," to listen.

When sitters who have functioned as primary caretakers plan to terminate, give the child as long as possible to adjust to the new sitter in order to minimize the pain of losing the current one. This is best done by gradually increasing the amount of time spent with the new sitter, while diminishing the time spent with the old sitter.

Guidelines for Leaving Children Alone. There are no hard- and-fast rules for leaving a child home alone without a sitter, as much will depend on his individual security as well as the safety of the neighborhood. When a child feels secure and is physically safe, he can be left alone with a slightly older sibling or friend for brief periods during the day at about seven to eight years of age or in the evening with a sibling from about eight or nine to ten years. He can be left alone for brief periods during the day from about eight or nine and for reasonably longer periods of time without a sibling during the day at about ten to eleven years. If he feels ready, he can be left alone without a sibling for brief periods at night anytime after ten to eleven years and for longer periods from about eleven to twelve years. These are merely general guidelines, and are not absolutes. Thus, it's important not to push a child who does not feel ready to stay alone, since doing this prematurely will increase his fearfulness rather than his independence. Moreover, if a child seems ready to stay alone earlier and wants to, these guidelines should not prevent you from acting on your own wisdom in the matter. The key is to ask the child how he is genuinely feeling about it and make sure that you don't rush him before he's ready or abuse his ability to manage by leaving him isolated for hours at a time. Be aware too that staying home alone for long periods of time without siblings can cause children to feel intensely isolated and ache for company. Thus, working parents would be wise to find alternatives to leaving their kids home alone after school or at night. Be aware that sometimes a child who has felt comfortable alone becomes fearful and no longer wants to be left. It's important to always listen to what your child has to say about it.

Baby Talk. The more "pretend baby talk" is ignored, the sooner it will go away. Furthermore, the best natural consequence is to make sure your child—rather than you—is the one to experience whatever extra effort is needed to communicate his ideas clearly. For example, if you genuinely can't understand him, ask that he repeat himself. If he's still unclear, and you are absolutely certain that he can do better, explain that you will be interested in what he has to say when he wants to make it clearer. *Never* use this approach with a child first learning to talk or with one who has not yet mastered how to speak clearly on a consistent basis. Thus, only if you are sure it's a game, make no further attempt to understand or inquire about what he's saying until it's clear enough for you to receive his message without straining to translate it. Remain calm and don't try to get him to stop using baby talk, since your irritation and resistance to it will only prolong this behavior. If genuinely unclear speech persists after three, see a speech pathologist. See **Babyishness**; **Passivity**; **Speech Problems**

Bad Behavior. See **Immature Behavior**; See Chapter 7

Bad Words. See **Swearing**

Bargaining. Parents who find themselves bargaining with their children have not learned effective discipline. See Chapters 6 and 7

Bed-making. Children can learn to make simple beds at about four years of age and should be fully managing this no later than their fifth year.

Bedtime. There will be occasions in our culture when the child is asked right from the beginning to be on his own for awhile, unless mother has elected to carry him in a body carrier at all times. Sleeping may be one of these times, if she hasn't also elected to allow him to sleep in their family bed and/or be nursed to sleep for the first six months to a year. This is a big decision for each family which should be made before attempting the following program. I would recommend that parents gather all of the ideas available on the subject and then listen to their own internal voices to make their final decision. (See **Carrying**; **Family Bed**; **Nursing**.) For those parents who have decided to have their child learn to sleep on his own, here are some guidelines for managing this with the most ease and least trauma to both parent and child.

Getting Children to Sleep. In preparation for helping your baby fall asleep on his own, strive not to nurse him all the way to sleep whenever possible after the first two to three months. (If he falls asleep naturally in the course of nursing, leave well enough alone, but don't make an effort to nurse him to sleep.) This allows him to establish an early pattern of dropping off to sleep on his own, rather than relying on you to put him to sleep. First, allow him to get sleepy during nursing, then put him into his bed while he's still slightly conscious so that he will know that he's going to sleep by himself, separate from you. In this way, he will learn to manage the final dropping off aspect of getting to sleep by himself, which will not only begin the important individuating process, but prepare him for knowing how to fall asleep on his own as he gets older. You can rest your hand on his back—or rock him gently back and forth—until he seems content to remain by himself and surrender to sleep.

Most babies will cry initially for a few minutes at this point before dropping off to sleep, so don't react too soon after putting your drowsy baby down unless he persists in crying and becomes agitated. You can first try softly talking to him to see if that's enough to assure him. If he doesn't settle down within a few minutes (about two to four) or begins to get agitated, go to him and put your hand on his back while briefly telling him that he's all right. You can remain in the room without further conversation with your hand on his back, or go into one nearby where he can hear you if he seems ready to accept that. If he cries again, wait another few minutes—or prior to his getting agitated—before going in again to reassure him. This repeated response will eventually teach your child that you haven't forgotten about him, but that it's the end of the day, time for him to go to sleep, and you trust that he can manage without you. The key is for you not to join him in becoming frantic about separating for the night. If a child is particularly fussy or colicky and does not seem to be a good candidate for this step, he may not be ready for this at two to three months. If either you or he (or both) are not ready, you can delay this step until three to five months. If you make the decision to wait, be aware that it will be harder to accomplish this—so don't overrespond to your child's normal levels of crying himself to sleep at that time. If you delay longer, be aware that by five months, you can feel confidant about letting him cry himself to sleep, even though he will have more energy to strongly protest at that point. If you are ready to do this, follow the guidelines under *Retraining*. If you are unsure about taking this step, don't do it, as you will probably back down and make matters worse in the long run. In such cases, wait until you can count on yourself to follow through.

Retraining. For those of you committed to dealing with the older child from five to six months or older who is unwilling to go to sleep by himself, you must now retrain him. Begin by putting him down with calming music to listen to at a regular time every day for naps and bedtime, since this adds to his security and ease of getting to sleep. If your child protests, wait at least five minutes before returning to assure him the first time, ten minutes the second time, twenty minutes the third, and thirty minutes for every interval thereafter. Stick with this until he makes the adjustment to his new reality. If your returning seems to be stimulating his crying or if this is still not working after a month, you may want to use the "cold turkey" method in which you let him cry it out, while all of your checking on him is done without his awareness.

Although the older child of two, three, four, or five can scream louder and longer, as well as run out of his room to find you, it's critical to get him to remain in bed as well. The first step is to become willing to spend about a week allowing him to challenge the new program, since it won't take any longer than that unless you back down (in which case you can count on it taking even longer than the original week required). Once you are committed, you must be prepared to *calmly* return him to his bed each time he leaves without any more conversation than an initial "I'll see you in the morning, sweetheart." (Once this is said, subsequent returns should be primarily in silence, broken only by an *occasional* "I'll see you in the morning" or something comparable, so that the silence does not become a point of struggle.) Returning him can take anywhere from fifteen to fifty times depending on how resistant your child is to facing the new regime. The key to his accepting it lies in your neutrality as well as your clarity about letting him go through his adjustment period while you make it clear that you neither plan to stay and entertain him nor lie down to help him get to sleep. With the older child of three, four, and five, you can draw a time line showing him that he will have to go to bed *earlier* the following night if needed to allow for the time he's using for his resistance, whereas if he can accept his bedtime, it will begin at the normal time the following night.

Be sure not to get angry or close a regular door—or lock it—with a child resisting bedtime, as this can trigger additional fears at a time when he's learning to release you and surrender to the dark and to sleep. Keep a hall light on in addition to his regular night-light if he seems more comfortable with the increase in light.

Parents unwilling to hold the higher—and preferable—standard of requiring that their child remain in bed should at the very least gate the door to his room or close the bottom portion and keep him contained there, rather than allow him to not only resist bedtime, but run freely about the house. Don't act interested or concerned if he cries about being confined. After all, he's supposed to be in bed! Again, the parent unwilling even to take these measures must, at the very least, calmly return their "escapee" every time he leaves his room.

Rituals. Meals, baths, quiet time, music, a night-light, and reasonable rituals such as calming bedtime stories (don't read scary ones even though they like them), a talk or review of the day, and a back, head, or foot rub before kisses and good nights all help to set the stage for sleeping. Be careful not to let your ritual-loving child of two and a half rope you into too many elaborate rituals, as these only serve to keep him tense and delay facing sleep. Also, once they get established, they are hard to eliminate.

Never Insist on Sleep. Requiring that a child fall asleep not only makes dropping off more difficult for him, but may trigger insomnia. Therefore, require that the child who has trouble releasing himself to sleep remain in bed, but allow him to have a night-light on, books to look at, and/or a calming music tape to listen to. Don't allow toys or story tapes that will keep him up even longer and delay his yielding to sleep. Once he accepts these terms, allow him to determine when he's ready to drop off to sleep without any prodding from you. The less you suggest that he get to sleep, the sooner it will happen.

Getting up for Drinks and Toileting. Allow your child to manage his own toileting and drinks (using tap water from a cup left in the bathroom) as many times as he wants. This prevents him from turning this activity into a social opportunity. However, should he use this time to play in the bathroom or peek in on the family, return him without interaction to bed and let him know that he won't be allowed to get up any more that night. If he gets up again, repeat the above response, and let him know—using a diagram—that if he gets up again, he must go to bed earlier the following night to allow for his delays. If this happens, return him to bed without conversation as many times as needed; then, wait for the following day to calmly show him the consequence that this extra time has earned him. Following through on this consequence will deter him from delaying again the following night.

Sleep, Amounts. When a child seems unhappy or crabby and is unusually difficult to manage, it's often because his parents are unaware of how much sleep he needs, and he's not getting enough rest. Consult your favorite baby care book to determine how much rest your child needs according to his age. It's often more than you realize! Be aware that adequate rest not only helps his disposition but contributes to the child reaching his optimal growth potential. Following is a brief guide for the approximate amounts of sleep your child will need:

- two years: twelve hours at night; one to two hours of nap
- two to six years: twelve hours at night; shorter nap periods varying with each child
- six to nine years: gradually decrease one hour of night rest to eleven hours; no naps except for required school rest periods
- nine to twelve years: gradually decrease another hour of night rest to ten hours; no naps
- teen years: the need for about nine to ten hours of sleep per night continues through the teen years until the child has stopped growing, since growth hormones are triggered after extended periods of rest; sleep requirements for adolescents who have stopped growing are parallel to adult needs

Bedtime for the Older Child. As your child grows out of infancy he should have a bedtime routine of a bath, bedtime stories, and perhaps a back rub as he settles down. You can then be firm but friendly about saying good night. Continued calming routines as he gets older—including a reasonable number of rituals—such as a quiet game or story and back rub before being tucked in with a favorite stuffed animal or tape and a kiss good night—offer your child the security of repetition and warmth before bedtime.

If a child falls asleep without problems, leave well enough alone. However, if he's worried about bedtime because he can't get to sleep, keep a hall or night-light on—or let him turn on a bedside lamp and read for as long as he desires while remaining in bed. He may also listen to a tape of restful music if he likes. If a child who has no real questions or problems calls for you, let him know one time that you won't answer his calls any further and will see him in the morning. Then, stick with it.

Some children resist bedtime due to the many fears that surface at night such as a fear of the dark, not waking up, monsters, and nightmares. You can talk about these worries to help desensitize your child to them, without adding to his concern with anxiety of your own. Other children simply want to stay up later, watch TV, or be with the family. All young children must have a firm bedtime that is not presented as a choice ("Are you ready to go to bed?") nor rigidly held (the young child can't tell time), but must be responded to when announced ("It's time to get to bed"). See **Adjustment Period**; **Carrying**; **Door Barriers, Gates**; **Family Bed**; **Individuation**; **Sleep Problems**; *Weaning* sub-entry under **Nursing**

Bed-wetting. Many children are able to sleep through the night without wetting between two to three years of age (68 percent), while many more are not trained until four, five, or six (20 percent). Although less common, it's still considered normal for a child to wet his bed after six, seven, or eight (10 percent) and in some cases throughout adolescence (2 percent). These delays may be due to something as simple as pinworms, bladder infections, or food allergies, or they may be due to genetic immaturities of the central nervous system or a bladder with limited capacity. In most cases, this delay simply requires patience; yet, parents of children still not trained by four or who show signs of itching, wakefulness, or painful or frequent urination might want to have them checked for a persistent bladder infection or a repeat of the pinworms. Ones not trained by seven should be medically checked as well. Children delayed in staying dry in the absence of medical problems have simply not developed enough bladder control or sphincter muscle strength to hold their urine or feces all night and sleep too deeply for the pressure to awaken them when they need to go. Parents can help such children by explaining why they aren't getting through the night, even though their peers are, and assure them that these muscles will grow in time. Some children can be successfully shown how to exercise these muscles. If it's a family trait, parents can also share various aspects of relatives' experiences with assurances that they all outgrew it in due course. It's vitally important that parents be patient, since any disappointment they show in this developmental delay shames the child and creates a far more serious problem for him than the original bed-wetting. Parents can further help their child develop his ability to stay dry all night by having him stop liquid intake after dinner and leaving a light on so that he can find the bathroom comfortably, if needed. It also helps to provide rubber sheets to minimize the mess for children too old for diapers, and thick training pants to keep him more comfortable.

If parents have mistakenly turned toilet training and bed-wetting into a battle, they must acknowledge their mistake and become even more patient than originally required, since their child will now have to get over his anger before he will be ready to cooperate.

When the four- to six-year-old has an accident, you can gently invite him to help clean himself and get his sleepwear and sheets into the wash. However, I wouldn't make an issue about this or turn it into a power struggle, since shame is often connected to delayed nighttime bladder control and is the primary thing you want to avoid as your child goes through this developmental delay. If a child who is reluctant to help is also resistant in other areas, I would address his general resistance first. See **"Challenging Child"**; **Passive Resistance**; **Resistant Child Loss of Bladder Control Once Gained.** If a child has demonstrated bladder control for several months, and then loses it, check again for pinworms or a bladder infection, as these are common contributors to losing bladder control. If the child is free of both worms and infection, you might consider psychological factors. If you suspect emotional problems, you must first respond to your child calmly and with assurance that it's all right. You can then gently investigate what changes he experienced just prior to his accidents. Is there a new baby? Did school just start? Did a teacher or friend yell at him? If necessary, you can present your child with a "menu" of hunches to choose from and use reflective interpretation (see Chapter 11) to help him uncover the problem. Once parents of children who wet for psychological reasons learn to remain neutral, while helping their child to address and resolve his problem, his wetting invariably stops. If you have trouble uncovering the underlying problem or resolving the bed wetting within a month or so, seek professional help. See **Professional Help**; **Toilet Training**

Biting. Initial biting of people in the young child of about two years of age can sometimes be viewed as a tensional outlet that he uses when he feels overwhelmed by the stimulation of play and managing toys at day care and preschool. In such cases, the school environment may be triggering his feelings of stress and this behavior may indicate that he's having trouble dealing with the pressures of school and its demands. For example, he may be too young for his classroom or to be left at school for so many hours each day. You should also check to see if he has been handled roughly by one or both parents or a sitter or if he has been exposed to aggressive television programming, both models of handling frustration aggressively. Once these underlying causes are investigated and addressed, you can assume that whatever biting remains is the child's way of working out dominance and submission with the other children. Or, if it's been going on for awhile, it may simply have become a habitual response for him when he feels the stress of not getting his way or because it has been reinforced by the way it's currently being handled.

Although the squabbles of children allow them to discover a balance between under- and overclaiming, whenever biting, scratching, or other such injuries occur, the adult must calmly interfere. Thus, the first step adults can take is to more carefully watch a child with this tendency and help him to better manage those times when he's feeling overwhelmed or unsure of how to handle things. By doing this, the adults have an opportunity to interrupt the child's biting behavior, immediately contract his freedom, and prevent his discovery of the illusion of power in biting.

If a child has managed to bite another child in self-defense, let him know that it's okay to defend himself but that he will need to use his hands, rather than his teeth to manage the problem. If he is the aggressor—or if it's his second offense as a defender—the biting child must be calmly put on a time-out and told during clearing that it's not a choice to cross the boundaries of others or bite them during disagreements. Thus, when he selects biting, he won't be free to be with the other children for awhile, since it's not an acceptable way of behaving with people. If this is handled neutrally and calmly the child will stop the biting behavior more quickly than when adults get excited about his biting and treat it like a "powerful" thing to do. It's not helpful to emphasize how hurtful the bite was for the other child, as this merely encourages his belief that biting is a potent weapon that puts him in control. If a child persists in biting at school, he can be sent home for the remainder of the day to parents instructed to make sure that he has a boring afternoon and evening. If a child is trying to avoid school, rather than being sent home, he can spend his time in an adult office at school. However, it's important to find out why a child who is avoiding school wishes to escape and then help him to resolve his problem. The key to remember is that a child will stop biting if he can see that it hurts *his* life in some way, rather than the life of his victim. See **Aggressiveness**; **Fighting**; **Habits**; **Hitting**; **Overclaimer**; **Tensional Outlets**; See Chapters 7, 8, and 10

Blame. Blaming is used as a defense against taking responsibility for our mistakes. Thus, it's not uncommon for those who fear error to resist facing their part in things and strive, instead, to project their mistakes onto others and feel superior in the process.

Parents who excuse their child when he transfers responsibility for his errors to others encourage this habit and retard his ability to handle life with greater honesty and clarity. Similarly, parents quick to blame teachers, neighbors, coaches, or peers for their child's problems are not facing what he needs to learn in order to grow in responsibility.

Thus, wise parents of children who have developed the habit of blaming others for their problems will look for ways to help them reduce their fear of mistakes and learn to face and accept their part in conflicts. They can do this by first holding their child to the truth and then remaining gentle, rather than disappointed or punitive, whenever he admits to his faults. Parents of defensive children with a tendency to blame others must consider ways to inspire their child to feel less competitive and more cooperative and caring in life and with others. See **Competitive**; **Error**; **Failure, Fear of**; See Chapters 4, 6, and 10

Bonding. Bonding is the term used to describe the powerful, loving connection that forms between parent and child when it's not broken by such things as abandonment, neglect, or abuse; unnatural or prolonged separations; loving the child with conditions; or pushing him too hard and early toward early independence and maturation. See **Access**; **Bedtime**; **Carrying**; **Comforters**; **Contact**; **Eye Contact**; **"In-Arms" Period**; **La Leche League**; **Lap-Sitting**; **Nursing**; **Reactive Attachment and Other Attachment Problems**; **Thumb Sucking**; **Touch**; See Chapter 5

Boredom. The child who complains of boredom has not yet learned to entertain himself and brings his boredom to you as an indication that he believes you should do something to remove it. This is a good sign that the child has been entertained too much, either by you or other adults, has an overabundance of toys, and/or has viewed too much television or played too often with electronic and computer games. The best antidote to boredom is to—lovingly—allow your child to experience it. This is best done by reducing the number of toys and electronic distractions from his more natural and genuine involvement in life. As a result of experiencing the vacuum, some urge toward an interest or activity will eventually stir in him.

Borrowing. Children can be taught from an early age that most people prefer not to be asked to loan their things, since this puts them in a position of having to either say "No" or to loan something they may not wish to release. As a result, people tend to feel less comfortable around persistent borrowers and may avoid them as a way to maintain control over their possessions. On those rare occasions when borrowing is either fun or essential, it's important to teach your child to promptly return the item in its original condition. You can also teach that he can refuse the requests of borrowers. See **Assertiveness**; **Overclaimer**; **Underclaimer**

Bottles. See **Carrying**; **Nursing**; *Weaning* sub-entry under **Nursing**

Boundaries. Parents must first teach children to respond to parental and societal boundaries. They must then teach them how to set and hold their own boundaries with others. See **Abduction**; **Abuse**; **Exploring**; **Overclaimer**; **Rules**; **Strangers**; **Underclaimers**; See Chapters 6 and 7

Boundaries, Healthy Between Parent and Child. Although ample doses of love for children are always healthy, the love between parent and child must never have sexual overtones. Neither should the child feel that he or she is Mommy's little boyfriend or Daddy's little girlfriend, even when this "romantic"—or dependent—relationship is nonsexual. Also important is that parents not burden children with their personal or emotional problems or use them as confidants with whom romantic problems and frustrations are aired. See **Abuse**; *Address Reality Fairly* subentry under **Divorce**; See Chapters 5 and 12

Bragging. The child who brags is not only caught up in the race to the top, but strives to improve his position by calling attention to his abilities. This becomes an unattractive personality quality and, like other competitive traits, separates a child from his peers, rather than creates the respect and friendship he's hoping to attain. Such a child can be helped to look for ways to feel more loving and connected, rather than separated, in his relationships. A bragging child must be differentiated from the child who's able to acknowledge his strengths, yet feels no need to impose an awareness of them on others. It's important to make this distinction so that we don't inadvertently teach children to suppress the fullness of their joy in their own beauty and magnificence in the process of teaching them not to insist that others constantly affirm their strengths. See **Competitive**; See Chapter 10

Brat Zone. Learning how to keep kids out of the brat zone is critical to good discipline. See Chapters 6 and 7

Breaking the Child's Spirit. Even and clear discipline—including requiring that a child yield to your rules—does not break his spirit as commonly believed. Only overdominance and excessively harsh and angry discipline can threaten a child's spirit. See **Overcontrol**; **Resistance**; **Rules**; See Chapters 1 and 3

Breast-feeding. See **Bedtime**; **Carrying**; **Nursing**

Breath Holding. Some children hold their breath, turn blue, and pass out in the middle of a tantrum. This is a frightening experience, and requires that parents get their child medically checked the first time it happens. However, if all is well and it's simply a breath-holding tantrum, subsequent tantrums that end this way must be handled with calm equanimity to let the child know that no matter how dramatic his tantrums, they still won't work. See **Tantrums**

Bribing. Parents who bribe are having problems with discipline. See Chapters 6 and 7

Brushing Teeth. Parents must teach their young child when and how to brush his teeth. During the early stage, they may do it for him or guide his efforts. Once a child knows how to brush, you can help him to develop the habit of brushing regularly by putting it on his schedule of responsibilities. If your child resists managing this chore, you can let him know that he's not free to do anything else until his teeth are brushed. It also helps to require a practice session and/or neutrally announce that he has lost his choice to brush his own teeth and calmly finish the task for him. Then let him know that he will be required to begin brushing earlier the following day to allow time for his resistance. When parents not only help their children understand that brushed teeth smell and feel better, but remain calm, yet clear, in the face of refusals to address it, their child eventually accepts toothbrushing as an accepted part of his day. See **Chores**; **Practice Sessions**; **Refusal to Comply**; **Resistant Child**; See Chapter 7

Bulimia. See **Eating Disorders** subentry under **Eating Problems**

Bully. Whenever a child regularly bullies others it's important to make it his problem, rather than view it as one for the child he's bullying or a problem between the two of them. In order for him to experience bullying as a problem for himself, the bully's freedoms must be contracted each time he behaves aggressively without provocation. During clearing, explore what things other than the desire to get his way may be motivating him. In some cases, a child who is teased and bullied by parents or older siblings copies this coveted role of dominator for use at school in order to get out of the powerless position he occupies at home. In other cases, the child has simply discovered this method of getting his way or being in charge as a result of his dominant size, superior strength, and/or a lack of effective adult supervision. Teaching a child the true result of this role—a loss of friends—helps some bullies to back off, whereas others need to be placed with older children who match their developmental level to get them back into balance. Still others, not ready for a more mature group, need to be consistently removed whenever they use dominance as a way of coping and taught to model on the more cooperative play of friendlier children. See **Abuse**; **Aggressiveness**; **Fear**; **Overclaimer**; **Television and Videos**

Car Behavior. If children are misbehaving in the car, the most effective approach is to pull over to the side of the road, and offer them a "crossroads" choice: they can either settle down so that you can continue driving to your destination; or they can choose not to settle down, and be returned home. (This includes getting rebuckled if they have unfastened their seatbelts.) If it's an outing they are interested in, the return home will be consequence enough. If not, get a sitter (no TV or entertainment), and finish the outing by yourself. If it's not possible to return home, let the children know that you're unwilling to drive with a ruckus in the car and will begin again only after they have settled down. Let them also know that they will receive a time-out at home for double the time it takes them to get quiet. If this isn't working, let them know that their behavior has not only cost them a time-out, but the next outing in the car. Follow through by planning an outing in the immediate future that the offending child or children must miss. If one child is causing the disturbance, only that child should experience a contraction of freedom. If a child who likes school (or other activity) is misbehaving in the car on the way there, stay on the side of the road or return home until he cooperates and take him late or not at all. If a child who doesn't like school (or other activity) is misbehaving, get him there and find another way to contract his freedom in a manner he cares about when he returns home. See **Car Seat**; **Consequences**; **"Crossroads" Choice**

Car, Seat Belt. See **Car Seat**

Car Seat. Young children must remain in car seats or buckled in their own places whenever the car is in motion. If you're as clear about this important safety procedure as you are that your child may not run into the street, he will succumb to this rule. In fact, it's critical that parents never start the car until their child is properly strapped in. Once the rule has been established and adhered to—even for short trips—it will no longer be a point of debate. Whenever your child feels ready to do his own buckling, allow him to do so unless he turns it into a problem. In that case, he loses the choice to buckle for this trip and may try again on the next one.

Caring. Raising caring children is one of the most important things parents can do if they wish to dwell on a living planet with caring people. Teaching children to feel sensitive in their hearts toward life and others is most effective during nonconflict times throughout the course of daily living. See **Access**; **Animal Care**; **Animals, Hurting/Tormenting**; **Bonding**; See Chapters 5, 8, and 10

Carrying. When we carry a child, we usually put him over our left shoulder, allowing our hearts to connect physically and emotionally. Carrying is a critical part of the bonding process and should not be viewed as "immature." Thus, when making decisions about how long to carry a child, we must remember that the goal of raising our children is not to find a way for them to achieve early independence and win the race to maturity, but to offer them an experience of love and a model of how to be caring people while guiding their personalities to come forth. Therefore, it's not important to get a child out of our arms and into the race as early as possible, but to look only in terms of how much to nurture him while enhancing his individuating process. Finding a balance between this combination keeps him healthy and functioning, while providing him with an experience of continuous love. In view of these criteria, it makes sense to use Jean Liedloff's more primitive model (*The Continuum Concept*, 1986) of allowing a child to remain in his parent's arms for as long as he likes during those times when he initiates a desire for it, yet without special attention focused on him.

Using this model, the period of most intense carrying will usually last until he's about six to eight months, at which time he learns to crawl, can nourish himself more independently, and likes to explore with his newfound mobility. It's useful to be aware of this juncture and allow the individuating process that nature has orchestrated to take place. You can support this step by requiring your child to sit in your lap to nurse or drink from his bottle, so that he can separate exploration from nursing and eating and make this natural transition toward his individuation process. Once the child is off exploring, his continued need for being carried gradually declines and comes only when he initiates it or you're en route somewhere. This desire can get prolonged, however, when parents either resist carrying him, become the initiator due to their need to overprotect, or excessively entertain him. Allowing the child who is outgrowing infancy to have continued full access—without entertainment—at all times not only allows him to individuate without being pushed, but to return for nurturing whenever desired.

When an older child, too big to be carried, asks to be held, offer to sit with him for a moment—without entertainment—before continuing on your way if you're en route. If this is impractical, let him know that he will simply have to manage. Understand that his fussing over this arrangement simply represents his adjustment to this reality. See **Access**; **Bedtime**; **Bonding**; **Contact**; **"In-Arms" Period**; **Independence**; **Individuation**; **Lap-Sitting**; **Nursing**; **Touch**; *Weaning* subentry under **Nursing**; See Chapter 5

Challenges. Although the adolescent rebellion is the challenge most talked and written about, it represents only one of many challenges a child poses to his parents throughout his development. When challenges are quelled, a cooperative effort between parent and child can take place in which they work together to give the child responsible control over his life. See **Adjustment Period**; **Consequences**; **Independence**; **Individuation**; **Rebellion**; **Refusal to Comply**; **Resistant Child**; **ToughLove**; See Chapters 7 and 12

"Challenging Child." The "challenging child" is one who seems oversensitive to life and has difficulty adjusting to a variety of things, probably due to some early trauma, including such things as difficulties at birth (fetal distress, prolonged labor, breech delivery, inducement drugs, cord wrapped around the neck, oxygen deprivation, delay in breathing); breaks in bonding (initial delay in being held by mother, prolonged delay after initial contact, infrequent time with mother throughout hospital stay, illness of child or mother, depression of mother, nursing difficulties, rapid return to work and premature child-care placement, interference on the part of relatives, other causes for early separation of mother and child); and/or a stressful, dysfunctional environment (excessive quarrels and fights, alcohol or drug use, immature, distracted, depressed, overworked, neglectful, angry, and/or physically/emotionally/sexually abusive parents).

These traumas may cause a child to respond with mild to moderate post-traumatic stress reactions while he is still preverbal and/or too young to express his distress. These reactions, although very subtle or even invisible to us, might include some of the classic post-traumatic stress symptoms such as reliving the experience of the anxiety originally felt; feelings of detachment, estrangement, and unreality; psychic numbing of responsiveness to the world and others; a desire to withdraw and avoid; repetitive autonomic reactions, thoughts, and behaviors; sleep disturbances including nightmares; and difficulty relaxing.

Moreover, these children may have made early—and therefore deep—decisions that life "hurts" or "overwhelms." Such decisions will cause them to begin very early to guard against life's pain while simultaneously wanting to participate and succeed in its activities. The part of them that fears life and wishes to withdraw manifests as excessive timidity, avoidance, and oversensitivity to life's normal encounters. The part that wants to participate and succeed is in conflict with the fearful self and creates an approach/avoidance conflict deep within them. Such conflicts may cause the child to seem fussy, difficult, and overly challenged in the face of new experiences. He may then defend against this conflict by attempting to anchor himself in rigid, obsessive responses, negative persistence, or outright avoidance. These defenses in turn cause him to be even more difficult to manage and motivate. Not surprisingly, these early traumas, and the defenses built around them, often lead to such problems as separation anxiety, problems with normal adjustment to new experiences and difficulties, and increasingly avoidant reactions to life's challenges.

The best way to help these children is to balance abundant doses of love with clear discipline, since balance helps to heal their initial traumas, calm them down, and bring their organisms back into better alignment. The worst thing to do is to get out of balance on either side of your parenting by overprotecting such a child, withdrawing your love from him because of his difficulties, or failing to provide him with adequate amounts of structure and discipline. Any of these responses will drive him further out of balance.

By the time the unhealed "challenging child" is a teen, he has not only spent years in conflict and resistance to life's offerings, but has developed defense mechanisms to hide his insecurities and deficits. Thus, he, too, can be helped by bringing love and discipline into balance in your home. In short, the key to raising the "challenging child" is to stick with the program. If more help is needed, seek professional help from someone skilled in EMDR (Eye Movement Desensitization and Reprocessing), a new technique for healing both old and current traumas. See **Anxiety**; **Attention Deficit Disorder**; **Compulsive Behaviors**; **"Immature Boss"**; **Learning Disability**; **Negative Persistence**; **Obsessive Thoughts**; **Post-Traumatic Stress**; **Professional Help**; **Refusal to Comply**; **Resistant Child**; **Tantrums**; **Tensional Outlets**; See Chapters 3, 4, 5, 6, 7, 9, 10, and 12

Charting. Charting a child's behavior helps parents understand any problems he's having. See Chapter 7

Chasing. Rather than chase the young toddler running away from you by merely bringing him back to where he was supposed to be in the first place, contract his freedoms in some way. You can do this best by requiring that he sit in your lap, hold your hand, be confined to a stroller or cart or—if he doesn't conform—returned home. This result will diminish his fun and subsequent interest in running away. See Chapters 6 and 7

Cheating. Cheating is a way for a child caught in the competitive race and wanting to be the best to avoid facing his "failures" and losses. Providing him with more unconditional acceptance, teaching him to embrace his errors, modeling a more caring, cooperative attitude, and showing him how to lose graciously can help. It's also important not to let him "win" with cheating but to have him experience less—rather than more—anytime he tries it. If cheating continues, seek professional help. See **Competitive**; **Error**; **Failure, Fear of**; **Professional Help**; See Chapter 4

Child-Care. See **Day Care**

Choices. Our choices of thought or action manifest themselves in our lives. Therefore, it's essential to teach our children how important and powerful their choices are. See Chapters 6, 7, 9, and 10

Chores. We have come a long way from colonial days when young children made substantial contributions to planting fields and maintaining households! In fact, modern parents often fail to assign their offspring any responsibilities whatsoever and do everything for them. They even avoid requiring them to make their own beds or clean their messes and rooms by closing their doors and viewing the mess as something the child "owns." Unfortunately, this not only prevents a child from learning to take responsibility for his messes, but undermines his ability to be organized and responsible. In truth, children actually feel better about themselves and closer to their families when they have been taught to contribute toward the care of their households. Following are some approaches to making this happen.

Before assigning chores, young children must first be taught to "full-cycle" their own personal messes as they go. This idea is more attractive to a child when he's told about the American Indian's understanding of completing the cycles of activity and the importance of cycling to the ecology and care of the earth. See Chapter 6.

Following are some general approximate guidelines for matching chores with your child's age:

- A child from two to three years old can begin to dress himself; pick up his books and toys; full-cycle his dishes; set the table with napkins and flatware; straighten magazines; dust; fold small items from the laundry pile; pick up leaves; and bring in the newspaper.
- A child from three to four years old can pick up his toys; put his clothes in the hamper; hang up his wet towel; set the table; clear his dishes; pick up his messes; wipe the table where he was sitting; begin to make a simple bed; help put groceries away; help with watering plants; dust the furniture; fold dish towels; do simple cooking tasks with supervision; and get the mail.
- A child from five to six years old can pour his own drinks; make his own cereal and sandwiches; help plan family meals; make a simple bed; keep his room ordered; scrub bathroom tubs, sinks, counters, and toilets; sort his own laundry by colors; answer the phone; help with marketing; help with pet care; sweep the kitchen floor and patio; and pull weeds.
- A child from six to seven years old can rake a section of the yard; pull larger weeds; sweep a sidewalk; empty the trash on a schedule; peel and chop vegetables; fold his own laundry; help wash the car; make his own school lunch; and cook simple foods such as pudding, pancakes, and scrambled eggs.
- A child from eight to nine years old can change his sheets; run the washer and dryer; make more complicated foods such as cookies—with minimal supervision; weed a flower bed; clean out the refrigerator; help with the dishes; clean bathroom mirrors; read to siblings; and water the plants.

- A child from ten to eleven years old can wash the car or dog on his own; take responsibility for a pet; mow a small lawn; cook a simple family meal with minimal supervision; keep his bathroom clean; sew and knit simple things; remain home alone or with siblings during the day; pack his suitcase; and do his own laundry.
- A child from twelve years old and up can be given additional personal chores such as doing his own laundry and added community chores such as helping to mow the lawn, vacuum, or clean a hot tub. He is also ready to take responsibility for such things as a paper route and staying with siblings in the evening.

As more chores requiring increased levels of responsibility and time are added to a child's required list of chores, some of his lesser chores can be eliminated. For example, when a child takes over mowing the lawn, he might be excused from his watering responsibilities.

Chore assignments work best when all of the chores are laid out according to degree of difficulty and kids select whichever chores most interest them from among the ones that match their age. I treat chores involving the family pets as a privilege available only to the more responsible children or the adults, so that animals don't starve while resistant kids are learning to be responsible. However, small caged animals that belong only to the child can be his responsibility. Be cautious about assigning the family dishes to children with loads of homework to manage each night, as this chore can interfere with study time. Delegating dishes to kids during the summer or on a free weekend night may work better. A useful guideline to use is that chores must not overwhelm a child's time for study, extracurricular activities, friendships, and relaxation, yet should give him a sense of contributing. Furthermore, chores for young children are best done before something desirable that follows. For example, it works well to have a child make his bed before breakfast each morning or mow the lawn on Saturday prior to pursuing his own activities. Chores are more likely to get done without resistance or "prolonged suffering" when parents are clear and not in conflict about assigning them and matter-of-factly assume the child will do them happily.

Parents shouldn't worry about keeping chores on an even scale or have children trade doing their chores each week to keep things "fair." Not only does this confusing system cause endless squabbles over whose turn it is to do which chore, it encourages kids to blame siblings for those not done. It also contributes to the worrying over fairness that develops in families striving to keep everything even. See Chapter 10.

When responsibilities are first assigned, parents should provide an interesting, clear, and playful period of teaching the child how to do each chore step by step with expectations that are realistically high, yet not so exacting that their child feels tense or overwhelmed. Once a child knows how to do a chore, his parents must help him establish a habit of managing it regularly, rather than forget about it themselves for several days and then scold him for not doing it. Once the habit has been established, they can check periodically to make sure that it's still in place. Only when they are confident that a child will do his chores without reminders is supervision withdrawn. Be aware this can take six months to a year or more!

Delay or refusal to do chores is best responded to by not allowing the child to go forward with other aspects of his life until the chore is done. Thus, a child who has not made his bed in the morning is not free to leave his room and join the family for breakfast. One who has not yet mowed the lawn Saturday morning is not free to leave the house except—in some cases— to participate in other responsibilities. Blocking his freedom in this way works better than repeated nagging, since the child eventually experiences that he hurts his own life and schedule when he resists doing his chores.

Never do a chore that your child has failed to do. Save it and require that he complete it before being free for his next activity, while gently adding an additional small chore to be done as well as docking part of his allotted payment. This pair of consequences makes it worth his while to attend to his chores. See **Cleaning**; **Full-Cycling**; See Chapters 6 and 10

Cleaning. Full-cycling one's own messes is an important skill that not only teaches respect for property, but helps a child learn to structure himself. This, in turn, affects such things as school-work and organizational skills. See **Chores**; See Chapter 6

Clearing. Full-cycling relationships is as important to clarity as full-cycling other messes. Clear-ing—or clarifying what wasn't previously clear between people—is the term I use to describe how this is done. See **Full-Cycling**; See Chapter 8

Clothes Selection. A good guideline for clothes shopping with kids is to select only those things that both the child and his parent like. In this way, the child doesn't feel pushed into attire he doesn't like and his parent doesn't purchase clothes of which he or she doesn't approve. A par-ent's open-mindedness to young styles and current looks enhances agreeing on things and makes for a fun time together, rather than one of tension and arguments.

You can organize a younger child's wardrobe by putting his playclothes in one area of his closet or drawers, school clothes in another, and dressy clothes in yet another. It's best to have him participate with this sorting in order to teach him about colors, why certain clothes fall into various categories, and to allow him to save any stained "treasures" from being tossed. After sorting is completed, your child has the option of selecting whichever outfit he would most like to wear on a particular day or for a specific event from the appropriate category. In this way, you honor his need to control what he wears within the context of a suitable structure. If he wants you to select his clothes, it's okay to do so, but don't get caught in the bind whereby he asks for your help, but then fusses over your selection. The moment this begins, drop out by letting him know that he's lost his choice to control the selection, since he wasn't managing it well. Thus, you will choose for today and he can try again tomorrow. Even if he has a tantrum, remain calm but stick with it. If you do, he will lose his appetite for initiating such "double-binding" interactions.

It's important to allow teens to pursue the standard fashions of their generation and to main-tain control over what they wear, so long as their selections are appropriate for the times as well as the occasion. When they fail to groom hygienically or are pushing for statements out-side of the standard of their own age-group, it's appropriate to draw some boundaries, since this usually constitutes a rebellion rather than a fashion statement. See **Dressing**

Colic. See **Crying**

Comforters. Comforters include such things as thumbs, blankets, and stuffed toys that children discover to soothe themselves. A child's need for an array of comforters may—or may not—indicate that he has experienced a bonding break or has not had enough nurturing. If this is the case, he would benefit from more lap time and touching. See **Bedtime**; **Bonding**; **Carry-ing**; **Lap-Sitting**; **Security Blankets and Objects**; **Touch**; **Thumb-Sucking**

Communal Sleeping. See **Family Bed**

Communication. Good communication occurs when listening becomes as active a part of the process as speaking. In this way communications are adequately sent as well as adequately received. See Chapter 11

Competitive. Parents often strive to motivate children by encouraging them to catch up or get ahead of their friends. Unfortunately, the belief that a child's superiority over others will strengthen and empower him is not only erroneous, but damages his relationships with the peers that he is trying to best. In fact, teaching kids to surpass their friends causes them to develop attitudes of superiority and intimidation. In reality, the skills and accomplishments of others have no effect on his personal ability to succeed. Teaching children otherwise makes them fear the good in the lives of others and causes them to minimize or undermine it. It may also result in their behaving with attitudes of superiority and intimidation in their effort to get to the top. Not only does such a competitive focus paralyze kids with the fear of losing the race, it encourages feelings of jealousy and separation that interfere with their ability to love and care for others. This approach to social encounters is self-defeating and is usually at the root of sibling and peer rivalry. See **Blame**; **Cheating**; **Jealousy**; **Sibling Rivalry**; See Chapters 2 and 10

Complaining. See **Negative Persistence**; **Sulking**; **Whining**

Compliance. Parents must create clear and fair rules and then require compliance to those boundaries. See **Adjustment Period**; **"Challenging Child"**; **Consequences**; **Refusal to Comply**; **Resistant Child**; **Rules**; **Safe-Holding**; **Tantrums**; See Chapters 6 and 7

Compulsive Behaviors. Compulsive behaviors are designed to reduce anxiety and include such repetitive activities as straightening, cleaning, touching, checking, washing, and counting. Tics can also be considered compulsive behaviors, and stuttering may fall into this category as well. Excessive rituals or rigidly insisting on such things as repeatedly wearing the same outfit may also fall into the category of milder compulsive behaviors. When a child compulsively repeats a behavior, he's anxious about something and uses the behavior to repetitively go back to fix the original trauma in hopes of making it turn out better this time. Unfortunately, this "flashback" mechanism not only fails to fix the original injury or reduce the anxiety or pain felt as a result of it, but traps the child in an ongoing state of hope that he can repair the event. To break free from the compulsive behavior—as well as heal the original injury—a child must stop resisting the pain of the trauma and find a way to accept the experience and the pain it generated in his life. Only then is he free to break through and complete whatever processing of the trauma is needed.

Parents can begin first to find out what their child's concerns are by asking how the behavior—for example, straightening his trucks in a row over and over again—will make him feel better or what worry it will help him to relax. In some cases, parents are already aware of the trauma and know the answer to this question. These might include such issues in the family as a serious illness or injury, addictions, violence, death, or divorce. In other cases, the trauma may go all the way back to a difficult birth, early bonding breaks, an accident, or other fear-evoking events. Thus, parents can reflect a "menu" of possibilities to their child. By doing this, they help him to examine what underlying unwelcome and resisted pain the repeated straightening is designed to fix. They can also help him to notice that the repeated behavior doesn't remove the problem or help him relax as hoped but makes him feel even more tense as he gets increasingly frantic about doing the behavior to ease the old pain. Once the child is able to see this, his parents can help him to change his mind about needing to resist the original pain and become willing, instead, to accept and embrace its reality into his experience. This step works most effectively when done with the help of a therapist trained in EMDR (Eye Movement Desensitization and Reprocessing), a new technique used to process old and new pain and trauma. If after he has released his resistance to the original trauma and its accompanying pain, he still has the residual of the compulsive habit, his parent—or the EMDR therapist—can teach him to bypass the urge to do the behavior by giving him an opposite one to do, conducting negative practice sessions to the point of satiation, and/or teaching him relaxation exercises. All of this should be done with his voluntary cooperation. If this doesn't help, seek further professional help. See **Anxiety**; **"Challenging Child"**; **Defense Mechanisms**; **Habits**; **Learning Disability**; **Lying**; **Negative Persistence**; **Obsessive Thoughts**; **Professional Help**; **Tics, Twitching**

Computer and Video Games. See **Television and Videos**

Conditional Love. Loving without conditions is critical to our bond not only with children, but with ourselves and others. See Chapter 5

Conflict Resolution. Whenever there are conflicts, they must be fully resolved in order for subsequent interactions to build on a clear foundation. See **Clearing**; See Chapter 8

Conscience. Children select from their higher self more often when they believe we not only know but care about what choices they make, much in the way we select higher choices when we believe a Higher Power knows and cares how we choose. Therefore, it's not only important to deeply care about the child, but to let him know that you are aware of his choices and honor his courage and clarity on those occasions when he chooses to be his highest self. A child's conscience also develops best when he surrenders his "immature boss" to the "mature boss" of his parents so that they can better guide him to reach for the higher choices while he's still young and immature. See **Egocentric**; **"Immature Boss"**; **Lying**; **"Mature Boss"**; **Stealing**

Consequences. Consequences teach a child to behave better by contracting his freedom or creating a loss for him each time he crosses his boundaries. This may be done by removing freedom or a privilege or perhaps requiring that he practice a behavior correctly. For example, the child who fails to come into the house when called may be calmly asked to practice repeatedly going outdoors and returning to the house, until he is able to do so responsively. Likewise, the child who won't brush his teeth may be given a practice session for brushing cooperatively. The child who delays in getting his bath must stop playing a half hour earlier the following afternoon to make up for his dawdling. The child who is asked to put away toys or clothes simply isn't free to do anything else until the task is done. And the teen who refuses to behave civilly to his family must lose his access to the phone as well as his freedom to leave his room until he's ready to be friendly and open again. Notice that in each example the uncooperative child's freedoms are neutrally contracted in a way that would cause him to prefer cooperation over resistance. Following are some additional samples of consequences for various infractions.

- When a child is causing a disturbance in one room of the house, he's simply required to leave that room. Depending on the circumstances and child, he may be required to go to another room until ready to settle down, or he may be asked to take a time-out in his own room. In either case, he's not free to rejoin other family members until he's ready to cooperate.
- When a child is creating a disturbance on an outing, contract his freedom by first creating a "crossroads" choice. To do this, gently have him sit on a bench at a mall, zoo, or park; remain on a towel at the beach; go to the lobby of a movie theater; or pull his chair back from the table at a restaurant, and let him know that he must stay in this contracted position until he's ready to settle down. If he cooperates, he may have his freedoms returned. If not, he must leave the mall, park, beach, zoo, movie, or restaurant and return to the car for a second opportunity to cooperate if this seems advisable. (Sometimes, it's best to teach a persistently uncooperative child that you mean what you say; in such cases, skip the second "crossroads" choice and return him home at this juncture.) If your child is still uncooperative after the second "crossroads" choice, he must be returned home to stay with a sitter—whenever possible—while the rest of the family returns to the activity. Do this calmly and gently and let the sitter know to withhold TV and entertainment. Clearing must be done after you return home from the activity or the following morning. If you are unable to return to the activity—though I strongly advise doing so—have the misbehaving child take a longer time-out than usual so that he experiences more loss than the other family members who have also been required to return home from the outing.
- When your children create a disturbance in the car while you are driving, pull the car over to the side of the road for your first "crossroads" choice and let them know that you won't continue until they have settled down. If they fail to cooperate, return home, get a sitter, and return to the outing by yourself. See **Contracting Freedom**; **"Crossroads" Choice**; **Refusal to Comply**; **Resistant Child**; **Rules**; See Chapters 7, 8, and 9

Consequences, Logical. See Chapter 9
Consequences, Natural. See Chapter 9

Consistency. Consistency is essential for successful discipline. See Chapters 6 and 7

Contact. Contact is critical to a child's feelings of being loved. Not only do we connect physically, but emotional contact is made through the heart, eyes, and voice as well. See **Access**; **Bonding**; **Carrying**; **Eye Contact**; **Lap-Sitting**; **Touch**; See Chapters 5 and 11

Contracting Freedom. Freedom can be contracted and expanded by degrees—much like the movement of an accordion—in response to a child's behaviors. When he's doing the right thing, his freedoms are maintained or expanded; when not, they must contract. For example, a young child who is not cooperating might be required to pull his chair back from the dinner table; hold his parent's hand at a park or shopping mall; sit next to his parent at the doctor's office, or on a bench at the mall; play indoors, rather than outside or be in his room, rather than the family area. By contrast, a young child who's cooperating might be allowed to walk ahead at the shopping mall or play at the park a reasonable distance from where his parents are sitting; leave the table to look at the fish tank at a restaurant; visit or play with other children at the doctor's office or park; or play freely outdoors or even walk by himself to the neighbor's house.

An older child who is not cooperating might lose his freedom to play with his friends for the day, ride his bike to the mall for a week, or use the family stereo or TV until he can abide by the rules. By contrast, when the older child is cooperating, he earns his parent's trust enough to allow him such freedoms as going to the mall or movies with his friends or having them over to the house without supervision after school; and the cooperative teen is given expanded freedoms such as a later curfew. See **Consequences**; **"Crossroads" Choice**; See Chapter 7

Control. See **Rules**

Cooperation. The more loved and nurtured a child is, the better he feels about himself and the more he wants to cooperate with the people who love him. Likewise, the more a child is taught to respect the boundaries of his society, the more he honors the rights of others. Thus, a balance between love and discipline engenders cooperation in a child. See **Caring**; **Sharing**; See Chapters 5, 6, 7, and 10

Counseling. See **Professional Help**

Cracking Knuckles. See **Habits**

Crawling. See **Exploring**

Crib, Climbing Out. Rather than let your child discover how to escape from his crib, take measures to prevent this from happening such as lowering the mattress as he gets older if your crib has this feature. In the event that your child has learned to climb out of his crib at about ten to twelve months (some never do), baby-proof and gate his room.

Critical. Critical families give their children the impression that every word or deed will be critiqued, which, in turn, makes them self-conscious, shy, and anxious about their performance. This is true even when the judgments are of people outside the family unit, since negative assessments of others implies a need to compete with them to get to the top. This not only causes a child to feel under pressure to win the race, but to generalize the negative assessments he has heard to include himself. See **Avoidance**; **Judgment**; **Shyness**; See Chapter 11

Crossing Streets. See Chapter 6

"Crossroads" Choice. When a child crosses a boundary that is measured by degrees such as getting too boisterous for a situation, running too far ahead, or using a voice that is too loud for the setting, it helps to first bring him back to the boundary. Then offer him *one* "crossroads" choice—rather than a series of warnings—from which he may choose to 1) settle down and return to his normal boundary or, 2) lose his freedom altogether. If he selects settling down, return his freedom. If not, contract it further. On occasion he is given a second crossroads, which differs from a reminder in that it contracts his freedom further than the first crossroads. For example, the first crossroads might entail having his chair pulled back from the table at a restaurant to give him a chance to settle down, while the second one includes going to the car to see if he will settle down there. Two crossroads at most are offered. If the child fails to cooperate at the second crossroads, all freedoms are contracted. See **Consequences**; See Chapter 6

Crying. Crying is something that all parents must listen to from time to time which will trigger varying reactions in them in accordance with their personal levels of tolerance for that particular noise. It's important to remember that nonmanipulative crying is your child's alert system telling you about his feelings of pain, discomfort, insecurity, and fear. When you respond to these problems without getting too concerned about the crying that he has used to inform you of them, he will learn to let you know when he needs help and will stop when he gains relief from his original problem. In short, his crying will be used as it was designed: to inform you that he has a problem and put you on alert that he needs help. However, if you dislike crying and get frantic whenever he cries, he learns that his distress is a more serious problem than he thought, and he may not only cry more intensely, but find new uses for his crying. Following are the five types of crying used by children.

- The first is due to any physical pain he's experiencing and lasts for as long as the pain feels intense. If you teach your child to fear and resist pain, the pain will frighten him more, and his resistance to it will cause both the pain and crying to last longer.
- The second type of crying represents your child's genuine grief and sadness over various losses, including such things as the loss of a friend, a pet, a parent (even temporarily), or an opportunity. If you allow him to feel his emotional pain, it will work its way through him, teach him whatever lessons are attached to the event, and come to a point of completion, relief, and release. However, if you teach him to fear his feelings of grief and pain over loss, he will learn to block them and the lessons they offer, rather than allow them to move through him to be processed.
- The third type of crying represents your child's adjustment period to the conflict he feels about wanting to achieve the next step in his independence, while also fearing giving up his dependence. If you allow him to experience his conflict and the tears that go with it, he is free to process his pain and move through it to the other side toward independence. However, if you fear his unhappiness and encourage him to withdraw from it, he fails to process his fears and venture toward independence, but gets stuck, instead, in feelings of helplessness and dependence.
- The fourth type of crying simply represents your child's period of adjustment to not getting his way. If you remain calm while he cries, his resistance winds down, and he feels adjusted to the limits imposed.
- The fifth type of crying develops when parents get confused about how to handle their child's fussing over his adjustment periods and either strive to save him from his discomfort or get angry at him for experiencing it or both. In such cases, the child learns to use crying to manipulate his parents' feelings in order to gain attention and/or get them to back down and give him his way.

Your job is to calmly reflect and/or console your child for his pain and losses, allow him the space he needs to fuss about his conflicts over becoming his own fulfiller, and let him cry until adjusted to those occasions when he is frustrated about being thwarted altogether. It's important, however, not to get angry about his crying or save him from his conflicts or adjustment period by fixing things for him, as these responses teach him to use crying to avoid and manipulate. Moreover, when parents who don't wish to listen to crying interfere with their child's adjustment period with overconcern or by trying to humor him or give him what he wanted, his ability to adjust to frustration is seriously thwarted. As a result, his crying periods will be more frequent and will last longer.

Babies, Crying/Colic. Crying is somewhat different for babies. When the young child under four to five months cries, he is usually hungry, tired, uncomfortable, or bored and must be tended to. In fact, when a baby is responded to and held during these early months, he usually cries less as a result of feeling secure. Some babies under four months will accept being put down, once their physical needs have been met, while others want continued closeness with their parents. When a young baby is fussy (see **Fussing**) or colicky, it can be difficult to comfort him, and parents would be wise to remain calm and find what works best for their particular child. Some colicky babies respond to rocking or walking or being patted. Others are calmed by being fed or bathed, taken for a car ride, or *safely* placed in their bassinets on the top surface of an unstacked, running dryer that creates enough of a vibration to soothe the baby without jiggling his bassinet off of the dryer. Certain kinds of music calm some babies, while others are relaxed by light. Still others like to be massaged or thumped on their backs with the heel of your hand. It's important not to get anxious or over-stimulate the colicky baby with either your anxiety or efforts to help. Remember that whenever a child is inconsolable, once you are sure that there's nothing medically wrong, your job is simply to figure out how to remain calm and loving in order to help both of you get through this challenging, but brief, phase of his life.

As a child gets past four months, it's important that parents continue to respond, yet not rush to their child so quickly with every whimper that he loses the opportunity to discover how to console himself. Instead, they must give him a little time to discover some self-comforting techniques which will enhance his individuating process. Thus, they can wait to see if he really needs them before going to him too quickly in his first moments of fussing. Use your internal voice of wisdom as your guide to help you respond appropriately. See **Adjustment Period**

Curfew. Curfews should be viewed as ways to help kids gauge time management, rather than serve as deterrents to uncooperative behaviors. See Chapter 12

Dark, Fear of. Fear of the dark and everything lurking therein begins at around three to four years of age, probably due to a child's increased awareness of the fearful programming of the world without equal time spent honoring his personal power to handle all that it entails. It's important not to respond by joining him in his fears and sweeping the monsters out from under his bed or chasing them out of his closet; but I would allow him to check if he wanted to assure himself that they exist only as an idea in his mind. Meanwhile, I would be sure to examine any negative programs he was adopting as well as any other stresses, emotions, fears, or struggles he was dealing with. Moreover I would make sure that people, TV programs, or the news were not supplying him with disquieting information too overwhelming for his unformed ego to manage. It's also helpful to keep a night-light on as well as demonstrate that dark is simply the absence of light and that everything in his room is the same with or without the light. See **Fear**; **Monsters**; **Nightmares**; **Strangers**; **Thoughtforms**; See Chapter 11

Dawdling. Dawdlers are children who demonstrate the dexterity of engineers when doing something they enjoy but look like overcooked linguine when asked to do things that they don't want to do. Children who dawdle often have parents who make a lot of suggestions while pushing and hurrying them through their tasks. A child handled in this manner feels overmanaged with no opportunity to take ownership of his own responsibilities. Thus, those of you with dawdlers must learn not to give so many instructions and then follow through on those things you have requested by requiring that your child complete the task before going on to other things. Once your child has discovered the power of dawdling, the best way to motivate him to function more effectively is to give the problem that his slowness creates back to him, while taking no interest in how long it takes him to respond. For example, if a child is walking slowly in a setting where it's safe to put some distance between you, calmly keep going and let him take responsibility for catching up. See **Passive Resistance**; See Chapter 7

Day Care. Although a society of working parents has great hope for improved day care programs, multiple problems result when children attend these centers at too early an age or for too many hours each day or week. Studies tell us that children under three left in day care for more than 30 hours a week without periodic visits from their parents are more likely to be uncooperative and unpopular and to have lower grades and diminished self-esteem by the third grade. Many parents of young children would prefer to spend more time with their children than jobs presently allow, and this practice would ensure adequate bonds as well as their child's emotionally secure development. Therefore, it would behoove us to look for alternate options to day care and sitters. If we look to other countries for solutions, we can see that a work week can be arranged to honor and accommodate family needs and that we—like other countries—could jump out of the currently rigid box we have established of uniquely long daily hours and extensive work weeks that fail to accommodate family needs.

It's apparent that options such as shared jobs, taking work home for pay, part-time work, working out of the home, and flexible schedules would offer better solutions for meeting childcare needs than the ones we are presently using. Arranging such alternatives is not only good for our families, but for the businesses that depend on a healthfully functioning society to survive. Thus, rather than passively accept being blocked by tradition, each family can take the initiative to create a method that blends work with family. Business would be wise to also embrace how much better our society would function as a whole—including economically—if we would raise healthier children in homes where parents are available to tend to the needs of their offspring. As more people claim this approach, the needs of children can be better met, and the family can regain the position of strength and value it once held in our society. Day care centers could then offer backup support, rather than the primary child care they currently provide. See **Parent Roles**; **Preschools**; **Single Parents**; **Working Mothers**

Daydreaming, Staring. Daydreaming is a child's way of meditating and can be useful for his sense of well-being and alignment with the peace of nature. However, if a child's daydreams prevent him from focusing or knowing what's going on during those times when it's necessary for him to do so or are interfering in other ways with his normal development and ability to participate, he may be using them to avoid coping with life's demands. If so, check to see why he feels a need to withdraw and gently help him to focus on his life and become more involved in it. Excessive daydreaming may also be a form of dissociation that he's using to escape the pain of some trauma or the chaos in his home. See **Meditation**; **Post-Traumatic Stress**

Death. Be aware that a death in the family can trigger such fears as separation anxiety and school phobia in children, particularly when the death is viewed as a tragic event over which the individual had no choice or control or is perceived as an annihilation of the spirit and self. It's particularly unsettling for children who believe that their own parents are weakened or ill enough to also be vulnerable to death. These ideas get rooted in children who have been given vague answers about a death in their family that cause them to suspect that adults feel too overwhelmed by the subject of death to even discuss it, much less help them to understand and process the event.

A young child can gradually be introduced to the concept of death whenever he encounters such things as dead bugs or animals or if one of his pets dies. If a child is exposed to an actual death of someone he is acquainted with, it's important to discuss it with him in a way that feels natural and open. If it matches your beliefs, you can explain that the person's living spirit has left the body behind in order to return to the place where he was before entering his mother's belly and coming to earth; and that this person will now live in this place that we can't see—much in the way we can't see the wind. (This place can be called Heaven if that fits with your belief system.) Yet even though we can no longer see them, we can still feel our connection to them—in the same way we could when they were still alive but in another location and out of view. Because we can feel this connection with them through the love we feel in our hearts when we think of them, it will help us to manage our missing them if we feel free to remember and talk about them or even write letters or draw pictures for them. For the older child, talking to the deceased person by writing a letter or journaling is very helpful, and he can even be taught how to ask for a letter in return by writing whatever comes to mind after addressing a letter to himself from his deceased friend. (Diagramming this concept helps the child to understand it.)

If compatible with your own beliefs, it's also helpful to point out that the individual who died was in some way finished with his life and ready to go to the next level of experience. This is clearer when the people who have died were old and the completion of their lives is more obvious. It can further be explained that when someone is ready to go to the next level of experience, they must shed their body, which they no longer need, in the same way a butterfly sheds its cocoon. However, they take their essence, their wisdom, and their love with them, all the things we could never see even when they were living on earth but could—and still can—feel through our bond with them.

It's important not to tell your child that the person was very sick or has gone to sleep, as this will make him afraid of both sleep and illness. It's more useful to connect death to something that usually comes with old age if this matches your beliefs. It's also helpful to say that the person who has departed as a young person probably had a prior arrangement for a shorter time on earth and is content to be returning to Heaven at this time. It's also helpful to assure your child that you do not plan to die because your plan is to remain with him until he is grown and old himself.

If your child has been exposed to an unexpected or violent death or has been given unsettling information about death, it's important that you keep the subject open so that he can draw appropriate conclusions and process the idea of death with your guidance and redirection if necessary. If he becomes anxious, develops separation anxiety and a school phobia, has sleep problems, or thinks about it more than seems normal, he may be suffering from post-traumatic stress. If so, consult a therapist trained in EMDR (Eye Movement Desensitization and Reprocessing). See **EMDR Therapy**; **Fear**; **Illness**; **Post-Traumatic Stress**; **Reluctance to Attend**; *School Phobia* subentry under **School**

Deceit. See **Lying**

Decisions and Vows. The decisions and vows we make about life shape our reality. See Chapter 9

Defense Mechanisms. Defense is a device we use to block out pain, and defense mechanisms are the psychological systems we develop within our personalities to help us defend against the pain of life's challenges. Some of these devices are useful, such as the shock we go into upon hearing bad news—designed to cushion us from the initial pain of the event until we are more ready to absorb it—or the denial we use as a buffer to unpleasant experiences. However, when we carry these mechanisms too far, they not only keep us separate from our pain and prevent us from processing and moving through it, but from our realities as well. Many of these mechanisms take root in our personalities when we are young and grow into elaborate tangles of defense against facing and feeling life's reality and its accompanying pain. Thus, when used to extreme, defense mechanisms can go beyond their initial purpose and serve, instead, to keep us emotionally unconscious and unhealthy. Therefore, we must not only unravel the tangles of defense that have grown too large within our own personalities and keep us from facing the truth of our lives, but help our children to embrace reality and its accompanying pain. Ironically, the opposite of resistance and defense—embracing the painful events of a lifetime—not only offers us more courage and greater strength for managing life's challenges, but gives us a way to feel more peaceful and serene. See **Anger**; **Anxiety**; **Compulsive Behaviors**; **Denial**;

Depression; **Error**; **Failure, Fear of**; **Negative Persistence**; **Obsessive Thoughts**; **Post-Traumatic Stress**; **Tics**; See Chapters 8, 9 and 10

Defiance. Persistent defiance is a symptom of problems with discipline and must be addressed. See **"Challenging Child"**; **Rebellion**; **Refusal to Comply**; **Resistant Child**; See Chapters 6, 7 and 12

Delaying Gratification. Children must learn the important life skill of how to delay gratification whenever it's necessary to do so. See **Adjustment Period**; See Chapters 3 and 7

Denial. Denial is useful when used to buffer us from overwhelming news or experiences. However, anytime denial is used to avoid ever facing these events altogether or to avoid facing errors or taking responsibility for them when appropriate, it keeps us separated from our truth and reality. This in turn blocks us from attaining higher levels of honesty, clarity, and emotional health. Children who have been taught to avoid and fear mistakes by parents intolerant of error use a great deal of denial. They hide their mistakes behind bad moods, hurt feelings, sulking, blaming, anger, or a refusal to discuss them. It's important not to be overly impressed with these tactics and require that your child confront his errors and work them out; then show him by your gentle, embracing response and actions that facing responsibility works better than avoidance. Those of you with children who fear error must also look at your own attitude toward mistakes as well as how you are presently responding to the ones your children make. See **Defense Mechanisms**; **Depression**; **Error**; **Failure, Fear of**; See Chapter 10

Dependence. A child who feels overly dependent on his parents has not learned to function separately from them. This can happen when families have been overprotective in hopes of shielding their children from life's pain. It also occurs when parents are overdirective, dominant, or critical in an effort to keep their kids from making mistakes. Thus, parents of dependent children would be wise to withdraw excessive protection as well as too much direction, correction, control, criticism, or advice. By doing this, they not only send a message that their child's attempts to manage can be trusted, but provide him the space he needs to practice handling things for himself. See **Fulfiller**; **Independence**; **Individuation**; **Separation Anxiety**; See Chapters 3 and 12

Depression. A depressed child will demonstrate feelings of hopelessness via a flat affect, a loss of normal interest in activities and friends, and withdrawing into lethargy or sleep. There are two kinds of depression. The first occurs when something so tragic has happened in a person's life that his heart is heavy with pain and his interest in life wanes as he strives to absorb the hurt of so much loss. This is the kind of depression that occurs when optimistic feelings have been flattened by life's events. The initial buffering from the painful event that the depression offers is useful and allows those with big losses to face their pain only when they have recovered enough from their shock to feel more ready to manage it. Yet, for children whose loss is one of feeling inadequately loved, this form of depression will be a deep and continuing problem until the lost love is either restored or accepted.

The second form of depression results when an individual becomes overly fearful and unwilling to face the truth about an event or the pain it offers. It's as though a pause switch in the brain has been pressed with the purpose of giving the individual a break from so much pain. However, when the pause switch is never released, the pain has no opportunity to be readdressed, confronted, and managed. Thus, the hurt gets stuck in resistance and the energies used to push it down are experienced as depression. This form of depression can also occur in those uncomfortable with allowing any pain whatsoever into their lives and thus go to great measures—including pushing down or depressing their feelings—to avoid it. Because of their inability to face or manage uncomfortable emotions, these avoiders get caught in the original pain and are unable to let it move through them and out. When too many issues get buried in this way, depression endures beyond its original usefulness and develops a life of its own. Thus, a child must be taught to gradually confront, embrace, and work through his pain if he's to remain clear and healthy. Once depression has taken hold, the best way to release it is to trace back to events taking place simultaneous to the onset of depression. Once you have traced the thing that triggered the depression, encourage your child to reopen the wound, face what happened, and begin to accept and process it. **See Sadness**; **Serious Behavioral and Psychological Problems**; See Chapter 10

Destructiveness. Young children often discover such diversions as writing on walls, getting into their mothers' makeup, or destroying a sibling's room. When parents react with frustration to such behaviors it gives the child a way to feel in control of his family, and he continues to do it. Parents would be wise to nip this behavior in the bud by first making it clear that it's not a choice to do such things and then closely supervising such a child. If he oversteps the boundary, make it clear that he created a problem for *himself*, rather than for his family, by removing him from the area or for a time-out. During clearing, he can be shown why he won't be allowed in the area he was misusing for the remainder of that morning, day, or week, depending on the age of the child and the severity of the problem.

Destructiveness, Persistent. When a child seems bent on damaging himself (accidents, drugs, suicide threats or attempts); property (breaking or destroying property, fire-setting); pets (injuring, tormenting); or relationships (disinterest, aggression), seek professional help. See **Professional Help**; **Serious Behavioral and Psychological Problems**

Development, Baby. Approximate timetables for basic development: Sits up: three to four months; crawls: six months; stands: six to seven months; walks: about one year; talks: ten months to two-and-a-half years. Drinks from cup: six months; can begin weaning: six to eighteen months. See **Bedtime**; **Carrying**; **"In-Arms" Period**; **Sleep**; *Weaning* subentry under **Nursing**; Consult favorite baby care book

"Difficult Child". See **Attention Deficit Disorder**; **"Challenging Child"**; **Negative Persistence**

Dinnertime. See **Eating**; See Chapter 11

Discipline. See **Rules**; See Chapters 6 and 7

Divorce. Whenever spouses develop problems, their children experience family life as problematic until they can resolve their differences and determine how to live together as loving partners once again. If they are unable to mend their relationship but remain in the marriage out of mutual dependency or for the sake of the children, their kids will live in a home lacking in love or filled with sacrifice and/or tension and battles. Unfortunately, the children will learn from this model how to endure loveless environments and will not thank their parents for teaching them to live life unhappily. By the same token, if these spouses decide that they are unable to live as loving partners and move forward to get a divorce, their children will also be deeply hurt by the dissolution of their family unit.

Deciding on a Course of Action. Couples with children would be wise to do whatever they can to mend their relationship, rather than continue to live together unhealed or move too quickly toward divorce. However, once spouses have genuinely tried but are unable to repair a broken relationship or when one discovers that their partner is too emotionally unhealthy, abusive, disloyal, or addicted to join in the healing process, divorce may be the healthiest option.

Telling Your Child. Before telling your children of the decision to divorce, you should be as certain as possible that this is what you intend to do, since going back and forth on the decision is confusing for them and triggers their yearning for reunification, rather than their adjustment to the reality of divorce. It's best to set up a family meeting to jointly tell the children about your divorce, using honesty and neutrality as your guides, while striving to explain both the implications and reasons for the divorce in clear, direct terms. You should explain that fighting and differences or even growing in separate ways without conflict can cause a change in the form of adult relationships but not in parent/child ones. You must also assure your child that he will continue to be "taken care of" by his parents and will always live with at least one of them, even when he has problems with them. This helps him to understand that even though differences can cause parents to dissolve relationships and decide to live separately, he doesn't risk abandonment if he has a difference—or even a fight—with either of them. (It helps to diagram these concepts.)

The Separation. If you are clear that divorce is inevitable, don't go through the motions of a long separation in hopes that it will help your children to adjust. Lengthy, drawn-out separations are harder on kids than divorce, since they cause them to resist, rather than adjust to the reality of the event. Once resistance is set in motion it can convert to a long-term yearning for reunification, which interferes with a child's ability to adjust. On the other hand, short separations give the child a buffer, as he begins the process of adapting to the reality that his family is breaking up. If this is already obvious, such buffers are not needed. When the couple plans to divorce, but will be living in the same house for an extended period, it's important to make it clear to children old enough to wonder what is going on that Mom and Dad are now living in the house as roommates, but will no longer remain married. You can begin at that juncture to work out how things will look once divorce is underway.

If parents plan to live indefinitely in the same home, it's important to keep bedrooms separate and any residual romance or indecision—both of which are common during this phase—to yourselves so the kids can see that you are clear about this. When one parent actually moves out, it's important to assure your child that the parent moving is separating from his or her spouse, rather than from the child and, in fact, will continue a relationship with the child. (See paragraphs on **Exceptions** and **The Absent Parent** for exceptions to this.)

It's equally important that your child is told that he's free to contact this departing parent at any time and is given explicit directions—and help—on how to do so. It's also helpful to have arrangements in place for ample contact with this parent on a regular basis, particularly if the parent and child are close. If the divorce is friendly, continuing to do things as a family unit from time to time is a possibility—as long as the outings don't cause the child to hold out hope that time together will lead to reunification. In fact, the best models of divorce are those couples who change the form of their relationship from partners to friends, rather than insist on a complete breakdown of positive feelings and continued interaction. Such mature resolutions to a marriage that has ended enhance their children's lives. Yet only when both partners have the maturity and inclination to accomplish this higher way of functioning is it successful.

The Impact of Divorce on Children. Not only do children of divorce have no say in the decision of something that so thoroughly turns their world inside out, they must often live by legal decisions that fail to honor their needs or rights—even to security and safety. Their economic status is typically lowered, and they are often required to change neighborhoods or schools as well as lifelong friends. Thus, children of divorce must sometimes adapt to the devastating loss of their family unit without the support of familiar neighbors, teachers, or friends. Children overwhelmed by this degree of disruption typically have trouble confronting their grieving over the death of something so important to them and often begin to act out their confused feelings in a variety of ways. Some experience anger and become demanding, combative, and defiant. Others are withdrawn and depressed and express their grief with silence, fearfulness, crying, or clinging. Young children often regress into immature behaviors which might include wetting, thumb-sucking, whining, fussing, sleep problems, aggression, and tantrums. Some show even more serious signs of injury to their sense of security by becoming withdrawn or hurting themselves.

Babies who have no other way of communicating may demonstrate their distress over separation from their primary parent during prolonged periods of court-ordered visitation—including overnights—by becoming withdrawn, sometimes staring into space, and avoiding eye-contact; becoming more clingy or fussy; having new difficulties with falling and staying asleep; or scratching, biting, and pinching themselves or pulling or twisting their hair.

Be aware that some children are not particularly affected by divorce, especially when there was tension and fighting in the intact family or when they live with a preferred parent and have little or no contact with a parent who was previously uninvolved, feared, or disliked.

Addressing Your Child's Needs. Once divorce is in progress, parents begin to face major personal challenges in their own lives. In a short period of time, they will experience the loss of their hopes and dreams for this relationship, the loss of the family unit they put so much effort into creating, and the loss of the financial and emotional security the intact family provided. In the middle of so much fear, sadness, anger, guilt, loneliness, grief, and increased responsibility, parents often forget to consider the parallel challenges they have created for their children. Thus, although your concerns are important, you must take care not to become so absorbed by your own needs for assurance and confidence-building during this period that you focus solely on new friends, mates, or careers, while ignoring the comparable needs of your children.

The most critical emotional needs that must be addressed from the outset are your child's fears that if one parent can leave the family, both might go; or that if one leaves, it's because the child was not "good enough" and must now strive to be perfect. Thus, addressing your child's needs must begin with an awareness of what decisions and vows he is making throughout the course of the divorce as well as guiding him in drawing the kinds of conclusions that will support rather than hinder his life. (See Chapter 9.) Following are some other areas to consider in helping your child through the challenge of divorce.

Developing Fair Custody Arrangements. Your child not only loses his primary family, but must confront such things as which parent he will live with, and how the house, the dog, and the TV will be divided up between the two halves of his previously whole family unit. Once again, he has little, if any, say in the matter and feels even more loss of control over his destiny. The following guidelines will help families to offer their child at least some measure of control.

Handling Custody with Maturity and Grace. Custody arrangements are best managed when the needs of the child are primary in the minds and hearts of both parents who, in turn, share this priority with attorneys and family court personnel. Generally, the most optimal plans are drafted when the child is neutrally encouraged to openly express his honest desires in the matter, rather than say nothing or champion whatever needs he feels pressured to express for the sake of one or both of his parents. In fact, parents would be wise to make it their first priority to work together to protect the best interests of their child. Since attorneys are trained to win the best deal they can get for their client and courts are known for their failure to rule with the best interests of children in mind, it works best when both parents can agree to put their child's needs ahead of their own.

I disagree with experts who avoid asking a child what would work best for him in the interest of not "putting him in the middle." The truth is, a child of divorce is already in the middle, and his opinion about where he feels comfortable is the most crucial information to be considered in deciding where his primary bedroom will be. In my experience, when children have been released from the caretaker role and are given permission not to side with parents or assume responsibility for the adults' insecurities, worries, and emotional needs, but to consider, instead, what will work best for them, I have found they have very definite opinions and tend to make the following requests.

- Children prefer to stay with the parent who has taken care of them most of the time; the parent they go to under stress and for comfort, communication, and problem solving; the parent they perceive to understand and care most about their needs; and the parent who represents "home" for them. This is the parent I refer to as the *primary* parent. In some cases, this includes both parents. See **Parent Roles**
- Children want to visit their *support* parent in proportion to the amount of involvement that parent had in their lives prior to the divorce.
- Children want to be free from requirements to go by themselves to visit feared or disliked parents, especially in cases where a parent has neglected, dominated, or abused them or suffers from addiction and other problems.
- Most children want to remain together with their siblings as the only aspect of their lives that remains stationary.
- *All* children want desperately to be free to love each parent—and their new partners—in their own way and without fear of hurting their other parent or making them angry. They also want to be free not to love them if that is what they choose, and dislike being coaxed to do otherwise.
- When bonds become stronger with secondary parents following divorce, children want the freedom to increase their time with these parents accordingly.
- Most children prefer to remain in the home they were in at the time of the divorce, if possible, and keep whatever pets were a part of the family prior to the divorce.

Assure Your Child Full and Frequent Access to Both Parents. If Mother acted as primary parent, she should have physical custody until the children are at an age when their primary parent is not of such great importance in their lives, perhaps sometime in their teens—depending on the child and circumstances. If Father acted as primary parent, he should be given physical custody, while Mother acts as support parent. The parent who is not the primary parent becomes the noncustodial or visited parent and must have continued access to the child in order to pursue an active support role so vital to the child's development. Only if this parent is unavailable, minimally interested, addicted to drugs or alcohol, dominates or abuses the child, or has other problems serious enough to interfere with the child's normal development is this access curtailed in any way. If the support parent has been minimally involved, it would be appropriate to have the children visit that parent in proportion to this involvement, at least initially. Thus, anywhere from one short visit per week to one evening midweek plus one to two days—with or without nights—every other weekend might be assigned to such parents, depending on the parent's interest in maintaining contact as well as the child's comfort and interest in visiting. Then, if their relationship develops more fully after divorce as it sometimes does, time together can be expanded. This possibility—if anticipated—can be included in the original decree.

When parents have coparented equally—and a child who has been consulted feels equally comfortable with both—physical custody is more difficult to arrange. Since children do best when they have one primary home as opposed to being split between two homes, preserving one stationary home while visiting the other for one night during the week—or two nights during the weeks when weekends will be missed—plus Friday through Sunday night every other weekend works best for the child. It also gives the visited parent close to half of the time with the child (twelve out of every twenty-eight days or four days less per cycle than the primary parent). Vacations can be alternated and summers divided, though the division of summers must be worked around the child's needs and should not interfere with camp and other programs or vacation travel.

Unfortunately, custody arrangements become even more complicated when parents are in conflict or live in different states. In working out these problems, the child's need to have access to both parents if desired, to be emotionally secure, to be amidst friends, and to be in security-building activities must be considered. Thus, support parents would be wise to take vacation time during summer visits or make sure that their children are in interesting activities during working hours, rather than left with sitters while a disinterested parent makes sure to "collect" his or her visitation time with the kids. Likewise, primary parents who block their child from enjoying a summer visit with an interested support parent who has taken the time to set up programs and make quality arrangements for the child during working hours betray their kids in order to take revenge or to appease their own emotional insecurities.

The Exception. When a parent has been either neglectful or abusive, this rule should change, since parents lacking in genuine responsibility toward their children should not maintain "parental rights." Neither should a child be made to feel he must learn to feel close to such a parent. Instead, measures must be taken to protect a child from the neglecting, addicted, or abusive parent. Sometimes this is difficult to perceive—or prove—but if a responsible parent is aware of such issues or a child attempts to report them, action must be taken by the courts to explore the charges sincerely and thoroughly and make custody and visitation arrangements accordingly. For example, such parents must not be allowed to succeed in using a struggle for custody and time alone with the child as a way to harass their ex-partner. Nor should they be allowed continued access in cases when time spent with the child is abusive or infected by their own addictions. Instead, every effort must be made to protect the best interests—and desires—of the child with such measures as minimal and supervised visitation for these parents.

The Absent Parent. In the event a parent is not physically and/or emotionally available to a child; has been given minimal, supervised visitation; fails to make custody payments; doesn't call on the child regularly; or fails to remember such occasions as birthdays, sports events, and other activities, it's important to face the reality of what this parent does and does not offer the child. Thus, the more involved parent would be wise not to plead with the uninvolved one to become a larger part of his child's life or purchase cards and gifts in his behalf in an effort to save the child from being hurt. When a child has been falsely led to believe that an absent parent is more available to him than is true, his disappointment is compounded once he matures enough to see through the deception. This is particularly hurtful to the child, since his hope and yearning for more connection with the absent parent has been artificially kept alive for an extended period of time. It further encourages his potential for romanticizing the absent parent. Because he remained hopeful for so many years, rather than face or feel the pain of his injury, the hurt has been delayed and prolonged, and it will now take longer for him to surrender to reality and heal. Consequently, it's preferable to allow the aloofness of an absent parent to be experienced from the outset, while gently helping the child to cope with that reality and complete his grieving over the loss it represents on those occasions when he introduces the subject or complains. For the child's sake, this should not be presented with anger or judgment but with compassion for the absent parent's loss of a relationship with the child. It's equally important to gently help the child to understand that the cause for a disinterested parent lies in the parent's lack of personal development, rather than any lack in the child. This helps the child to avoid concluding that it was his unlovability that drove his parent away. In explaining this deficit, it also helps to explain why it's there if you understand it, yet to also let the child know that this parent would be wise to face and work on this weakness within him- or herself. It's critical to also highlight the strengths of such a parent, so that the child can feel good about this parent within his heart. This not only helps the child to come to terms with his own roots, but helps him to put his loss in a compartment that's balanced with understanding and acceptance, rather than disappointment, anger, and resentment. Remember that whatever feelings your child selects about this loss will be carried deeply within him and will thus affect his emotions, relationships, and life.

Deadbeat Dads (or Moms). This term has become a common one due to a pervasive lack of paternal (sometimes maternal) responsibility to offspring following divorce. Yet, as important as a parent's loving and responsible presence is to a child's well-being, a parent's presence without these elements has negative repercussions. Thus, social systems and courts focused on bringing parent and child together at all costs can create a secondary problem for a child worse than his original problem of a broken family. The notion that there should be no connection between parental responsibility and visitation, for example, fails to consider the needs of the child or protect his rights over those of his parents. To do better, courts must first rule on fair custody and payment arrangements based on a full investigation of all factors and charges. They must then assure that parents accept their responsibilities in order to maintain visitation rights. In short, deadbeat dads (or moms) should be held accountable *before* they are allowed to claim parental "rights."

Free Your Child to Love Both of His Parents and Their Partners. Statistics show that otherwise healthy parents who fight over where their child lives or vie for his love have children who make very poor adjustments to divorce. By contrast, children who make the best adjustments to living in two households do so when both parents are mature enough to create two separate homes in which their child receives both nurturing and discipline and is free to love everyone included in each home without guilt or concern for the missing parent.

Thus, allowing your child to continue to freely and openly love his other parent if he chooses is the greatest gift those of you involved in divorce can offer your child. This permission not only enhances his adjustment to divorce, its absence seriously threatens his normal and healthy development. Furthermore, any parent who indulges in using his or her child's head and heart to battle with an ex-spouse eventually loses his or her child's respect if not his love. When a child whose feelings have been tampered with in this way grows old enough to see what has been done, he generally turns against the parent who manipulated his love and favors the one who had the maturity to allow him to love both parents without guilt.

Keep Things as Similar and Stable as Possible. Parents would be wise to keep the lives of children as similar to their predivorce arrangement as possible. For example, living in one residence with a primary parent, while visiting one night a week plus every other Friday through Sunday at the home of the support parent, is a common arrangement for children with two fully responsible parents. If a new primary household is established, it's critical that the family pets and cherished possessions are accommodated, as their loss at this time would be too overwhelming for the child to absorb. It's also best to stay in the same neighborhood, if possible, so that the kids can remain in the same school with familiar friends and teachers.

Address Reality Fairly. Once malicious or competitive efforts to win a child's love are put aside, there are times when a certain amount of communication must take place in families who have attending psychological traumas in addition to the divorce. Not talking about these challenging subjects can be extremely damaging to a child, since he will know that something is wrong, but in the absence of communication has no opportunity to label it or process it emotionally. Thus, rather than unrealistically suggest that parents say nothing about such issues as manipulativeness, alcoholism, abuse, mental illness, and violence or feel guilty for speaking of them, it's more helpful to offer realistic guidance on how to address these important aspects of a family's reality. Parents need to feel free to discuss such topics with their children, since a failure to do so makes the child's world even more illogical and crazy. The key is to insure that all discussions have the goal of helping the child to not only better understand his world, but to feel compassion and caring for the parent with a genuinely serious problem. Children must never be burdened with the inference that it's their job to take over and provide either the primary source of strength for their family or to become the caretaker, singular friend and confidante, or partner replacement for a wounded or lonely parent. See **Boundaries, Healthy Between Parent and Child**

Free Your Child from Taking Care of the Emotional Needs of His Parents. Whenever an immature parent feels dependent on a child and uses guilt to get him to call more often or to fix his parent's pain, such an expectation becomes a psychological burden to the child who is already struggling with his own adjustment to the difficulty of divorce. Because this is so emotionally overwhelming to a child, it's permissible for his other, healthier parent to clarify that it's not the child's job to keep either of his parents happy. That parent can further explain that it's both parents' job to find friends, work, activities, and new partners that are fulfilling and to manage their own emotional needs and life. Furthermore, although telling a child the truth about his family's problems at the level he can manage is critical to his ultimate well-being, using him as a sounding board for unresolved and confused negative feelings toward his other parent is dangerous to his emotional adjustment. A guideline to use in deciding how much to share with a child is to first determine if the information is helping him to understand and manage his world better; if it's honest information that hasn't been distorted by emotional biases; and if it's being given in a neutral, sensitive, and fair manner that encourages the child to not only face reality but to feel increased love and compassion for his other parent.

Assist Your Child to Manage Any Problems He's Having with His Other Parent. If a child shares—unprompted—that he does not like to visit his other parent, the parent confided in must gently, without judgment or upset, probe to see what the problem is. This parent must not be too quick to assume that the other parent is in error, but to listen carefully for whether or not the child is playing one parent against the other. For example, if the child's complaints are simply about strict, yet appropriate levels of discipline, the parent confided in would be wise not to treat him like a victim, but to support the other parent's style as ultimately helpful to the child. If his complaints are legitimate ones about a nonabusive, yet overbearing or frustrating parenting style, it's best to teach him how to approach this parent, rather than coach his other parent on how to behave. For example, the parent confided in might calmly assist the child in ways to discuss the problem with his other parent. If the child is too insecure or afraid to do this, he can be helped to be more assertive in this relationship. If this doesn't work, the parent confided in might offer to help with the communications or to have a professional guide the child and his other parent through them.

Larger Problems. If a problem seems too big for the child to handle or involves undue levels of control or abuse by a parent or stepparent, the parent confided in should never suggest that the child try to handle it by himself. Instead, that parent must act as an advocate for the child and seek professional help.

Confidentiality. It's *essential* that a parent confided in *never* disclose any of the information to the offending parent without the child's consent! Such a betrayal would not only cause the child to lose control and be subjected to the wrath of his other—usually immature—parent, but he would stop sharing his secrets and lose his much-needed confidant. This in turn would block all avenues for the child to get the help he needs in such important matters.

When Advocacy Is Needed. One of the most disruptive and cruel side-effects of divorce is when one or both parents behave immaturely and irresponsibly. Such a parent may do such things as use battles over custody and visitation of the child to harass his or her ex-spouse when, in fact, he or she is not truly interested in the child; refuse to provide child support; try to win over the child's loyalties by gossiping maliciously about the other parent; distort the truth about the other parent; or tell the child outright lies about the situation. This causes children to turn against parents who are actually healthy role models and interested in relating to their children. This interference in the child's relationship with a healthy parent by the less mature, jealous, and angry parent seriously affects the child's development. I have seen good kids not only become difficult, angry, and disruptive as a result of these confusing manipulations, but develop eating disorders, drug habits, and other serious problems. Thus, whenever a parent becomes aware that the other parent is threatening a child's development with dishonest betrayals, he or she must intervene as early as possible and act as the child's advocate. Divorce attorneys and the courts must also be accountable to the children in their family law practices and be willing to help the child to be placed in a safe, secure, and psychologically healthy home.

Getting Professional Help. The best way to deal with the problematic components of a family breakdown is to engage a qualified counselor willing to maturely address whatever issues each family member must confront. The goal is to help the child to face and deal with his reality in a fair way, rather than encourage his denial of what is truly happening in his life or to simplistically turn against one or both parents for not being perfect.

Working It Out Alone. For families who can't afford professional counsel or otherwise choose not to use this option, it's essential that they address these matters *responsibly*. For example, it's important not to discredit the other parent or turn the child against him or her. Always speak about the other parent with compassion and with the goal of helping the child to love and understand that parent, including whatever painful effect his or her behavior has had on the family. This can best be done by pointing out the positive traits this parent possesses as well as the problems that have hurt him or her. In this way, the problems and the parent's resistance to addressing them—rather than the parent—are seen as the troublemaker. When this information is presented lovingly, the child does not feel a need to defend this other parent's behavior and can move out of denial and begin to face the reality that parent offers. It's valuable to also present the child with an honest list of your own strengths as well as the areas where you, too, need to improve so that he can see that all people have both strengths and weaknesses and that the goal of life is neither to judge these issues nor to hide them from yourself, but to confront and heal them.

Hammer Out the Details. It's critical that all arrangements be drawn up in detail, rather than left to chance, as most couples who have been unable to maintain a marriage will be equally incapable of working out such sensitive issues as "reasonable" custody and visitation or financial arrangements for their child on an ongoing basis. Thus, all such issues should be hammered out in detail at the time of the divorce, including such specifics as when and how transitions will be made from one home to the other. Although whatever legal arrangements are agreed upon need not be strictly followed if both parents prefer to do otherwise, whenever there are disagreements, the decree offers clear guidelines to fall back on. Following are some of the issues that should be included in the decree.

Handling Transitions Graciously. It's essential that a child's needs be considered primary during transitions from one home to the other. Parents can help their child most by being prompt for pickup and delivery as well as by acting in a courteous manner toward one another and saving any unresolved issues for later. Furthermore, a child's fatigue, sadness, or disrupted rhythm must be expected following transitions and cannot be automatically interpreted as a result of poor caretaking on the part of the other parent. If a parent misreads these moods to mean the child was not handled properly and thus fights with the other parent about management, this response will trigger additional emotionalism and transitional problems for the child. On the other hand, if a child seems unduly withdrawn, aggressive, or out of sorts after every transition, it could be a sign that there are some problems in the other home or that the other parent is undermining the child's love for you. Yet it could also be that your child feels upset about returning to you, in which case your own handling must be honestly assessed.

Parents who suspect they are being undermined must bring this possibility out into the open with the child, rather than with their ex-spouse, as soon as possible. The scorned parent can gently reflect, "It seems as though you are getting caught between your Dad (or Mother) and me, and I get the feeling that it's making you feel less comfortable with me than you used to feel. Is that because of something I'm doing or is it because of something you have been hearing about me?" That parent can further explain in a neutral way, "You need to be aware that it's not uncommon for divorced parents to talk against their ex-mate because they are so mad at them or hurt about breaking up, but often what they say is in anger and isn't really true. So if you are hearing things about me that make you feel angry or sad or confused about my actions, I hope you will ask me about it. If something is true—even if I'm not proud of it—I will tell you. If it's not true, I will clear that up for you as well. And I promise I won't go back to your other parent and let him or her know what you have shared with me. I will only work it out privately between you and me so that we can feel clear with one another again. You have my word on that." The only thing worse for a child than having one parent manipulate his feelings toward the other is not to have these issues put on the table and opened up for calm, yet honest, discussion and clarification.

Honoring the Child's Privacy During Visitations. Although the ideal arrangement would be for parents to agree on such things as diet, baths, and bedtimes, if this becomes a point of disagreement, it's best to let it go. When neither parent is addicted, abusive, or damaging to the child, his time at each house is best respected without interruptive phone calls from the absent parent, inquiring about schedules and diet. The older child should be told that he can reach his other parent whenever he wishes, and unless he initiates a call, his time with the parent he is visiting goes better if not constantly interrupted by calls from his other parent. Furthermore, as long as both parents are psychologically healthy, their individual approaches to parenting should be accepted without complaint by the other. Thus, whenever a child is at one of his parent's homes, it's best to allow that parent the room to determine his or her own parenting style without coaching from the other parent. If parenting skills are minimal—yet not abusive—the child must be neutrally shown that he will meet with different standards in the two homes and must make the adjustment between them with each transition, much as he does to the differences at school or at Grandmother's. On the other hand, if desired by the child, one phone call per day can be scheduled at a mutually agreed upon time.

Only if a child demonstrates by his behavior or by openly complaining of being frightened by the activities at his other home or of abusive behavior should advocacy for the child be initiated. The only other exception to becoming involved in such management issues is in regard to the child's bedtime, since not getting his rest will affect his school days as well as his time in your home. Teachers who have noticed the problem can be asked to talk directly to this parent about bedtime. Or doctors can be enlisted to help. It's also okay to mention it yourself, without anger and accusations. However, if the other parent is unreceptive to making an adjustment, rather than fighting indefinitely over it, elicit the child's help. Teach him that regular sleep not only improves his health and moods but enables him to grow to his full height. Thus, if a child is going to bed late at his other house and is exhausted when he returns to you, he can be gently told that because he is so tired, he will have to go to bed extra early to catch up on his rest. (Use diagrams to help the young child understand this concept.) If he would rather go to bed at a more regular time in both homes—rather than extra late in one and extra early in another—then he should inform his other parent of his decision and/or put himself to bed at an earlier hour at that house.

Special Problems of the Noncustodial Support Parent. Because noncustodial support parents— usually fathers—have lighter visitation schedules and less time during which close feelings can naturally surface, they often feel under pressure to make each moment with their child count. As a result they create a circus atmosphere during the time they have with too much entertainment and too little structure or rules. Although support parents would have more successful relationships with their children if they responded in a more natural and balanced manner, their approach is understandable and should not be criticized—or controlled—by the primary parent or used as a reason to keep the child away.

In addition to a deficit of time, the noncustodial parent often notices how much the child dislikes interrupting his normal activities and time with peers to fulfill visitations and may withdraw from following through with them. However, rather than give up his relationship with the child, the support parent would be wise to keep visitations as scheduled but oper- ate exactly as the primary parent does during her time with the child. In doing this, he might stop treating visitations as times when the child must focus only on the visit with him, but allow the child, instead, to simply base at his home while continuing to pursue his usual activities, which might include an overnight with a friend. Not only does this style more closely simulate the more natural environment of his custodial home, it allows the child to feel more comfortable in his secondary home. Furthermore, by being with the child in the course of normal daily living, the support parent soon discovers how often the low-key sit- uations create better opportunities for connecting than a weekend of frantic activity and high entertainment.

Helping Children Let Go. Many children get stuck in the first phase of their grieving process, which consists of their denial of their new reality. This normal reaction is designed to cush- ion the shock of the event and allow the child time to gradually filter in the pain of so much loss at a level that can be psychologically tolerated. It's a good mechanism, unless it gets overused to the point that the dissolution of his intact family is never faced nor the pain of the loss experienced and processed.

I have worked with a number of children, adolescents, and adults who have traced their unhappiness and general resistance to life to the day they were told about the divorce in their family. When I ask them to go back with their eyes closed, become the child again, and tell me how they decided to cope, they consistently express their resistance to the event and their unwillingness to let it in. This is often accompanied by a feeling that the parent would not have left if the child had been more adequate. From that day forward, the child experiences a deep and constant yearning for life to be different than it is, accompanied by the feeling that his own adequacy could once again be restored if the missing parent would return. This may be expressed by his efforts to get his parents to reunite, by acting out with anger, espe- cially toward any new partners that prevent reunification, or by rebelling against life in gen- eral. This wishful thinking prevents him from surrendering to the reality of the split in the original family and embracing the two new family units that have been formed. In short, yearning for reunification of mother and father prevents his adjustment to the divorce. Con- sequently, if a child has failed after about six months to accept the divorce in his family, seek professional help. See **Day Care**; **Parent Roles**; **Professional Help**; **Single Parent**; **Step- parenting**; **Working Mothers**

Dominance/Dominated Child. See **Overcontrol**; See Chapter 1

Door Barriers, Gates. Parents not only need brief breaks from tending to active toddlers, but may need to keep them safe while showering or while on the telephone or restricting the child during time-out. Gates used in doorways help to keep a young child contained in a room while allowing him to see out and still feel secure. A playpen or the tallest gate you can find or two stacked on top of each other offer the best arrangement for preventing your child from climbing over his barrier. For the older toddler who requires containment, Dutch doors allow parents to keep their child confined, while maintaining visual access through the open top half of the door when the bottom half is closed. See Chapter 7

Dressing. Learning to dress is one of the many individuating experiences that children go through. Between one to two years a child begins to remove clothing items; from two to three he puts on simple things; and from four to five he learns to manage buttons, zippers, and laces. The process is a long one and requires careful teaching and patience on the part of parents. The key is to give your child a strategy to use, sit nearby to support him, allow him to take the time he needs to manage it, and get involved only if invited and to the degree the child wishes. The child will periodically master a task and then want his parent to continue to do it for him. The best response is to neither refuse to help nor take it over for him, but to cheerfully assist him in managing whatever he doesn't feel ready to handle on his own. See **Clothes Selection**; See Chapter 6

Driving/Driver's License. See Chapter 12

Drugs. Since the use of drugs and alcohol creates a false sense of power and social competence, it offers the preadolescent and adolescent a way to avoid confronting the challenges of growing up. A recent National Department of Health survey reveals that approximately 80 percent of families with teenagers ought to assume that their child is involved with drugs or alcohol at some level. Not only is this activity pervasive, but drug experimentation is more potent and potentially dangerous than in prior years. Thus, parents would be wise to encourage their kids while they are still young and receptive to not only want to keep their brains, emotions, and mental health clear and safe from the effects of alcohol and drugs, but to know how to stand up to peer pressure, a key factor in developing a problem with substances. The three keys to guiding kids through this potentially dangerous minefield is to remain friends, inform, and do whatever you can in a credible way to disempower the illusionary "cool" and "potent" images of alcohol and drugs. Kids with histories of ADD(H) are particularly at risk for drug use with potentially more intense negative results to their chemical balance. Following are some of the more common drugs used by kids.

Alcohol. There are two types of alcohol addiction. The first, less common type occurs when an individual takes his first drink and becomes immediately addicted. The second, more common type of alcohol addiction develops slowly over a number of years, beginning first with abuse and culminating in addiction if not treated. However, due to the early and excessive use of alcohol by young people today, the kind of alcohol problems that once took one or two decades to develop are now manifesting within one to five years in young people. Even more than with other drugs, early and excessive use of alcohol is so common among adolescents today that teens perceive this activity as normal behavior and fail to see its short- or long-term dangers. Because the pressure to use alcohol among youth is so intense, the problems of abuse must be taken as seriously as abuse with other drugs. Moreover, excessive use of alcohol can lead to increased vulnerability to using other drugs as well. Sixty drinks per month is the new criteria for determining when drinking has become problematic. Check with local Alcoholics Anonymous and Al-Anon programs in your community to help you determine if there's a problem and get the appropriate help.

Marijuana. Although experts now realize that there's no such thing as safe drug use, this news is trickling out very slowly. Psychoneurologist Dr. Robert Gilkeson's research on the dangers of marijuana—most often thought to be the safest drug—explains how its oily content causes it to adhere to the fatty cells so abundant in the brain, interfering with their normal functioning and eventually causing them to die. Without these cells the brain loses its ability to run its more complicated functions, including higher levels of thought, analysis, judgment, and planning for the future. Thus, if they know what to look for, kids can see the early damaging effects of marijuana use in friends whose language, plans, relationships, and goals have become more simplistic.

Although little known and less common, marijuana is also capable of inducing such psychological problems as panic attacks, paranoia, depression, or delusions and can even trigger psychosis. Again, when kids understand that these symptoms reflect a drug-induced breaking down of personality structure, they can better recognize in friends—and themselves—what is happening when such things as early signs of paranoia begin.

Cocaine. Cocaine, once thought to be a safe recreational drug, is now considered—along with its derivative *crack*—a dangerous, dependence-producing drug. Not only does it inhibit the ability to experience pleasure as a result of draining the body of its endorphins, it causes physical and mental deterioration, depression, paranoia, hallucinations of touch, sight, taste, or smell, cocaine "psychosis," sexual dysfunction, violent tendencies, suicidal thoughts, convulsions, seizures, respiratory arrest, and abrupt heart failure. The onset of deteriorating functioning develops within one to four years of use, and the more cocaine consumed, the greater chance of slipping into a pattern of uncontrolled use. In addition, cocaine puts anyone with a propensity for mental illness at great risk. The side effects of cocaine derivatives are even worse and happen faster. At least one out of every three people who try cocaine is addicted after their first time. Another third become addicted within six months to two years, and all users eventually get caught in its web, even when it takes longer than the one- to five-year period. Cocaine and its derivative crack create a drug hunger so strong that they are considered some of the most difficult drugs to overcome.

Hallucinogens. Hallucinogenic drugs such as *LSD* and *ecstasy* can cause unmanageable levels of anxiety and hallucinations or even trigger psychosis.

Ice. Ice—also known as crystal meth—is a smoking derivative of methamphetamine and not only causes intense symptoms of agitation, anger, and violence, it's one of the most addictive drugs available.

Symptoms of Drug Use. Symptoms of general drug use include mood swings ranging from generalized to dramatic; nervousness; secretiveness, paranoia; failing to act like themselves; lacking in motivation; dropping out of activities; falling grades; hanging out with new, rebellious friends; lying; stealing; breaking rules; or other changes in normal patterns and behaviors. If you suspect drug use, be alert and ask your family doctor to order comprehensive drug tests, as drug abuse is best confronted and treated as early as possible. If there is a problem, contact local Alcoholics Anonymous and Narcotics Anonymous programs as well as community or hospital-based drug inpatient and outpatient treatment programs. See **Adolescence**; **Emotional Illness**; **Family Dysfunction**

Dysfunctional Families. See **Emotional Illness**; **Family Dysfunction**

Eating. Eating will be a pleasant experience for both you and your child if you handle it effectively. When a child is young, he will reject a number of foods, simply because his palate is more sensitive than it will be as he develops. His appetite will also vary at different ages in accordance with his growth spurts. If he is coaxed—or forced—to eat more than he wants during the times when his appetite is reduced or he doesn't like a food, a generalized loss of appetite and undereating as well as specific food aversions may develop in some children. In others, learning to ignore the signal that they are full develops, and they begin a habit of overeating. Therefore, it's critical to allow your child to determine what amounts and which foods his own body signals him to eat, so that he doesn't lose touch with this important internal mechanism provided by nature to determine when to start and stop eating. Thus, your only job will be to provide a variety of nutritious foods at mealtimes. Although it's okay to require that he try a minuscule sampling of new foods, it's important never to force him to eat. Not only do uncoaxed children become the most normal eaters, but a lack of discussion about food allows the entire family to enjoy other topics of conversation and feelings of pleasure, fun, and connection during mealtime. This, in turn, evokes positive associations with eating, rather than negative feelings of tension during meals.

If your child seems to be an unduly picky eater, without comment, reduce the size of his snack if it consists of nonnutritious food to allow for the nutritious foods to be included in his small menu. When your child is taking an inordinate amount of time to eat, you can sit with him for a reasonable period before excusing yourself from the table. It's important that you neither mention how slowly he's eating nor how tired you are of waiting for him to finish. At this point, the hungry child will stay at the table alone to finish, whereas the one manipulating the family to wait for him will simply clear his place. If your child is playing with his food or misbehaving at the table, it's a good time to calmly end his meal. If he's hungry later, it's okay to give him some juice to tide him over until the next meal, but don't prepare something special at this point, or he won't learn to take responsibility for eating during mealtimes. It's also helpful to have nutritious foods such as fruit and cheese available on low shelves in the refrigerator and cupboards that your kids have access to during those times between meals when they are hungry. If these do not include sweets, children will eat simply what their bodies require without going overboard or using these foods in place of meals. Moderately nutritious foods—including such things as frozen yogurt, fruit popsicles, dried fruits, pudding, popcorn, cereal snack mixtures, or carrot sticks and other vegetables with dip—are best served at one time of day only, preferably as an after-school snack. I would avoid introducing the more extreme forms of junk food and candy so that your child doesn't get used to these excessively sweet or artificial tastes. It works best not to serve dessert after meals, as this is an unnecessary time for additional food and causes conflict in the minds of parents as to whether their child ate enough of his meal to qualify for dessert. This determination puts both parent and child into a struggle about how much the child is eating and can create eating problems as well as unhealthy attitudes about "deserving" nonnutritious foods. If your family ends a meal with fruit, allow your child to participate in this—without comment and regardless of how much dinner he ate—since fruit qualifies as a nutritional food. When the family has dessert on special occasions or when there are guests, the child should be allowed to have some, again without comment and regardless of how much of his dinner he has eaten. Parents would also be wise to require that their child sit down to eat meals as well as snacks, rather than allow him to run around as he eats. If he gets up, he can be given one "crossroads" choice to return to his meal or have his place cleared. If this becomes a nightly ritual, skip the "crossroads" choice, and let him know that if he gets up, his meal will be over. Finally, parents can ask their child about his preferences, but must avoid acting as a short-order cook, since this arrangement is not good for either the child or parent.

Eating in Restaurants. Dining out at places appropriate to a child's age and ability to manage should merely be an extension of what happens at home. When children misbehave in a restaurant setting, rather than nag and remind, parents would be wise to act. The first step might be to calmly pull his chair back from the table—or, if it's a booth, have him stand next to the table—until he is ready to cooperate. If he continues to be disruptive, he must be taken to the rest room or car by a neutral parent until he's ready to calm down. If he's unwilling to get back in control, he can wait in the car with a calm parent or preferably be taken home to a sitter, while the rest of the family remain to finish their meal at the restaurant and the parent who drove the child home returns to join them. See **Family Time**; **Manners**; **Weight Problems**

Eating Problems. Because there are so many serious eating disorders among young people today, parents are well-advised to understand the roots of these problems and to strive to bypass them.

Undereating. When parents are fearful about how much their child is eating and coax him to have more, he stops responding to his own body's signals for when to eat and how much. Moreover, a coaxed child often eats more than he needs to please his parents or less than he needs to worry them. In doing this, he either draws extra attention and "love" to himself or gains control over his family's emotions. Parents who have become entangled in a struggle with their child over eating must realize that young children will eat normally when their families withdraw their interest and concern over the amounts they consume.

Overeating. Twenty-five percent of our children are overweight, and the figures are growing. The cause of this unfortunate problem is complex. At the foundation, we can observe that children who have been coaxed to eat learn to ignore the internal device that tells them when they are full. Thus, parents must not only withdraw coercion but teach those who have forgotten how to listen to this mechanism to pay attention to it once again.

Lethargic children who have no playmates and spend their time in front of television or electronic toys often develop the habit of grazing and snacking and thus eating too much while getting very little exercise. Parents of such children would be wise to buy less automated toys, help their child to find more involved activities and friends, and limit computerized game time and TV watching to no more than approximately one to one-and-a-half hours a day, beginning in the evening (after dinner) along with other family members. They would also be wise to make more nutritious foods available and cut back on "recreational" ones—particularly such things as candy, artificial baked goods, sweet cereals, ice cream, soda, and chips. Moreover, it's critical that they refrain from talking excessively about foods as caloric, oily, fatty, and fattening or of the need to cut back, as studies show that once the body hears such repeated messages, it begins to crave increased amounts of food, particularly the taboo ones. As a result, parents would be well-advised to simply make better foods available while increasing their child's activity and connection to others.

Once the eating mechanism has been disturbed, eating without hunger becomes a habit that can be activated by such things as boredom, associated activities such as television, and feeling down or depressed. Since eating releases endorphins and acts as a mood elevator, this habit is rewarded and gets repeated and is especially dangerous to the person who has learned to eat without hunger.

Eating Disorders. A serious threat to the normal development of young people—particularly girls—lies in eating disorders. Concerns about eating—when, how much, and how to get rid of the food or exercise it away—consume the mind of a young girl with an eating disorder. This problem is showing up in children as young as seven to eight or nine years old, and some estimates put the number of girls suffering from eating disorders by the time they are in high school or college as high as 25 to 30 percent. Furthermore, doctors now say that young men are also at risk.

Symptoms. Whenever a highly intelligent, perfectionistic child who likes to please, hates criticism, denies her feelings, is shy or fearful of people, and rarely causes problems becomes concerned with body image and weight, parents must wake up and look for the following signs of a developing eating disorder: does she control and ritualize her food intake, resist eating with others, worry excessively about calories and the nutritional value of food, exercise obsessively, have sudden swings in mood, or look sallow and ill? Does she strive to keep caloric intake under 600 calories a day? Has she lost her sense of humor, missed some menstrual cycles, experimented with vomiting after losing control and bingeing, or lost 25 percent of her normal weight?

Since early intervention is essential to success in treating eating disorders, it's important to seek professional help immediately if your child has two or more of these symptoms. Failing to do so may result in a severe and complicated disorder that can take years—or a lifetime—to heal. It's best to find someone who specializes in this disorder, has a reputation for success, and understands the need to include the family in treatment, since inadequate intervention delays getting the help that is needed and can worsen the situation. In some cases, a therapist may also be eating disordered and, thus, incorrectly teach his or her client to be overly concerned about when, what, and how much food to eat. Untreated and inadequately or improperly treated eating disorders can result in dangerous laxative abuse, tooth loss, damage to the esophagus, dangerously low potassium levels, life-threatening heart problems, obsessive thinking, clinical depression, paranoia, and severe psychiatric problems including serious suicide ideation and attempts.

How It Begins. Young people vulnerable to developing eating disorders may come from families burdened with one or more problems involving one or more family members. These problems include such things as physical or emotional illness; drug and alcohol abuse; family anger and violence or abuse; feelings of personal or business failure; financial worries and problems; divorce; problems with one or more of the children, including learning disabilities; or a death in the family. These issues are severe enough to disrupt family life and distract parents from their parenting as well as cause feelings of depletion and powerlessness in family members, including the children.

In response to these problems, the eating-disordered child may feel as though her emotionally depleted family relies on her to help them cope and believes that if she's not strong enough, her family will collapse. Such a child not only senses that she is required to be stronger than she's emotionally ready for, but believes she can count only on herself to manage things, regardless of how young and insecure or inadequate she feels.

Relying prematurely on herself in this way forces her to turn within and become answerable to her own "infantile boss," which demands that she be perfect and behave in such a manner that she can successfully avoid all criticism. Yet in spite of operating with such high levels of responsibility, because adult life seems so overwhelming, she also fears genuinely growing up and having to manage on her own. Yet rather than admit to the impossibility of coping without help, she attempts to gain control over life by controlling such things as her intake of food. Once dieting is begun, it becomes obsessive and consumes enough of her energies to take the attention off of her problems and offer an illusion of avoiding her pain. Moreover, the effect diet control has on her body—thinness and lack of sexual maturation—meets her need not to grow up by actually blocking her physical maturation. This cycle is often triggered during times when her need to grow up and cope independently are most challenged. Thus, going to camp or on a trip alone, off to college, or out into the world to manage independently may activate an eating disorder.

Eating disorders also surface in families with parents who cross their children's boundaries by dominating them, overprotecting them, or not allowing them to act as individuals with feelings and ideas separate from their families. The eating disorder offers the child raised in such a family an arena of control and is used to claim dominion over her sense of self and boundaries as well as a way to say "No" to overprotective or dominating family members who don't tolerate her individuality and independence. She also uses it as a way to distract herself from inner pain, assuage the feelings of guilt and shame she feels about being dominated, and to create a sense of internal order.

Others develop eating disorders as a result of extreme feelings of insecurity, shyness, and fear of people due to living in competitive families critical of family members and/or judgmental toward people outside of the family unit. Still others trigger eating disorders as a result of going on a diet and getting hooked on the urge to control food intake.

Many young people with eating disorders come from homes in which parents are overly concerned about body image, exercise, weight gain, dieting, the fat and nutritional content of food, and calorie counting. These kids learn from their families to view food as more of an enemy, aimed at destroying their appearance, than a nurturing provider and friend. Viewing food in this negative way is further intensified for kids in dance and aerobic programs where fellow students and teachers are concerned about thinness; health classes in which nutritional "do's and don'ts" are stressed; and sports programs with coaches who are obsessive about exercise or weight control. Unfortunately, those encouraging young people to control their caloric intake usually fail to also teach that once the body experiences a deprivation of calories, it not only craves more food, but becomes overefficient in its use of it, causing more weight to be gained on less intake. This sets up a devastatingly long-term problem for the person who has forced her body to operate at this level of efficiency through diet and intake control. When the eating disordered person begins vomiting in her effort to counter those times when she loses control and binges, the vomiting experience eventually becomes addictive, and the problem is compounded.

The eating disorder obsession—as with all obsessions—uses a repetitive thought or behavior as a way of going back to an earlier trauma (such as the family trauma; strong feelings of insecurity and fear of people and their judgments; the pressure of needing to individuate; the belief that gaining control over dangerous foods is required in order to control weight) in order to redo it and make it turn out less painfully. Although the obsessive thoughts and compulsive behaviors fail to repair the earlier problem, they bind together all of the child's energies, attention, pain, and anxieties and place them in an envelope of obsession where they can't be felt. However, the obsessive/compulsive eating pattern eventually becomes far more painful than the original problem and can be converted to a serious psychological problem.

To get well, the eating-disordered child must eventually confront the painful feelings she was hoping to bypass in the first place and learn to experience and process them. In doing this, she learns to include all of life's agenda, rather than create an elaborate, destructive mechanism for avoiding the painful parts of a lifetime. To begin, she must have professional help, as she's unable to work this out by herself. In more advanced cases, she will need some form of residential or hospital care to break the eating obsession cycle and do some deeper healing. See **Anxiety**; **Competitive**; **Compulsive Behaviors**; **Defense Mechanisms**; **Fear**; **Obsessive Thoughts**; **Post-Traumatic Stress**; **Praise**; **Professional Help**; **Shyness**; **Weight Problems**; See Chapter 11 (Reference: *Treating and Overcoming Anorexia Nervosa* by Steven Levenkron, 1983; Remuda Ranch, Residential Treatment, Tucson, AZ 800-825-2624)

Education. Those of you caught up in the race for your child's superiority will force information down his gullet as though education were a pie-eating contest. Unfortunately, this will not only snuff out his desire to learn, but can damage his bond with you. Thus, it would be more effective to teach him things that naturally emerge out of what is happening in the course of daily life together. This is best done by asking him questions in the Socratic style to access his own self-knowledge and thinking, rather than providing him with answers to digest and repeat back. Children taught in this way not only feel closer to their parents, they are considerably brighter than those who have been pushed to learn concrete bits of information, basic math facts, and reading at early ages. In short, learning to explore, examine, ponder, and think make a far greater impact on a child's intelligence than memorizing the basics. See **Intelligence**; **Motivation**; **Study**

Egocentric. Children who fail to surrender their "immature boss" to the "mature boss" of their parent sometime between two and three years of age remain stuck at this earlier egocentric stage of development during which they continue to think that they must have everything their way. A failure to make this critical surrender keeps a child stuck in resistance which, in turn, interferes with his normal movement out of ego-centered concerns toward caring for others. See **Conscience**; **Immature Boss**; See Chapters 6 and 7

Embarrassment. Because parents are the managers of their child's development, they often view his behavior as a reflection on them rather than an indicator of his own level of development. This causes them to feel embarrassed by their child's behavior which in turn triggers their impatience and anger. Thus, parents must learn to view their child's immaturity as a normal aspect of his development and include it on life's daily agenda. See **Pride**; See Chapter 4

EMDR Therapy (Eye Movement Desensitization and Reprocessing). EMDR is a new, effective therapeutic technique designed for healing both past and present emotional traumas and pain and is particularly helpful in releasing old negative programming and reducing anxiety and stress. It must be performed by a therapist also certified in using the EMDR technique. For referrals, call 408-372-3900, then interview those trained in the technique for overall counseling skills. The combination of a skilled therapist using this technique can be very helpful.

Emotional Illness. When emotional illness runs in a family, children may have a slight predisposition to it—although, thankfully, the stronger, more dominant genes will tend to prevail. Moreover, this predisposition can be neutralized by raising children with clarity. Thus, if you have family members who have suffered with depression, bipolar or other emotional illness, suicidal tendencies, drug addiction, or psychosis you would be wise to raise your children with as much clarity as you are able, since clarity can serve as an antidote to the expression of these illnesses. This does not mean that you should become fearful of provoking emotional illness in your child or respond with overprotection or backing down from discipline, but strive, instead, to provide a clear balance between love and structure in your home.

When an immediate family member has an active episode or has been hospitalized for any of these disorders, the family loses its normal balance and goes into chaos. Children are deeply affected by such traumas even when they cushion themselves with denial and don't immediately show the effects of their pain. Unless it goes on for too long, this denial serves the useful purpose of easing their initial shock and allowing the pain of the experience to penetrate in more manageable doses as they feel ready to confront it. Fear, anger, depression, guilt, loss of confidence, concern for their own mental health, feelings of depletion, and a need to be strong for the sake of the family unit are some of the side effects that often surface. Consequently, children in families with members who have endured serious emotional problems would benefit from an opportunity to work with a professional to sort out these issues both individually and as a family. See **Eating Disorders**; **Family Dysfunction**; **Professional Help**

Emotions. When our emotions are neither denied nor exaggerated they offer valuable feedback about how we feel in various situations. When we feel violated, they tell us to speak up for ourselves. When we are the transgressors, they cause us to feel appropriately guilty and to back down. When we experience loss, we feel genuine sadness. On the other hand, if we ignore or deny our emotions to avoid the pain they bring, we experience being out of touch with our own truths and reality. The more we deny these personal truths, the less we can see what is going on with us or what needs correcting and thus fail to achieve increased clarity and emotional health. Consequently, children must not only be allowed to experience their emotions— without exaggeration, drama, or an attempt to manipulate others—but helped to identify, express, and examine them and the message they offer. For example, if a child feels angry about his parents' protection of baby sister while asking too much responsibility of him, helping him to examine his underlying emotions can enable him to clarify for himself and his parents how abandoned he feels. On the other hand, if a child feels angry because he was not able to prevail in overclaiming his boundaries, rather than encourage him to hit a pillow or verbally vent his anger, he can be helped to reevaluate his view that he needs to have everything go his way. When we carefully examine the cause of our emotions for content and clarity, they make wonderful guides for living a clearer life.

Error. Nobody tries to be his worst self or to do his worst job. Our natural urge is to always be a little better than we already are, but it's critical that we are also comfortable with ourselves in the process of getting there. Thus, the mistakes we make on a daily basis must be accepted as we continue to love who we are in the course of becoming better. See **Blame**; **Denial**; **Failure, Fear of**; See Chapters 4 and 10

Explaining. Parents who overexplain need help with discipline. See Chapters 6 and 7

Exploring, the Young Child. Somewhere around six to eight months a child begins to crawl and becomes mobile enough to move himself around. By the time he's about a year or so, he learns to walk and gets increasingly mobile and into more things. Because this exploration is a valuable learning period for him, it's important to safety-proof the house as much as possible and allow him to enjoy his discoveries free from too much restraint or repeated warnings about not touching things. On the other hand, certain items can't be removed, and your child will need to learn about his first parameters. For example, a stereo, TV, or hot oven must not be touched; glass shelves and coffee tables cannot be banged; and lamp cords, dog's ears, and cat's tails must not be pulled or bitten. If your child crosses these boundaries, he needs to be told, "That's not a choice" and removed from the forbidden object.

The young child first getting around is rather easily distracted and usually forgets about returning to the object. However, if he does return, he can be removed again for as many times as it takes him to understand the message. If he's determined to examine the forbidden object, you can calmly restrain his hands or hold him in your lap until he is ready to relent. Some children of ten to eleven or twelve months, particularly those who have learned to walk, may be even more persistent and knowingly challenge the rule by repeatedly returning to the banned object. Other children don't begin this until they are about fifteen months old. No matter when it begins, such a child needs to have his freedom contracted by gently restraining him in your lap or, if he persists, removing him to a playpen or behind a gated door for a minute or so after his crying has stopped. Only hold him in your lap if you are able to remain calm and hold love for him in your heart as you restrain him. He can then be released with a reminder not to touch the object. If he touches it again, the cycle repeats until he relents. Be sure not to get angry or you will confuse the lesson and lengthen the time it takes your child to learn about boundaries. Over time, he will begin to understand that his freedom to explore will be contracted when he crosses boundaries, whereas it will be preserved or expanded when he follows the rules and that your love for him will remain constant no matter which he chooses. Eventually, he will learn that cooperation works best. See **Adjustment Period**; **Compliance**; **Door Barriers, Gates**; **Playpens**; **Redirecting**; See Chapters 6 and 7

Extracurricular Activities. Extracurricular activities not only encourage children to overcome any reluctance they might have to trying new things, but help them to develop organizational and social skills, become more disciplined, discover their strengths and talents, and learn to be more cooperative and caring. Because extracurricular activities are just as important to a child's development as academics, the enthusiastic participator should be allowed to try as many activities as he wants to pursue. Furthermore, he should not be viewed as a quitter if something he has tried proves not to be as interesting as he had thought. Thus, after a reasonable period of exploring a new activity, a child should be allowed to quit without being made to feel like a failure. However, if he's jumping around too much from one idea to another, he can be helped to confront any fears he may have about pushing through the hard times in various activities, particularly when he is in the middle of learning the beginning skills required for them. This is particularly true for the child who has trouble being the nonknower in the middle of learning something new. The reluctant participator should be required to join at least one outside activity during the school year and have his summers structured in some way to include such activities.

However, within these parameters, a child should not only be allowed to choose his own general areas of interest—such as sports, music, drama, or art—but which specific activity within these areas he would like to pursue.

I disagree with the popular notion of requiring a teenager to succeed in the academic arena before allowing him to participate in extracurricular pursuits. Not only are these activities critical to his development, they ultimately support his academic success by teaching him the skills he needs in the academic arena, including how to organize, push through the difficult parts, and get excited about life and its successes. It should be noted that many successful people not only initially failed in school, but found success through these outside channels. See **Motivation**; **Study**

Eye Contact. There are a number of children who become uncomfortable with eye contact. In some, this is due to unconnected feelings as a result of inadequate bonding and broken relationships with parents. In others, eye contact is avoided as a result of being overly sensitive, fearful, or shy due to having been overprotected, overcontrolled, or criticized by parents or hearing family judgments of others. In still others, eye contact is absent due to uncooperative and hostile attitudes as a result of having been treated with impatience and anger or having been indulged in immature behaviors and attitudes.

A failure to hold eye contact serves as a barrier to your child's closeness to people and social development. As a result, those of you with children who avoid eye contact would be wise to address whatever barriers have developed between you. The first step will be to heal any emotional breaks that seem to be injuring your child's spirit and causing him to feel emotionally distant. The next step will be to reestablish physical contact by finding more time to sit and make yourself available to the child still interested in snuggling. If your child has become uneasy with physical contact, give him a foot or back rub, neck massage, or head scratch, even if this is done only briefly in passing or while he's watching TV. Once any injuries to his spirit or your relationship are repaired and some physical contact is reestablished, eye contact will be easier to resume. This can be done by voluntarily playing such games as "stare-down" in which parent and child look into one another's eyes with the winner being the one who resists looking away—or laughing—first. Bets can be placed with stakes including such things as foot massages, or doing—or not doing—the dishes. See **Attention Deficit Disorder**; **Bonding**; **"Challenging Child"**; **Touch**; See Chapters 5, 6, 7, and 11

Fads. Adolescents must be allowed to follow the most common fads, passages, and rituals of their peer group in order to feel a sense of belonging. In fact, blocking this is so frustrating for them, it may trigger a rebellion. Thus, it's important to listen to your teen's needs without closing your mind to whatever is new and different from when you were young and allow him to use the general styles of his peer group. It's only when teens refuse to groom their hair or bodies altogether and go to the outer limits or beyond the norms of their own peer group that you must assess whether they're genuinely asserting their individuality or acting out resistance and rebellion. If it's rebellion, you must reestablish your authority, since letting this go often leads to increased levels of resistance and rebellion. See Chapter 7

Failure, Fear of. The child who fears failure doesn't experience himself as fully loved without conditions or critical judgments and views errors as something that will diminish his value. As a result, he fears making mistakes and becomes so afraid of failure that he avoids participation altogether. See **Errors**; See Chapters 4 and 10

Fair. Children do better when parents stop trying so hard to make everything fair and even for them. See **Jealousy**; See Chapter 10

Family Bed. I've learned from parents that a great many families allow their children to sleep with them, and many are interested in the pros and cons of returning to this primitive practice as a way of helping children feel more secure. Tine Thevenin (*Family Bed*, 1987) confirms my informal observation of how common a practice this is and offers interesting support for the benefits of doing so. Studies reveal that children sleep with their parents for at least the first year or so in most non-Western cultures. When welcomed into their parents' bed, children in Western society also sleep with their parents and leave on their own accord when they are between two to five years old and do best when they move in with siblings as a transition out of their parents' bed. It's hypothesized that the benefits of allowing your child a connection with you at night are similar to the ones obtained during the day; thus, the child who is allowed a full measure of physical contact and bonding both day and night seems to grow up securely, with considerably less crying and more cooperation and caring for others. It is also reported that cultures who allow this have fewer sexual hang-ups and problems.

Yet in spite of the potential for so many positive results in allowing children to sleep with them, there are a number of concerns that arise for Western parents considering the family bed option: parental lovemaking; fear of sexual feelings between parent and child; incest; overdependence on the part of the child; and a lack of desire to commit to such a prolonged period of sleeping with one's child.

- *Parental Lovemaking*. Because adults often report having felt disturbed as children by overhearing parental lovemaking, parents inviting children into a family bed must find alternative times for lovemaking.
- *Sexual Feelings*. Sexual feelings between parent and child are a concern for individuals uncomfortable with physical closeness and touch with their children. Their discomfort and lack of ease with such close physical proximity is usually a result of not having been touched or loved abundantly when they were children, and touching for them has come to be associated only with sexual touch. It's important for these parents to realize that even though they may have fleeting sexual feelings or thoughts while in close physical proximity with others—including children—mature people never view such moments with children as sexual possibilities, nor do they mentally pursue these thoughts or act on them in any way. It's also useful to consciously learn to enjoy touch without associating it with sexuality. If a child becomes overly interested in his parent's body, the parent must gently explain the inappropriateness of this and shift the focus to something else. (Be aware that nudity or seductive nightclothes would be inappropriate options for the family bed.) If the child persisted, he would lose his chance to remain in the family bed until he's willing to cooperate. In effect, a parent would handle this crossed boundary in the same way they would handle any crossed boundary taking place in any room in the house.
- *Incest*. Incest is a serious problem inflicted on children by people who have not been maturely loved or treated with respect as children. When they become parents, they often assume the coveted position of control and create a "secret" bond with their child, while crossing his personal and sexual boundaries, usually in the same way theirs were crossed. Although problems can develop when parents aren't mature in their handling of physical and nonphysical sexual boundaries with children, a private incestual pattern of behavior would not seem to be supported by a family bed environment in which both parents are including their child into a total family system of love and caring. Nevertheless, it's a factor that must be considered when deciding on sharing a family bed.
- *Overdependence*. Because sleeping alone in one's own room seems more precocious than

sleeping with parents, the idea of inviting a child into their bed makes many parents fear that he will become too dependent on them. Furthermore, experts have suggested that children who sleep with their parents may develop such intense, dependent relationships with them that it becomes difficult to gain emotional separation and individuation. Thus, parents must decide if they believe access to them at night—as well as during the day—will help their child to feel more secure and subsequently independent, or if the additional connection between them will intensify his attachment to them and handicap his individuation. I suspect the additional connection a family bed arrangement offers would work best in those families in which parents are calm and clear in their relationships with their children, rather than anxiously attached and worried about them or fearful of letting them go.

- *Unwillingness to Commit to Long-Range Sleeping with Your Child.* A number of parents are still undecided about what benefits or ill effects family bed will have on a child in Western society and, therefore, don't wish to try it; others believe they can have secure children without taking this step; and still others simply don't want to sleep with their children.

Although the jury is still out on the concept of the family bed, I believe it's an important enough subject for parents to investigate before making their decision. Some will want to incorporate the family bed—and already do—while others will reject the idea, which is equally acceptable. Still others will want to find a solution somewhere in the middle. For example, many parents prefer that their children come into their beds sometime between 5:00 to 6:00 A.M., to provide an opportunity for a cozy family connection and cuddling in the early hours of the morning or while waking up, rather than spend the entire night together. (This option offers the opportunity for both closeness and individuation.) Interestingly, children are able to awaken themselves at the approximate time they will be welcomed. However, if a child has awakened himself too early, you can ask that he go back to his room—or gently escort him if necessary—and let him know that he needs to wait a little longer. Still others will allow their children to fall asleep in their bed, then carry them to their own rooms for the night and allow them back into the family bed once they awaken or during the early hours of the morning. I think it's important—whether or not the family bed is used—that parents not feel obliged to lie down with their child to help him get to sleep.

When children switch—usually sometime from one to two years of age or older—out of the family bed, they generally prefer to sleep in their siblings' rooms. Under such circumstances, I would recommend allowing them to sleep in the same room with siblings whenever they wanted—as long as they were cooperating—but in separate beds. If a child has not switched by three or four, and his family is ready for him to do so, the attraction of his own big bed—popular with the older toddler—can create a bridge from his parents' room to his own room or his sibling's.

The key is for parents to decide for themselves what will most fulfill their children's needs in a way that is harmoniously aligned with the requirements of their own family unit. See **Abuse**; **Bedtime**; **Carrying**; **Family Cohesiveness**; **"In-Arms" Period**; **Incest**; **Individuation**; **Internal Voice of Wisdom**; **Nursing**; *Weaning* subentry under **Nursing**

Family Cohesiveness. Psychologists are concerned about families that are so distant and separate from one another that there is no feeling of closeness, bonding, or healthy attachment to other family members. On the other hand, it's also considered unhealthy for families to become so enmeshed that members are discouraged from pursuing individual time, thoughts, or activities and friends separate from the family unit. Yet we cannot become so concerned about avoiding these two extremes that we lose our understanding of the value of healthy cohesive families that allow for abundant feelings of love, bonding, touch, and closeness, yet also encourage individuality and differences, independent thinking, separate activities and friends, and as much time to oneself as desired. In short, we don't have to choose between enmeshment to feel close or distance to feel independent. A balance between the two offers the most fulfilling and healthy family style. See **Individuation**; **Privacy**; **Secrecy**

Family Dysfunction. Families experience a breakdown in function whenever one or more members has a significant problem—particularly when the problem is not being treated. Thus, problems involving things ranging from poor communication, anger, marital problems, and difficulties in parenting to lying, infidelity, emotional illness, eating disorders, drug addiction, abuse, and violence cause family systems to break down and function chaotically, rather than clearly. Parents would be wise to seek help in resolving their family problems and striving for improved individual and collective functioning. See **Emotional Illness**; **Professional Help**

Family Meetings. Family meetings provide opportunities for families to discuss rules, problems, and plans as well as any good news or strategies for personal growth or improving family relationships. Meetings are best arranged on a regular basis to allow family members opportunities to connect regularly and plan for the good in their lives as well as resolve their problems. In addition, special meetings can be called whenever a family member feels the need for expanded communications, addressing a problem, or healing an injured relationship. Children should be included as full participants in these functions, and it's important that parents listen deeply and value their ideas. Although it's not a good idea to create pseudo-democratic standards in which parents aren't allowed to make decisions without the consent of their offspring, it's important that children have ample opportunity to provide input toward decisions that will affect them, including such things as moves, trips, selection of schools, family pets, and summer plans. My favorite format is to go around the circle and have each family member express what ways he or she can improve and help the family before sharing opinions on how other family members might change or contribute more. Family meetings also provide children an opportunity to participate in solving individual and family as well as community and world problems. Such communications develop a child's thinking and problem-solving skills. See Chapters 8 and 11

Family Time. A feeling of closeness and connection simply has no opportunity to develop in families who are never together. Thus, in busy times, parents must consciously create opportunities for their family to spend time together. Dinnertime offers an optimal time for families to convene on a daily basis. For a longer discussion on how to create family time, see Chapter 11.

Family Trips and Vacations. See **Family Time**; See Chapter 11

Fathers and Mothers, Roles. See **Parent Roles**

Fear. Fear heightens our alertness and learning in situations that require careful management. Thus, a normal amount of fear serves to produce enough adrenaline to help us manage new and challenging situations with increased awareness. The natural course is for the fear to rise and then settle down, once the fear-evoking situation has been confronted and addressed. However, anytime there's too much fear to manage, we become overwhelmed by it, and rather than simply handle the situation and learn the lessons contained in it, we become afraid of feeling our fear. As a result, we often strive to avoid similarly challenging situations in the future, rather than face our fear and proceed anyway. This is true for our children as well. Thus, anytime parents become overly afraid of fear and respond by protecting their child from new and challenging encounters, he too becomes overly avoidant of new situations that might provoke his fears.

Not surprisingly, learning to avoid fear in this way is problematic since fear will surface naturally throughout a child's development, especially during those times when he's encountering new experiences and challenges. Therefore, it's critical to a child's normal development that his parents teach him to embrace rather than resist fear, take it in stride, and use it to catapult him forward and accelerate his learning as it is designed to do.

Following are some normal patterns of fear a child in Western culture will encounter and how we can help him to manage.

As a result of his increased awareness at about five months a child demonstrates a fear of strangers when they look directly into his face, approach him too quickly, or when he loses sight of his parents in their presence. Thus, helping him to get acquainted with others works best when he is given the time he needs to adjust. At eight months he becomes even more alert to strangers and is less willing to have them invade his space or to be left alone with them; respecting his need to take it slowly helps him to get connected to others during this phase. His concern about strangers is intensified at twelve months as he ventures out even further into life, yet still feels dependent on his parents for solace between his spurts of independence. Taking his hesitancy into account by neither overprotecting him nor flooding him with too many new experiences will help him to tolerate new situations and people. At two and three he's often asked to manage in play groups or day care and preschool and needs time to adjust to making these leaps of independence. Around this time, the two-year-old is also becoming more attuned to his lack of influence on the world and is thus more fearful of such things as loud noises and large animals. The three-year-old is further aware of the possibility of "evils" lurking in the dark whose frightening images symbolize his conflict about going out on his own yet still feeling dependent. At ages four and five children continue to be fearful of the dark and such things as their parents' leaving—or dying—but also add more real concerns about daily living to their list of worries.

Just when parents think that their child should be outgrowing his fears, he becomes even more afraid during the years from seven to eleven. At this point, he develops an awareness of the possibilities of being robbed or attacked, fire or war breaking out, cars and planes crashing, or his family going through a divorce or death. His increasing awareness, coupled with his own sense of helplessness, makes him afraid of the dark and the attackers who might come in the night. These may be in the form of real burglars, gunmen, and kidnappers, or represented by witches and ghosts. Because of his increased ability to think and imagine, shadows become dancing horrors in his mind, while under his bed lies a "kidnapper" waiting to strike.

As he grows older, a child gets worried about things like his performance and acceptance, and some become extra fearful as a result of being conditionally loved by praising or critical parents. Others develop fears due to overprotectiveness and being cautioned too much against such things as risks and germs. And still others become fearful as a result of being exposed to too much drinking and fighting among the adults in their homes; excessive exposure to violence on television and in the movies; or too much information given to them about burglary, kidnapping, rape, murders, and death before they are ready to deal with such overwhelming possibilities.

Although a certain amount of fear must be confronted and assimilated as a child moves toward increasing levels of independence, the first step in helping children process their fear is not to overexpose them to so many fearful images and possibilities, but to highlight the positive potential for people and the world. Next, we must allow our children to express their concerns without minimizing or exaggerating them, yet look for ways to help them better manage their fear. For example, if a child's fear is part of the normal developmental fear he encounters as he faces his next level of independence, our job is to teach him not to focus on the fear and get sidetracked by it, but to take it in stride as something that will surface whenever he challenges himself to reach the next level of development. On the other hand, if his fear has gone out of control, we must help him get it into more realistic perspective, which sometimes requires the help of a professional, preferably one trained in EMDR. See **Dark, Fear of**; **Death**; **Failure, Fear of**; **Ghosts**; **Monsters**; **Post-Traumatic Stress**; **Professional Help, Shyness**; **Strangers**; See Chapters 2 and 10

Fighting. Have you ever wondered why all of the babies from the animal kingdom wrestle and tumble with one another while they are young? If we stand back to look, we will see that the fights of young children look exactly like those of the other babies of the animal kingdom. Children have these battles with one another in order to organize—at an experiential level of learning so important to the young child—how to get along with others without fearing their dominance or becoming the dominator. Moreover, because he feels comfortable with his ability to handle things, he has no need to fight unless unduly provoked, and even then responds without the charge of fear, attachment, or anger. He simply deals with his intruder. As a result, his confidence is felt by others, and they are less likely to attempt to dominate or bully him. In this way, he contributes to a more peaceful world by neither attracting bullies to dominate him nor wanting to dominate others. Moreover, because this knowledge of how to protect his boundaries and respect the boundaries of others is obtained through *experience*, it's woven into the fabric of his personality or fulfiller.

However, in order to weave this important lesson of how balanced boundaries work into the structure of a child's personality, he must be allowed to mix it up with his peers and learn through these early experiences how to both respect and hold boundaries. Children who have not been allowed to do this are often out of balance on one side or the other. Some feel weak and become underclaimers who must later learn to stand up to others in order to maintain their rights and hold their personal boundaries. Others are overclaimers who cross the boundaries of others and must learn to back off from taking so much control. Both underclaimers and overclaimers can use childhood squabbles and the lessons they learn from these encounters to discover how to better establish and hold fair and appropriate boundaries. Ironically, when children are allowed to work this out and get into better balance deep within themselves, it results in their interacting with one another harmlessly. See **Overclaimer**; **Underclaimer**; **Violence**; See Chapter 10

Firesetting. See **Destructiveness, Persistent**; **Serious Behavioral and Psychological Problems**; **Reactive Attachment and Other Attachment Problems**

Focusing. Children who are unfocused and overly busy often live in families that overvalue "doing," accomplishing, and praising for success and thus lack enough "being" time in their homes. "Being" time—or opportunities to simply sit, "hang out," and feel peaceful—helps these children to bring their energies into better balance and focus. You can interest a busy and active child in "being" time simply by sitting down and allowing him to join you without introducing activities that might interfere with calm and quiet time together. A child who is reluctant to join you in this more passive experience can initially be enticed by a gentle book, read to him in quiet tones, while refusing to do other, more active activities with him. Once he's used to spending this calmer time with you, he will be more receptive to "being" with you without any distractions other than chatting. If, after taking these measures, he is still unable to sit and/or focus, you may want to explore other possibilities for why he's unfocused as discussed under the following entries: **Attention Deficit Disorder**; **Hyperactive**; **Relaxation**; See Chapter 5

Following Directions. See **Compliance**; **Focusing**

Forgetting. Parents must remember that children who regularly say they "forgot" as an explanation for not meeting obligations are using "forgetting" as a defense against facing and accepting responsibility. Parents must teach such children that part of being accountable is choosing to remember and that forgetting will not excuse them from responsibility. In short, a forgotten duty is a choice the child has made not to be responsible, and parents should not be fooled by this euphemism.

Remembering. Children can be taught to remember by "looking ahead of themselves" when going somewhere and "looking behind themselves" when leaving. For example, if a child is going to school, he can "look ahead" to see what classes he will have and therefore what books he will need. Similarly, when he's leaving the classroom he can "look behind" to see what needs to be gathered together to take with him.

Forgiveness. Forgiveness is critical to keeping relationships clear. See **Acknowledging**; **Clearing**; See Chapter 8

Freedom. See Chapters 7 and 12

Friends. Friends are essential to a child's social development and are the primary indicator of how well he is adjusting. Although a child can impress adults with his precocity and can get along with a parent who gives him his way on things during play together, peers require higher levels of development and social skills. Thus, parents would be wise to provide their children with ample opportunities for making friends their own age and practicing appropriate social skills. In many cases, exposure is all that a secure, well-behaved child who is close to his family will need to learn socialization. His security will help him to be both outgoing and caring, while his ability to yield to rules will make him a cooperative friend. By contrast, the child who feels insecure will timidly withdraw from friendship, while the one who competes with others to feel better about himself will view peers as adversaries and thus behave competitively, or perhaps even aggressively toward them.

Parents with a reluctant child who is having trouble making friends would be wise to get him to school early each morning and enlist the help of teachers to pair him with a potential friend in seating and activities. Families can also encourage their child to invite a classmate home to play after school or go on a family outing. Once a child has made a connection with a child from school in the comfort of his home, he feels more secure at school as a result of this friendship and is better able to branch out to form additional relationships. Parents helping their aggressive child with socialization skills must teach him impulse control and how to surrender to boundaries. He must also realize that other kids neither want to watch him play or dominate the activities, nor do they want him to boss them around. Both shy and aggressive children can be taught how to become better friends by teaching them to model on socially skilled peers.

The child or teen who is still unable to make friends would benefit from counseling with someone skilled in helping him to uncover what he does that is not working for him and how to correct his error. It's best to do this before problems with friendlessness cause him to feel rejected and insecure, which will, in turn, create additional barriers to friendships. See **Neighborhood**; **Peer Clusters**; **Rebellious Friends**; **Rudeness**; **Socializing**

Frustration. The ability to tolerate frustration is an essential life skill. See **Adjustment Period**; **Crying**; See Chapters 2, 3, and 4

Fulfiller. See Chapter 2

Full-Cycling. In full-cycling we show children how to complete the cycles of all their activities, messes, and relationships which, in turn, teaches them the value of full-cycling everything on the planet. See **Clearing**; See Chapter 6

Fussing. Fussy infants may have experienced a difficult birth or bonding break or may have medical problems or allergies to a formula or food. Once these things have been checked, parents can best console irritable babies by determining how much verbal reassuring, stroking, and holding is helpful to them without becoming overstimulating. When babies won't be consoled in this way, they may be helped by measures used with colicky babies. See *Babies, Crying/Colic* subentry under **Crying**; **Bonding Break**; **Whining**

Ganging. When we teach children to be competitive, they exclude other children in their attempt to get ahead socially. This, in turn, makes them realize that they, too, can be excluded. Thus, they become increasingly anxious about their own acceptance and begin to exclude others ever more vigorously to assure themselves a place in the group. Parents equally worried about their child being left out teach such things as "three is a crowd" and suggest that their children avoid playing in groups. By the time kids get to junior high, they are more sophisticated and one girl often has the power to manipulate her entire group to gang against one of its members. A good way to resolve this problem is to point out that three or more *can* get along and that those who are unwilling to make this work—even those who seem to hold the power—will eventually have their turn on the outside of the group. It also helps to point out to junior high girls that as the group gets even more sophisticated they will grow less interested in the members of their group who are manipulating and ganging. Once kids are motivated by their awareness of such possibilities, they are able—with a little help from adults—to figure out how to get along. Of course, the greatest antidote of all to this unpleasant practice is to help the group access their higher selves and purpose on this planet—which is to add caring and kindness to the world, rather than detract from it. See Chapters 10 and 12

Gangs. Gangs are the groups that some teens like to identify with more than with their own families or other peer groups. Kids who have experienced serious bonding breaks; a serious lack of discipline; or a combination of both are vulnerable to gangs. Moreover, a child from a family that never joins together or unites in common values and thus fails to provide a unit the child can love and learn from will look desperately for a group he can claim as his family; unfortunately, gangs often form to meet this increasingly unmet need. Having been formed around a desire to rebel and strike out as a result of not being loved enough, disciplined enough, or both; a loss of hope that they can become a part of the societal scramble to the top of the ladder; these gangs become dangerous to the child who joins them as well as to society. Moreover, the model they provide to our youth for how to cope with a sense of alienation further endangers our society. Thus, we not only need to heal the issues of family and societal unity at its core, but must find ways to unite the gang energy toward positive causes or to break it up and disperse its energy. See **Peer Clusters**; **Violence**; See Chapter 12

Gates. See **Door Barriers, Gates**; **Time-Out**

Ghosts and Spirits. Some children are afraid of ghosts and monsters; others may possess the kinds of abilities recorded in biblical times when angels were seen and prophecies heard, also reported today by increasingly more people. These children do not fear—but enjoy—their visions and may be trying to describe such things as auras and angels that they see but do not fear. If so, and you are open to such possibilities, investigate before assuming that your child is afraid and/or discouraging his ability to see in this potentially expanded and refined manner. If, on the other hand, he fears the traditional ghosts and monsters of childhood, help him to confront and address his fears. See **Dark, Fear of**; **Fear**; **Monsters**

Gossip. See Chapter 10

Grades. A child is more important than his schoolwork. Thus, parents would be wise not to sacrifice their child's feelings about himself to vent their frustration over his grades in a naive effort to inspire more study. See **Extracurricular Activities**; **Motivation**; **Study**

Grandparents. Grandparents and other relatives offer a child important segments of his bridge to the outside world beyond his primary family unit. Thus, a child who has loving grandparents and relatives interested in his well-being, learns to feel secure in a gradually expanding world that is both safe and loving. Involved grandparents often have more faith than parents in a child's goodness and can better see the butterfly within as he slowly emerges from the caterpillar and chrysalis stages of his development. Disinterested grandparents miss this special opportunity and create a loss for both themselves and their grandchild. (See **Absent Parent** for guidelines in helping a child adapt to this loss.) Those grandparents who have the capacity to love their grandchild without conditions become a unique blessing in his life. However, this special relationship between grandparents and grandchildren can also pose certain problems for the child as well as his parents.

Ideal grandparents not only love their grandchildren unwaveringly, but are willing to provide them with structure and discipline. Such elders are a great help to their own offspring in using this approach, while also providing a mature model for their grandchildren of how life works at its best. Unfortunately, there are other grandparents who not only ignore this balance and prefer only to spoil their grandchildren, but feel that it's their privilege to do so. Although there's some truth to this viewpoint, it can damage a child's development when taken to extreme. The best way to handle this is to allow grandparents who see their grandchildren occasionally to be left alone to enjoy spoiling them, if that's what they are determined to do. In such cases, parents can simply teach their child to distinguish between the more permissive boundaries of his grandparents' home from the normal rules of his own home, school, and other environments. On the other hand, when grandparents who serve as regular child-care providers are determined to spoil their grandchild, the time the child spends without rules in their home creates some serious problems for him. Often, when grandparents are made aware of their grandchild's poor adjustment at school or unpopularity with friends as a result of the confusion they are creating for him about rules, they become more willing to adjust and provide additional structure. This is more likely to happen when grandparents aren't personally attacked or blamed for the problem but are told about it gently. However, there are a number of elders who resist making this adjustment, no matter how it's presented. In such instances, it's important that parents not fight with them over this, but simply find alternate regular child care, while providing ample opportunities for shorter visits with these loving, though indulgent grandparents.

Discipline Differences. Whenever children and their parents are visiting, grandparents should allow the parents to discipline their own children without interference. If grandparents have trouble tolerating this and thus interfere, one parent can leave the house with the child requiring discipline, handle the problem, and return only after disciplining is complete.

In some cases, it's the grandparents who are frustrated by the lack of discipline that their grandchild receives and are concerned that he will become spoiled and bratty as well as unpopular. Such grandparents have every right to keep their grandchild within normal boundaries while he's in their home; yet they don't have a right to spank him if his parents disapprove of this approach to discipline. Although parents may resist the stricter styles of discipline recommended and modeled by such grandparents, they would be wise to remain open to the possibility that more control over their children is needed and develop a discipline style compatible with their own views for achieving it. See Chapters 6 and 7

Greed. When children want everything they see advertised or in the possession of others, they are becoming overly focused on material things and anxious about satisfying their desire for them. Such children will feel more relaxed and happy if their focus is brought back to the essence of life as experienced in their relationship to animals, nature, friends, and others through a heart filled with caring. See **Toys**; See Chapter 11

Grooming. See **Fads**; **Manners**

Grounding. Grounding is a commonly used term for a contraction of an adolescent's freedom. Once a teen is grounded, whether it's for an afternoon, a weekend, or a week, he must fully acknowledge his transgressions and demonstrate his willingness to behave responsibly before regaining his freedom. If he does this early, he can sometimes get off restriction sooner. If not, he will be required to remain grounded for the full duration of time originally allotted before given the option to clear. See Chapter 12

Growth. In addition to adequate rest and nutrition, such things as touch, love, massage, and holding contribute to a child's optimal physical and emotional growth. See **Touch**

Guilt. When guilt is used to motivate better behavior, a child is taught to feel obligated to respond to the emotional needs of others and feels guilty whenever he fails to do so. As an adult, this makes him vulnerable to trying to meet the demands of spouses and friends, even when they are unreasonable. Thus, it's best not to manipulate your child's emotions as a way to get him to hold to your rules.

Habits. Children often develop a number of habits such as sucking a pacifier or their thumb, hair twisting, nail biting, knuckle cracking, nose picking, teeth grinding, masturbating, or an array of tics. These are generally unattractive, yet normal behaviors which begin as tensional outlets to help the young, immature child cope with a build up of tension. These tensional outlets usually disappear as the child matures and develops better ways to manage the normal stresses of life. The best response to your child's need for tensional release is to search out underlying causes for excess tensions and do what you can to reduce them. (Be aware that for sensitive children, both positive tension—good news or a birthday party—and negative tension—a spelling test or fight with friends—can trigger a need for tensional release.) It's always helpful to allow children—while they are still young—more lap time where they can sit in the calm frequency of your heartbeat while you are at rest. As they practice matching their energies to your quieter energy, they learn to select relaxation without the aid of tensional outlets. This not only offers them quiet time to bond with you, but helps them to manage their stress more appropriately.

In some cases, tensional outlets become habitual, and the child begins to use them all of the time, even when he's not under stress. As unpleasant as they are, I wouldn't try to stop these habits unless one was particularly irregular or unattractive enough to interfere with the child's social acceptance. The reason for this is that eradicating a habit is tricky and requires consistent, gentle follow-through since any upset or anger will increase the intensity of the habit. Thus, I would let most habits go initially and would only address one if it seemed to be getting persistent. Once I made a clear decision to deal with a habit I thought might cause a child social rejection and/or interfere with his normal development in some way, rather than nag at him about it, I would begin by consistently and calmly confining him to doing the habit in his bedroom as the most benign way of helping him to break the pattern. You can present this by offering your child a "crossroads" choice between continuing to do the habit in his room or remaining with the family. Because most children prefer to remain with others, requiring that he choose between his habit and the group usually motivates a child to surrender the habit. I would keep this up—without emotion—for several months to give the habit an opportunity to gradually release.

If this didn't help, I might have the child do the habit in front of a mirror so that he could see its true effect and become more motivated to stop. Next, I might teach him ways to relax his body without tensional outlets (see **Relaxation**) or show him more socially acceptable, competing, or substitute behaviors such as finger twiddling, foot shaking or quietly stroking the top of a thumbnail. A child can also be taught that when he "starves" a habit by not succumbing to its demand, it slowly loses its strength, and the urge to do it eventually releases and goes away. A dentist should be consulted to check the bite of a tooth-grinding child, since the grinding is often an attempt to correct an irregular bite. See **Hair Pulling and Twisting**; **Head Banging**; **Masturbation**; **Nail Biting**; **Nose Picking**; **Rocking**; **Stuttering**; **Sucking**; **Tantrums**; **Tensional Outlets**; **Tics**; **Whining**

Hair. See **Fads**

Hair Pulling and Twisting. Hair pulling and twisting are generally harmless tensional outlets unless they become habits severe enough to cause the child to develop bald patches. In such cases, it would be helpful to intercede by searching out and eliminating sources of stress, providing more connection or lap time, and requiring that the child do the behavior only in private. See **Habits**; **Tensional Outlets**

Head Banging. Head banging is a rhythmic motion that serves to relieve tension for a child, often to help him go to sleep. Although it seems as though the child has something psychologically or medically wrong, usually this is a harmless comforter to the child and does not require medical intervention unless he seems to be hurting himself or has other signs of headache and pain. Children who experience mild to severe cases of neglect may also express their discomfort with a lack of touch and connection by head banging. It's as though they are trying to feel more connected with the world by creating touch boundaries around them in order to compensate for a lack of bonding. As with all tensional outlets, scolding and spanking make head banging worse, whereas more bonding, touch, lap-sitting, rocking, and body-rubs offer the connection these children seem to be seeking—and may thus improve the situation. If the head banger appears to be in physical pain or rubs his ears, head, or eyes regularly, seek medical help. See **Bonding**; **Carrying**; **Habits**; **Rocking**

Hitting. See **Aggressiveness**; **Biting**; **Bullies**; **Fighting**; **Overclaimer**; **Underclaimer**; See Chapter 10

Holding. See **Access**; **Bonding**; **Carrying**; **Contact**; **"In-Arms" Period**; **Lap-Sitting**; **Nursing**; **Touch**; *Weaning* subentry under **Nursing**

Home Alone. See *Guidelines for Leaving Children Alone* subentry under **Baby-Sitters**

Homework. See **Grades**; **Motivation**; **Study**

Homosexuality. See **Sexual Identity**

Honesty. See **Family Cohesiveness**; **Integrity**; **Lying**; **Secrecy**

Ho'oponopono. Ho'oponopono—a Hawaii-based method of healing misunderstandings—is becoming increasingly recognized as a uniquely successful approach to mediation and is being considered for use in a number of states for divorce and other court-related family mediation. For a full explanation of how it works, see Chapter 8.

Hormones, Adolescent. See Chapter 12

Hyperactive. Hyperactive defines a child who is neurologically injured in a way that seriously interferes with his ability to calm his energies. The diagnosis of true hyperactivity should include a child whose energies are so stimulated that his movements are persistently active throughout the day as well as many nights. He can't seem to sit still and is in perpetual motion. He also appears to need less sleep than other children and has trouble falling—or staying—asleep, although occasionally he may sleep well and for long hours. This physiological overresponsiveness to both external stimuli (activity, clutter, noise, television, toys, excessive amounts of focus on the child) and internal stimuli (sensitivity, sugar, excitement, stress) causes hyperactive kids to get into trouble as well as to develop learning problems. However, before a diagnosis is made, check to see if your child has the more common symptoms of an overactive or unfocused child (see following).

Overactive Children Misdiagnosed with ADD(H). There is another, more common category of "hyperactive" child who is neither neurologically damaged nor as easily overstimulated in the same way that the truly hyperactive child is. He either suffers from a bonding break, which makes him frantic for a connection; has not been disciplined enough to have gained control over his impulses; and/or has been so excessively the object of adult attention, praise, and criticism that his behavior has become self-conscious and attention-demanding. The result is that he not only lacks impulse control and the ability to be self-contained, but has not learned to accept not getting his way. These kids look and act very much like hyperactive children, though they are able to remain calm in environments that clearly require it or for activities that interest them, and they sleep soundly through most nights. I refer to this type of hyperactive response as "learned hyperactivity." The danger in misdiagnosing these children as ADD(H) is that this label not only disguises their lack of emotional balance and impulse control, but sends their families down the wrong roads for solutions. Help for these kids lies in strong, connected bonds, merged with a good dose of clear, firm discipline. Thus, before a diagnosis of ADD(H) is made, a child should be provided a consistent balance between love and discipline for at least six months to see if this quiets him down. In my experience, the majority of these children are able to get back into balance and harmony within a few weeks, *if* their parents apply such a program.

In addition, there are children who have what I refer to as "psychologically induced nonfocusing." As a result of being constantly yelled at or living in homes filled with tension and anger, or even violence, they freeze and become emotionally "paralyzed" when around adults, spoken to, or given directions. As a result, they are unable to attend carefully and miss receiving much information. These children look different from truly attention deficit disordered (ADD) children in that they seem tense, fearful, and frozen or paralyzed when spoken to, rather than relaxed and happily distracted by other things. The best antidote to this problem is for families to heal the tension and anger in their homes and learn to speak to their children with love and gentleness (see Chapters 5 and 11). These children are also helped to interrupt their pattern of freezing when spoken to by being lovingly held or gently touched during communication as well as addressed in soft and quiet tones. See **Attention Deficit Disorder**; **Focusing**; **Impulse Control**; **Overactive Energy**; **Relaxation**; **Surrender**; See Chapters 5, 6, 7

Ignoring. Ignoring is a generally ineffective response to children's unwanted behaviors, since in order to clarify for children what activities are a choice and which ones are not, adults need to respond to those behaviors that are not a choice. This not only makes it clear to a child what his choices are, but interrupts any maintainers of a behavior that a child may be enjoying other than parental responses. There are two situations in which this does not apply. One is when a child is whining and fussing or having a tantrum. Because ignoring him in these situations prevents the child from getting the concern or capitulation he wants from you, he will eventually realize that he's wasting his time. The other time ignoring is helpful is when a child being sent to his room is calling out that he hates you. Since you can't further contract the freedom of a child already on his way to his room, nor can you stop him from protesting, it's best to ignore these claims as well as his resistance. Address his declaration of hate during clearing only if he brings it up again as a genuine issue. See **Maintainers**; See Chapters 6 and 7

Illness. If a child is truly sick, it's important to be there for him, while also exploring the stressors in his life that have made him vulnerable to illness. When children complain regularly of headaches, stomach pains, and vague symptoms with no fever on school days only, it's important to let them know that if they're sick enough to stay home from school they will need to be in bed, rather than the TV room. You can be nice, but boring, and let the sick child entertain himself with quiet activities. You can also spend some time inquiring about what he might want to avoid at school. Is his teacher cranky? Is he struggling with schoolwork? Is he having trouble making friends? If there's been an illness or a death in the family or any other traumatic experience, the child may be developing a school phobia or symptoms of post-traumatic stress. See **Accident-Prone**; **Damaged Child**; **Death, Fear of**; **Post-Traumatic Stress**; **School, Reluctance to Attend**

"Immature Boss." The child who has not yet surrendered to the "mature boss" of his parents and still uses his own immature or "infantile boss" to guide his life usually lacks impulse control; is often overactive, interruptive, intrusive, and aggressive; dislikes and resists the ideas and approaches of others; is typically inflexible and stubborn; tends to be fussy and particular about things; and not only defies directions and refuses to respond to requests made of him, but sulks, screams, throws things, and has tantrums when he doesn't get his way. When a child behaves this way, his parents often view him as "strong-willed" and "difficult" and fail to see that he is acting this way due to their inability to get him to yield to their love or boundaries, or both. When their child also has features of the "challenging child," parents tend to confuse the two issues and believe that they are unable to gain surrender due to his earlier traumas and sensitivities. Although gaining surrender can be more difficult with the "challenging child" or one trying out his "immature boss," if it's done with both kindness and conviction, it's not only possible to achieve, but helps such a child to develop more clearly. See **"Challenging Child"**; **Independence**; **Individuation**; **"Mature Boss"**; **Resistant Child**; See Chapters 5, 6 and 7

Immaturity. Children are by definition immature. Thus, raising them involves gently guiding—rather than rushing them—toward the next level of maturity. When a child has been permissively raised and overly indulged, he will fail to stretch to the next level of maturity, and his development will not only fall behind the normal pace of his peers, they will be less interested in associating with him. On the other hand, when a child has been pushed too quickly toward maturity, he becomes overwhelmed, and his ego strength collapses under so much pressure. As a result, his development is also arrested and he appears immature. In still other cases, a child is immature due to physiological causes that hold back his development. Whatever the cause, it's important to uncover why an unusually immature child is not developing at a normal rate. See **"Immature Boss"**; **Serious Behavioral and Psychological Problems**

Impulse Control. "I want what I want when I want it; I want it now; and I want you to get it for me." This is the foot-stomping attitude of a child who has not yet achieved impulse control. Gaining impulse control is a critical aspect of maturation, and children who lack this ability will behave immaturely. Impulsive behavior—or a lack of impulse control—can be an early indication of hyperactivity or learning disabilities or it can simply indicate a lack of parental structure. Whenever a child's ability to control his impulses is developmentally lagging, his parents would be wise to create more structure and follow-through in their discipline. If a lack of structure is the problem, the child will gain more impulse control once discipline is in place. However, teaching a hyperactive or learning disabled child to control his impulses will take more patience and effort. In fact, parents of such children will need to take the following steps: 1) make the environment as uncluttered as possible, removing such things as background television noise, then address one activity or conversation at a time; 2) make instructions brief, concise, and consistent; 3) when talking to a hyperactive child or one with an attention deficit disorder, make sure that you have—and keep—his attention; and 4) follow through consistently on holding your boundaries. See **Attention Deficit Disorder**; **"Challenging Child"**; **Focusing**; **Overactive Energy**; See Chapters 3, 6, and 7

Impulsive. See **Impulse Control**

"In-Arms" Period. Jean Liedloff (*Continuum Concept*, 1986) writes about the "in-arms" period of the South American Yequana Indian in which they welcome their babies in their arms for as long as the child desires. When we give up the race to maturity, we no longer feel a need to push our children out of our arms and laps toward early independence and can consider the benefits of this "in-arms" period for Western children. See **Access**; **Bonding**; **Carrying**; **Lap-Sitting**; **Nursing**; **Touch**; *Weaning* subentry under **Nursing**

Incest. Statistics suggest that one in every three children is an incest victim and that an equal number of girls and boys are affected. Incest includes any sexual abuse of a child—including voyeurism, exhibitionism, inappropriate touch, masturbation, rape, sodomy, and ritualized torture in cult settings—by a relative. Incest differs from violations inflicted by strangers in that the child cannot run home to get away from his tormentor. As a result, he is not only more severely damaged psychologically, but is subject to regular, ongoing violations. Because the child is so confused by the acts and threats of this "trusted" person, he often keeps the secret as he was told. Therefore, it's up to other family members, child-care providers, and courts granting custody arrangements to be alert to recognizing and helping victims of incest. Some symptoms include irritations and injuries to the mouth, urethra, vagina, and anus; bed-wetting and soiling and other regressions and symptoms of insecurity; symptoms of post-traumatic stress; fear of everyone of the perpetrator's gender; nightmares and/or sleep loss; compulsive masturbation; precocious sexual knowledge and sexual acting out; defiant, incorrigible behavior and running away in the older child; and ultimately anger, depression, and suicide attempts. See **Abuse**; **Post-Traumatic Stress**

Independence. The purpose of childhood is for the child to grow out of his dependence on his parents and to eventually attain independence. This is accomplished through a process of increasing individuation, leading to the child's eventual readiness to accept responsibility for full management of his own life. See **Bedtime**; **Carrying**; **Compliance**; **Family Bed**; **Family Cohesiveness**; **"Immature Boss"**; **Individuation**; **"Mature Boss"**; *Weaning* subentry under **Nursing**; **Rebellion**; **Refusal to Comply**; **Rules**; See Chapters 2, 3, and 12

Individuation. A child's individuation from parents is attained in incremental steps as he moves from being only a wanter to also becoming his own fulfiller and ultimately learning to manage on his own well enough to feel ready for independence. As each stage of this unfolding process is complete, he is prepared to go on to the next stage of his development, which is designed to strengthen his ego function and help him to meet the ultimate goal of childhood— his independence. For example, the child who feels loved and secure as a result of being held and nurtured without refusal, resistance, or anger for the first six months or so will feel ready— once he is able to crawl, drink from a cup, and eat solid foods—to give up wanting primarily to be carried about by parents or sitting in mother's lap to nurse. Instead, he will become interested in beginning to venture out on his own. If he is allowed to do this without being taught to fear the world he's exploring or made to feel unwelcome when he wants to check back with his parents, the success of his explorations will cause him to feel braver, more competent, and increasingly curious. The same is true as he goes through his elementary and teen years, during which time he becomes anxious to go to school, make his own friends, find his own interests, and expand his horizons on such outings as sleep-overs and camp-outs. As an adolescent, he will want to drive, select his own course of study, and plan his own activities, future, and eventual departure from living with his family. As he's encouraged to go forward, yet not discouraged from touching base with his family, his courage and confidence continue to strengthen. And so it goes. Each stage of individuation sets the foundation for the next and increases the development of the child's fulfiller as he gradually grows toward independence. Yet even full independence must allow for touching base with family, both for pleasurable connections and in times of need. In fact, adult children who are blessed enough to feel close to family should not be made to feel that they must now break those bonds in order to grow up. Because connection, rather than separation, is the goal of the fully realized individual, the healthfully individuated person feels a strong connection to his family, friends, and the whole of humankind. See **Bedtime**; **Carrying**; **Family Cohesiveness**; **Independence**; *Weaning* subentry under **Nursing**; See Chapters 3 and 12

Inflexible. See **"Challenging Child"**; **Compulsive Behaviors**; **Negative Persistence**; **Obsessive Thoughts**

Injuries. See **Accident-Prone**

Insecurity. Insecurities often develop in children who fail to get their nurturing needs met, while others become insecure as a result of joining their overprotective parents in worrying too much about them. Still others become fearful and insecure when parents are demanding and punitive or strive to coerce them into submission through bullying. In yet other cases, insecurity develops as a result of earlier traumas, which have caused the child to feel vulnerable and fearful. See **Authoritarian Parents**; **Nurturing**; **Overprotection**; **Permissive Parenting**; **Security**; **Structure**; See Chapters 1, 2, 3, 4, 5, 6, and 7

Integrity. According to the late Dr. David Viscott, our emotional health lies on a continuum between our ability to tell the truth and our urge to lie and deceive ourselves and others. Because concealing the truth, even in the form of "white lies," can no longer be considered acceptable, we must teach our children a higher level of integrity that creates a foundation for their emotional health.

When parents are comfortable with their own errors and are able to acknowledge and openly discuss them, they help their children to feel comfortable with mistakes. Kids who come from such homes not only see that honesty is valued, but that it is safe to express the truth. Once your child shares his truth with you, it's critical to make honesty work for him. Thus, it's important not to be shocked and angry or scold him for the information he offers, but to gently guide him through it. This is best accomplished by remembering to put your child on the agenda, embrace and calmly address all of the information he shares with you, and understand his need to have ideas of his own and to do activities with his peers, separate from the family. See **Lying**; See Chapter 8

Intelligence. In addition to using the Socratic style of teaching (see **Teaching, Socratic Style**) in which answers are pulled from the student, even higher levels of intelligence and wisdom are accessed by tapping into the clarity that comes when we strengthen our ability to experience ourselves as part of the larger whole. It's said that Albert Einstein formulated many of his theories during meditation, then later worked out the math to prove them. Buckminster Fuller also received much of his brilliance during meditation and would often stop in the middle of lectures before live audiences to achieve a meditative state before continuing. Robert Bly suggests that our highest levels of learning and intelligence are located in a third hemisphere called the "third brain" or place of wisdom, which can only be accessed through the opening of the heart. The Heartmath Institute and other brain researchers are finding that research supports this hypothesis. With this in mind, it appears that the best way to enhance your child's intelligence and wisdom is to not only talk to him in the Socratic way that demonstrates your deep and genuine interest in him and his ideas, but to love him deeply; teach him to love himself, nature, and others deeply; and to help him reach within himself to access his deepest levels of love and wisdom. See **Internal Voice of Wisdom**; **Motivation**; **Study**

Internal Reinforcer. See Chapter 11

Internal Voice of Wisdom. The best authority for your life is your own inner guidance during those times when you sincerely ask for your highest self to act in behalf of the highest good for all. Therefore, it's important after gleaning the knowledge of others to return to your own internal voice of wisdom and listen to the direction it suggests. This voice can be accessed by shifting your awareness to your heart and can be distinguished from the confused and distressed voice of fear by its calm sense of clear "knowing" without question or confusion.

Interrupting. Children's communications and questions interjected in the middle of adult conversation should not always be viewed as interruptions, since waiting for grown-ups to complete their conversations is unrealistic. Thus, it's better to teach children not involved in an adult conversation to give a signal when they would like to talk. The young child can put his hand on your arm, whereas the older one can be taught how to wait for a pause in the conversation before interjecting his question. Children can also be taught how to join adult conversation rather than dominate it or continuously change the subject. A child who is demanding attention from adults and insisting that they focus singularly on him should be told that his interruptions will cause him to be removed if he continues. See **Telephone Rules**

Irritable. See **Pinworms**; *Sleep, Amounts* subentry under **Bedtime**; **Whining**

Jealousy. Jealousy is the insecure feeling we get when we believe that others are more attractive, talented, powerful, or successful than we are. We then exaggerate their strengths in our minds while minimizing our own. Rather than compete with people who provoke jealousy in us, we can focus, instead, on which qualities they possess that we would like to claim for ourselves and then focus our attention on achieving them. Thus, parents can help a child who feels jealous to determine what qualities he values in the other person, help him to sincerely honor and rejoice in that person's gifts, and learn to claim and strengthen those qualities in himself as well. See **Competitive**; **Sibling Rivalry**; See Chapter 2

Judgment. Our judgments represent the beliefs and attitudes that we have adopted about life that are projected onto the world and others. Thus, they have more to say about us and what fills our minds than the person we are judging. As such, they serve no purpose other than to show us what kinds of thoughts and ideas make up our personal reality. If we find ourselves to be highly judgmental and angry at the world and others, our irritations can show us where we need to accept and forgive more. When children are raised in homes filled with judgment, it not only makes them judgmental, but causes them to shrink into insecurity and shyness in order to avoid being judged by others. In this way, the very judgment we give out is brought back to us—and to our families—in the form of our fear about being judged, our assumption that others are judging us as much as we judge them, and the subsequent feelings of concern about judgment and ways we use to avoid it. See **Critical**; **Praise**; **Shyness**; **Thoughtforms**; See Chapter 11

La Leche League. La Leche League is an organization designed to encourage nursing as well as to help mothers succeed in this important nurturing process. For information, call 1-800-638-6607. See **Bonding**; **"In-Arms" Period**; **Nursing**

Lap-Sitting. Lap-sitting is critical to a child's sense of well-being and is best continued for as long as the child is interested. It not only helps to mend earlier bonding breaks and incomplete "in-arms" experiences, but continues to fill the child's ongoing need for nurturing. When I counsel with adults striving to heal the wounds of incomplete love in their lives, the thing that most often moves both men and women alike is an opportunity during meditation to find a lap to surrender into as they imagine themselves being rocked and held in loving arms. See **Bonding**; **Carrying**; **"In-Arms" Period**; **Nurturing**; **Touch**; See Chapter 5

Latchkey Kids. Leaving elementary-aged children home alone after school is a serious national problem. Not only do they get lonely and often frightened, they are simply not mature enough to provide their own discipline to do chores or homework. Moreover, the time alone without direction creates an opening for them to learn troublemaking patterns if they have tendencies in this direction. Not only is it unrealistic for parents to expect full self-responsibility of their child, it's unfair to feel disappointed or punitive toward him for his failure to manage completely on his own. As a solution to this problem, I suggest that parents look for alternatives to keeping children home alone. If they can't arrange to have their child with them at work or in an after-school program, they can carefully select a relative, adult, or paid teenager to look after him alone or with a small group of children.

If a preteen—too mature for supervision—is left home alone, he can be told that getting his responsibilities handled before his parents return will free him to do such things as go for a family walk or bike ride, shopping, out to dinner, play a game, watch a family sitcom, or simply enjoy his freedom. If he elects not to handle his responsibilities, he won't be free to do anything once his parents have returned home, until his chores and homework are completed. The older adolescent should be allowed to begin his own management of time for handling chores and homework. See **Baby-Sitters**; **Day Care**; **Study**

Laziness. A child who appears to be lazy may have been taught to fear work as a result of being criticized for his earlier efforts and mistakes or given another task each time he accomplished something. Such a child may procrastinate as a result of feeling his workload can never be completed to satisfaction. Thus, anytime your child approaches activities reluctantly, you would be wise not to discourage him with your own behavior as well as help him to examine what fears and beliefs are standing in the way of his full participation. See **Procrastination**

Learning Disabilities. Learning disabilities are a result of brain abnormalities ranging from minor to moderate or severe that cause specific learning functions to be weakened. For example, a child may have trouble with visual or auditory discrimination or memory; fine or gross motor coordination or eye-hand coordination; assimilating or processing information received; problems expressing what is understood; or a combination of these or other disabilities.

Causes may include such things as alcohol, drugs, or illness before or during pregnancy; early birth traumas (including drugs used for labor and delivery); or by other unknown factors such as medications and environmental contamination. Other post-delivery causes may include such things as a fall or other head injury; effects of yelling, anger, and violence which cause the brain to "freeze" or close down under stress which interferes with the cortical plasticity needed to allow new information to penetrate and provide ongoing learning; a lack of love and bonding so severe (common with drug-addicted parents) that the mechanisms designed to be triggered by love and touch fail to ignite properly, resulting in damage to skills for processing information.

Symptoms to look for if you suspect a learning disability include signs of physical and/or neurological damage; uneven development; impulsiveness; immaturity; easily stimulated; distractible; poor ability to remember directions; seemingly disorganized and scattered; poor gross or fine motor coordination; poor eye-hand coordination; mixed dominance; difficulty with language—either in speaking, reading, or writing; difficulty with math and spatial relations.

The child with learning disabilities often has a problem learning in the traditional school environment and may require special help in overcoming his weaknesses. In some cases the disability is minor, and the child is able to enter regular classrooms as he outgrows his delays or after a brief period of special help. In other cases, the disability is more severe and interferes with the child's ability to understand increasingly complex information. In such cases, it's best for him to remain in a special learning environment. When parents or teachers suspect a learning disability, it's critical to find a qualified professional to test the child and make recommendations. If a learning disability is indicated, it would be a good idea to obtain a second opinion, since learning disabilities can be tricky to assess and may be over- or underevaluated.

Be aware that the learning disabled child not only has problems with academic learning, but with acquiring social skills. Thus, it helps to break down useful social behavior into skills that he can understand as well as hold him to the social boundaries you create. Learning disabled kids usually do best when given a chance to practice their social skills with children a little younger than themselves or with familiar siblings and cousins.

Some learning disabled children seem unusually stubborn or stuck on ideas and ways to approach things, often bordering on compulsivity. The best way to handle this is to get them to surrender their "infantile" boss's approach to your more "mature" and competent boss. This will make guiding them through life a more mutually cooperative process. It's equally important to remain loving with them to help bring them into balance.

One of the interesting things about learning disabled children is their unevenness in development. Although a child may have trouble learning to read, he may do quite well in such things as piano, sports, art, or woodworking and carpentry. Therefore, it's critical that an opportunity to pursue special interests and talents be made available to these children, since such activities are crucial to their ability to develop their own unique and precious talents, maintain positive feelings about themselves, and give them something meaningful in life to pursue and enjoy.

Speaking gently but openly about the disability is important to the whole family, since it gives both the disabled child and his siblings an opportunity to understand his experience and allows his siblings to feel free to help, yet pursue their own abilities without guilt. However, these explanations must always provide a positive picture for the family to hold of how the disabled child's special program is steadily strengthening him and his life. See **Attention Deficit Disorder**; **"Challenging Child"**; **Compulsive Behaviors**; **"Immature Boss"**; **Negative Persistence**; See Chapters 4, 5, 6, and 7

Learning Problems. See **Learning Disabilities**; **Motivation**; **School, Adjustment Problems**

Lenient. See **Permissive Parenting**; See Chapters 2, 3, and 4

Listening. See Chapter 11

Logical Consequences. See **Consequences**; See Chapter 7

Losing Things. It's important to understand that all kids lose things well into their teens. Nevertheless, you can help your child to outgrow this by teaching him to "check behind himself" whenever he leaves one place to go to another. When a child repeatedly loses things, it's helpful to have him participate both physically and financially in the replacement of these objects. A child who is not yet dependable shouldn't be allowed to borrow items from other family members, as this is part of the natural consequence of not being more reliable. See **Planning Ahead**

Lying. Lying reflects a denial of reality and serves as a defense against the truth. Yet even though telling the truth is critical to a child's emotional clarity and health, kids will experiment with lying from time to time as they are growing up. If these falsities are handled properly, they can serve to strengthen a child's urge to tell the truth and ultimately enhance his development. If not, they can interfere with his healthful and clear functioning and launch him into a serious and long-term habit of lying.

Lying in the Young Child. Young children believe that their parents are omniscient and have the ability to see, hear, and know everything. This belief not only motivates a child to do the right thing and stay out of trouble, but supports the development of his conscience. Thus, it's essential that you resist prematurely announcing to your child that you don't know what he is doing on those occasions when he's out of your view and must rely on him to tell you. You should strive, instead, to extend his belief in your omniscience by acting as if you know what's going on for as long as possible. The more children believe that you know everything, the more they will track on you and the lessons you teach.

Once a child discovers his ability to get away with things that his parents don't seem to know about, his belief in their omniscience begins to wane. When this belief weakens gradually, it serves as a bridge between the child's selection of the right behavior based on external control and his choice to do the right thing as a result of having internalized his parents' standard of behavior. Here's how it works.

Children first begin to break a few rules and then lie to cover up what they have done sometime between three to five years of age. This happens when they first realize that their parents are not as omniscient as they had previously believed and begin to test just how far parental awareness actually extends. As a result, they question whether they must continue to do as their families ask when they are not in view. At this point, they are at a crossroads and must determine whether or not they will internalize their parents' values and continue to use them on their own volition. As your child begins to process this decision, he will experiment with not following the rules as you have defined them. When he then discovers that he's still at risk of getting caught from time to time, he will lie to cover up what he has done, making the morality issue worse for himself.

What happens at this juncture is critical to the decision he will make and his subsequent choices about whether or not to do the right thing and tell the truth. In effect, if a decision to do the wrong thing—and then conceal his actions—works for him, he will most likely continue to choose deception. If not, he will return to his family's standard of behavior. Consequently, it's important that parents neither become fearful nor act helpless when they discover a lie, since their child will experience both responses as reinforcing. Instead, they must calmly find a way for his choice to impact on him. Thus, parents would be wise to calmly require that their delinquent child not only backtrack and redo his behavior correctly, but experience that he has created additional losses for himself as a result of concealing the truth. For example, the child who decided not to address his homework before sitting down to watch television must gently be interrupted in the middle of his program to do the assignment. Moreover, if he not only failed to address this responsibility, but then falsely claimed that he had, he must lose the privilege of watching television for the remainder of that evening as well as the rest of the week. (I like to make losses for lying substantial enough to discourage this behavior at the outset, since it can be so difficult to uncover and curb, once it's underway.) His parent can explain that, had he been willing to admit to his avoidance of homework, his losses would have been substantially less, but that failing to be open is what had cost him the bigger loss. Over time, such a child will begin to feel uncomfortable—or appropriately guilty and anxious—about getting caught when he doesn't do as he is supposed to. As a result, he will internalize a desire to do what is right in order to protect his feelings of comfort as well as his freedom.

By contrast, when parents get excited and angry or express feelings of helplessness ("I'm worried about your lying and don't know what I'm going to do with you"), their reaction distracts the child from the lesson that lying causes the kinds of problems for him that he would rather avoid. Instead, he sees that he not only controls his parents' emotions, but that they can't get him to behave now that their lack of omniscience is exposed. Many children will use this juncture as a starting point for doing the wrong thing and then lying about it to conceal this choice. In such cases, rather than internalize a good conscience as they are developmentally supposed to be doing during this period, they reject "doing the right thing" and test to see how much they can get away with. When parental responses are filled with anger and emotional loss of control, they often trigger an even stronger desire in the child to rebel against family values.

Thus, parents would be wise not to react to their young child's lying with dramatic helplessness nor angry drama but with more neutrality while continuing to act as if they do, in fact, know what is going on and how to handle it. For example, rather than tempt your child to lie by asking if he has done his chores or completed his homework, check these things for yourself. Likewise, if he's having a problem with a sibling, don't ask what happened, but say, "I can see you are having a problem here that we need to discuss." Neither should you ask the child with an empty ice cream cup under his bed if he has been eating in his room. Respond, instead, to your discovery by announcing his consequence for breaking the rule ("I want you to know that I won't be purchasing ice cream for several weeks, since you haven't been following the rules for where to eat it"). Don't share how you discovered this broken boundary but simply let him experience how much better following his rules will work for him than breaking them. I remember my mother saying that she had eyes in the back of her head whenever we would inquire how she knew about various things during this stage of our development, and my sisters and I were tempted to check under her hair! The less you expose about why you know things, the longer the child believes that he had better do as you say.

When your child is a teenager, anytime you discover information that indicates that he has lied, don't tell him what you know or how you got the information. Simply let him know that it has come to your attention that he has not been truthful and gently announce that he will lose *all* freedom (including phone access to friends) until he can level with you. By doing this, you not only keep your source of information to yourself, he may tell you more than you already know. For example, if you have found evidence of your teenager's lying about where he has gone, it's critical not to disclose how you made the discovery, but only that the gig is up and that you require a full disclosure before any freedoms are resumed. It's critical that you present this gently yet with firm clarity and confidence.

Lying in the Older Child. Elementary and high school kids may lie to avoid harsh criticism and punishment; gain normal privileges from overly strict parents; avoid constant nagging about responsibilities; bypass the lectures or punishment they receive whenever they share the truth with their families; or create a more successful, though false, image of themselves in an effort to live up to the demanding expectations of their families or society. These kids do not outgrow lying, as hoped, but get worse whenever their lying behavior is not interrupted. Therefore, parents must determine what is motivating their child's lying and determine what will help.

The first step is to make sure that your parenting is in balance and that you offer your child love without the condition of high performance; that you are able to see his point of view in things; and that you offer fair—rather than dominant and controlling—rules and responses to the information he shares. If your family has the serious kinds of dysfunction that cause your child to escape into a better world woven by fantasy, seek professional help to heal these issues. Once family balance is in place and it's safe for your child to be real with you, lying will tend to disappear of its own accord. However, if your child continues to flirt with deceit or seems to have developed a habit of lying, be on the alert and find ways to make this unfortunate behavior backfire on *him*—rather than you—so that he will lose his appetite for it.

Making the Truth Work. Kids continue to lie only when lying works for them better than honesty. By contrast, they will tell the truth when doing so doesn't cost them their freedom or provoke punishment and problems for them. As a result, you can encourage the truth by making sure that it works for your child whenever he exposes a part of himself or his activities to you. Thus, rather than punish your child for something you don't like, but wouldn't have known about if it weren't for his honesty, make his truth safe. Talk about the situation that he has shared, ask how it made him feel, and gently explore what he wishes he had done or might do differently in the future. Don't be in a rush to slap a lesson on him. Instead, treat him as a friend and move slowly enough with your feedback for him to discover the higher road for himself. You can then reflect the relief—and greater emotional stability—we all feel when we expose the truth of things, look for solutions, and allow ourselves to see that mistakes are both understandable and correctable. In this way, you are able to gently guide your child through whatever truths he tells, while making it clear that concealing things threatens his freedom not just in his interactions with you, but in his relationships with his friends and society. You can help him to understand, for example, that peers and their parents are less interested in inviting kids they can't trust into their homes and lives. Thus, lying can affect his happiness in ways he won't always see. Children can be further encouraged to be truthful by modeling on family members who are forthright and honest, rather than succumb to defensiveness and denial.

Healing a Lying Habit. Once lying has started, you can help your child to heal it by sitting down with him, becoming soft and gentle, acknowledging your own errors that helped to trigger the habit (taking too much control over his freedom, not making the truth safe, overfocusing on success and disapproving error), and letting him know how it will hurt his life and cause serious loss of friendship and the trust of others. Next, invite him to work with you to change the habit by simply beginning to risk telling the truth; then teach him with your safer responses how well this works. Finally, help him come to terms with the truth of who he is, including his deficits and errors, so that he can begin to feel more love for his true, raw self, devoid of deceptions. You can do this best by offering your own acceptance of him, including his immaturities and mistakes. See **Compulsive Behavior**; **Conscience**;

Drugs; **Family Cohesiveness**; **"Immature Boss"**; **Individuation**; **"Mature Boss"**; **Motivation**; **Peer Cluster**; **Post-Traumatic Stress**; **Professional Help**; **Rebellious Friends**; **Secrecy**

Maintainers. *Maintainers* are consequences or results that serve to support a particular behavior a child has selected and encourage him to select it again. For example, if a child with minimal access to his parents is cuddled following a scolding or punishment, the cuddling might maintain his undesirable behavior in spite of the fact that he was scolded or punished for it. Maintainers can be internal, such as the good feeling a child has when he sucks his thumb, or external, such as the closeness he feels to his friends when he plays cooperatively. Some maintainers surprise us, as in the case of a child's enjoyment in causing his parents to lose emotional control—even when this loss includes his getting yelled at or even hit. Thus, parents must remain alert to eliminating whatever results are maintaining their child's negative behaviors. See Chapters 7 and 9

Manners. A child develops manners over time, usually beginning around three to four years of age. Modeling and teaching manners in friendly, innovative, and interesting ways at nonfriction times is more effective than scolding a child for violating some rule of conduct. Parents can further inspire their children to be gracious and courteous by making their expectations clear. Thus, asking a three- or four-year-old child to eat while sitting up reasonably straight, filling his mouth moderately full, and using the proper utensils is helpful to the development of his manners. Preparing a child ahead of time to say "hello" or "thank you" or reminding him privately to do so teaches him to express appreciation. However, saying this openly in front of others may draw a refusal. If a child refuses to express friendliness or gratitude, it's best to ignore his reluctance and put your focus on the other people present, while modeling friendly, appreciative behavior. You can later gently share the effect on both him and others when he fails to express these positive attitudes and require that he now send a note to fulfill this important social requirement. It helps to realize that his failure to speak up is often a result of his inexperience or shyness and that providing him with more opportunities to socialize is useful. Helping the older child remember such things as hygiene, expressing thanks, taking care of the property of others, and helping to clear and clean while in their homes all contribute to good manners. See **Shyness**

Masturbation. Masturbation is a natural activity that some children discover quite early, while others never do. This discovery is most common when diapers have come off and toilet training begins. Once discovered, masturbation can serve as a tensional outlet for children. If it becomes a habitual response for your child, you would be wise not to make a scene and cause him to feel shamed, guilty, or fearful about it, but provide him, instead, with clear enough guidelines to help him determine appropriate parameters for this behavior. Thus, parents might calmly let their child know that playing with his genitals is not done in public or social situations, much in the same way going to the bathroom or picking our noses is done privately. If your child persists with public stimulation, he can gently be sent to his room until he's ready to use the social parameters you have established. Although most children will prefer to remain with the group, some will choose masturbation. Such a child is usually more tense, under too much pressure, or overindulged and less socially adjusted and may need to heal broken bonds with his parents, be provided more structure, have demands and stressors reduced, and/or interrupt the habit and refocus on other interests and activities to absorb his energies. If a child seems overly interested in masturbation or sex play, underlying problems should be investigated, including such things as family tensions and possible sexual abuse. Teens may begin to masturbate as a result of their sexual development. However, if their lives are filled with other interests, friends, and activities, this behavior will stay within appropriate bounds. See **Habits**; **Relaxation**; **Sexual Abuse**; **Sexuality**; **Tensional Outlets**

"Mature Boss." A child must initially surrender his "immature boss" to the "mature boss"—or guidance—of his parent in order to learn socially civilized and appropriate behaviors. Paradoxically, once he has made this surrender, he is given increasingly expanded choices and freedoms—so long as he handles them responsibly. These expanded choices, in turn, give him the opportunity to develop and strengthen his own "mature boss" which will ultimately take over and guide his life. See **Adjustment Period**; **Compliance**; **"Immature Boss"**; **Immaturity**; **Independence**; **Individuation**; **Redirecting**; **Refusal to Comply**; **Resistant Child**; **Rules**; **Tantrums**; **Time-Out**; See Chapters 3, 6, 7, and 12

Meetings, Family. See **Family Meetings.** See Chapter 11

Messes. See **Cleaning**; **Full-Cycling**

Misbehaving. See **Compliance**; **Consequences**; **Refusal to Comply**; **Rules**; See Chapters 6 and 7

Mistakes. See **Error**

Money Management. Money represents an exchange of energy and should be treated as such. Yet many parents hand over funds to their children and teens as needed, regardless of whether or not they have exchanged any energy for it. This tends to keep their offspring in a childish, dependent position and unable to begin the process of earning and managing money on their own. Other parents allow their kids to collect an allowance and save gift money, yet hang onto control over how they will spend it. And still others go so far as to not only control allowance and gift money, but whatever income their child has earned from various jobs. So much control over the management of a child's or teen's money—whether it's from gifts, his allowance, or has been earned—is highly frustrating to him as well as inappropriate.

By contrast, allowing kids to manage their allowance, reasonable amounts of gift money, and the wages they have earned gives them an opportunity to plan their needs; make decisions about what is important to them; and live with the results when they have been unwilling to do the work required to earn some funds or manage them well. Allowing this process teaches kids such things as the true results of making a bad purchase, loaning money to unreliable friends, losing or breaking things, or spending all of their money at the beginning of the month or on frivolous things. The key, of course, is for parents not to provide additional funds for kids who refuse to work or who mismanage their money, but to allow them to feel the pain of their mistakes and learn from them.

In addition, the older adolescent who is given an opportunity to manage his own checkbook and learn to make withdrawals and deposits will have the skills necessary to manage all of his money by the time he's in college or living on his own. Not only does this management of his financial affairs enhance a child's development, it allows him to feel that he has control over an important part of his life. See **Allowance**

Monsters. Monsters tend to visit the minds of children four to six years of age, due to their fears of things they are becoming more aware of but have no power to control. The best way to deal with these visitors is to have the child calmly confront them and the fear they represent—rather than avoid and run from them in a state of panic. Thus, parents can guide their child to close his eyes and look into the face of his monster, describe it, and explain how it's feeling or what it wants. This act of facing the monster and whatever parts of the self have been projected onto it help both the parent and child see which of the child's fears are represented in the monster. For example, a child who stops running from his nighttime visitor to stop and look into its eyes and heart may discover that the monster is chasing him because the monster needs a friend. This could represent the child's wish to make more friends, while fearing that he's not very good at it. Thus, once the monster is befriended, wise parents will help their child to see the feelings he has in common with the monster and feel understanding for him, rather than fear. The monster—if asked—might even have some ideas for the child on how to make more friends.

Whenever we face our fears we not only dissolve the anxiety and feel more courageous, but learn the lessons available to us when we confront our problems. See **Fear**; **Ghosts and Spirits**; **Nightmares**

Moodiness. See **Sulking**

Morning Routine. See Chapter 6

Mothers and Fathers, Roles. See **Parent Roles**

Motivation. When we urge our children to pursue the interests of their ego-based worldly selves over those of their higher selves, they become competitive and develop a fear of failure. Once this fear is active, they often withdraw from the activities that they would normally pursue. Thus, pushing our kids to perform backfires and becomes demotivating, rather than motivating. How do we reverse this trend and inspire our kids to find their passions, pursue their bliss, and fulfill their potential? A newborn doesn't lie on his back and wait there until he is ready to die. Instead, a passion within motivates him to squirm, turn over, scoot, and eventually crawl and walk in his desire to meet life's adventures and partake of its offerings. Because a child's desires constitute the force that drives his life, parents must take care to nurture, rather than destroy these inborn passions. They must not, for example, meet all of his needs before he has had a chance to move toward fulfilling them on his own. Nor should they push him too fast or hard toward things that don't inspire him or criticize his efforts or the arenas he has chosen to pursue. The most valuable way to inspire a child is to expose him to life's smorgasbord of possibilities and encourage him, by example, to fully enjoy its offerings. Once he is allowed to pursue his own interests and passions, your only job is to assure that he associates enough positive feelings with his participation and efforts to ignite his passion and keep his desire to remain involved alive.

When a child seems unmotivated, parents must investigate what decisions he has made about himself and life that have caused him to withdraw his passion for involvement. What fears—of criticism, failure, rejection or pain—has he associated with participation that cause him to now reject further involvement as a way to avoid these fears? Once his motives for avoidance are understood, your job will be to help him make a new decision. You can do this by asking gentle questions about how well his avoidant approach is working, rather than give him a lecture about the need to participate. For example, you might ask when he made the decision that he can't handle life's effort, errors, pain, and rejection? Is that decision meeting his goals, or is he feeling bored, left out, and lonely? Does he notice that others are more willing to include these aspects of life in order to remain free to participate? Would he like to get his courage back now that he's older and try participation once again? It's also important that you remove any maintainers you may be contributing to his decision to withdraw. For example, does he get extra concern and attention from you for his avoidance? Once he decides to try participation again, make sure that you offer positive rather than negative associations with his efforts.

Motivating Positive Qualities in Children. Tony Robbins, the king of motivation, pays attention to what *neurological associations* are being made with various behaviors and strives to *consciously flood* the individual with *positive associations* connected to *rewarding behaviors* and *negative associations* connected to *unrewarding behaviors*. For example, when a child is being industrious, honest, and caring, it's important not to criticize his efforts, even if they fall short, since the association you hope he will make when trying out these qualities is that they are rewarding. Likewise, don't give extra attention or make proclamations about the power of his negative choices during those times when he is uncaring, dishonest, or procrastinating. Instead, reflect the negative associations that he is creating for *himself* as well as provide some additional ones if the natural associations are too subtle. If you think in terms of strengthening the kinds of associations that will support your child in choosing rewarding behaviors, while helping him to make negative associations with behaviors that don't serve him, your child will become increasingly motivated to "do the right thing." See **Extracurricular Activities**; **Practicing**; **Procrastination**; **Study**; See Chapter 9

Music, Teen. Pay attention to the words and messages of teen music and be willing to ban selections that are whispering rebellious ideas into your adolescent's head. Aside from these, teens should be allowed to select the beat they enjoy, whether or not you can relate to it. See **Television and Videos**; **Video and Computer Games**

Musical Instruments. Children should be allowed to choose which—if any—musical instruments they would like to play; to learn at their own pace; to have practice arranged and supervised by a teacher known to inspire; and to be encouraged to freely enjoy the instrument at other times. The same is true for all artistic and extracurricular pursuits. See **Extracurricular Activities**; **Practicing**

Nagging. Nagging occurs when parents consider a behavior to be important that their child has not yet accepted responsibility for integrating into his personality or life. The issues that most often provoke nagging are room cleaning, chores, practicing, studying, posture, nail biting, manners, attention to hygiene and grooming, and overall development of the social graces. Because these behaviors take an indefinite period of time to develop, parents aren't able to draw clear parameters around them, take a stand, and follow through on their execution, so succumb, instead, to nagging. Unfortunately, repetitive nagging over a period of time represents a problem for both parent and child that can seriously undermine their relationship. Here's why.

Although parents feel compelled to nag their child about behaviors important to his maturity and to gaining social acceptance, the child resents so many ongoing parental instructions and often ignores or resists them, no matter how useful they may be. Thus, parents would be wise to refrain from issuing a multitude of irritated directives, but, instead, remain conscious, calm, and gentle, while more precisely pointing their child toward his studies, overseeing his grooming and manners, supporting his involvement in activities, reminding him to express his appreciation, and guiding him to reach within to be his best and highest self.

Nail Biting. Nail biting is a normal, yet unattractive tensional outlet. Thus, rather than get angry at the child who does it or see him as unduly nervous or immature, it's better to see if this tensional release will run its course while you search for ways to reduce stress in his life. If it becomes a persistent habit, you can require that it be done privately in his room, rather than attempt the difficult task of eradicating the activity altogether. This approach takes your focus off of the behavior and allows it to run its course without your further involvement. You can best help your child to develop his own desire and ease in stopping the habit by giving him manicures to remove tempting snags and by making his hands more attractive. Eventually, all children will want to break their nail biting habit and will have their own internal motivation to do so. When that time comes, they may ask that you put bitter potions on their nails, remind them not to bite, and/or supply them with emery boards. I would caution parents not to allow this normal activity to become a source of serious friction between you and your child. Be aware that a good diet, rich in calcium, will produce strong nails, less susceptible to biting. See **Habits**

Name-Calling. See **Swearing**

Napping. Because children generally require sleep during the day until about four years of age, it's best to require that they rest—at least for a quiet period in their rooms—until that age. Moreover, since most schools require rest periods through the first or second grade, parents would be wise to help their children accept the idea of a nap while they are still young. Many children will have periods when they will resist resting, but if you calmly stay with it, they will eventually learn to surrender to this part of their day. Although it's important to require that a child remain on his bed during naptime, he should not be required to sleep. It's okay for the older child outgrowing daytime sleep to pass the time listening to soothing music or a story tape and/or have some books available to browse through. If the child gets off of his bed, he must be calmly returned without conversation for as many times as it takes him to surrender. Your clarity about this will encourage most young toddlers of one to two years of age to stop resisting and often even surrender to sleep as a result of relaxing. Because a child this age does, in fact, need the rest, it's best not to introduce the distraction of books or story tapes, though soothing music can be helpful. With the older toddler, begin the rest period only after he has settled down, and show him how this works on a timeline to motivate him to shorten his period of resistance. He may or may not sleep, but the quiet time is, nevertheless, important for both of you. See **Sleep**

Natural Consequences. See **Consequences**

Negative Persistence. Some children seem to be unduly stubborn and persistent in their effort to get their way. Thus, rather than be flexible and yield to life's realities, they often respond to situations with negative persistence. For example, when they are dressing, they may have trouble selecting an outfit and become inordinately frustrated as they go back and forth on a decision. They want assistance with their "no-win" approach to things but fail to gain relief or feel satisfied by the help given. As a result, they complain further, whine, or throw a fit. Assistance and suggestions never seem to help, and the more you try, the worse the situation gets. They may want a particular seat in the car and cannot let go and yield when it's not available. Instead, they will persist in trying to get their way, even to the point of aborting the outing. These children have often had early traumas such as difficult births, bonding breaks, or other emotional or physical assaults to their little beings, and some have minimal learning disabilities. As a result, they tend to be more sensitive and persistent about things, sometimes bordering on the inflexible rigidity common in children with mild imbalances. (This repetitive/obsessive response may be a mild form of an ongoing post-traumatic stress response to an early trauma or an attempt to bring order to a world that has been thrown out of balance in some way.)

These children should be distinguished from the ones who have never surrendered their "immature boss" to the "mature boss" of their parents and have learned their resistant response from parents who back down and give them their way on everything.

The best response for both types of children is to let them know that if they persist in trying to get their way, they will be given less freedom—usually a time-out—until they are willing to yield to their reality. If you are stuck in a car with a child engaged in negative persistence, simply announce that you are no longer interested in the subject or willing to participate in the conversation, and then drop out until you get home, no matter how persistent he is in trying to engage you. If your child is still going at it by the time you get home, contract his freedom to his room until he is ready to release it. The sooner you recognize that your child has launched into negative persistence and respond by dropping out, the sooner he will stop using this less fruitful approach to life. During clearing, reflect how the persistence is causing him loss, rather than gain. Then, help him to explore avenues for relieving his tensions and concerns. Be sure to investigate if his underlying concerns are connected to an earlier trauma. If so, seek help for healing post-traumatic stress. See **"Challenging Child"**; **Compulsive Behaviors**; **"Immature Boss"**; **Impulse Control**; **Obsessive Thoughts**; **Oppositional Child**; **Post-Traumatic Stress**; **Refusal to Comply**; See Chapters 5, 6, and 7

Negotiation. Do not begin negotiations with a child until he has first learned to surrender to your authority. See Chapter 6

Neighborhood. Living in a supportive neighborhood is one of the greatest gifts you can give a child, since neighbors not only offer your children adult support, but opportunities for interactions and play in natural settings with their peers. See **Friends**; **Socialization**; See Chapter 11

Nightmares. Nightmares—common in children—are a result of a child's feelings of powerlessness in the face of fear-evoking ideas and events and surface during sleep as he struggles to work through how he will manage these various challenges. Thus, the child of two-and-a-half to three just starting preschool will dream of separation and abandonment, while the four- to six-year-old will dream of ghosts and monsters as he strives to come to terms with how little independence and strength he actually possesses. Although a child's nightmares may drop off for a while at about six years of age, they resume again sometime between the ages of seven to eleven as a result of worrying about divorce or illness in his family, betrayal or abandonment by friends, or concerns about the kinds of things he is exposed to on television.

The best approach to a nightmare is to help your child to calm down and go back to sleep, if he's not fully awake, and discuss the material in the morning. However, if he's too overwrought to get back to sleep, it helps to turn on an indirect light and calmly help him to confront the things he fears and sort out his concerns about them. This can be done by helping him understand that the dream is a movie he created in his head with a message contained in it to help him examine the things he hasn't yet come to terms with or resolved.

As with adults, whenever a child's fears are confronted, the feeling of fear is reduced or eliminated, and safe and loving feelings are able to fill the vacuum again. Parents can help their child confront the dream and describe how he was feeling in the face of the thing that frightened him; for example, was he feeling worried, sad, afraid, powerless, or helpless? This information leads to the core of the issue for him and reveals whatever fears he's not yet resolved in his life. It also helps at this point to invite a comforter, such as a favorite stuffed toy or blanket, to keep him company and help him feel safe. His parent can then unobtrusively stay with him awhile in silence as he gets drowsy again—or suggest that he turn on a light to read, if it seems as though he can manage on his own. If your child has not fully awakened and goes right back to sleep, save the discussion of the nightmare—if he remembers it—for morning. See **Fears**; **Ghosts and Spirits**; **Monsters**; **Sleep Problems**

Night Problems. See **Bedtime** and **Sleep Problems**

Night Terrors. Night terrors may be more terrible for the parent than the child, who is asleep but with his eyes wide open while he sits up or walks around, often crying or flailing his arms. In contrast to nightmares which occur in the second half of the night during the lighter REM sleep—allowing the child to wake up easily—night terrors occur during the deeper non-REM sleep, which takes place within the first few hours after falling asleep. The child who has night terrors (usually between three to six years of age) is generally undeveloped in his ability to make the transition from deep to light sleep and then awakening. He often cries out, has a wild look in his eyes, and may claw at the bed or kick you away as his heart races frantically. Because of his agitation, combined with his inability to wake up, it's difficult to help the child in this state. Fortunately, most fall back asleep on their own after the episode is over—with no memory of it in the morning. Night terrors can last anywhere from three to forty-five minutes. If they are short, it's best just to let the child fall back to sleep if he will. If he goes on for longer or doesn't settle down until after awakening, parents can hurry up the process of waking him with a wet face cloth. Older children ten, eleven, or twelve having night terrors tend to sleepwalk as well. Thus, precautions must be made for their safety. Although rare, night terrors can indicate a neurological problem which should be checked in children who have them regularly. In children seven or older, night terrors can be a symptom of problematic emotions that are not being expressed fully enough during the day and thus surface at night.

Help for Night Terrors. Dr. Bryan Lask, consulting psychiatrist for Hospital for Sick Children in London, suggests that parents note what time the terrors take place for five nights in a row; then wake the child ten to fifteen minutes before the terror usually occurs; and keep him awake for about five minutes before letting him fall asleep again. This reprograms the brain's sleep cycles that are causing the terrors and often stops them within a week. See **Sleep Problems**

Nonchoices. Nonchoices represent those things a child elects to do that are designated to be out of bounds for him. See **Choices**; Chapters 6 and 7

Nose Picking. Nose picking is a tensional release that has become habitual and is one of the less attractive behaviors of children. Thus, parents would be wise to gently have the child who is picking his nose in public be made aware of what he is doing, how it looks, and its social implications; then matter-of-factly have him go to the bathroom to manage it in private with the help of a tissue. If it persists, introduce the practice technique. See **Habits**; **Practice Technique**

Nursing. Nursing is the most natural way for a mother to create deep bonds with her child, while offering him the most healthful diet available. However, she can run into problems that will interfere with this special experience if she doesn't educate herself on how to optimize her nursing success. Thus, she would be wise to consult one or more of the many books that guide mothers through successful nursing or contact La Leche League (information under separate listing).

When nursing is not selected, parents would be wise to treat bottles as though they were breasts, rather than use them for propping or allow the mobile child to walk around with them. In this way, bottle feeding more closely simulates the advantages of nursing.

Once successful nursing is established, many Western mothers will continue to nurse on demand, yet will wisely put a drowsy baby down before he falls asleep at the breast whenever possible. Parents using bottles would be wise to follow this approach as well, as it teaches their child to experience nursing and sleeping as separate activities. This distinction makes it easier for him to learn to fall asleep on his own.

Most Western mothers also figure out a combination of demand and scheduled feedings by offering options other than nursing during those times when they know their child is not really hungry, but is feeling fussy. When a baby wakes up for a night feeding and truly eats, it's important to allow him to nurse, since research shows that a child who genuinely eats at this hour needs the nourishment and reaches his full growth potential if he's allowed to have it. On the other hand, if a child is only nibbling in the middle of the night, his mother might want to begin weaning him from this feeding.

Weaning. At about six months a child can begin to drink from a cup and is learning to crawl. With these two events, he has been prepared by nature to leave mother's lap and begin some exploration on his own. Some babies will be ready to begin the process of giving up nursing at this natural juncture, whereas others will want to continue for another six months. Still others prefer to wait until about eighteen months to two or three years. Whether or not to use this event as a time to wean is an individual choice, and mothers would be wise to consult baby care books and La Leche League as well as their own hearts and internal voices in making it.

Planned Weaning. Whenever a mother selects a weaning time before her child is ready to wean on his own, she can begin by gradually eliminating one daily feeding. This gives both mother and baby time to adjust. Some babies, comfortable with the cup and solid food, will wean without substitutes, whereas those with a strong need to suck will find another outlet, such as a pacifier, thumb sucking, or a bottle if it's offered. During this period, it's best not to offer the breast; but also not to refuse it. Mother can provide extra time to replace the closeness they shared while nursing as well as a variety of new things and activities to distract him. Mother can also ward off an anticipated request for nursing by offering a special snack about that time, then heading for the park or other popular outing. Once he has accepted this, Mother can eliminate a second feeding in the same way.

When weaning your child from his bottle, it works best if you make sure that he takes all of his feedings sitting in your lap, rather than wandering around the room with his bottles. In this way, he will be more willing to give up the bottle and leave it behind in order to free himself for his growing independence and need for exploration. On the other hand, if he's allowed to drag a bottle around with him, he won't have to choose and will later have trouble giving up the bottle.

Whether you are weaning your child from the breast or bottle, the last evening feeding will be the hardest for most babies to give up, but even this will go better if you haven't used feeding to put him to sleep. Check with La Leche League and your favorite baby care books for different approaches on how to proceed. See **Access**; **Bonding**; **Carrying**; **Contact**; **"In-Arms" Period**; **La Leche League**; **Sleep**; **Touch**

Nurturing. Learning how to provide nurturing balanced with discipline is the key to your child's healthy development. See **Access**; **Bonding**; **Contact**; **"In-Arms" Period**; **Insecurity**; **Lap-Sitting**; **Nursing**; **Touch**; See Chapter 5

"Oak Tree." The oak tree is an image used to remind parents to be calm and at the same time strong and rooted when dealing with their children.

Obsessive Thoughts. Obsessive thoughts include recurrent and persistent ideas, thoughts, images, or impulses that intrude on the consciousness of the individual and are used as a defense mechanism against anxiety. These thoughts vary but often include such things as doubt, violence, or contamination. Rather than face the initial problem or feel the original feeling, the person focuses on the obsessive thought, which is repeated over and over again in a symbolic attempt to go back and repair the original trauma. In the same way, compulsive behaviors such as alcoholism, gambling, and eating disorders are repeated in an effort to fix the original pain, while also serving to distract the adult or child from his or her real problems. A child with obsessive thoughts or behaviors requires quality professional help. See **"Challenging Child"**; **Compulsive Behaviors**; **Eating Disorders**; EMDR **Therapy**; **Professional Help**

Oppositional Child. An oppositional child is one whose development is interrupted by a pattern of disobedience and opposition to authority. This is often a result of weak discipline, but can also be a result of bonding breaks, early traumas—including such things as neglect and abuse—or learning disabilities. If you have an oppositional child, work first to establish a balance between love and authority, since this is the best response to the oppositional child, no matter what the original cause of the behavior. Once you are in balance, if your child continues to be oppositional, apply directions under **Resistant Child**. If that doesn't work, seek professional help to uncover possible traumas that are motivating this response. See **Abuse**; **Adjustment Period**; **Bonding**; **Compliance**; **"Challenging Child"**; **"Immature Boss"**; **"Mature Boss"**; **Negative Persistence**; **Overactive Energy**; **Refusal to Comply**; **Resistant Child**; **Rules**; **Tantrums**; **Time-Out**; See Chapters 1, 3, 4, 5, 6, and 7

Overactive Energy. Many overactive children have simply not been taught to bring their energies to levels within their bodies that are appropriate to various situations. For example, when outdoors at a park, the sky is the limit, whereas at a restaurant, a child would be required to contain his energies at a quieter level. Parents must first get clear what energy levels they require in various situations, rather than wait until their child's exuberance gets out of hand. When children are shown the difference between loud and quiet energy and are asked to note these levels in others as well as in their own bodies and hearts, they are able to reproduce the quieter energy at will. If they fail to use the energy level you require, they must have their freedom contracted until they have calmed down. In this way, they are motivated to conform to the various energy levels each situation requires. Children who persist in overactive energy after being taught otherwise may do so as a result of having experienced an early trauma or bonding break, or they may watch too much television or suffer from allergies or other medical problems. In other cases, a child may be overactive because his home is emotionally chaotic or lacks discipline, and he has thus failed to surrender his "immature boss" to the "mature boss" of his parents. All of these possibilities should be honestly examined and corrected before giving a child the neurological label of hyperactive. See **Attention Deficit Disorder**; **Bonding Breaks**; **Focusing**; **Impulse Control**; **Oppositional Child**; **Relaxation**; See Chapter 7

Overclaimer. An overclaimer is a child who aggressively claims things that are already in use or belong to others. Such a child is focused only on his own desires and is unaware of the rights and boundaries of others. See **Fighting**; **Underclaimer**; See Chapter 10

Overcontrol/Overdirection. Overcontrolling parents seize too much control over the decisions and management of their child's life and direct too many of the details of his day-to-day functioning. They constantly remind their young child not to forget his shoes or jacket, awaken their teen every morning for school, and then feel disappointed that their child is not more self-starting and self-reliant. When parents overcontrol and overdirect, their child's internal reminder not only atrophies, he has little opportunity to develop his own fulfiller and feelings of personal competence and ego strength. Thus, overdirective parents would be wise to allow their child to use his own fulfiller, even during those times when his efforts are immature and clumsy or he forgets. Most children respond to overdirection by passively—or passive/aggressively—resisting, although some may openly rebel against so much parental involvement once they are old enough to do so. See **Overprotection**; **Passive-Aggressive**; **Passive Resistance**; **Passivity**; See Chapters 1 and 12

Overnurturing. See **Overcontrol/Overdirection**; **Overprotection**; **Permissive Parenting**; See Chapter 1

Overprotection. Some parents are so afraid that their child will be hurt by life that they buffer him from its blows by living it for him. These parents fear that their child can't handle things and, thus, overmanage for him. They may, for example, cut out their young child's circle, finish his picture, or push the pedals on his bicycle. They may do their junior high schooler's science project or order prom flowers for their high schooler. The child handled in this way soon joins his parents in their fear that he can't manage on his own and must rely, instead, on their more effective fulfiller to cope in his behalf. This undermines his belief in his own fulfiller and ego strength and robs him of the opportunity to develop his own abilities, courage, and strength. Thus, overprotective parents must learn to let go and give their child more opportunities to practice managing things for himself as well as experience whatever results he elicits, including life's pain. See **Fulfiller**; **Overcontrol/Overdirection**; **Permissive Parenting**; See Chapter 1

Overweight. See **Eating Problems**; **Weight Problems**

Pain, Emotional. See Chapter 10

Pampered child. See **Permissive Parenting**; **Resistant Child**; See Chapters 1 and 2

Parent Roles. Although the lines are blurring some between mothers' and fathers' traditional roles, a distinction continues to persist between what I refer to as *primary parenting*, which mother usually assumes, and the secondary or *support role* more typically provided by father.

A child first establishes a sense of security and belonging in the world through a nurturing relationship with his *primary caretaker* and first object of love and bonding, usually his mother. This caretaker becomes his primary parent, since she is the first one available to him, and he initially feels most dependent on her. If she meets his needs with love and caring, he feels securely connected—or attached—to her. This, in turn, causes him to feel safe and trusting enough in the world and its people to explore his horizons further. Thus, a good relationship with his primary parent is not only critical to a child's development but serves as the foundation for a good relationship with his *secondary* or *support parent* as well.

Mother as Primary Parent. In the animal kingdom it's generally the mother who provides for and teaches her young. And true to form, the primary caretaker in our society is usually the female. I can remember prior to having my own children watching a pregnant friend struggle on the beach to get comfortable as she acknowledged Mother Nature's ingenious method for preparing her for the burden of responsibility ahead of her. Although I laughed know-ingly, it wasn't until having a child of my own that I understood the deeper meaning of this seasoned mother's comment! As a result of these encumbering nine months, it's the mother who is most prepared to accept the newborn's intrusion into her personal life. She is also the one who nurses and provides for him during his first six months to a year and thus gets closest to him. This observation is merely a statement of reality and is not right or wrong, good or bad, and doesn't make women more capable parents than men. However, it does provide a plausible explanation for why statistics continue to describe mother as the one who surfaces as primary parent to the developing child.[9]

Father as Primary Parent. Although rare, some fathers assume primary responsibility for rais-ing their children. Because these fathers have missed the gradual introduction to the burden of child care that pregnancy provides, they must learn to include their child's demands after he is born. Yet any father committed to twenty-four-hour duty with a newborn—as well as primary responsibility for the next eighteen years—is perfectly capable of managing the job. Some fathers assume this responsibility in the absence of a mother in the home due to death, abandonment, or divorce, while others do so to compensate for an ill, addicted, or inade-quate mother. Still others assume responsibility simply because their children are of great personal interest, and primary parenting is a priority for them.

The Primary Couple. Also rare—but increasing in numbers—is the couple who shares equally in the responsibility of primary parenting, which doesn't include one of the parents reluc-tantly dealing with children only after being urged to do so by the other. Assuming full respon-sibility means being alert—without prodding—to the child's many needs as well as being willing to interrupt one's own life to fulfill those needs on a continuous basis day by day, year in and year out for eighteen years. This level of commitment also includes a willingness to provide for surrogate care when needed or to stay home from work or up all night with a sick child. Thus, in order to qualify as a *primary couple*, both parents must be equally will-ing to accept this complete range of responsibilities. As lovely as this arrangement sounds, couples fully sharing child-rearing responsibilities continue to be the exception.[10]

Support Parenting. The parent who is not a child's primary parent becomes his secondary or support parent and is the second person with whom the child connects and forms a mean-ingful bond. Although second in line, this relationship is aligned in value to the child's devel-opment with the role of primary parent, as it offers him his first bridge away from a relationship solely with his primary parent outward to an expanding world full of people and experiences.

Father as Support Parent. Those fathers who don't assume the position of primary parent— or couple—are usually more comfortable in the support role and should not be made to feel as though they're not doing their job. From this secondary position fathers have a profound influence on their children's lives and make a meaningful contribution to their development. Yet father in the support parent role often doesn't provide the same amount or kind of nur-turing as mother during those early years. Instead, he offers his child an opportunity to ven-ture further into the world, once the child is fulfilled enough by his mother's nurturing to feel ready to do so. In this way, Mother addresses more of the internal, dependent, survival needs of her child's wanter, while Father provides the child's fulfiller with a bridge to the external world. The combined roles of both parents are essential to the child's security as well as his ability to manage in the larger world, independent of his parents. Thus, ideally both parents will fulfill their roles.

Moreover, mothers must understand that although a father's parenting style may be dif-ferent from hers, it's of equal value and helps their child to overcome his hesitancy and fear in trying new things. Not surprisingly, it's this difference between his mother and father that explains why young children often do better when taken by their fathers to school—or other new experiences—to face the challenges of the expanding world. It's also the reason a child runs to his mother at the end of the day when he has had enough of the rigors of the world and is ready to be shielded once again by her protective arms. It further explains why children with fathers who eagerly expose them to the larger world tend to be more outgoing and less shy or withdrawn.

As a child grows older, his father can continue to provide an increasingly wider bridge to this expanding world by teaching him steadily more about it and encouraging him to venture further and further into it, while still remaining safe.

Dads who pay little attention to their children and fall under the statistics that report fathers communicating with their kids as little as one to ten minutes a day—usually in regard to some discipline issue—create an enormous vacuum in their children's lives. Thus, not only would fathers be wise to recognize the importance of the contribution they can make to their child's development, mothers would be wise to honor—rather than battle—the form it takes when fathers fulfill it.

Blending Primary and Support Parenting. Mothers typically assume the job of nurturing and civilizing the child, while tuning him into such things as his feelings, artistic sensitivities, and an interest in caring relationships, pets, the environment, and others. Fathers more characteristically go on to inspire their nurtured, sensitive, and civilized child to explore the world, seek adventures, extend himself in various situations, and act on the world and contribute to it in positive ways. When both mother's and father's roles are honored and expressed, the child is the beneficiary of a growing balance between the male and female energies within himself. It's this combination of internal feelings—and control over them, as needed—plus external interests and activities that keeps him even in his development. This balance is best assured when mother not only embodies her more nurturing, protective female qualities but is balanced by male energies within herself and thus offers her children a model of a courageous, outgoing approach to life. Likewise, father is most balanced when he expresses his male exuberance but also possesses sensitivity, self-control, and nurturing components within his personality. Moreover, it's helpful when a child views his parents as a loving couple, respectful of the male and female energies within one another. This combination provides him with balanced role models that help him to become a more balanced individual. See **Working Mothers**

Parenting Goals. See Chapter 2

Passions. Wise teachers encourage us to follow our bliss and pursue our passions in order to find success in life. Our passions and bliss can best be found in the things of intense interest to us. Thus, if a child shows an interest in something, wise parents will do what they can to help him explore it, rather than serve as barriers to the discovery of his passions in life. See **Artistic Pursuits**; **Extracurricular Activities**; **Musical Instruments**; **Practicing**

Passive-Aggressive. A passive-aggressive child is one who not only responds passively but with aggression. For example, he resists what is being asked of him by substituting an aggressive behavior such as spilling his paints instead of cleaning them, spitting out his food instead of eating it, or urinating on the carpet instead of getting ready to leave. A child's passive-aggressive behavior is symptomatic of an angry child who needs his relationships with his family healed and balanced in both love and discipline. See **Overcontrol/Overdirection**; **Passive Resistance**; **Passivity**

Passive Resistance. The passively resistant child is one who ostensibly agrees to cooperate but then passively, by dawdling and delaying, refrains from doing so. Such a child can be helped by not allowing his passivity to control you—and your emotions—but to let it impact on *him* instead. For example, if he's not ready to leave on time, the car goes anyway and he must gather himself together as best he can—ready or not. Your job is to remain calm as you continue to go forward with the day. See **Overcontrol/Overdirection**; **Passive-Aggressive**; **Passivity**

Passivity. A passive (inactive, bored, or babyish) child is one who may have overcontrolling and angry parents who have intimidated him; parents who are so overprotective and concerned about his safety and well-being that they never allow him to manage things for himself; parents who swing between overprotection and angry, critical control; and/or parents who have taught him not to defend himself with other children. Parents must first understand that the passive child's development is out of balance; then seek to understand why he is responding to life with such timidity; and finally, address bringing him and his world into better balance.

Such parents can help their child by withdrawing their intimidating anger, overdirectiveness, and control as well as their debilitating overprotection. By doing this, they help him to experience feelings of adequacy as a result of his own interactions with life and the practice he gets with problem solving. Parents would be wise not to entertain the inactive or bored child or to sit him in front of television, but allow him, instead, to experience his boredom until he is moved to respond to life in some way. Once he does become involved, they must allow him the space he needs to figure out how to manage things for himself. See **Anger**; **Fighting**; **Overcontrol/Overdirection**; **Overprotection**; **Passive-Aggressive**; **Passive Resistance**; See Chapters 1, 7, and 10

Peer Clusters. When two or more young people hold the same point of view—such as that drugs are harmless or that it's okay to lie to parents about plans—this shared opinion makes them part of a *peer cluster* that is so powerful that adults will find it difficult to counter. Parents should be aware of the peer cluster their child spends time with and what beliefs and attitudes that cluster holds, since those ideas will soon be the ones their child will most likely champion. When a negative cluster is in its early formation, parents can strive to befriend, and influence the ideas of, the whole cluster. If the cluster is both established and determined to remain rebellious, parents would be wise to steer their child toward new friends, before he gets too involved and becomes highly identified with the negative cluster. Or they can let their child know that he may spend time with this group only if he's able to hold onto their family's standards. This option can only work when a minority of the members of a cluster are rebellious, while the majority maintain higher standards of behavior. When an entire cluster is rebellious, most kids will follow suit. Consequently, parents must consider the option of restricting their child from spending time with a group determined to rebel. See **Peer Pressure**; **Rebellious Friends**; See Chapter 12

Peer Pressure. We are all affected by peer pressure, and so are our children. In short, we all want to fit in and do what others are doing, since those activities become the norms of our times. Fortunately, peer pressure can be just as positive as it can be negative, since genuine friends interested in being their best have a positive influence on us as well as on our children. Not surprisingly, our children will tend to pick more positively oriented friends if they have been treated well at home, have good relationships with family members, and are used to living with openness, honesty, and high standards. On the other hand, children who have lived in homes filled with fighting chaos or have broken familial relationships and thus sneak and lie to their families will be most vulnerable to the influences of negative peers. In short, the closer your child feels to you and the more he shares himself openly with you, the more he will pick friends that share your values and approach to life.

When a child experiences pressure from his peers, it's helpful to acknowledge how difficult it is for him to go against the group. It's also important that he realize how critical it is that he not betray his own standard of behavior in order to keep such friends. In fact, when friends require that of him, the value of their friendship becomes questionable. Help your child understand that friends don't want to go against his ideas or give up his friendship any more than he wants to lose theirs and that he has more latitude for individual behavior and holding to his values than he realizes. See **Peer Clusters**; **Rebellious Friends**; See Chapter 12

Perception-Checking. See Chapter 11

Performance Anxiety. Performance anxiety develops when there is too much attention focused on what a child does and how well he does it. Children actually perform best when they engage in activities without self-consciousness, concern about the outcome, or doubt in their ability to keep others happy with their results. See **Praise**; See Chapters 3, 10, and 11

Permissive Parenting. Permissive parenting occurs when the urge to nurture gets so out of control that parents lose sight of when to say "No," and fail to provide equally important requirements for boundaries and discipline. This results in hesitant, pleading, submissive, and powerless parents left without tools for dealing with rude, uncooperative children. See **Nurturing**; **Overprotection**; See Chapter 1

Persistent. See **"Challenging Child"**; **Negative Persistence**; **Resistant Child**; **Rigid**

Phobias. See **Anxiety**; **Death, Fear of**; **Fear**; **Illness**; **Post-Traumatic Stress**; *School Phobia* subentry under **School, Reluctance to Attend**; **Separation Anxiety**

Pinworms. When a child's behavior seems irritable, particularly in the evenings, combined with itching in the anal or vaginal area or a loss of bladder control after prior success with toilet training, check for pinworms. (This is best done with a stool sample, rather than invading the child's anal area with searches and swabs—which only reveal *active* egg-laying worms and thus offer insufficient results.) Pinworms are common, particularly among preschool and elementary children as they get passed among kids in sandboxes and on playgrounds. Those who are sensitive or have allergies are most bothered by them and may seem emotionally fussier and less stable as a result of the stress they experience from the parasites. See **Toilet Training**

Playpens. Playpens give parents of a newly mobile child brief breaks from watching him and can be used to keep him safe during those times when parents are on the telephone, cooking, or showering. However, it's best to avoid using playpens for long stretches of time, since the child needs time to crawl and explore as part of his developmental process. When your child has outgrown playing in the pen around the time he begins to walk and becomes even more mobile, it can be used as a place for time-outs on those occasions when he doesn't want to voluntarily accept the boundaries you have set for him. However, once it is used for time-outs, the playpen should no longer be employed for play or parent breaks. Instead, you can gate your child in a safe room while you are showering or are overly distracted by such things as phone calls. See **Door Barriers, Gates**; **Exploring, the Young Child**; **Safe-Holding**; **Time-Outs**

Polarizing. Polarizing results when each parent moves to the extreme end of the parenting continuum between structure and nurturing in an effort to balance the parenting style of their mate who is on the opposite end of the scale. Polarizing not only causes each parent to go out of balance and parent ineffectively, but creates a triangle in which the two are fighting over the management of the child, with each one viewing him as a victim in need of saving from the other. A child raised in such a triangle usually identifies with the victim role in life and recreates it in settings outside of his home.

Post-Traumatic Stress. When a child has had a frightening or traumatic experience—including such things as a serious illness, brush with death, or death in the family; a car or other serious accident; a violent storm, hurricane, or earthquake; a robbery, abduction, abuse, molestation, or violence—he may develop symptoms of post-traumatic stress, including flashbacks (or flooding of memories of the event accompanied by the original intense emotions that took place at the time of the event); emotional numbing of responsiveness to the world and others, blunting, extensive daydreaming, and detachment (all used to dissociate or distance himself from the pain and fear of the event); sleep disturbances in both falling and staying asleep; hypervigilance and inability to relax; an increased startle reaction and other anxiety reactions; impaired memory, concentration, and functioning; an increase in withdrawing and avoidance; and obsessive and repetitive thoughts, and/or compulsive behaviors (designed to go back and redo the experience as a way of gaining control over the outcome of the event in an attempt to reduce the anxiety that goes with it). Any stimulus that is similar to the triggering event or by association reminds the child of it can trigger these symptoms. Often triggers become progressively generalized as well as autonomic and thus create a great deal of free-floating anxiety for the child.

I noticed in my counseling practice that even the less dramatic "traumas" such as disquieting newscasts; disturbing television programming; overly aggressive programs for teaching stranger-awareness to children too young to handle it; being picked up unduly late from school; or being harshly spanked, yelled at, or criticized can also trigger symptoms of post-traumatic stress in young children. This observation helped me to realize that sensitive children often experience an ongoing underlying post-traumatic reaction to these common events that were experienced earlier as traumatic for them. When post-traumatic stress is ongoing and long-term it seems to serve the purpose of repeatedly going back to the original event to redo the intolerability of the experience or find a way to gain control over managing the trauma of it better. When post-traumatic stress is involved, a child needs to understand that the anxious feelings come only when he is reminded in some way of the original thing that frightened him and that his body now braces itself—often even releasing adrenaline—to prepare him for a recurrence of the scary event. This anxious response is autonomic and out of his control until he changes his mind about the intolerability of the event.

Thus, it's useful to teach the child to communicate with his body to let it know that the trauma isn't going to happen again, and that his body doesn't need to continue to get prepared for the event or figure out how to cope with it; nor does he need to erase or redo it. His job is to accept that it happened, that he got through it, and that it's over. Sometimes the event and his response have become so deeply ingrained in his neurology that he will need professional help to reprogram his reaction.

The sooner this cycle of going back over a feared event—and reexperiencing the fear without any improvement in the situation—is broken, the better chance a child has of not becoming even more afraid in an increasingly generalized way of life's events or his anxious response to the fear they evoke. If this doesn't help within a couple of weeks, seek professional help (preferably with someone trained in a technique called EMDR, which is particularly effective for this type of problem). See **Anxiety**; **"Challenging Child"**; **Compulsive Behaviors**; **Death, Fear of**; EMDR; **Fear**; **Habits**; **Illness**; **Negative Persistence**; **Obsessive Thoughts**; **Professional Help**; **Sleep Problems**; *School Phobia* subentry under **School, Reluctance to Attend**; **Strangers**; **Tensional Releases**; **Tics**

Practice Technique. When a child resists doing such things as coming in from play, brushing his teeth, feeding the cat, or emptying the dishwasher when asked, he can be required to *practice* responding to such requests until he seems willing to respond without resistance. See **Consequences**; See Chapter 7

Practicing. Be open to letting your child discover his artistic and other interests without thwarting his explorations during those times you view his practice levels as insufficient and uncommitted. Also be careful not to become angry should he discover that any of the explored activities prove not to be of continuing interest to him. View pursuits and lessons, instead, as a way for him to discover his interests and talents. Yet also help him to understand that higher levels of accomplishment in these areas will require the discipline of practice as well as an ability to push through those times when he's going from the novice to the knower. Next, help your child select activities that will be manageable for someone his age and then find a good teacher or coach, known for both inspiring and holding the interest of his or her students. At that point, you would be wise to leave the requirements for practice up to the teacher and simply support what he or she requires. It's also important to let your child help select his practice times as well as allow time to merely enjoy the music, art, sport, or dance media he has selected. If a child decides he wants to quit his activity or lessons, carefully find out why by offering him a "menu" of possible reasons. If he's withdrawing from effort or errors, show him the problem with this approach to life, and encourage him to stick it out. However, if he has truly lost interest in an activity, allow him to let it go. If he finds it too stressful to practice something like dance or an instrument at the levels required for optimal performance, ask if he would like to continue his lessons with reduced practice time. Children allowed to continue to learn about music, dance, and art, even when they've decided they don't want to strive for top performance, will gain more than the child who's required to withdraw from any activity he views only as a hobby. Children who learn a little bit from a variety of areas end up with increased knowledge and talent as well as improved feelings about themselves. By contrast, kids who are forced to quit due to their lack of ambition or discipline are made to feel like failures. The child who wants to commit to an art form and reaching the top can be shown how to structure the amount of practice needed to fulfill his goal. The key is not to interfere with a child's passions, but to support him in keeping his interest in activities alive. See **Artistic Pursuits**; **Musical Instruments**; **Passion**

Praise. Constant praise can make children feel that normal behavior is so unexpected that it requires unusual measures to encourage it. See Chapter 11

Preschool. Preschool constitutes one of your child's most important school experiences, since it gives him either a positive or negative experience of people outside of the family unit as well as his first impression of school and the learning experience. I believe that preschool teachers should be among our most talented and highly paid and that both teachers and programs should be carefully examined before enrolling your child in school. They should also include a strong social-emotional development program and an innovative learning approach, rather than focus only on a traditional academic-readiness program.

Pride. Parental pride causes parents to focus on what their child can do, rather than on who he is, and puts pressure on him to either perform in a way that evokes pride in them—or its opposite, shame. Thus, it's best when parents realize that their child's activities and accomplishments ought not to be connected to their pride but should, instead, be expressions of his own life. See **Embarrassment**

Primary and Secondary Parenting. See **Parent Roles**

Privacy. Privacy is healthy, whereas secrecy is not. When children who enjoy family connections and fun are allowed to have private time and thoughts, they feel balanced between closeness and individuality and have no need to go underground with hidden secrets. See **Secrecy**; **Lying**

Problem Ownership. If a child is creating a problem, let him know how it impacts on *him*, rather than on other family members. For example, if a child is moving slowly, don't tell him that he will make others late. Let him know, instead, how his lateness will impact on *him*. For instance, you can point out that he will have to go with you, ready or not; that he will lose his choice to join the family if he's not ready and will either be left with a sitter, or, if he is old enough, asked to stay home alone; or, if he's able to get himself to the event, that he will have to come when he's ready and arrive late by himself.

Problem Solving. Children who are encouraged to participate in discussions about how to solve their problems and differences with others; how to reach for their best and highest self; and how the world can be a better place develop skills in thinking and problem solving. Although invitations to participate in solutions must always be included at family meetings and during clearing, it's also useful to include such discussions at dinner and other times. See **Family Meetings**; See Chapter 8

Procrastination. Procrastination develops when an individual acquires an urge to avoid addressing and accomplishing things normally of interest to people and easily handled by most. Not only does this urge to avoid life's activities block the procrastinator's successes in life and damage his or her relationships, it's hard for such a person to feel good about himself when he's letting himself and others down. Since procrastination offers such painful results for the procrastinator and those involved with him, let's examine how this nasty habit gets rooted in the fabric of a personality.

Procrastination is usually a habit that a child develops as a result of being overdirected and overcontrolled by parents or teachers; given too much homework; and/or asked to do too many chores and then given additional chores or assignments once the original ones are completed. Moreover, the procrastinator has often been criticized for the work he has produced. The child in this position feels so overwhelmed by the abundance of directions and projects given to him and the potential for failure they represent that he grows to fear that he won't be able to manage. Thus, he resists addressing tasks in an effort to escape feeling overwhelmed and defeated by them. Before long, the procrastinator focuses on how hard and threatening a task will be, rather than on how interesting and fun it is or on his desired results. These images further overwhelm and worry him, which in turn cause him to recoil ever more diligently from the tasks before him. Although a child's desire to resist and delay doing work under such circumstances is understandable, this reaction prevents him from participating in many pleasurable activities and thus interferes with his personality development and enjoyment of life. If the procrastination habit works for him, the urge to resist and delay deepens within his neurological programming and puts the child at risk for increasingly less participation in life's activities. This, in turn, results in such things as emotional problems, low self-esteem, and the use of drugs and other avoidance mechanisms designed to help him escape even further from life's work, the potential for failure, and the pain he feels about being a procrastinator.

Parents and teachers can assist a child to overcome procrastination by first acknowledging and then withdrawing their dominant and critical styles or unrealistically heavy workloads. They must then be sure to allow him to experience the results of his procrastination, rather than bail him out. Next, they can help their child to see—and feel at the neurological level—that he is missing involvement in life and the pleasure and success that go with work and participation. They can further help him to recognize—and weave into his internal neurological programming—that procrastination is a self defeating habit that he adopted to protect himself from such things as overdirection, extra work assignments, an excess of criticism, and a feeling that he is a failure no matter what he does. He can then reexamine procrastination's role in his life and make a new decision about his attitude toward work and his ability to manage it as well as tolerate any errors he might make in the process. If procrastination is already deeply rooted in his personality structure, seek help from a therapist, preferably one trained in EMDR. See **EMDR**; **Motivation**; **Professional Help**; See Chapter 10

Professional Help. When seeking professional help, get several referrals from friends and doctors, select the therapist who is the most frequently and highly recommended, and then try that person out. You should feel good about your counseling experience and clearer as a result of the direction you are getting. If the experience feels enlightening, continue. If not, keep looking. I recommend that parents who have child-management problems enter into counseling to improve their parenting skills, rather than send their child for help. Similarly, if a young child under six or seven has a problem with such things as confidence, friendships, assertiveness, schoolwork, fear, anxiety, sleep problems, grief, loss, depression, eating disorders, tics, phobias, or general insecurities, I would want to work with his parents first to see what adult strategies could be employed to help him. If his problems persisted or he was older, I would include the child in counseling. By working with the entire family, the therapist not only has an opportunity to deal with family dynamics, rather than view the family from only the perspective of one family member, but families learn what the therapist is teaching their child and how this is accomplished. The exception to this plan is when one parent suspects child abuse or molestation. In such cases, the suspecting parent should act as an advocate for the child and seek individual counseling for recommendations on how to proceed. Counselors can also be alert to such possibilities and have periodic individual sessions with the child—not to suggest that this is happening—but to set the stage for the child to share in the event that it is. Parents must be careful not to allow a therapist to form an alliance with their child or teen against them, since this may serve the counselor's needs for popularity, but is not therapeutic, and can be damaging to the child's development and family relationships. Consequently, families must be informed about what goals are being accomplished, and periodic time for family sessions and with parents alone must be set up in cases when a child is seen individually. A skilled therapist is able to bring families together, rather than cause them to feel more separated during the counseling process; thus, if this isn't happening, reassess if you are with the right practitioner. I would also look for a skilled therapist trained in a useful healing technique called EMDR (Eye Movement Desensitization and Reprocessing). See **Abuse**; **Eating Disorders**; EMDR; **Fears**; **Post-Traumatic Stress**; *School Phobia* subentry under **School, Reluctance to Attend**; **Serious Behavioral and Psychological Problems**

Protecting Family Property. It's important to be clear with your child that you expect him to protect family property when his peers are visiting and that friends are welcome in your home as long as he's able to stand up to anyone damaging it. If he needs help with this, let him know that you will support him by role-playing or modeling how to speak up and say something to his friends. Or the two of you can agree that you will talk openly about the problem to the guest in the presence of your child during his next visit.

Psychological Problems, Serious. See **Serious Behavioral and Psychological Problems**

Punishment. Your goal as parents is to teach your children to want to behave better because it's rewarding to do so, rather than to simply vent your disappointment or inflict angry punishment on them for the times when they fail to do so. See **Consequences**; See Chapters 2, 6, and 7

Quality Time. See Chapter 5

Reactive Attachment and Other Attachment Problems. When bonding breaks are early, severe, or extensive, the child not only fails to surrender to love and guidance, but feels untrusting and rageful. His mistrust and rage prevent him from responding to subsequent attempts to bond with him which further prevent him from becoming bonded. This no-win cycle is called Reactive Attachment Disorder and can be healed with attachment therapy, a uniquely effective treatment for seriously unbonded children who may exhibit some of the following symptoms in response to this break: uncuddly; lack of eye contact on parent's terms; indiscriminately affectionate with strangers; charming but unconnected; inappropriately demanding; destructive to materials, animals, self, and others; lacking impulse control, cause and effect thinking, and a conscience; demonstrating crazy lying without purpose; unpredictable and poor social relationships; abnormal eating; delayed speech; learning lags; and a preoccupation with fire. Other attachment problems in varying degrees often produce similar, though less severe, symptoms and are equally important to treat. Attachment Therapy Centers for treatment: Northwest-206-889-8524; CO-303-674-1910; AZ-602-912-5340. See **Abuse**; **Adoption**; **Bonding**

Reading. How early a child learns to read is completely immaterial, and rushing this process can damage his ability to read as well as his feelings about himself. Young children who have books that are well matched to their ages and interests read to them learn to love reading. Moreover, the better quality a book, the more likely it is to engage a child's sense of magic about language and the written word. Many parents read a bedtime story to their child until he learns to read and then stop this ritual. However, continuing to read books above your child's reading level, but matched to his comprehension and interests, allows him an opportunity to continue to be exposed to good works—whereas when he is relegated only to books at his own reading level, his exposure to literature is limited.

Rebellion. Wise parents, balanced in their parenting, don't accept or allow their teens to be rude or to steal freedoms; instead, they remain in charge while allowing their teens to enjoy progressively more control over their lives in a cooperative, nonrebellious process. Moreover, they rejoice in their teen's increased management of his own life, his eventual independence, and his new attachments outside of the family unit. Thus, rebellion is not only destructive, but an unnecessary aspect of adolescence. See **Challenge**; **Rebellious Friends**; **Refusal to Comply**; **Resistant Child**; **Secrecy**; See Chapter 12

Rebellious Friends. When a child's friends are rebellious, they can have a strongly negative influence on him. Thus, parents would be wise to intercede in such friendships at the outset whenever possible. For details of how to do this, see Chapter 12. See also **Peer Clusters**

Redirecting. Redirecting is a technique used by parents to pull their young child's focus away from an activity that is off-limits toward something he may do. Although this works well for the distractible younger child, it doesn't confront the older one with the reality that he must accept boundaries. Thus, when your toddler first demonstrates his refusal to comply with your efforts to redirect his focus by continuing to go back to the object, he is giving you a signal that it's time to help him realize that there will be occasions when he must accept being thwarted. Under these new circumstances, redirecting no longer works, and you must shift to thwarting him from returning to the desired object, while allowing him to cry as he adjusts to his awareness of this limit. See **Adjustment Period**; **Compliance**; **Exploring, the Young Child**; **Refusal to Comply**; **Resistant Child**; **Rules**; **Tantrums**; **Time-Out**; See Chapters 6 and 7

Reflecting. See Chapter 11

Reflective Interpretation. See **Active Listening**; See Chapter 11

Refusal to Comply. The child who ignores instructions must have his freedom contracted in some way. For example, if a young child refuses to go to his room or come indoors from play, his parent must gently let him know that he has a choice to remain in control of his own body and take himself to the required place or have his parent do it for him. The older child who has failed to come in from play when called must be required to miss the first half-hour or so of play with his friends the following day, and the one who fails to clean up his mess is simply not free to do anything else until he has done so. A child refusing to comply may also be asked to do a *practice* session of responding to instructions. The teen who refuses to comply is more difficult to handle and may require a more complex solution (see Chapter 12) or professional help if taking a stand doesn't result in his surrender. See **Adjustment Period**; **Compliance**; **Exploring, the Young Child**; **Oppositional Child**; **Practice Technique**; **Professional Help**; **Rebellion**; **Redirecting**; **Resistant Child**; **Rules**; **Safe-Holding**; **Tantrums**; **Time-Out**; See Chapters 6, 7, and 12

Regression. Spurts of growth and moving toward independence are generally followed by periods of regression in children. Parents anxious to have their child develop precociously will have trouble accepting these regressed periods of behavior and often feel impatient and angry at him for his immaturity during these stages. This causes him to lose trust in the reliability of their love, and he becomes less secure. Wise parents learn, instead, to accept these periods of regression and embrace the child who wants to check back with them or sit in their laps in order to shore up his courage to go out into the world once again. See **"In-Arms" Period**; **Lap-Sitting**; See Chapters 3 and 4

Relaxation. Relaxation is best achieved by giving your young child a lot of "hang out" time in your lap. You can guide a particularly active child to consciously tune into your calmer energy and match his to it. This can be facilitated by putting your hand gently on his hand or leg or over his heart so he can experience your calmer energy through touch. You can further focus on breathing calmly and slowly together, like ocean swells rising and falling. He can put his hand on his abdomen to feel the "wave" within him rise and then fall. Gazing at burning candles (under supervision), an aquarium tank, or into a fireplace also helps overactive children to relax. Older children who still require practice can listen to meditation tapes that provide soothing music or nature sounds. Once a child has practiced learning how to relax, he can call on this ability during times when he's feeling worried, stressed, or just plain "hyper."

Reminding. There are two parts to a chore: 1) telling oneself to do it, and 2) doing it. When parents are required to take responsibility for the telling part through reminders, their child owes them an additional chore in return. This additional chore creates a useful consequence for children who wait for reminders to fulfill responsibilities. See **Consequences**; See Chapter 6

Resistant Child. Many parents teach their children to resist directions by first putting pressure on them to do more than they can manage and/or failing to follow through on those directions or tasks that they have assigned. In other cases, children become resistant and avoidant as a result of fearing mistakes and effort or because they have never been required to do anything they don't like. Once resistance takes hold in the personality, it becomes a problem for the child, as he not only resists rules and boundaries, but may resist cooperating with peers or participation in general. Parents who overpressure and overdirect must back off; those who don't follow through must reverse this tendency; and all parents of resisters must help their child to make new decisions about effort and error in life, rather than remain stuck in his avoidance pattern.

Remedy for Resistance. Regardless of how it began, resistance must be addressed and compliance attained. Thus, if you are clear to consistently contract freedoms for broken rules in a neutral manner, yet your child continues to resist, an additional contraction of freedom for the resistance should be applied to the program. (These can include the kinds of things he likes that you would be happy to be rid of such as the loss of a negative computer game or questionable TV program.) If he's still resisting, apply a second loss, then a third. If he's still resisting, have him call it a day or remain in his room with no further freedoms except to prepare for a meal in his room and bed early. No matter how much he rebels, stick with it while remaining impeccably calm so that he experiences these losses as *his* rather than *yours*. Once he surrenders, clear. Then allow him to assume normal freedoms. Because you will not return any of the possessions that he lost while he was resisting, be sure to take only those things that have a negative influence on his behavior. Refer to Chapter 12 for how to handle the special problems of resistant teens. See **Adjustment Period**; **"Challenging Child"**; **Compliance**; **Lying**; **Negative Persistance**; **Oppositional Child**; **Passive Resistance**; **Procrastination**; **Rebellion**; **Redirecting**; **Refusal to Comply**; **Rules**; **Safe-Holding**; **Tantrums**; **Time-Out**; See Chapter 7

Respect. Respect for adults should not be blind. Neither should it be lacking. Instead, it should develop out of mutual caring between parent and child. Kids who are not allowed to mistreat parents, siblings, or property feel better about themselves than those who sass their families, are rude to them in front of friends, and allow teen guests to destroy family property. Likewise parents who are respectful of the genuine needs of their children, treat them fairly, and allow them ownership and choice over as much of their own lives as possible have the most rewarding relationships with their offspring. See **Rudeness**

Responsible. When a child refuses to use his rules and clean his messes or comply with agreements and requests, he's not behaving responsibly. This is a behavior that is learned from parents who don't know how to maintain their boundaries. Thus, parents of such children must learn to create a framework in which their child's freedoms expand with responsibility, but contract whenever he fails to act reliably. See **Compliance**; **Consequences**; **Resistance**; See Chapters 6 and 7

Restrain. See **Compliance**; **Exploring, the Young Child**; **Playpen**; **Rules**; See Chapters 6 and 7

Results. See **Consequences**; See Chapters 6 and 7

Rewards. Rewarded children tend to focus more on their reward than the task and strive to figure out what minimal level of performance will produce the prize. See **Praise**; See Chapter 11

Rigid. See **"Challenging Child"**; **Compulsive Behaviors**; **Negative Persistence**; **Obsessive Thoughts**

Rituals. Simple bedtime rituals help children to feel more ordered and secure in life and are useful if kept within reasonable bounds. See **Bedtime**; **Sleep**

Rocking. Some children like to rock themselves in their beds as a way to release tension prior to going to sleep. Parents can view the rocking itself as a rather harmless tensional release that usually runs its course sometime between three to four years of age and does not require intervention. Yet because the rocking implies that the child is attempting to nurture himself, parents would be wise to heal any bonding breaks or other underlying problems the child may have that cause him to use this tensional release. See **Head Banging**; **Security**; **Tensional Release**

Roles, Parent. See **Parent Roles**

Room Cleaning. Cleanliness and orderliness are part of discipline and have been recommended by many of the great teachers throughout civilization. Thus, requiring that a child keep his room reasonably clean and ordered is important to his self-discipline and personal development.

Rudeness. Children should not be allowed to be rude to other family members, as this not only breaks down positive family feelings and mutual respect, but makes the child feel bad about himself. A child should also be made aware that his friends become uncomfortable when he's rude to his parents in front of them, and that his friends are most drawn to those homes where there are good relationships between family members. See **Respect**; **Sassing**

Rules. Rules define parental boundaries for children and must be reasonably drawn and then adhered to. Many parents erroneously believe that they can avoid problems with their children by keeping tight controls over them. Such parents allow their kids very narrow parameters of movement that don't match the purpose of their growing-up years and end up with kids who respond with resistance and noncooperation to rules they know are unfair.

Thus, rather than use restrictive rules as a way to prevent problems, parents would be wise to make a conscious effort to expand their boundaries to match the needs of their child and temporarily contract them only when such ample freedom is being misused. In this way, parents with rules that allow their child the freedom he needs to manage his life, explore his own interests, and practice decision-making create an environment in which his urge for independence can flourish, while he practices responsibility and cooperation. See **Boundaries**; **Compliance**; **Consequences**; **Exploring, the Young Child**; **Redirecting**; **Refusal to Comply**; **Resistant Child**; **Time-Out**; See Chapters 6, 7, and 12

Running. Running is the term used for teens who run away from home and stay either with friends or on the streets. Once a teen has an experience of running that has successfully worked in getting him out of school and responsibilities, he not only repeats it, but may become addicted to it. Running is an indication of serious problems, and professional help should be sought. See **Professional Help**

Running Away. See **Chasing**; **Running**

Sadness. The sad child who cries frequently, rarely laughs, and responds only minimally to life does not experience himself as fully loved in a world balanced with structure. As a result he does not believe in himself and may become depressed. See **"Challenging Child"**; **Depression**; **Whining**; See Chapters 1 through 5

Safe-Holding. Safe-holding is a method used to restrain a child during those times when there are no alternate places for him to remain during time-out or when controlling his body is critical to his safety or the safety of others. Safe-holding is accomplished by restraining a child in your lap, while immobilizing his arms by folding them across the front of his body. You may also need to put one leg over the top of his legs to immobilize them, as well as take preventative measures so that he's not able to bang his head into your face or bite your arms. It's critical to remain calm and loving while gently letting the child know that you will release him as soon as he's ready to settle down. Once he relaxes his resistance and begins to surrender, partially release your hold to see if he's ready to cooperate further. If not, return to holding him. If so, continue to gradually release your hold until he will remain surrendered in your lap without any restraint. Once this is accomplished, begin to clear with him. See Chapters 7 and 8

Sassing. The child who sasses is generally trying out the parameters of his power. The more you react with emotional helplessness, the more he believes in your weakness and the acceptability of being rude to you. Thus, you must let him know early that you don't collude with his view of you as foolish and incompetent and that using a disdainful and sassy approach will only cause him to lose his freedom to be with you and others until he's in a more cooperative frame of mind. Let him know that you're always available for a genuine two-way communication, but that a rude approach will never work for him. A sassy child who has been sent to his room can resume normal freedoms and privileges only after clearing. See **Rebellion**; **Respect**; **Rudeness**; **Swearing**; See Chapter 12

School, Adjustment Problems. Many bright kids do poorly when they are the youngest in their classrooms. Thus, their previously well-adapted socialization, learning, and adjustment skills become weakened in these settings, and their self-image is threatened. Consequently, when children are having adjustment problems at school, check first to see if they are in the right grouping. A good formula for determining if a child will be able to keep up with his group is to make sure that he has a minimum of two or more plus ratings out of three sets of criteria as follows. 1) *Chronological Age:* Does the child fall in the top two-thirds of his class in terms of chronological age? If he's in the bottom third, I would give him a −1 rank. These younger children can manage in the setting *only* if they are strong in the other two areas. Thus, the youngest children in a classroom should have +1 ratings in the other two categories. 2) *Developmental Age:* Does the child fall in the top two-thirds of the class in terms of his developmental skills and abilities? These would include such things as his physical coordination and skills; his general knowledge and information; his ability to attend, absorb information, and process it normally; and his readiness for doing the kind of work that will be addressed in his particular group. 3) *Emotional Age:* Does the child fall in the top two-thirds of the class in terms of his emotional maturity and strength? This would include such things as his ability to tolerate frustration, cooperate with others, attract friends, resolve social problems, and genuinely care about others as well as himself. Any child with two or more minus scores should be considered for the next youngest grouping.

School, Reluctance to Attend. In cases where parents are satisfied that a school is good; have acknowledged and resolved their own ambivalence about their child being there; and are sure that he is not too young for his class, they can have the parent with the less intense feelings of attachment between parent and child (usually the father) take him to school; drop him off matter-of-factly with the teacher (so that she can assist him if needed); cheerfully say good-bye (never slip away); and without lingering, leave the room, even if he cries. Parents can further support their child in making his adjustment by getting him to school early while social groups are still forming; inviting candidates for friendship home to play in the context of a more secure environment; and staying in touch with his teacher for information on where the gaps in his adjustment are closing and where he still needs help.

School Phobia. Occasionally, a child will develop a school phobia and not only resist going to school, but will seem unduly anxious and worried about leaving his parents. When there has been undue stress, illness, or a death in the family, the child generalizes that his parents could become overwhelmed by life or illness and die while he's at school. Such a child will make it his job to stay home and protect his parent, usually his mother. He believes that if he can see her, she will be all right, whereas if he loses touch with her, she will be vulnerable. Thus, the child becomes anxious about separation in the same way that he did as a younger child. However, when he was young, he feared separation because he wasn't sure he could get through the day without his mother. Now, it's a defense against how he would feel if he lost his parent altogether. Thus, it's important to be aware of false illnesses and other excuses he will use to stay home and not succumb to these, as it makes his phobia worse when he succeeds in staying home to guard mother. However, it's also critical to help him understand why he has become so worried as well as to clear up the distortions he has about illness and death. For example, it's important to help him understand that people don't usually die until they are old and tired of living or for some other reason feel ready to die, and that his family members are healthy, aren't ready to die, and clearly plan to stay with him. In the unlikely event that this does not turn out to be true, the child will be required to confront that real loss (and the broken promise) at that time, rather than the imagined one he is presently experiencing. In other cases, a child will become fearful about separating from his parents as a result of post-traumatic stress. When school phobia persists beyond a few weeks after first being addressed, seek professional help, since it can develop into a serious anxiety disorder if not treated. See **Anxiety**; **Death**; **Fear**; **Illness**; **Post-Traumatic Stress**; **Professional Help**; **Separation Anxiety**

School, Schoolwork. See **Grades**; **Homework**; **Study**

Scratching. See **Biting**

Seat Belts. See **Car Behavior**; **Car Seats**

Secrecy. It's important that families not keep secrets, since this creates a confusing world for their children. Because children are intuitive and can sense what is happening around them, they know when there is a problem. If it's not fairly explained to them in a clear and open manner, they will not only fill in the details for themselves, but will imagine that the problem is too horrible to share and will assume the worst. Moreover, the only thing worse than having a problem in life is to not know what it is or how to deal with it. This is why conscious awareness and truth are considered to be at the core of mental health, whereas hidden and denied material leads to emotional confusion and illness.

Secrets in families are problematic, whether they are the family's secrets from the world, the parents' secrets from the children, or the children's secrets from their parents. (See **Integrity** for a broader treatment of the problem with secrets.) Children allowed to be separate and different from other family members and have their own friends, life, and activities in addition to the time they spend at home don't feel a need to hide themselves in order to gain individuality. However, when this freedom to function as an individual is denied, kids become secretive and deceitful. Thus, families with kids who have gone underground would be wise to look at how they handle their child's truths to see if they are giving him enough freedom to do those things of interest to him and his age-group that are generally allowed by other families. See **Honesty**; **Integrity**; **Lying**; **Overcontrol**; **Overdirection**; **Privacy**; **Truthfulness**; See Chapter 12

Security. A young child feels secure when he has received ample doses of bonded love and has not endured any big traumas. As he gets older, this initial security is maintained by having structure a part of his life as well. Once security is established, it's easier for the child to remain secure, even in the face of life's difficulties. By contrast, when children have experienced early bonding breaks and trauma and are insecure from the outset, they require remedial experiences of being loved in order to heal the earlier wounds. This is why access, lap-sitting, and touch are so powerful in helping children to heal previously broken bonds with their parents as well as early childhood traumas. Sometimes this connection with love is not experienced until the child is grown to adulthood and visualizes a loving lap to sit on during meditation. See **Access**; **Bedtime**; **Bonding**; **Carrying**; **"In-Arms" Period**; **Insecurity**; **Lap-Sitting**; **Nurturing**; **Touch**; See Chapters 1, 2, 3, 4, 5, 6, and 7

Security Blankets and Objects. Because young children often become attached to security blankets and other objects, it's best to have a plan to help them gradually release them. For example, if a child is developing a connection with a blanket and a stuffed animal, you might let him know that the blanket is for the bed only, but the animal may go other places. Moreover, because self-stimulating behaviors such as thumb sucking, or hair twisting often accompany the security blanket or object, parents of children over two to two-and-a-half may want to require that the object be used in this way only when the child is in a cuddle corner, or in his room. On the other hand, if he's willing to just hold the object, it may remain with him in other, more social and interactive situations as well. Once he's ready for preschool, use the rules of his school. Most will allow the object to come to school and remain in his cubby until naptime. If your child is able to take a similar object to school and leave it there, he has less of a chance of losing his treasured object in transit. Make this clear to him and let him decide. Most kids are ready to give up these objects when leaving the house by the time they are about three to four years old and keep them on their beds for nighttime comfort or when they are having a problem or have been sent to their rooms. If a child hasn't done this naturally by the time he leaves preschool, a new parameter can be drawn for him. At this point, he might be required to leave his security object at home unless he's going overnight to Grandmother's or on a family trip. If a child is having trouble during rest time in kindergarten without his comfort object, he might want to consider a smaller, less conspicuous alternative to tuck into his sleeping mat. See **Comforters**

Self-Centered. See **Egocentric**

Self-Esteem. Self-esteem or feeling good about oneself comes from serving both the needs of the higher and world self. Thus, if we both teach our kids to choose the kinds of values that will please the higher self and teach the skills for living out those values that will satisfy the world self, they will feel good about the kinds of choices they make and their ability to manifest those choices. This, in turn, will cause them to feel good about themselves and experience high self-esteem.

Self-Image. See **Thoughtforms**

Self-Righteousness. The need to be right all of the time causes problems for the child, since it prevents him not only from admitting to his errors and correcting them, but from being honest and open with himself and others about his humanness. A child who feels a need to hide the truth of his errors becomes a defensive person who values winning over all else, including relationships. Wise parents will not only release their child from the race to the top, but will help him to become more comfortable with his mistakes as a way to release self-righteousness as well as the self-loathing that surfaces during those times when he realizes that he's falling short. See **Blame**; **Competitive**; **Denial**; **Error**; **Failure, Fear of**; **Jealousy**; **Sibling Rivalry**; See Chapters 2 and 4

Separation. The more balanced the love a child receives, the more secure he feels and the better able he is to separate from his parents. In addition, the more friends and relatives he's exposed to in social situations, the more comfortable he becomes with a variety of people, and separating from his family gets increasingly easier. See **Baby-Sitters**; **Independence**; **Individuation**; **Separation Anxiety**

Separation Anxiety. Parents who are close to their kids, yet also get anxious about their well-being, are more likely to have children who develop separation anxiety. Sometimes this anxiety develops gradually in a child whose parents feel anxious about separation, but most often it begins when there is an illness or death in the family that causes the child to become concerned about the safety of other family members.

Children who experience opportunities to be with others while their parents leave for short periods, as well as those allowed to explore their world without raising their parents' anxiety, are better prepared to separate from family for increasingly longer periods. During the years prior to preschool, a child still unable to separate from his parents can practice doing so by first staying with relatives or a reliable baby-sitter for a few hours until this is comfortable for him, then for an afternoon and later for an evening. The child who learns to manage these short separations gains confidence from his experience that although his parents may leave him, they always return. Such a child will learn over time not to feel so dependent on parents as a result of this opportunity to gradually cope without them. As a result, he won't be so traumatized by staying at school for several hours when he's around two-and-a-half to three years of age, since he will know how to relax enough to adjust to teachers and peers. By contrast, parents who have never allowed others to stay with their child raise kids who often feel dependent and anxious when it's time to separate. This is particularly true when parents haven't resolved their own feelings of anxious attachment. Parents who resist separating from their child are often the ones who don't trust his ability to manage and do much of his managing for him. This too keeps the child more dependent on his family.

Although short periods of separation strengthen a child's ability to manage without his parents, long periods without family are stressful to the young child. Thus, parents with children under three (or four with sensitive children) would be wise not to leave their child in school for more than thirty hours a week or take trips away from him, since such lengthy separations from both parents may raise his anxiety and increase his insecurity.

When a baby-sitter or day care center are new to the child, provide ample time for him to become familiar with them before leaving. However, if he gets upset and begins crying, rather than spend this time becoming familiar with his new setting, you may have to leave, since staying at this point only adds to his anxiety, drags out the painful part of the separation, and gives him false hope that you will change your mind. Be assured in knowing that the crying represents his adjustment period to separating from you and will eventually stop. In fact, once he accepts the situation, he usually enjoys himself. However, when young children are strongly protesting separation, it's an indication that they are not ready for a long break from you. Thus, returning after a few hours initially will help to build up his tolerance for separation without overwhelming him.

Parents often make separation from their child worse by their own anxieties about it, which the child picks up intuitively. He might not have been so concerned, but becomes so when he senses that his parents are worrying about leaving him. Thus, parents must realize that leaving their child from time to time makes him a more flexible and independent person and is good for him, so long as they keep the separations brief for the young child under two and moderate for the child under three, unless he requests staying with friends or at school longer.

Sneaking Away. Be sure *never* to sneak away from your child after he has fallen asleep or is distracted, since the child who later notices that you are missing feels betrayed. His anxiety about your leaving is raised because he now feels that he has no way of knowing when it will happen next. Thus, it's essential to face the child with the reality that you are leaving, even if it provokes a lengthy crying period as he adjusts to it. See **Anxious Attachment**; **Dependence**; **Independence**; **Individuation**; *School Phobia* subentry under **School, Reluctance to Attend**

Serious Behavioral and Psychological Problems. The following behaviors in children and teens should be taken seriously and professional help sought: obsessive pattern of thinking; repetitive, compulsive behaviors; repeated masturbation; school or other phobias; extensive and persistent tantrums; a sudden change in behavior (including a drop in grades, insomnia, loss of or increase in appetite, drastically different friends); change in appearance (including sloppy dress, red eyes, weight loss, and negative attitude); full-scale defiance and rebellion; persistent lying and/or stealing; persistent aggressiveness; enduring feelings of hopelessness (a flat affect, excessive sleep); intense concerns about weight, food intake, and compulsive exercise.

Other symptoms of even more serious proportions include prolonged sadness and crying, referring to self negatively, and alluding to suicide; paranoid concerns about people watching him or plotting against him; constant hopeless and negative thoughts; persistent sleep disturbance; hearing voices; hallucination; delusions; inappropriate laughing; conversations that don't make sense or sound as if he's talking to someone within a dream sequence; serious, persistent suicide threats—including details of how to do it and actual attempts; persistent cross-dressing; persistent wishing to be the opposite sex; persistent fire setting; persistent cruelty to animals; persistent acting out; persistent destructive behavior; urinating or defecating in inappropriate places; persistent feces smearing; eating plaster or other nonedible things; engaging in fetishes or unusual sexual behaviors; and long-term eating disorders. See **Professional Help**; **Reactive Attachment and Other Attachment Problems**

Sex Education. See **Sexuality**

Sex Play. Sex play involves children exploring their sexual parts with one another, sometimes including stimulation. Parents must not shame and frighten children or make them feel guilty for this very normal exploration. On the other hand, it's best to redirect the play and let the children know that it's not a choice to continue to do this. If the sexual explorations continue, calmly let the children know that they need to find other things to do and are not free to play behind closed doors. In rare instances, a young boy will attempt to penetrate a young girl's vagina. This is usually the result of having been overexposed to adult sexual activity or adult television and should gently be explained as something done only by adults. If a child persists in sex play after you have provided him with gentle guidance, additional supervision, and structured activities, it may indicate that he is a victim of sexual molestation. Seek professional help. See **Masturbation**; **Professional Help**; **Sexuality**

Sexual Abuse. See **Abuse**; **Sex Play**

Sexual Identity. Most boys naturally identify with being male, while most girls identify with being female. However, young children can get confused about their own sexual identity when parents go too far in their efforts to blur gender differences. Thus, in homes where sex-typing is strenuously avoided or a young boy is encouraged to wear female clothing on a regular basis and is allowed free access to such things as his mother's underwear and makeup drawer for dress-up, he may become a bit confused about his sexual identity. This is particularly true when such a boy has been very closely identified around the ages of three to six with a more visible, more powerful, or more beloved mother and does not have a strong relationship with an absent or weaker, less valued father or another male. When his sexual identity as a male is made clearer and he has more opportunities to identify with his father or other males, many of these boys become identified with being male once again. Some theorists believe that girls with sexual identity problems are also lacking in close relationships, primarily with their fathers and possibly with their mothers as well—rather than just with their mothers (or parent of the same sex) as seen with boys. When a child's gender differences no longer remain blurred, and he or she has more opportunities to relate to father—or mother if she, too, is part of the missing parent picture—gender identity confusion may resolve itself. Yet in cases when a child's sexual identity confusion persists after these measures have been taken, it's a good idea to seek professional help to explore any additional conflicts that may be involved or to help both the child and his family accept this difference in him. See **Professional Help**

Sexuality. When parents are not embarrassed about sexuality, they are able to more naturally and freely talk about it as one of life's many topics. For example, naming bathroom and sexual parts honestly while offering basic information about them—such as that your urine leaves your body through your penis or babies get out of their mother's uterus through an opening called the vagina—as well as fully answering any of the child's specific questions would be the most natural response. Furthermore, if a young girl notices her brother's penis and asks her mother what it is, mother must not assume that since her daughter has not asked for more detailed information that she only wants the name for the penis. This is a natural opportunity to teach her child something about the names and function of genital parts.

Taking cues from their particular child is key, and parents would be wise to listen carefully to his questions, as they provide information regarding what he is both interested in and ready to learn more about. On the other hand, when parents use their child's sexual questions as an invitation to tell him the whole story about sex, they are going too far in the same way they would be going too far if they told the child interested in a cow the whole story of dairy farming, the nutritional components of milk, and how it's marketed. Be aware that a child is more comfortable with sexual information when parents don't personalize sexuality between themselves but refer to sexual experience in terms of a man and a woman. When parents are matter-of-fact about sexual topics, the child feels informed yet not overly stimulated by the information. When children become too focused on their genitals, parents must not only consider what's motivating this, but supply appropriate boundaries. See **Masturbation**

Talking to the Older Child About Sex. Once parent and child have established a foundation on which to build continued sexual information as the child grows into it, the child feels comfortable discussing sexual topics with his parents, rather than relying only on the limited, often incorrect, information of peers. When your teens are ready to learn more about sexuality, they may explore this subject with you or they may prefer to get their information elsewhere. Thus, your job is to be willing to keep the topic open in the event that they feel more comfortable learning from you as well as provide them with other sources of information such as books and tapes. At this point, it's useful to share with your adolescents the value of waiting until they are old enough to emotionally handle a sexual relationship as well as being sexual only with partners with whom they are in a serious and long-term relationship—and perhaps even waiting until marriage. It's also critical to emphasize the importance to the success of all intimate relationships of knowing and caring for the other person at a deep level before becoming sexually intimate. It's important for young people to understand that this approach is not only more rewarding, but that relationships based on the foundation of friendship are more lasting.

In the event a teen does become pregnant, it's critical that her parents are able to remain calm and mature in helping her confront this very serious matter and the profound decisions facing her. It's important to note that families with calm, open communication around the topic of sexuality are less likely to find themselves confronting such problems. In fact, statistics show that kids who have had an opportunity to discuss sexual matters with their families do not become promiscuous as some parents fear, but actually delay their sexual experiences and are more likely to use caution and contraception. See **Masturbation**; **Sex Play**; **Sexual Identity**

Sharing. Rather than ask the child using a community activity to share it, it's more effective to ask the child fussing about having a turn to look for something that is not in use and available. This reduces the anxiety each child feels about the kind of sharing that requires a child to surrender his activities to others who are asking to use them. Releasing this rule for required sharing results in far fewer squabbles among children. It's also important to help children distinguish between the kind of sharing that requires giving up activities to jealous friends and the kind that supports using games and activities with friends because it's more rewarding than playing with them alone. See **Cooperation**; See Chapter 10

Shyness. The shy child is one who has become overly focused on himself and his performance, often as a result of parental expectations and praise. His parents have given him so much feedback on his behavior, either by praising or criticizing him that he fears he will be judged either positively or negatively for everything he does. Being in the spotlight like this makes him self-conscious and anxious to withdraw from the agony of so much focus. Families of shy children often judge others outside of the family unit as well, which causes their child to view judgment as pervasive and something that will be turned on him. As a result, he feels even more fearful of the judgments of others and worries not only about how he is doing, but how he is being perceived. These concerns make him afraid of failure which, in turn, causes him to feel self-conscious, competitive, and defensive, while simultaneously anxious to withdraw in order to avoid any judgment of his mistakes. Over time, shy kids become avoidant, low risk-takers. Thus, parents of shy children would be wise to withdraw so much fuss over them, whether it be in the form of expectations and praise or directing, correcting, and criticizing their performance. They would also be wise to curb their judgments of others outside their family unit and bypass the debilitating feelings of separation from others that judgment creates.

With the exception of babies first getting used to people, I ignore the signals that shy children send out not to get too close, but slowly and gently desensitize them to my presence. Yet when I am close, I am also careful not to focus on them so much that they feel a need to withdraw. In this regard, it helps to remember that a shy child is like a turtle. When he comes out of his shell a bit, it's critical to approach him slowly and sideways rather than frontally and boldly. Thus, it works best initially not to ask him too much about himself but about other things such as animals, teachers, friends, and activities while looking together at some common object. When people offer gentle friendship to a shy child, his parent would be wise to allow time for a connection to develop, rather than answer for the child as though his silence was a problem and a better "performance" was required.

Shy children also become more outgoing after developing closer relationships with their fathers. This happens, in part, because father serves as a secondary matrix or bridge to the outside world for the child, but also because his less protective, more rough-and-tumble style helps the child to overcome his sensitivity and fears of the larger world. See **Critical**; **"Challenging Child"**; **Eating Disorders**; **Judgment**; **Parent Roles**; **Resistant Child**; See Chapter 10

Sibling Rivalry. When I checked one morning to see how some birds nesting on my patio had survived a stormy night, I saw that the mother had left the nest, while one of the babies had his wing spread over his weaker sibling, who later died. I was struck by this protective gesture and felt vindicated in my belief that the natural state of siblings is to care for one another. Expecting siblings not to get along and "compete" for love is a problem in our society and often results in a self-fulfilling prophecy. I think we can change this outcome by establishing different expectations as well as handling siblings differently. When we consider the higher goals of humanity and the purpose of a lifetime, learning to get along with one another is at the top of the list. If such a goal is valid, it becomes apparent that uncovering how to get along with our own family members is of critical importance. Following are some typical problems and new ways to approach them.

It seems that parents who worry most about their older child managing his jealousy of a new baby are the ones whose children are the least resolved in their feelings of jealousy and competition. Ironically, fears about being loved as much as the baby often get started when parents feel a need to insist on how loved and special the older child is, while minimizing or hiding their love for the baby. Rather than help their oldest to relax, this gives him the feeling that his parents are capable of loving their children unevenly. Thus, even though he may currently be in the alleged preferred position, he realizes that this could shift, and he could become the one who is out of favor.

Parents can better help their children to relax the scales over which child is loved the most by not joining them in this concern or hiding their love of one from the other. Children do better when their parents openly and abundantly demonstrate their love for all of their children, as this helps them to release any concerns they might have that love is so fragile or limited that it must be parceled out in secret. When you love the baby openly, while treating the older child as lovingly as you always have, the older one begins to adjust to the reality that love is not reserved only for him as he had hoped, but neither is it lost to only the baby as he had feared. This message can be further reinforced by not engaging in reassurances or arguing against his doubts about being loved. Instead, you can help him during a one-time discussion to clarify his distortions about how love works. Ask such questions as, When you're petting the dog do you still love the cat? And when you're with Grandma do you still love me? What happens to your love? Does it expand in your heart to include everyone you care about or do you run out of love? By this line of questioning you help your child to realize that love is not meant to be focused singularly on one person. In fact, it's not only unlimited, but is most enjoyable when expressed abundantly.

Another error parents make is to remain overly protective of the baby. In fact, rather than let the older child be fully involved right from the beginning, they often resist letting him hold or play with the baby as much as he would like, somehow not trusting his intentions and thinking that his handling will be harmful. Showing the older child, instead, how to handle the baby and then trusting him to manage—just as you have had to do—allows them to bond and feel closer to one another from the beginning. Leaving him out of this phase of the experience cuts him off from the positive feelings he was all set to share with the baby.

Such overprotection of the "baby" often continues as the children get older, and many parents require only their older child to follow the rules and be responsible. This overzealous protection of the younger sibling leaves the older one defenseless to protect his things or himself, and he is typically blamed for every problem between them or assigned to clean up their messes. Moreover, although the older one is often put in charge of the younger sibling, he's given no authority to manage him, and is then reprimanded for not keeping things under better control. This interrupts the natural flow of love between siblings, as the older child learns to view the younger one as a pest who gets him into trouble. He feels angry at all the things the "baby" gets away with and often retaliates by teasing, hurting, and rejecting him. Thus, it's also a losing proposition for the younger sibling, who would love to be friends with his big brother or sister.

The situation is worsened when parents view the older child as a troublemaker whenever there is a problem and hold him responsible for keeping the peace, since he's the older and more reliable child. The less successful the older child is in keeping the peace, the more his parents blame him. Consequently, their feelings toward him steadily fill with annoyance, and the younger child often begins to be genuinely favored. This is the most injurious thing parents do to destroy positive relationships among siblings. Thus, parents guilty of this would be wise to not only confront their own feelings and actions, but heal them if they are unjust or uneven.

In yet other situations, sibling rivalry grows out of a child's distorted view that the love and success his siblings experience will prevent the love and success he will have. Assuring such a child that he is, in fact, loved only increases his anxiety over this issue, since he senses that his parents are joining him in his concern about his lovability. It's also fruitless to try to give each child special time alone with you, since his world now includes a sibling and he must begin to adjust to that reality. Besides, the goal of life is not to hang onto the myth that we can have the love of our parent—or one other person—all to ourselves. We must learn to join in love—rather than divide and compete—and our family unit is a good place to start.

Don't concern yourself with keeping things equal. It's simply a fact of life if the younger one gets more privileges than the older one did at that age. On the other hand, if he's not managing these early freedoms, don't contract the privileges of your older child to make the baby feel better about having his reduced. Likewise, if only the older one is ready for some additional privileges, don't hold him back to wait for his sibling.

Siblings get along best when they are allowed to control when their sibling may enter their bedroom or side of a shared room. In this way, a child is required to use the rules of his sibling—which include not handling personal toys unless permission to do so has been granted—in order to remain in his sibling's personal space. If he doesn't conform, he may lose his choice to stay.

Finally, trying to adjudicate sibling fights in order to determine which child needs punishing puts parents in the middle and reinforces the fighting behavior. The more parents interfere or take sides in sibling relationships, the more intense the feelings of jealousy and rivalry between siblings become. Thus, when parents withdraw their interference in sibling squabbles and help only when kids get stuck or ask for help—or when the wrong lesson is being learned—a child no longer feels that he stands to either gain or lose his parent's love each time he has a disagreement with his sibling. Although siblings will continue to have their differences, these battles will lose both their intensity and frequency. See **Competitive**; **Fighting**; **Jealousy**; See Chapters 5, 9, and 10

Single Parents. Almost half of families today are headed by single parents. Although many of these have interested stepparents or family members such as grandparents, aunts, or uncles to help, others hold the responsibility for raising their children entirely by themselves. In many cases, these single parents have also been left with full responsibility for the economic support of their children. When you add one or both of these components to the challenge already inherent in raising children, it can become a rather overwhelming experience.

Another, often overlooked, category of single parent is the parent who lives with a spouse who fails to provide any help whatsoever and may add to child-rearing problems by failing to help financially and/or obstructing the efforts of the parent who is taking responsibility for the children. These parents not only hold full responsibility for raising their children, but are often actively sabotaged while trying to do so. These are the parents who would be wise to face that they are already parenting alone, rather than remain in destructive relationships while clinging to the illusion that they have the support of a spouse.

Although many of the problems of single-parent families are similar to the normal challenges of parenting, the single parent faces the additional problem of doing everything for him- or herself as well as the loneliness of doing such a difficult job alone. Furthermore, mothers—or fathers—with children to support on modest incomes, without adequate child support or other resources, have the overwhelming challenge of managing full economic support of a family. These parents have the greatest challenge of all and would be wise to reach out to uncover any support systems that might be available to them. It's also critical that they utilize whatever family, friend, and economic resources are available to them to establish some competent backup care to give themselves an occasional break from such full-time responsibilities. Many parents in this position benefit from uniting with other single-parent family units to create a larger fam-

ily unit or to go on outings together or to trade services and resources. Others join such organizations as Parents Without Partners or other family oriented groups in order to join with other
like-minded people to share their experience.

Yet as painful as their challenge is, it's important that single parents not use the difficulty of
managing alone as a point of primary focus that further depletes their energies or as an excuse
for not managing at all. Not only do more parents than they realize in dual homes also quietly
parent alone, but confronting the job with commitment and a balance between nurturing and
structure is their *only* hope of meeting the challenge with success. See **Day Care**; **Divorce**;
Parent Roles; **Stepparents**; **Working Mothers, Working Parents**

Sleep Problems.

Nightmares. See separate listing under *Nightmares*

Sleeping with Parents. The jury is still out on whether or not sleeping with parents is harmful to children. (See **Family Bed** for a more thorough discussion of this option.) Be aware
that once a child develops the habit of sleeping with his parents throughout the night, it's
difficult to talk him out of it. Therefore, parents who really don't want their child in bed with
them would be wise not to let the habit get started, even on nights when the child is sick or
awakened by a nightmare. On those occasions parents can return their child to his room,
attend fully to his needs, and then return to their own bed for the remainder of the night.
However, if parents don't mind having their child sleep with them for an extended period of
time, it's okay to allow him into their bed if he needs tending in the middle of the night.

Sleeping in the Child's Room. Parents who abandon their own bed and partner to sleep with
the child give him a confused message about his position in the family and relationship to
that parent. The same confusion is created when parents who don't sleep together invite a
child into their bed. Thus, parents in these situations would be wise to gently attend to their
child's nocturnal needs before returning to their own bed alone for the remainder of the night.
This does not apply to the single parent, since no confusion is created by allowing the child
into the family bed of a single parent household as long as their relationship is healthy, rather
than based on excessive fears, anxious attachment, or seeing the child as a surrogate partner.

Sleeping with Siblings. Although sleeping in separate beds in the same room is acceptable,
sleeping in the same bed with siblings on a regular basis should not be encouraged, since
because it is not supervised as in the case of the full family bed, it can lead to sexual stimulation and play. Thus, children who prefer to have company for the night can sleep in the
same room with their siblings—if they are cooperative—but preferably in separate beds.

Sleepwalking. Sleepwalking runs in families. It indicates deep sleep and may be associated with
other nighttime activities such as bed-wetting and night terrors in which the child appears
to wake up but continues in an agitated dream-state with a sense of terror that is difficult to
calm. (See **Night Terrors**.) All such sleep symptoms may occur when the child is overly
fatigued or under stress or as a result of certain medications. Or, sleepwalking can be a family trait with no psychological impetus behind it. The key is to find ways to keep the child
safe during his nocturnal meanderings. Such things as bells on his bedroom door and latches
on main doors and windows will help to keep him safe.

Sleeplessness. If a child has trouble sleeping, don't focus on what time he drops off to sleep
or put pressure on him to do so. Urging a child to sleep inhibits his natural ability to drop
off and causes him to think and worry about whether or not he's asleep—which of course
keeps him awake. Take both the focus and the pressure off by allowing him to have a night-
light for reading or to listen to music tapes until he feels drowsy and ready to sleep. Don't
check on him or suggest that he'd better get to sleep. With the pressure off, he will eventually learn to fall asleep again without worry.

Wakefulness. When a child awakens in the middle of the night, it's important that parents remember to keep their tending to him low key and boring, so that he won't want to train himself to awaken the following night to be entertained. Thus, if you prefer that he not develop a wakeful habit or begin joining you in bed, rather than bring an awakened child into bed with you, it's best to go to his room to assure him that all is well, that it's still nighttime, everyone else is sleeping, he can go back to sleep, and you'll see him in the morning. If he has trouble with this, allow him to turn on his reading light and look at books or listen to a restful tape. If he continues to call, wait another five or ten minutes before returning to tell him briefly that you're sleeping and will see him in the morning. If he continues to call or cry, wait twenty minutes, then thirty, before returning to his room to again briefly say you'll see him in the morning. Continue thereafter returning every twenty to thirty minutes until he gives up or the sun rises, whichever comes first. If wakefulness continues even when the child is not reinforced for it, check for pinworms or other physical problems. Never require a child to sleep nor talk or worry about whether or not he's able to fall back asleep. Focusing on the need to sleep on command can cause him to become self-conscious and worried about this very natural behavior, both of which are the primary causes of insomnia.

Weaning Your Child from Dependency on You to Fall Asleep. Parents who elect not to use the family bed approach, but who have laid down with their child each night as he drops off to sleep (I do not personally recommend starting this habit), eventually get to the point when they want him to fall asleep by himself. In order to wean their child from this arrangement, parents can let him know he's at an age to manage this by himself and invite him to take this next step in his maturity. They can let him know that they will be in the next room, and that he may use a night-light, a music tape, or books until he feels drowsy enough to fall asleep, but that he must remain in bed, and toys are off-limits. A new or special stuffed animal may help him feel that he has company in the absence of his parents. If such a child should then come out of his room, his parents can—without upset or conversation—take him back and restate that they will see him in the morning. The key is to believe that the child can do it and remain committed to the program, even if his adjustment to it includes crying.

Persistent Sleep Problems. If sleep problems are persistent and/or the onset of sleep problems has followed a stressful or traumatic event, the child may have symptoms of post-traumatic stress. If so, this can develop into a more serious problem if not handled and, therefore, must be addressed. See **Bedtime**; **Family Bed**; **Night Terrors**; **Post-Traumatic Stress**

Snacking. A child should be free to eat throughout the day, rather than be controlled by his parent's timetable. Thus, healthful snacks can be left within the child's reach in a cupboard and/or the refrigerator. See **Eating**

Socializing. See **Friends**

Spanking. Although I believe that parents must use dominance to get resistant children to surrender to limits, there are so many ways—other than spanking—to accomplish this, that hitting a child is simply unnecessary. It is better to give uncooperative children painful losses of freedom and privilege, while allowing them to maintain or expand their freedoms during those times when they are holding their boundaries. Moreover, when angry parents use spanking to discipline, they often lose control and cross the line over to abusive discipline. Ironically, 90 percent of parents disagree with spanking, while 95 percent end up using it. This demonstrates that if parents would take the time to learn the system described in Chapters 6 and 7, they would be more in alignment with the form of discipline they would prefer to use. See **Abuse**; See Chapters 6 and 7

Speech Problems. Speech develops as early as eighteen months in some children and as late as two-and-a-half in others. Both ends of this continuum fall within the normal range, so it's important not to get too concerned if your child is a late talker. Following are some guidelines for determining if a child's speech development is delayed enough to seek a professional opinion: If the child uses mostly vowel sounds in his speech after one year; if the child is unable to name familiar objects, follow brief one-part commands, and is not using simple phrases by the age of two; if the child is unable to follow simple two-part commands, cannot name common objects and body parts, uses no sentences, has many omissions of initial consonants, or speech is largely unintelligible after age three; if there is consistent and frequent omission of initial consonants and substitutions are made for difficult sounds at four; if word endings are consistently dropped, sentence structure is consistently faulty, and the child is embarrassed by incoherent speech after age five; if the child is distorting, omitting, or substituting any sounds after age seven; if the voice is monotone, extremely loud, largely inaudible, or of poor quality and nasal resonance; if the pitch is high and not appropriate to the child's age and sex; if the child does not take turns to speak or consistently echoes what is heard rather than responds to the content; if the child looks confused or blank when spoken to. See **Stuttering or Stammering**

Spitting. Spitting at someone is in the same category as biting, since it's something that others are appalled by and don't want to put up with. Thus, when a child spits, he must be calmly removed from the group and made aware that he will be able to join others only after he is clear about how to behave in a socially appropriate manner. See **Biting**

Spoiling. See Chapter 1

Sports. Children should be encouraged to choose which—if any—sport they would like to participate in, go at their own pace of learning, and quit if they are no longer interested in pursuing it. See **Extracurricular Activities**; **Grades**; **Motivation**; **Skills**; **Study**

Stealing. The young child of two to three takes things because he wants them and does not yet understand ownership. This is certainly not stealing, and a child this age needs only to be gently taught about possessions and ownership, while supervised closely enough to make sure that he's not developing a habit of helping himself to the possessions of others. The more deliberate stealing of a child of four to five is usually a result of not having learned to control the impulse to take something he sees and wants, even though he now knows that it's not his to take. Not only would having these things be of interest to him, he believes that they will help him to be a part of the group he's learning to identify with. Teaching them to control the impulse to take these attractive things is the best antidote to stealing in young children. Thus, alert parents who notice a foreign item among their child's possessions will require that it be confronted and returned, yet, without making too big a fuss over the event. It's important not to ask a child if he has taken something when you know that he has, since this gives him an opportunity to lie about it and compound the problem. Simply start with your awareness of what has happened and begin to remedy it by requiring that he return the object.

Moreover, if something is damaged, the child must work off the bill with chores. If it's a second infraction, in addition to returning the goods, I would require that he not be allowed to play at the "burgled" house until he is very clear about controlling his impulse to possess the things he sees. Wise teachers will remove a child from the area where he took something for a few days.

When an experience fails to provide a child with additional objects—but gives him some loss instead—it's usually not repeated. On the other hand, if he receives a great deal of attention for this deed—even if it's negative excitement—he may be motivated to repeat the behavior. If stealing continues past the second infraction, it's important to help the child understand the effect on *him* of not being trusted—or liked—by others when he fails to respect their property. He must also be made to understand that such a reputation will result in his getting *less* of life's invitations and bounty, rather than *more*.

There are other children who take things as a result of needing more love and fulfillment in their lives, and they attempt to stuff their internal voids with material things as well as food.

Such children improve if their parents learn to heal bonding breaks and bring love into better balance in their parenting. If the problem continues after these measures are taken, seek professional help. See **Conscience**; **"Immature Boss"**; **"Mature Boss"**; **Professional Help**

Stepparenting. Parents must allow their child the freedom to enjoy—and freely love—any steppeople who are brought into his life, since the one positive aspect of divorce is the child's opportunity to enjoy two expanded families. Not only is it cruel for jealous parents to block these relationships, but allowing them enhances the harmony in the child's other home which, in turn, helps his adjustment to the divorce.

By the same token, natural parents bringing stepparents into their child's life must take care to include only those people who are able to care enough about him to offer him mature love. Any stepperson who suggests a natural parent choose between their child and the stepparent is adding further hardship to the child's already disrupted life. Parents would be wise to take a very hard look at anyone who subtly implies or openly requires that such a choice be made. They must further protect their child from a potential or actual stepparent who dislikes their child, constantly criticizes him, verbally or physically abuses him, or seems capable of sexually molesting him.

Problems Between Stepparent and Child. Cinderella is no fairy tale, as many children with stepparents will tell you. It's a story reflecting the many problems and emotions that occur today in the millions of homes involving stepparents and their stepchildren. Although it's painfully difficult to admit, many stepparents—like the wicked stepmother—are not only partial to their own children, but actively dislike their stepchildren or feel jealous of the close relationship the stepchildren have with their natural parent. Likewise, a stepchild can make life unbearable for the most loving of stepparents trying to integrate into the family unit by rejecting them outright or engaging them in confusing power struggles. Because each new stepfamily is built on the foundation of so many old bonds and unresolved feelings, it has a number of obstacles to overcome.

Many problems between a stepparent and child begin with a reluctant child who has already experienced so much loss and unresolved grief as well as a secret yearning for the reunification of his original family that he doesn't dare give his stepparent a chance to get close to him. Or, he may view this new person as the one who displaced his own parent and is now trying to steal his love away as well. Many children feel guiltily disloyal to their natural parent if they happen to like their stepparent and thus strenuously fight against any contact or communication that might lead to positive feelings between them. In some cases, this is their own idea, whereas in others it has been fueled by their displaced natural parent. Others may view the stepparent as an intruder to the exclusive bond they have formed with their natural parent, especially during the period since the divorce.

Other problems begin when a naive or childless stepparent is capable only of loving a stepchild who is perfectly behaved and adult-like or has the maturity to be the first to offer a gesture of love. Others compete with their stepchild for the love of their spouse or feel disloyal to their own children whenever they get close to a stepchild or do anything nice for him. And, still others feel like outsiders, not really a part of the tight family unit that was formed out of the ashes of divorce prior to their arrival. Unable to discipline or find a clear-cut role, such stepparents soon feel out of place, ignored, and hurt, and often withdraw their love. These many complex factors usually result in either the stepparent or child—or both—not being willing to form a relationship.

Solutions. The only way such difficult problems can be resolved is for the adult to put justifiable hurts and irritations aside and maturely begin the process of loving the child without conditions or expectations of love in return. Although the child will rarely have the maturity to initiate making friends, very few children are able to resist being loved unconditionally for very long. Thus, once love and friendship are genuinely—and consistently—offered by a stepparent, the barriers begin to slowly melt away. The following guidelines will help any stepparent dedicated to overcoming the barriers to loving their stepchild.

Earning Love and Claiming Authority. Unlike natural parents, stepparents cannot assume that either love or authority exists in their relationship with the stepchild and must carefully nurture both. Thus, stepparents, ready to give up their own barriers to a relationship, must begin by gaining their stepchild's love. However, before a connection between them can be achieved, the child's natural parent must be willing to help!

The natural parent must first make a concerted effort to integrate the stepparent—and any children that stepparent brings to the new unit—into the bond that has already been established between the natural parent and child, while assuring the child that loving this new stepparent does not reduce his ability to love his other natural parent. In this way, a new bonded unit is formed that offers the child more people in his life to love and enjoy. In addition, he must clearly be given permission to bond with all the people in the new unit his other parent forms as well.

It helps enormously if the child is given permission by his other parent to freely love his new stepparent without guilt. However, when an immature parent is unable to grant this freedom and is determined, instead, to undermine the child's love for the new people in his life, it's important that the immaturity of this parent be exposed to the child in a neutral, nonattacking manner by his other natural parent. When the message is given with compassion, the child is able—without defense or protection—to see the insecurity motivating this other parent's behavior.

Once a child is no longer afraid to love the people in his new family unit, his stepparent must carefully and gently help him to feel safe in their relationship. In order to accomplish this, the child can neither be hurried nor disciplined at the outset, but given the time he needs to slowly develop trust and friendship. When the child's natural parent—the counterpart to the stepparent—is still in the picture, a stepparent would be wise to assume the role of friend, while actively supporting the value of the child's natural parent. However, when the natural parent is out of the picture and the child has released all hope of reclaiming that parent, the stepparent who is willing to assume a full parent role can help the child to complete his grief and replace his loss by stepping into the void created by the absent parent.

In addition, it's critical that the stepparent's spouse—the child's natural parent—be willing to provide clear yet loving boundaries for the child and discipline him whenever necessary—since it would be premature for a new stepparent who has not yet established a friendship with the child to do so. This management of boundaries is essential to the success of a positive relationship between the child and his new stepparent, as it shows the child a united bond between his natural parent and new stepparent. The child who resists rules or courtesy must be gently separated from the family unit by his natural parent each time he crosses these boundaries and then taught that it was his behavior—rather than the new person—that caused him this isolation. Once a child can see that he will be required to behave, he begins to settle down and can better accept the reality of his new family unit.

By contrast, when natural parents erroneously sidestep disciplining their child, they create a feeling of excluding the stepparent while aligning with the child in his rude and uncooperative behavior. This reinforces old bonds formed between them prior to the arrival of the stepparent and blocks any opportunity for new family systems or connections between members of the new unit to form.

On the other hand, firm discipline only works when the child is being irresponsible; it backfires when a natural parent succumbs to meting out unfair rules and punishments under pressure to do so from a jealous or angry stepparent. As we can see, this early period is a sensitive and trying one for any family forming new bonds and must be handled with maturity and care by both natural and stepparent.

The wise stepparent who is backed by discipline from the child's natural parent will work first on achieving friendship before applying discipline. In this way, when the time comes for discipline to be added, it will be delivered with genuine love. However, anytime a child blocks this friendship, yet challenges boundaries that his natural parent is either unwilling or unavailable to uphold, stepparents must move quickly to claim their authority, even if their friendship with the child has not yet been established. However, this should only be done in response to crossed boundaries and must be handled maturely, with calm neutrality. Whether done early or later, at some point stepparents must lovingly claim their authority with the stepchildren in their lives.

The stepparent who is willing to love another's child and offer him fair boundaries while he is still immature and imperfect, without the condition of expecting love to be returned, offers the child a special gift. Although it can take some time and require the help of the natural parent, when this approach is used, most stepchildren will eventually succumb to the power of this unconditional love. See **Divorce**

Strangers. Introducing the idea of how to handle strangers to the very young child of three to five or even six to seven will not keep him safe on his own in public, since studies are showing that even after such training, children will go with a stranger with an interesting enough ploy. Consequently, the very young child should always be under the supervision of an adult while in public and never be required to deal with strangers on his own, since he's neither physically nor psychologically equipped to manage. In view of this, I question the validity of introducing safety programs to children in this age-group. Not only do such programs create deep levels of anxiety and fear in the young child, often resulting in post-traumatic stress disorder (PTSD), they provide early programming of deep feelings that people are dangerous, rather than safe and loving. This sets up a very negative image of an unsafe world and triggers deep mistrust of anyone who is not yet known to him. The image is not a useful one for all of us to carry in our heads and bring into manifestation. For the older child who will not always be in the physical presence of an adult, the basics of not eating candy or food provided by a stranger, not getting close to an individual or the car of someone who has stopped to talk or ask for directions, and never getting into the car of a stranger—no matter how convincing their story—is important information. Nevertheless, even this information must be given in the context that although it must be taken very seriously in order to protect the child from the rare person who has not developed properly and is capable of hurting others, the planet is filled primarily with people who are deeply kind and caring. This image of the hurtful person as unusual in a sea of wonderful humanity is a better image for us to collectively carry in our heads and bring into manifestation. See **Abduction**; **Professional Help**; **Sexuality**; **Thoughtforms**

Stress. See **Fear**; **Habits**; **Post-Traumatic Stress**; **Tensional Outlets**; **Tics**

"Strong-Willed Child." I don't believe that "strong-willed children" are born but that they are created by traumatic births, bonding breaks, unbalanced parenting, parental insecurity with authority, and suggestions about their "willfulness." I suspect most willfulness develops when a child is repeatedly asked to do things; yet when the child fails to do them, nothing happens except another reminder. This pattern trains children to resist responding to instructions and results in the strongly defiant or temperamentally strong-willed child. Other strong-willed children seem to have other bases for their rigidities. To better understand these, see **"Challenging Child"**; **Negative Persistence**; **Resistant Child**; See Chapters 5, 6, and 7

Structure. Structure is critical to balanced parenting. See Chapters 1, 2, 3, 6, and 7

Stubborn. See **"Challenging Child"**; **Negative Persistence**; **Resistant Child**

Study. Only manageable amounts of useful and interesting work should be given to kids by teachers willing to follow through on work not completed. Yet once a child is in a situation where homework is required, even if it's excessive, he will fare better in life if he learns to address it, rather than program himself with a deep dislike of the work and a habit of avoidance and resistance to it.

Accepting Responsibility. Kids who resist doing what is asked of them and refuse to clean their rooms or do their chores are going to have a problem responding to the activities and work given to them in the form of academic assignments. Thus, if your child is still resistant to work and chores in general, you must get him to surrender to including them in his daily living. To do this, you will need to go back to the basics of discipline and gain his cooperation. See **Compliance**; **Refusal to Comply**; **Resistant Child**; **Rules**; See Chapters 6 and 7. Simultaneously, work on the academic problem as follows.

Setting Standards. There are a surprising number of families who are afraid to establish academic standards for their children; thus, they don't require their kids to respond to homework and may even brag of the poor grades they received in their youth. Others announce their acceptance of poor grades so long as their child is doing "his best," implying that his best won't amount to much. Not only is this lack of belief in the child an insult to him, a goal that has never been set will certainly not be reached. Thus, kids in homes with hazy academic goals don't put much effort into their schoolwork. Instead, they develop the habit of ignoring what is asked of them and eventually become desensitized to the bad grades that result. Although these children are spared the criticisms of overly ambitious parents, they are nevertheless damaged by the hidden feelings of failure they experience throughout their school years. They are further injured by their lack of investment in those years and are later baffled to find many doors of opportunity closed to them. Ironically, parents of these young people are disappointed in them for failing to live up to the parent's secret hopes for greater success.

Other families set unrealistic goals for their kids, expecting levels of achievement neither they nor anyone they know has achieved. Even if their child brings home a string of "A's" they focus on his few "B's" or one "C." If he stumbles in his track meet or play performance, they upbraid him for his "failure." Such messages are extremely undermining to a child's self-esteem and desire to keep trying.

The Elementary Years: Developing a Habit Pattern. Parents can help their young child to establish a study habit by consistently, yet supportively, clarifying that homework must be done before free time begins each afternoon. Parents may, for instance, pick their child up from school, stop somewhere or go home for a snack and a leisurely chat together, before setting the child up at a desk or table at home or the office where he is expected to complete his homework. Most young children prefer to do their work at the kitchen table with a parent nearby to help with such things as explanations for how to do their math, spelling help, and word selection. I recommend accommodating these requests, rather than adding to your child's frustration by suggesting that he look everything up. Parents would also be wise to demonstrate a tolerance for error so that anytime their child makes a mistake, he simply corrects it and learns from it without fear of criticism. After a child's schoolwork is finished he is free to play with friends or begin other free-time activities.

It's essential that a child not play in his room or outdoors while his parent periodically nags at him to begin his homework, as this sets up a nag/resistance response to homework between parent and child. Such a pattern gets internalized and ensnares the child in an endless conflict between a need to do his homework and a desire to resist it—which is the beginning of a procrastination habit that can plague him throughout life. By requiring that he sit at a study table until his work is done, his parent can stop all reminding and coaxing and leave it completely up to the child when he wishes to be free again. Eventually, the child discovers that it's in his best interest to address his homework without delays.

It's equally essential that parents not add additional jobs to the ones assigned by school, as the child given extra work after completing an assignment feels discouraged and defeated. He soon learns to delay completing his assignments as a way to prevent more work from being given, a tactic that engenders even more procrastination in his personality structure. Furthermore, parents who add extra assignments to their child's workload would do well to release their attachment to this excessive focus on academic success and notice, instead, how interesting their child is beyond his ability to memorize, recite, compute, or regurgitate predigested facts. See **Teaching, Socratic Style**

The Older Child. The older child of eight, nine, or ten who has clearly established a habit of doing his homework without resistance or a need for prompting and is now faced with increasing amounts to do, should be given an opportunity to play first with siblings or neighborhood friends before tackling this increasingly time-consuming task. Thus, parent and child can work together to select a study time that will work best for the child. Some children will elect to do their homework upon returning home from school, whereas others will want to do it before or after dinner.

If the child who chooses the later study time addresses his homework as planned, he can maintain his new schedule. If he resists and procrastinates, he must do it the following afternoon before play. If he then eliminates the delay that afternoon, he will be given another chance the following day to see if he's ready to play first and do his homework in a timely fashion that evening. If he doesn't cooperate at that point, he should do it before play for the rest of the week and try again the following week to see how he does with the new schedule. If it continues to be a problem, wait for another three to six months before trying it again. All of this must be conveyed neutrally without anger. Such an accordion between freedom and structure, depending on the child's level of responsibility, will help to motivate him to address his schoolwork promptly no matter what time of day it has been put in the schedule.

Furthermore, as a child begins to pursue music, dance, and art programs; joins a club or committee; or plays a sport, he must always be free to participate in these activities, even if he hasn't finished his homework, since these are every bit as important to his sense of responsibility and overall development as academics.

The Junior High Schooler. Any student in junior high who voluntarily accepts responsibility for doing his work and maintains grades to match the standard set by his family must be left to manage his studies on his own. This includes when and how he does his work, even if he gets a late start or is sprawled out on his bed with music blaring.

Furthermore, it's essential that parents never send a child to bed who is tardy in starting an assignment and plans to stay up late to complete it, as this forces him not to finish his assignments and teaches him to function at a reduced level of responsibility. It's also destructive to get angry at him for his late start, as that simply pushes him into hiding such errors in the future by going to bed and not dealing with the assignment. I would serve him a cup of cocoa, instead, or perhaps read late in my own room to support him in his urge to stay up and push through. If he complained of fatigue, I would gently share that I had learned from similar late nights how much I preferred the feeling of completing assignments earlier and getting the rest I both needed and enjoyed. I would let him know that I respected his ability to hang in there and get the assignment done. When parents allow a child to manage his own schedule and learn from the discomfort of a late start, he eventually figures out that he would rather begin assignments earlier and get a full night's rest.

The junior high student who does not demonstrate the maturity to address his schoolwork must be handled differently and should be put back on a home study hall program similar to the one required of the younger child. This approach can be used successfully with the high schooler up to about the second semester of his sophomore year.

The High Schooler. By the time a child reaches high school, rather than continue to be managed as he has in the past, he must begin to confront the results if he chooses not to address his schoolwork. Thus, at this point all that is left for parents is to lovingly teach, guide, and motivate their child to want to do better. One way to do this with the teen is to help him to more consciously select the kind of future he wants for himself and to determine if his approach to school is, in fact, helping him to keep doors open to that future. It's also important to make it clear that he will be expected to assume responsibility for his own life, once he reaches adulthood, rather than be subsidized indefinitely by you. This is only effective when it's done in a genuinely caring manner, rather than with an angry, threatening approach. My children, who were college-bound, inadvertently benefited during a family vacation from seeing the kinds of schools they could get into with their current grades. Without much discussion, their grades went up considerably after that sojourn. The key is not to lecture but to help your kids confront the reality ahead of them.

A freshman or first-semester sophomore in academic trouble usually responds to being required to return to a study hall, especially when this is presented calmly and with love and when motivation is in place. A sophomore or junior in academic trouble may, after a discussion about his future, voluntarily accept the study hall structure. However, when this structure is resisted by high school students who are not otherwise rebelling, they should be allowed to create their own approach with continued communication and loving guidance from you. If there is an accompanying rebellion with poor academic performance, the rebellion must be addressed first. See **Academics, Accelerated**; **Grades**; **Motivation**; **School, Adjustment Problems**

Stuttering or Stammering. Stuttering is a halting speech pattern that includes a repetition of beginning sounds or words or prolongations of sounds, syllables, or words. It's a normal developmental phase that young children learning to speak go through and may last up to about five years of age. Even in cases when it persists past this age, it usually continues to diminish as the child's speech becomes increasingly fluent. Thus, only about 1 percent of the population are still stuttering as adults. Consequently, the main thing most parents can do during this phase is to remain calm, and create a relaxed atmosphere in which their child has time to speak without interruption and feels patiently listened to. It's important never to finish his words or ideas for him or to ask him to slow down. And, it's critical not to mention the stuttering or make him self-conscious about it, as impatience and criticism can turn this normal developmental pattern into a serious speech disorder.

Because tension and criticism exacerbate the problem, eliminating criticism and reducing tensions in your home are the best things parents can do to help these children. The key is to make sure that your parenting is balanced between love and authority and that you are gentle, calm and patient, rather than angry and harsh in your approach with him. This will create the kind of environment that can best support him in resolving the nonfluency in due time.

The child about five years or older who is still stuttering may begin to feel tense and worried about it—especially if he's receiving negative feedback—and becomes anxious as he approaches the words he usually gets stuck on. He may even develop tic-like facial and body movements designed to help push the words out. The problem with stuttering is that it feeds on itself and becomes a habitual response to the troublesome situations or words that initially induced it. Thus, early intervention becomes important once it appears that the child may be developing a more persistent pattern.

Some children will respond within a few months to a number of techniques that can be taught at home, whereas others will need professional speech therapy. Only embark on helping your child yourself if you are able to remain completely calm and loving while doing so, since impatience will worsen the problem. The two most important things you can teach him are to learn to relax his shoulders, chest, and throat and become aware of his breathing by putting his hand on his abdomen to see how the breath goes in, raising the chest, and then leaves, letting the chest drop. The second step is for the child to take air in (raised chest) before saying a short phrase and then softly say the words as he lets the air out (chest down). This successful use of air may explain why stutterers can be fluent when singing. Moreover a softer voice will enable him to retain more of the air in his lungs that he will need to get the words out. Anytime the child blocks, it's important not to stay on that word, as this creates a habit of getting stuck. Instead, he should stop and begin again. Your gentle assurance at these junctures is critical. If these techniques fail to work, don't delay in getting professional help. See **Compulsive Behaviors**; **Post-Traumatic Stress**; **Professional Help**; **Speech Problems**

Suicide. There are two kinds of suicide threats. The first and most common is used in the same way a temper tantrum is used—to manipulate. These threats often begin when a person isn't getting his way, makes a threat, and then sees the impact this has on the person thwarting him. Often that person will become concerned and back down. This is a highly reinforcing experience for the person already poorly adjusted to not getting his way. Thus, whenever a suicide threat is made during those times when a person has not gotten his way on something, it's important to stay alert, but not allow the threat to serve as blackmail or cause you to change your mind or behavior. When reinforced by the people they were aimed at, these threats— although initially designed only to manipulate—become more and more real and serious as a result of having worked. Over the years, they can become addictive and eventually even acted out—sometimes successfully. Therefore, no suicide threat can be taken lightly, but how it is responded to will depend on the circumstances. If it's manipulative, it's important not to back down and give the person—or child—what they wanted. Moreover, the person must be taught over time to better tolerate not getting his way. Since most parents will find it difficult to decide if the threat is serious, it's best to seek professional help.

In other more serious cases, the person who is feeling suicidal is not simply trying to get his way, but is genuinely discouraged and so filled with loss of hope and despair that— sometimes as a result of a long-term emotional problem or eating disorder—he is in a chemical or clinical depression. Symptoms leading up to this level of despair range from depression, loss of appetite, isolation, minimal or excessive sleeping, to acting out with violence. These people need professional help immediately as their threats are neither manipulative nor empty. See **Professional Help**; **Serious Behavioral and Psychological Problems**

Sulking. A child who is sulking is usually trying to manipulate his family into worrying about him in order to gain extra attention or to get them to give into him on something. Parents who fear their child's pain mistakenly rush to help him or attempt to talk him out of the sad faces he puts on. This solicitous attitude toward his unhappiness causes him to produce even more unhappiness in order to get increased attention or to get his way. Parents would be wise to note their child's unhappiness without comment, rather than plead with him to cheer up or rejoin the family. Such a child will usually come around when nobody takes an interest in his staged unhappiness. Although a child should not be asked to stop his sulking or to smile, instead, it's appropriate to inform him that the energy he is using is not a socially useful one and does not allow for problem solving. Thus, he should experience his mood in his bedroom for as long as it interests him, which can take as long as he likes. Parents should not follow him into his room to request that he hurry through his mood or stop it; nor should they pursue what is wrong. After the child has decided to join the family again, he must clear first. If he has a legitimate concern or complaint, he's more than welcome to voice his concerns, put his feelings and thoughts on the table, and look for genuine solutions. Often sulkers don't have legitimate concerns that will hold up when brought into the open for airing, which is why they prefer sulking to talking things over. In sulking they play on the emotions of the parent they are blaming for their unhappiness while drawing them in with guilt. This only works, however, when you are willing to feel guilty for absolutely nothing, just because your child has chosen to feel unhappy, and you do him a disservice to encourage this style of managing his relationships and life. See Chapter 12

Summers. Children who have some form of structure during their summer break do better than those who are completely unstructured. Yet it's also best when summer activities offer kids a break from academia and an opportunity to pursue other interests and to develop skills in a variety of areas. See **Work**

SuperCamp. SuperCamp is a motivational program for teens. Learning Forum SuperCamp, 1725 South Hill Street, Oceanside, CA 92054-5319, 800-228-LEARN (5327) or 800-527-5321. See **Adolescence**

Super-Learning. Super-learning is a modern teaching method that engages multiple senses and aspects of self simultaneously for learning and can be most exciting when enhanced by extensive technical media. Some super-learning techniques that can be used at home are 1) listening to the same musical piece played during study periods, since the association of that piece with study suggests concentration and enhances memory; 2) using stories, visual diagrams, or pictures to describe a concept, as the image created evokes a memory of the entire concept each time it's revisited; 3) reviewing notes shortly after hearing a lecture or taking notes from a reading assignment, since this step will allow you to retain a considerably larger percentage of the material. Going over it again that night before bed increases retention dramatically.

Support Parent. See **Parent Roles**

Support People. Relatives, teachers, coaches, neighbors, counselors, youth leaders, ministers, and doctors offer another segment of a child's bridge to an expanding world and provide him with the impression that the larger world beyond his family is either safe and loving or cannot be trusted. Consequently, the contribution of these leaders is greatest when they offer children love and caring as well as clarity, inspiration, encouragement, excitement, and challenge. The more support people contribute to the lives of each child they encounter, the more love and caring there will be in the lives of all children.

Surrender/Surrendering. See **Adjustment Period**; **Compliance**; **"Immature Boss"**; **Impulse Control**; **"Mature Boss"**; **Refusal to Comply**; **Resistant Child**; **Rules**; **Time-Out**; See Chapters 4 and 7

Swearing, Cursing, Name-Calling, "Bad" Words. It's important for parents to first distinguish in their minds what is and what is not a choice before responding to their child's use of "bad" words. If the child includes swear words in his growing vocabulary, it's important to help him to see that it's understandable that kids explore this use of words among themselves but that it's not considered clever or acceptable when children use them in the presence of adults. If he then persists in swearing, calmly let him know that this isn't what people in social settings want to listen to, so he will have to continue it in his room for as long as it interests him. The most important thing for parents to remember is not to be shocked or emotional about swearing in young children, since a big reaction is what causes them to persist in using these kinds of words, beyond their initial curiosity about them. As your child gets older, he and his friends may enjoy the freedom of using the "strong" language of swearing. It's important not to try to control this, but to merely share the parameters that you think will work best for him. For example, a teen who overuses swearing or uses it in settings other than with his peers is giving out messages of insecurity, rather than the strength he assumes such "grown-up" language is creating for him. Swearing that is used aggressively toward family should never be tolerated. See **Sassing**

Tantrums. There are two types of tantrums; one is used as a tensional outlet in the face of too much stress and the other is used to manipulate. Parents must learn to bypass the one used to release tension and ignore the one used to manipulate.

The Tensional Tantrum. The tantrum used to release tension occurs during those times when parents have stretched their young child beyond his limits, and he's feeling overwhelmed and overwrought. The result is a tantrum to release the buildup of tension.

Thus, parents must first be aware of what their child can and cannot developmentally handle. For example, if your young child is not getting enough rest (see *Sleep, Amounts* subentry under **Bedtime**); does not have enough opportunity to snack between meals; is too confined physically as well as in what he's allowed to do; is overloaded with too much stimulation; or is bored and understimulated, he will build up tension and may have a tantrum to release it. Furthermore, most young children can't get through an evening of formal dining in which the meal is brought in courses. Likewise, a hungry and tired child who has already put in an hour or more of shopping cannot be asked to hold up for one last store before going home. You must also make sure that you're not adding to his frustrations by treating him gruffly or overcontrolling the management of his world.

Bypassing the Tensional Tantrum. By becoming more aware of your child's needs and being sensitive to meeting them, you will bypass many of the tensional tantrums that emerge when a child has been asked to stretch beyond his limits. On those occasions, when you are not able to bypass such a tantrum, don't provide your child with excuses for his behavior by telling him or others that he's tired or hungry. This inadvertently teaches him that he's not expected to learn increasingly higher levels of coping but is excused from managing during those times when he's not feeling his best. Thus, rather than provide him with excuses, simply handle the tantrum and be more alert to trying to bypass them in the future.

The Manipulative Tantrum. It's not uncommon to see a young child whose parents are ignoring his tantrum call out, "I'm crying!" Crying is lots of work, and a child hates to expend so much energy when there is no payoff for his efforts.

The eighteen month to two-and-a-half-year-old wants more than he's able to assume responsibility for; yet his immature perspective does not allow him to understand why he must be thwarted. Therefore, he throws himself on the floor and screams in frustration in a primitive effort to get his way. If this works and his rules are changed, he will learn to act in this manner as a way to gain control over his parents—and life—as he coerces those around him to respond to his desires. However, if his parent is unimpressed by his tantrums and is willing to ride them out until he's too tired to cry anymore, he learns from the experience that his "immature boss," with its limited perspective, is not yet ready to be in charge. Therefore, he must yield for a period of time to the larger perspective—and "boss"—of his parent. Along with this surrender, the temperamental self is relinquished and a more flexible self emerges. By contrast, if a child's tantrums work to delay some requirement, get him what he wanted, win him additional attention, or upset his parents and put them in conflict about discipline, he will continue to have them. And, his temperamental or challenging self will grow strong within his personality structure.

Don't Bypass the Manipulative Tantrum. Parents who anticipate a tantrum during those times when they must thwart their child in some way would be wise not to attempt to bypass his frustration. Such a bypass would only delay his ability to confront the normal disappointments in life and adjust to the frustration they create for him. For example, when parents suspect that their child will tantrum when he hears that it's time to leave some activity to return home, they must not attempt to bypass his tantrum by suggesting that they leave to go get some ice cream. They serve his development better when they confront him with the reality that it's time to leave their activity and then allow him to protest with tantrums and tears for as long as he wants to express his frustration over this reality. Once he's finished, he will be better adjusted to the reality of such frustrations. Your only job while he's going through this period of adjustment is to remain calm and keep him moving in the direction of home. See **Adjustment Period**

Handling Tantrums. Even when parents believe that their child is overtired and overstimulated or that they may have contributed to a tantrum by being too controlling, unfair, or angry, they must not respond to his fit with apologies, alter requests made of him, change their minds, or give in to his demands.

The only thing to do when your child is having a tantrum—no matter whether it's due to tension or manipulation—is to give him no reaction or response whatsoever. Attempting to plead with your child to stop—or reason with him, console, or distract him—while he's in the middle of his tantrum are not only inappropriate responses for the occasion, but will cause him to repeat this method of coping in the future. Thus, after getting him to his playpen, room, the back seat of the car, or another safe place away from your direct observation, allow him to cry for as long as it takes him to figure out that the tantrum is not producing anything. Even if he bangs his head, kicks the walls, pulls his room apart, or holds his breath and turns blue (he will breathe again as soon as he passes out if not before)[11], trust that these too will pass if you have the fortitude to ignore it all! You can view this crying period as an opportunity for you to get calm and/or handle some chores. Although you will want to check on the tantrumming child periodically, do so discreetly, since your presence will only fuel his anger.

After he has finished crying and has been quiet for several minutes (approximately two to four minutes for the young child or five to ten for the older one), you may go to him. If he resumes hard crying, you will have to leave, whereas if he's merely sobbing in emotion upon seeing you, it's okay to stay. Get him to move to the living room, where he can sit in your lap or next to you in order to clear. Then, even if you agree with his frustrations and requests, help him to understand that tantrumming is not the way to get his needs met and that he will get better results if he expresses them directly. (If he did try to express his needs and you ignored him, you will need to acknowledge this and promise to do better next time— but that he will nevertheless be more successful in getting through to you if he asks again rather than having tantrums.) If you don't agree with his complaints, lovingly ask him if the crying helped him to get his way or if things are still the way they were before the crying. Don't be afraid to confront this for fear of triggering another tantrum, since facing and acknowledging the truth will not only help him to adjust, but to get past using tantrums as a tool for getting what he wants.

If a child is having frequent tantrums over little things, there may be an underlying physical or emotional reason for his wanting to cry so often and hard. If you suspect this, check out potential physical causes first. Then, determine in your own mind what is new and different or potentially disturbing for him emotionally and present him with a "menu" of your hunches during clearing.

Tantrums in Public. When a child gets to the point of having a tantrum at a mall or in a restaurant, it's best to calmly take him home. If you have stretched his limits, returning home without upset is all you will need to do, since this tantrum was a result of your misjudgment. If the tantrum is a manipulative one, calmly return him home, call a prearranged sitter, lovingly announce that you will return after the activity is complete, and clear with him after you return or—if he's asleep—in the morning. This consequence is preferable to having him pay several weeks later by not being allowed to go to dinner with the family. In two weeks, he may be in a completely different, delightful phase and it will seem out of place to punish him for past infractions. Although this method is drastic, it's also the most effective. The parent who doesn't have a sitter—or the heart to get one—can take the child home to finish his tantrum in time-out, clear, and give him some contraction of freedom. If he wanted to remain at the restaurant, mall, or other activity, the return home can serve as the contraction. However, if he wanted to leave, then some loss is needed to make him feel that his strategy didn't work to get him what he wanted. For example, if it's later in the day, he might be required to miss the evening activities and prepare for bed early—since he had demonstrated that he was too tired to cope. If it happened earlier in the day, he might be required to lose certain privileges, such as playing outdoors or watching TV for the rest of the day. Since there is no logical connection to this consequence, he would need to be told that you were providing this restriction so that he could learn that the reality of tantrums is that they give him less, rather than more in life. The key is to remain calm and loving while giving him some experience of loss as a result of the approach he used. See **Breath Holding**; **"Challenging Child"**; **Compliance**; **"Immature Boss"**; **"Mature Boss"**; **Negotiation**; **Refusal to Comply**; **Suicide**; **Tensional Outlets**; See Chapters 6, 7, 8, 9, and 11

Tattling. It's important to note that all tattling is not bad and should not automatically be reprimanded. For example, if a child tells his mother that the baby is playing with her pincushion or the toddler is smearing makeup all over the carpet, that child is protecting the baby's safety and the family's carpet. Other children tattle about important issues such as stealing and lying in an effort to get their parents to apply the rules that have been established. In such cases, a child's worry that rules are being broken and inconsistently held is a legitimate concern. Moreover, parents who indulge in favoritism must take inventory of their own behavior, since this is confusing not only to the child required to mind the rules, but to the one being let off the hook as well. Thus, the child who occasionally reports information to a parent can be thanked and assured that the adult will handle the problem.

By contrast, some children tattle with a desire to cause problems for a child they envy or hope to get into trouble, while others like to be in control of things and simply want to be the boss. Thus, wise parents will consider what has motivated tattling and perception-check their hunch with the child. For example, a parent may inquire, "Are you worried that I won't see what Johnny is doing or that I won't make him stop, or are you feeling that it's your job to make sure that all the children are doing the right thing? Or, are you a little angry at Johnny and hoping that he'll get into trouble with me?" Once the child admits to worry, jealousy, anger, or a desire to control, the adult can then release him from being in control of the other child's consequence and assure him that she will do her job responsibly.

Teaching, Socratic Style. Socrates is one of history's greatest teachers, known for asking the kinds of penetrating questions that pulled answers to life's mysteries from the hearts and minds of his students. When we discourse with our children as Socrates did, we not only respect their intelligence and tap the wisdom carried within them, but further stimulate the questioning and expansion of their minds. I liken the image of pulling answers from children to a magician pulling scarves from his top hat. The results are not only informative but surprising, entertaining, and delightful. See **Intelligence**

Teasing. As any person being teased will tell you, teasing is an aggressive behavior, disguised as fun. Adults who tease children not only use dominance unjustly but are being disrespectful of the child as an important person whose wishes must be listened to. Teased children often turn the aggression they have received at home on others by becoming the teasers at school. Other children who are the recipients of teasing at home or are overprotected by their parents become oversensitive and timid and thus draw the dominance—and teasing—of others to them.

Although most adults deal with children who tease by striving to control the teaser's behavior, it's more effective to teach the teasee to withdraw his reaction in order to stop attracting the teaser to him. Thus, it helps teased children to be shown with puppets or drawings how exciting it is for a teaser to torment someone who fusses and sobs over the teasing, whereas a teaser finds it quite unrewarding to tease someone who can remain bored and disdainful of his efforts. Demonstrating this with puppets or pictures is effective with young children. Sometimes the teasee needs simply to learn not to be so impressed by life's pain and not to withdraw so timidly from normal activities in his effort to avoid it. While helping teasees not to respond to teasing, adults should also be alert to the role of the teaser; anytime he teases so much that his behavior seems generalized and bullyish, he can be treated as a bully and be temporarily removed from social settings. See **Bullies**; **Overprotection**; **Permissive Parenting**; See Chapter 10

Telephone Rules. Parents must clearly define telephone rules with their young children. You can let your toddler know that he may sit on your lap while you are talking, but may not interrupt you. If he likes to talk to callers, you can create prearranged signals with him, indicating whether or not the caller is someone he may speak to; you must also give him the rules for waiting and letting go of the phone when you ask for it. If he fusses about waiting his turn, won't get off once he has the phone, fusses about talking when it's not a choice, or is too young to understand this system and is crying, you must get off the phone and put him on a time-out. Only after your child has completed his time-out and has cleared should you attempt to get on the phone again. In addition, emergency signals with kids four years and older can be created for problems that require immediate attention. Then if your child indicates he has an emergency, you must respond. However, if he cries "wolf," he must experience some contraction of his freedom. It's also important that you not spend excessive amounts of time on the phone while blocking your child's access to you for prolonged periods of time.

Answering the Telephone. Tell children first learning to answer the phone exactly what you want them to say. It's best to instruct them not to give out personal information, including unlisted names, numbers, or addresses to someone they don't know. If the caller continues to pester, teach them to hang up and refrain from answering the phone for awhile if it rings again.

Instruct them not to tell anyone that they are home alone. Instead, they should tell all callers that you are busy, and they will take a message, rather than supply details of what you are doing. If a caller interrogates them, they can repeat their message. If this doesn't work, they can hang up and not answer the phone again for awhile.

Kids on the Telephone. Children learning parameters for their own telephone use should be treated with respect as well. Their calls are important too, and they should be given ample time to talk to friends and make their personal arrangements. Kids have a genuine need to connect with their peers, and in this day of limited neighborhoods, the telephone is one way they have to do it. Thus, a responsible child should be able to enjoy this activity without undue control and supervision. Moreover, if your teen is sociable and likes to spend time on a phone needed by other family members, consider getting a second line—if affordable—for the sake of the entire family. If not, allow ample time for telephone use, rather than restrict his calls. When teens are not cooperating with telephone—or other—rules, removing phone privileges is a powerful consequence for them.

Television and Videos. The average American preschooler sits in front of his family television set for a little more than four hours a day, staring at a one-dimensional world he cannot touch or interact with. Studies demonstrate that hours of such passive viewing interrupt the development of a child's neurological, social, and emotional competencies as well as his ability to think and learn. It's apparent that excessive viewing interferes with a child's opportunity to participate in a variety of outside activities, play, socializing with peers, and developing his tal-ents, which, in turn, results in excessive passivity, an inability to be intimate with others, and a failure to live his own life. Not only does this cause disuse of his body, it subtly inhibits the development of his inner world of initiative, creativity, communication, and motor skills, as well as his reasoning ability. Some specialists believe this deprivation of development—as well as the negative effect TV has on a young child's brain waves and mental development—is the cause of learning disabilities in increasing numbers of children with this disorder.[12]

Thus, parents would be wise never to put television sets into their children's bedrooms for indiscriminate watching and passive withdrawing from other aspects of life. Moreover, due to the effect on his neurological development, experts suggest that a child under two should not be watching television at all. With children from two to six, parents can easily control the amount of viewing and create a habit pattern of minimal watching. Their children can be helped to select from one-half to one-and-a-half hours of favorite programming per day and be allowed to watch this selection only. These should include good family programs that teach positive val-ues and ought to begin in the evening and be watched with other family members as a socia-ble family activity. Once programs are selected, it's critical that the TV is turned on for these programs only, then turned off when they are finished. During the time the television is off, the family will have an opportunity to talk to each other, play games, make plans and gener-ally "hang out" together. On school nights, TV should not be turned on until homework is com-pleted, if it's turned on at all for special programming only. If a child turns on the TV during times other than what is allowed, he must be restricted from going into that room or watch-ing television for the remainder of the day. If he breaks that rule, he should be required to first remain in his room and then clear before returning to any of his normal freedoms in addition to losing all television for several more days or the remainder of the week.

Programming. Whatever we see and hear that we accept as true gets converted to ideas and beliefs which are stored in our neurological structure and programming. We then act on these pictures and expectations of how life works and manifest them in the material world as real-ity. (See **Thoughtforms.**) Thus, parents must be aware of the power of the television pro-gram content they allow their children to watch. For example, the news alone evokes within us an enormous collective experience of a negative, unsafe world and imprints additional feelings and fears about an uncertain future. Moreover, studies now indicate that the violent content of television programming provokes aggressiveness and rebellion in kids and may even incite violent acts in all age groups. Moreover, 73 percent of TV violence goes unpun-ished, leaving kids with the false impression that aggression not only pays off, but carries no consequence. Only recently have we begun to face that excessive viewing of such aggressive programs causes hyperactivity and disobedience in the young child, stimulates twice as much violence in the elementary-aged child, and creates a foundation for rebellion in teens and antisocial behavior in adults. Thus, parents would be wise to supervise program selec-tion and limit viewing to only those programs that provide positive values and lessons.

It's also best to provide a model for your child of turning on the television only for spe-cific, valuable programs, giving the show your attention, and then turning the set off when the program is over. This not only teaches family members to attend to each others' con-versations during times when the TV is off, but to attend to the planned program when it's on as well. This is preferable to only partially attending to either the TV or other family mem-bers, while both vie for the floor.

Video and Computer Games. We now know that video and computer games can become addic-tive. Moreover, parents with children addicted to these games report that they not only inter-fere with their desire to be a part of the family or socialize with others, but often provoke hyperactive and aggressive behavior as well as a poor attention span. It seems they interfere with development more than contribute to it; yet if families have them, they are best limited to use for no more than a half-hour a day—possibly longer if a sibling, friend, or parent is playing the game with the child. Although well-selected software can offer educational and logic challenges, the primary problem with them is that they can capture the child's attention away from entertaining himself as well as from developing his own talents and social skills in play with siblings and friends.

Tensional Outlets. Habits such as biting, hair pulling or twisting, head banging, head rolling, nail biting, rocking, temper tantrums, thumb and finger sucking, whining, and masturbating serve as tensional outlets for children. The best way to reduce your child's need for tensional release is to look for the underlying stressors in his life and work to reduce them. See **Habits**; **Individual habits listed under their names**; **Post-Traumatic Stress**; **Security**; **Tics**

"Terrible Twos." The "terrible twos" are merely the first in a series of challenges a child will wage as he goes through various stages of development. See **Challenges**

Therapy. See **Professional Help**

Thinking. See **Family Meetings**; **Problem Solving**

Thinking, Magical. There is a period from about six to nine years of age when a child believes that his thoughts will become reality. Because this belief has not been understood or valued in our society, we think of it as a stage of development, label it magical thinking, and assure the child that this belief is not true. In other cultures, this strength of belief in manifesting what is thought to be true is valued and used to teach children how to use the power of their minds to help them create and manifest their dreams. In fact, this is the basis for Uri Geller's spoon bending with his mind and the children of Bali being taught to fire-walk without getting burned. Because our culture devalues this use of the mind, it is not used and thus atrophies in our children; only a few pick it up again later to develop this skill. Because science is now uncovering why the power of the mind is so useful in manifesting our goals, it's important that parents more carefully guide children to understand this power contained in their minds and put it to good use.

Thoughtforms. Because both the positive and negative messages parents communicate to their children are so strong, a child will invariably develop the traits that have been repeatedly projected onto him throughout his childhood.

The mechanism for how this process works can be rather easily understood. As a way to maintain our sanity and to not be overwhelmed by all of the sensory input and information available to us, we each have built into our perceptual mechanism the capacity to block out superfluous input and focus only on those things we've selected as important and useful. Although this prevents us from being bombarded by too much data, it also causes us to narrowly select only that information that we have been taught to accept as valid or that supports our personal belief systems and hypotheses about life and ourselves.

Consequently, if our belief about a child is that he is quiet and shy, we will consistently ignore or block out his bolder, more outgoing traits and focus only on his timid, reserved qualities. As we then tell him and others how quiet he is, they, too, will notice the reticent part of his personality to the exclusion of his more outgoing moments. When we share this view of him with our spouse, friends, his teachers, and anyone else who will listen, we lock the child into a perceptual box—or thoughtform—from which it will be very difficult for him to escape.

A Harvard study[13] supports this concept in its demonstration of how randomly selected children given a perceptual image of themselves as particularly bright actually made significant IQ gains by the end of the school year. Because their teachers had been informed that these children were highly intelligent, they perceived them accordingly. The children, in turn, performed at very high levels. Such results can best be explained by understanding that once the teachers were told to expect bright behavior from these children, they not only sent forth affirming energies supporting their brightness, but tended to block out all of their average or below-average ideas or actions. Moreover, the teachers' responses to the children caused them to perceive themselves as bright, and they acted accordingly! Similarly, children who are raised with a great deal of criticism, or are told that they are stupid and can't do things, develop into adults who feel deeply within themselves that something is very wrong. As a result, they feel and act as though they are incompetent and worthless.

It's important that parents take an inventory of the labels they presently use to describe their children and reevaluate whether or not those labels are ones they want to see manifested in the child.

Threats/Threatening. Parents who use threats have a problem with their discipline. See Chapters 6 and 7

Thumb Sucking. I'm not sure we know why children get so attached to sucking in addition to the sucking required to eat. It could simply represent a developmental need that, in some cases, starts in the womb. Or, it could be a result of bonding breaks or unfulfilled needs for nurturing. Another possibility is that fear is present in all new experiences that stretch us toward independence. Thus, even though babies desire independence, they may feel somewhat disquieted during their first moments alone without Mother or when they are challenged to not only be the wanter but their own fulfiller as well. They often find their fingers, a blanket, or an ear to massage in order to "comfort" and relax themselves during these times of normal stress or as a way of withdrawing from the challenge for awhile. Dependence on these comforting objects is high from birth to two to three years of age, and gradually decreases thereafter. This could be a result of a learned response to stress or a continuing effect of birth trauma or unfulfilled nurturing needs.

When this early desire to self-comfort and reduce tension becomes habitual, it gets used in increasingly more situations. Thus, when a child hasn't outgrown his need for sucking by about three years of age, it has probably become a strong habit. Parents with these habitual suckers may want to first determine if there are any underlying reasons why their child feels a need for self-comfort and to resolve any problems they uncover. They would also be wise to provide him with ample opportunities for lap-sitting (without sucking). If, after taking these steps, his sucking is still habitual, they may want to restrict the times and settings in which they allow their child to suck his thumb. To do this, they can let him know he may do his sucking anytime he wishes, but that it's something he must now do while alone in his room during those times when he's feeling in a dreamy, sleepy mood—but not when he's socializing or participating in activities (including television-viewing). Preschools wishing to contain this behavior can have a dreamy corner—devoid of other activities—for children wishing to suck their thumbs and/or use their other comforters. In this way, there's no struggle to get the child to stop his sucking behavior; yet this habit is used as it was originally designed: to serve as a time for withdrawing from independence. Thus, he must choose between the two, rather than take his withdrawing mechanisms out into the world with him. This also gives him a way to contain the habit within socially acceptable parameters until he outgrows it.

Although there are conflicting reports regarding whether or not thumb sucking damages a child's bite, there's evidence to support that a good bite is not affected by it, whereas a poor bite may be worsened by thumb sucking. See **Comforters**; **Habits**; **Tensional Outlets**

Tics, Twitching. Tics and twitching are repetitive movements that are common in children from about five to six years of age and older. The most common tics include head shaking, eye blinking, turning the head to the side, tongue clicking, throat tightening with or without noises, and shoulder jerking. Tics can be more difficult to manage than other habits, as they sometimes run in families and may have a genetic correlation—seen most often in boys—and manifest as a strong urge in the child to tighten the muscles in some part of his body as a way of responding to stress. Children with tics may be flashing back to earlier traumas incurred during difficult births, bonding breaks, or other physical and emotional stressors that cause them to reexperience an approach/avoidance conflict and thus freeze and tense anytime the original stimulus is activated. Because most tics run a short course of from several weeks to a month or so, parents would be wise to initially allow the tic to run its course without any mention of it.

The best thing to do during this waiting period is to reduce tensions and conflicts in the child's life while helping him to embrace—rather than resist—the fear-evoking situation this time around. You can also examine any earlier stressors that might have triggered the tic behavior in the first place. By doing this, you help him to understand the earlier trauma as well as the more recent stimulus that go with this pattern of fearing and, thus, resisting new or tense situations. For example, a child with tics may experience current conflicts between such things as wanting to socialize, yet feeling afraid; wanting to speak up, but feeling too shy; or wanting to play on a team or have a girlfriend, yet feeling inadequate. Because the tic probably represents an approach/avoidance conflict that he started while very young, parents would be wise to see if they can trace the onset of the habit to the original event, perhaps of being yelled at. If they uncover the original conflict, they can help him to revisit and reexamine that trauma without the presence of the original fear. In this way, he can release the original trauma and stop bringing the fear that goes with it into present situations. Sometimes the original trauma is so deeply programmed in the child's neurological structure—as in the case of a traumatic birth or other traumatic physical or emotional experiences—that professional help is required to release it. (See **EMDR**; **Post-Traumatic Stress**)

Only if a child's tic persists for several months and appears to be developing into a strong habit should parents strive to interrupt it before it becomes a deeply ingrained habitual response to tension. As with other persistent habits, in order for a child to overcome tics, he must first want to stop. He must also understand that—as with drug hunger—each time the tic is denied an opportunity to express itself, the urge to do it diminishes. Next, he must become aware of doing tics as the first step in gaining control.

One way to accomplish this goal is to have him do the tic in front of a mirror. This not only makes him aware of what he is doing and how it looks, but gives him an opportunity to control the activity by doing it on command. He can also use the mirror to practice the tic, followed by an alternate, competing behavior. Repeating the tic until the child hates doing it is also effective in making the habit feel aversive, rather than relaxing to him, although this exercise should only be done voluntary. It's also helpful to teach the child with tics how to relax in other ways (see **Relaxation**); meditation is particularly helpful for such a child. It's critical that parents are patient with the child who has tics and become his ally in learning to stop the behavior. This might include requiring that he go to his room or have a practice session in front of the mirror, but these should only be done with calm neutrality and gentle compassion and if a prior agreement to work together in this way has been made between parent and child. Anger, continual nagging, and threats will only make the tension and tics worse.

If a child's tics seem extremely unmanageable or are accompanied by sounds and/or swearing, the child should be given a medical check, as this can be a symptom of a more serious neurological problem called Tourette's syndrome. See **Anxiety**; **Compulsive Behaviors**; **Habits**; **Post-Traumatic Stress**; **Professional Help**; **Tensional Outlets**

Time-Out. Time-out is a technique that uses contraction of a child's freedom as a form of discipline. It should only be used, however, when there are no other ways to contract the freedoms he enjoys that are connected to his infraction. See **Adjustment**; **Compliance**; **Door Barriers, Gates**; **"Immature Boss"**; **"Mature Boss"**; **Playpens**; **Redirecting**; **Refusal to Comply**; **Resistant Child**; **Rules**; **Safe-Holding**; **Tantrums**; See Chapter 7

Toilet Training. It's critical that parents not view toilet training of their child as part of the race to maturity, since rushing him will not only delay this developmental experience, but can create a struggle that may unfavorably affect the parent-child relationship and delay toilet training. Thus, parents would be wise to assume the attitude that their child—like all other children—will eventually get trained, and that how old he is when it happens has no bearing on his IQ or future.

Toilet training can only happen when the child has developed physiologically to the degree that he's beginning to hold more urine in his bladder and has less frequent bowel movements—and is thus dry and clean for longer periods. This usually happens sometime between one and a half to three years of age. As a result of his increased capacity, he is also becoming more aware of when he's eliminating this larger amount or when it builds up in his body, and he feels the need to go again. Until these two things are happening, a child has very little chance of gaining control over his elimination functions. Therefore, parents would be wise not to rush this process. Neither should they delay it once this period of more elimination less often has begun.

The first thing your child will probably—but not always—give up naturally is his nighttime bowel movements. He will then become more aware of his bowel movements during the day and will be ready to begin to control them. Learning to control his urination will most likely come next, first during the day and then at night. However, the control of urine may come first, followed by the control of bowel movements.

Thus, the first step in toilet training involves helping your child to gradually develop his awareness of when he is dry and when he is wet or soiled by gently describing this when it happens. Next, you can help him to become more aware of when he is actually having a bowel movement or wetting by cheerfully labeling it for him as he is completing doing it as well as when he is being cleaned up. When your child hears you provide him with the vocabulary and information describing this act in a friendly way, he feels safe in talking about it and remains comfortable doing it in front of you.

The next step is to introduce the idea of the potty, while explaining to your child that big people prefer to put their urine and feces in it because they don't like to get their clothes and bodies all wet and stinky or take the extra time to clean up the mess. You can then show him how it's used and let him practice sitting on it. If you talk about the potty as a convenience that is used with maturation and never express anger or disappointment in your child on those occasions when he fails to use it, your child never learns to view using the potty—or not using it—as an emotional weapon he has against you. On the other hand, it's important not to avoid the subject of learning to use a potty altogether in an effort not to traumatize him. The key at this juncture is that you explain to your child that as he grows bigger, he can feel the urine and feces coming and thus has a choice to put it in a more convenient place.

For the unmotivated child you can add to this awareness that it also saves time for some of the extra things that he likes to do. Never make a specific plan for doing something special that you will do only if he uses the potty, since if he fails to use it, not following through on this activity will seem like a punishment. Nonetheless, when the unmotivated child does use the potty, point out that the time he saved by doing this has given you more time to play a special game and ask what game he would like to play.

A Word of Caution. Never punish a child for not using the potty or take away an activity that has been planned. This serves as a punishment, rather than an enjoyment of time that has been saved by his growing-up process.

Next, you can choose between having your child sit—voluntarily—on the potty for awhile at the time he normally goes, while you sit with him, reading or talking; or, you can simply watch for when he seems about ready to go and cheerfully recommend that he put it in the potty; or, you can use a combination of styles. It's best when suggesting the potty just before he's ready to go that you not ask if he would like to do this, since this question usually draws a refusal; it's better to suggest that it would be fun to do it in the potty, while providing some motivation for doing so, such as he won't need to do the cleaning if it goes in the potty. You can then express how impressed you are and let him know that it's a sign of growing up. I think it's important to give him natural, relaxed feedback that he has succeeded in the task without making too much of a fuss about it or intruding your own personal pleasure—or displeasure—into the event. Once he has experienced some successes and understands the connection between these body functions and the potty, you can also offer him the option of turning in his diapers for training pants. Once this is accomplished and in place, you can introduce the idea of using the potty on his own whenever he feels ready to go. Whenever your child has an accident, he can lovingly be asked to help clean himself up and reassured that he will have another chance to try it in the potty when he feels ready.

Parents must understand that even after a child's initial successes, he will continue to miss from time to time. Thus, whenever your child reports that he has just wet or soiled his diaper, you must respond positively—rather than with the attitude that he has failed, since this reporting represents his growing awareness of his elimination experience and his interest in getting to the toilet in time. It also helps to clean him up immediately so that he begins to value being clean.

Parents must further understand that some children feel afraid to let their bowel movements fall away from their bodies or dislike seeing them flushed away. The fear of flushing can become intensified in unknown toilets or the noisier public toilets or ones at school, once he begins preschool. To help with this fear of releasing the feces, you can explain that the bowel movement comes out of our bodies because it is not needed—much like the trash left over from our lunch or the banana peel portion of a banana.

Other children become worried about falling into the toilet and being flushed away or simply dislike the noises of the flushing toilet. You can help to curtail these fears by letting your child practice sitting on the potty or using a separate, smaller one of his own. You can further desensitize your child to the noises of flushing by waiting until he feels ready for flushing or perhaps decides to do it himself. Still others develop more intense fears as a result of experiencing pain during elimination and must be assured that such pain is rare and won't happen again. Adjusting your child's diet, including adding vegetable oils to it, to prevent constipation and the hard feces that cause pain will allow you to keep this promise. (If the fear is intense, your child may need professional help to release it.)

Once training begins, you must remember to let your child know when he has succeeded; acknowledge that he is doing it just like Mommy and Daddy; ignore his accidents; neutrally clean your child, following an accident, to help him value cleanliness; and ignore any negative comments he makes about toileting or requests for going back to diapers, once he has had a period of success.

The entire process usually takes a couple of months and is most successful when parents are able to understand that this is simply an expected part of the learning process and are able to put toilet training on their "agenda" for as long as the child needs to master it.

If your child seems resistant and is still not trained by three years of age, you must first check to see if you have been too laid-back or overly anxious or firm about your toilet training, or if your child's ability to control is simply undeveloped. If any of these is the case, you must bring yourself into balance or wait until he has matured. If not, you can motivate your child to want to bypass a mess in his diapers by having him help to clean it up. This is not done with anger, but in a very gentle, matter-of-fact manner while you explain that you prefer to put the mess directly into the potty as a way to bypass this cleaning step. If he refuses to help, you can gently move his hands through the motions while remaining neutral.

In other cases, the child is simply not motivated enough to give up his diaper or training pants. In such cases, it's helpful to let him know that more of the grown-up things that he would like to do that require dry pants, such as attending a movie, can be done once this skill is mastered; then, be sure to expand his horizon by taking him to an appropriately screened movie or to some other coveted event that requires greater maturity once he makes his first deposit in the toilet.

Relapses. Once a child is toilet trained, it's normal for him to lose control periodically, particularly within the next year. Never shame the child who has had an unexpected accident, as this behavior is normal, and demeaning him can result in emotional problems and further delays in mastering toileting.

The child who is having regular wetting accidents after initial training may have developed a bladder infection or be bothered by pinworms. These possibilities must be checked before pursuing other angles. Or, he may be too involved in his activities to break for bathrooming or fear the larger, noisier commercial toilets at school. Parents can address the fear of commercial toilets by first desensitizing their child to different public toilets. They can also show their child the school toilets—and desensitize him to their flushing action—before leaving him there alone to discover these noises by himself. Wise teachers will be alert to this possibility and help new children under their care by remaining with them as the toilet flushes.

A child who is fully trained and deliberately defecates on the carpet or sprays the bathroom walls with urine must calmly be required to thoroughly clean it up. This should include whatever number of times it takes to genuinely remove the stain and smell as well as provide any disinfectants you plan to use. This gives him an honest experience of why it's easier to use the bathroom facilities. In short, let the child do everything you would do if you were the one cleaning up the mess, while you remain calm and neutral. Parents who mistakenly react and show their child what a powerful way this is to upset them will invariably have to deal with this behavior again and again!

Once the child with prolonged toileting problems has been checked for pinworms and bladder infection, reminded to take a break from play to handle toileting, and has been discouraged from going in the wrong place, psychological reasons can be investigated. If emotional problems are suspected, parents must first respond to their child calmly and with assurance that it's all right. They can then gently investigate what antecedents their child has experienced just prior to this accident, including their own behavior and discipline style. Is he afraid it will hurt? Did school just start? Did a teacher yell at him? Did a friend reject him? Is he feeling anxious about something such as an impending divorce? If necessary, they can present him with a "menu" of hunches to choose from and use reflective interpretation (see Chapter 11 on "Communication") to help uncover the problem. Once parents of children who wet for psychological reasons learn to remain neutral, then uncover and resolve the underlying problems, their child's wetting will invariably stop.

The child who soils himself regularly has usually developed a problem with constipation and impaction of feces which then causes leaking into his underwear. Such a child should be seen medically and is usually given dietary aids and mineral or olive oil to break the impaction. Painful defecation during a period of constipation often causes a child to fear—and thus resist—elimination to this degree. When this is explained to a child, letting him know that the original pain he felt is not only rare, but would not bother him now that he's older, he often becomes willing to resume allowing his feces to pass without further resistance. Such children often feel more secure if they can hold a diaper to them as they eliminate, and this helps them to break their habit of holding back. If there are no medical problems and the child persists in being fearful or oppositional, it would be valuable to seek professional help for guidance in completing his toilet training and treating other parent/child conflicts as well. See **Bed-Wetting**; **Oppositional Child**; **Pinworms**; *Reflective Listening* subentry under **Active Listening**

Touch. Touch stimulates the development of the child at both the physiological and psychological levels, beginning in infancy and continuing throughout his development. In fact, touch is at the core of bonding and is critical to a child's overall healthy development. Touch is not only an antidote to illness, but can stimulate healing in people who are either physically or emotionally diseased or distressed. Touch is also a source of contact that enhances continuing bonds between parent and child. I would suggest that parents not only provide ample, noninvasive and nonsexual touch, stroking, and massage for their infants, but continue this happy experience throughout their children's growing-up process. (Ashley Montagu, *Touching, The Human Significance of the Skin,* New York: HarperCollins, 1985.) See **Access**; **Bonding**; **Carrying**; **Contact**; **"In-Arms" Period**; **Lap-Sitting**; **Nursing**

ToughLove. ToughLove helps parents to bring moderately rebellious teens back under control. P.O. Box 1069, Doylestown, PA 18901, 800-333-1069

Toys. Children today are provided with excessive numbers of toys and diversions. Not only do so many activities keep their rooms a mess and their energy "busy" and overactive, they teach them to relate to things instead of people. Too many toys further prevent children from developing their own imaginations and ideas of what to do by dictating the direction of their play during those times when they are alone. Because the child with so many toys feels he must be excited by his latest purchase and "doing" something with it, he loses touch with how to simply "be" in the more natural world around him. This material orientation often keeps him so occupied that he isn't motivated to find a friend or to play cooperatively enough to keep friends interested in him. In this way, toys can cause children to overvalue material things, while undervaluing the true treasures of life found in nature, real life adventures, and genuine friendships. See **Greed**

Toys, Full-Cycling. Young children still learning to put things away learn best when they are required to return each activity to its original condition before going on to the next. Once they can do this easily, two activities may be added. Although this early teaching initially takes more supervision, it trains the child to view his activity and its return to the shelf as a complete unit of activity. This Montessori technique is useful in teaching children not only to clean up after themselves but to understand and value the concept of full-cycling everything on the planet. In this regard, parents would be wise only to purchase environmentally friendly toys and teach their children to do the same. See Chapter 6

Traditions. Traditions are important to keeping families bonded. See Chapter 11

Transgressions. Transgressions against others must be acknowledged in order to keep relationships clear. See Chapter 8

Trauma. See "Challenging Child"; **Post-Traumatic Stress**

Travel, Parent. It's best not to leave children too young to understand what is happening with baby-sitters while parents travel, since the time seems like an eternity to them and causes them to feel abandoned. If travel can't be avoided, it's preferable to take the child with you or to at least have one parent remain at home if the trip lasts longer than one or two days. As your child gets older and can better understand that you will return, he can manage the separation for a brief period, but trips longer than a week will tax the child under three to four years of age, depending on who stays with him and how comfortable he is with separation. A child of five to six will be better equipped to manage his parents' absence for a week or so.

Triangling. Triangling is a common dynamic in families in which two or more parties unite against a third party. This opens the way to teasing, gossip, and ganging or even to more seriously unkind and unfriendly patterns of relating within family systems. Thus, families should become aware of such patterns, interrupt them, and learn new, more inclusive styles of relating. See **Family Meetings**

Trips. See **Family Time**; See Chapter 11

Truancy. Truancy occurs when a teen heads off to school but then never gets there and spends the day elsewhere. This differs from a teen openly taking an occasional day off from school. If nothing happens when a child is truant for a day or so, he will repeat the behavior, and, before long, he will become addicted to truancy. In most cases, truancy signals a larger problem and is cause for families to seek counseling. See **Professional Help**; **Running**

Truthfulness. See **Honesty**; **Integrity**; **Lying**

Unconditional Love. Unconditional love is what results when parents learn to fully accept their child and embrace all of who he is. See Chapters 4 and 5

Underclaimer. An underclaimer gives up things he owns or is using to other children taking them from him, rather than claim his right to have or use them. Underclaimers are generally passive children. See **Fighting**; **Overclaimer**; See Chapter 10

Underprotection. Parents who refuse to support their child in handling tasks that he's not yet ready to manage put him in situations beyond the capacity of his ego development to cope. They should remember, instead, to teach, guide, and support their child in managing things he does not yet feel ready to handle.

Vacations. See **Family Time**; See Chapter 11

Values. See Chapter 2

Victim. Children who are rarely allowed to practice using their own power feel helpless and powerless and experience themselves as victims. The more such a child is trusted to use his own ideas in managing his life, the more in charge and powerful he will begin to feel. Because victim feelings are opposite to ones of power, they interfere with feelings of strength. Other children grow to feel like victims as a result of being overprotected or when families feel sorry for them whenever life is challenging. See **Accident-Prone**; **Illness**; **Overcontrol/Overdirection**; **Polarizing**

Video and Computer Games. See **Music**; **Television and Videos**

Violence. The increase in aggression and violence in our children and youth stems from the combination of an increase in bonding breaks and a decline in discipline in our homes. This, in turn, influences our public and political attitudes and methods of dealing with people and problems. Thus, a break in our ability to care about people, combined with a disregard for rules is permeating our families, schools, businesses, professions, legal system, and government. Moreover, in accordance with the discoveries of our brightest scientists that we create what we focus on, the excess of violent images we create on the screens of our minds and media result in increasingly more violent manifestations. To reverse this trend, we must strive to heal the bonding breaks within our families and organizations; improve discipline at home and societally; embrace more positive pictures in our daily lives and media; and design more optimistic predictions for our future. See **Bonding**; **Fighting**; **Rules**; **Television**; **Thoughtforms**; See Chapters 9, 10, and 13

Voice, Tone. The tone of voice parents use must convey kindness if they are to have credibility with their child and model maturity as they guide him through life. See **Anger**; See Chapters 4 and 11

Wanter. See Chapter 2

Warning. Don't set up in a child's mind all the possible things he might do wrong with a string of warnings. Instead, address only those things that genuinely need managing as they arise. See **Reminders**; See Chapter 6

Weaning. See *Weaning* subentry under **Nursing**

Weight Problems. When a child is overweight, it's best not to make him self-conscious about it or suggest a diet. It's better initially, at least, to investigate for yourself what you think the problem is. If he's eating too much junk food, eliminate it without fanfare from your grocery list, while substituting more interesting, nutritious foods. If he's underactive and watches too much television, set new rules about TV watching and inspire him to join more activities. If he has little access to playmates, support him in locating some. Or if he has trouble making friends, help him to develop this very important life skill. If you use his excess weight to alert you to other developmental problems and then follow through on helping him to resolve them, you will probably never have to address the weight directly. If he's still overeating, seek professional help. Interview someone by yourself first to explore a plan for handling it, since mismanagement can trigger more serious eating disorders. See *Eating Disorders* under **Eating Problems**; **Professional Help**

Whining. Before whining can be considered a behavior management problem, parents must first investigate any underlying health or emotional problems that may be causing it. These might include such things as earaches, illness, allergies, pinworms, or some unresolved problem. A child also whines when his parent has a wall up, and he can't get love or help by asking for it directly. Such children feel unheard and unattended to unless they create a problem. Others feel overdirected and overcontrolled and express their feelings of weakness and helplessness by whining. Still others are bored by their routines and need more opportunities to socialize with peers.

Whining is very hard on the nervous system and usually gets a quick response from parents who were previously ignoring their child—and may even cause a frazzled parent to back down on some rule. This combination of responses trains the child to use his whiny voice when talking to parents, and this annoying behavior soon becomes a habit. Thus, parents must be sure to respond to their child's appropriate requests for being with them, obtaining their help, or being listened to, rather than respond only when he begins to whine. They can further support a normal speaking tone by calmly letting their whiner know that they will listen to him when he uses his regular speaking voice. If he continues to whine, he can be further ignored or calmly put in his room until he's ready to use a normal voice tone. The latter is not a time-out, and the child is not asked to stop whining. Instead, it's gently explained that the rest of the family is enjoying a quieter, more cheerful energy and doesn't wish to listen to the whiny sound. It's also explained that he is free to join them when he's bored with the whining and doesn't want to do it anymore. In clearing he can be told that he may use that tone for as long as he likes while he's in his room, but that he will need to use his regular voice if he wants to be with the family. See **"Challenging Child"**; **Fussing**; **Negative Persistence**; **Tantrums**; **Tensional Outlet**; See Chapters 5 and 8

Why. When young children ask the question "why" to serious questions, make sure to answer them to the best of your ability, since this is a stimulating period in their development when they genuinely want answers. It's also helpful to ask them what they think the answer is. However, when a child asks why he has to do this or that, he's merely challenging your rules with intelligent sounding questions. This questioning must be handled by letting him know that you will be happy to discuss it after he has completed the task. If he insists on asking why, he must then take a time-out, do the task requested, and then clear. At that point, if he's still interested in why he had to do the thing requested, it's okay to tell him. See **Compulsive Behavior**; **Negative Persistence**; **Resistance**; Chapters 6, 7, and 8

Willful Child. See **Resistant Child**

Winners' Camp Foundation. Winners' Camp is a program designed to enhance personal growth in young people, 1292 Maleko Street, Kailua, HI 96734, phone 808-263-0177, fax 808-261-3429. See **Adolescence**

Work. Kids who have work experience become more mature and responsible than those who don't. Thus, requiring that kids gain work experience once they are old enough during summers when they are out of school is a very important part of their development. See **Allowance**

Working Mothers/Working Parents. Having both parents work outside of the home fails to deal with the needs of the children or the general management of the household; neither does this arrangement contribute to feelings of warmth and nurturing nor issues of child management and discipline in the home. Nobody has wanted to admit it, but this trend has been a real blow to the family unit!

The answer is not for every woman to scurry back to the home on a full-time basis, while shunning career interests and goals. That would be a step backward for women and an economic blow to their families. Although the issue is no longer one of women having to prove their capabilities, there remains an urgent need to address how to meet the needs of the children with two working parents. The time is long overdue to honestly assess the effect women in the work force has had on the family.

It's important to first reaffirm and honor the roles of women (or men) who by preference and economic ability choose to stay in the home to pursue its management and child-rearing as their primary focus. While these women (or men) feel that home management and child-rearing keep their lives full, yet balanced, there's also time for meaningful volunteer work, a serious hobby, or other goals to make the job even more complete and rewarding.

Something that enables all parents to save time and energy is to have children who are both secure and well-behaved as a result of having been raised with the balance between love and structure recommended in this book. Thus, nonworking as well as working parents would be wise to get a handle on their parenting in order to gain time in their schedules. In this regard, it's important to understand that although the time required to make connections with children and follow through on discipline with them offer the illusion of taking extra time, in truth, once time has been invested in creating this balance in your parenting, the better behavior of your children will save you an immeasurable amount of time, especially the time required for negative interactions with misbehaving kids.

Next, it's important that we get honest about just how challenging it is for a woman—or man—to handle a full-time career and provide for all of the home management and child-rearing as well. The women who tried this when women first entered the work force as well as the ones still trying to make it work strive to look like superwomen with everything amazingly under control. In most cases their personal interests and needs are overlooked during the years when career, child-rearing, and home management demands are at their peak. In fact, it's not uncommon for even minimal needs for exercise, relaxation, reading, social contact, or rest to go unmet. The women who do seem to get it together are whirling dervishes for a period of time—but eventually experience burnout, stress, and health problems after a number of years in this mode. Not surprisingly, 84 percent of women responding to a *Woman's Day* magazine survey reported feeling overworked and tired.

Although managing both work and the home front are challenging to mothers, the real problem lies in the fact that their schedules are simply not good for their young children, a fact mothers are painfully aware of. Not only do the babies of working mothers lose their opportunity for the consistent, primary bonding, so critical during the first two years of life to the child's security and emotional health (see **Bonding**), the developing child is often required to handle more on his own than he feels ready for. Latchkey children who spend eleven hours a week or more on their own after school report aching with loneliness and are twice as susceptible to substance abuse as children with someone at home to care for them. Clearly, whenever both parents work, meeting the children's initial and ongoing needs for bonding and connection becomes a serious challenge.

What can be done? Part of our reality today is that women are in the work force. They are doing a good job there, and many thrive on it. Now that a choice truly exists for women to work or not, some have discovered that they would prefer to work part-time or not at all. Yet for many this is neither a desire nor a realistic financial option.

Once women begin to more honestly state how difficult it is to work full time and manage the home and children as well, they can begin to squarely face that they are, in fact, holding down two jobs. Rather than continue to ignore this as a serious national issue that greatly affects family life and children, it's time that we confront this critical problem and seek workable solutions to it.

The key is to remember that by putting women into the job force we have created the unusual situation in which we are asking two individuals to fulfill the responsibilities of three full-time positions—the mother's job, the father's job, and the home and child management job. It's no wonder that there are feelings of confusion, resistance, and resentment over the division of labor in fulfilling the requirements of so much work! It's time to explore better solutions to this unresolved problem!

The most viable solutions we have developed so far lie in more business-based day care programs that allow parents access to their children throughout the day, more part-time work opportunities with flexible schedules, and men getting more genuinely involved in sharing child care and home management responsibilities.

But this is only a small beginning. We need to go further and examine our priorities to determine whether or not we are willing to begin to make the larger changes needed to truly honor the family and place it at the center of our lives. For example, it's apparent that options such as shared jobs, taking work home for pay, part-time work, working out of the home, and flexible schedules would offer far superior solutions for meeting the needs of families than the ones we are presently using. Arranging such alternatives is not only good for children and families, but for the businesses that depend on a healthfully functioning society to survive. Thus, rather than passively accept being blocked by tradition, each family can take the initiative to create a method that blends work with family. Business would be wise to also embrace how much better our society would function as a whole—including economically—if we would raise healthier children in homes where parents are available to tend to the needs of their offspring. I personally like the European approach in which work is simply not so all encompassing. Not only do they take two hours out of the middle of each day, their workdays and weeks are shorter. America used to have shorter workdays and weeks as well, a system that was part of the nostalgic 1950s. If we are serious in our concern for the needs of our children and families, this would be one of the simplest things to resurrect, especially since Parkinson's Law in which the work expands into the time allotted is probably at work during the increasingly long hours we are spending at our jobs.

As more people claim new approaches to this very real problem, the needs of children can be better met, and the family can regain the position of strength and value it once held in our society. See **Day Care**; **Divorce**; **Parent Roles**; **Single Parents**

End Notes

1. In psychological terms, the *wanter* represents the *id* while the *fulfiller* represents the *ego*.

2. It's important that parents realize this response is not always appropriate following tantrums. For a deeper understanding of what transpired during this experience, refer to Chapter 7 on "Holding Boundaries."

3. For further understanding of how this works, refer to Chapter 7 on "Holding Boundaries."

4. Information about Ho'oponopono is drawn from M. Pukui, E. Haertig, and C. Lee, *Nana I Ke Kumu*, vol. 1 (Honolulu: Hui Hanai, 1972); lectures at Mental Health Association of Hawaii given by L. Paglinawan, Honolulu, Hawaii, 1972; and E. Victoria Shook, *Ho'oponopono* (Honolulu: East-West Center, 1985).

5. *Clearing*, in this context, is based on an ancient Hawaiian technique and is not associated with the clearing used in Scientology.

6. Although it is easier to practice forgiveness when someone has admitted to their transgression, learning to forgive, even when this piece is missing, is an important quality to develop.

7. Charting the ABCs of behavior is an important contribution made by learning theorists. I have added the D and E.

8. The subject of violence in our society is complex and includes problems with broken bonds; neglected, abused, and undisciplined children; violent media images; and a poor model for containing agression in the adult world. Thus, my discussion here is limited only to the effect that inhibiting developmental childhood battles has on the larger picture.

9. Sandy Dornbusch, Ph.D., quoting Shirley Feldman, Ph.D., in "Adjustment in Early Adolescence," The Stanford Center for the Study of Families, Children and Youth, in cooperation with Stanford News and Publications Services, published as a supplement to *The Stanford Observer*, February 1988.

10. *Critical mass* is a term used by physicists to describe the point at which an idea has been accepted by enough members of a group to penetrate the thinking of the entire group, even though the number accepting the idea does not constitute the majority. Ken Keyes, Jr., *The Hundredth Monkey* (Coos Bay, OR: Vision Books, 1986).

11. Genevie, Louis and Margolies, Eva, *The Motherhood Report* (New York: MacMillan, 1987), "Fathers are still not participating much in household maintenance or childrearing. Mother is still ultimately responsible for the custodial care of children. This was true even when a woman was working full-time" (p. xxiv).

12. Genevie and Margolies, *The Motherhood Report*, 1987. Only 10 percent of the women responding felt their husbands assumed a fair share of household and child-rearing responsibilities (p. 336).

13. Although it's unlikely that anything is physically wrong, parents would be remiss not to have their child checked by a doctor if he has done this behavior. Furthermore, knowing he's medically sound will enable them to find the strength to ignore it.

14. Jerry Mander in *Four Arguments for the Elimination of Television* (York: Quill, 1988) has some fascinating arguments for how television replaces real experience, causes sensory deprivation, blocks thinking, and evokes hyperactivity.

15. Robert Rosenthal and Lenore Jacobs, *Pygmalion in the Classroom* (Boston: Harvard University Press, 1958).